THE AUCTION COMPANION

THE

AUCTION

COMPANION

Daniel J. Leab
and Katharine Kyes Leab

HARPER & ROW, PUBLISHERS, New York
Cambridge, Hagerstown, Philadelphia, San Francisco,
London, Mexico City, São Paulo, Sydney

1817

FIRST EDITION

Designer: Sidney Feinberg

Library of Congress Cataloging in Publication Data

Leab, Daniel J
   The auction companion.
   1. Auctions—Handbooks, manuals, etc.
I. Leab, Katharine Kyes, joint author. II. Title.
HF5476.L4   658.8′4   80–8208
ISBN 0–06–012556–X
ISBN 0–06–090850–5 (pbk.)

81 82 83 84 85 10 9 8 7 6 5 4 3 2 1

Contents

PART THREE: APPENDIXES

Foreword

People and plunder were the subjects of the first auctions. In the fifth century B.C., Herodotus wrote of the auctioning off of maidens for matrimony in Babylon. (The very brave—or perhaps foolhardy—auctioneers sold the maidens in order of beauty, the prettiest first.) Slave auctions of prisoners of war were not uncommon in the ancient world, nor were auctions of goods plundered in the course of battle. It was a Roman soldier who gave the name *auctio* to the method whereby the victors disposed of "increase" or spoils: hurling a spear into the ground point first, piling loot around the spear, and then calling for bids.

From these beginnings, auction has had a double-edged development, so that the word calls two images to mind: the shameful sheriff's sale, where a house or business is sold off because of bankruptcy, and the glamour and high romance of a paintings sale at Sotheby's or Christie's, where a single canvas can fetch millions, while elegantly dressed ladies and gentlemen gossip in low, rounded tones and applaud discreetly as one or another buys a Cézanne for $3.9 million, or a Van Gogh for $5.2 million, a Picasso for $3 million, or a Turner for $6.4 million. (These prices were fetched at Christie's and Sotheby's in New York in the merry month of May 1980, and the $6.4 million paid for J. M. W. Turner's luminous *Juliet and Her Nurse* was the highest price ever paid anywhere for a work of art.)

These days, the auctioning off of household "effects," a wonderful word which means anything that might be found in a house, from a Formica-top table to a stuffed alligator, is no longer considered a mark of shame. Rather, it is a clever way to take advantage of the world "collectibles" mania. There are collectors of beer cans, barbed wire, prisoner-of-war memorabilia, etiquette books, erotic scrimshaw, motorcycles, and what have you. In short, one man's household effect is another man's passion, and auction is often the best way to convert one to the other.

Although the media are always focusing on Old Masters and Gutenberg Bibles sold for millions, in fact the majority of fine arts lots sold by auction houses go for less than $500. As *Punch* writer Basil Boothroyd has pointed out in a masterly piece of advertising for Phillips Auctioneers: "A young couple furnishing a house, say, can find an antique piece at Phillips, of high quality, costing much less than its equivalent in a show-room of modern furniture. . . . Their children may grow up amid beauty and craftsmanship after all, and the modern manufacturer, of less exacting standards, be put on his mettle to improve his ways."

Auction is buying and selling as theater. It happens in public; it has a script and a plot, and if successfully produced, should have a driving pace and build to a climax. There are elements of spectacle—the bidders are like contesting gladiators and only one will be left standing to be acknowledged the winner by the auctioneer.

Most people are fascinated by the idea of auction, but many are wary of participating or vaguely afraid of becoming unwitting participants and through some unconscious gesture winning that stuffed alligator they neither want nor can afford. Many people also worry about auctions being rigged, about being "taken" in public. It is true that some of the auctioneers of an earlier era were little more than snake oil salesmen or confidence men. Today, partly because of legal constraints and partly because the sort of person who becomes an auctioneer has changed, buying and selling at auction often is safer than obtaining or disposing of objects by other means. And sale at auction can determine fair market value to the satisfaction of tax authorities. The authors of this book have been "taken" by building contractors, bathroom designers, politicians, magazine publishers, and bankers, but not by auction houses. Using a good dealer as agent when buying anything expensive at auction goes a long way toward dispelling any potential dangers, as we shall see.

Another form of uneasiness about auction was expressed by a friend of ours who easily makes daily decisions affecting tens of thousands of shares of stock but asked us to go with her to Sotheby's because she did not want to go alone. "It's like credit cards," she explained. "Even though you know you have the money, there's that awful moment when you almost expect the public humiliation of being told that your credit is no good."

Because auctions take place in public and because auction customs vary from place to place, people who wish to buy or sell at auction need information to be effective and to escape embarrassment. That is why we have written *The Auction Companion:* to provide information on auctions—of fine arts, crafts, and domestic goods, but not of horse or tractor sales—and their procedures throughout the world. The auction market today is an international market, and the collector or auction enthusiast needs to know which auction house excels at what specialties, how to read a catalogue without bedazzlement, when to buy personally at auction and when to use a dealer, and how to decide whether a collection should be consigned to an auction house or to a dealer. Accordingly, the book provides information on buying at auction, on selling at auction, and on the multinational auction houses— Sotheby's, Christie's, and Phillips. These introductory chapters prepare you for the country-by-country listings of the auction houses in the world's principal auction centers, which contain information about each firm's procedures, charges, specialties, services, and guarantees. The information in these listings is correct as of January 1, 1981, and is based on lengthy questionnaires completed by officials of the auction houses in question. Occasionally we will give a country short shrift even though a number of auction houses are located there. Examples are Italy, where it is worth your life to export any work of art, and France, where the system is such that we cannot recommend bidding by amateurs. Should these situations change for the better, we will give full listings for such countries in later editions. Please remember, this book is a companion, not an encyclopaedia of auction houses. It is selective and well-verified but does not attempt to be all-inclusive. Write us if you have any candidates for the next edition.

All the auction venues have been assigned a code number. At the end of *The Auction Companion,* you will find sample contracts and conditions of sale, and a list of specialties, such as silver or art nouveau, with the code numbers of the auction houses which emphasize these specialties.

Now let's go and sell something at auction.

PART ONE

WHY AND HOW
TO USE THIS BOOK

1

Selling at Auction

Selling at auction can be an excellent way to settle an estate without incurring tax problems, a means of cashing in on the "collectibles" mania, a release from the fear of being burgled, a method of raising money or of cleaning out the attic, a shortcut to the achievement of immortality as a collector, or a pain in the neck. Our job in this chapter is to help the would-be consignor to avoid the last possibility while enjoying one or more of the others.

We begin with a story about selling. It is set at Christie's, but in outline and principle it applies to other auction houses, both great and small.

Miss Rosemary Spencer, lecturer in medieval Welsh at the University of London, had just retired and was going through the tiresome process of reviewing all her worldly goods as she moved house from a spacious London flat to Ivy Cottage in Berkshire. While sorting things out, she came across two allegedly valuable china figurines which had been given her by her eccentric uncle Sacheverell. Having never liked them much, she decided to part with them. She had never been to an auction house, but she had seen a television program about them called "For Love or Money" on the Omnibus series, and she remembered liking the look of Patrick Lindsay of Christie's. After a few moments' thought, she telephoned Christie's to make an appointment.

On February 20, 1980, when Miss Spencer appeared at Christie's King Street premises, a serious young woman at the front counter ushered her into a very small room and shut the door. Miss Spencer couldn't help feeling caged in that tiny room, and she was considerably relieved when the door opened and in stepped Roger McIlroy of the European Ceramics Department. After a swift examination of the pieces, he expressed real interest in the Berlin figure of a sportsman and polite interest in the Parian figure of a young lady kneeling before a cross. Miss Spencer decided then and there to leave the figures with this nice young man for sale.

Christie's gave Miss Spencer a receipt showing the stock number assigned to her consignment ("BM830"), indicating her Value Added Tax status, and describing the figures as "1 porcelain figure" and "1 Parian figure"; the receipt also included Mr. McIlroy's initials, the identification of the department ("Porc"), and a notation that Christie's would advise her of the reserves and the insurance values would be set at £500 and £80 (she would have to pay .05 percent of these insurance valuations as a premium). On the reverse side were printed Christie's "Terms for Selling Works of Art by Auction at our Great Rooms," which set forth all the information Miss Spencer needed about charges, reserves, storage, buy-ins, and payment.

Miss Spencer made her good-byes, and her two figures were carried downstairs to the basement warehouse area, where objects are stored by type—Chinese porcelain, European porcelain, and so on. There they were handed over to the European Ceramics Department's warehouse porter, whose function is far more important than his title suggests, since he is responsible for maintaining order among objects belonging to a great many people. He entered in his log the reference number ("BM830") from the house copy of the receipt, the description of the item, and its location in a specific warehouse room. (In many instances, the object will remain in the warehouse room until it is taken upstairs for exhibit and sale. Although some objects are moved to the departments for cataloguing—books, for instance— many are catalogued in the warehouse rooms.)

On February 26, a member of the European Ceramics Department wrote to Miss Spencer.

Madam:

We have now had an opportunity to examine the two items which you left with us under the above stock number.

We would be delighted to include the Berlin figure in a specialised sale of Continental porcelain here at King Street on 11 May and would suggest a protective reserve price of "about £300" be placed on this, although at the time of sale we would expect it to realise in the region of £300–£400. Perhaps you would be kind enough to let us know if you are agreeable to this suggestion.

With regard to the Parian figure, although models of this appear in Derby biscuit, yours is of Staffordshire origin and would date from the mid-19th Century. As such its probable value at auction would be in the region of £20–£30. We would be delighted to transfer it to our South Kensington salerooms at 85 Old Brompton Road for inclusion in a specialised sale there on your behalf, and enclose a transfer form for your authorisation.

We look forward to hearing from you and hope we will have very successful sales on your behalf.

The enclosed transfer form gave the original stock number ("BM830") and a reference number ("1642") which would become the stock number at Christie's South Kensington, and it informed Miss Spencer that the Parian figure would be transferred to South Kensington "unless we hear from you to the contrary within a week," that it would be sold there in an appropriate sale as quickly as possible without a reserve (unless instructions were received to the contrary), and that proceeds would "normally be sent within 14 days of the sale, provided payment has been received from the buyer." The charges would be 15 percent of the sum realized if the lot sold, 5 percent of the highest bid if it failed to sell, and 10 percent of the approximate value if she withdrew the figure before the sale.

Miss Spencer was delighted with this turn of events. She sat right down and wrote Christie's to say that a £300 reserve was agreeable to her, as was the sale of the Parian figure at South Kensington.

On receipt of Miss Spencer's letter, arrangements were made to transfer the Parian figure to South Kensington. A notation of the "1642" number was made in the warehouse porter's logbook, and the figure was wrapped and placed in the Christie's truck that shuttles back and forth between King Street and Old Brompton Road each day.

At South Kensington (a place which fairly crackles with the combined energy of the very young, very eager people who work there), the Parian figure was taken to the area set aside for European ceramics and was catalogued almost instantly for inclusion as lot 52 in the March 13 sale of European ceramics. A copy of the catalogue reached Miss Spencer on Tuesday, March 11, along with a presale advice which gave the stock number ("1642"), the sale number with the year of sale appended ("130380"), and the lot number ("52"), and reiterated the information about reserves and payment of the proceeds as stated in the transfer form.

Busy as she was with settling into Ivy Cottage, Miss Spencer did not call London to find out what the Parian figure made at the sale. At the end of March, the postman brought her a Christie's envelope containing a Settlement Statement and a check dated March 24 (a scant month after her visit to Christie's). The statement noted that the hammer price for the figure had been £50. After deductions of £7.50 as commission, £1.13 for VAT service (VAT is now chargeable on commission at 15 percent), and £1 for insurance, she received a check for £40.37 drawn on the South Kensington branch of Lloyds Bank. She was delighted to receive more than double the £20 she had anticipated and just a bit shocked to see that 20 percent of the hammer price had gone to fees and VAT.

Back at King Street, the catalogue manuscript for the May 19 sale of Fine Continental Porcelain was taking form. As each item was catalogued, the resulting description was added to those already on the clipboard in the warehouse room. When all the work was done, they would be given lot numbers, and the completed manuscript would be sent off to the printer. (Black-and-white photos can be taken for catalogue illustrations at Christie's discretion. The seller might be charged for an illustration Christie's doesn't recommend, or if he insists on color instead of black and white.) Any lot that was to be photographed would be the subject of an in-house request form so that the object would not get lost during the trip to the photographic studio (also in the basement) and back to its spot on the shelf. Every item was either tagged or stickered with its lot number.

Miss Spencer's Berlin figure remained securely on its shelf until late in the day on Tuesday, May 13, when it was moved upstairs to the exhibition and saleroom area and was placed in a showcase with several other objects (had it been super-important, it might have had a showcase to itself). The figure was on exhibit with the other lots in the sale on the Wednesday, Thursday, and Friday preceding the auction of Fine Continental Porcelain. And it was well placed in the sale, about midway through the 350 lots.

Not long before the figure went on exhibition, Miss Spencer received a copy of the sale catalogue, along with a notice (in duplicate and with translations into French, German, Italian, and Spanish on the reverse side of the original) showing the stock number ("BM830"), the sale number ("01784"), the lot number ("180"), and that a reserve of £300 had been agreed upon in writing. The notice had a second column, for recommended reserves, which did not apply to Miss Spencer but which she found interesting. Of recommended reserves, the notice said (in red ink): "These must be confirmed in writing. Please sign the pink copy and return it to us. Should no instructions be received before the sale, your property will be bought in on your behalf and the appropriate commission rate charged." And the notice added: "Your property will be offered subject to the notice and conditions of sale which is shown in every sale catalogue."

This time Miss Spencer did not have to wait for her check to learn how her lot had fared. That very week, she received an After Sale Advice, which conveyed the happy news that Uncle Sacheverell's Berlin figure had sold for a thwacking great £900 (the commission rate was 10 percent).

And how had her Berlin figure gone from the showcase to the new owner's hand? On May 19 at approximately 12:36 in the afternoon, the figure, which had been removed from its showcase by a saleroom porter and placed behind the rostrum with the other objects in lot order, was held aloft so that the bidders could see it clearly. When the bidding ended, the figure was taken almost immediately to Christie's central delivery room (in European ceramics sales, objects usually go to the central delivery room in batches of, say, fifty lots). After the buyer had paid the cashier (located adjacent to the central delivery room), the figure was packed, wrapped, and taken away.

About a month after the sale, Miss Spencer received a Settlement Statement (the last time that stock number "BM830" would be used) detailing charges of £4.50 for insurance, £90 as commission, and a nasty £13.50 VAT on the commission. The net proceeds of £792 meant that just about 11 percent of the hammer price went to charges. The check accompanying this statement was a lovely pink and white check drawn on the St. James's Street Branch of Lloyds Bank. Thank you, Uncle Sacheverell.

Miss Spencer's experience is a fairly typical one. What bothers us about her story—and about many stories of auction consignors—is her passivity throughout the whole process. Except for going into the auction house with her figurines, she was virtually a spectator. And she never bothered to find out even the approximate values of her figurines. Fortunately for her, the auction house was honorable and the expert was bright. Had she gone to, say, the New Clear Auction House in Amchitka, she might not have fared so well. This is not to say that one is necessarily better off at Christie's or Sotheby's, but rather that there is no excuse for a consignor not to know whether the value of an object is in the 10s, 100s, or 1,000s before consigning it to auction. Stories about an auction house selling an object for $180 which later turned out to be worth thousands, or, conversely, about somebody bringing in an old piece which the auction house discovered to be worth £200,000, impress us not at all, for they are stories of laziness on the consignor's part.

People today seem to be far more aware of the values of business objects than of cultural artifacts. A person who would never dream of sending 100 shares of IBM stock off to his broker for sale without some idea of its worth may well send a work of art worth thousands to the auctioneer without the slightest attempt to find out anything about its value.

Admittedly, the auction market is not the stock market. Stock prices do not depend on the condition of the certificate or whom it might have belonged to years ago. But in terms of 10s, 100s, or 1,000s, one *can* determine the value of an object and thus be able to make rational arrangements with an auction house. There are reference books available in a variety of collecting fields, from *American Book Prices Current* for books and autograph material to *Print Prices Current* for prints to *Art Auction Records* for paintings. All these cover auctions in several countries. There are auction catalogues (some museums and libraries have long runs of them) to be checked for similar sales. There are shops and galleries selling similar objects. And there are museum curators and librarians to consult; people who buy for institutions on tight budgets often know a good deal about current market conditions. None of these sources can provide a precise measure of auction value—factors like condition and provenance do affect auction prices—but you can get some idea of what you have before you talk to anyone at the auction house.

And the proper handling of a sale can make a very great difference indeed. Consider this example:

In the mid-1970s, the heirs of Henry Hubbard Middlecoff, delighted by their lawyer's handling of the Middlecoff estate and knowing that he liked old books, presented to him a copy of Herman Melville's *The Whale* (in three volumes), which is the first edition of *Moby Dick*. The lawyer, a supremely honest man, refused the gift, for he recognized the unique value of this particular copy and what its sale at auction could mean to the Middlecoff heirs. Melville had inscribed this book to "his old shipmate and watchmate" Henry Hubbard on the *Acushnet*. Moreover, the characters Pip and Stubb are identified in Hubbard's hand. The lawyer, being both bright and careful, secured no fewer than three appraisals from local California dealers before approaching the major auction houses about selling the book. Then he sent clear and fully descriptive letters to several auction houses, describing the copy and its provenance. The final result: the Henry Hubbard Middlecoff copy of *The Whale* sold at Sotheby Parke Bernet in New York on January 26, 1977, for $53,000. But for the lawyer, the book's value might have gone unrecognized or it might have been sold privately for a fraction of its worth.

Notice that the lawyer did not "shop" the book. One mistake often made by amateurs is that they take an object from place to place endlessly, trying to sell it to a dealer for a high price. Then they consign it for auction. By the time such an object comes up for auction, the trade is thoroughly sick of it and its consignor, and frequently the object has to be bought in.

Another mistake that was avoided in the case of the Melville was the imposition of too high a reserve. Some houses will not accept a reserve. Others will expect you to abide by their suggestion. And still others will go along with your suggested reserve, provided it is not outrageous. When a consignor unreasonably insists on a sky-high reserve and the object then fails to sell, the object is referred to as being "burnt" or as a "cripple." Should this happen, moreover, it costs the consignor money. His cost—known as the buy-in charge—is usually a percentage (the normal range is 2.5 to 5 percent) of the reserve or of the highest bid under the reserve. Be certain that the auction house does not put too low a reserve on the object, especially if the house has a buyer's premium. In that case, a buy-in means that the house gets nothing from the buyer, and often the money made on that premium is the house's margin of profit. Houses that have buyer's premiums tend to cut seller's commissions in order to get the objects they want for sale. The buyer's premium thus becomes increasingly important to the house and creates a tendency to try and set very low reserves so that everything will sell. If despite your and the house's best efforts an object fails to sell, you may be able to put it into a later sale if it is a chest or a table, but if it is an oil painting or other expensive work of art, it should be retired from public view for at least a decade.

The Middlecoff lawyer—and the Parke Bernet Book Department—

also made some intelligent decisions with regard to photographs, advertising, and viewing of the Melville. A black-and-white photograph may cost the consignor money, but it can make a whale of a difference in the price an object brings at auction. A friend of ours once demonstrated this to us by putting in a catalogue an illustration of an object that had never sold for more than $50 though it sold often and was usually rated in fine condition. Sure enough, the object sold for $250. Similarly, a press release or the mention of an object in the advertising for a sale will tend to boost its price, as will its careful positioning in the exhibition prior to the sale. The Middlecoff Melville benefited from all these techniques, which, combined with the efforts of Book Department members to ensure that collectors, dealers, and institutions knew this unique book was coming up for sale, probably added at least $10,000 to the sale price. And another 5 percent of the price may have been the result of John Marion's having acted as auctioneer that day. A superb auctioneer like Marion can easily make a 5 percent difference in the price realized.

In the case of the Middlecoff Melville, the obvious choice was auction. But how do you decide whether to sell something at auction or privately to a dealer?

Certain specialist fields really are outside the expertise of auction houses. If you wish to sell a Hebrew manuscript, for instance, a specialist dealer is the likely choice for a buyer. With rare exceptions, auction houses do not do a good job with them. (We know of one instance where not a character of Hebrew could be read by the cataloguer, who, however, was canny enough to know that a spot catalogued as a wine stain tended to enhance rather than detract from the value of the manuscript.)

Another reason for selling to a dealer is an urgent need for cash on the barrelhead. Dealers pay less, but they pay immediately and at a fixed price. An auction house may take anywhere from a few weeks to several months to pay the consignor, and some houses now make payment to the seller contingent on the receipt of payment from the buyer. This is a trend to be resisted; if you are paying an auction house a commission, the least they can do is be sure they are selling to reliable people.

Sometimes an auction house may in fact *be* a dealer. This is common practice in Germany and elsewhere. As Sotheby's former chairman Peter Wilson has explained it: "If somebody comes to us with a collection, or we hear of a collection, and they say they will not sell it at auction because they think the risks are too great . . . we say, 'Well, would you accept a guarantee?' and we explain how that works, which is that they pay a somewhat higher commission but they are absolutely dead certain of getting a minimum price that we mutually agree on. Sometimes they will not do that because they want the money here and now, and in that case we are prepared, but only after having offered the other two alternatives, to say, 'Well, in that case we will offer so-and-so for the collection,' or for the picture, or whatever it is." How often this is done varies widely: William Doyle Galleries in New York buy privately and resell about half the time; Christie's say they never do. Whether or not auction houses should buy and sell on their own account is a moot point. Many do, and even their most vocal critics (the dealers) seem to buy when these houses sell objects for their own account which are desirable or in demand.

If, however, the auction house you are using does sell for its own account, you should be certain that it does not hog the best spots in the catalogue or on the exhibition floor. You do not want your object to be in the first or last twenty lots, for many people come late, overspend in the middle, and leave early. Be certain that your object is well displayed and that the objects grouped with it enhance rather than detract from its appearance. Try to see it again right before the sale to be certain that it has not been damaged. Should there be damage, raise Cain right then and there. Traditionally, the auction house has been on your side because you were the consignor paying the fees. Where there is a buyer's premium, this loyalty has been diluted.

Using an auction house to dispose of a large collection of furniture and fine arts or the entire contents of a household can have a number of advantages over other methods of selling. The auction house often will take on everything, which means paying the movers only once—or not at all if the sale takes place on the premises—and avoiding storage costs and a great stream of dealers. But do not simply call the movers and then let the auction house know that a consignment is coming. Telephone or write the house or, in the case of the larger ones, their closest representative to arrange for a valuation inspection. There may be a charge for that inspection; certainly the firm will expect to be reimbursed for the inspector's out-of-pocket expenses, although if the property is consigned, the inspection fee is often waived or at least reduced.

Unless the property is so desirable that the auctioneer lusts to obtain consignment for the firm, the consignor must bear the cost of removing the goods to the saleroom—and often he must make all the arrangements as well. The length of time that goods are stored in the auction house depends on their quality and quantity. Usually, the bigger the house, the longer the wait. Smaller firms look for a quick turnover, but often have a longer interval between specialized sales—and, if your property is to be sold in such a sale, check to see how long the wait will be. Generally, you should pay no fee for warehousing unless the objects go unsold and you do not reclaim them.

You must choose your venue carefully. If you have unexceptional furniture and a super carpet collection but want to sell both, the furniture might be consigned locally and the Oriental rugs sent to, say, Edelmann Galleries in New York. Or the rugs might be used as the carrot to get the local auction house to take on 126 plastic-topped tables. If you have a small specialized collection and are not disposing of any "effects," then before making any move to sell you should spend some time in gossip with dealers, curators, writers, and others involved with auction houses to determine what is the very best venue for your collection. Right now, for instance, illuminated manuscripts should go to Christopher de Hamel at Sotheby's in London, and autograph letters of the late actor James Dean should be sold at Charles Hamilton's in New York. But there are no such hard-and-fast guidelines to deciding whether jewels should be sold in Switzerland or New York or whether Chinese porcelain must be sold in Hong Kong to reach the best (i.e., highest-paying) markets. The situation can change quickly if an expert changes jobs, or if, say, Japanese buyers leave the market. So-called auction consultants usually base their advice on which auction house will give them the best finder's fee for bringing in your goods. They should be avoided.

Estate lawyers often turn to auction because in several countries auction value is recognized as being equivalent to fair market value for estate tax purposes. Sometimes an executor will even submit a sale catalogue with the prices realized instead of a formal estate tax appraisal. Moreover, sale at auction provides a defense against possible charges by squabbling heirs that more could have been realized. Sometimes the executor's life is made easier by the existence of a thorough insurance appraisal, but overdependence on such a valuation can be disastrous. Time after time, we have seen estates settled by some of America's less energetic estate lawyers simply by selling the listed insurance objects and dumping everything else. If the insurance appraisal has been made by an auction house, it may be inclusive. But most people tend to insure haphazardly and to list individually only those things for which they have paid a great deal of money. Thus the "everything else" that gets dumped can include books, art objects that are not conspicuously valuable, and all sorts of things that, with a little care in the handling, might bring in a fair amount of money. Unhappily, not all estate lawyers are like the Middlecoff lawyer.

Some of the larger auction firms have estate departments which have been set up specifically to smooth the way for executors in everything from filling out forms and assessing alternate ways to compute tax to coordinating the sales of whatever is in the estate, be it furniture or wine. This can be helpful but also lulling. The executor must keep an eye on the progress of the estate through the auction house in the same way that an individual does, whether it be checking the exhibition and the sales the objects are to appear in or reviewing the reserves.

The thinking estate lawyer is likely to insist on making a few changes in a standard contract. Recently Henry Anon, executor of the estate of Mabel and Roy Ymous, arranged for the sale at Christie's East in New York of a group of some thirty household objects that the heirs did not want, including chairs, chests, tables (all reproduction), light fixtures, and a screen. By so doing, he was able to clear out the Ymous's cooperative apartment in Manhattan and thus get it ready to go on the market quickly. Mr. Anon's modifications of the contract included having the precise date and place of the sale written into the contract and inserting a clause to the effect that all lots would be sold at no less than the minimum appraisal by Christie's East. In this instance, the consigned items were sold within a month, with the exception of one piece which Mr. Anon and Christie's East agreed was worth saving for inclusion in a specialty sale. The only fees were .05 percent insurance on the objects and 10 percent commission. Everything sold within the estimate range except for one unsold table, which, by the terms of contract, was popped into a sale seven weeks later, when it found a buyer. Altogether, it took about three months for the matter to be wrapped up, and the estate realized about $10,000. In England, where many auctioneers are chartered surveyors, the residence and the contents might have been sold by one firm.

At the other end of the spectrum is the "name sale." On one level, this means that names like Joan Crawford and Gypsy Rose Lee will bring in people to pay high prices for such absurdities as false eyelashes and G-strings. On another level of celebrity, there can be sales like the Edgar and Bernice Chrysler Garbish sales held by Sotheby Parke Bernet in New York and on the premises at "Pokety" in Maryland to the tune of $20.4 million in 1980. Sometimes a superb collection will make its late owner's name known to the world at large, as was the case with the peerless Robert von Hirsch collection of paintings and other fine art objects, which sold at Sotheby's in London on June 20–27, 1978, for £18,468,347.

The von Hirsch sale was decades in the making, from the care taken in appointing a Sotheby representative in Zurich to the annual visit to von Hirsch of Sotheby's chairman to the actual work of the sale. The sale preparations were backbreaking: cataloguing, advertising, renting space at the Westbury Hotel for the overflow crowd (the assemblage at the sale filled three auction rooms at Sotheby's plus space at the Westbury plus a remote hookup to Parke Bernet in New York). Part of the collection was exhibited in Germany, in Zurich, and at the Royal Academy in London, involving packing, moving, setting up, security, and entertaining of potential buyers. Representatives visited and sent letters or made phone calls to hundreds of potentially interested individuals and institutions, making the telex lines hum with inquiries to branch representatives throughout the world. Huge credit lines for dealers had to be arranged (it has been said that an auction house lives or dies on two factors—supply and credit arrangements). The press was showered with press releases and photographs. And the results were spectacular, in terms not only of money but also of publicity. The von Hirsch sale became news—almost sporting news. Major television outlets throughout the Western world reported each day's "scores" somewhat breathlessly. Such a sale brings glory, money, and—most important—many future consignors.

If you have a world-class collection of anything from motorcars to textiles or if your name is a household word, you hardly need worry about how to approach an auction house about selling it. Chances are that auction house experts know about you, and in these times of short supply, the merest indication of interest in selling confided to the wall of your own study will bring them to your door.

Auction house employees spend much of their time working to get supply, and they have evolved some wonderful and subtle methods. An example is what might be called the worm-in-the-apple technique. A dashing friend of ours recently went into Stalker and Boos in Birmingham, Michigan, to buy a gift (they have a retail operation as well). She was greeted by one of the principals, who, as they chatted, just happened to remember that she had been the underbidder on a set of Flora Danica dinnerware at the Anna Thompson Dodge estate sale at Rose Terrace in Grosse Pointe in 1971. And he just happened to remember that she had stopped bidding at $10,000 and the lot had sold at $10,500, and that she had so much Flora Danica of her own (his firm had done an appraisal of her household contents) that she could hardly miss having the Dodge pieces. But just out of curiosity, he had recently checked to see how much the Dodge Flora Danica would be worth today. Just for the fun of finding out. And that lot would be worth $94,000 today. Just shows you how the world is going. And the conversation flowed on to other subjects.

Now, there was an auction house principal doing his job superbly well, combining a splendid memory with research and market savvy. And you can bet that he knows precisely who is collecting Flora Danica these days. He won't push; he'll simply bide his time. She may think about it and decide to sell several years from now. Whether somebody from an auction house is on his own ground or at a party or doing an appraisal, the same sort of gentle attempt to pry loose a desirable collection goes on daily throughout the world. To function, auction houses need good collections and single works of art. Whether you are a private individual or a museum, they are only too happy to help you move things their way. And so long as you keep your wits about you, know the approximate value of what you have to sell, and are prepared to keep an eye on reserves, cataloguing, exhibition, and sale, the pitfalls are few. Moreover, selling at auction can be great fun. We once asked a major collector what it felt like to see the paintings he had bought for comparatively little money sell for huge amounts in a record-breaking sale. "It was like Tom Sawyer's funeral," he said. "I sat up in the balcony and watched men who had laughed at my taste and my own work in this field over the years. Now they were scrabbling to buy." The sale made this collector a sort of immortal: he had unswervingly bought what he knew to be good without regard to fashion, and it brought him the satisfaction of being proved right in public. That is the supreme joy of selling at auction.

2
Buying at Auction

There are two ways to buy at auction. For most people, commissioning a dealer or other agent to buy an object is the best and safest way. In terms of value for money, the 10 percent you pay a dealer to buy for you at auction is a real bargain. The saving in paperwork alone is almost worth the price. If you are in the market for an Oriental rug or a piece of Mayan pottery or if your institution has a prime collection of, say, arms and armor and a sale of interest to you is coming up, the dealer may notify you well in advance of the public announcement of the sale so that you can have funds available for a major purchase. Some eminent dealers receive galleys of auction catalogues before the catalogues are printed, bound, and distributed. This gives them and their clients a head start over the rest of us.

Most auctions are in fact like town meetings of dealers. A major sale in particular brings out many of the expert dealers in a given fine arts area. They meet and talk, exchanging pointed gossip and using various forms of gamesmanship on each other; they do other business—we have been at some fairly dull auctions when much more business was transacted in the hall than in the saleroom. Most important, dealers use their sense of timing and their knowledge to play the auction game itself.

Yet another reason to use a dealer when you buy at auction is that a practiced eye will look at the object you think you want in order to be certain that it is in fact what you want. And should you purchase the object and then find something wrong with it, you will have a much easier time returning it to a dealer under his guarantee than you will to the auction house. As an individual, you may be held to the most literal reading of the auction house's conditions of sale. A dealer, however, can return an object with considerable ease—he has a continuing relationship with the house, for he spends thousands there each year.

Three other services performed for you in return for the dealer's 10 percent commission are sitting through the auction for you, thereby saving you time (and you don't pay anything if the dealer is unsuccessful); paying the auction house—the dealer bills you, which gives you more time to pay than if you paid the auction house directly; and taking care of the removal, packing, and shipping of the object.

One cautionary note: Be certain that your dealer is representing only one client for any given lot in an auction catalogue. Occasionally in London an object will be knocked down—that is, the bidding will come to a close—at, say, £350, whereupon the successful dealer calls out "£520 for that lot." The reason, of course, is that he has taken multiple bids, but the practice is an unsavory one.

To illustrate the process quickly, let us recount the story of one of our purchases at auction. Among other things, we collect early editions of the works of John Gay, who is best known as the author of *The Beggar's Opera.* We knew that the first sale of Corning Glass heir Arthur Houghton's books, to be held in June 1979 at Christie's in London, would include a presentation copy of the large-paper issue of the first edition of Gay's *Shepherd's Week.* Because it seemed like the copy to have and because we did not plan to attend the Houghton sale ourselves, while in London six months earlier we talked at length with the late eminent dealer Dudley Massey of Pickering and Chatto, and our conversation was twofold: (1) about the copy itself and its worth, taking into account other copies and their known prices; and (2) about the Houghton sale and its effect on the market, taking into account such factors as whether the Conservative or the Labour party would win the general election.

At this point, Mr. Massey had seen the book and we had not. The following day, we went to Christie's to look at the Houghton books. Note that they were not yet on exhibition; Christie's allowed us to see them early because we would be listing them in *American Book Prices Current* and because we would be writing articles on the Houghton sale for various magazines. Nonetheless, we did not tell them of our interest in the Gay, for we wished to avoid the mistake made all too frequently by collectors and curators who conspicuously concentrate their presale attention on one specific lot. When an auction house is thus alerted to a potential buyer's interest, it is honor bound to take this interest into account in its efforts to get as much money as possible for the consignor and thus for itself.

Having seen the book, we met again with Dudley Massey and made a final determination of what his bid on our behalf would be. We stated our limit in terms of the hammer price (not in terms of the hammer price plus the 10 percent buyer's surcharge levied in London and elsewhere) and made it clear that we do not subscribe to the custom of "plus one," according to which the dealer has the latitude to put in one bid beyond the limit you have given him. (Be certain that you and your dealer understand each other on this point.)

The book now is ours—at twice the auction house's high estimate of what it would fetch. But as that charming old fox of a dealer put it in a letter to us after the sale, "You will be happy to note that I obtained the book at a figure that was less than our estimate"—which was true, whereas most of the Houghton books went for triple the presale estimate. Moreover, we picked up the book and paid for it two months after the sale. Clearly, in this instance, using a dealer at auction was well worth the 10 percent fee.

But before our dealer colleagues smile too broadly at our counsel, we must say that if you have developed real expertise in a collecting area (or if you simply don't care what something is so long as it is well made and fits into your home) and if you have the time to attend auctions, bidding for yourself is enormously satisfying, even thrilling.

In discussing how to buy at auction, let us pretend that you live near a major auction house and that you have read and read and read about your special interests and have visited museums and restorations to see as many examples of, say, Sheraton chairs as you possibly can. Keep an eye on your local newspaper so that you will know when the auction house is having an exhibition that interests you. The more presale exhibitions you attend, the better prepared you will be when you want to bid on something. To develop an "eye," you have to use your mind and your senses often and intensely. And you should not depend on anybody else for information on the general run of sales. If your budget permits, subscribe to auction house catalogues in your area of interest—the listings in the geographical section of this book tell you where, how, and how much. Some catalogues are fun to read—provided that you remember at all times that the traditional job of the auction house is to represent the consignor or seller. Thus a recently sold missal whose binding was in disgraceful shape became in the catalogue description a missal whose binding was "worn and rubbed—by devotional kissing?" Not a misrepresentation; just a few words to stir the imagination.

Do not be intimidated by the perfectly dressed, faintly sneering young persons who initially deal with the public at the large firms. If they tend to make you feel unkempt and unworthy, just keep in mind that they work for a purveyor of secondhand goods. For many years, the presence of second sons and third-rate titled daughters at the front desk was thought to make the very rich feel comfortable and to keep out the time-wasters. Gradually the auction houses have come to realize that this approach made many people with ready cash feel unwelcome. Accordingly, they now are trying to project a friendlier image.

Once inside the auction house, you should pick up a catalogue (unless you're a subscriber and brought it along) and proceed to the exhibition area. On the way, if you pass by a saleroom with an auction in progress, stop for a moment and see what's going on. With the exception of a very few major sales which are held at night and for which tickets are issued, auction sales are open to the catalogue-carrying public. It is not unusual to see people inspecting objects in a saleroom while a sale of totally different objects is going on. We once were almost demolished by an overeager examiner of wood paneling while we were attending a book sale. He tugged very hard indeed on what turned out to be a false door and very nearly brought a sixty-foot section of paneling down upon us.

When you reach the exhibition area, look around to see whether there are dealers examining the objects and how they do it. It has been said that the novice handling art objects is very like the novice holding a baby: he doesn't hold it tightly enough and he looks as if he's afraid it's going to bite him. The dealer doesn't gaze moonily at a chair—he turns it upside down to examine it thoroughly for wear and construction faults. Occasionally a dealer might be doing more than examining a piece, a notorious example being the dealer in porcelain who wielded a wicked pencil at the exhibitions. His marks looked precisely like hairline cracks. Until this ruse was discovered, he always got the lots he wanted at low prices. Then he erased the "cracks" and sold the pieces at a handsome profit.

While examining objects in your field of interest, try to guess values before looking at the estimate lists, and always remember that estimate lists are not reliable as bidding guides. All you can learn from them is what the highest possible reserve may be. The reserve, or lowest price at which the consignor will sell the item, should not be more than the estimate or than the high estimate if a range is given; otherwise, the house is playing a dishonest game. Especially at the big houses, estimates (and reserves) tend to be low. If you can't live without the object, double the high estimate will almost always get it for you, except in "name" sales, where the sky's the limit.

In examining the catalogue, you should pay attention to provenance. If the catalogue says "Property of a lady," for instance, the convention is that it was consigned by a private person rather than by a dealer. As such it is more likely to be "fresh," rather than having been limping exhaustedly around in the marketplace. The name of a famous collector attached to the piece may raise the price, unless the collector was known to have no judgment at all. Try to find out what you can about a named collector.

You also should be certain to refer to the conditions of sale in the catalogue in order to check for the possible use of code in the catalogue entry. This is most likely to occur in sales of paintings, prints, porcelain, and Oriental art. For example, in Christie's catalogues of Oriental ceramics and works of art, you will find the following explanation:

The name of a ruler or dynasty	In our opinion made during or shortly after that dynasty or the reign of that ruler
"In the style of" followed by the name of a ruler or dynasty	In our opinion probably a copy or imitation of pieces made during that dynasty or the reign of that ruler
Where reference is made to a mark and to a period	In our opinion made in that period
Where reference is made to a mark but not to a period	In our opinion probably not made in the period of that mark

Should you find the chair or netsuke or book of your dreams, try to see it on more than one occasion before the sale, and if it is fragile try to see it as close to the sale time as possible to be sure that nobody has damaged it. How does it compare with examples in the shops of antique dealers in terms of condition and possible price? Ask one of the saleroom staff whether the expert responsible for the sale is available to answer questions. If so, you almost certainly will find that he or she is extremely pleasant and helpful. Remember—do not ask about one lot only. Often the auction house expert knows an enormous amount about his or her areas of specialization. This is because the experts see huge numbers and varieties of objects—which they have to identify and catalogue in very short order. Those experts who survive the pressure of this sort of time-dominated work do so because they study hard and develop an "eye" as a result of their constant exposure to objects in their area of specialization. But you can beat these experts and competing bidders if your eye and your scholarship are good enough.

Even at a highly publicized sale like that of the contents of Mentmore, the Rothschild-Rosebery estate in Buckinghamshire—a nine-day sale in May 1977 which realized £6,389,933—the clever researcher can find bargains, for occasionally the auction house and other experts miss a beat. This is more likely to happen in a big sale which has many lots and stretches out over many days. He who keeps his eye clear when others' are getting glassy may win a real prize. At the Mentmore sale, the canny art expert David Carritt paid £8,000 for what turned out to be a misattributed painting. What everybody but Mr. Carritt missed was that this particular painting, which was badly in need of a cleaning, was a Fragonard. The painting, after having been cleaned and thoroughly tested for authenticity, was sold to the National Gallery for a rumored price of £400,000 (neither Mr. Carritt nor the National Gallery would confirm or deny that figure).

David Carritt has reason to understand the difficulties that time limitations place upon the scholarly researches of auction house experts and what temptations can arise as a result of the frustrations inherent in the expert's job. While just such an expert at Christie's in 1964, he even invented an artist called Van Essabel, whose name he derived from that of Virginia Woolf's sister, Vanessa Bell. According to Carritt: "A particularly revolting flower piece appeared. I decided it might be nice to invent a painter who might eventually find her way into one of those dictionaries of artists. What amazes me is that nobody penetrated it." And two Van Essabels sold as lot 145 in Christie's sale of December 1964.

Having made a thorough examination of the object you want to buy and having decided that you still want to buy it, the next step is to establish credit. It helps if you carry a bank reference about your person, but most of us don't. Find the desk or office where you register and proceed to establish your bona fides. Some houses will check with your bank; others take credit cards. All houses will be glad to explain their specific procedures. If you are far away from home and the auction is about to begin, you may be asked to demonstrate that you have sufficient cash or traveler's checks to pay for whatever you might buy. If the firm uses the "paddle system," where each would-be bidder registers before the auction and receives a numbered paddle or card with which to bid, you may have to pay a desposit on the paddle. Too many people thought that a paddle makes a fine souvenir and walked off with them; hence the deposit.

Should you be unable to attend the sale, you can leave a bid with a member of the auction house staff, a so-called *order bid*. Some firms will also allow you to bid by mail. An order bid represents the highest price you are willing to pay. If competition falls away before that price level is reached, then you will pay less. That is, if you are the successful bidder at $150, you will pay $150 (plus the buyer's premium if there is one) even if your order bid was for $200.

If you decide to do your own bidding, be prompt when sale time comes. Many auctions start late, but if you are on time, you can eavesdrop on the gossip in the halls and check to see whether a *saleroom notice* has been posted, withdrawing a lot or amending a catalogue description. Then find yourself a good seat in the saleroom. A good seat is one where you can clearly see both the auctioneer and the other bidders in the room. The extreme right side near the front is usually our choice, and we have been known to stand up and lean against the wall for a better view. Do not sit in the first or the last row of the saleroom—you may be trespassing on the traditional preserve of a dealers' clique and they may bid you up (which means bid against you for the hell of it just so that you will have to pay more) for trespassing. Back in the days when the salerooms were almost exclusively dealer preserves, the amateur was likely to be bid up just as a matter of habit. The practice has virtually ceased because there are too many amateurs and unknown dealers in the saleroom to make the practice worth it. A dealer will, however, keep bidding on something he does not want if there is a risk of its going for such a low price that the value of his own stock of similar objects will be endangered. We well remember a strained moment at a sale in 1976 when it became apparent that there was nobody in the room who wanted a First Folio of Shakespeare's plays and that the auctioneer would have to make a great deal of noise to cover up the fact. Riding to the rescue came one of the world's foremost book dealers, who put on a show of bidding up to $35,000 and then left it to the house to buy it in. It would not have done for a First Folio to be retired from the floor at, say $4,000; that could have cast a pall over the whole antiquarian book trade. Right after the sale, several dealers called the auction house and offered to buy the First Folio at private treaty, for this copy was a bargain in the $35,000 range and there certainly is a market for First Folio Shakespeares (in 1980, the Houghton copy sold for £80,000).

By sitting where you can see both the auctioneer and the other bidders, you may be able to determine whether or not the auctioneer is taking bids "off the wall." As Patrick Lindsay, auctioneer and Christie's Old Masters expert, explains the phrase:

"Say we've got a reserve of five thousand pounds for a picture; now it is my job as the auctioneer to cap any bid in the room until that five thousand is reached. So I have to bid the owner's reserve for him and in the same way I do this for the bids in the book—if you leave a bid I bid it for you. Rather than look down at the book each time one takes a genuine bid there (and the person whose bid it is isn't in the room), it's a little bit of theater in a way to pretend the chap is there rather than give the impression that he is not there or that the bid is always in the book or the reserve. . . . It can only be unethical if you do it beyond the reserve. It is quite unethical to do it just as a means of boosting the price with imaginary bids; that is quite wrong."

There is one other ethical reason for taking bids "off the wall." In an unreserved auction, it is the only way that the auctioneer can try to protect the consignor from dealers "ringing" a sale. From time to time, a group of dealers will make a secret agreement not to compete for an object but rather to allow one of their number to buy it for a low price. After the sale, the ring of dealers meets for a private auction in which the winner gets the object and the other members of the ring split the difference between the public auction price and the amount the winner bids at the private ring auction. All this is hideously illegal, but it happens nevertheless. Ringing is less common than it used to be because there are so many more private bidders at auctions and because auctioneers strike back by taking bids off the wall. Ringing can also work backward, especially in photographica sales. On some occasions, dealers have concertedly bid up the prices of photographs so that their own stocks of photographic material would increase in value. The auctiongoer should be aware of these practices, but they are not something to be worried about in the general run of sales. If you know what you are willing to pay for an object and you stick to your limit, you will not be affected by off-the-wall bids, rings, or reverse rings.

And just how do you bid? You raise your hand or your catalogue or your pencil. Now, you can make arrangements with the auctioneer for a secret signal—wiggling your ears or scratching the right side of your neck with your left hand—but most of the time this sort of signaling is silly and amateurish. At times it can be downright counterproductive, as when Norton Simon made the following bidding arrangements: "When Mr. Simon is sitting down he is bidding. If he bids openly he is bidding. When he stands up he has stopped bidding. If he sits down again he is not bidding until he raises his finger. Having raised his finger, he is bidding until he stands up again." The upshot of all this fancy arranging, which took place before Christie's sale of March 19, 1965, was that Rembrandt's *Portrait of Titus* was knocked down not to Simon but to Marlborough, causing Simon to raise a public fuss, whereupon the picture was put up for sale a second time and was knocked down to an openly bidding Simon for 760,000 guineas.

Dealers often mark entries in their catalogues to jot down their intended bids, using a letter/number code—either a ten-letter word with no repeated letters or a nine-letter word and an *x* for zero. (This code may also be used in marking objects in their retail establishments to remind them of how much they paid.) As an example:

Q	U	A	T	R	E	F	O	I	L
1	2	3	4	5	6	7	8	9	0

Using a code enables the dealer to sit next to his chief competitor during the sale without divulging how much he is going to bid. For "200," write "ULL," for "750" write "FRL," and so on. If you bid often enough, then you should use a code. Besides, it's fun.

Before you start bidding on a lot that interests you, be certain that you have checked the catalogue so that you know what the bidding increments are, whether or not there are export restrictions on what you want to buy, whether or not you have to pay a buyer's premium on top of the knockdown price, and whether you are bidding on the correct lot. The inattentive bidder may have to take a white elephant home to dinner. It is also wise to be certain that you do not communicate your intense interest in a lot to possible competitors. The eminent French auctioneer Maurice Rheims notes in his memoirs (*The Glori-*

ous Obsession, London: Souvenir Press, 1980) that in the saleroom, "the main physical movements are very slight, just a sway this way or that from the waist—until something suddenly happens. Someone moves differently, though the difference is barely perceptible. My mind instantly registers this inchoate disorder denoting perturbation, excitement; and almost invariably, the man who gives himself away like this will start bidding on the next lot to come up." Not all auctioneers are as sensitive as Maître Rheims. Accordingly, the first time that you bid, you may have to make a fairly large gesture. Should you join the bidding late, the auctioneer probably will wait until one of the two original contestants drops out before recognizing you. Once the auctioneer is aware of your interest, he will come back to you until you become the buyer or until you shake your head "no" to signal that you do not wish to top your competitor's bid. In a large and crowded auction room, there may also be "spotters," auction house employees who point out bids that the auctioneer might not be able to see.

Should you be successful in buying an object, a member of the auction house staff may ask you to sign a form or even to put money on deposit. After the sale—or, as auction houses computerize, after the sale of the lot but while the auction is still going on—you will have to pay for the object, and if it is large, arrange for its packing and shipping. Firms that do not have packing and shipping facilities will usually give you the name of somebody who can perform these services for you. Be sure to allow enough time for the dreary business of paying and picking up. It usually takes longer than you would have thought possible. But your purchase is worth the wait. Auctiongoing is a blood sport, the fun of the chase being surpassed only by the exhilaration of the kill. And every time you sit on the chair, or look at the painting, or wear the necklace, or use the fish knives, you will remember the joy of the hunt and the feeling of victory.

3

Auction International

In the past twenty-five years, Sotheby's, Christie's, and Phillips, all fine old English firms, have changed the nature of the fine arts market by becoming international auction houses. The old jest had it that Christie's was composed of gentlemen pretending to be businessmen, while Sotheby's was composed of businessmen pretending to be gentlemen. Now it can be said that Sotheby's and Christie's are multinational public companies pretending to be private firms, while Phillips is a private firm pretending to be a public company.

The international auction houses today are remarkable examples of what economists call vertical integration. The New York venue of the Sotheby Parke Bernet Group, for example, will appraise your goods, pack them, insure them, transport them, arrange for you to get a loan on them if your consignment is valuable enough, photograph them in their own in-house photography department, advertise and publicize them through their own in-house agency, sell them wherever in the world they will sell best, provide you with protection against international currency fluctuations while you await the proceeds of the sale, and then act as real estate agent in the selling of your now-empty house or apartment. Finally, your homeless children can enroll in Sotheby's fine arts training course in London or even New York and learn whether the firm has treated you properly. With these resources, it's no wonder that the 1980 turnover at Sotheby's Madison Avenue alone was $196 million. In London, a consignor might not have been able to unload his real estate through Sotheby's, but he would have received the additional services of having oil paintings restored and reframed by James Bourlet Frames, the comprehensive services of Artscope International Insurance Services ("a comprehensive service covering security, valuations and insurance principally for owners of works of art"), and a formally organized Taxation Advisory Service.

In terms of companies, divisions, decentralization, and overall organization, Sotheby's has come to look more like a smaller version of General Motors than like a traditional auction house. Christie's and Phillips have remained more centralized operations, though international, but they, too, have come a long way from their beginnings in 18th-century England.

Samuel Baker, whose firm evolved into Sotheby's, began his business with the sale of the library of Dr. Thomas Pellet in the mid-1740s; James Christie, with the household effects of "a Noble Personage (Deceas'd)" on December 5, 1766; and Harry Phillips (who had been James Christie's head clerk), with a sale of "neat and elegant" household furniture on April 23, 1796. And there is a sense in which these three first sales defined the character of the three firms for many years.

Samuel Baker was a bookseller and publisher as well as an auctioneer, and books remained the substance of Sotheby's business throughout the 18th and 19th centuries, although prints and coins and such were sold from time to time. The firm evolved into Leigh & Sotheby in 1780 (Sotheby was Baker's nephew), and into Sotheby, Wilkinson & Hodge in 1864, and between those two incarnations it moved house to Wellington Street, near the Strand. After a horrible fire in the new quarters, the firm recovered and kept on selling books, and in fact, would-be consignors of pictures and other large works of art or pieces of furniture would be referred to Christie's.

This pattern might have continued forever if Edward Grose Hodge had made a will. But he died intestate in 1909, and his son Tom had to sell the business. Fortunately for the subsequent history of Sotheby's, he sold it to Montague Barlow, Geoffrey Hobson, and Felix Warre, who became the Mr. Outside, Mr. Inside, and Mr. Finance of Sotheby's. World War I caused the virtual suspension of the firm's activities; Tom Hodge bowed out completely in 1916, and with the lease on Wellington Street due to expire in 1917, the remaining partners took a calculated risk which was the making of the modern Sotheby's. They decided to move the firm to New Bond Street in the West End, which had become a fashionable area and a center for the selling of fine art. Moreover, they decided to charge a higher commission rate than Christie's because they would offer unmatched expertise. Hobson combined the mind of the scholar with formidable organizational skills, and he set about building expert departments, securing experts as employees or consultants. Such men as C. F. Bell of the Ashmolean Museum and Tancred Borenius became fine arts advisers, and for many years Sotheby's experts in a number of fields were unequaled by those at other houses. (Sotheby's to this day lists the name of every principal expert in its catalogues.) Hobson himself became internationally known as an expert on bindings, and the firm became stronger than ever in books and manuscripts as he built up reference files of autograph specimens and research files for other departments. Sotheby's soon began to hold general sales, the first ones of note being the 1917 sales of armor, Old Master drawings, engravings, and paintings from Wilton House, the home of the Earl of Pembroke.

James Christie's first sale was typical of the firm he founded in that it auctioned off the effects of a "Noble Personage." Christie from the beginning worked to make his firm the auction house favored by England's aristocracy. An economic history of the English nobility could be written on the basis of the appraisals and other documents in the muniments room in Christie's basement. Christie himself came from nowhere, but he was tall and mannerly, handsome and a captivating talker. Fashionable ladies found him overwhelmingly charming, and his men friends included David Garrick, Sir Joshua Reynolds, and most important, Thomas Gainsborough.

Christie began in premises in Pall Mall, and his neighbor and sometime adviser Gainsborough painted a portrait of him which is one of the firm's chief assets to this day (though the portrait itself is now in the Getty Museum). It is one of the most lovable, trust-inspiring portraits ever painted. Small wonder that Christie's International in New York reproduced it on the cover of the booklet it used to introduce their new operation and staff to New York in 1976.

For a number of years, James Christie was one among many auctioneers. Then in 1778, he was chosen to arrange the sale to Catherine the Great by private treaty of part of the Walpole painting collection at Houghton. Being thus singled out made him the preeminent auctioneer in London. He also sold Madame Du Barry's jewels, and did better on the deal than she did, for she was guillotined after having been convicted of selling state treasures.

Since James Christie's time, the firm has enjoyed an orderly succession in terms of management, as summarized in almost biblical fashion by I. O. Chance in his chairman's letter in the prospectus for the 1973 public offering of Christie's shares:

James Christie died in 1803 and was succeeded by his son, James Junior, who was succeeded on his death in 1831 by his two sons, James Stirling and George Henry. They took as their partner in that year William Manson, who died in 1852 to be succeeded by his brother Edward, and in 1859 Thomas H. Woods joined the partnership to create the firm of Christie Manson & Woods. James H. B. Christie, grandson of James Christie junior and a member of the partnership until he retired in 1889, was the last member of the founder's family to serve with the firm. In that year my great uncle, Walter Agnew, and Lance Hannen, grandfather of Guy Hannen, the present Managing Director, joined the firm and began the family connection which exists to this day. Sir Henry Floyd became a partner in 1928 and his cousin, J. A. Floyd, is the present deputy Chairman. . . . For many years, just as sons and nephews consigned to Christie's, so sons and nephews ran it.

In 1823, Christie's moved to King Street, to the premises that have been its headquarters ever since (except for the period from 1941, when the Great Rooms were destroyed by an incendiary bomb, to 1953). Throughout most of that period, it was cock of the walk, holding sales for such persons of rank as the Duke of Buckingham, whose sale at Stowe took forty days. It was not until the 1950–51 season that the turnover at Sotheby's exceeded that at Christie's, and the firm had to face squarely the fact of competition.

And what of Harry Phillips and his "neat and elegant" household furniture? His first sale was a "house sale," held in Crown Street, Westminster. Phillips had just resigned, at age thirty, as James Christie's chief clerk, and he could not afford a venue of his own. Phillips was amiable and able and a great entertainer, both in the rostrum and at the evening receptions he began to hold soon after he established a venue at 73 New Bond Street late in 1797. By the time he died, in 1840, he had sold everything from harrows to goods that had belonged to Beau Brummel, the Duke of Buckingham, Marie Antoinette, Napoleon, Talleyrand, and a host of more ordinary people. The high-water mark came in 1823, with his sale of the contents of Fonthill Abbey, formerly the home of William Beckford. The sale took thirty days and was the social event of the season.

On Harry Phillips' death, his son William Augustus became head of the firm, and he ran it successfully for forty-seven years. Then the firm was taken over by W. A.'s son-in-law Frederick Neale (by then the firm name had been changed to Phillips, Son and Neale), and

Neale soldiered on until 1922, when his son Philip succeeded him. The firm's fortunes had declined in the late 19th and early 20th centuries, and finally, in 1937, Phillips, Son and Neale was bought by G. Hawkings, who had an auction room in Lisson Grove. The energetic Hawkings began to turn the firm around, but his energies were severely tested in 1939, when the firm's headquarters were destroyed by fire. Missing only one sale, Hawkings moved into smaller quarters at Blenstock House. But although Glendining and Co. had joined Phillips after World War II and Phillips had acquired Puttick and Simpson in 1954, nobody would have guessed in the 1940s and early 1950s that Phillips would become an international auction house.

What happened to change these three very English firms into the monoliths they are today? Briefly put: World War II. The possibility of a truly international fine arts market opened up about 1954, when price, import, and currency controls were lifted. Thus consignors from any country could be paid in their own currency, and bids—say, on furniture—were not limited by price control regulations. Add to this the growing availability of air transport, and the scene was well set for internationalism. By mid-1955, Sotheby's had opened a small office in New York, with the urbane John Carter at its head. Christie's followed with offices in New York and Rome in 1960, and with a larger operation, including a saleroom, in Geneva at the end of 1966.

For Sotheby's, the first realization of major change came with the Goldschmidt sales of Impressionist and modern paintings in 1956 and 1958. In the first sale, fifty-six paintings which had been in Berlin and New York fetched £326,000 in London; and in the second, seven paintings made £781,000. After the second sale, the whole world knew that fine art was big business and big news. The second and more important event for Sotheby's was the acquisition of Parke-Bernet in New York in 1964.

For Christie's, the sale of the Anna Thompson Dodge estate in 1971 was the first major incursion into large-scale internationalism (though the Geneva sale of Nina Dyer's jewelry in 1968 for Sfr7,498,000 provided a splendid rehearsal). Their experts descended upon the Dodge estate, Rose Terrace, in the Detroit suburb of Grosse Pointe, to divide its contents into three parts: jewels for Geneva; major art and fine French furniture for London; and "choice residue" to be sold at Rose Terrace in association with the local firm of Stalker and Boos. The total of £1,564,000 for the remaining contents of the house in Grosse Pointe hardly conveys the excitement of this trinational sale. Not only was this the first time that Christie's had sent a whole planeload of furniture and artworks to London from the United States, but it also was Christie's first "house sale" in America. All Detroit came and bought and bought.

The mid-1960s and early 1970s were a time of enormous expansion in fine arts auctions, thanks to such factors as the apparent readiness of the Japanese to buy any available Impressionist painting and to outbid each other for jewelry; changes in the tax laws (an example being the 1965 Capital Gains Act in Great Britain); the expanding world economy; and Elizabeth Taylor's craving for the Cartier diamond ($1,050,000 at auction before Richard Burton bought it for her). By 1973, the year in which Christie's became a public company, a single jewelry sale in Geneva was bringing in Sfr15,869,000, a substantial sum indeed. Christie's also held the world record for Old Master paintings: in 1970, they had sold Velázquez's *Portrait of Juan de Pareja* to the Metropolitan Museum of Art for $5,544,000. This record stood until May 1980, through a whole decade of inflation and collecting madness, when Sotheby Parke Bernet in New York won the blue ribbon with the sale of Turner's *Juliet and Her Nurse* for $6,400,000.

When sales totals dipped in 1975, however, Sotheby's and Christie's were ready with a new economic weapon—the 10 percent buyer's surcharge levied on all goods sold in London. The surcharge, plus the rise of Islam in the fine arts market, meant that the Sotheby Parke Bernet Group's pretax earnings, which had been £2,450,000 for the 1973–74 auction season and £1,099,000 for the 1974–75 season, rose to £3,346,000 at the end of the 1975–76 season. And for the first time, in the 1975–76 season, sales in the United States and Canada accounted for a greater percentage of Sotheby's sales volume than did those in London—43.5 percent for America and 38.6 percent for London. In June 1977, Sotheby's followed Christie's suit and became a public company.

While all this was going on, Phillips, too, were enjoying the expansion of the late 1960s, keeping their overhead low, dealing in everything from "the Furniture and Effects" of Cliveden House to Staffordshire pot lids and the contents of old Printing House Square after the *London Times* moved to new headquarters. In the mid-

1970s, under the direction of its superdynamic new chairman, Christopher Weston, Phillips became like a terrier, nipping through the feet of the slower and more regal hounds, not catching the largest prey, to be sure, but making off with much of the smaller game. When Sotheby's and Christie's announced their surcharge policies in 1975, Phillips countered by lowering their consignor's fee to 10 percent and conspicuously *not* imposing a surcharge. This policy was rewarded with a leap of about 40 percent in their total sales, to £15,750,000 in 1976 (by contrast, in 1971 their sales total had been £4,000,000).

The Phillips approach was so successful that Sotheby's responded by beefing up their Victoriana outlet, Sotheby's Belgravia, and Christie's took an even more important step in 1975, taking over Debenham and Coe's premises to establish Christie's South Kensington for "works of art in the lower price ranges," as their press release put it. South Kensington was a radical departure for Christie's and its huge success resulted in its director, Paul Whitfield, being sent over to King Street to become managing director.

The rest of the story to date sounds like a game of tag. Phillips followed Christie's to America in 1977 and saved themselves all sorts of agony by moving into Christie's old Madison Avenue premises in the Rhinelander mansion after Christie's opened a full-scale operation on Park Avenue. With a tiny but valiant staff, Phillips began holding sales, gently reminding Americans that they could come to Phillips for serious jewel or porcelain buying or for fun—as in the sales of old toys from the Marx Company. Similarly, they made Douglas Fairbanks, Jr., happy by selling his toy soldier collection. By 1980, Phillips' sales in the two New York venues (they also have rooms at the other end of East 72nd Street) were close to $13 million, and they could boast of world records for posters ($52,000 for a Lautrec Moulin Rouge) and for Lalique ($39,000 for a cire perdue figure of a cougar). And Phillips' international turnover reached £33,700,000, with rooms or offices in London, the four corners of England, Scotland, Dublin, Geneva, The Hague, Ottawa, Toronto, Boston, and New York.

Meanwhile, Sotheby Parke Bernet and Christie's International, Inc., were (and are) slugging it out for domination of the upper reaches of a burgeoning New York market, enriched in part because of the influx of European and Latin American flight capital. Christie's introduced the 10 percent buyer's surcharge to New York in the hope that they could undercut Sotheby Parke Bernet by lowering fees to consignors.

Sotheby's, declaring the surcharge an abomination and refusing to institute it, thereby enabled Christie's to woo some consignors with lower commission fees and thus gain a firm footing in the United States. (Sotheby's changed their mind and instituted the surcharge.) The end of the 1979–80 season saw Christie's in New York with a sale total of $113,000,000 against Sotheby Parke Bernet's $196,000,000 at its Madison Avenue venue alone. London totals were £98,000,000 and £82,600,000 for Sotheby's and Christie's respectively, and worldwide totals something like $500,000,000 and $300,000,000. The strategies of the two houses were diametrically opposed—Sotheby's spreading out into regional networks and multiple venues, with decentralized units in competition with each other; Christie's rejecting the idea of regional networks and emphasizing more centralized control. From the figures, both seemed to be right for the moment.

Not that the sky was cloudless. All agreed that the middle had dropped out of the market, though the top and bottom were strong—a physical impossibility perhaps anywhere but in the auction market. More serious was the suit brought against Sotheby Parke Bernet & Co. and Christie, Manson & Woods Ltd. by British dealers' groups alleging that the introduction of the buyer's premium was the result of collusion between the two firms and that the premium is consequently illegal because the alleged agreement had not been registered under the 1976 Restrictive Practices Act. The case is set for hearing in October 1981, and its outcome may have a dramatic impact on the auction market. Then, too, something has been sacrificed in the drive for bigness by these auction houses. The financial men have become more important than any expert, and the advertising men possibly most important of all.

For all these clouds, the formation and development of the multinational auction houses is overall a sunny achievement which has brought a wide range of services to buyers and sellers all over the world and has served to make the world at large more conscious of its cultural artifacts, and thus, perhaps, more eager to preserve them.

PART TWO

AUCTION HOUSES

United States

"Never on Sunday" does not apply to the auction market in this country. On Sundays and every other day in the week, dozens of auction sales are taking place in the United States. During the 1970s, an auction fever swept the land, and this fever has continued unabated. What *Time* magazine described as "auctionphiliacs" are everywhere. And everywhere there is a sales venue of some kind waiting for them.

The largest and best known auction houses in the United States are Sotheby's and Christie's, and they speak to the public with an English accent. They are not only preeminent in New York City—the center of the fine arts auction market in the United States—but very active elsewhere in the country. Sotheby's has a flourishing Los Angeles branch, has begun to hold auctions in such cities as West Palm Beach and Chicago, and has established a series of regional offices that blanket the United States and facilitate consigning and bidding for many people who may never see the inside of a Sotheby's saleroom. Christie's is content for the moment to limit itself to the occasional (and spectacular) house sale outside New York City and to an increasing network of representatives who, like their Sotheby's counterparts, solicit consignments, facilitate bidding, and otherwise further the fortunes of the house.

Phillips has also limited its activities for the present. But it got off to a smashing start with its first American house sale in 1978, when the firm auctioned the household contents and antique shop stock of a man who had been brutally murdered on the premises just a few months earlier. The sale exceeded the none too conservative estimates by almost 30 percent.

To describe the next tier of American auction houses as "second rank," as has often been done, is to do them a great injustice. Their annual turnover, admittedly, is not nearly so large as Christie's or

Sotheby's, but many of them do a highly professional job of serving the area in which they are located, and they also manage to attract a national and international clientele.

Some do so because of intelligent specialization—like the New York City firms of Swann (which emphasizes books) and Hamilton (mostly devoted to autographs); indeed, these firms flourish in the very shadow of the giants. Some do well because they recognize the special needs of their area and in so doing have dramatically improved the level of their consignments and thus attracted a more sophisticated type of bidder. Firms such as Morton's in New Orleans, Robert Skinner in Massachusetts, and C. G. Sloan in Washington, D.C., have not only benefited from the auction boom but helped to foster it as much as their multinational colleagues. You can now go to these houses and others like them and be sure of finding world-class objects. These firms may not be setting world price records, but they are selling lots that attract national and international interest from buyers and consignors, as well as a plethora of commission and absentee bids.

The glamorous items sold by the larger firms understandably attract public attention, thanks in part to what critic Robert Hughes has described as "the largest gaggle of public relations people ever to batten on the flank of culture." But *all* these firms (including the multinational houses) also sell large numbers of lots at the lower end of the price spectrum. Many important houses hold a few first-rank sales annually, and weekly sales of a variety of low-priced merchandise. The kind of catalogue available for a sale often types it: Sotheby Los Angeles, for example, produces detailed, well-illustrated, glossy-paper catalogues for its big sales, and minimal listings which are not even mailed out for its other kinds of sales.

Lower-priced lots are the staple of the numerous auction firms to be found in large cities and small towns, in the country and in the suburbs, which hold weekly, semiweekly, or biweekly auctions. The cataloguing is minimal or nonexistent. Hundreds of lots are auctioned off at each sale, and seldom are guarantees or warranties offered. But these local auctions offer bargains galore. You may have to compete with the legion of dealers whose elbows are everywhere, even at the small country auctions, but if you know your stuff, have staying power, and are not afraid to compete, you can do well.

Most auction operations (large or small) in urban or even small-town areas used to adhere to a schedule in which sales were held from the end of September to the middle of June. These dates marked what was known as the auction season, and indeed, figures are still compiled according to that schedule rather than the calendar year. That is why in July you will read in the press how well, or how poorly, a company has done over the past twelve months. Country auctions used to be held mostly in the late spring, the summer, and the early fall. No more. The holding of sales has become a year-round affair for most auctioneers.

The largest houses are now holding sales through the summer, although the number does slacken toward the end of July. Smaller firms in the cities are following suit, and in the country, sales are now held as the occasion demands, be it winter, spring, summer, or fall. Two very useful guides to the changing auction calendar are the monthly *Art & Auction* (250 West 57th Street, New York, NY 10019), whose schedule of sales each month highlights the activities of the larger firms across the country, and *Antiques and the Arts Weekly* (Newtown, CT 06740), whose ad pages seem to contain sale notices from just about every country auctioneer in New England, and a good many elsewhere; they also carry ads from many of the larger firms. Saleroom aficionados desirous of up-to-the-minute information about New York City auctions can dial *Auctionline* at (212) 977-2579; its recorded announcements prepared by *Art & Auction* staff are updated daily.

At most auctions, you have to register before you can bid. Usually you are given a numbered card or paddle in return. The auctioneers want you to bid, but they also want to know who you are and to keep auction junkies and other undesirables from bidding. Therefore, they ask you to register. The use of numbered cards or paddles also helps to speed the auction along; no need to stop and ask the spelling of your name for the sales record.

Registration usually entails showing your driver's license or some other piece of identification. You may also be asked for a "paddle deposit" (perhaps $20–$30) and/or a deposit (10–25 percent) on the amount that you intend to bid. This deposit—which is refundable and which establishes your financial bona fides—usually has to be paid in cash, traveler's checks, or a certified check. Increasingly, credit cards (generally MasterCard and Visa) are accepted in payment of purchases—mostly for amounts over $50.

The buyer's premium, although not yet universal by any means, has been widely adopted since its introduction to the United States in the late 1970s, and is now found on every level of the American auction market. Whether at one of the multinational firms, at a good regional auction house, or at a country auction, you should be prepared to pay an additional 10 percent on your winning bid. And note that sales tax is usually charged on the purchase price (that is, the hammer price plus the buyer's premium).

It may well be that you want to bid on a lot but cannot attend the auction in person and do not want to commission a dealer to act for you. No problem. Many auctioneers, both large and small, accept absentee bids, although if you are not known to the auctioneer, you may be asked to put up a 25 percent deposit on your absentee bid, and in most instances telephone bids have to be confirmed in writing prior to the sale. Once an auctioneer gets to know you, it may well be possible for you to forgo the deposit (if such is required), and despite all strictures to the contrary, it may even be possible for you to obtain credit—a chance to pay in thirty days or longer, or to establish a revolving credit line. Be realistic, however, in your bidding: where the catalogue indicates estimates and states that reserves are accepted, you can assume that a bid 75 percent below the estimate has no chance of success. Even where reserves are not accepted, there is always the chance that the auctioneer in fulfilling his responsibility will reject an excessively low bid.

You should note that many houses in the United States sell "as is/ where is" without any guarantees or warranties. Thus you are strongly urged by them (and by us) to look at the item you are bidding on, or to have someone look at it for you. It is easy enough to make a mistake when present, but nothing beats a personal inspection, given the minimal cataloguing that is general and the possible mistakes in even the most detailed catalogue by even the most meticulous, best-intentioned cataloguer, under the pressure of getting ready for a sale.

Generally speaking, it is true that where there is ample parking available, the auctioneer offers some kind of food service as well. By this we don't mean the kind of special catering that often is found at a fancy house or estate sale, but simply a snack bar, the chance to get a bit of something to eat or drink during a long sale. Most times, "ample parking" means that the area has space but relatively few other amenities close by.

The increasing competition for auctionable material as well as the widespread adoption of the buyer's premium has meant that you now can take advantage of an opportunity formerly offered only to a limited number of dealers and institutions, and certain private individuals: the negotiation of the consignor's commission. In the past, a select few were able to negotiate deals with regard to the consignor's commission, but because that commission was almost the auctioneers' only source of income, a limited number of such deals could be offered. The adoption of a buyer's premium, which ensures the auctioneers a certain amount on every lot sold, also gives them more flexibility, and auctioneers on all levels are willing to cut their announced standard commission rates for an important or exciting prospective consignment. You should be prepared to take advantage of this situation if you believe that you have a consignment of value. But remember that what may seem of value to you, such as an old family Bible, may have no worth in the open market.

You may, incidentally, have wondered about the large number of "colonels" to be found in the auction trade, especially in the country. An old American tradition dubs country auctioneers "colonel" even when they don't have a nodding acquaintance with the armed forces, and a variety of stories attempt to explain this tradition. One has it that a man who actually had been a colonel in the U.S. Army became an auctioneer in Kentucky and was always referred to as "the colonel" by the local citizenry and the outsiders who came to bid. These outsiders also began to refer to auctioneers elsewhere as "colonel" and soon the designation spread, and the national auctioneers association adopted the term when referring to their members throughout the United States.

Taxes: As yet there is no value added tax or national sales tax in the United States. Each state and locality has the authority, however, to impose sales taxes and few have forgone the opportunity.

Such taxes are levied on the purchase price (i.e., the hammer price plus the buyer's premium). The auctioneer must collect sales tax from you unless you are exempt and can demonstrate this exemption, by, for example, presenting a registered resale number issued by a local taxing authority. This number indicates that you are making a purchase not as a collector who intends to keep the object, but as someone who intends to sell it.

Shipping a purchase out of state or to another locality does not always ensure that sales tax can be avoided. Regulations differ widely from state to state and must be carefully checked. The requisite sales tax as of 1980 in each of the jurisdictions in which the auctioneers function is found under each listing in the pages that follow.

1.   American Art Galleries Ltd.

6001 North Lincoln Avenue   Tel. (312) 271-8800/1/2
Chicago, IL 60659

American Art Galleries has recently moved closer to its suburban clients and has located in pleasant quarters in the "Suganash" area of Chicago. This part of the city, which is not too far from the boundary between Evanston and Chicago, is euphemistically called a "stable area."

The house holds 8 sales yearly, as well as special sales when necessary. During the summer, sales are often held on the premises of individuals. It is a good, middle-range auction house.

Contact person: O. C. Sline

Days/hours of operation: Mon.–Sat. 9 A.M.–6 P.M.

Areas in which general auctions and special sales are held:

Americana	Etchings
Dorothy Doughty and Boehm Birds	Paintings
Drawings	Porcelain
Engravings	

Sales are advertised via a mailing list which you can request to be put on, and in local and New York City newspapers.
Catalogues are available singly for each sale and by subscription ($150 annually for all catalogues).
Usual viewing procedure: Exhibition is 2 days before the sale during regular business hours.

Bidder Information

Auctions are held both on and off the premises.
There is no buyer's premium. Accounts must be settled within 5 days after a sale. Mail order bids are accepted. Credit terms are available (30–60 days).
The house offers packing and shipping services, at the buyer's expense.
The house will accept return of goods that prove to be not as catalogued.
State and local tax: 6 percent.

Consignor Information

Potential consignors should contact the house in writing or by telephone. There is no minimum value for acceptance.
The usual commission charged consignors is 10 percent. It is negotiable, depending on the situation.

Consignors pay for catalogue illustrations ($25 per photo), but do not pay for warehousing or insurance of consigned property.

Reserves are accepted. The buy-in charge to the consignor is $10 per lot.

Goods consigned are usually sold within 30–45 days; settlement is 35 days after the sale.

Appraisal service is available; the cost is $75 for the first item and $5 "for every ensuing item."

American Art Galleries Ltd. belongs to the Appraisers Association of America and the American Society of Appraisers.

The firm does buy and sell on its own behalf.

2. Associated Appraisers Inc.

915 Industrial Bank Building   Tel. (401) 331-9391
Providence, RI 02906

A general-purpose auction house, which is also very active in the appraisal business. This firm ranks among the foremost appraisal firms in New England.

Auctions are held whenever "we have an Estate or Estates worth selling," usually in rented halls. The firm occasionally holds special sales, and for these, catalogues are available. For each sale the firm issues an illustrated brochure which in general terms describes what is to be sold and depicts a few of the most important items.

Contact person: N. D. Scotti

Days/hours of operation: Mon.–Sat. 9 A.M.–5 P.M.

Areas in which general auctions and special sales are held:

Americana	Jewelry	Prints
Books	Manuscripts	Rugs
Clocks and Watches	Paintings	Silver
Furniture	Pewter	Toys
Glass	Porcelain	

Sales are advertised in area newspapers, such as the Boston *Herald* and the Providence *Journal,* as well as in more specialized publications, such as *Antiques and the Arts Weekly.* Announcements are mailed to interested parties; write to be put on the mailing list, at no cost.

Usual viewing procedure: Day before the sale, 2–8 P.M.

Bidder Information

All sales are held off premises.

There is no buyer's premium. Buyer must pay 6 percent sales tax unless in possession of a valid dealer's tax number. Credit cards are not accepted.

Credit is not available. Settlement is "by 7 P.M." day of sale.

"All property is sold as is and with no recourse. It is an AUCTION."

State sales tax: 6 percent.

Consignor Information

Persons wishing to consign property should contact the firm in writing or by
telephone. There is no minimum value for acceptance of property; the
only requirement is "just good quality."

Commission is 25 percent plus moving and packing charges. It is not negotiable. There is no separate rate structure for dealers.

Consignor must carry own insurance. There is no charge for warehousing.

Settlement is made in less than 30 days after sale; usually in 2 weeks.

Reserves are not accepted. Only charge for unsold property is packing and
shipping charges to return it.

Appraisal service is available. For probate, inheritance taxes, and liquidation,
the cost is 3.5–4 percent of value; for insurance purposes, 1.5 percent.

The firm will pay a finder's fee of 10 percent for property "we buy outright."
There is no finder's fee on consignments.

Associated Appraisers does buy and sell on its own behalf, and "is always
willing to purchase estates, collections, estate residues, libraries & other
property."

3. Astor Galleries
1 West 39th Street   Tel. (212) 921-8861/473-1658
New York, NY 10018

Founded near the beginning of the Great Depression, in 1931, this privately
held, unpretentious firm has survived hard times, war, and urban renewal. It
was forced out of its original quarters at Astor Place in downtown New York
City at the beginning of 1979, when the owner of those quarters decided that
new apartments were worth more than a veteran auction saleroom. Astor relocated to its present quarters, across the street from Lord & Taylor, in March
1979.

Astor Galleries, part of whose management is now second generation, is a
good, middle-rank auction house, most of whose consignments are relatively
inexpensive. The house is intelligently run and its owners are not afraid to
take a chance. Astor has, for example, run a sale of firehouse memorabilia.
The house tries to be "flexible" with bidders and consignors. Sales are approximately every 3 weeks.

Cataloguing is minimal (e.g., "Louis XV Petite Three Drawer Commode"),
lots must be viewed; estimates are not given; prices are relatively low. Since
1976, bidding has been done with a numbered paddle. Prior to a sale, you
register at the front desk and in return for a $2 deposit receive a paddle, with
which you bid. The deposit is refundable, of course, whether or not you purchase a lot.

Contact persons: Joseph Liebson/Ralph Levy

Days/hours of operation: Mon.–Fri. 9 A.M.–5 P.M.

Areas in which general auctions and special sales are held:

Americana	Paintings
Clocks and Watches	Prints
Furniture	Porcelain
Glass	Silver

Sales are advertised in the *New York Times* and in the trade press, such as *Antiques and the Arts Weekly*.

Catalogues are not available by subscription but are available singly for each sale, upon written request with a self-addressed stamped envelope, or at the auction house.

Usual viewing procedure: Exhibition is usually 2 weekdays before the sale, during regular business hours.

Bidder Information

Most sales are held on premises, but Astor does hold house sales.

The buyer's premium, which was instituted in 1979, is 10 percent.

Accounts must be settled within 3 days of sale; a 25 percent purchase deposit in cash, at the time of sale, is generally requested if the bidder is unknown to the house. Credit cards are not accepted.

Mail order bids are accepted, but the item should have been inspected previously by the bidder.

Astor does not offer guarantees of authenticity: "ALL GOODS SOLD AS IS." Astor will "cancel any purchase if the catalogue statement is incorrect."

The house offers packing and shipping services, at the buyer's expense.

State and local sales tax: 8 percent.

Consignor Information

Persons wishing to consign property should write, enclosing photographs and a description. There is no minimum value for acceptance.

Consignor commissions are 10 percent of the hammer price for items fetching $500 and over, 15 percent for those under $500. The terms on very-high-value items are negotiable.

Commissions are negotiable; there is a lesser rate for institutions.

Consignors do not pay for catalogue illustrations, warehousing, or insurance. They do pay for packing and shipping of the consigned property.

Reserves are not accepted. The buy-in cost is "negotiable."

Consignments from dealers are not accepted.

Appraisal service is available: "The cost is flexible" and should be negotiated.

Astor buys and sells on its own behalf: "We ... actively compete on any estates for sale."

4. Auctions by Theriault
P.O. Box 174   Tel. (717) 945-3041
Waverly, PA 18471

Only dolls are auctioned by the Theriaults. Sales are held once a month, except in July, August, and December, at various locations in the United States. Usually they are held at easily accessible locations in metropolitan areas, but away from the downtown sections. Thus sales have been held at the Sheraton Inn, Newark International Airport, and at the Dulles Marriott Inn, Dulles International Airport (between Baltimore and Washington). Sales, which begin at 11 A.M., tend to be 2-day affairs.

The catalogues are splendidly and fully illustrated. Indeed, during 1980, an exhibition—"Photography and the Doll"—sponsored by the Theriaults and made up in the main of photographs used to illustrate their catalogues, traveled across the United States. The catalogue descriptions are full (and interesting); however, estimates are not included.

The Theriaults have evolved a fascinating and useful auction tool: the Gold Horse Guarantee. It is extended to what the catalogue describes as "only the most special items"; these are so designated because of "their singularity and/or fine condition, regardless of their monetary value." The Gold Horse Guarantee, usually extended to about 5 percent of the lots in any auction, was developed by the Theriaults to "promote investor interest and buyer confidence." According to the terms outlined in each catalogue: "Auctions by Theriault will guarantee to the original purchaser . . . after 90 days . . . the full purchase price paid. . . . This guarantee may be consummated by outright reimbursement of purchase price, or by full credit toward purchases at future auctions."

At each auction there are some lots that fetch thousands of dollars, but most dolls sell for much less. Typical is the 1980 auction where the most expensive lot sold for $8,000, but nearly half of the over 300 lots went for $250 or less. The firm reports an annual turnover in excess of $1 million.

Contact persons: George and Florence Theriault

Days/hours of operation: Mon.–Fri. 8:30 A.M.–5 P.M.

Area in which special sales are held: Dolls

Sales are advertised regularly in the local press of the area where the sale is to be held and in specialty periodicals, such as *Antiques World*. To be placed on the mailing list for announcements of sales free of charge, write to the Theriaults.

Catalogues are available singly for each auction at the sale and by order ($12–$13). There is also a standing order plan by which you will receive catalogues as they are issued, and the cost includes "prices realized," which sells separately for $2.

Usual viewing procedure: On the day of the auction, a 2-hour preview.

Bidder Information

All sales are held off premises.

There is no buyer's premium. All accounts must be settled immediately following the auction. Absentee bidders must pay immediately after receipt of invoice. The firm charges a $5 handling fee per lot for such bids. Credit cards accepted: MasterCard, Visa. Payment must be with credit card, cash, or certified check. Bidders must register before the auction.

The firm offers buyers packing and shipping services.

Absentee bids are executed, but as the catalogue points out, "in the case of identical final bids from attending bidder and absentee bidder, preference will be given to attending bidder."

There is no guarantee of authenticity, but the firm does "guarantee the catalogue descriptions of each and every one of the dolls included in our catalogues. If the doll does not fit the catalogue description we will accept a return."

State sales tax: 6 percent.

Consignor Information

Prospective consignors should write to the firm and include Polaroid pictures if possible, as well as any information found on the back of the doll's head.

Commission is 25 percent.

Consignors do not pay for catalogue illustrations, warehousing, insurance, or packing and shipping.

Consigned items are usually sold within 2 months. Settlement is made after 30 days.

Reserves are not accepted.

There is no charge for buy-ins: "We have not had this happen."

Appraisal service is available: "Costs are determined by needs."

Auctions by Theriault belongs to the National Auctioneers Association and the American Society of Appraisers.

The firm does buy and sell on its own behalf.

5. Barridoff Galleries

242 Middle Street   Tel. (207) 772-5011
Portland, ME 04101

Rob and Annette Elowitch began Barridoff Galleries in 1976 as a retail operation selling European and American art. The establishment of Barridoff and its subsequent history reads like an engaging Horatio Alger story. Husband and wife return to Maine after living in New York City; he becomes dissatisfied with his role in the family business; they open an art gallery and succeed dramatically; interested in enlarging the scope of their business—which, although sophisticated and profitable, is very much a "mom and pop" affair—

the Elowitches decide to initiate art auctions, and these do very well also. The story is not yet finished, but the outcome promises to be glowing.

Barridoff Galleries, which began holding auctions in 1979, is located in a pleasant brick building, all four floors of which are given over to the business: first floor, modern art; second floor, pre-20th-century art; third floor, framing and offices; fourth floor, storage. For the thrice-yearly auctions, the lots to be sold are exhibited on the first and second floors; sales are held on the first floor, which has space to accommodate more than 100 people.

Bidding is by numbered card. Bidders register before a sale. About 100–500 lots are put up for auction. There are in each sale a few very expensive items, but the bulk of the lots sell for between $900 and $2,500. Sales are usually held on Saturday evenings.

Contact persons: Annette and Rob Elowitch

Days/hours of operation: Mon.–Sat. 10 A.M.–5 P.M.

Areas in which general auctions and special sales are held:

> Paintings
>   19th c. European
>   Early 20th c. American

Sales are advertised regularly in newspapers (both locally and elsewhere) and in the trade press. Barridoff also mails announcements of forthcoming sales to anyone who requests placement on the mailing list.

Catalogues are not available by subscription but can be obtained singly for each sale (the cost is approximately $10), either through mail order or at the house.

Usual viewing procedure: Exhibition is on the day of the sale, 10 A.M.–5 P.M.

Bidder Information

All auctions are held on the premises.

The buyer's premium is 10 percent.

Buyer must settle accounts upon receipt of goods, usually at conclusion of sale.

Mail order bids are executed. "All items are sold 'as is' and requests for refunds will only be considered on the grounds of authenticity . . . within 15 days of the auction and must be supported by the written testimony of at least two recognized experts in the field with respect to the specific artist involved."

The house offers packing and shipping services, at the buyer's expense.

State sales tax: 5 percent.

Consignor Information

Potential consignors can request an appointment for the paintings to be viewed, or, upon receiving permission to do so, can ship them to the gallery.

Commissions generally are 10 percent and are not negotiable.

Consignors pay for color illustrations in the catalogue, but not for black-and-white ones. Consignors are not charged for packing, shipping, or warehousing of their property, but are charged for insurance.
Settlement is made within 2 weeks of the auction.
"Reasonable reserves are accepted in certain very specific instances."
A buy-in costs the consignor 10 percent plus insurance during storage.

Appraisal service is available; the cost is $25 per hour "if we have to make a house call; otherwise, free of charge."

Barridoff Galleries belongs to the Maine Antique Dealers Association.

6. Berman's Auction and Appraisal Service
75 Bassett Highway   Tel. (201) 361-3110
Dover, NJ 07801

Edward Berman has been in the auction business in New Jersey since the middle 1950s. He started with a small saleroom in Union, moved to bigger quarters in Hanover, and then settled in a large converted barn in Dover, which was popularly called "Berman's Barn." It, too, proved too small and Berman moved to the firm's current facility, which provides more than 10,000 square feet of space and has a seating capacity of nearly 400.

Berman holds sales 3–4 times a month, mostly on his premises on Saturdays, though some are on-site estate sales. The energetic Berman advertises that "our phones are open 24 hours a day and if you leave a message with the answering service we try to return your call within the hour." A specialty of the house is American art pottery.

Contact person: Edward Berman

Days/hours of operation: "Available 7 days a week"

Areas in which general auctions and special sales are held:

Clocks and Watches	Jewelry
Coins	Paintings
Etchings	Old Master
Furniture	Modern Art
Glass	Pottery

Sales are advertised regularly in the local press, newspapers such as the *New York Times,* and trade outlets such as *Antiques News* and *Antiques and the Arts Weekly.* There is no charge to be placed on the mailing list for announcements of forthcoming sales.
Catalogues are not available by subscription but can be obtained at a sale ("no charge").
Usual viewing procedure: Exhibition is from 10 A.M. until the sale begins.

Bidder Information
Sales are held both on and off the premises.

The house has a buyer's premium of 10 percent, instituted in June 1980. Credit cards are not accepted. Credit terms are not available. Accounts must be settled on the day of the auction.

The house will accept mail order bids and will provide packing and shipping services, at the buyer's expense.

The house will accept return of goods within 13 days if "verification" makes that necessary.

State sales tax: 5 percent.

Consignor Information

Prospective consignors should call or write and "set up an appointment."

There is no minimum value for acceptance of consignment.

Consignor's commission: 15 percent on any item from $1 to $50; 10 percent on any item from $51 to $500; 6 percent on any item over $501.

The commission is negotiable in "special situations."

Consigned property is usually sold within "maximum 30 days" and settlement is within 14 days.

Reserves are accepted. "All property will be sold subject to a reserve determined by Berman's in its absolute discretion. If this reserve is not met, there will be no charge to seller except for furniture, which will be $25. *No* reserves will be accepted under $200."

Berman's Auction and Appraisal Service belongs to various trade organizations, including the National Auctioneers Association, the New Jersey Society of Auctioneers, and the American Cut Glass Association.

Appraisal service is available: "Minimum $25; maximum usually $200."

The firm buys and sells on its own behalf: "We do at times purchase outright."

Butterfield & Butterfield

7.   1244 Sutter Street   Tel. (415) 673-1362
         San Francisco, CA 94109

8.   660 Third Street
         San Francisco, CA 94103

In the years from its founding in 1865 to the end of the 1960s, Butterfield & Butterfield had developed into a somewhat staid, stuffy, northern California auction house of some reputation but with little drive. In 1970, new owners (a private corporation) bought control and began to remake the firm. It has become a house marked by energy and has been staffed by an aggressive, ambitious, hardworking crew of young men and women who have created new buyers' and sellers' markets for Butterfield & Butterfield. A recent innovation is the use of videotape and colored slides to illustrate to buyers during an auction what's for sale. This speeds up the proceedings.

The auction house is no longer content with just serving northern California and has reached out to the east and north. Representative offices have been established in Portland, OR [P.O. Box 966, zip 97207, tel. (503) 223-4273], Kent, WA [P.O. Box 5506, zip 98031, tel. (206) 631-0500], Santa Barbara, CA [P.O. Box 2311, zip 93101, tel. (805) 969-3087], and Pacific Groves, CA [P.O. Box 330, zip 93950, tel. (408) 372-7495]. The representatives solicit consignments, explain the philosophy of the auction house to buyer and seller, assist in bidding, etc.

Sales are held every Tuesday and Wednesday; sessions are at 10 A.M. and 1 P.M. Most auctions are 2-day affairs of 4 sessions. The sales are held alternatively, one week at Sutter Street and one week at Third Street, the latter an extensively renovated large warehouse put into operation in 1980, to facilitate fast turnover of less valuable merchandise, sold in either mixed lots or specialized sales. The Sutter Street operation remains the venue for more traditional quality mixed-lot or specialty merchandise. During 1980, the annual turnover exceeded $10 million and an average of 2,500 lots was sold every 2 weeks.

Contact persons: John Gallo/Peter Fairbanks

Days/hours of operation: Mon.–Fri. 9 A.M.–5 P.M.

Areas in which general auctions and special sales are held (incl. some contact people):

Arms and Armor (Robert Haynes)	Paintings
	18th c. British
Books (Piers McKenzie)	19th c. European (Eleanor Notides)
Chinese Works of Art (Boris Benado)	Pre-20th c. American (B. A. Osher)
Coins	Porcelain
Furniture	Pre-Columbian Art
Glass (John Gallo)	Rugs (Paul Novak)
Japanese Works of Art (Boris Benado)	Silver
Jewelry (Denise Highet)	Toys
Netsuke (Boris Benado)	Victoriana

Sales are advertised regularly in the local press and in specialty periodicals.
Announcements of sales are mailed on a monthly basis; there is no charge to be placed on the mailing list.
Catalogues for each sale are available at the house or by mail order, at $5–$10. Catalogues are also available by subscription: all catalogues cost approximately $185 in 1979–80; by category—general merchandise, $60; Oriental auctions, $30; special painting auctions, $25; silver and jewelry, $35; carpets and tapestries, $35.
Usual viewing procedure: Exhibition is 2 or 3 days before the sale, depending on the quality and quantity of the lots (Saturday, 10 A.M.–5 P.M.; Sunday, noon–5 P.M.; Monday, 9 A.M.–7 P.M.).

Bidder Information

All auctions are held on premises.

A buyer's premium was instituted in 1978 and is 10 percent. Accounts must
be settled within 5 days of sale. Credit cards are not accepted. Mail
order bids are executed. Successful absentee bids are not acknowledged;
the bidder "should telephone the following day to confirm auction
results."
All goods are sold "as is," but the house does offer buyers the opportunity
within 30 days to return goods that prove to be not as catalogued: "We
stand behind our catalogue descriptions."
The house offers packing and shipping services at buyer's expense.
State and local sales tax: 6.5 percent.

Consignor Information

Persons wishing to consign properties should contact the house. The minimum
value for a consignment, be it a single item or a group of objects, is
$500.
Consignor's commission is as follows: 10 percent on lots over $500, 15 percent
for lots $100–$500, 25 percent for lots under $100.
Consignors do not pay for warehousing, but do pay for insurance, packing and
shipping, and illustrations in catalogue. Costs for insurance are 0.75 percent of selling price. Costs for illustrations are $50 for black-and-white
photos, $250 for color.
Reserves are accepted. If buy-in is result of a reserve suggested by Butterfield
& Butterfield, there is no charge; otherwise, charge is 5 percent of
reserve.
Consigned goods are usually sold within 30–60 days; settlement is after 21
days.
Commission rates are negotiable, depending on the situation.

Butterfield & Butterfield pays a finder's fee of 5 percent of the selling price.

Appraisal service is available: cost is 1.5 percent of the first $50,000 and 1
percent of the balance.
The house does buy and sell on its own behalf: "Less than 2 percent of the
items marketed."

9.   California Book Auction Galleries

358 Golden Gate Avenue   Tel. (415) 775-0424
San Francisco, CA 94102   Cable: BOOKS, S.F.

Branch office (part time):
1749 North La Brea Avenue   Tel. (213) 850-0424
Hollywood, CA 90046

Despite its name, California Book Auction Galleries sells more than books.
Once or twice a year, California Book holds print and graphics sales. And
manuscripts, autographs, maps, etchings, engravings, and photography are
frequently included in the book auctions. The house prides itself on its cookery
and gastronomy book sales. The flourishing of this house (which does an an-

nual turnover in excess of $400,000) in an area not noted for its devotion to the printed word is a tribute to Maurice Powers, the ambitious veteran director of the galleries' operations.

Contact persons: San Francisco—Maurice Powers
Hollywood—George Houle

Days/hours of operation: San Francisco—Mon.–Fri. 9 A.M.–5 P.M.; Sat. by appt.
Hollywood—by appt. only

Frequency of auctions: 10–12 times a year, at least once a month except August

Areas in which general auctions and special sales are held:

Autographs	Manuscripts
Books	Maps
Engravings	Photographica
Etchings	Posters
Graphics	Prints

Sales are advertised regularly in the California press (including San Francisco *Examiner* and Los Angeles *Times*), as well as in specialized magazines, such as *AB Bookman's Weekly.*

Catalogues are available singly for each sale; the price varies. Yearly subscription cost: $25 North America; $30 Europe/South America (incl. airmail postage); $35 rest of the world (incl. airmail postage). Postcard announcements are available for those who identify their special interests.

Usual viewing procedure: Exhibition begins week prior to sale, Monday–Friday, 9 A.M.–5 P.M.; Saturday hours vary.

Bidder Information

All auctions are held on premises.

The buyer's premium is 10 percent. Mail order bids are accepted. Buyer must settle when picking up goods or upon receipt of invoice, essentially within 10 days of sale. Credit cards are accepted: Visa, MasterCard.

The house guarantees items as catalogued, including authenticity where applicable. The house does its own packing and shipping, charging buyers for the service. Items that prove to be not as catalogued are accepted for full refund "without question."

State and local sales tax: 6.5 percent.

Consignor Information

Potential consignors should send a letter of inquiry indicating the nature of the material they plan to consign. If the material is appropriate, the house will ask for more information—e.g., with books, a short-title list of authors, titles, dates, and places of publication, and then will notify as to which items are acceptable. For large collections, the house will send a representative to visit. Minimum value accepted is $25–$30.

Commission structure is on a sliding scale: 30 percent on items to $100, 25 percent $100–$1,000, 20 percent $1,000–$5,000, etc. The commission is negotiable, depending on the situation.

The packing and shipping of consigned property is the consignor's responsibility. If consignors can apply already existing insurance to consigned goods, they can save on cost of insurance; otherwise, house will arrange for insurance and charge consignor. There is no charge for warehousing or for illustration in catalogue.

Settlement is made 30 days following auction.

If property is unsold, there is no charge, unless consignor insisted on a reserve, in which case the charge is 10 percent of the reserve.

Reserves are accepted.

Goods are sold 60–120 days after receipt of consignment.

Appraisal is available. The cost is $25 per hour plus travel expenses.

The house buys and sells on its own behalf: "We sometimes buy books outright and sell them through our catalogues. Often an owner is unable to wait 60–120 days for money and insists on selling right away."

10. C. B. Charles Galleries, Inc.

825 Woodward Avenue   Tel. (313) 338-9023
Pontiac, MI 48053

Although its mailing address is the unfashionable factory town of Pontiac, C. B. Charles Galleries is located on the fringes of that community not far from the posh suburb of Bloomfield Hills. Charles was organized in the early 1950s as a retail operation, but has since that time been holding auctions too. Sales are usually on weekend afternoons, 2–3 times a month, at the gallery or, if the auction is a house or estate sale, on location. The gallery sales may be both general purpose or specialized (e.g., rugs, jewelry).

One of the more unusual and successful specialized sales undertaken by C. B. Charles was the 1979 auction of the Oriental art collection of Carrie Lee. Ms. Lee (who died shortly after the auction) had for years operated a Chinese restaurant in the fashionable Detroit suburb of Birmingham. There seems to have been some disagreement about the quality of the food served there, but it was the only game in town, and did a good business. However opinions about the food differed, there was a mistaken consensus that the decor was "not much." A goodly portion of that decor, however, was made up of Ms. Lee's admirable collection, which, when sold, fetched many thousands of dollars.

All Charles sales are catalogued, except for the annual Christmas Gift Auction, just before the holiday, which gives bidders a chance to enjoy themselves at what is normally a spirited auction, while performing the onerous task of Christmas shopping.

Contact persons: C. B. Charles/Dorothy Matsel

Days/hours of operation: Mon.–Sat. 10 A.M.–4 P.M.

Areas in which general auctions and special sales are held:

Chinese Works of Art	Paintings
Furniture	18th c. British
Glass	19th c. European
Japanese Works of Art	Pre-20th c. American
Jewelry	Porcelain
Netsuke	Rugs
	Silver

Sales are advertised in local newspapers and in specialty periodicals, such as *Antiques Magazine* and *Antiques Monthly*. There is no charge for being put on the mailing list for announcements of forthcoming sales.

Catalogues are not available by subscription, but can be obtained singly for each sale either by mail or at the gallery.

Usual viewing procedure: "Exhibition hours are set according to size and scope of collection being auctioned; can vary from one day to one week."

Bidder Information

Auctions are held on the Charles Galleries' premises and on location for house and estate sales.

There is no buyer's premium. Accounts must be settled at the end of the sale "unless prior arrangements have been made." Credit cards are accepted: American Express, MasterCard, Visa.

The house offers packing and shipping services at the buyer's expense and will execute mail order bids. Charles does not offer guarantees of authenticity.

State sales tax: 4 percent.

Consignor Information

Persons interested in consigning property should contact the house in writing or by phone. No minimum value for acceptance of property.

The consignor's "commission is negotiable depending upon size and $ value of collection and any agreed-upon reimbursable expenses."

Consignors do not pay for catalogue illustrations, packing or shipping, insurance, or warehousing.

Settlement is within 45 days.

Reserves are accepted.

Buy-ins cost the consignor "only agreed upon reimbursable expenses."

Appraisal services are available; "cost depends upon location of appraisal."

C. B. Charles Galleries belongs to the National Auctioneers Association.

11. Christie's East
219 East 67th Street
New York, NY 10021

Tel. (212) 570-4141

Christie's launched its auction operations in the United States in the late 1970s. Their success made clear to management the need for a venue in New York City like Christie's South Kensington in London. "South Ken" very successfully served as a saleroom for moderately priced properties and for certain kinds of specialties, such as photographica.

The absence of such an outlet in New York created problems—not insurmountable, but problems nonetheless. For one thing, when Christie's North America accepted an entire estate, the firm would find it necessary to consign the more moderately priced properties to another New York City auction house (not Sotheby's, of course). Such a practice is not unusual in the trade, but Christie's did want to provide as full a range of integrated services in the United States as in the United Kingdom.

The result was that some 24 months after the opening of Christie's North America, the firm established Christie's East in the spring of 1979. It is located on a typical New York street, sandwiched between a TV studio and a Buddhist temple, and down the block from a glass-sheathed high-rise apartment building. Once a six-story parking garage, Christie's East has two galleries and offices on the first two floors, the rest of the building being given over to storage. The renovated public space is a fascinating blend of tasteful gray carpeting, white walls, modern business furnishings, and architectural remnants of the building's former purpose. Giant elevators that once took automobiles to overnight resting places now are used to transport a wide range of objects.

Christie's East is far from being a dumping ground. Less than 18 months after its opening, this branch could claim an annual turnover in excess of $10 million. During 1980, the average lot price was $460. And Christie's East has more than fulfilled the plans of its designers with regard not only to general sales but also to specialty auctions. These specialty sales (at which a number of world record prices have been achieved) range from designer clothes to the disposal of a collection of stuffed animals from Yale University's Peabody Museum.

The chief operating officer of Christie's East since the beginning of 1980 is J. Brian Cole. An engaging, no-nonsense Briton with considerable real estate and auction experience, he came to the United States in the mid-1970s to establish Phillips' American operations. Although Christie's East is "a secondary auction house," it is a most active one. General sales are held once or twice a month on Tuesdays, at 10 A.M. and sometimes at 2 P.M. as well. Specialty sales are held as necessary, and this proves to be quite often. Indeed, the number of specialized sales is constantly increasing. And the emphasis, under Cole's energetic direction, is away from the general toward the selective. Christie's East is even being utilized for more expensive sales that once might have taken place at the Park Avenue operation.

Occasionally the galleries on the first floor (where usually general auction sales are held) and the second floor are used simultaneously for different sales. The catalogues for the general sales are nowhere near as detailed as the ones for the specialty sales, but provide just enough information without too much detail. A new feature, begun in the fall of 1980, is that some 10 percent of the catalogue, which even with the computerized printing used by Christie's East closes about a month before the sale, is left open for items that demand a quick turnover. A special mimeographed addendum is provided for these lots, which, of course, are on view during the regular exhibition schedule.

Contact person: J. Brian Cole

Days/hours of operation: Mon.–Sat. 9 A.M.–5 P.M.

Areas in which general auctions and special sales are held (incl. some contact people):

Americana	Paintings (Ann Berman)
Art Deco	Old Master
(George Mathysen-Gerst)	17th & 18th c. British
Art Nouveau	19th c. European
(George Mathysen-Gerst)	Pre-20th c. American
Chinese Works of Art	Modern Art
(Martha Wright)	Contemporary Art
Clocks and Watches	Photographica (Dale Stulz)
Costume (Julie Collier)	Photographic Instruments
Dolls (Julie Collier)	(Dale Stulz)
Drawings (Nancy Green)	Porcelain (Anne Leighton)
Embroidery	Posters
Engravings	Pre-Columbian Art
Etchings	(Sabina Adamson)
Furniture (Phillips Hathaway)	Prints (Nancy Green)
Glass (Anne Leighton)	Rugs (George Bailey)
Islamic Art	Silver (Delphine Espy)
Jewelry (Shelley Hullar)	Toys (Julie Collier)
Musical Instruments	Vintage Cars
Netsuke (Martha Wright)	(Warren S. Cresswell)

Sales are advertised regularly in newspapers, such as the *New York Times,* and specialty periodicals, such as *Antiques and the Arts Weekly* and *Antiques Magazine.* For information about subscriptions to announcements of forthcoming sales and the quarterly newsletters, please see information listed under Christie, Manson & Woods International.

Catalogues to Christie's East general sales and specialty auctions are available at the house and by mail. The cost for general auction catalogues is usually $1 at the house and $2 by mail. The cost of the specialty auction catalogues varies from $3–$4 to $12 and up. Usually, under $10, the mailing charge is only $1; $10 or above, the mailing charge is $2 or more.

Usual viewing procedure: Exhibitions are Tuesday–Saturday 10 A.M. to 5 P.M.

and until 2 P.M. on the day preceding the sale; late viewing is possible on
Thursday until 7:30 P.M.; Monday by appointment.

General and specialty sales fit their viewing into this exhibition schedule. Thus
lots for sale at a general auction go on display from the preceding Thursday. The amount of time the lots in a specialty sale are on display depends on their quality and quantity, and ranges from a few days to a
week.

Bidder Information

Some house sales are held, but most auctions are on the premises.

The buyer's premium is 10 percent. It is not negotiable and credit cards are
not accepted. Credit is available "with arrangements; dealers may be
given up to 30 days."

Mail order bids are acceptable.

Buyers must settle accounts "within 7 days unless other arrangements are
made."

The house offers packing and shipping services at the buyer's expense.

All lots are sold "as is," but "if within 4 days after the sale Christie's has
received from the buyer . . . notice in writing that the property is a forgery and within 4 days after such notification the buyer . . . returns it to
Christie's in the same condition as when sold and within a reasonable
period thereafter satisfies Christie's that the property is a forgery . . .
then Christie's will rescind the sale and refund the purchase price."

State and local sales tax: 8 percent

Consignor Information

Prospective consignors should arrange through either the mails, the phone, or
a personal visit to have their property examined by an expert.

Consignor's commission is as follows: 15 percent on items valued at $500 or
under, 10 percent if over $500; the rate for dealers is 6 percent, and for
institutions 8 percent.

Consignors do not pay for warehousing. Consignors do pay for illustrations in
the catalogue (black and white, $30; color, by negotiation), usually pay
for insurance (unless they have own coverage) and generally pay for
shipping, although sometimes, depending on the property, shipping is
paid by Christie's East.

Consigned goods are usually sold within 3–4 weeks, and settlement is after 1
week.

Reserves are accepted; there is no buy-in charge.

Finder's fees are paid: 40 percent of the Christie's commission.

Appraisal service is available; the cost varies with the property; for information, contact the chief operating officer of Christie's East.

12. Christie, Manson & Woods International

502 Park Avenue   Tel. (212) 826-2888
New York, NY 10022   Telex: int. 620 771/dom. 710-581-2325
                                      Cable: CHRISWOODS

REPRESENTATIVE OFFICES

CALIFORNIA:
9350 Wilshire Boulevard   Tel. (213) 275-5534
Beverly Hills, CA 90212   Telex: 910-490-4652
    Donelson F. Hoopes (general manager)
    Christine Eisenberg (automobile and special sales)
    Anne Johnson
    Michael Lampon (jewelry)

FLORIDA:
225 Fern Street   Tel. (305) 833-6592
West Palm Beach, FL 33401
    Helen Stedman Cluett

MID-ATLANTIC:
638 Morris Avenue   Tel. (215) 525-5493
Bryn Mawr, PA 19010
    Paul M. Ingersoll

WASHINGTON:
1422 27th Street N.W.   Tel. (202) 965-2066
Washington, DC 20007
    David Ober

MIDWEST:
46 East Elm Street   Tel. (312) 787-2765
Chicago, IL 60611
    Frances de Brettville Blair

Will London remain the center of the international fine arts auction market or will it be displaced by New York City, which has become a center for flight capital from the non-Communist world? The establishment of a vibrant Christie's operation in North America may tip the scales in favor of the American metropolis that O. Henry called "Baghdad on the Hudson." Christie's had opened offices in the United States in 1958, but only with the establishment of the Park Avenue salerooms in the spring of 1977 did the auction house begin full-service operations in the United States.

And the results have been little short of sensational. Christie's has changed the auction scene in the United States drastically. At the end of its first (curtailed) season of operations in New York, Christie's had a turnover that was estimated in July 1977 at about $8 million. By summer 1980, when the figures for the 1979–80 season were released, Christie's had increased its turnover by 1500 percent to more than $113 million (and this sum does not take into account sales held by Christie's East, a companion operation established in

1979—see preceding entry). In less than 40 months, Christie's had become a driving force in the North American auction market, real competition to Sotheby Parke Bernet, until then the unchallenged leader. Keep in mind that turnover is not the same as profitability, but that is not the main concern here—we are interested in the fact that Christie's has become a viable alternative.

Christie's Park Avenue salerooms are located in the former Delmonico Hotel at 59th Street, cheek by jowl with the posh, snobby nightclub Regine's. Until that club adjusted its acoustics, one could occasionally hear, faintly but clearly, the beat of disco music at evening auction sessions. Christie's has the first four floors of what used to be Delmonico's and is now expensive apartments. Christie's has thoroughly and quite intelligently renovated and modernized that portion of the building it occupies. Delmonico's expansive mirrored grand ballroom is now the main saleroom, and it can hold up to 1,000 people for a major auction, or through the judicious use of partitions can easily be made smaller. There are also a smaller saleroom, two floors of exhibition space, offices and storage areas (Christie's, it should be noted, also has warehouse space elsewhere in the city). The style of the public space is attractive but subdued. You can browse here with ease.

Under the intelligent direction of David Bathurst, the president of Christie, Manson & Woods International, an able, hardworking, spirited, and generally young team of specialists and administrators hold sales Tuesdays through Saturdays. These sales may be of Oriental porcelain, or of Russian works of art, or of jewelry, or of American sculpture—all of which may be sold within the same week. Sales are usually held at 10:30 A.M. and 2 P.M. Evening sessions are scheduled only for more important sales. Rarely are tickets required for admission to any exhibition or sale. You can call (212) 371-5438 anytime, day or night, for recorded information about sales and exhibitions.

Christie's offers a wide range of services. At the front counter of the Park Avenue salerooms you can present objects for a free oral estimate of the prices they might bring at auction; where necessary, an appropriate specialist is called in to render an opinion. Christie's also takes this service to the general public in other parts of the country by offering "appraisal days." These are often held for the benefit of a local institution or charity. The only costs to the sponsor are the travel expenses of the Christie's specialists. The appraisal fee, usually a nominal $5 per item, is donated by Christie's to the sponsoring institution. And more often than you might think, an object brought in for appraisal finds its way to the auction floor, perhaps after years of neglect.

In its promotional literature, Christie's—with some justification—boasts about being "the world's most experienced auction house in holding house sales." It has with considerable success conducted such sales for years in Ireland, Scotland, and England, and such ventures have also proved successful in the U.S. Indeed, in one of its first international house sales, in 1978, Christie, Manson & Woods sold the contents of Ravenscliff—the estate of the late Charlotte Dorrance Wright in St. Davids, Pa., a suburb of Philadelphia on the Main Line—for approximately $1.9 million, setting what was then a record for American house sales.

Christie, Manson & Woods International has built an impressive record in the United States in only a few years. The firm has established some world price records, as in the May 1980 sale in which $25.5 million was realized for a single sale of works of art. But the bulk of the lots sell for much less than might be expected. As David Bathurst told the *New York Times* in July 1980: "While we sold several pictures for more than $1,000,000, the average price fetched per lot was $4,000, a clear indication of the broad range of our services."

In addition to its New York salerooms on Park Avenue and at Christie's East the firm has established representative offices in various parts of the United States. This network of "qualified representatives" (to use Christie's words) is designed to "assist potential buyers and sellers and to facilitate clients' business with the New York salerooms and with Christie's auction galleries around the world." Each of these representatives can "offer advice on appraisals, on consigning objects for sale, and on bidding by mail or phone."

Contact person: Elizabeth Shaw (she is in charge of public relations and she or one of her staff can direct you to the proper person within the large staff employed by Christie's)

Days/hours of operation: Mon.–Sat. 10 A.M.–5 P.M.; closed Sat. in July and August

Areas in which general auctions and special sales are held (incl. some contact people):

Americana (Dean Failey)
Art Deco
    (Nancy McClelland)
Art Nouveau
    (Alastair Duncan)
Autographs
    (Stephen Massey)
Books (Stephen Massey)
Chinese Works of Art
    (Anthony Derham)
Clocks and Watches
    (Winthrop Edey)
Dolls
Drawings (Susan Seidel)
Engravings
Etchings
Furniture (American,
    Dean Failey;
    European, E. Charles Beyer)
Glass
    (Victor Bernreuther)
Japanese Works of Art
    (Anthony Derham)

Jewelry (François Curiel;
    Alison Bradshaw)
Judaica
Manuscripts
    (Stephen Massey)
Medieval Works of Art
Musical Instruments
    (Charles Rudig)
Netsuke
    (Anthony Derham)

Paintings
  Old Master
    (Ian G. Kennedy)
  17th c. British
  18th c. British
  19th c. European
    (Henry M. Wyndham)
  Pre-20th c. American
    (Jay E. Cantor)
  Impressionist
    (Christopher Burge)
  Modern Art
    (Christopher Burge)
  Contemporary Art
    (Martha Baer)

Porcelain (Victor Bernreuther)
Posters
Pre-Columbian Art
  (David Crownover)
Prints
  (Nicholas G. Stogdon)
Rugs (George Bailey)
Russian Art
  (Bronislaw N. Dvorsky)
Sculpture (Alice E. Levi)
Silver
  (Anthony M. Phillips)

Sales are advertised regularly in the national press, such as the *New York Times,* and in specialty periodicals, such as *Antiques Monthly.* A monthly preview of all Christie's sales everywhere in the world is available on subscription ($36); *News from Christie's,* a quarterly newsletter detailing forthcoming sales as well as other information, is available for $2 a year in the U.S. and $3 elsewhere (subscribers to Christie's catalogues receive the newsletter free of charge). To subscribe to either the preview or the newsletter, write Faith Wolf, Catalogue Department, 141 East 25th Street, New York, NY 10010.

Catalogues for each sale are available at the house and by mail. The price varies with the sale ($5–$20). A subscription to all Christie's Park Avenue catalogues costs approximately $750 (including a 10 percent reduction in price for a "block subscription"). You can also subscribe to all catalogues of any special subject, such as art nouveau and art deco ($55).

Usual viewing procedure: Exhibition is usually 5 days prior to the sale, 10 A.M.–5 P.M. Tuesday–Saturday; Monday by appointment.

Bidder Information

Most sales are held on premises, but Christie's does hold on-site house and estate sales.

The buyer's premium is 10 percent of the hammer price. Credit cards are not acceptable. Credit is available "by special arrangement." Buyer must settle accounts 7–10 days after the auction; the trade has 30 days.

Absentee bids are executed.

Christie's "warrants for a period of six years from the date of sale that any article in this catalogue unqualifiedly stated to be the work of a named author or authorship is authentic and not counterfeit. The term 'author' or 'authorship' refers to the creator of the article or to the period, culture, source, or origin, as the case may be. . . . The buyer's sole remedy under this warranty shall be the rescission of the sale and refund of the

original purchase price paid for the article." Despite the limitations expressed in this warranty, Christie's in effect does offer guarantees of authenticity and does stand ready to offer refunds for lots that prove to be not as described.
State and local sales tax: 8 percent.

Consignor Information

Interested persons should bring in objects or write. Objects to be auctioned are evaluated and terms discussed with the consignor before a contract is signed.
The standard consignor's commission is 10 percent of the hammer price over $500 and 15 percent of the hammer price $500 and under. The commission is negotiable, depending on the situation.
Consignors are charged for catalogue illustrations, insurance, packing and shipping, and warehousing. The firm reports "all charges and terms are stated in contract which consignor signs—all terms can be negotiated."
The length of time before consigned goods are sold is "variable."
Settlement is 35 days after the sale.
Reserves are accepted. If there should be a buy-in, "all costs paid by consignor—negotiable."
There is a separate rate structure for dealers (6 percent of hammer price over $500, 9 percent $500 and under) and institutions (8 percent of hammer price over $500, 12 percent $500 and under).

13. Clements

P.O. Box 727   Tel. (214) 226-1520/3044
I-20 East at FM Road 740 exit
Forney, TX 75126

Located just "20 minutes East of Dallas," Clements of Texas began in the early 1970s as a retail operation and as an outgrowth of Clements Antiques of Tennessee (see *Northgate Gallery*). The Texas operation started holding occasional auctions in 1976, and since then has developed to the point where auction sales are held the second Saturday and Sunday of each month.

As with the Tennessee operation, Clements of Texas is family run. And Charles W. Clements has a large family; the directors of the burgeoning Texas operation are his three sons-in-law.

This firm sells properties that, in the words of a company spokesman, are "of investment value in the art world." Each sale is catalogued and these catalogues are available at the saleroom free of charge at the time of the auction. In addition, the house produces a slick, colorful, and interesting brochure which illustrates the highlights of a given sale (it is from this brochure that many of the firm's absentee bids come).

The firm being in Texas, one certainly can expect that people would fly in for the auction, and so they do, although the bulk of the bidders come from the Dallas–Fort Worth area. However, the firm gets consignments where it can and these come from all over the country, even from New York. Each month, about 600 lots are sold over the sale weekend.

Contact person: Norman Garrett

Days/hours of operation: Mon.–Fri. 9 A.M.–5 P.M.

Areas in which general auctions and special sales are held:

Art Deco	Furniture	Porcelain
Art Nouveau	Glass	Prints
Chinese Works of Art	Jewelry	Rugs
Clocks and Watches	Paintings	Silver

Sales are advertised regularly in daily newspapers in the Dallas–Fort Worth area, and in trade publications, such as *Antiques Monthly.*

Catalogues for each sale are available at the house at the time of the auction, free of charge. An illustrated brochure presenting highlights of a forthcoming sale is obtainable at an annual subscription cost of $18 for 1 year, $30 for 2 years, $36 for 3 years. The cost is refundable "in the form of credit toward any future purchases at a Clements Auction."

Usual viewing procedure: Exhibition is the Thursday (9 A.M.–9 P.M.) and Friday (9 A.M.–5 P.M.) preceding the sale, as well as 2–3 hours before it begins.

Bidder Information

Sales are held on the premises of Clements and also on site for house sales.

There is no buyer's premium. Buyer must pay local taxes unless exempt. Credit cards are accepted: MasterCard, Visa, American Express. Mail order bids are acceptable. Accounts must be settled at once.

Clements does not offer packing or shipping services or guarantees of authenticity. Returns will be considered only if the catalogue has inadvertently contained a blatant misrepresentation.

State and local sales tax: 5 percent.

Consignor Information

Those wishing to consign property should contact Clements by phone or in writing.

The consignor's commission is negotiable, depending on the situation. There is no minimum value for goods to be accepted.

Consignors do not pay for catalogue illustrations, insurance, or warehousing, but do pay for packing and shipping of consigned property.

Consigned goods are usually sold within 30–60 days, and settlement is within 1 week.

Clements does buy and sell on its own behalf.

Appraisal service is available; contact Clements for cost.

14. William Doyle Galleries, Inc.
175 East 87th Street   Tel. (212) 427-2730
New York, NY 10028

The saga of Doyle Galleries reads like one of the better manifestations of the American Dream. At the beginning of the 1970s, Bill Doyle, then in his early thirties, ran a profitable but small retail operation—one of many such operations—on a side street on the Upper East Side of Manhattan. Then, supplementing his capital with small sums borrowed from more than 35 people, he established an auction house in 1973. Since then, Doyle, who no longer has a retail operation, has flourished as an auctioneer. In 1980, the house's gross was estimated to be in excess of $15 million. Doyle Galleries has a good reputation and an eager, youngish staff. Furniture remains an important part of Doyle's operation, but paintings have begun to play a significant role. The firm estimates that "in our current fiscal year we will have sold more than three million dollars' worth of paintings, representing approximately 2,000 individual canvases, with several paintings exceeding $50,000."

Since 1973, Doyle Galleries has been located in an old-fashioned, nondescript building which has begun to undergo extensive renovations. Some thought had been given to moving from 87th Street, but the ultimate decision was to remain and renovate. And 87th Street, while not overflowing with charm, has at least one other site besides Doyle Galleries worth a look: taking up a good quarter of the block and diametrically opposite the auction house is a splendid six-story art nouveau parking garage.

Doyle Galleries holds sales every two weeks on Wednesday, except during the summer, when sales are held a bit less frequently. Bidding is done with numbered paddles, received at the front desk after registration. There is no paddle deposit, but bidders unknown to the house whose identification is less than superb may be asked to pay a 25 percent deposit on the hammer price during the sale, this sum to be in the form of cash or certified check.

Prices achieved at these sales vary considerably. At a recent painting sale, a few of the 165 lots went for more than $10,000 and a few for less than $1,000. Most sold for between $2,000 and $8,000. At furniture sales, the price range tends to be narrower and less expensive. In addition to holding sales on its premises, Doyle Galleries runs a significant number of house sales. Recently and with some success, Doyle has begun to hold "discovery days" in New England, where thousands of dollars' worth of items are appraised (many are consigned ultimately to Doyle Galleries), some of which the firm purchases outright ($20,000 changed hands in one 1980 Connecticut session) and later places at auction.

Contact person: William J. Doyle

Days/hours of operation: Mon.–Fri. 8 A.M.–6 P.M.

Areas in which general auctions and special sales are held (incl. some contact people):

Americana (Jeffrey Werner)
Arms and Armor
Chinese Works of Art
Clocks and Watches
Dolls
Drawings, all periods (Susan Powell)
Furniture (Wendy Gold)
Glass
Japanese Works of Art
Jewelry (Wendy Carhart)

Paintings (Susan Powell)
   Old Master
   17th c. British
   18th c. British
   19th c. European
   Pre-20th c. American
Pewter
Porcelain
Prints
   18th–20th c.
Rugs
Silver

Sales are advertised in the local and international press, as well as in many trade journals. Write to be put on the mailing list for announcements free of charge.

Catalogues are not available by subscription, but can be obtained singly for each sale, either by mail order or at the house.

Usual viewing procedure: Exhibitions are held for 4 days before the sale (Saturday 10 A.M.–5 P.M.; Sunday noon–5 P.M.; Monday 9 A.M.–7:30 P.M.; Tuesday 9 A.M.–5 P.M.).

Bidder Information

In addition to sales held on its premises, Doyle Galleries also runs numerous house sales.

The buyer's premium is 10 percent. The New York sales tax of 8 percent will be charged on the invoiced price (i.e., hammer price plus premium) unless the buyer has an exemption or a resale number. Credit cards are not accepted.

Settlement must be made by the end of the day after the sale.

The house offers packing and shipping services at the buyer's expense.

"Every lot is sold 'as is' and without recourse." Doyle Galleries "is not held responsible for the correctness of the description, genuineness or authenticity of any lot, and no sale will be set aside on account of incorrectness, error of cataloguing or any imperfection not noted."

State and local sales tax: 8 percent.

Consignor Information

Persons wishing to consign property should contact the house.

The basic commission rate is 10 percent. It is negotiable, "depending on the consignment."

The minimum value for a consignment, of however many items, is $1,000. Consignments from dealers are not accepted.

Consignors are not charged for catalogue illustrations, insurance, warehousing, or packing and shipping.

Reserves are accepted.

The cost of a buy-in to a consignor "varies on situation."

How long before consigned goods are sold "varies on the type of object."

Settlement is made within 10 business days.

Appraisal service is available; the cost is hourly and varies.

Doyle Galleries buys and sells on its own behalf: "we purchase outright as well as take on consignment." Indeed, much of what Doyle sells has been purchased outright from estates, dealers, etc., as well as at its "discovery days." At the end of the summer 1980 Doyle Galleries opened a representative office on the West Coast, staffed by a local person active in the fine arts and appraisal fields there:

Howard Zellman
Suite 205
8380 Melrose Avenue   Tel. (213) 653-1424
Los Angeles, CA 90069

15. DuMochelle Art Galleries
409 East Jefferson   Tel. (313) 963-6255
Detroit, MI 48226

Detroit, a city once described as "a desert of cars and bars," has proved to have few lasting institutions. DuMochelle, however, can lay claim to being one of these. Located in the same six-story building since 1927, this family-dominated business has served generations of Motor City families, who have been both bidders and consignors. The firm is in fact a landmark to many Midwesterners, who have bought and sold there. Its operations have been enhanced by the fact that Detroit's innovative attempt at urban renewal, the prestigious Renaissance Center, was built in the late 1970s just a few hundred feet away from the galleries.

Auction sales are held at the DuMochelle Galleries once a month, usually on the third weekend, on Friday night and Saturday and Sunday afternoons. During these 3- or 4-session sales, well over 1,000 varied lots are generally sold. DuMochelle also holds specialized sales (e.g., jewelry or books), as well as house and estate sales.

The cavernous first-floor saleroom, with its balcony (an ideal roost to use for spotting friends and bidders), is used for auctions. The rest of the building is given over to offices, storage, and DuMochelle's retail operations. Once a year, usually in July, DuMochelle holds a flea market to clear out all the unsellable odds and ends that have accumulated during the preceding 12 months. Valet parking is available and useful, since Detroit is not a city known for public transit. Given its location, DuMochelle, which is less than 20 minutes from Grosse Pointe and the fancy apartment complexes that have sprung up along the lakeshore, attracts many people from those areas to auction sales. But clever residents of such suburbs to the west of the city as Birmingham and Bloomfield Hills also find their way to DuMochelle with some regularity.

Contact person: Niki Konas

Days/hours of operation: Mon.–Sat. 9:30 A.M.–5:30 P.M.

Areas in which general auctions and specialized sales are held (incl. some contact people):

Americana	Furniture
Art Deco	Japanese Works of Art (Ernest
Art Nouveau	DuMochelle)
Books	Jewelry
Bronzes (Mary Joe Caleal)	Paintings (Lawrence DuMochelle)
Chinese Works of Art	Porcelain (Mary Joe Caleal)
(Ernest DuMochelle)	Rugs (Lawrence DuMochelle)
Coins	Silver
Etchings (Richard Federowicz)	Toys

Sales are advertised locally in the Detroit newspapers and nationally in publications such as *Antiques Monthly, Connoisseur,* and *Antiques and the Arts Weekly.* Announcements of forthcoming sales are sent free of charge to persons who request placement on the mailing list.

Catalogues are available singly for each sale ($4 postpaid) or by subscription ($20 yearly for all catalogues).

Usual viewing procedure: "Previewing commences exactly seven days before the auction and is maintained during regular store hours."

Bidder Information

Sales are held on the premises or on site for house and estate sales.

There is no buyer's premium. Buyers must settle accounts within one week of sale. Credit cards are accepted: American Express, MasterCard, Visa. Sales tax must be paid unless buyer is exempt.

Mail order bids are executed: "a deposit check, 25 percent of the total bid, is required."

DuMochelle's offers packing and shipping, at the buyer's expense. The house also reports that "when we have certificates, etc., of authenticity, we do offer clients these documents."

State sales tax: 4 percent.

Consignor Information

Those interested in consigning should "call and describe merchandise, or write, sending description, preferably with photograph." Minimum value $25.

The standard commission for consignors is 25 percent, but it is negotiable, "depending on the individual situation."

Consignors pay for packing and shipping, but not for insurance, catalogue illustrations, or warehousing.

Goods consigned are "normally" sold within 1–3 months and settlement is made usually 30 days after sale.

Reserves are accepted, and the cost for buy-ins is cartage and "any cleaning, refinishing, etc., involved."

The house does buy and sell on its own behalf.

Trade association memberships include the American Society of Appraisers.

16. John C. Edelmann Galleries, Inc.

123 East 77th Street   Tel. (212) 628-1700/1735
New York, NY 10021

Edelmann Galleries—"America's only auction house specializing in rare Rugs, Tapestries and Textiles"—was established in 1979. John C. Edelmann, in his mid-thirties, had resigned his position as head of Parke Bernet's rug department because he wanted to run his own show. He has done so with some verve.

Sales are usually held on Saturday afternoons; Edelmann experimented with weekday evenings, but found them a bit awkward. Sales are in effect run on a two-tier level, with the catalogue furnishing a guide to the quality of the sale. Six to 7 sales a year are held without formal catalogues, and while the lots are interesting, the prices generally are low. Another 6–7 sales are held each year for which elaborate, marvelously illustrated, glossy-paper catalogues are issued; lots offered are of a very different quality and price.

The saleroom is conveniently located less than 10 steps from a subway station, and next to a very fancy butcher. Indeed, the location, across from a hospital, is in a way incongruous, but the saleroom is spacious and light, and is a fine venue for both exhibitions and sales.

Contact person: John C. Edelmann

Days/hours of operation: Mon.–Fri. 9 A.M.–5 P.M.

Areas in which sales are held:

     Books (about rugs and textiles, etc.)
     Rugs
     Textiles

Sales are advertised regularly in newspapers, such as the *Wall Street Journal* and the *New York Times,* as well as in specialty periodicals, such as *Antiques Magazine, Connoisseur*, and *Antiques and the Arts Weekly.*

Catalogues are available singly at the house and by mail order ($12 U.S., $13 elsewhere), as well as by subscription for the more important sales ($100 U.S., $120 elsewhere); price lists are sent to subscribers. Mimeographed or otherwise informal catalogues are available at the house for other sales.

Usual viewing procedure: Exhibition is usually for a week before the sale (Monday–Friday 10 A.M.–7:30 P.M.; Saturday 10 A.M.–6 P.M.; Sunday noon–5 P.M.)

Bidder Information

All auctions are held on the premises.

The buyer's premium is 10 percent. Buyers must settle accounts within 1 week after the auction. Credit cards are not accepted.

Mail order bids are executed.

Packing and shipping services are offered, at the buyer's expense.

The house warns that "Bidders should personally inspect all property to determine its origin, age, condition, size, and whether or not it has been repaired or restored . . . all property is sold 'as is.' "

State and local sales tax: 8 percent.

Consignor Information

Prospective consignors should "either send us a photo or bring in property." No minimum value on property accepted.

Commissions for dealers are 6 percent on lots sold under $500, 10 percent on lots sold for $500 and above; for all others, the consignor's commission is 10 percent.

Consignors are not charged for packing and shipping of property nor for its warehousing. Consignors are charged for catalogue illustrations (black and white: $50 half page, $100 full page; color: $100 half page, $400 full page). And consignors are charged for insurance on consigned property.

Commissions are negotiable, depending on the situation. There is a separate rate for institutions, as for dealers (see above).

Reserves are accepted.

The length of time it takes for goods consigned to be sold "depends on what type of sale pieces are going into. Could be two weeks or two months." Settlement is made after 2 weeks, "providing lots have been paid for."

John C. Edelmann Galleries does buy and sell on its own behalf.

Appraisal service is available; the minimum fee is $100. For terms and conditions, contact the galleries.

17   Robert C. Eldred Co., Inc.

Box 796   Tel. (617) 385-3116/3377
East Dennis, MA 02641

Upon his discharge from the armed forces at the end of World War II, Robert C. Eldred established the company which now bears his name and which today has an annual turnover in excess of $2 million. Eldred lives picturesquely in an elaborate old sea captain's house, behind which the auctions are held, either under a tent or in the gallery, a converted barn.

These premises are located on Route 6A just inside the town of Dennis and are about 90 minutes driving time from Boston. Eldred holds auction sales on Saturdays 2 or 3 times a month between September and June. During July and especially during August, sales are held with much more frequency. The Oriental art auction, first held in 1967, which usually takes place in August, with afternoon and evening sales, has over the years become a multisession, multi-day event drawing people and bids from all over the world. These sales offer such diverse objects as Chinese snuffboxes, Korean ceramics, and Paul Jacoulet prints (art by a Frenchman done in the Japanese manner).

Bidding at all Eldred sales is by numbered card. Prospective bidders not known to the management are expected to establish their financial bona fides with a 25 percent cash deposit, a bank letter, etc. "Trippers" (i.e., tourists on the Cape) are neither encouraged nor discouraged, but Eldred is not a country auction at which to pick up cheap souvenirs.

Contact person: L. W. Schofield

Days/hours of operation: Mon.–Fri. 8:30 A.M.–4:30 P.M.

Areas in which general auction and special sales are held (incl. some contact people):

Americana (Robert C. Eldred, Jr.)	Paintings
Art Deco (Alfred Cali)	18th c. British
Art Nouveau (Alfred Cali)	19th c. European
Chinese Works of Art (John H. Schofield)	Pre-20th c. American
Clocks and Watches	Marine Art
Dolls	Pewter
Furniture	Porcelain
Glass (Alfred Cali)	Rugs (Alfred Cali)
Japanese Works of Art (Jill Maher)	Scrimshaw
Jewelry	Silver (Robert
Netsuke (John H. Schofield)	C. Eldred, Jr.)

Sales are advertised in the local and regional press, in specialty publications, such as *Antiques and the Arts Weekly, Arts in Asia,* and *Antiques Magazine,* and through a mailing list, which you can join free of charge just by asking to do so.

Catalogues are not offered by subscription. They are available singly for each sale, but the style of catalogue varies with the sale—for the more important sales, such as Oriental art, catalogues are quite elaborate (cost is $12–$15 at the house, more by mail).

Usual viewing procedure: Exhibition is 2 days before each sale, the first day 10 A.M.–5 P.M. and the second 10 A.M.–8 P.M.

Bidder Information

Most sales are on the premises, but Eldred also conducts house and estate sales.

There is no buyer's premium; credit cards are not accepted; accounts must be settled immediately after the auction.

The house accepts mail order bids, provides packing and shipping services, at the buyer's expense, and will accept return of goods that prove to be not as catalogued.

State sales tax: 5 percent.

Consignor Information

Persons wishing to consign property should contact the firm either in writing or by telephone. The minimum value for acceptance of a single item or a series ranges between $40 and $100, depending on the object.

The commission structure varies, depending on the situation.

Consigned goods are "held for appropriate sale—10 days to 10 months." Settlement is made within 10 days.

There is a separate commission structure for dealers.

Reserves are accepted subject to a 10 percent charge if the property fails to sell.

Consignors do not pay for catalogue illustrations, packing and shipping of consigned property, or its warehousing, but do pay for insurance on consigned property (cost: 1 percent of estimated value).

Appraisal service is available: the cost is "generally, but not always" 1.5 percent of total value.

18. Samuel T. Freeman & Co.

1808-10 Chestnut Street   Tel. (215) 563-9275
Philadelphia, PA 19103

As its publicity claims, Samuel T. Freeman & Co. is "the oldest auction firm in the world under continuous management by one family." The firm was founded in 1805 by Tristram B. Freeman, and there are still a multitude of Freemans active in the firm—the current president is John M. Freeman.

Over the years since its founding, Freeman's has become a Philadelphia institution. At one time or another, the firm probably has sold the contents of just about every important Main Line estate and some not so important homes elsewhere in the area.

Freeman prides itself on being a "full service auction house," and one of its strong points is that it will take on consignment everything in a home or location, not just the good items. The less valuable merchandise it will dispose of quickly (paying out quickly as well), and the better properties it will save for specialized sales. The sale schedule reflects the philosophy of the house. At its quaint but serviceable five-story-and-basement quarters in downtown Philadelphia, three general-purpose mixed-lot auctions are held each week: Tuesday on the mezzanine—costume jewelry, linens, appliances, power tools, etc.; Wednesday on the first floor—"Good to Better than Average" furniture, bric-a-brac, porcelain, silver, etc.; Thursday in the basement—odds and ends, part sets of china, pottery, kitchenware and kitchen furniture, "Collectibles of Every Nature and Description." In the gallery, in an attractive if somewhat old-fashioned setting, sales are held every 5–6 weeks, except during July and August, of fine arts, fine furniture, Oriental rugs, etc. Special sales of books, jewelry, and valuable collections are held as necessary. Freeman's may be a bit stodgy, but it performs a very valuable function for buyers and consignors in the Delaware Valley.

Contact persons: John M. Freeman/George C. Freeman

Days/hours of operation: Mon.–Fri. 8:30 A.M.–5 P.M.

Areas in which general auctions and special sales are held (incl. some contact people):

Americana (Samuel M. Freeman II)	Paintings
Autographs	18th c. British
Books (Gordon Hollis)	Pre-20th c. American
Clocks and Watches	Impressionist
Coins	Contemporary
Dolls	Porcelain (Richard Wolf)
Drawings	Postcards
Furniture (Samuel M. Freeman II)	Posters
Jewelry	Pre-Columbian Art
Manuscripts (John M. Freeman)	Prints
Maps	Railroadiana
	(Daniel W. Freeman)
	Rugs (Richard Wolf)
	Silver
	Toys

Sales are advertised regularly in New York, Pennsylvania, Delaware, and Washington, D.C., newspapers, in local magazines, such as *Philadelphia,* and in specialty periodicals, such as *Antiques Magazine.* Mailings are made to a list of over 8,000 persons; you can be placed on that mailing list free of charge by writing to the Mailing Department.

Catalogues for specific sales are available at the house and by mail order; the price varies. Catalogues are also obtainable by subscription ($70 annually, including prices realized). Contact George C. Freeman III.

Usual viewing procedure: For weekly sales, exhibition is 9 A.M.–5 P.M. the day preceding the sale. For gallery and specialized sales, exhibition is 9 A.M.–5 P.M. 2–4 days prior to the sale.

Bidder Information

Not all sales are held on site; the occasional specialized sale is also held off premises—e.g., the railroadiana sales at Philadelphia's 30th Street Station.

There is no buyer's premium. Credit cards are not accepted. Buyer must settle accounts within 48 hours.

Absentee bids are accepted; a 25 percent deposit must accompany mail order bids. Packing and shipping is occasionally available by special arrangement, and at the buyer's expense. John Freeman reports that "if cataloguing is our error we return your purchase price within a reasonable time from claim."

State sales tax: 6 percent.

Consignor Information

Prospective consignors should write or phone the house; John Freeman believes that "telephone arrangements are usually adequate."

The standard consignor's commission is 20 percent, with a sliding scale as follows: 15 percent on any single item bringing in excess of $5,000, up to and including $10,000; 12.5 percent on any single item bringing in excess of $10,000 to $15,000; 10 percent on each item that brings over $15,000.

Commissions are negotiable, depending on the situation.

Consignors do not pay for catalogue illustrations or for warehousing; consignors are to pay for shipping and handling and for insurance (if the consignor wants special insurance).

Reserves are accepted "under certain circumstances and within the limits of our estimate." There are no buy-ins, for according to George Freeman, "everything is sold."

Consigned goods are sold in the weekly sales 1–2 weeks after arrival at the house; gallery and specialized sales can take 2–3 months. Settlement is made within 30 days.

Appraisal service is available, for estate tax and fair market prices only. The cost is $250 per man-day, $125 per half day, with a minimum charge of $100. If the appraised items are consigned to Freeman's, the appraisal fee is rebated. Contact Miss Bonnie Dawson.

Samuel T. Freeman & Co. belongs to the Pennsylvania Auctioneers Association and to the National Auctioneers Association.

19. Garth's Auctions, Inc.
2690 Stratford Road   Tel. (614) 362-4771/369-5085
Delaware, OH 43015

Located approximately 20 miles north of downtown Columbus, Garth's Auctions was established in the early 1950s by antiques dealer Garth Oberlander. Subsequently he took into partnership Tom and Carolyn Porter, who upon his death in 1974 assumed control of Garth's. The young and energetic couple have surrounded themselves with an equally young and energetic staff. And this dedicated group has made Garth's an important regional auction house in the tristate area of Indiana, Ohio, and Pennsylvania—so much so, that the firm's 1979–80 annual turnover of approximately $2 million placed it among the top 15 firms in the country in terms of sales.

Garth's Auctions is composed of two buildings on the same property, not far from each other:

The Stratford Auction Center, a spacious, modern one-story building, at which the lots sold comprise post-1850 items, has sales the first or third Friday of the month. Mostly not catalogued, these sales offer mixed lots of collectibles and Victoriana. About 400 lots are sold at each session, which begins at 5 P.M. and runs as long as is necessary.

Garth's, a renovated large old-fashioned barn, is devoted to the selling of pre-1850 items—all of which are catalogued—and the sales are usually a mixture of antiques, although as Tom King reports: "We try to group things into areas of specialization—e.g., American furniture and accessories; Oriental, or English, or French furniture and accessories." Sales are usually held Saturdays from 10 A.M. to 4 P.M. About 100 lots are sold each hour.

Included in the firm's statement of "our policy" is one paragraph that may be of interest to you: "Pools are an association of dealers or collectors formed with the purpose of keeping down auction prices for the benefit of its members. They are illegal in England, but flourish in Eastern United States. They have never occurred at our auction and under no circumstances will they ever be permitted."

Contact person: Tom King

Days/hours of operation: Mon.–Fri. 9 A.M.–5 P.M.

Areas in which general auctions and special sales are held:

Americana	Dolls
Arms and Armor	Furniture (18th & 19th c.)
Art Deco	Glass
Art Nouveau	Indian Relics
Chinese Works of Art	Toys
Coins	

Sales are advertised regularly in the local and regional press, as well as in specialty periodicals, such as the *Tri-State Trader* and *Maine Antique Digest*.

Catalogues are available by mail or at the house for certain sales: Americana, early American glass, French and English furniture and accessories, all cost $2–$4, with $1 mailing costs and $1 for prices realized. The catalogues or illustrated brochures for guns, Indian relics, art glass, and dolls are free and available on request. Subscription to catalogues for which a fee is charged is $30 per year with prices realized and $25 without.

Usual viewing procedure: Preview the day before Saturday sales, the afternoon before Friday-evening sales.

Bidder Information

Most auctions ("99 percent") are held on the premises. Occasionally Garth's will hold an estate or a house sale.

There is no buyer's premium. Credit cards are not accepted. Settlement is immediately after the sale session.

Absentee bids are accepted and executed.

Packing and shipping services are offered, at the buyer's expense.

The catalogue states: "we guarantee the age, condition, and authenticity of each item to be as represented in the catalogue." In catalogue sales, the firm offers buyers their money back if goods are not as catalogued.

State and local sales tax: 4.5 percent.

Consignor Information

Potential consignors should get in touch with the house in writing or by phone:
as at most houses, "generally a telephone call or mail is followed by a
visit from . . . staff."

Standard consignor's commission is 20 percent of items sold for $50 and over,
and 25 percent for goods under $50. Commission is negotiable, depend-
ing on the situation.

Consignor is not charged for catalogue illustrations, warehousing, packing and
shipping, but is charged for insurance. "Insurance is optional and available through our agent. We will deduct premiums from check."

Reserves are not accepted. Minimum time for a consignment to be sold is 6
weeks. Settlement is 14 days after sale.

The firm does pay a finder's fee, usually 20 percent of gross.

Appraisal service is available; the cost "varies." Contact Tom Porter.

20. Charles Hamilton Galleries, Inc.

25 East 77th Street   Tel. (212) 628-1666/7/8
New York, NY 10021

Charles Hamilton began collecting autographs before World War II, when he
was 15. Since then he has turned his hobby into a very profitable business—
first as a dealer, and then since 1963 as the innovator of auctions devoted
almost exclusively to autographs.

Hamilton's sales are held approximately every 6 weeks at the Waldorf-
Astoria. The catalogues are snappy, thorough, scholarly, and fascinating to
read. Hamilton's cataloguers have a real sense of humor as well as great
knowledge. Who can resist this description of a Joan Miró lot: "Spanish modern artist. Interesting U.S. $1 bill on which Miró has heavily drawn, in black
paint, a drawing which resembles a surrealist fish. Miró was probably trying
to convey the fishiness of the debased dollar."

Each sale, which usually is held in the evening, contains about 200–250
lots. Autographs predominate, but Hamilton—who is one of the main auction
outlets in New York for World War II Nazi material of the memorabilia
type—has also sold Göring's silverware, Goebbels' books, and Hitler's sketch-
es. The auctions have included such oddities as an autographed violin with
literally dozens of signatures, including Franklin D. Roosevelt's and Greta
Garbo's. Although there are a few high-priced lots in each sale, most items
sell for less than $250, and many for less than $100.

An expert and a scholar, Hamilton is also a master promoter, and is very
good at advertising his field: his numerous television appearances include a
stint on the one-time hit children's show *Wonderama*. He was among the first
to understand and to publicize the fact that government officials, including
the President, were using "auto-pens"—mechanical devices which saved them
from personally having to sign letters and the like. His book on President John
F. Kennedy's use of the auto-pen is a standard work for collectors and
scholars.

Contact person: Charles Hamilton

Days/hours of operation: Mon.–Fri. 9 A.M.– 5 P.M.

Areas in which general auctions and special sales are held:

    Autographs   Manuscripts

Sales are advertised regularly in the press, such as the *New York Times*.
Catalogues for each sale are available singly at the house and by mail (the
cost is $4–$6, with $2 for the prices realized). Catalogues are also available by subscription, including prices realized: $40 U.S., $80 elsewhere,
by airmail.
Usual viewing procedure: Exhibition 10 days prior to sale during regular business hours at the Hamilton Galleries.

Bidder Information

All sales are held off the premises.
Since 1979, there has been a buyer's premium of 10 percent.
Credit cards are not accepted.
Absentee bids are executed.
Settlement must be made within 10 days by floor bidders, and within 2 weeks
by absentee bidders.
Packing and shipping services are available, at the buyer's expense.
All autographs are "unconditionally guaranteed to be genuine." This warranty, however, is not extended to non-autograph material, but if "any substantial defect not described in the catalogue is found by a purchaser
who was unable to examine the lot or lots prior to the sale, the material
in question may be returned within three days of receipt."
State and local sales tax: 8 percent.

Consignor Information

Prospective consignors should "bring material in or mail registered and insured for examination." Commission is negotiable.
Minimum value for consignment to be accepted is $75.
Standard commission is 25 percent, "less for important collections or valuable
items."
Consignors do not pay for catalogue illustrations, insurance, or warehousing.
Consigned goods are usually sold within 3–4 months; settlement is within 90
days after the auction.
Reserves are accepted; there is no charge for buy-ins.

Appraisal service is available; the cost is $100 and up.

Charles Hamilton Galleries, Inc., does buy and sell on its own behalf.

21. Kelley's Auction Service

P.O. Box 125   Tel. (617) 272-9167
Woburn, MA 01801

Warehouse:
553 Main Street   Tel. (617) 935-3389
Woburn, MA 01801

One of many such general auction houses scattered across the United States, Kelley's Auction Service serves as an outlet for the sale of estate properties of various kinds, much of it furniture of no special value. Kelley's is unusual in that it also specializes in interesting areas such as dolls and "military collectibles."

The objects for sale under this rubric range from weapons (e.g., Bowie knives, Mauser pistols, Japanese carbines) to propaganda posters in several languages, uniforms and helmets from various armies, orders and decorations from assorted countries, as well as photographs and books.

Auctioneer Harold Kelley is an engaging, energetic man who conducts whirlwind sales 30–50 times a year.

Contact person: Harold Kelley

Days/hours of operation: Mon.–Sat. 9 A.M.–5 P.M.

Areas in which general auctions and special sales are held (incl. contact people):

     Arms and Armor (Harold Kelley, Paul Ciampo)
     Dolls (Mary Kelley)
     Furniture
     Medals (Paul Ciampo)

Sales are advertised in Massachusetts newspapers, such as the Boston *Globe*, in antiques/auction outlets, such as *Antiques and the Arts Weekly*, and in specialty magazines, such as *Shotgun News*.

Catalogues run about $3 each per sale. They are not available by subscription, but send your name and address and Kelley's will put you on the mailing list and let you know when a catalogue is ready.

Usual viewing procedure: Exhibition takes place day of sale, usually beginning 2–3 hours before sale commences.

Bidder Information

Most auctions are held at the American Legion Hall in Woburn; estate sales are held on the premises of the consignor.

There is no buyer's premium.

Credit cards are not accepted. Mail order bids are executed. Accounts must be settled right after the sale, except for mail order bidders, who have 10 days from the receipt of invoice. If two or more mail bids are at the same price, the earliest postmark shall decide which is the winning bid.

Kelley's offers guarantees of authenticity, the opportunity to return goods that prove to be not as catalogued, and packing and shipping services (on small items there is no charge for packing; for large items or if special packing is requested or necessary, there will be a charge).

All federal and state laws apply to the purchase of modern guns, which have to be shipped to a federally licensed dealer in the bidder's area for collection.

State sales tax: 5 percent.

Consignor Information

Those wishing to consign property should call or write. There is no minimum value for acceptance, but Kelley's wants "no junk."

Commissions are generally 20 percent, except on major items, and are negotiable, depending on the situation. There is no separate rate structure for dealers.

Consignors are not charged for catalogue illustrations, insurance on consigned property, or warehousing.

Consigned property is auctioned 1–8 weeks after receipt by Kelley's, and settlement is generally the day after the sale.

Reserves are not encouraged, but are accepted though usually only in the case of items being sold at specialized sales.

Appraisal service is available, the cost depending on the number of items and the time it takes.

Kelley's Auction Service pays finder's fees—either 10 percent or a set fee, depending on the items.

Kelley's belongs to the Massachusetts Auctioneers Association, the National Auctioneers Association, and the Appraisers Association of America.

22. Morton's Auction Exchange

701 Magazine Street
New Orleans, LA 70190

Tel. (504) 561-1196
Toll-free: 1-800-535-7801
Telex: 460076
Cable: MORT

Morton's, which advertises itself as "the largest auction house in the South," was begun shortly after World War II by Morton Goldberg, whose father and father-in-law were both auctioneers. Since then, especially in recent years, Morton's Auction Exchange has experienced phenomenal growth. According to the authoritative *Gray Letter* ("the every-week 'Insider's' report serving the Fine Antiques community"), Morton's annual turnover increased by 400 percent between the auction seasons of 1977–78 and 1979–80: the turnover between July 1, 1977, and June 20, 1978, was $1 million; between July 1, 1979, and June 30, 1980, it was $6 million.

In 1980, the firm extensively renovated one of the two buildings it owns on

Magazine Street and centered its auction operations there. (The other building, next door at 643 Magazine Street, houses Morton's Antique Department Store—a retail operation selling both antiques and reproductions, as well as a "to the trade only" wholesale business.) The two-story 701 building, offering 40,000 square feet of space for sales, exhibitions, offices, and storage, is, like many of the buildings in this one-time commercial warehouse district—by the river, close to the French Quarter and to the downtown business area—of some architectural interest: it has a mezzanine and stretches back from the street.

Also at 701 is the Side Door Gallery, a space in which Morton's, because of the warehouse situation, is able to sell goods minimally catalogued (i.e., mimeographed or Xerox-copied) for fast turnover. Bidding there and at the more important, catalogued sales is by paddle obtained for a refundable $5 deposit upon registering before the sale. On the average, somewhat more than 30 auctions a year are held, about 3 a month except in the summer months, when fewer sales are held. Auctions usually take place on a Tuesday, Thursday, or Saturday, sometimes at night and sometimes during the day.

Morton's offers tours of the 701 building, and "has arranged to take reservations to personally guide interested visitors through . . . the rambling 19th century building. Visitors will . . . learn how to bid, use auction terminology, and appraise antiques at the pre-sale exhibition . . .; a glimpse of the vast . . . gallery from atop the auctioneer's podium will be part of the behind-the-scenes tour." If you're interested, get in touch with Della Graham.

Part of Morton's auction success derives from its offering of lots that are of interest to buyers in the prosperous sun belt region. The firm draws buyers from all over, but especially from the South. In an attempt to draw consignments from the North, Morton's opened a representative office in New York City in 1980; it is staffed by a personable antiques dealer in his mid-thirties:

Greg Hubert
115 East 82nd Street   Tel. (212) 628-2922
New York NY 10028

Hubert, who has had considerable experience in the antiques trade, feels that because Morton's has "been so successful in bringing high prices for Victoriana furniture, decorations, and silver, we have every reason to believe that our New York office can provide a valuable and timely service to individuals from New York and New England."

Contact person: David Goldberg

Days/hours of operation: Mon.–Sat. 8:30 A.M.–5:30 P.M.

Areas in which general auctions and special sales are held (incl. some contact people):

Americana	Dolls
Art Deco	Furniture (Morton & David Goldberg)
Art Nouveau	Orientalia

Paintings	Pewter
Old Master	Porcelain (Clive Howe)
19th c. European	Prints (John Fowler)
Pre-20th c. American	Rugs
Impressionist	Silver (Carey Mackie)
"Local paintings,	Victoriana (Neal Alford)
Southern U.S.A."	

Sales are advertised in the local and international press, as well as in American and international specialty periodicals, such as *Antiques* and *Connoisseur*. To be placed on the mailing list for announcements, just write to Morton's.

Catalogues are available singly for each sale (the price ranges from $3 to $8), both at the house and by mail. All the more important catalogues can be had by subscription ($25).

Usual viewing procedure: Exhibition is usually for 6–8 days prior to the sale, during regular business hours.

Bidder Information

Most sales are held on premises, but house and estate sales are held.

Most lots are free of buyer's premium, but according to Morton's Vice President David Goldberg, "we have a few lots in each sale" with a buyer's premium of 10 percent.

Credit cards are not accepted, but a buyer can have up to 30 days to pay if credit has been established. Otherwise settlement must be made immediately.

Absentee bids are executed.

Packing and shipping services are available at the buyer's expense. Morton's offers delivery in the immediate New Orleans metropolitan area in its own trucks "for very reasonable rates."

The firm offers buyers the opportunity to return goods which prove not to be as catalogued.

The house does buy and sell on its own behalf.

State and local tax: 6 percent.

Consignor Information

Persons wishing to consign property should call or write.

The consignor commission varies and is negotiable: the basic charges are 16 percent to institutions and the trade, and 20 percent to all others.

Consignors are not charged for catalogue illustrations, insurance, or warehousing. Consignors are charged for packing and shipping, but David Goldberg points out: "we offer the service of picking up any consignments in our trucks; we charge, but it is usually quite below public rates."

Out-of-state consignors pay no taxes; in-state consignors pay 0.5 percent for the charity hospitals tax.

Consigned goods are sold within 1–3 months; settlement is made after 30 days.

Reserves are accepted.
Buy-ins cost 3 percent.

The house pays finder's fees; how much varies.

Morton's Auction Exchange belongs to the National Auctioneers of America and the American Appraisers Association.

23. Northgate Gallery
5520 Highway 153   Tel. (615) 842-4177
Chattanooga, TN 37443

Located about 8 miles from downtown Chattanooga, Northgate Gallery holds auctions the first Saturday of every month. The location ensures ample parking. The founder of this auction operation is Charles Clements, who has been involved in auction sales since the end of the 1930s, when he was in his teens. Clements, who also runs a highly successful and large retail operation (Clements Antiques of Tennessee) in the suburb of Hixson, began Northgate Gallery in the mid-1960s. It is family run, the directors being his son and his son-in-law. Clements is very family oriented: the Texas operation established by him is directed by his other three sons-in-law (see *Clements*).

Northgate sells an average of 500 lots at each sale, with an average price of less than $300 per lot. About half the lots are catalogued in a splendidly illustrated brochure which serves as both an announcement of the forthcoming sale and a partial catalogue. A much less splendid addendum, cataloguing the rest of the lots, is available at Northgate on the day of the sale. Bidding is done by numbered cards, which one receives upon registering before the sale. Northgate bidders (whether dealers or "civilians") tend to be regulars and the firm therefore only asks for bank letters or cash deposits from bidders who are not known. The main specialty of Northgate is fine English furniture, but each auction has mixed lots of varying objects. Northgate also holds estate and house sales.

Contact persons: Charles Clements/Virginia Norris

Days/hours of operation: Mon.–Fri. 9 A.M.–5 P.M.

Areas in which general auctions and special sales are held:

Americana	Jewelry
Chinese Works of Art	Paintings
Clocks and Watches	Porcelain
Drawings	Prints
Furniture	Rugs
Glass	Silver

Sales are advertised regularly in the local newspapers and in specialty periodicals, such as *Antiques Monthly*. An illustrated brochure cum partial catalogue is available free of charge; just ask to be placed on the mailing list.

Catalogues are not available by subscription, but are obtainable at the house for each sale. The highlights of the sale are in the brochure mailed out prior to the auction.

Usual viewing procedure: Exhibition is 2 days before the sale takes place.

Bidder Information

Most sales take place on the premises, but Northgate also holds estate and house sales.

There is no buyer's premium.

Credit cards are not accepted. Settlement is immediately after the auction. Mail order bids are accepted.

All property is sold "as is."

State and local tax: 6.25 percent.

Consignor Information

Those wishing to consign property should get in touch with Northgate in writing or by telephone.

Commissions are negotiable. The maximum is 25 percent. There is no minimum value for acceptance of goods.

Consignors do not pay for catalogue illustrations, insurance, or warehousing, but do pay for shipping and packing of consigned property.

Goods are usually sold within 30 to 60 days; settlement is within 1 week.

Reserves are not accepted; there is no charge for buy-ins.

Northgate does buy and sell on its own behalf.

24. O'Gallerie, Inc.

537 S.E. Ash Street   Tel. (503) 238-0202
Portland, OR 97214

O'Gallerie began operations in 1972, when Dale O'Grady, then in his mid-thirties but a veteran real estate man, bought out a small auction house and began a dual retail-auction operation. O'Grady, a shrewd and ambitious man, is a collector who has turned his avocation into a highly impressive vocation.

Over the years, O'Gallerie has been very successful and has become "the largest auction operation between San Francisco and the Canadian border." The firm moved in 1976 to its present location, a four-story red-brick building built in 1927 and once utilized by UPS. The first floor (about 10,000 square feet and able to seat over 500 people) is given over to auctions; the second and third floors to retail sales (the merchandise is advertised as "an excellent offering of American and Continental furnishings. . . . The Northwest's finest display of roll-top desks, outstanding bookcases, conference table and chair sets . . . 'for the trade only' "). The gallery is about a 10-minute walk from downtown Portland.

Auction sales are held approximately every 5 weeks, and are 3- to 4-day affairs, with sessions held on successive evenings, beginning usually on Monday nights. The Tuesday-evening session, described as "funky collectible night," has seen the auctioning of such oddball items as a barbed-wire collection, but the house is moving away from such nights, into general sales of mixed lots.

About 900 lots a month are sold, and the annual auction turnover is estimated at over $1 million. Although a significant number of high-priced lots are sold, the average lot sells for less than $150. O'Gallerie is very much a family affair; both Dale and his son Tom are auctioneers, Dale's wife is an expert, and their grandson runs the snack bar on sale nights.

Contact person: Dale T. O'Grady

Days/hours of operation: Mon.–Fri. 10 A.M.–5 P.M.

Areas in which general auctions and special sales are held:

Americana	Maps
Arms and Armor	Medals
Art Deco	Musical Instruments
Art Nouveau	Paintings
Books	Pewter
Coins	Photographica
Dolls	Porcelain
Drawings	Posters
Engravings	Prints
Etchings	Rugs
Furniture	Silver
Glass	Stamps
Jewelry	Toys

Sales are advertised regularly in local and regional papers, as well as in specialty periodicals in the U.S. and overseas. Announcements are mailed to over 11,000 persons on the mailing list, which you can be placed on if you request it in writing.

Catalogues are available by subscription but are ready only at the time of the sale preview. Catalogues are also available singly (for $1) at the house during the preview and the sale.

Usual viewing procedure: Exhibition is Saturday and Sunday prior to auction, noon–5 P.M.; days of sale, 5–7 P.M.

Bidder Information

All sales are held on the premises; house sales are not held. Since April 1979, there has been a buyer's premium of 10 percent. Accounts must be settled within 2 days of the auction. Credit cards are accepted: American Express, Mastercard, Visa.

Mail and phone bids are accepted (about 10–15 percent of the lots at any sale have absentee bids). Indeed, O'Gallerie "welcomes your Absentee Bids," but the catalogue warns: "our policy regarding Absentee Bids is that the Auctioneer will favor a bid from the floor over an Absentee Bid: thus a bidder in the audience may be the successful buyer for the same amount

of the Absentee Bid." A 25 percent deposit is requested of absentee
bidders.

Packing and shipping services are offered at the buyer's expense.

No guarantees of authenticity are offered except on gemstones and gold. All
goods are sold "as is" and sales are final ("no refunds"), "excepting
jewelry when the gem has been determined by a reputable jeweler not to
be as stated in the catalog, or when not 14 or 18K Gold as stated; on
gold coins, determined by a reputable coin dealer as counterfeit."

Bidding is in set increments ranging from $5 between the opening bid and
$50, to $100 between $1,000 and $2,000.

Consignor Information

Prospective consignors should deliver small items to the gallery and write or
phone about larger ones.

Consignor's commission is as follows: $100 or under, 25 percent; $100–$500,
15 percent; over $500, 10 percent.

The minimum value for a consignment is $25 per item.

Consignors do not pay for shipping and packing, warehousing, or insurance.

Consigned goods are usually sold within 3–6 weeks.

Settlement is after 14 days.

Consignors cannot set reserves; they "are accepted but only at the low estimate or below."

Buy-ins are 5 percent of the reserve selling price.

Appraisal service is available: "1–5 items in the gallery by appointment, $25.
Over 5 items, minimum of $50 or 1½ percent of appraised value up to
$50,000; 1 percent thereafter." There is a partial rebate for property
consigned to O'Gallerie for auction within a year following the appraisal.

Absentee bidders must call for results.

Phillips

25. 867 Madison Avenue   Tel. (212) 570-4830
New York, NY 10021   Telex: 126 380

26. 525 East 72nd Street   Tel. (212) 570-4852
New York, NY 10021

REPRESENTATIVE OFFICE

6 Faneuil Hall Marketplace   Tel. (617) 227-6145
Boston, MA 02109
Lynne Kortenhaus

An aggressive, intelligent grasp of the realities of the British auction scene
enabled Phillips in the late 1960s and early 1970s to expand dramatically in
its home market and to become a real force there. In 1977, as a logical outcome of that expansion, Phillips established a base of operations in New York
City, and held the first sale there just prior to Christmas. Under the able

direction of J. Brian Cole (who has since taken charge of Christie's East), Phillips got off to a cracking good start. The annual turnover for its first full season (1978–79) was approximately $9.5 million, and the next season, that turnover increased to approximately $12.9 million. But for all its success, and despite the fact that Phillips ranks among the top ten American auction houses in terms of annual turnover, the firm has failed to achieve the luster in the United States that marks its operations in the United Kingdom. Phillips has established itself in the United States—no easy task—but the firm has yet to establish its presence in America the way other English firms have.

Phillips in the United States has received the close attention of the energetic, forceful Christopher Weston—the operating head of the parent English company. Weston, who travels tens of thousands of miles annually in overseeing Phillips operations everywhere, spends 1–2 weeks of every month in the United States. This commitment of time is an indication of the importance that Phillips places on its American operations. The principles under which these operations are carried on have been summed up by the Phillips official in New York City who has been candid enough to admit that "world records in themselves are meaningless," but also was intelligent enough to recognize that while intrinsically such records may be meaningless, "success breeds success." And Phillips has been geared in New York City to establish some world records of its own—one it already holds is for a piece of Lalique glass.

During the winter of 1980, Phillips purchased the five-story Madison Avenue mansion one floor of which had served as the firm's American headquarters since the beginning of 1977. A registered landmark, this building was erected in the mid-1890s for the fashionable and wealthy Mrs. Gertrude Rhinelander Waldo. Built in the style of a French chateau, it has also in recent years served as quarters for Olivetti and for Christie's (before it moved to its present location). Phillips undertook a careful but extensive modernization of the interior of the mansion. The firm now occupies all five floors. In addition to three salerooms, the mansion houses most of Phillips' specialists and administrators. Sales of smaller items, such as glass or jewelry, are held there twice a week. Go to a Phillips sale or exhibition even if you do not intend to bid; the mansion is worth a visit.

Phillips' other saleroom, at 525 East 72nd Street, was, of all things, once a Polish vaudeville theater. It was also for a while the home of Coleman Auction Galleries, which went out of business before Phillips took over the premises. These are very utilitarian premises and serve well for sales of larger items, such as rugs and furniture, held about twice a week.

The representative office in Boston is staffed by Lynne Kortenhaus, a savvy, attractive woman in her thirties, who has been much involved in trust and estate work. She arranged for Phillips' first big New England operation, the Steven Straw bankruptcy auction, held in the Copley Plaza Hotel in May 1980, a million-dollar sale.

Contact person: Cintra H. Huber (she is in charge of public relations and either she or one of her staff can assist you to find the right person)

Days/hours of operation: Mon.–Fri. 9 A.M.–5 P.M.

Areas in which general auctions and special sales are held (incl. some contact people):

Americana
Arms and Armor
Art Deco
Art Nouveau
Autographs (Larry Rutter)
Books (Larry Rutter)
Chinese Works of Art
   (Dean Schwaab)
Clocks and Watches (Susan Volk)
Coins
Dolls
Drawings
Engravings
Etchings
Furniture (Edward J. Herguth,
   David J. LeBeau)
Glass
Japanese Works of Art
   (Dean Schwaab)
Jewelry (Eric A. Manasse,
   P. Joyce Jonas)
Manuscripts (Larry Rutter)
Musical Instruments

Netsuke (Dean Schwaab)
Paintings(Ann LaPides,
   Joan Dearborn)
Old Master
   17th c. British
   18th c. British
   19th c. European
   Pre-20th c. American
Impressionist
Modern Art
Contemporary Art
Photographica (Penelope Dixon,
   Crary Pullen)
Porcelain
Posters
Pre-Columbian Art
   (Tara Ann Finley)
Prints (Meg Hausberg)
Rugs (Dean Schwaab)
Silver (Susan Volk)
Stamps
Toys
Toy Soldiers (Tara Ann Finley)

Sales are advertised in the New York and national press, as well as in specialty periodicals, such as *Antiques and the Arts Weekly.* Phillips also publishes *The Auctioneer,* which 3 times yearly lists sales and other information about Phillips auctions; a subscription is $3 per year.

Catalogues for each sale are available at the house and by mail (the price varies from $3 to $10; add $1 for mailing). Catalogues are also available by subscription: all in a given specialty may cost between $15 and $60; in 1980, an annual subscription to all Phillips catalogues for sales in New York cost $350 in the U.S., and an additional $15 outside the U.S. for airmail postage.

Usual viewing procedure: 1–3 days before sale, 10 A.M.–5 P.M.

Bidder Information

Most auctions are held on premises, but house and estate sales are also held on location.

There is a buyer's premium of 10 percent. Credit cards are not accepted. Absentee bids are accepted and executed. Buyers must settle accounts within 3 days after the sale. Credit is available on application.

Guarantees of authenticity are not offered. But, states a Phillips employee, "we stand behind our attributions." Notwithstanding that all lots are sold "with all faults and errors of description" and that the "auctioneers disclaim all responsibility for authenticity, age, provenance, origin, condition, or quality," a refund will be given if the purchaser within 10 days gives notice the lot is a forgery and if within a subsequent 10 days proves that fact.

The house will assist buyers at their expense to obtain packing and shipping services.

State and local sales tax: 8 percent.

Consignor Information

Prospective consignors should contact the appropriate specialist in writing or by telephone.

The standard consignor's commission is 10 percent, but is negotiable, depending on the situation.

Consignors are charged "sometimes" for catalogue illustrations, and also for packing and shipping, insurance, and warehousing.

Consigned goods are sold within 1–3 months.

Settlement is made 30–35 days after the sale.

Reserves are accepted; buy-ins cost the consignor 2 percent of the reserve price.

There is a separate consignor's rate for dealers; it is negotiable, but usually is 6 percent.

Phillips pays a finder's fee, normally 4 percent of price realized.

Appraisal service is available: the cost is 1.5 percent of the first $50,000 and 1 percent of higher amounts; the per diem rate is $750. The minimum is $150 plus travel. Contact Teri N. Towe.

27. Plaza

406 East 79th Street   Tel. (212) 472-1000
New York, NY 10021   Cable: PLAZAGAL NY

Except for the dog days of summer, when many New York City auctioneers desert the Big Apple, Plaza holds sales every Wednesday, Thursday, and Friday. Wednesday is given over to jewelry; Thursday to furniture and the decorative arts; and Friday to "collectibles," which Plaza has described as "toys, mechanical banks, books, porcelain, prints, and other similar items which have become very popular with special and young collectors." Plaza also periodically holds sales of "Unredeemed Pledges Sold by Order of the Provident Loan Society of New York," at which some highly unusual items which were left as collateral for loans may turn up to astound auctioneers, bidders, and visitors.

Plaza has a 24-hour "hot line" [(212) 472-3939], which provides continuously updated information about forthcoming sales. Each session averages 300–400 lots, and the average price per lot is about $300—although some very expensive items are auctioned at each sale. The attractive main saleroom is located in a pleasantly decorated, recently renovated four-story building on the edge of Manhattan's posh Upper East Side. This building also has a secondary saleroom for smaller sales, as well as storage and offices.

The firm claims to be "the largest American owned Art Auction House"—which means that its annual turnover until recently has been more than other American-owned auction houses (but still only about 10 percent of Christie's annual turnover and less than 5 percent of Sotheby Parke Bernet's). That claim, however, may no longer be true. Plaza, despite its considerable annual turnover, which was in the neighborhood of $15 million for the auction year 1979–80 (i.e., July 1–June 31), had enough problems that the question of its possible bankruptcy surfaced in the July 25, 1980, *New York Times*. The retiring chairman dismissed the question as unfounded rumor.

However, Barry K. Hookway, a man with considerable auction experience in the United Kingdom and Canada, who at that time succeeded to control of the firm's auction operations, determined to change some of the more traditional policies. Hookway has embarked on a policy of organizing more special sales and ending the jumbling of lots in such general-purpose auctions as those devoted to collectibles. However, financial problems persisted and the firm found it necessary to operate under Chapter XI. But Plaza did remain an important part of the American auction market.

Contact person: Barry K. Hookway

Days/hours of operation: Mon.–Fri. 9 A.M.–5 P.M.

Areas in which general auctions and special sales are held:

Americana	Engravings	Pewter
Art Deco	Etchings	Photographica
Art Nouveau	Furniture	Porcelain
Books	Glass	Prints
Chinese Works of Art	Japanese Works of Art	Rugs
Clocks and Watches	Jewelry	Silver
Dolls	Musical Instruments	Toys
Drawings	Paintings	

Sales are advertised regularly in newspapers such as the *New York Times* and the *Wall Street Journal*, as well as in specialty periodicals, such as *Antiques Monthly*. Announcements are also sent to the more than 10,000 people on the mailing list; if you would like to join that number, write to Plaza.

Catalogues for each sale are available singly at the house and by mail (the price varies between $3 and $15). Catalogues are also available by subscription: the complete set, approximately 100 catalogues per year, is $300. Catalogues are also available on the following basis: all furniture and decoration, $200; all jewelry, coins, and virtu (including Provident Loan Society), $75; all fine paintings and prints, $50; all collectibles (toys, dolls, books, etc.), $100. To all subscription orders outside the U.S., $25 should be added for airmail postage and handling.

Usual viewing procedure: Exhibition varies with the sale but is usually at least 3 days, including one evening, which is divided between private buyers and the trade.

Bidder Information

Most sales are on premises, but Plaza does hold house and estate sales.The buyer's premium is 10 percent. Accounts must be settled within 3 days of the sale. Credit cards are not accepted. Absentee bids are executed.

The house does not offer packing or shipping services.

No guarantees of authenticity are offered, and all goods are sold "as is," yet notwithstanding these conditions, "if within 7 days of the sale . . . the purchaser gives Plaza notice in writing that the lot so sold is a forgery and if, within 7 days after such notice, the purchaser returns the lot to Plaza in the same condition as sold, and proves beyond a reasonable doubt that the returned lot is in fact a forgery and that this was not indicated by a fair reading of the catalogue, Plaza . . . . will refund the purchase price."

State and local sales taxes: 8 percent.

Consignor Information

Consignors should phone or write the firm.

The consignor's commission is 10 percent.

Plaza charges the consignor for catalogue illustrations, insurance, packing and shipping, but not for warehousing.

Reserves are accepted (not more than 40 percent of the estimate on items under $500 and two thirds of the estimate for items over $500). There is a buy-in charge of 5 percent.

Consigned goods are sold within 2–6 months; settlement is after 35 days.

Plaza does buy and sell on its own behalf.

Appraisal service is available: the cost is 1 percent of the gross evaluation or $300, whichever is greater.

Robert W. Skinner, Inc.

28. Main Street   Tel. (617) 779-5528
Bolton, MA 01740

29. 585 Boylston Street   Tel. (617) 236-1700
Boston, MA 02116

The story of the rise of Skinner's as one of the more important regional auction houses in the United States is an American entrepreneurial success story of the kind that has become all too rare lately.

Robert W. Skinner, Jr., conducted his first auction in the summer of 1962 and for the next 8 years, while continuing in the antiques business, also held auctions on site, in rented halls, and as benefits. Having done reasonably well, Skinner and associates decided to build their own gallery. And in 1971, as reported in a promotional piece of literature issued by the firm, "we acquired a 17 acre tract of land in Bolton, built the gallery, and incorporated. The new building was one of the few in this country to be designed for the sole purpose of conducting auctions, having such innovative features as revolving stages for the display of furniture." Over the next years, Skinner's continued to flourish, holding more sales, selling ever finer properties, establishing some world auction price records, and expanding the gallery by adding additional thousands of square feet. It was among the first to "computerize the major portion of its invoicing, cataloguing, inventory, sales, bookkeeping, and accounts." And in 1978, Skinner's opened its Boston gallery, designed for the exhibition and sale of smaller items, such as books, jewelry, and paintings. The firm's annual turnover has now grown to the point that at the end of the 1979–80 season, it was among the top seven in the United States and well over $6.5 million.

The Bolton gallery is located 25 miles west of Boston, a half mile east of I-495, and is an attractive, functional, spread-out one-story building. There is an auction room, which can seat approximately 500 people, 3 exhibition rooms, offices, and extensive storage areas, as well as ample parking space. The Boston gallery is on the second floor of a building by Copley Square. It is staffed with experts who conduct appraisals, accept consignments, and assist with bidding for sales held either in Boston or in Bolton. The Bolton gallery holds auctions just about every week; the Boston gallery has monthly sales. At both venues, bidding is done with numbered cards, which can be obtained by registering before the auction.

Contact person: Nancy Skinner

Days/hours of operation: Bolton—Mon.–Fri. 9:30 A.M.–4:30 P.M.
                           Boston—Mon.–Fri. 8 A.M.–4 P.M.

Areas in which general auctions and special sales are held (incl. some contact people):

Americana (Stephen L. Fletcher)	Paintings (Kathryn Corbin)
Books	19th c. European
Clocks and Watches	Pre-20th c. American
Coins	Photographica
Dolls	Porcelain
Furniture (Karen Keane,	Prints
Mildred Ewing)	Silver
Glass (R. W. Skinner, Jr.)	Vintage Automobiles
Jewelry (Sara Ellen White)	

Sales are advertised regularly in the local and national press, as well as in specialty periodicals, such as *Antiques and the Arts Weekly*. Announcements of forthcoming sales are sent monthly to a mailing list of over 6,000 people; if you want to be placed on that mailing list free of charge, just write.

Catalogues are not available by subscription, but are available singly for each sale at the Bolton and Boston galleries ($3–$5) or by mail ($6–$8).

Usual viewing procedure: Nancy Skinner reports that "major sales have previous day viewing from 2 to 7 P.M. All sales have preview from 8 to 9 A.M., with sales starting at 10 A.M."

Bidder Information

Most auctions are held on the premises, but some house and estate sales are held on site.

The buyer's premium of 10 percent was instituted in September 1979. Credit cards are not accepted. Credit is offered "only in very special cases." Accounts must be settled immediately after the sale, "unless previous arrangements have been made with the auctioneer."

Absentee bids are executed.

Packing and shipping services are available, at the buyer's expense.

Skinner's does offer buyers the right for a limited period of time to return lots that prove to be not as catalogued, but the firm is very careful both in the catalogue and at the sale to describe all faults, "even to the extent of listing damage."

State sales tax: 5 percent.

Consignor Information

Persons wishing to consign property should get in touch with Skinner's either in writing or by phone.

The standard consignor's commission is 10 percent for items bringing $500 and over; 15 percent for items bringing under $500. Commissions are negotiable.

There are no other charges for insurance, warehousing, or catalogue illustrations—these are all included in the consignor's commission. Also included are transportation costs on lots valued in excess of $10,000.

Appraisal service is available: the cost per appraiser is $500 per day or $50 per hour, travel time included. Contact Mrs. Jean Butler in Bolton.

Robert W. Skinner, Inc., does buy and sell on its own behalf; Nancy Skinner estimates that "about 10 percent of goods sold are owned by the gallery."

30. C. G. Sloan & Co.

715 13th Street N.W.   Tel. (202) 628-1468
Washington, DC 20005   Toll-free (eastern U.S.): 1-800-424-5122

Branch office:
403 North Charles Street   Tel. (301) 547-1177
Baltimore, MD 21201

C. G. Sloan & Co. has been in continuous operation since before the Civil War, having serviced the Washington community since 1853 under a succession of owners. The most recent are David Webster, a veteran of the antiques trade, and J. William Middendorf II, attorney, government official, and print and book collector extraordinaire. They took control in 1976, with Webster in active control of day-to-day operations.

Since then, Sloan's has been revitalized, has once again assumed a premier position in the nation's capital in terms of annual turnover, and has surged to new glories in a series of exciting sales. Typical was the September 23, 1979, sale of a Salomon van Ruisdael landscape; this painting was sold to a London art dealer for the highest price ever paid to that date at public auction in the metropolitan Washington area ($185,000 plus a 10 percent buyer's premium). Sloan & Co. is located, as it has been since 1922, in a 5-story building just 3 blocks from the White House. There is ample parking nearby. Since 1976, the Sloan building has undergone extensive modernization, and in 1980 a second saleroom was created there, as well as a Baltimore office, to serve the affluent suburbs that lie between metropolitan Washington and Baltimore. Essentially, this firm runs a two-tier operation. At one level are the catalogued sales, internationally advertised, of finer properties. These auctions are 4-day affairs, and are held approximately every 6 weeks, Thursday through Sunday, except July and August. About 600 lots are sold at each session. At the other level are the sales, usually on alternate weekends, that offer mixed lots of household merchandise, etc. The average lot price at these sales hovers around $60, and 1,000–1,500 lots are sold during each all-day session.

Contact person: David Webster

Days/hours of operation: Mon.–Fri. 9 A.M.–5 P.M.

Areas in which catalogued general auctions and special sales are held:

Americana	Paintings
Art Deco	Old Master
Art Nouveau	17th c. British
Chinese Works of Art	18th c. British
Clocks and Watches	19th c. European
Drawings	Pre-20th c. American
Engravings	Pewter
Etchings	Porcelain
Furniture	Prints
Glass	Rugs
Japanese Works of Art	Silver
Jewelry	

Sales are advertised in the local and national press, as well as in American and international specialty periodicals. Free illustrated brochures are available; to be placed on the mailing list, write to the Catalogue Department.

Catalogues are available by subscription (approximately $90 annually). They are also for sale singly at the house (about $12) and by mail (about $15 U.S., about $18 elsewhere).

Usual viewing procedure: 5-day public exhibition 10 A.M.–6 P.M. prior to the sale (Thursday–Monday).

Bidder Information

Not all catalogued auctions are held on the premises; Russell Burke reports that "we occasionally hold sales on the premises" of the consignor.

Sloan's has had a 10 percent buyer's premium since September 1979.

The firm does not accept credit cards. Accounts must be settled immediately after the sale. Absentee bids are acceptable: "We have an employee who handles all absentee bids and is our only employee who is privy to the amount."

Buyers are offered packing and shipping services for a fee. The firm will accept return of goods that do not prove as catalogued. Burke reports that there is a "5 year guarantee of authenticity backed by their right to return."

Local sales tax: 5 percent.

Consignor Information

Prospective consignors should contact Sloan's in writing or by phone.

The standard consignor commission is 10 percent on items over $500 and 15 percent on items $500 and under.

Consignor commission is negotiable; the rates vary with the "value of consignment."

Consignors pay for illustrations in the catalogue (black-and-white photos $40; color $125).

Consignors pay for packing and shipping and for insurance (50¢ per $100 of value).

Consignors do not pay for warehousing.

Consigned goods are sold within 6–10 weeks; settlement is "within 35 days."

Reserves are accepted; buy-in costs "vary."

Appraisal service is available; the cost is $75 per hour.

Sotheby Parke Bernet, Inc.

31. 980 Madison Avenue   Tel. (212) 472-3400
New York, NY 10021   Telex: 232 643
                                            Cable PARKGAL

32a. 1334 York Avenue
New York, NY 10021

32b. 171 East 84th Street
New York, NY 10028

REGIONAL OFFICES

NEW ENGLAND: 232 Clarendon Street   Tel. (617) 247-2851
               Boston, MA 02116
               Patricia Ward

MID-ATLANTIC:	1630 Locust Street	Tel. (215) 735-7886
	Philadelphia, PA 19103	
	Wendy T. Foulke	
WASHINGTON:	2903 M Street N.W.	Tel. (202) 298-8400
	Washington, DC 20007	
	Joan Fleischmann Tobin	
	(fine arts)	
	Sam Beach (real estate)	
SOUTHEAST:	155 Worth Avenue	Tel. (305) 658-3555
	Palm Beach, FL 33480	
	Elena Echarte (fine arts)	
	Rodney A. Dillard (real estate)	
MIDWEST:	700 North Michigan Avenue	Tel. (312) 280-0185
	Chicago, IL 60611	
	Catharine C. Hamilton	
SOUTHWEST:	Galleria Post Oak	Tel. (713) 623-0010
	5015 Westheimer Road	
	Houston, TX 77056	
	Flo Crady	
NORTHWEST:	210 Post Street	Tel. (415) 986-4982
	San Francisco, CA 94108	
	Andrea Comel di Socebran	
PACIFIC AREA:	Aina Haina Professional Building	
	Suite 117	Tel. (808) 373-9166
	850 West Hind Drive	
	Honolulu, Hawaii 96821	
	John Marr	

SPB is the result of a 1964 merger between two prestigious, proud, highly successful auction houses on opposite sides of the Atlantic. One firm was Sotheby's, whose founding in London in 1744 antedates the declaration of American independence. The other firm was Parke-Bernet, which since its founding in 1938 had come to dominate the New York fine arts auction scene.

Just before the merger, a guidebook to New York City described the Parke-Bernet Galleries as "New York's favorite and most elegant attic," and categorized "any afternoon's audience . . . more likely than not, to be straight out of the latest edition of the *Social Register.*"

Much has changed since then. SPB has become a department store (admittedly one with occasionally some very high-priced wares) catering to all kinds of buyers, be they insatiable bargain hunters or swishy interior decorators. Despite the occasional arrogance displayed by some of the younger SPB staff members, remember that SPB wants *you* to come, to view, to bid, and to consign. All the publicity about la-di-da sales to the contrary, you are welcome and SPB is geared to modest incomes as well as posh ones. In 1968, PB84—a branch on a side street a few blocks away—was opened to attract younger and less affluent buyers. PB84 achieved enormous success with its general-purpose mixed-lot auctions and with its specialized sales emphasizing such new interests as collectibles, Victoriana, and 19th- and 20th-century decorative arts.

Today, despite increasingly formidable competition from Christie's, Sotheby's bestrides the American auction scene in much the same fashion that the Colossus dominated the harbor of ancient Rhodes. In a striking break with tradition, SPB ran sales all through the summer of 1980 and in effect extended the auction calendar to the whole year. Northern American sales of SPB (i.e., including the Los Angeles salerooms and Canadian operations) during the 1979–80 auction season reached the staggering total of nearly a quarter of a billion dollars. This figure represented more than a 50 percent increase on the previous year's turnover, and was greater than the combined total sales of 9 of the next largest firms in the North American auction market. Mind you, annual turnover is not the same as profitability, but whatever SPB's net, the gross represents tens of thousands of items sold.

This continuing increase in volume and the need for more auction space resulted in 1980 in a restructuring of SPB's operations. It opened a second major auction facility, at York Avenue and 72nd Street, and divided the location of most expert departments and the sales they held between this new facility and the older one at Madison Avenue. The operating principle governing the relocation was that the decorative arts were to be centered at York Avenue and the fine arts at Madison Avenue. PB84, a "victim of its own success," to use the words of one SPB director, was integrated into both locations. The PB84 premises were completely renovated and given over to the sale of autographs, books, coins, manuscripts, and stamps. Although there continues to be some shifting, the following breakdown will give you the overall picture of where an SPB expert might be located and where certain kinds of sales are held:

1334 York Avenue:	African and Oceanic Art	Islamic Art
	American Decorative Arts	Japanese Works of Art
	American Folk Art	Medieval Works of Art
	American Furniture	Musical Instruments
	American Indian Art	19th & 20th c. Works of Art
	Antiquities	
	Art Deco	Paperweights
	Art Nouveau	Porcelain
	Chinese Art	Portrait Miniatures
	Clocks and Watches	Pre-Columbian Art
	Collectibles	Rugs and Carpets
	Costume	Russian Art
	Dolls	Silver
	English Decorative Art	Snuff Bottles
	English Furniture	Toys
	European Decorative Arts	Victoriana
	European Furniture	Vintage Vehicles
980 Madison Avenue:	Ballet and Theater Arts	Jewelry
	Drawings	Photographs

	Prints Sculpture	Paintings American Contemporary European Haitian Impressionist Latin American Mexican Modern Old Master
171 East 84th Street:	Autographs Books Coins	Manuscripts Stamps

Sales are held 3–4 times a week at the Madison and York Avenues locations. Mostly the sales are held on Tuesdays, Wednesdays, and Thursdays. Morning sales usually begin at 10 or 10:15; afternoon sales begin at 2; and evening sales, when held, start at 8. No matter when a sale is held, viewing always includes a Saturday. There is still the occasional elegant sale where a ticket of admission may be necessary, but this occurs very infrequently.

The Madison Avenue building, which takes up the blockfront between 76th and 77th streets, has four stories and contains a main saleroom that can comfortably seat 600 people. There are also ancillary salerooms, offices, exhibition space, and storage. The main entrance is always filled with little knots of people talking animatedly about what they have bought or will bid on. You can feel the pace in all the public areas, where there is a hustle and a bustle. Collectors, dealers, curators, and the curious are all there. The main saleroom has special lighting, a stagelike setting, and over the auctioneer's pulpit-like podium, an electronically operated currency conversion board, which tells the audience instantaneously just how much that dollar bid is in pounds, marks, and yen. SPB, like all auction houses, has good auctioneers and bad ones; among the best in all the trade is John Marion. A showman supreme, he can keep an auction moving along rapidly and still bring humor, tragedy, and yet another bid to the fore, all the while making it seem effortless. In his forties, he is the chairman of SPB, Inc., and the son of the man who helped build up Parke-Bernet.

The York Avenue building, which occupies the blockfront between 71st and 72nd streets, is also four stories high; its facade is of gray Canadian granite; and it has more than twice the space of the Madison Avenue building. According to SPB, "the York Avenue Galleries have more exhibition, auction, and storage space than any other auction facility in the world—nearly an acre of space per floor for a total of 160,000 square feet." Built in 1922 and originally a cigar factory, the building was occupied before SPB by Kodak, which used it for a distribution center. SPB has modernized the structure. Movable partitions make it possible for the firm to create intimate space for small sales, or to open up the saleroom to accommodate huge crowds. Auxiliary services in the building include a first-class restaurant. The 84th Street facility has been completely redecorated. It has special exhibition space to enhance the viewing of smaller objects such as books, coins, and stamps. A small brown Mercedes bus shuttles back and forth several times a day between the various facilities.

Absentee bids play an important role in SPB auctions. The house estimates that it receives over $90 million annually in "order bids" from persons who cannot or do not want to attend auctions. Of this figure, about one fourth represents successful final bids.

The regional offices are staffed with representatives who solicit and accept goods for consignment, help bidders, and otherwise make SPB's services known in the region. Auctions by the house are also coming to the regions. SPB held its first sale in Chicago in September 1980, and plans to hold more.

Incidentally, the last syllable in Sotheby Parke Bernet is pronounced to rhyme with "get."

In addition to holding auctions and conducting appraisals of fine art properties, SPB is involved in diverse corporate activities. Among the most interesting is the Sotheby Parke Bernet International Realty Corporation (Charles H. Seilheimer, Jr., president), which offers marketing and brokerage services for luxury residential, estate, and farm properties. Look at what they offer for sale or rent and you will feel like the child with its face pressed against the store window, staring at unattainable goodies. These properties are offered by the superrich for the superrich, but thanks to SPB's advertising of them, we can all get a peek at such things as a Rockefeller private island or a Henry Ford II high-rise triplex.

Contact person: Nancy Tremaine, director, Marketing and Communications, can steer you to the right person.

Days/hours of operation: Mon.–Sat. 10 A.M.–5 P.M.

Areas in which general auctions and special sales are held (incl. some contact people):

Americana (Nancy Druckman)	Japanese Works of Art
Arms and Armor	(D. Martin Lorber)
Art Deco	Jewelry (Denis Scioli)
Art Nouveau	Judaica
Autographs (Fanny Neville-Rolfe)	Manuscripts
Books (Jerry Patterson)	Maps
Chinese Works of Art	Medieval Works of Art
(James G. Lally)	Musical Instruments
Clocks and Watches	(Lauren Boucher)
Coins (Jeremiah Brady)	Netsuke
Dolls (Pamela Brown)	
Drawings (Linda Silverman)	
Furniture (American: William	
Stahl; English: Gerald Bland;	
European: Thierry Millerand)	
Glass	
Islamic Art (Michael Jones)	

Paintings
  Old Master (Brenda Auslander)
  17th c. British
  18th c. British
  19th c. European (Susan Bodo)
  Pre-20th c. American
  (Peter Rathbone)
  Impressionist (John Tancock)
  Modern Art (Shary Grossman)
  Contemporary Art
  (Linda Silverman)
Paperweights (Lynne Tillman)
Pewter

Photographica (Anne Horton)
Porcelain (Letitia Roberts)
Pre-Columbian Art
(Claudia Giangola)
Prints (Marc Rosen, Ruth Ziegler)
Rugs (Michael Grogran)
Russian Art (Gerard Hill)
Scientific Instruments
Silver (Kevin Tierney)
Stamps (Andrew Levitt)
Toys (Pamela Brown)
Vintage Vehicles (Chris Landrigan)

Sales are advertised regularly in the *Wall Street Journal,* in the New York press, and in specialty periodicals around the world. Sotheby Parke Bernet also publishes a newsletter 8 times a year, at approximately 6-week intervals (subscription is $3 for the U.S., Canada, and Mexico; $5 elsewhere), which can be ordered from Subscription Dept., 980 Madison Avenue, New York, NY 10021.

Catalogues for each sale are available singly at the house and by mail; the price varies from sale to sale, tending to range from $5 to $25. Catalogues are also offered by subscription, either in a particular specialty, such as Chinese snuff bottles ($35 U.S., Canada, and Mexico; $50 elsewhere, sent via airmail), or for all the categories in which SPB has sales and catalogues (in 1980, a subscription to all New York catalogues cost $980 for the U.S., Canada, and Mexico, and $1,334 elsewhere). On all orders totaling $100 or more, there is a 10 percent discount. The *Newsletter* is sent free to all catalogue subscribers. Post-sale results are sent without any extra charge.

Usual viewing procedure: Exhibition is 3–5 days before a sale and almost always includes a Saturday (Mon.–Sat. 10 A.M.–5 P.M.; Sun. 1–5 P.M.). Presale exhibitions close at 3 P.M. the day immediately preceding the auction. During July and August, hours are Mon.–Fri. 10 A.M.–5 P.M.; Tues. to 7:30 P.M.

Bidder Information

Most sales are held on premises, but SPB does hold house and estate sales, as well as benefit auctions on location, and an occasional sale in another city.

There is a buyer's premium of 10 percent. Credit cards are not accepted. Buyer must settle account "immediately, unless credit has been arranged." Credit arrangements for qualified buyers are made "through the corporate treasurer's office."

SPB offers a limited guarantee of authenticity—"the identity of the creator, the period, culture, sources of origin of the property, as the case may be, as set forth in the BOLD TYPE HEADING of such catalogue entry." This guarantee runs for 5 years, and if during that time "it is established that the ... BOLD TYPE HEADING of the catalogue description of such lot (as amended by any posted notices or oral announcements during the sale) is not substantially correct based on a fair reading of the catalogue including the terms of any Glossary contained ..., the sale of such lot will be rescinded and the original purchase price refunded." In effect, SPB is guaranteeing the lot for 5 years and offers buyers the opportunity to return goods that prove to be not as catalogued.

Packing and shipping services are offered, at the buyer's expense.

State and local sales tax: 8 percent.

Consignor Information

Persons wishing to consign property should "call or write to set up an appointment; or write, sending photographs and pertinent information."

The standard consignor's commission is 10 percent on lots sold for more than $1,000, and 15 percent for lots sold for $1,000 or less. But it is negotiable, depending on the situation. There is a separate rate structure for dealers and institutions: "reduction from the usual varies with value of property and whether the institution allows use of name."

Consignor pays for insurance, packing, and shipping to SPB premises, catalogue illustrations (black and white: full page $80, half page $50, quarter page $30; color: $600), and special advertising.

Consigned goods are sold within "several months."

Reserves are accepted; if not mutually agreed on, the reserve will automatically be "60 percent of our low estimate published prior to the auction."

Consignors should work out a reserve with SPB, since the Consignment Agreement allows SPB: (a) to "sell the property at a price below the reserve provided that we pay you on the settlement date the net amount to which you would have been entitled ... had the property been sold at the reserve (that is, the reserve less our selling commission and reimbursable expenses)"; and (b) if a lot fails to reach its reserve, "you authorize us, as your exclusive agent, for a period of 14 days following the auction to sell the lot privately for a price that will result in a payment to you of not less than the net amount ... you would have been entitled [to] ... had the lot been sold at a price equal to the agreed reserve."

Settlement is made after 35 days.

Buy-ins cost 5 percent of the reserve.

Appraisal service is available; the cost varies and is negotiable. "A partial rebate will be made on any property subsequently consigned" within a year of the appraisal. Call Marjorie Crodelle at (212) 472-3452.

The house does buy and sell on its own behalf: "occasionally when sellers wish to sell outright rather than through auction, company will purchase; such ownership is always indicated in sales catalogue."

33. Sotheby Parke Bernet Los Angeles

7660 Beverly Boulevard
Los Angeles, CA 90036

Tel. (213) 937-5130
Telex: 677 120
Cable: ABINITIO

The Los Angeles division of Sotheby Parke Bernet started holding auctions in 1971. Before that, the SPB presence had been as a representative office. In 1972, Peter McCoy, a native Californian and a collector in his late twenties, was chosen to head the Los Angeles operation. That same year, Marvin Newman, a veteran California auctioneer with over 30 years experience in the antique and auction business (he was then in his early fifties), closed his auction house and joined SPBLA in order to work with McCoy. Together they have built up an impressive operation, one whose 1979–80 annual turnover of approximately $24 million represented about 10 percent of SPB's total North American turnover. McCoy joined the Reagan administration after the 1980 election, and was succeeded as head by Newman.

Quarters for SPBLA is a 1940s Southern California–style spread-out building—it once housed an aeronautical space institute—that has about 40,000 square feet of usable space. SPBLA renovated the building, converted the lecture auditorium into an attractive saleroom, and added exhibition space. The inside and exterior of the building can be seen in the 1979 movie *American Gigolo*.

Sales are held on two levels. There are monthly sales in the decorative and fine arts, for which catalogues are available only over the counter ($2 each). These are mixed-lot general-purpose auction sales. And 3–4 times a year, SPBLA holds multisession sales of better properties—paintings, or rugs, or jewelry, or furniture of various styles and periods—for which illustrated glossy-paper catalogues are prepared. The multisession sales, which often do quite well, have attracted a considerable amount of interest in Japan and a significant number of Japanese participate, either as floor bidders or as absentee bidders. In June 1979, SPBLA sold a George Caleb Bingham painting, *Jolly Flatboatman*, for $980,000 and established a world record for an American painting (a record that lasted until spring 1980, when SPB in New York City broke it). Although these better-quality sales always include such high-priced items, SPBLA still sells a significant proportion of lots for under $500.

SPBLA runs very independently of the New York operation. There is an interchange in expertise between New York and Los Angeles, but that is similar to the exchange between London and New York. Not only are the 65 people employed by SPBLA involved in sales in that city, but the division oversees the San Francisco representative office and coordinates the sales held by SPB in Vancouver. For all the romance of auctioneering, the corporate setup is as mundane as that in any other middle-sized company.

Contact persons: Marvin Newman/Tracy Schrick

Days/hours of operation: Mon.–Fri. 9 A.M.–5 P.M.

Areas in which general auctions and special sales are held (incl. some contact people):

Arms and Armor (Terry Parsons)	Paintings (John E. Parkerson)
Art Deco	Old Master
Art Nouveau (Jane Campbell)	17th c. British
Books	18th c. British
Chinese Works of Art	19th c. European
(Peter Malone)	Pre-20th c. American
Dolls	Impressionist
Drawings	Modern Art
Engravings	Contemporary Art
Etchings	Photographica (Tessa Helfet)
Furniture (Kenneth Winslow,	Photographic Instruments
Joseph Kuntz)	Porcelain
Glass	Posters
Japanese Works of Art	Prints (Tessa Helfet)
(Peter Malone)	Rugs (Kenneth Winslow,
Jewelry (Rene Atlass)	Joseph Kuntz)
Medieval Works of Art	Silver (Jane Campbell)
Netsuke	Toys

The better-quality sales are advertised in the American and European press as well as in specialty periodicals, such as *Arts in Asia*. Other kinds of sales are generally advertised only locally. SPBLA sales are also previewed in the SPB *Newsletter* ($3 for an annual subscription).

Catalogues for the monthly sales are available only at the counter just a day or two before the sale; the cost is $2. Catalogues for the better-property sales cost $10–$16 and are available at the house and by mail, as well as by annual subscription, which costs $75 for all such catalogues and includes prices realized.

Usual viewing procedure: Except in summer, exhibition is 3 days prior to the sale, noon–5 P.M., including Saturday and Sunday. Summer hours are Monday–Friday 9 A.M.–5 P.M.

Bidder Information

SPBLA holds house and estate sales, but most sales occur on the firm's premises.

The buyer's premium is 10 percent. Credit cards are not accepted. Buyer must settle accounts immediately after auction.

Packing and shipping services are offered, at buyer's expense.

Guarantees of authenticity are not offered, but goods that prove to be not as catalogued may be returned. The catalogue conditions of sale state that although all goods are sold "as is," if "within 21 days of the sale of any lot, the purchaser gives notice in writing to us that the lot is counterfeit and if within 14 days after such notice the purchaser returns the lot . . .

and demonstrates that the lot is counterfeit, we will refund the purchase
price."
State and local sales tax: 6 percent.

Consignor Information

Persons wishing to consign property should contact the house for a no-obliga-
tion estimate. Minimum value for a consignment is $500.
The consignor's commission is basically 15 percent to $500 and 10 percent for
over $500. But the commission is negotiable, depending on the situation.
And there are separate rates for dealers and institutions: 8 percent to
$500; 6 percent over $500.
Consignors do not pay for warehousing, but do pay for catalogue illustrations
($45–$70), insurance ($6 per $1,000), and special advertising (0.5 percent of the selling price).
Consigned goods are usually sold within 90 days; settlement is made 35 days
after the sale.
Reserves are accepted; buy-ins cost 5 percent of the reserve.

Appraisal service is available: the price varies. Contact Rupert Fennell in the
Appraisal Department.

Sotheby Parke Bernet Los Angeles, according to Peter McCoy, does "not usually" buy and sell on its own behalf.

34. Stalker and Boos, Inc.
280 North Woodward Avenue   Tel. (313) 646-4560
Birmingham, MI 48011

This firm's direct predecessor began as a company involved in liquidating
businesses in Detroit and the surrounding area. David Stalker became involved with the firm while still in his twenties during the 1950s, and later
brought into it his childhood friend Frank Boos III (pronounced "bows," as in
"buttons and . . . "). What became Stalker and Boos grew apace, and in 1976,
the company Stalker and Boos, Inc., moved to its present location on the
ground floor and lower level of the sleekly modern Great American Insurance
Building in the affluent Detroit suburb of Birmingham.
  Stalker and Boos conducts both a retail operation and an auction business.
The retail operation, on the ground floor, sells rare books, fine crystal, good
reproductions, gracious antiques, etc. The tastefully decorated saleroom and
exhibition space for the auctions is on the lower level; sales are held approximately 5–6 times a year. The first really fine auctions were held after the firm
moved to this location. Since then, the firm has been co-auctioneer with Christie's at the fabulous Dodge estate sale at Rose Terrace in Grosse Pointe, another Detroit suburb, and has auctioned some splendid pieces for very high
prices—including the study for Frederick Church's *Icebergs* (the finished
work was among the most expensive paintings ever sold at auction).
  The saleroom can seat 250–275 people. Sales are usually held Saturday and

Sunday afternoons. Bidding is with black-numbered yellow cards, which can be obtained by registering. Everyone is welcome to attend a sale, but prospective bidders must register.

Contact persons: David Stalker/Frank Boos III

Days/hours of operation: Mon.–Sat. 10 A.M.–5:30 P.M.

Areas in which general auctions and special sales are held:

Americana	Furniture	Pewter
Drawings	Glass	Porcelain
Engravings	Jewelry	Prints
Etchings	Paintings	Silver

Sales are advertised in the national and local press and in specialty periodicals as well as via direct mail. To be placed on the mailing list, write La-Verne C. Short.

Catalogues are not available by subscription but are available singly for each sale at the house ($6) and by mail ($7.50). Prices realized costs an additional dollar.

Usual viewing procedure: Exhibition the Thursday (3–8 P.M.) and Friday (10 A.M.–4 P.M.) before the sale.

Bidder Information

Most auctions are held on the premises, but house and estate sales are also held.

A buyer's premium has been in effect since 1979 and is 10 percent.

Credit cards are not accepted. Absentee bids are executed. Settlement is 1–3 days after the sale.

Guarantees of authenticity are not offered, but a person has 21 days "to return goods if they have been misrepresented" inadvertently in the catalogue.

Stalker and Boos will assist the buyer to obtain shipping and packing services.

State sales tax: 4 percent.

Consignor Information

Prospective consignors should contact Stalker and Boos either in writing or by phone.

The consignor's commission varies: "the higher the value, the less the commission"—the rate ranging from 12.5 to 20 percent.

Consignors are not charged for insurance or warehousing, but are charged for photographs for the catalogue ($15).

Consigned goods are sold "within a few months."

Settlement is 21 days after the sale.

Reserves are accepted; buy-in charges depend on the situation, but there are "generally none."

Appraisal service is available: the cost is $20 verbal; $60 written; $375 or 1 percent of the total to come to the home.

35. Swann Galleries, Inc.

104 East 25th Street   Tel. (212) 254-4710
New York, NY 10021   Cable: SWANNSALES

Benjamin Swann, a New York book dealer and no relation to the noted English bookman Arthur Swann, held the first sale at the auction house that bears his name in 1942. An angry Arthur Swann threatened to sue, but later changed his mind. Under Benjamin Swann's direction, the firm had a checkered but generally profitable career as a somewhat low-level book auction house. Thirty years later, in 1972, George Lowry bought control of the firm, and he has worked wonders with it. Lowry was not a bookman per se, although his wife, Judy, was and is intimately involved in the direction of Argosy Bookstore, an important wholesale and retail book operation. But George Lowry did bring to Swann Galleries enthusiasm and energy, and under his intelligent administration Swann has fared very well.

In 1975 it moved to its present attractive quarters on the fourth floor of a nondescript office building; considerable thought went into the renovation. The firm has steadily increased the quality, quantity, and type of lots offered. In addition to books, Swann now sells prints, posters, and photographica, as well as other items. And in 1980, Swann fell only a few thousand dollars short of holding a million-dollar sale. The annual turnover is now well in excess of $2 million. At a time when many auctioneers of literary properties are complaining of lack of product to sell, Swann has an enormous backlog and has found it necessary to rent storage space in the building next door.

Sales are held weekly on Thursday afternoons. The catalogue is thorough and gives realistic estimates. The sales are fun to attend. There is at most sales a kind of "old shoe" quality to the bidders, all of whom seem to know each other and are known to the auctioneer. Lowry has computerized much of his operation and is well in advance of much of the book trade, which seems to look on the computer as the weapon of the devil.

Contact person: George S. Lowry

Days/hours of operation: Mon.–Fri. 9 A.M.–5:30 P.M.; Sat. by appt.

Areas in which general auctions and special sales are held:

Autographs	Manuscripts	Postcards
Books	Maps	Posters
Engravings	Photographica	Prints

Sales are advertised in the local press, such as the *New York Times*, and in specialty periodicals, such as *AB Bookman's Weekly*. A quarterly schedule is available; just write to be placed on the mailing list.

Catalogues for each sale are available singly by mail or at the house (the price is between $3 and $5). Catalogues are also available by subscription (the cost for catalogues and prices realized is $75 U.S., Canada, Mexico, and $65 for catalogues only; elsewhere the cost is $100 for catalogues and price lists, or $75 for just the catalogues).

Usual viewing procedure: Exhibition is always 3 days preceding sale, 9 A.M.–5 P.M.

Bidder Information

All auctions are held on Swann's premises.

The house instituted a buyer's premium of 10 percent in September 1980.

Bills are due upon receipt for mail order bidders; all others must pay immediately after the sale, unless other arrangements have been made prior to the auction. Credit cards are not accepted.

Absentee bids are executed.

Packing and shipping services are available at the buyer's expense.

All lots are sold "as is" and Swann makes no guarantees or warranties, but asserts in the catalogue: "notwithstanding the preceding condition, property may be returned by the purchaser, the sale rescinded, and the purchase price refunded under the following conditions: 1) printed books which upon collation prove to be defective in text or illustrations (provided such defects are not indicated in the catalogue or at the sale), and 2) autographs which prove not to be genuine (if this can be demonstratand if not indicated in the catalogue or at the sale)." Written notice must be received by the firm within 7 days of receipt of the property that is in question.

State and local sales tax: 8 percent.

Consignor Information

Prospective consignors should write "with list of material. Once list is approved material may be mailed in or brought in."

Minimum value for a consignment is approximately $50 for a single lot and $1,000 for a bunch of items.

The standard consignor's commission is as follows: 10 percent for items realizing $300 or more; sliding scale below $300—25 percent to $100, 20 percent to $200, 15 percent to $300.

The commission is negotiable, depending on the situation.

Consignors pay for insurance and packing and shipping; consignors do not pay for warehousing.

Consigned goods are sold within 6–9 months; settlement is made 45 days after the sale.

Reserves are accepted; buy-ins cost $10.

A photograph of any item for sale can be obtained for $3; payment must accompany the request.

Appraisal service is available; the cost is $300 per day.

Trosby Auction Galleries

36. 81 Peachtree Park Drive   Tel. (404) 351-4400
Atlanta, GA 30326   Toll-free (eastern U.S.
except Georgia): 1-800-241-8502

37. 905 North Railroad Avenue   Tel. (305) 659-1755
West Palm Beach, FL 33401

38. 1110 Bucknell Avenue   Tel. (305) 358-0014
Miami, Fl 33131

Originally a small retail antiques store in Palm Beach, Trosby was taken over
by Milton Freshman in 1948, and began holding auctions that year. Since
then, Trosby—which is now devoted almost entirely to auctions and appraisals—has greatly expanded.

This expansion has come in the main under the direction of Richard J.
Ramus, who married Freshman's granddaughter, and who for some time
worked with him and with his father-in-law, Robert Freshman. In 1974, in an
amicable transaction, Ramus bought out the Freshman interests.

In addition to the occasional house sale (and Trosby has built up an enviable reputation for handling the estates of Northerners with second homes in
south Florida), the firm holds approximately 3 sales a month of mixed lots at
3 different locations. These are:

Atlanta: Trosby had been holding sales here at different locations until
             1980, when it moved into its present quarters, which are situated
             about 4 miles from the city's downtown, about midway between
             that area and Atlanta's northern suburbs. These quarters, which
             are now the firm's headquarters, offer ample parking, as well as
             office facilities, storage space, and a good-sized saleroom. Trosby
             estimates the annual turnover at the sales it holds in Atlanta to be
             well in excess of $1 million. No sales are held here in August.

Miami: Since 1975, Trosby has been holding sales here at the Bayfront
             Auditorium (499 Biscayne Boulevard), just about every other month.

West Palm Beach: Trosby moved to its present quarters, an attractive 3-
             story building with office space, storage facilities, and a
             saleroom, in 1976. And this building served as its head-
             quarters until 1980. Sales are usually held here from
             January through the beginning of April, a period when
             the tourist season is at its peak.

Sales at all Trosby locations are held generally on weekday nights. Most auctions are at least 2-day affairs and sometimes they stretch to 3 days. Approximately 200–350 lots are sold at each session. Bidding is by numbered paddle,
obtained by registering upon arrival. All sales are catalogued, with addenda
issued at the time of the sale announcing corrections and additional lots.
Trosby is among the largest art and antiques auction firms in the South.

Contact person: Richard J. Ramus

Days/hours of operation: Mon.–Sat. 10 A.M.–6 P.M.

Areas in which general auctions and special sales are held:

Americana	Chinese Works of Art
Art Deco	Clocks and Watches
Art Nouveau	Drawings

Engravings	Pewter
Etchings	Porcelain
Furniture	Posters
Glass	Prints
Japanese Works of Art	Rugs
Jewelry	Sculpture
Maps	Silver
Musical Instruments	Toys
Paintings	

Sales are advertised regularly in local newspapers, such as the Miami *Herald* and the Atlanta *Constitution*, as well as in specialty periodicals, such as *Antiques Magazine* and *Art & Auction*.

Catalogues are available singly for each sale, either by mail or at a Trosby office; the usual cost is $6. Subscriptions to all catalogues issued are available, contact Judith Miske at the Atlanta office.

Usual viewing procedure: Exhibition 2 days before the sale, 2–9 P.M.

Bidder Information

Auctions are held both on and off the premises.

The buyer's premium is 10 percent. Credit cards are not accepted. Credit is available, depending on the situation. Buyer must settle account within 3 working days from time of sale or of notification.

Mail order bids are executed.

Trosby offers packing and shipping services, at the buyer's expense.

All goods are sold "as is," but goods that prove to be not as catalogued may be returned within 7 days.

Consignor Information

Prospective consignors should contact a branch of the house. The minimum value for a consignment is $100.

Consignor's commission is 10 percent, but it is negotiable, depending on the situation. There is a lower commission for dealers, 6 percent, and for institutions, although exactly what that commission is depends on "what's being sold."

Goods are usually sold within 60 days; settlement is made within 30–45 days.

There is no charge for warehousing or insuring consigned property; catalogue illustrations are $40 each. There is a charge for packing and shipping of consigned property.

Reserves are accepted, but "are usually only placed on items of over $500 valuation"; there is no charge for buy-ins.

Appraisal services are available: contact George Hall at the Palm Beach office or Paul Sternberg at the Atlanta office. Cost is 1 percent of the first $100,000 and ½ of 1 percent thereafter.

In 1981, Trosby filed for reorganization under Chapter XI.

Trosby does buy and sell on its own behalf.

39. Young Fine Arts Gallery
56 Market Street
Portsmouth, NH 03801

Tel. (603) 436-8773

Young holds monthly European and American paintings sales, monthly antiques and modern prints sales, and twice-yearly book, autograph, and paper documents sales. These sales are each between 100 and 200 lots, and while they include some expensive items, most lots sell for less than $300. The catalogues are not detailed, but occasionally have a refreshing candor; in referring to quality of the estimates, the catalogue states: "we'll probably be wrong as often as right." In 1980, the gallery moved to somewhat improved quarters at a new location.

Contact person: George M. Young, Jr.

Days/hours of operation: Mon.–Sat. 10 A.M.–5 P.M.

Areas in which general auctions and special sales are held:

Autographs	Paintings
Books	19th c. European
Drawings (all periods)	Pre-20th c. American
	Modern Art
	Contemporary Art
	Prints

Sales are advertised regularly in Boston and Portsmouth newspapers, as well as in specialty periodicals, such as *Antiques and the Arts Weekly*. Announcements are mailed free of charge to those requesting to be put on the mailing list. Catalogues are available by subscription ($36 for 12 monthly catalogues of either the painting or the print sales). Catalogues are also available for a specific sale, at the house ($3) or by mail ($3.50).

Usual viewing procedure: Exhibition 3 days prior to the sale, 10 A.M.–5 P.M.

Bidder Information

All auctions are held on the premises.

There is no buyer's premium. Accounts must be settled immediately by buyers present, and within 3 business days by absentee bidders. Mail order bids are executed.

Credit cards are accepted: American Express, MasterCard, Visa.

All goods are sold "as is," but the gallery will consider requests for refunds based on authenticity, provided that such a request is made within 7 days of the sale and that the property is returned to the gallery within 30 days of the sale, accompanied by written proof: "the refund will apply only to the hammer price and not to the 10 percent buyer's premium added to the hammer price of each lot."

Consignor's Information

Prospective consignors should get in touch with George Young either through the mail or by phone. The minimum value for a consignment to be accepted is $100.

Consignor's commission is $10 for any item selling for less than $100, and 10 percent for any selling for $100 or more.

Commission is negotiable, depending on the situation; "exceptions made for consignments of greater quantity and/or value than usual."

Goods consigned are usually sold in about one month; settlement is made after one week.

Consignors do not pay for insurance on consigned property or for its warehousing, or for catalogue illustrations, but do pay for packing and shipping of consigned goods.

Buy-in charge is $20 a lot.

Reserves are accepted.

Appraisal service is available: "$40 per hour with $40 minimum; if travel is required, $40 per hour and 20 cents per mile."

Young Fine Arts Gallery does buy and sell on its own behalf: "approximately 5 percent of lots sold in each auction are owned by house."

United States: also worthy of note

40. Aalten's Galleries
411 Main Street   Tel. (201) 674-2535/6
East Orange, NJ 07018

This firm was founded in 1914 in Newark by the grandfather and developed by the father of the present owners—Sanford and Jerome Holover. The firm has operated out of East Orange for many years, and is now located in air-conditioned premises 6 blocks west of Exit 145 of the Garden State Parkway. Sales are also held "on occasion at locations."

The on-premises sales are held monthly or every 5 weeks, usually on Mondays, and if necessary on Tuesdays, beginning at 11 A.M. These mixed-lot sales include AMERICANA, ART DECO, ART NOUVEAU, FURNITURE, GLASS, JEWELRY, JUDAICA, PAINTINGS, RUGS, and SILVER. They are advertised in the *New York Times*, the local press, and specialty periodicals. Announcements are sent out in the mail as well; if you wish to be placed on the mailing list, just write.

Catalogues are available only at the time of auction; the cost is $1. A buyer's premium of 10 percent was instituted at the beginning of 1980. Viewing is 8:30 A.M.–5:30 P.M. the Friday before the sale, as well as 8:30–11 A.M. the day of the sale. Absentee bids are not accepted. There are no guarantees of authenticity. Buyers are not offered packing and shipping services. Goods that prove to be not as catalogued may be returned. Buyers must settle accounts within 24 hours of the sale. State sales tax: 5 percent.

The consignor's commission ranges between 10 and 25 percent. Generally, consignors are not charged for packing and shipping, insurance, or warehousing. Consigned goods are sold in approximately 30 days. Settlement is made after 30 days. Reserves are not accepted. There are no buy-ins: "all items are sold regardless of price."

The house does buy and sell on its own behalf.

Appraisal service is available. The cost varies with the time involved.

Aalten's Galleries belongs to the New Jersey Society of Auctioneers and the National Association of Watch and Clock Collectors.

41. Joseph P. Adzima, Auctioneers and Appraisers

80 Shelton Road   Tel. (203) 275-1095
Trumbull, CT 06611

This is a general-purpose auction company whose scope ranges from business liquidations to estate consignments. Among its specialties are AMERICANA, ART DECO, ART NOUVEAU, BOOKS, DOLLS, JEWELRY, POSTCARDS, SILVER, and TOYS.

Auctions are held "as often as necessary" and advertised in local newspapers in Connecticut and New York, as well as in trade newspapers, such as *Antiques and the Arts Weekly.*

Adzima holds house sales. Announcements of forthcoming sales are available. Requests for catalogues, which are not available by subscription, should be sent to the above address.

The commission structure for consignors is a "sliding scale on gross sales," and is negotiable, depending on the situation. There is no buyer's premium. Mail order bids are executed. The usual viewing procedure is "2 hours prior to the sale, or by appointment."

Buyers must settle within 30 days. Credit terms are not available. The firm buys and sells on its own behalf: "information is available at the above address." State sales tax: 7.5 percent.

Adzima belongs to the Connecticut Auctioneers Association and the National Auctioneers Association.

42. Atlanta Galleries

2050 Hills Avenue   Tel. (404) 355-0755/1267
Atlanta, GA 30318

D. C. Moore, James Moore, and D. W. Richline run this firm, whose specialties include AMERICANA, FURNITURE, GLASS, PORCELAIN, and RUGS. Annual turnover is estimated to be about $1 million.

A general-purpose auction house, Atlanta Galleries holds sales approximately twice a week, on the premises. These are announced in the local newspapers. Catalogues for single sales are available on request. The usual viewing procedure is exhibition 3 days before the auction takes place.

There is no buyer's premium. Accounts must be settled within 5 days "unless prearranged." Credit is available for "possibly 30 days on large buys."

Mail order bids are not accepted. State and local sales tax: 4 percent.

Consignor's commission "varies with the value of the goods" and is negotiable. Dealers and institutions are charged a "slightly lower" rate. Goods consigned are sold within 2–4 weeks and settlement is within 2–3 weeks. Consignors pay insurance and packing and shipping.

The house pays a finder's fee of 10 percent.

Atlanta Galleries does buy and sell on its own behalf: "we purchase an estate because they will not wait for it to be auctioned."

43. Auction Service of Vermont
140 Church Street
Burlington, VT 05401   Tel. (802) 864-0043

This firm holds auctions 2 or 3 times a month on the premises of those who choose to use its services. Although, as owner Poncho Camire puts it, "quality is screened," the firm sells everything from real estate to FURNITURE. Contact person for antiques is Keith Manning.

Sales are advertised locally via newspaper advertisements and fliers. Announcements of forthcoming sales are also mailed. Catalogues are not available. There is no buyer's premium. Consignor's commission, which is negotiable, varies from 10 to 25 percent, "depending on the situation." State sales tax: 3 percent.

Viewing is usually the day before and one hour before the sale. Buyers must settle immediately, "unless prearranged." Accounts are usually settled with consignors within 24 hours.

The annual turnover of the firm is in excess of $500,000. It belongs to the Vermont Auctioneers Association.

44. C. T. Bevensee Auction Service
P.O. Box 492
Botsford, CT 06404   Tel. (203) 426-6698

Located in a very small town in Fairfield County, Connecticut, C. T. Bevensee is an auctioneer and estate liquidator. He holds sales as required on the premises of his clients or at venues like the American Legion hall in Norwalk. He does not issue catalogues, and sales are mainly advertised locally. The usual viewing procedure is exhibition 2 hours before the sale, and buyers must settle their accounts "immediately." The firm does buy and sell on its own behalf. State sales tax: 7.5 percent.

45. Bowers & Ruddy Galleries, Inc.
Suite 600
6922 Hollywood Boulevard   Tel. (213) 466-4595; (800) 421-4224
Los Angeles, CA 90028   Cable: PHOTOGRADE USA

A subsidiary of General Mills, this firm holds sales 6–8 times a year. Among the items auctioned are COINS, MEDALS, and STAMPS.

Sales are held in various parts of the United States, mostly in hotels. Announcements of forthcoming sales are available, and are free; just write to the firm. Catalogues are available for each sale ($5 to $10) and on an annual basis (U.S., $15; elsewhere via airmail, $37). Sales are advertised in specialty publications. Prices realized cost $1 for each sale except to catalogue subscribers.

There is no buyer's premium. The usual viewing procedure, according to Dr. George Fuld, the auction manager, is "9–4, one week minimum" in the area where the sale is to be held. Mail order bids are accepted and encouraged. Shipping and packing services are available at the buyer's expense. Accounts must be settled immediately after the auction, but credit terms are available. Credit cards are accepted (American Express, MasterCard, Visa). State and local sales tax for sales in Los Angeles: 6 percent.

The basic commission structure is 20 percent "including pictures, full design." There are no extra charges for catalogue illustrations, insurance, or warehousing prior to sale. There is a separate commission structure for dealers. Goods consigned are generally sold within 2–3 months. Settlement is usually 45 days after the sale. The minimum value for a consignment is $2,000. Reserves are accepted. The consignor's costs vary when property is not sold.

Appraisal service is available. The "fee is waived if goods auctioned."

The firm, which ranks among the largest coin dealers in the world, does buy and sell on its own behalf.

46. Bridges Antiques and Auctions
Highway 46, 1.5 miles east of I-4
P.O. Box 52A   Tel. (305) 323-2801/322-0095
Sanford, FL 32771

In central Florida, not too far from Disney World, the husband-and-wife team of Bill and Mary Bridges run an auction house/retail operation. Sales are held the last Saturday of each month, and exhibition is usually 10 A.M.–5 P.M. the day before. Sales are advertised regularly in the Orlando, Sanford, and Daytona Beach newspapers, as well in as such trade papers as *Antique Trader* and *Southern Antiques*.

Bridges is a general-purpose auction house, but it does have some specialties, including GLASS, JEWELRY, and TOYS. All auctions are held on the premises. Announcements of forthcoming sales are available at "no charge" to those who "sign up for our mailing list." Catalogues are "not usually" available.

There is no buyer's premium. State and local taxes must be paid unless the buyer is exempt or has a resale number. There is no guarantee of authenticity as such, but "if Bill guarantees anything, then he stands behind this." Property for consignment should be valued at least at $50. The commission scale is flexible and negotiable. Standard rates are: 20 percent for furniture brought in by consignor, but 25 percent if Bridges has to arrange the pickup; 25 percent on "small items," etc. State sales tax: 4 percent.

Buyer should settle at the sale. Credit cards are accepted: MasterCard,

Visa. Consignors' property is usually sold "within the same month" and settlement is made the Wednesday after the sale.

The house buys and sells on its own behalf: "we buy antiques and sell them."

47. Brookline Auction Gallery

Proctor Hill Road, Route 130   Tel. (603) 673-4474/4153
Brookline, NH 03033

Sales are held on the premises and on site where estates are being liquidated. To be placed on the mailing list for announcements of sales, write to Roland Pelletier; there is no charge for announcements or for catalogues. Brookline Auction Gallery is a general-purpose auction house, with some specialties: ANTIQUE TOOLS and TOYS.

Sales are held on the average twice a month. There is no buyer's premium, and mail order bids are not accepted. The commission charged consignors "depends on what is consigned." Reserves are not accepted. Items are sold 4–6 weeks after being consigned; settlement is made 5–7 days after the sale. Brookline does buy and sell on its own behalf: "we will either accept merchandise on consignment or we will buy it outright and sell it through the auction ourselves."

48. R. W. Bronstein Corp.

3666 Main Street   Tel. (716) 835-7666/7408
Buffalo, NY 14226

Bronstein specializes in real estate, but from time to time it auctions antiques and household inventories as well as collectibles. Sales are advertised in the local papers and through mailings. You can be placed on the mailing list free of charge by request. There is no buyer's premium. State and local sales tax: 7 percent.

49. Brzostek's Auction Service

2052 Lamson Road   Tel. (315) 678-2542
Phoenix, NY 13135

Established in 1978 in central New York State, Brzostek knocks down between 8,000 and 10,000 items per year (for a gross of approximately $400,000 annually). Sales are held, usually on the weekend, 20–30 times a year, mostly on the auctioneer's premises, though there are some house sales.

Bernard Brzostek reports: "we sell primarily antiques and collector's items," such as FURNITURE (early Victorian, oak), GLASS, CLOCKS AND WATCHES, PAINTINGS (pre-20th c. American), COINS, LAMPS, QUILTS, MUSIC BOXES, etc. Most lots sell for under $75.

There is no buyer's premium, and credit cards are not accepted. Settlement is immediately following the sale; "except on large amounts, buyers may place

25 percent down, with balance due within 17 days." State and local taxes: 7 percent.

Sales notices are sent to anyone who requests them, enclosing a self-addressed stamped envelope. For $5 a year, the firm will place your name on its mailing list. Catalogues are not available by subscription, but can be obtained from the firm for single sales. The usual viewing procedure is 2 hours before the sale, but, reports Brzostek, "on large 2-day estate sales we provide viewing the day ahead at the site."

The consignor's commission is negotiable, "ranging from 10 to 30 percent, depending on the amount of merchandise to be sold, value, work to be done, etc." Settlement is 48–72 hours after the sale.

The house accepts no reserves, pays finder's fees of 5–10 percent, and will execute mail order or phone bids on which a 25 percent deposit has been paid. However, "all items are sold 'as is,' with no returns."

Brzostek belongs to the National Auctioneers Association.

50. Buckingham Galleries, Ltd.
4350 Dawson Street Tel. (714) 283-7286
San Diego, CA 92115

High-level estate liquidations are the goal of Chester J. Whalen, the president of Buckingham. In addition to the usual items auctioned off by such a firm, it also specializes in ARCHITECTURAL ANTIQUES, which are sold for commercial restaurant interiors. Sales are held 8–10 times a year and are advertised in newspapers, on West Coast radio and TV, and via direct mail.

Most sales are held on-site, but some take place in hotel ballrooms. Catalogues are available only at the auction. Exhibition usually is 1–2 days prior to sale, noon–8 P.M. There is no buyer's premium. Accounts should be settled "as soon as possible." State and local sales tax: 7 percent.

Consignor commissions are 25 percent per lot valued under $50,000, negotiable thereafter. Dealers and institutions are charged 23 percent. Reserves are accepted only if an item is valued at $5,000 or more. Consigned goods are usually sold within 30 days and settlement is made within 7 days of sale. There is no cost if a lot is bought in. The house does buy and sell on its own behalf.

51. Bushell's Auction
2006 2nd Avenue Tel. (206) 622-5833
Seattle, WA 98121

Bushell's is a general-purpose auction house which holds sales every Tuesday, sometimes in the evening. Viewing is generally on the day before the auction, during business hours. All sales are held on the premises, and are announced in the local newspapers. Sales are not catalogued. There is no buyer's premium. Accounts should be settled within 3 days of the sale. State sales tax: 4.5 percent. Consignor's commission: 40 percent on items sold for $50 or less; 20

percent on those selling for more than $50. The only other cost for the consignor is the shipping and packing of property to be auctioned. The house does buy and sell on its own behalf, "on very rare occasions. We prefer to sell consigned items." In 1979, Bushell's auctioned approximately 22,000 lots, for a gross of over $750,000.

52. Canton Barn Auctions
79 Old Canton Road   Tel. (203) 693-4901/379-0500
Canton, CT 06019

All auctions are held on the premises, Saturdays at 7:30 P.M. and Sundays 10 A.M.–5 P.M. Auctioneer Richard E. Wacht does not accept consignments: "we own all items" for sale. There is no buyer's premium. Canton Barn Auctions does not accept mail order bids and does not offer packing or shipping services. Sales are not catalogued. Viewing is possible prior to the sale and often during the week before the auction takes place. Credit cards are not accepted, but personal checks are, "as long as we are notified prior to the sale." State tax: 7.5 percent.

53. Fred Clark Auctioneer, Inc.
P.O. Box 124, Route 14   Tel. (203) 423-3939/0594
Scotland, CT 06264

This firm specializes in "on-site estate sales" and these are usually held weekly during spring, summer, and fall. In the winter, Fred Clark "works from hotel-restaurant banquet rooms." Sales are advertised in local weeklies, such as the Norwich *Bulletin*, and in the trade papers, such as *Antiques and the Arts Weekly*. There are no catalogues available for these sales. There is no buyer's premium. Buyers must settle "on the spot." Viewing is possible "1–3 hours prior to the auction." Consignor's commission "varies." Goods are usually sold within 60–90 days; settlement is made within "10 banking days." State sales tax: 7.5 percent.

54. Cockrum Auctions
2701 North Highway 94   Tel. (314) 723-9511
St. Charles, MO 63301

This firm was started by Betty Cockrum and her ex-husband in 1960. The auctioneer is Paul Ernst, Ms. Cockrum's son.

Sales are held every Friday and Saturday night, on the premises, a one-story brick building connected to two other structures, which are used for storage space and offices. Mostly these sales feature household goods of one sort or another, such as FURNITURE. Once a month, antique collectibles of higher value are auctioned. Both types of auction are advertised in suburban and St. Louis newspapers, as well as in specialty periodicals.

Most sales are uncatalogued. Bidding is done by numbered cards. There is no buyer's premium. Accounts must be settled as soon as the sale ends. Credit cards are accepted: MasterCard, Visa. State and local sales tax: 4⅛ percent. Consignor commissions are flexible. Goods are sold within 30–45 days and settlement is made in 10 days or less. Reserves are not accepted. There is no charge for buy-ins, nor is it likely there will be any. The firm does buy and sell on its own behalf.

55. George Cole, Auctioneers and Appraisers
14 Green Street   Tel. (914) 338-2367
Kingston, NY 12401

Sales are held by Cole "at least once a month," "on location" or at the Ramada Inn, Route 28, Kingston. Cole includes among his specialties AMERICANA. Announcements with brief descriptions of lots for sale are available for a self-addressed stamped envelope. When a sale is catalogued, that catalogue must be paid for in dollars; foreign currency is not accepted. State and local sales tax: 5 percent.

There is no buyer's premium. Settlement is the day of the auction. Mail bids are accepted, but there are no guarantees of authenticity, no packing or shipping services available, and no chance to return goods that prove to be not as catalogued. The usual viewing procedure is "at least 2 hours" before the auction, "unless it is a special sale."

The consignor's commission, which is negotiable, depending on the situation, is normally 20 percent, which "includes pickup, cleaning, advertising, and selling." A buy-in costs the consignor 20 percent of the last bid. Reserves are accepted only if "it is super merchandise" or a "quality item." Settlement is made within 10 days of the sale. The house does buy and sell on its own behalf "when the situation arises."

George Cole has been vice-president of the Ulster County Antique Dealers Association and is a member of the National Auctioneers Association.

56. Conestoga Auction Company, Inc.
P.O. Box 1   Tel. (717) 898-7284
Manheim, PA 17545

This company holds auctions at its premises and "on location." Sales are announced through recorded telephone messages, by brochures mailed out to anyone who wishes to be put on the mailing list, and in local newspapers, such as the Lancaster *New Era*.

Sales are held weekly, one sale a month being given over to antiques. The buyer's premium, which was instituted in 1980, is 10 percent. Buyers must settle up immediately. Consignor's commission is 15 percent for any item selling for less than $50; 10 percent, $50 and above. State sales tax: 6 percent.

Conestoga head Walter Bomberger reports that reserves are not accepted and finder's fees are not paid. Catalogues are available for single sales and may be obtained upon mail request to the auction house. Mail order bids will be executed.

57. Cook's Auction Gallery

Route 58   Tel. (617) 293-3445/866-3243
Halifax, MA 02338

Louis A. Cook has held more than 4,000 auctions since his beginnings at the
end of World War II. Currently he conducts auctions every Saturday, usually
in the afternoon but sometimes in the evening. About half of these take place
on the premises; the rest are held wherever the properties to be auctioned are
located.

Cook's is a general-purpose auction house whose specialties include AMERI-
CANA, CLOCKS AND WATCHES, DOLLS, FURNITURE (all periods), MUSICAL IN-
STRUMENTS, PAINTINGS, PEWTER, PORCELAIN, POSTCARDS, RUGS, SILVER, and
TOYS. But Cook's also has an unusual specialty. In the spring and fall, usually
5 times each season, Cook—an avid horticulturist and a past officer of the
national rhododendron society—holds SHRUBBERY auctions, featuring plants,
shrubs, and the like.

All sales are advertised in the local and Boston press, as well as in trade
newspapers, such as *Antiques and the Arts Weekly* and *Yankee Auction
News.* Announcements are sent out only for the occasional special sale, for
which catalogues are available.

There is no buyer's premium, and mail order bids are not executed. Viewing is usually the morning before the sale. Bidders register before the auction
and are given numbered cards, which they use to identify themselves if they
capture a lot. You can bid any way you want: by voice, by signal, or by
waving your card. During the auction, a successful bidder not known to the
house will be approached by one of the young women in stewardess-like uniforms who are spotted around the room, and she will ask him to pay 25 percent of the knockdown price. The rest can be paid after the auction.

Consignor commissions are 25 percent of the knockdown price of a property. Goods consigned are usually sold within a month of being received and
settlement is the week following the sale. There are no reserves and no charge
for buy-ins. State sales tax: 5 percent.

Cook's belongs to the National Auctioneers Association and the Massachusetts State Auctioneers Association.

58. Dairy State Auction Service

412 North Washington Street   Tel. (414) 671-3013
Milwaukee, WI 53203

Also known as "Colonel John," the Dairy State Auction Service holds about
40 auctions per year, with John D. Haynes presiding over estate and liquidation sales.

These sales are uncatalogued and are advertised in the local press. There is
no buyer's premium, and consignor's terms are negotiable, "depending on the
situation." Settlement is made with the consignor the day after the sale; the
buyer settles up at once. "Colonel John" reports that he "never knowingly

misrepresents; if we do make an error, then we will refund." State and local sales tax: 4.5 percent.

Dairy State Auction Service also buys and sells on its own behalf.

59. Douglas Galleries
Route 5   Tel. (413) 665-2877
South Deerfield, MA 01373

This firm is a general-purpose auction operation. Its "on-site estate sales" are held approximately once a week; Douglas Bilodeau is the auctioneer. Sales are advertised in the local, Springfield, and Boston press, as well as in papers such as *Antiques and the Arts Weekly*. Brochures for some sales are available and can be requested from Douglas in writing. A few sales are fully catalogued; most are not.

There is no buyer's premium. Buyers must settle accounts immediately, and pay sales tax unless exempt. The consignor's fee "varies according to the value of consignment." Goods are sold usually within 1–3 weeks of consignment; settlement is 30 days after the sale. State sales tax: 5 percent. The usual viewing procedure is exhibition a few hours before the sale.

Douglas Galleries buys and sells on its own behalf: "we are prepared to purchase estate contents if that is the type of settlement desired by the heirs, executor, etc." Trade Association memberships include the National Auctioneers Association, the Massachusetts Auctioneers Association, and the Certified Auctioneers Institute.

60. Empire Galleries, Ltd.
2722 North Main Street   Tel. (714) 547-7384
Santa Ana, CA 92701

A general-purpose auction house, Empire holds sales approximately 4 times a month. It is open for business Tuesday–Saturday, 1–5 P.M. It emphasizes CLOCKS AND WATCHES, FURNITURE, and JEWELRY.

The house instituted a buyer's premium of 10 percent in 1980. Viewing is usually available 2 hours before the sale. Sales tax is charged on the invoice price (hammer price plus buyer's premium), unless the bidder has a proper resale number. Buyers must settle up within 30 days of the auction, but in any event must pay one third at the time of the sale. Credit cards are accepted: MasterCard, Visa. State and local sales tax: 6 percent.

Sales are uncatalogued, but announcements are available free of charge to anyone who wishes to be placed on the mailing list.

Prospective consignors should get in touch with Carl Marcus. The usual commission for consignors, which is negotiable, is 20–25 percent. There is no charge for buy-ins. Consigned goods are sold within 30 days.

61. The Fine Arts Company of Philadelphia, Inc.
2317 Chestnut Street   Tel. (215) 564-3644
Philadelphia, PA   Cable: FACPA
19103

This firm holds auctions approximately every 2 months. These sales, many of which are house and estate sales, usually consist of mixed lots, including AMERICANA, FURNITURE, JEWELRY, and the like. These sales are held on the premises of the consignor, or at public venues (such as the M. C. Benton Convention Center, Winston-Salem, N.C.), or in institutional settings (such as the Historical Society of Pennsylvania, in Philadelphia).

Sales are advertised in the local press and in specialty periodicals, such as *Antiques Magazine*, as well as through an extensive mailing list to which announcements are sent. You can be placed on this mailing list free of charge by writing to the firm.

The sales are catalogued and the price of the catalogue ($10 up) depends on the size and quality of the sale. There is no buyer's premium. State sales tax: 6 percent. Viewing is usually 2 days before the sale. Goods are sold "as is"; the firm will consider claims, however, made within 30 days of the sale. Credit cards are not accepted. Buyer must settle within a week after the sale. Consignor's commission is usually 10 percent but is negotiable, depending on the situation. Reserves are accepted. On such items there is a 10 percent buy-in charge. Goods consigned are usually sold within 2 months; settlement is made 30 days after the sale.

Appraisal service is available; it is the "major part" of the firm's business. Minimum is $125 if appraisal is for estate or tax purposes, $250 if the appraisal is for insurance purposes.

62. George S. Foster III
Route 28   Tel. (603) 736-9240
Epsom, NH 03234

Billed as "the Complete Auction Service," Foster holds about 4 auctions a month, wherever the properties to be auctioned off are located. Sales are advertised in New Hampshire newspapers and in the specialty and trade press. Foster reports: "we generally run a mixed auction covering many categories; we travel and do on-site auctions, estates, real estate, business liquidations, commercial sales."

Catalogues are produced only for very special sales, but announcements are available at no charge upon request.

The usual viewing procedure is exhibition 1–2 hours before the sale or by appointment the evening before. There is no buyer's premium. Foster "auctions everything as is, but if an item should somehow be misrepresented," he "would be most happy to receive [it] back." Settlement must be made immediately after the auction takes place. Consigned goods are generally sold within 3 weeks and settlement is within 4 days. Foster asserts that "all property consigned is sold. We don't reserve or place minimum bids on items. We run a true auction."

63. Fred's Auction House
92 Pleasant Street   Tel. (617) 534-9004
Leominster, MA 01453

Fred R. Tousignant holds uncatalogued auctions once a month. These are advertised in the local papers and consist of mixed lots. Annual turnover for Fred's Auction House is about $100,000. There is no buyer's premium. Consignor's commission is 20 percent on goods delivered, 30 percent if they have to be picked up. Buyers have 1 week to settle accounts; consignors are paid 10 days after the auction. The consignor's commission is negotiable. State sales tax: 5 percent. The firm buys and sells on its own behalf: "I auction my own goods which I choose to sell. Some I market, some I auction."

64. Col. K. R. French and Co. Inc.
166 Bedford Road   Tel. (914) 273-3674
Armonk, NY 10504

French's motto is "Have Gavel, Will Travel," and he sells "whatever comes along" at auctions held every other week or so. He does not charge a buyer's premium. The commission for consignors is negotiable. State and local sales tax: 5 percent. French holds sales "anywhere," and that includes the consignor's premises. Sales are advertised in local newspapers and specialty periodicals, such as *Antiques and the Arts Weekly*. The usual viewing procedure is 9 A.M. to the time of sale. French is licensed, bonded, insured, and a member of the National Auctioneers Association.

65. Gilbert Auctions
River Road   Tel. (914) 424-3657
Garrison, NY 10524

Richard S. Gilbert is the fourth generation of his family to be involved in the auction business. He holds on-site estate sales approximately twice a month. From time to time, he rents space for general-purpose auctions.

The mixed lots available at both types of sales include CLOCKS AND WATCHES, FURNITURE, GLASS, PORCELAIN, RUGS, and SILVER. Illustrated brochures announcing the sale are available free of charge; just ask to be put on the mailing list. Sales are advertised in the local press and in specialty periodicals, such as *Antiques and the Arts Weekly*.

Viewing is 1 day and 1½ hours prior to sale. Listings are available at the time of the sale. Bidding is by numbered card, and a $50 deposit is required after the first successful bid. There is no buyer's premium. Sales are usually held midweek or on the weekend. Settlement must be made by the following Monday. Credit is available if "suitable arrangements are made." State and local tax: 5 percent.

Commission for consignor varies with the size of the estate and the value of items to be sold. Commissions are negotiable. Reserves are accepted only "on exceptional pieces." There is no charge for buy-ins. Settlement is made after

30 days. Minimum value for on-site sale is $50,000; less if consignment is to be sold elsewhere.

Appraisal service is available: cost is approximately $500 for the average house, but the fee varies.

66. Grandma's House

4712 Dudley   Tel. (303) 423-3640/534-2847
Wheatridge, CO 80033

Owner John White holds estate sales as the need arises. The entire contents of a house are put up for sale. Everything is done on site.

Announcements are to be found in the local press and in specialty periodicals, such as *Mountain States Collector*. Also, announcements are sent in the mail. Just ask to be put on the mailing list.

Grandma's House accepts consignments "in entirety only." The consignor's commission is 30 percent. Though commissions are not negotiable, White reports "we try to be philanthropic to churches, etc." Reserves are accepted, "but on a *very limited* basis." State and local sales tax: 5.5 percent.

The usual viewing procedure is a preview the day before the sale. Attendance is by invitation only, but the invitation is very easily obtained: each announcement flier contains one. Buyers must settle accounts within one day of the sale. Credit is offered in only very rare circumstances, but credit cards are accepted: MasterCard, Visa. Packing and shipping services are offered, at the buyer's expense.

67. The William Haber Art Collection, Inc.

139-11 Queens Boulevard   Tel. (212) 739-1000
Jamaica, NY 11435

Mr. Haber, according to the *New York Times*, "began selling paintings and antiques in the Bronx" in the late 1940s, and opened his operation in the New York City borough of Queens in 1961. The Jamaica gallery has been the site of his auctions for some years now.

Sales are held approximately every 2 months, including a "traditional" summer sale. The gallery can easily accommodate over 100 people.

Each auction is advertised in the local press, such as the *New York Times*, and in specialty periodicals, as well as by direct mail. You can be placed on the mailing list at no charge by writing to the firm.

Sales are occasionally held off the premises "to benefit institutions in Florida and New York." Catalogues are not available by subscription, but are available for each sale and can be obtained from the house either by mail or in person.

Graphic art is the specialty of the house and lots sold include ART DECO, ART NOUVEAU, DRAWINGS (19th & 20th c.), ENGRAVINGS, ETCHINGS, POSTERS, and PRINTS. Most sales are of over 150 lots, and most of these lots sell for less than $600. There is no buyer's premium. The usual viewing procedure varies with the sale and is "as advertised." Packing and shipping services are offered, at the buyer's expense. Guarantees of authenticity are offered; the catalogue states: "This art collection is guaranteed to be genuine as described." Settlement must be made within 5 days after the sale. State and local sales tax: 8 percent.

The commissions charged consignors varies between 10 and 25 percent. Consignors are not charged for insurance, warehousing, or packing and shipping. There is a separate rate structure for dealers and institutions. Reserves are accepted. There is no charge for buy-ins. Goods are sold within 30–45 days, and settlement is 10 days after the sale.

68. Charlton Hall Galleries, Inc.

930 Gervais Street   Tel. (803) 252-7927/779-5678
Columbia, SC 29201

This general-purpose auction firm's specialties include French and English 18th and 19th century FURNITURE and PORCELAIN. Persons to contact with regard to such properties or any other are Roland B. Long or Charlton F. Hall, Jr. Sales are held approximately every 2 months, at the premises or, in the case of house sales, at the consignor's. Announcements are available without cost, but catalogues are not available. Viewing is 2 days before each auction, 9 A.M.–6 P.M. There is no buyer's premium.

Authenticity is not guaranteed, nor are potential buyers offered the opportunity to return goods that prove to be not as catalogued. Buyers must settle the day of the auction. Commissions for consignors "are determined by the amount of items consigned and whether the auction is held at our gallery or elsewhere." Settlement is within 2 weeks and there is no charge for buy-ins. Sales tax: 4 percent.

69. Harbor Auction Gallery

238 Bank Street   Tel. (203) 443-0868
New London, CT 06355

A subsidiary of the Harbor Management Company, the gallery holds mixed-lot sales "as available." A specialty of the firm is PAPER. Sales are advertised in specialty periodicals, such as *Antiques and the Arts Weekly*. Though sales are not catalogued, fliers are available; just write to be put on the mailing list. There is no possibility at the moment for absentee bids. Auctioneer William Petersen reports that "items are returnable for any reasonable doubt." There is no buyer's premium. Credit cards are accepted: MasterCard, Visa. Viewing is either the day preceding the sale or 2 hours before it.

Consignor's commission is 25 percent under $500, and 10 percent for $500 or over. The commission is negotiable, depending on the situation. Goods consigned are sold within 3 months. Settlement is made 1 month after sale. State sales tax: 7.5 percent.

Mr. Petersen also reports that the house does buy and sell on its own behalf: "we sell our own merchandise, which may or may not be under reserve."

70. Harmer's of New York, Inc.

6 West 48th Street   Tel. (212) 757-4460
New York, NY 10036   Cable: HARMERSALE NEW YORK

71. Harmer's of San Francisco, Inc.

49 Geary Street   Tel. (415) 391-8244
San Francisco, CA 94102   Cable: HARMERSALE SAN FRANCISCO

Harmer's is an international firm primarily given over to the sale of STAMPS at auction. The firm also deals in a small way with AUTOGRAPHS, MAPS, and POSTCARDS.

One of the largest philatelic auction firms in the world, Harmer's—which began holding sales in London in 1918—had its first sale in New York City in 1941 and opened its San Francisco branch in 1977.

Bernard D. Harmer, a philatelist with long experience selling at auction, is in charge; Christopher R. Harmer, a young man previously active in the New York office, runs the San Francisco branch.

Harmer's has won for itself an enviable reputation over the years, and has handled the collections of President Franklin D. Roosevelt, the actor Adolphe Menjou, and Alfred H. Caspary (which in 1955–58 sold for the then-record sum of $2,895,000). During the 1979–80 season, both Harmer's branches had a turnover of more than $9.5 million.

In New York, sales are held on the firm's premises several days every 2 weeks between mid-September and mid-July. Exhibition is several days before the sale during regular business hours. Sales of several days' duration are held by the San Francisco branch 4 times a year. These take place at the Jack Tar Hotel in San Francisco and occasionally at a hotel in Los Angeles.

Harmer's auctions are advertised in national and international philatelic journals, specialty periodicals, and the local press. Catalogues are available free for each sale at the gallery offices, or can be obtained by mail (usual cost is $1). The catalogues are also available by subscription ($20 for both New York and San Francisco sales, including lists of prices realized; $40 outside the U.S., including airmail postage).

There is a buyer's premium of 10 percent. Mail order bids are executed. Buyers are offered packing and shipping services for low cost. Harmer's offers guarantees of authenticity and permits buyers to return goods that prove to be not as catalogued. Settlement is after sale or upon receipt of invoice. Credit cards are not accepted. Credit is available for 30 days to "credit-established clients." Sales taxes are 8 percent in New York and 6.5 percent in San Francisco.

The standard consignor's commission is 10 percent, but it can be negotiated, depending on the situation. There is a separate rate structure for dealers, "subject to negotiation." Consignors do not pay for catalogue illustrations, insurance, or warehousing, but do arrange for packing and shipping to Harmer's. Reserves are not accepted. There is no buy-in charge. Consigned goods are sold within 3 months; settlement is normally 5 weeks after the sale.

Appraisal service is available. The cost is 2.5 percent on the first $50,000 and 1.5 percent on the portion in excess of $50,000; this is refunded if the item is sold through Harmer's within 24 months.

72. Harris Auction Galleries
873-875 North Howard Street   Tel. (301) 728-7040
Baltimore, MD 21201

Occupying 3 floors of a brick building in a series of shops in downtown Baltimore that is advertised as Antique Row, Harris Auction Galleries holds 2 kinds of sales. Every other week, there are mixed-lot sales, in which household goods such as FURNITURE dominate. Every 5 or 6 weeks, the firm holds Collectors' Auctions, catalogued, at which are offered such items as AUTOGRAPHS, BOOKS, PAPER AMERICANA, PHOTOGRAPHICA, PRINTS, and the like.

Subscriptions are available to the Collector's Auction catalogues; the first-class U.S. cost is $23 with prices realized (there are cheaper rates if you do not want the prices or are willing to gamble on bulk mail); elsewhere in the world (via airmail), $39.

Both kinds of sales are advertised in the local press; the Collectors' Auctions are also advertised in specialty periodicals. Catalogues are available singly at the house or by mail (just write or phone).

In 1980, Harris instituted a buyer's premium of 10 percent. Barr Harris, the director of the galleries—a hustler in the best sense of the word—who has built up the operation in recent years, reports that "items are always on view the day prior to the auction and on auction day up to time of sale." Credit cards (MasterCard, Visa) are accepted on purchases over $50. Bidding is with numbered paddles; there is a paddle deposit of $20. Bidders unknown to the house are expected to make a 10 percent deposit in cash. Settlement is within 48 hours after the sale for floor bidders and within 5 days of receipt for absentee bidders. All goods are sold "as is," but "all autographs are guaranteed to be genuine." Barr Harris reports that buyers are offered the opportunity to return goods that prove to be not as catalogued.

Consignor's commission for Collectors' Auctions is as follows: 20 percent for lots selling for $100 or less; 17.5 percent for lots selling from $105 to $200; 15 percent for lots selling for more than $300. Goods consigned to the Collectors' Auctions will be sold within 60–90 days. Reserves are accepted for the Collectors' Auctions; buy-in charge varies. Settlement is within 30 days of the sale date. For household sales, the settlement is made within 10 days.

Commissions for the regular sales are negotiable, depending on the situation, and there is a different rate for dealers. Buy-ins are charged $2 at regular sales. State sales tax: 5 percent.

Harris Auction Galleries does buy and sell on its own behalf, "only to a very minor degree, though we advise seller to consign and gamble that he or she will profit more. However, there are some who cannot wait for an auction and settlement thereafter."

Appraisal service is available: home appraisal is $50 per hour—minimum, 2 hours including travel time (portal to portal). Appraisal of small items brought into the gallery costs $15–$25, "depending on the research necessary." Harris reports that "home appraisals include photographs of the major items."

73. William F. Hill Auction Sales

Route 16   Tel. (802) 472-6308
East Hardwick, VT 05834

Mr. Hill holds sales on his premises (in northern Vermont), known as Bill Hill's Warehouse, and on location for house or estate sales. He sells the usual goods offered by a general-purpose auction house, and these include FURNITURE and GLASS.

Not all of Hill's sales are catalogued. In any event, the catalogues are not available by subscription, but they can be had on request.

There is no buyer's premium; there are no guarantees or warranties. Payment must be made immediately, unless arrangements were made prior to the sale. The viewing procedure varies with the sale and can be anywhere from 3 days to 1 hour.

The standard commission varies with the sale and with the type of merchandise being consigned. Consigned goods are sold as soon as possible. Reserves are not accepted. Settlement is made "almost immediately." State sales tax: 3 percent.

William Hill belongs to the Vermont Auctioneers Association.

74. The House Clinic

P.O. Box 13013A   Tel. (305) 859-1770/851-2979
Orlando, Fl 32859

Auctioneers Marvin F. Levy and Marvin F. Larvison, who have worked together for 10 years in the Florida area, are veterans in the auction market. Levy for some years held auctions in Canada, and Larvison's career includes holding surplus property auctions for the Dallas Police Department.

Their motto, like that of some other auction houses, is "Have Gavel, Will Travel," and they hold sales on Saturdays every other week in central Florida and elsewhere. Most of these sales are not catalogued. They are advertised in the local press and in specialty periodicals, such as *The Bargain Trader.* Mostly general-purpose sales, these auctions are made up of mixed lots that include BOOKS, FURNITURE, JEWELRY, and RUGS. Advance sale notices are mailed out at no cost to those requesting to be put on the mailing list. Viewing is the day prior to the auction or that morning.

The firm does not accept credit cards. Buyers must settle immediately. Terms are "cash or check with proper ID and acceptance by management." Buyers are offered packing and shipping services "through local movers." Buyers have the opportunity to return goods "if misrepresented—or contrary to auctioneer's calling. We tape most auctions for just such reasons, as well as verification in the event of a dispute, etc."

Consignor's commission depends on merchandise, value of the lot or items, location. Goods are usually sold at next auction. Settlement is within 72 hours "maximum." Reserves are not accepted: "our auctioneer's pride means that we pass on improper bids." State and local taxes: 5 percent.

The firm does buy and sell on its own behalf: "We are liquidators, we buy, sell, swap, trade, barter. No man can survive by bread alone. Commission does not pay the bills; investments do."

75. International Antique and Auction Center, Inc.

7415 Hillcroft Avenue   Tel. (713) 495-5463
Houston, TX 77081

Under the direction of Sami and Melinda Shehata, this firm holds auctions approximately 6 times a year. Sales are both general-purpose auctions of mixed lots and specialty sales of properties such as AFRICAN ART. The Shehatas also auction "quality reproductions in walnut coming out of London."

Sales are announced in the local press, such as the Houston *Chronicle*. Announcements of forthcoming sales are also mailed out. To be placed on the mailing list free of charge, just write to the firm.

Sales are not catalogued. Mail order bids are not accepted at this time. Buyers have the opportunity to return goods that prove to be not as described. The usual viewing procedure is exhibition 2 days before the sale. Buyer must settle accounts within 1 week after the sale. Credit cards (MasterCard, Visa) are accepted. The firm does buy and sell on its own behalf. State and local sales tax: 6 percent.

The consignor's commission is basically 25 percent but is negotiable, depending on the situation. Goods consigned are sold in a week to 6 months; settlement is 1 day to 1 week after the auction. Reserves are accepted.

76. Iroquois Auctions

Box 66, Broad Street   Tel. (518) 942-3355
Port Henry, NY 12974

Billing itself as "the largest antique auction house between Montreal, Canada, and Albany, New York," Iroquois holds 10 "major auctions" annually. These sales are held in rented space, such as the Port Henry High School gymnasium and the Glens Falls Sheraton Inn. House and estate sales are also held. Sales are advertised in *Maine Antiques Digest, Antiques and the Arts Weekly,* and local newspapers.

Illustrated brochures are available for all sales. To be put on the mailing list free of charge, just write to Iroquois. Some sales are catalogued and some are not. Most sales are of mixed lots and include, at one time or another, AMERICANA, ART DECO, ART NOUVEAU, CLOCKS AND WATCHES, FURNITURE, GLASS, PORCELAIN, SILVER, and TOYS.

There is no buyer's premium. Absentee bids are accepted with 10 percent deposit. Packing and shipping are offered, at the buyer's expense. The sales are usually held on Saturdays, and viewing is from noon to 7 P.M. the previous day, as well as 2 hours prior to the sale. Accounts must be settled immediately. State and local sales tax: 7 percent.

The basic consignor's commission is 15 percent, but it is negotiable. There is a different rate for dealers. Consignors are not charged for insurance or warehousing, but must pay for packing and shipping. Reserves are accepted. How long it takes before consigned goods are sold "depends on the type of merchandise consigned," according to owner Gerald Petro. Settlement is made 10 days after the sale. The minimum value for a consignment is $50.

Iroquois Auctions pays a finder's fee "based on the merchandise." Appraisal service is available; the cost is $50 per hour.

77. Steve Ivy Numismatic Auctions, Inc.

Suite 800, 7515 Greenville Avenue   Tel. (214) 692-5531
Dallas, TX 75231   Toll-free: 1-800-527-6810
                                      Telex: 732 587

An affiliate of the Steve Ivy Rare Coin Co. (a retail operation), this auction firm holds quarterly sales of COINS and PAPER MONEY.

Under the energetic direction of Bob Merrill, Ivy Auctions holds sales in "major hotels in large cities." Catalogues are replete with color illustrations (indeed, the firm prides itself on its "all-color auction catalogs"). Viewing is not limited to the city where the sale is to be held: "Steve Ivy Numismatic Auctions puts your coins on display in at least one major coin show in a major city before they go to auction." Viewing at the sale site is usually 2 days prior to sale, all day.

Sales are announced in local newspapers and specialty periodicals, such as *Coin World* and *Trusts & Estates,* as well as via direct mail to an extensive mailing list. If you want to be placed on the list, just write the firm. Catalogues are $5–$10 each, and an annual subscription is $20.

There is no buyer's premium. Absentee bids are executed. New bidders unknown to the firm must establish their financial bona fides or deposit 25 percent of their total bids with the firm in advance of the auction. Coins may be returned if not authentic (Mr. Merrill points out that "this has never happened"). Cost of shipping is added to mail purchaser's invoice. Buyers must settle account within 10 days of the sale.

The basic consignor's commission is 18–22 percent. It is negotiable, depending on the situation. Consignors are not charged for catalogue illustrations, shipping and packing, insurance, or warehousing. Consigned goods are usually sold at the next sale, within 90 days. Settlement is made after 45 days. "All auctions are unreserved—everything is sold without a minimum bid." State and local sales tax: 5 percent.

Steve Ivy Numismatic Auctions, Inc., sells hardbound catalogues (including prices realized) of its past auctions. The firm estimates its annual turnover as well in excess of $1 million.

78. Julia's Auction Service

Route 201, Skowhegan Road   Tel. (207) 453-9725
Fairfield, ME 04937

James D. Julia holds 24–30 auctions a year. Some are catalogued, most are not. A few are on-site sales; usually the auction is held on Julia's premises. Julia is a general-purpose auction house and the mixed lots sold at its auctions include AMERICANA and FURNITURE.

Sales are advertised as warranted, in either the local or the national press, and/or in specialty periodicals. Announcements are available; just indicate your interest by writing to Julia's and you will be placed on the mailing list free of charge.

Since catalogues are not produced for all sales, they must be ordered individually. There is no buyer's premium except on the specialized fall BOOK auction, when it is 10 percent. Viewing is usually day of sale, 2 hours prior to the beginning of the auction. Buyer must settle accounts immediately after the end of the sale.

Consignor's commission varies: "increases for inexpensive items, decreases for expensive items." Consignors do not pay for warehousing or insurance, but do pay packing and shipping charges on goods delivered to Julia. Goods are usually sold in a "few weeks to a couple of months." Reserves are accepted, but are "not commonplace." There is no charge for buy-ins. Settlement is made "usually within 14 days." State sales tax: 5 percent.

Appraisal service is available. The cost is 1–1.5 percent of the total value. Julia's Auction Service belongs to the Maine Auctioneers Association.

79. Kennedy Antique Auction Galleries, Inc.

1088 Huff Road   Tel. (404) 351-4464
Atlanta, GA 30318

This somewhat unusual operation is "owned by a group of four antique dealers from the U.K." Sales, held every Monday night at 7:30, are advertised in the local newspapers. Viewing is on the Friday, Saturday, and Monday prior to the sale, 10 A.M.–5 P.M.

All auctions are on the premises. Announcements are not sent out, nor are catalogues obtainable by subscription, though occasionally they are available singly: "for special sales featuring higher-end items (about 5 per year) we have a mailing list for dealers."

There is no buyer's premium. Kennedy offers no packing and shipping services, guarantees of authenticity, or opportunity to return goods. Buyer must settle immediately after auction. Credit cards (MasterCard, Visa) are accepted. State and local tax: 4 percent.

Kennedy does buy and sell on its own behalf: indeed, "all merchandise sold is the property of Kennedy Antiques." Specialties of the firm include FURNITURE (Georgian, 1930s), GLASS, PRINTS (mid-Victorian–1930s), and RUGS. The annual turnover, reports general manager James S. Rogers, is "100–125 40-ft. containers."

80. Kinzle Galleries Auction Service
1002 3rd Avenue   Tel. (814) 695-3479
Duncansville, PA 16635

Two to 8 sales a year are held by the Kinzle Galleries, which are located in a small community in western Pennsylvania, about 20 miles south of Altoona.

Sales are of mixed lots and include AMERICANA and FURNITURE, as well as PAINTINGS and PRINTS. Catalogues are available from the firm; just call or write. The cost is usually $5. Sales are held on premises or, in the case of house sales, on site. Sales are advertised in "daily papers within 50 to 100 mile radius" and "in larger city and state papers when advisable," as well as in "most antique publications."

Viewing is during evening hours the day before the sale as well as one hour prior to the sale. There is no buyer's premium. Buyers must settle accounts immediately after the sale. Kinzle does not offer guarantees of authenticity. State sales tax: 6 percent.

Consignors are not charged packing and shipping, or warehousing or insurance. The commission for consignors varies, "depending on value." Reserves are accepted; buy-ins cost the consignor 10 percent. Settlement is made 10 days after the auction.

Dorothy Kinzle reports: "we operate a full-time antiques business," and that the firm does buy and sell on its own behalf at auction.

81. R. L. Loveless Associates, Inc.
4223 Clover Street   Tel. (716) 624-1648/1556
Honeoye Falls, NY 14472

This firm, which is located in a suburb of Rochester, reports that "most every type and kind of merchandise is handled." Sales are held frequently at various locations and on site. A number of sales are held each year at the Monroe County Fairgrounds. Sales are advertised in local newspapers and specialty periodicals, as well as via direct mail. Illustrated brochures are available for most sales, free upon request with self-addressed stamped envelope.

Catalogues are not available by subscription. Only specialty auctions, such as those that sell GLASS, are catalogued. Most sales are of mixed lots that include FURNITURE, RUGS, and "our famous 'Box Lots.' "

The usual viewing procedure depends on the kind of sale, but "yes, there is always a viewing time." There is no buyer's premium. Accounts must be settled right after the sale. Credit is not available. The firm will execute absentee bids of $50 or more, but "we much prefer not to handle same and suggest that other arrangements be made." No guarantees of authenticity are made; goods that "are not received as described at the time of sale, during auction, i.e., damaged or whatever, will be resold immediately."

The consignor's commission is normally 15 percent plus expenses, but is negotiable, depending on the situation. Consignors must have their own insurance. They usually do not pay for warehousing, but do pay for packing and shipping: "Pickup charges are made at a per hour basis." Goods consigned are usually sold within 3 months. Settlement is "usually within 30 days, large consignment sales are prorated, settlement is made within 60 days. Partial checks are always available." Reserves are not accepted. State and local sales tax: 7 percent.

The firm does not pay a finder's fee.

82. Lubin Galleries
30 West 26th Street   Tel. (212) 924-3777
New York, NY 10010

A veteran auction firm, Lubin Galleries moved to pleasant new quarters in the summer of 1980. The firm's policy has remained consistent: general-purpose auctions of mixed lots are presented every other Saturday. These lots include AMERICANA, CHINESE WORKS OF ART, ENGRAVINGS, ETCHINGS, JAPANESE WORKS OF ART, JEWELRY, JUDAICA, PAINTINGS, PORCELAIN, RUGS, and SILVER.

Sales are advertised in the local press, such as the *New York Times,* and specialty periodicals, such as *Antiques and the Arts Weekly.* All auctions are held on the premises. Catalogues are not available by subscription but can be obtained at the exhibition. Viewing is usually the Thursday (10 A.M.–7 P.M.) and Friday (9 A.M.–3 P.M.) before the sale, as well as Saturday before the sale, which usually begins at 11 A.M.

There is a buyer's premium, instituted in 1980. Credit cards are not accepted. No guarantees of authenticity are offered. Packing and shipping services of smaller items, such as silver, are offered at the buyer's expense. Accounts must be settled by 6 P.M. the Tuesday after the sale. Absentee bidders must deposit 25 percent of their bid "in certified check." State and local sales tax: 8 percent.

The consignor's commission, reports Alex Boné, "depends on the merchandise and the nature of the consignor." Consignors are not charged for insurance or for packing and shipping, but will be charged storage if unsold merchandise is not picked up "in a reasonable amount of time." Consigned goods are usually sold within 2 weeks. Settlement is made within 3–4 weeks. Reserves are accepted. Buy-ins cost nothing if there was no reserve; "unsold reserved merchandise is subject to handling charges, depending on the piece." There is a separate commission rate for dealers.

Lubin belongs to the Appraisers Association of America and the National Auctioneers Association.

The firm does buy and sell on its own behalf.

83. Maison Auction Co., Inc.
128 East Street   Tel. (203) 269-8007
Wallingford, CT 06492

Auctions are held by this firm "usually every other week, sometimes more." Sales are advertised in local papers, such as the Meriden *Record,* and in specialty periodicals, such as *Antiques and the Arts Weekly*. All sales are held at the Maison gallery; they are not catalogued.

Most auctions are mixed-lot sales and include among other items AMERICANA, CLOCKS AND WATCHES, and PRINTS. There is no buyer's premium. Viewing is 4 hours the day preceding and 2 hours the day of the sale. Accounts must be settled the day of the sale. The house does not accept credit cards. State sales tax: 7.5 percent.

According to partner Laraine Smith, absentee bids are not accepted and guarantees of authenticity are not offered, though Maison will accept return of goods if these have inadvertently been misrepresented.

The consignor's commission varies (20–30 percent), depending on the situation, and is negotiable. Consignors are not charged insurance, packing and shipping, or warehousing. Goods are usually sold within 4–6 weeks. Settlement is "within 2 weeks." There is a separate commission structure for dealers, "depending on the value of the consignment." Reserves are not accepted.

The house pays a finder's fee: "a percentage of the sale."

Maison Auction Company does buy and sell on its own behalf; it does "purchase private collections and contents of homes" and place these at auction.

The firm belongs to the National Auctioneers Association and the Connecticut Auctioneers Association.

84. Joel L. Malter and Co., Inc.

Suite 518, 16661 Ventura Boulevard   Tel. (213) 784-7772/2181
Encino, CA 91316   Cable: MALTER COINS

"Ancient" is the key word in the auction offerings of this firm. They have held sales of ancient COINS, ancient GLASS, and ancient JEWELRY, as well as PRE-COLUMBIAN ART.

Begun as a retail operation at the beginning of the 1960s, the firm started to hold auctions a decade later but with no great frequency. Sales are now held approximately 6 times a year, in various hotels, such as the Pasadena Hilton or the Beverly Wilshire. Viewing is for 2 weeks prior to the sale, Monday–Friday, 9:30 A.M.–5:30 P.M., or by appointment. Properties are also on view in the saleroom during the auction.

There is no buyer's premium. Bidders unknown to the firm must establish their bona fides or deposit 25 percent of the sum of their bids. The catalogue "terms of sale" indicate that "all floor sales are final. No lot may be returned for any reason by floor bidders. Any claims for adjustment from mail bidders must be made in writing within 5 days of the delivery of the goods."

Catalogues are available by subscription ($20 annually) and individually either by mail or at the sale ($5).

The consignor's commission varies between 20 and 25 percent. The commission is negotiable, depending on the situation. Consignors are not charged for catalogue illustrations, but must pay shipping and packing as well as insurance. Consigned goods are usually sold within 3–4 months. Settlement is between 30 and 45 days after the sale. Reserves are accepted. State and local sales tax: 6 percent.

Joel L. Malter and Co. also publishes the *Collectors' Journal of Ancient Art.* A joint subscription to it and a season's worth of catalogues is available at the money-saving rate of $25.

The firm does buy and sell on its own behalf; Joel Malter reports that "we buy and sell coins, wholesale and retail."

85. David W. Mapes, Inc.

82 Front Street   Tel. (607) 724-6741/862-9365
Binghamton, NY 13905

In operation since the middle 1960s, Mapes holds general-purpose auction sales whose mixed lots include AMERICANA, CLOCKS and WATCHES, DOLLS, FURNITURE, RUGS, and TOYS.

Most sales are not catalogued. Announcements of forthcoming sales are available free of charge to anyone who requests placement on the mailing list. Sales are advertised in the local press and in specialty periodicals, such as *Antiques and the Arts Weekly.*

There are approximately 20 sales a year, in the American Legion Hall, on Legion Road in nearby Vestal, about 8 miles west of Binghamton.

There is no buyer's premium. Buyers must settle immediately after the sale. No guarantees of authenticity are offered. Absentee bids will be executed. Packing and shipping services are available, at the buyer's expense. Viewing is 1–2 hours before the sale. State and local sales tax: 7 percent.

The consignor's commission varies. Consigned goods are sold as soon as possible. Settlement is made after 10 days. Buy-ins cost 5 percent. Reserves are "sometimes accepted."

Appraisal service is available at $25 per hour.

86. Matthew's Galleries

186 Veterans Drive   Tel. (201) 768-9241
Northvale, NJ 07647

Located in northern New Jersey, not far from the New York state line, Matthew's is a typical regional house which holds general-purpose mixed-lot sales "about every 3 weeks," according to its owner, Matthew Gerber. A typical sale might include JEWELRY, PAINTINGS, SILVER, and various kinds of decorative arts objects.

Sales are held on the premises and on location. They are advertised in the *New York Times,* the local press, and specialty periodicals. "Card of announcement is sent to currently active clients and potential clients at no cost. Contact Adrian Gerber."

Catalogues are not available by subscription, but they can be obtained singly at the sale and by mail (these mimeographed catalogues are free, but "a small fee may be requested for catalogues covering large auctions of significant works of art").

The usual viewing time is 10 A.M.–5 P.M. the day before the auction and 1–2 hours before the auction begins. There is no buyer's premium. "All bidders must register and get a bidder's number." Everything is sold "as is, where is." But items including "gold jewelry, diamonds, precious gems, sterling silver, bronze, handmade carpets, paintings, and objets d'art are guaranteed to be such as stated." They can be returned within 10 days of the sale. Credit cards are not accepted. Payment must be in cash, certified check, or traveler's checks. Buyers must settle immediately, unless other arrangements have been made. State sales tax: 5 percent.

Consignors are responsible for arranging delivery of their property to the gallery. There is no charge for warehousing. Insurance is a negotiable item. Minimum value for a consignment is $25. The standard commission ranges between 10 and 25 percent. There is a separate rate for dealers and institutions, depending on the situation. Consigned goods are sold within 1–8 weeks. Settlement is 30 days after the sale. Reserves are accepted. Buy-ins cost 5 percent.

The firm does buy and sell on its own behalf.

Appraisal service is available. Contact Matthew Gerber or Edward Wintringham. "Fees are flat rate and vary according to circumstances."

Matthew Gerber belongs to the National Auctioneers Association.

87. Mechanical Music Center, Inc.

25 Kings Highway North   Tel. (203) 655-9510
Darien, CT 06820

This firm auctions MECHANICAL MUSIC INSTRUMENTS. These include, in the words of the head of the firm, W. H. Edgerton, "mechanical music, music boxes, barrel organs, piano rolls."

Sales, which are "infrequent," are held at various locations. They are advertised in the "antique press." Announcements of forthcoming sales are not available. Catalogues may be obtained "by request" for a particular sale.

There is no buyer's premium. Mail order bids are accepted. Guarantees of authenticity are not offered, but buyers can return goods that prove to be not as catalogued. Packing and shipping services are available, at the buyer's expense. Accounts must be settled usually on "the same day as the sale," but buyers may have "longer for larger purchases." Credit cards are not accepted. State sales tax: 7.5 percent.

The consignor's commission "varies depending on location, condition, quantity." Consignors are not charged for warehousing or for packing and shipping. They are charged for insurance if they want it or they may carry their own insurance. Consigned goods are sold within a reasonable time; settlement is made 1 week after the auction. Whether or not reserves are accepted "depends on item and value." Buy-ins do not cost the consignor anything, except "in rare cases."

Mechanical Music Center, Inc., does buy and sell on its own behalf.

88. Milwaukee Auction Galleries

4747 West Bradley Road   Tel. (414) 355-5054
Milwaukee, WI 53223

How many auction houses are there in the United States that are directed by a Ph.D. candidate in the History of the Decorative Arts? This firm is one of the very few that are. Janice Kuhn, whose dissertation deals with the design evolution of Chinese jade, is a veteran of the auction business. She and her partner bought this firm in the late 1970s, but Ms. Kuhn had previously been employed there as manager and auctioneer.

A good regional house, with a turnover estimated to be in excess of $1 million, Milwaukee Auction Galleries hold 8 multisession auctions each year. These usually are on Tuesday–Friday evenings, as well as on Saturday and Sunday afternoons, as the occasion demands. The mixed-lot sales range widely among: AMERICANA, ART DECO, ART NOUVEAU, CHINESE WORKS OF ART, CLOCKS AND WATCHES, ENGRAVINGS, FURNITURE, GLASS, JEWELRY, PAINTINGS, POSTERS, RUGS, SILVER, TOYS, etc. About 300 lots are sold at each session; Ms. Kuhn estimates about 90 percent sell for $300 or less.

Sales are advertised nationally in specialty periodicals, such as *Antiques and the Arts Weekly,* and in the Milwaukee and suburban press, as well as through mailed announcements, sent free of charge. To be placed on the mailing list, write office manager Janet Remstad.

Catalogues can be ordered for individual sales ($4 at the house; $5.50 by mail) or by subscription ($40 per year for 8 catalogues). Estimates are not given in the catalogue but they are available separately, as are prices realized (each is $14 per year). There is a buyer's premium of 10 percent, instituted in 1979. Bidding is done with numbered paddles. Absentee bids are executed. All items are sold "as is." There are no guarantees of authenticity and buyers are not offered the opportunity to return goods that prove to be not as catalogued; further, "any and all claims of a purchaser shall be deemed waived and shall be without validity unless made in writing to the Galleries within 21 (twenty-one) days after sale." For goods whose purchase price is more than $180, credit cards (MasterCard, Visa) are accepted. State and local sales tax: 4.5 percent. The firm does not provide packing and shipping services, but will help make arrangements for these. Viewing is for 4 days before the sale: Friday (1–9 P.M.), Saturday and Sunday (1–5 P.M.), and Monday (1–9 P.M.); also for 2 hours before each auction. Settlement must be made by 5 P.M. Wednesday after the last Sunday sale.

The standard consignor's commission is 15 percent (to the usual 10 percent commission is added 5 percent for "insurance, printing the catalogue, and advertising"). There is no charge for storage, and important items will be photographed free of charge. The galleries advise consignors that "for items of fine antique quality, a minimum reserve may be set." On such items there is a buy-in charge of 15 percent of the last bid before the reserve. Minimum value for a consignment of any size is $250. Goods are usually sold within 1–2 months; settlement is 35 days after the sale.

Appraisal service is available from an affiliate company, Chestnut Court

Appraisal Associates, Ltd., whose staff is largely drawn from the galleries' personnel. The cost is $50 per hour.

89. Wayne Mock, Inc.

Box 37   Tel. (603) 323-8057
Tamworth, NH 03886

Located in central New Hampshire, Mock holds auctions biweekly "or as items warrant sale," between May and December. Sales take place at the Chocura Auction Gallery on Route 16, just a few miles from Tamworth. Mock sells a wide variety of objects in general-purpose mixed-lot sales that include FURNITURE, JEWELRY, PORCELAIN, RUGS, and SILVER. Occasional house and estate sales are also held.

These sales are advertised in the local press, in Boston newspapers, and in specialty publications. To receive, free of charge, Mock's illustrated brochure announcing sales, please write or phone.

There is no buyer's premium. Absentee bids are accepted. Packing and shipping services are available or "can be arranged." No guarantees of authenticity are offered, and Mock reports that "on occasion," buyers may return goods that prove to be not as described. Viewing is usually the morning of the sale or by special arrangement. Buyer must settle account immediately after the sale.

The standard consignor's commission is "generally 20 percent for fine antiques." It is negotiable, depending upon the situation. There is no minimum value necessary for a consignment. Settlement is usually "within a few days." Consigned goods are sold "usually within 60 days." Reserves are accepted, "but not encouraged."

Appraisal services are available. The cost is $25 per hour "plus secretarial services."

Wayne Mock, Inc., is a member of the New Hampshire Auctioneers Association.

90. William F. Moon and Company

12 Lewis Road, RFD 1   Tel. (617) 761-8003
North Attleboro, MA 02760

"Colonel" Bill Moon holds weekly auctions offering everything from AMERICANA to TOYS, in estate sales, liquidation sales, and what have you. Many of his sales are held a bit far afield from North Attleboro; others are held in local motels and in the Veterans of Foreign Wars hall in that town.

These sales are advertised in the local press, the Boston newspapers, and specialty publications. To get on a mailing list for printed brochures, write to the colonel. Announcements will indicate which sales are catalogued and the catalogues' cost if any.

There is no buyer's premium at Moon's sales. Packing and shipping services are available at the buyer's expense. Buyers have the opportunity to return goods that are not as described. Backing up this guarantee is the colonel's "code of ethics." Viewing is usually just before a sale. Settlement must be made "forthwith." State sales tax: 5 percent.

The consignor's commission depends on "the quality of the merchandise." Consignors are not charged for insurance, but are charged for packing and shipping, and warehousing if necessary. Consigned goods are sold within 7–10 days, and settlement is within 24 hours. Reserves are accepted. The firm does buy and sell on its own behalf.

91. NASCA

Suite 53, 265 Sunrise Highway   Tel. (516) 764-6677/6678
Rockville Centre, NY 11570

Sales are held 7 times a year at various locations in New York City. Specialties of Douglas B. Ball and Associates, who do business as NASCA, include COINS, PAPER MONEY, and MEDALS. Announcements of sales are to be found mostly in specialty periodicals, such as *Coin World*. Catalogues are available for single sales ($4) or by subscription ($15 U.S.; $25 overseas).

Since 1976, there has been a buyer's premium of 5 percent. Buyers have up to 5 days after the auction to settle accounts; credit is available, subject to negotiation and the situation. Consignor's commission varies, depending on the situation. Goods are usually sold within 3–6 months. Settlement is 45 days after the sale. State and local sales tax: 7 percent. There is a separate rate structure for dealers and institutions who consign property. Exhibition of lots to be sold is "at our offices during the previous week and on sale days at place of auction sale."

92. New England Rare Coin Auctions

89 Devonshire Street   Tel. (617) 227-8800
Boston, MA 02109   Toll-free: 1-800-225-6794

Advertising itself as "the effective auction company," New England Rare Coin Auctions is a division of New England Rare Coin Galleries, Inc., and holds 4 or 5 2-3-day multisession auctions per annum at various hotel locations in Boston, New York City, and Orlando, Florida. For sale at these auctions are COINS, MEDALS, and PAPER MONEY.

Sales are advertised in the national press, such as the *Wall Street Journal* and the *New York Times,* as well as in specialty periodicals, such as *World Coin News* and *Trusts & Estates.* Sale schedules are published each year; to be placed on the mailing list for these announcements free of charge, just write to Susan Bradley. The well-illustrated comprehensive catalogues are available singly for each sale, either at the office or through the mail ($5), and a subscription for a year's sales catalogues costs $15.

Since July 1980, there has been a buyer's premium of 10 percent of the hammer price. Absentee bids are accepted. The firm reports that "we guarantee all coins to be genuine in the terms of the sale; coins are shipped registered mail once payment has been made; may return within three days stating reason." Packing and shipping services are available, at the buyer's expense. Usual viewing procedure is the week of the auction, in the firm's offices in the Boston financial district, during business hours. Goods to be auctioned are also displayed at two major coin shows prior to the sale. All payments must be made within 30 days of sale, but arrangements can be made for extension of payment. State sales tax: 5 percent.

The standard consignor's commission is 10 percent. It is negotiable, depending on the situation. The dealer's rate is usually 8 percent. Consignors are not charged for catalogue illustrations, packing and shipping, insurance, or warehousing. Reserves are not accepted. The firm reports that "all material is sold—if, in the event, the material is returned, we will attempt to sell to the underbidder or place in the next auction." Consigned goods are sold within 3 months. Settlement is made 45 days after the sale. The minimum value for a consignment is $1,000 per lot. The consignment coordinator is Bruce Laing.

New England Rare Coin Auctions does buy and sell on its own behalf: "We do supplement sales with house material to give a full and diverse sale."

93. Park City Auction Service
925 Wood Street   Tel. (203) 333-5251
Bridgeport, CT 06604

The mixed lots sold by Park City Auction Service, a general-purpose auction house, include FURNITURE, GLASS, and SILVER.

Sales are held once or twice a month, usually at the Knights of Columbus Hall in Fairfield, Connecticut (333 Unquowa Road). Sales are advertised in the local press, such as the Bridgeport *Post* and the Westport *News,* as well as specialty periodicals, such as *Antiques and the Arts Weekly.* Announcements of forthcoming auctions are available to anyone who requests placement on the mailing list, free of charge, of course.

Auctioneer A. Zetomer reports that "a preview is provided 1–2 hours prior to each sale." Credit cards are not accepted. There is no buyer's premium. Buyer must settle accounts immediately after sale. State sales tax: 7.5 percent.

Consignor's commission is usually 25 percent—"our basic fee." Commissions are negotiable. Reserves are accepted, but the "general practice is no reserves." There is no charge for buy-ins. Sale of goods is generally 4–6 weeks after consignment and settlement is 7–10 days after the sale.

Park City Auction Service belongs to the National Auctioneers Association and the Connecticut Auctioneers Association.

The firm does buy and sell on its own behalf.

94. Pennypacker Auction Centre
1540 New Holland Road   Tel. (215) 777-5890/6121
Kenhorst, Reading, PA 19607

On Wednesdays every week, the Pennypackers sell household goods, which include FURNITURE and much else. Every second month, they hold an "antique sale"—i.e., an auction of better property, which includes some specialties, such as CLOCKS AND WATCHES and FOLK ART.

Both kinds of sales are advertised in the local press; the antique sale is also advertised through direct mail. An illustrated brochure to all such sales is $15 annually.

There is no buyer's premium. Credit cards are not accepted. Absentee bids are accepted. Buyers are offered the opportunity to return goods that prove to be not as catalogued. Cathy M. Pennypacker Andrews reports that "conditions of sale on the back of our catalogue are self-explanatory." Buyer must settle account within 30 days of the sale. State sales tax: 6 percent.

The standard consignor's commission is 25 percent for the Wednesday sales and 20 percent for the others; however, the commissions are negotiable, depending on the situation. Settlement is within 10 days for the Wednesday sales, and 30 for the antiques sales.

Viewing is Sundays (11 A.M.–5 P.M.) prior to the antique sales, and Tuesdays (9 A.M.–4:30 P.M.) for the Wednesday sales.

95. Quickie Auction House
Route 3   Tel. (612) 428-4378
Osseo, MN 55369

Located on Highway 152 some 6.5 miles west of Osseo, a Minneapolis suburb, Quickie Auction House conducts sales 3 times̄ a week on the premises, and usually once a week on site. According to Dave Christian, head of the firm, these off-premises sales are held "wherever our customers need to be served! Usually a fine hotel or inn." But they have also been held in roller rinks.

Quickie Auction House, which started in business in 1967, sells mostly "floor samples, unclaimed and damaged freight repossession, appliances, sporting goods, misc. items," household merchandise, stock of bankrupt companies, etc. But once a month, the firm holds sales not just of FURNITURE and the like, but of AMERICANA, much of which is collectibles but some of which is AMERICAN INDIAN ART.

All sales are advertised in the Minneapolis newspapers. In 1980, the firm computerized its operations and established a mailing list; you can be placed on this list free of charge by writing to Quickie. Basically, sales are not catalogued. Sales at the house are held Monday and Saturday, 6 P.M.–midnight, and Wednesday, 3 P.M.–midnight. There is no buyer's premium. Viewing is 1–3 hours before the auction starts. Buyer must settle accounts immediately. Credit cards are not accepted. Packing and shipping services are available, at buyer's expense. State sales tax: 4 percent.

The consignor's commission is generally 25 percent, but it is negotiable, depending on the situation. Consigned goods are usually sold within 30 days. Settlement is made after "5 working days." Buy-ins cost consignors $5 per item. Consignors do not pay for warehousing, insurance, or packing and shipping.

Quickie Auction House buys and sells on its own behalf: "We buy private collections." The firm belongs to the National Auctioneers Association and the Minnesota Auctioneers Association.

96. R & S Estate Liquidations
Box 205   Tel. (617) 244-6616
Newton Center, MA 02159

This firm holds general-purpose sales several times a week. Sales are held on location and items auctioned include FURNITURE, GLASS, JEWELRY, SILVER, and just about anything else that someone wants to sell. Ronald Viselman, the head of the firm, reports that it has held sales in 15 states.

Sales are advertised in the local press and in auction periodicals. Announcements of forthcoming sales are available free of charge; just write to the firm. Catalogues are available for specific sales, but not by subscription. There is no buyer's premium. Absentee bids are accepted. Packing and shipping services are not available. Guarantees of authenticity are offered on jewelry. The usual viewing procedure is 2 hours prior to sale. Buyer must settle accounts immediately after the sale. Credit cards are accepted (MasterCard, Visa). State and local taxes depend on the venue.

The commission structure for consignors is "varied" and is negotiable depending upon the situation. Reserves are accepted. Consigned goods are usually sold within 30 days. Settlement is made 7 days after the sale.

Appraisal service is available; the cost "varies."

R & S belongs to the National Auctioneers Association.

97. Bill Rinaldi Auctions
Bedell Road   Tel. (914) 454-9613
Poughkeepsie, NY 12601

Bill Rinaldi and his partner, Mike Fallon, began as truckers at the end of the 1960s, servicing auctioneers and others who needed art and antiques moved carefully. Becoming interested in the auction business, they decided to set up their own firm, and have conducted auctions since the mid-1970s with some success, while continuing to truck selectively.

Sales are held once a month in a converted, renovated, heated barn some miles from the center of Poughkeepsie. There is ample parking. In addition, some 3–4 times a year the firm holds estate or house sales on site. The firm does buy and sell on its own behalf.

Rinaldi Auctions does not hold catalogued sales. There is no buyer's premium. Everything is sold "as is." No guarantees of authenticity are offered. No absentee bids are accepted. Viewing is 3 hours prior to the sale. Buyers must settle their accounts the day of the sale.

The consignor's commission varies from 15 to 25 percent, depending on the situation. Consignors do not have to pay insurance, packing and shipping, or warehousing. Consigned goods are usually sold within a month. Settlement is made after 2 weeks. Reserves are not accepted. Should there be a buy-in, the consignor is not charged. State and local sales tax: 7 percent.

The firm does pay finder's fees. As in most country auctions where mixed lots are sold, the properties run the gamut and include FURNITURE, PORCELAIN, RUGS, and what have you.

Since 1979, the firm has run a call-in radio show on Saturday mornings (10–11 A.M.) on WWWI-AM and its sister station, WJIB-FM, both of which broadcast out of Hyde Park, New York. *The Incurable Collector* attempts to answer questions about what an item is, how much it is worth, and where it should be taken for sale.

98. Roan, Inc.
Box 118, RD 3   Tel. (717) 494-0170
Logan Station, PA 17728

Quartered in a small town some 4 miles north of the somewhat bigger town of Williamsport, in central Pennsylvania, Roan's is a family firm which holds auctions as the occasion demands (usually 4–5 times monthly).

Bob, Chuck, and Rich Roan advertise their sales in the local press and in specialty periodicals, such as *The Antique Trader,* as well as by direct mail; to be placed on the firm's mailing list free of charge, write to Chuck or Rich.

Their sales include the standard objects auctioned by a firm that holds mixed-lot sales, such as CLOCKS AND WATCHES and FURNITURE.

There is a buyer's premium of 10 percent. Credit cards are not accepted. Viewing is the day before the sale, 2–8 P.M. There is a catalogue. Absentee bids are executed. Packing and shipping services are available, at the buyer's expense. Goods may be returned if not as described: Rich Roan reports that "we pride ourselves in being honest and fair and will do whatever is humanly possible to keep customers satisfied."

The standard consignor's commission is 10 percent for dealers and 15 percent for private individuals. Commissions are negotiable. Consigned goods are sold as soon as possible, "depending on value, etc." Reserves are not accepted, thus there are no buy-ins and no buy-in charges. Settlement is made 30 days after the sale. State sales tax: 6 percent.

Roan's does buy and sell on its own behalf.

Appraisal service is available: the cost is $50 per hour, with a $50 minimum.

99. Rockland Auction Services, Inc.
72 Pomona Road   Tel. (914) 354-3914/2723
Suffern, NY 10901

Under the direction of Sy Cohen, Rockland Auction Services conducts approximately 2 auctions a month. Sales are held off premises, either on site or at the Holiday Inn–Holidome in Suffern, New York, and the Sheraton Hotel in Hasbrouck Heights, New Jersey.

Sales are advertised in local newspapers, such as the Bergen *Evening Record* in New Jersey and the Middletown *Record* in New York, as well as in specialty journals, such as *Antiques and the Arts Weekly.* Announcements of forthcoming sales are also sent to those who ask to be put on the mailing list. Absentee bids are accepted.

Catalogues are not available by subscription, but "are given to registered attendees at sale." Each "Exceptional Auction" is made up of mixed lots, which often include FURNITURE, GLASS, and SILVER. Catalogue descriptions are sparse but adequate. There is no buyer's premium. Packing and shipping services "can be arranged for a fee." All sales are "as is," but the catalogue states these conditions of sale: "If within 10 days of the sale . . . the buyer gives notice in writing . . . that the lot is not as represented and if within 4 days after giving such notice the buyer returns the lot in the same condition as it was at the time of sale . . . and shows that considered in the light of the terms of the catalogue the lot sold is not as represented, RAS will rescind the sale and refund the purchase price." Credit cards are accepted: MasterCard, Visa. Viewing is usually 1–1½ hours prior to the sale.

The "basic" consignor's commission is 20 percent, but it is negotiable, depending on the situation. Consignors are not charged for insurance, warehousing, or packing and shipping. Goods consigned are sold within 2–4 weeks and settlement is made 48–72 hours after the sale. Reserves are accepted. The buy-in cost is 5 percent. State and local sales tax: 5 percent.

Rockland Auction Services belongs to the New York State Auctioneers Association, the New Jersey Auctioneers Association, and the National Auctioneers Association. The firm pays finder's fees, "depending on size (dollars) of the consignment."

100. Rose Galleries, Inc.
1123 West County Road B   Tel. (612) 484-1415
Roseville, MN 55113

The community of Roseville lies just north of St. Paul, Minnesota. In this pleasant community, Rose Galleries holds sales every Wednesday and every other Monday. These sales, which are advertised in the regional press, over the local radio, and through specialty periodicals, include GLASS, JEWELRY, RUGS, and TOYS. An unusual specialty of the house is BUTTONS.

Catalogues are not available by subscription but can be obtained the day before the sale. There is a buyer's premium of 5 percent, instituted in 1979. "Inspection" is on the day of the sale from 11 A.M. to 6 P.M., when the sale starts. There is also inspection on Sunday from 2 to 8 P.M., for the Monday sale.

The conditions of sale relating to warranties and guarantees are interesting and worth repeating in part: "It is our intention to call out any defects that we know about. However, with this many items we may miss something. Be sure to inspect all items you intend to bid on. All items will be sold as/is, where/is. Know what you are buying! . . . We disclaim any responsibility for any opinions on the value of any item whether expressed by the auctioneers or others. This catalog is for the purposes of identifying the merchandise . . . the auctioneers make no warranty or guarantee, expressed or implied, as to the accuracy of the information contained in this catalog. All glassware and china bringing a price of $10 or more each will be guaranteed to be free of cracks, chips, and/or repairs, unless otherwise noted in this catalog. . . . All jewelry is guaranteed to be as catalogued." Credit cards are accepted: MasterCard and Visa. Settlement is same day. State sales tax: 4 percent.

The consignor commission structure is as follows: $5 and 10 percent on articles sold for over $50; $1 and 25 percent on articles sold for $50 and under. Consignors are charged for packing and shipping, but not for insurance or warehousing. Consigned goods are sold within 3 weeks; settlement is 1 week after the sale. Reserves are accepted on items valued at over $1,000. Items bought because of a reserve are charged 5 percent of that reserve.

Deborah Kaufhold reports that appraisal service is available, at $30 the half hour.

101. Rosvall Auction Company
1238 & 1248 South Broadway   Tel. (303) 777-2032/722-4028
Denver, CO 80210

Rosvall is a family firm (father and son), founded in 1941. Sales of FURNITURE and general household merchandise are held every Wednesday at 7 P.M. at the 1238 building. Sales of mixed lots of what Rosvall calls "antiques" and that include AMERICANA, COINS, JEWELRY, and RUGS are held on Mondays twice monthly at 1248.

Sales are advertised in the local press, such as the Denver *Post* and the *Rocky Mountain News*. The majority of sales are held in these two salerooms, but the firm also conducts house and estate sales on site.

Announcements are available, but these sales are not catalogued. There is no buyer's premium, absentee bids are not executed, and there are no guarantees of authenticity. Viewing is on the day of the sale only, starting at 10 A.M. Buyers must settle their accounts within 48 hours. State and local sales tax: 3.5 percent.

The consignor commission is 25 percent. Consignors are not charged insurance, but are charged $20 an hour for packing, hauling, and cleaning. According to Mrs. Charles W. Rosvall, "If items must be held for a period of time, we charge" storage. Consigned goods are generally sold within a week or less. Settlement is made with the consignor 2 days after the sale. There are no reserves and no charge for buy-ins—there are none, as "everything is sold." The firm does buy and sell on its own behalf.

102. Sigmund Rothschild
27 West 67th Street   Tel. (212) 873-5522
New York, NY 10023

Mr. Rothschild, who is best known for his appraisal work, holds auctions "as required," at "various galleries and on location."

Announcements are made when a sale is scheduled. Catalogues generally are not available.

Rothschild will not accept consignments from dealers. The standard consignor's commission is 10 percent of gross. Reserves are not accepted. Settlement is made within 2 weeks of the sale. State and local sales tax: 8 percent. There is no buyer's premium, and no guarantees of authenticity are offered. The viewing procedure is "variable." Buyer must settle within 48 hours of the sale.

The press release accompanying Mr. Rothschild's response to our questionnaire emphasized his activities as an appraiser and made no mention of recent auction activities.

103. Vince Runowich Auctions
2312 4th Street North
St. Petersburg, FL 33704

Tel. (813) 895-3548

Runowich is a general-purpose auction house which holds sales of mixed lots once a month as well as on-location auctions as necessary. The general-purpose auctions, which include JEWELRY and GLASS, are held in the banquet room of Jerry's Restaurant, in the Best Western Motel by I-275, near Haines Road and 54th Avenue North.

Sales are advertised in the local press and via direct mail. Just write to be placed on the mailing list. Catalogues are prepared only for large estate sales. Most sales are, according to the owner, "country style and low profile."

There is no buyer's premium, although at press time the owner was "considering" its implementation. Viewing is the day before the sale and 1 hour before the auction begins. Absentee bids are accepted. There are no guarantees of authenticity, and buyers are not offered the opportunity to return goods that prove to be not as catalogued. Settlement must be made immediately. Credit cards are accepted: MasterCard, Visa. State sales tax: 4 percent.

The consignor's commission "is generally 25 percent, however some commissions can be negotiated." Consignors are charged insurance, "in some cases" are charged packing and shipping, and "sometimes" are charged for warehousing. Consigned goods are sold within 2–4 weeks. Settlement is made 24–48 hours after the sale. "Most auctions are absolute," but occasionally a reserve is established at 10 percent of lot value. Reserved items are charged a 10 percent buy-in fee "up to sensible limits."

The firm does pay finder's fees, but as the owner points out, "finder or bird-dog fees vary as to my profit from sale."

Vince Runowich Auctions is "a family operation . . . and we are not interested in being millionaires. We left the corporate rat race 20 years ago and want to keep it that way."

104. Sage Auction Gallery
Route 9A
Chester, CT 06412

Tel. (203) 526-3036

Approximately 10,000 lots a year are sold by this firm, which is under the direction of Mrs. Gloria N. Twomey and her son. Sales, held every other

Friday evening, "year round," are announced in local newspapers, such as the Middletown *Press,* the New London *Day,* and the Hartford *Courant,* as well as in specialty periodicals, such as *Antiques and the Arts Weekly.*
AMERICANA, FURNITURE, and RUGS are among the items sold at Sage's mixed-lot auctions. These sales are uncatalogued. There is no buyer's premium. Absentee bids are executed. Viewing is 10 A.M.–5 P.M. on the day prior to the sale, as well as 1 hour before the sale. Buyers must settle accounts within 24 hours. State sales tax: 7.5 percent. There are no guarantees of authenticity, etc. As Mrs. Twomey points out, "The buyer has ample time to inspect . . . all sales final."
The consignor's commission is generally 30 percent. Consignors are not charged insurance, packing and shipping, or warehousing. Consigned goods are sold within 2–4 weeks. Settlement is made after 1 week. Reserves are not accepted.
The firm does buy and sell on its own behalf: "We buy lots or estates if the owner would rather dispose of it that way rather than send it on consignment."
Appraisal service is available; the cost is $75 an hour.

105. San Antonio Auction Gallery

5096 Blanco   Tel. (512) 342-3800
San Antonio, TX 78216

Sales, uncatalogued, are held almost every Friday night at the gallery. Offered for auction are a variety of mixed lots typical of the kind of properties a general-purpose auction house offers, including ART DECO, ART NOUVEAU, FURNITURE, GLASS, JEWELRY, PORCELAIN, RUGS, and TOYS. John W. A. Jones, who has owned the gallery since 1973, reports that he has also sold a boa constrictor and a Model-T-Ford . . . in separate sales.
Sales are advertised in the local press, such as the San Antonio *Express,* and via direct mail; contact the office to be placed on the mailing list.
There is no buyer's premium. The terms of sale vary, but in the main these Friday-night sessions offer properties "as is." Viewing is possible right up to the time of the sale, all through the week during regular business hours. The best time to come to view the lots is Friday afternoon, for by then everything is in the gallery. Buyers must settle accounts at the end of the sale. The firm accepts credit cards: MasterCard, Visa. State and local sales tax: 5.5 percent.
The consignor's commission varies: "35 percent—junk, 25 percent—dealers, 20 percent—antiques, 15 percent—commercial liquidation."
Consignors are not charged for shipping and packing, warehousing, or insurance. Goods are sold as fast as possible; settlement is made after 6 days. Reserves are accepted sometimes. There is no minimum value for acceptance of a consignment.
The house pays a finder's fee. San Antonio Auction Gallery, which belongs to the National Auctioneers Association, buys and sells on its own behalf: "If the price is right we will buy anything."

106. San Francisco Auction Gallery
1217 Sutter Street   Tel. (415) 441-3800
San Francisco, CA 94109

Auctions are held once a month in a wide range of areas, mostly in the lower price ranges, including FURNITURE ("1800 up"), JEWELRY, CLOCKS AND WATCHES, and RUGS. Sales are advertised in local newspapers. Catalogues are available. There is no buyer's premium. Credit cards are accepted. State and local sales tax: 6.5 percent.

Viewing begins 2 days prior to auction. The commission structure for consignors is flexible, with a lower rate for dealers. Reserves are accepted on "valuable items only."

Hours of operation are 9 A.M.–5 P.M. daily. The house buys and sells on its own behalf. The contact person is Perry Omidvar, the owner.

107. Emory Sanders
New London, NH 03257   Tel. (603) 526-6326

House and estate sales held on site are Mr. Sanders' métier. New England country furnishings are his stock in trade, items such as FURNITURE, GLASS, and SILVER, although he has also sold horse-drawn vehicles and a collection of miniature elephants.

Sales, held "on demand," are advertised in the local press and in specialty journals, such as *Antiques and the Arts Weekly*. Announcements of forthcoming sales are catalogued only if the sale warrants it. To obtain a catalogue to such a sale, you must "respond to advertising."

There is no buyer's premium. "Telephone/mail bids are accepted," and packing and shipping services are available, at the buyer's expense. There are no guarantees of authenticity and no opportunity to make returns. You buy as is and that's it. Viewing is usually 1 hour prior to the sale. Settlement must be made immediately. Credit cards are accepted at some sales.

The consignor's commission varies, depending on the consignment's value. Consignor pays for moving goods to the auction site. Goods are usually sold within 2–4 weeks. Consignors are not charged warehousing or insurance. Reserves are not accepted. There is no buy-in charge: "Consigned property is sold." Settlement is made with the consignor within 24 hours after the sale.

108. Sandwich Auction House
15 Tupper Road   Tel. (617) 888-1926/5675
Sandwich, MA 02563

Sales by this general-purpose auction firm are uncatalogued, but are advertised in the local press, such as the Cape Cod *Times,* and in the Boston newspapers. There is no mailing list. Among Sandwich Auction House's specialties are AMERICANA and GLASS. The firm estimates it has an annual turnover of $500,000.

Sales are held once a week, in the evening. Viewing is 2–3 hours prior to the sale. There is a buyer's premium of 10 percent, instituted in September 1979. Buyers must settle accounts "ordinarily, immediately," but "special arrangements can be made." Sandwich Auction House offers buyers packing and shipping services, at the buyer's expense. Partner Janet Johnson indicates that "returns are allowed within one hour of each sale (after that consignors are owed their money)." State sales tax: 5 percent.

The consignor commission is 15 percent to $200 and 10 percent thereafter. Reserves are not accepted. Goods consigned are sold within 1–3 weeks and settlement is made 14 hours after the sale.

109. Schafer Auction Gallery

82 Bradley Road   Tel. (203) 245-4173
Madison, CT 06443

A general-purpose auction house, Schafer sells mixed lots including AMERICANA, FURNITURE, and RUGS. Sales are held once or twice monthly in a 3,700-square-foot building erected in 1978; the firm is much older.

Sales are also held on site, "under tent upon location." Schafer's sales are not catalogued. They are advertised in the local press, such as the New Haven *Register,* and in specialty periodicals, such as *Antiques and the Arts Weekly.* Fliers are also mailed out. If you want to be placed on the mailing list free of charge, just write.

There is no buyer's premium. Viewing is the day before the sale and 2 hours before the auction begins. Buyers must settle accounts immediately after the sale. Absentee bids are not accepted. Schafer will assist buyers with packing and shipping. State sales tax: 7.5 percent.

The consignor's commission varies from 20 to 35 percent, depending on the amount of merchandise and its quality. Consignors are not charged for insurance or warehousing, but are charged for packing and shipping. Goods consigned are sold in 3–8 weeks. Settlement is made with dealer consignors in 3 days, with all others in 30 days. Reserves are accepted.

Appraisal service is available at $25 an hour, or a fixed cost can be negotiated.

Schafer Auction Gallery belongs to the National Auctioneers Association and the Connecticut Auctioneers Association.

The firm also buys and sells on its own behalf. D. J. Schafer, head of the gallery, reports that "we buy merchandise outright and sell outright either at auction or directly to individuals."

110. Schmidt's Antiques

5138 West Michigan Avenue   Tel. (313) 434-2660
Ypsilanti, MI 48197

When this firm moved to Ypsilanti in 1939, after having been in business in Detroit since 1911, Neils Schmidt, just turned 20, joined his father in the business. Today the firm, under Neils Schmidt's sound direction, is involved in various operations. Schmidt's Antiques sells wholesale "to the trade," it sells retail to anyone, and it holds auctions "the first Saturday of each month and the Friday preceding." It also holds estate and house sales, as well as special catalogued sales as necessary.

The center for these activities is two buildings joined by a long gangway. In one of these buildings is the saleroom for the auctions, mostly mixed-lot sales of such items as AMERICANA, CHINESE WORKS OF ART, and the like. These general-purpose sales are not catalogued, in the main, but announcements are sent to a large mailing list, on which you can be included free of charge by writing the firm. When issued, the catalogue costs about $5.

Schmidt reported in 1980 that "as yet" there was no buyer's premium. Absentee bids are accepted, "with a 20 percent deposit," and the firm "will pack and ship for a charge." No guarantees of authenticity are offered and buyers are not offered the opportunity to return goods. Viewing is 1–2 weeks on the premises and 1 day on site. Credit cards are accepted: MasterCard, Visa. State sales tax: 4 percent. Schmidt's Antiques does buy and sell on its own behalf; as Neils Schmidt points out, "We also run a shop." Buyers must settle "right away."

The consignor's commission is 20–35 percent, depending on the situation. There is no charge for warehousing or insurance; there is a charge for packing and shipping. Consigned goods are sold within 1–3 months. Settlement is made "within 45 days." Reserves are not accepted. For buy-ins there is a "minimum handling charge, depending on the size of the item."

Schmidt's Antiques is a member of the National Auctioneers Association and the Michigan Auctioneers Association.

111. Schrader Galleries
211 Third Street South   Tel. (813) 823-5657/4701
St. Petersburg, FL 33701

Mixed-lot auctions are held every other month. Among Schrader's specialties are ART DECO, ART NOUVEAU, DOLLS, JEWELRY, PORCELAIN, and RUGS.

Sales are advertised in local newspapers and specialty publications, as well as in international journals. Most sales are held on the premises, but the firm does hold house sales. Announcements are sent out free of charge to anyone who requests to be put on the mailing list. Catalogues are not available by subscription, but can be obtained singly for each sale at a fee.

There is no buyer's premium. Mail or telephone bids are accepted. The usual viewing procedure is generally a week or more, during normal office hours, including Saturday. The house does not offer packing or shipping services. "We have a week or more preview so an individual may make up his mind or bring in any experts he wishes; all items sold as is, no refunds or returns, no guarantee made per catalog description."

The consignor's commission is 30 percent, but it is negotiable, depending on the situation. Consignors do not pay for insurance or warehousing, but must pay for transportation of consigned property. Goods are sold at the next available auction. Settlement is in the days following the sale as everything is picked up and paid for. There are no reserves or buy-in charges, since "every-thing is sold." State sales tax: 4 percent.

The firm does buy and sell on its own behalf: "We generally purchase the items to be auctioned and then auction them off."

112. Shore Galleries, Inc.
3318 West Devon   Tel. (312) 676-2900
Lincolnwood, IL 60659

ARMS AND ARMOR, COINS, and MILITARIA are the specialties of this firm, which is located in a suburb of Chicago.

Sales are held "once or twice a year or when necessary," and are advertised in the press and specialty periodicals, as well as through the mail (there is no charge for placement on the mailing list).

Catalogues are $1 each. Viewing is "usually the day before the sale." All sales "as is." Potential buyers cannot return goods that do not prove as catalogued. Settlement must be within 1 week. State and local taxes: 5 percent.

Consignor's commission "varies according to items and quantity." Settlement is made in "4 weeks or less." Reserves are not accepted.

The firm does buy and sell on its own behalf.

113. Shute's Auction Gallery
70 Accord Park Drive   Tel. (617) 871-3414/238-0586
Norwell, MA 02061

Although not specializing in any particular categories, Shute's mixed-lot auction sales include AMERICANA, ART DECO, ART NOUVEAU, CLOCKS AND WATCHES, GLASS, PAINTINGS, PORCELAIN, and SILVER.

Sales are held approximately every 2–3 weeks at the gallery, located in a smallish town 25 miles south of Boston. There is ample parking.

Sales are announced in the local press, such as the Boston *Globe* and the Boston *Herald,* as well as in specialty journals, such as *Antiques and the Arts Weekly.* Fliers are sent by direct mail; you can be placed on the mailing list free of charge by writing the firm.

Catalogues are available at the door, but not by subscription. Since 1979, there has been a buyer's premium of 10 percent. Usual viewing procedure is 7–9 the evening prior to the sale, 3–6:30 the afternoon of the sale, usually held in the evening. Buyers must settle accounts immediately. Shute accepts credit cards: MasterCard, Visa. State sales tax: 5 percent.

The consignor's commission is 15 percent for an item selling for $300 or under, and 10 percent for an item selling in excess of $300. Consignors are charged insurance, as well as the cost of packing and shipping consigned property. Consigned goods generally are sold within 1 month and settlement is made after 2 weeks. Reserves are accepted, according to general manager Samuel Collins, "on very rare occasions." Minimum value for a consignment: $50.

Shute does buy and sell on its own behalf, since there are estates, collections, and individual items whose owners do not wish to wait for auction results.

114. Robert A. Siegel Auction Galleries, Inc.

120 East 56th Street   Tel. (212) 753-6421/2/3
New York, NY 10022

This firm conducts 18–20 auctions per year, primarily of STAMPS but also of AUTOGRAPHS and COINS. Sales are mostly held on Siegel's premises, though a few take place in hotels in other cities or in New York.

Sales are advertised regularly in specialty journals, such as philatelic magazines. Catalogues are available singly or by subscription ($7.50 annually, including prices realized).

A buyer's premium of 10 percent was established in May 1979. Absentee bids are executed. Packing and shipping services are available, at buyer's expense. Guarantees of authenticity are offered and buyers can return lots that turn out to be not as catalogued. Buyers must settle within 3 days after sale or receipt of invoice. Credit can be established. State and local sales tax: 8 percent.

The standard consignor's commission is 10 percent. The commission is negotiable, depending on the situation. Goods consigned are sold within 6–10 weeks. Settlement is made 35 days after sale. Consignors do not pay for catalogue illustrations, warehousing, or insurance. Reserves are not accepted. There is no buy-in charge; Robert Siegel reports that "everything is sold."

Appraisal service is available; the "2–3 percent appraisal fee is returned if we handle for owner," reports Siegel.

The firm belongs to the American Stamp Dealers Association.

Annual turnover is estimated to be well in excess of $7.5 million.

115. Christopher L. Snow

12 Auburn Street, Box 28   Tel. (617) 465-8872
Newburyport, MA 01950

Mr. Snow conducts sales approximately once a month, at "on-site location when feasible, but rented halls are used during winter months or whenever an on-site sale is impossible (parking problems, neighbors, etc.)."

Sales are advertised in the Boston newspapers, the local press, and in specialty periodicals, such as *Antiques and the Arts Weekly*. To be placed on the mailing list costs $1; write the firm.

The uncatalogued mixed-lot sales include FURNITURE, GLASS, PAINTINGS (pre-20th c. American), and SILVER. There is no buyer's premium. Absentee bids are not accepted. There are no guarantees of authenticity. Packing and shipping services are not available. Mr. Snow reports: "Previews always before an auction, either the day before by appointment at times, and always immediately before the auction begins." Buyer must settle account directly after the sale. State sales tax: 5 percent.

The basic consignor's commission is 20 percent; it is negotiable. Consignors are not charged for anything, since there is nothing to charge them for—the goods are not moved, or if they are, the move is a limited one. Reserves are not accepted. There is no buy-in charge. Dealers are given "a slightly lower commission rate."

Christopher Snow buys and sells on his own behalf.

He belongs to the Massachusetts Auctioneers Association.

116. Stack's Rare Coin Auctions

123 West 57th Street   Tel. (212) 583-2580
New York, NY 10019   Telex: 666125

A well-known and long-established rare-coin dealer, Stack's also holds monthly sales in the Sheraton Hotel, at 56th Street and Seventh Avenue, around the corner from the firm's offices.

At these auctions, the lots offered include COINS, MEDALS, and PAPER MONEY. The sales are advertised in specialty journals, trade periodicals, and on the stamp/coin pages of the American and occasionally the European press. Catalogues are available singly at the firm or by mail, for an average cost of $3–$5 per copy. Catalogues are also available by subscription: $15 per year sent third class, $25 per year sent first class.

There is no buyer's premium. Absentee bids are executed. Bernard Stack, the managing partner, reports that "all items sold are guaranteed genuine . . . we are quick to correct errors on our part" in the catalogue. Viewing is generally 3 weeks prior to the sale dates, in the firm's offices Monday–Friday, 10 A.M.–5 P.M. Payment is due after sale when invoice is presented; "in some cases of substantial purchases, extended arrangements can be made." State and local sales tax: 8 percent.

The consignor's commission is variable: 10 percent, 12.5 percent, 15 percent, etc., "depending upon what may be involved and the expenses to be projected." There is no charge for catalogue illustrations, insurance, or warehousing. Consigned goods are sold within 6 months. Settlement is made 30–45 days after the sale. Reserves are not accepted. Mr. Stack reports that "everything is sold! We absorb any returned merchandise, and settle at the printed price realized." The minimum value for a consignment is $10,000. Consignments are not accepted from dealers.

The firm does not buy and sell on its own behalf in auctions; "only in retail division—not at any public auction (strict rule of house)."

117. Sterling Auction Gallery

62 North Second Avenue   Tel. (201) 685-9565/464-4047
Raritan, NJ 08869

Gerald and Celia Sterling, the directors of this firm, hold sales approximately once a month. These are usually on the premises, though the firm also holds house sales.

These sales are advertised in the *New York Times,* local suburban newspapers, and specialty periodicals, such as *Antiques News*. Catalogues are available during viewing and at the sale. The usual viewing procedure is on the day before and the morning of the sale (which is always held on Sunday).

The Sterling auctions sell mixed lots and these include AMERICANA, CLOCKS AND WATCHES, DOLLS, FURNITURE, PAINTINGS (pre-20th c. American), PHOTOGRAPHICA, and VICTORIANA. There is no buyer's premium. Absentee bids are not executed. Packing and shipping services are not offered. Goods may be returned only "in errors of identification, i.e., gold or silver proved not as catalogued." Credit cards are accepted: MasterCard, Visa. Buyers must settle accounts immediately. State sales tax: 5 percent.

Consignor commission "varies depending on the quality and the value." Consignor pays for cartage to the gallery, but not for insurance or warehousing. Reserves are accepted but not generally; only if a "very good piece" is involved. Goods consigned are usually sold within 1 month and settlement is made "within 10 business days." Minimum value for a consignment is $100.

118. Stremmel Auctions, Inc.
2152 Prater Way   Tel. (702) 331-1035
Sparks, NV 89431

Located not far from Reno, Stremmel is a general-purpose auction firm which also handles real estate. Among its auction specialties are AMERICANA, FURNITURE, PAINTINGS, PORCELAIN, and RUGS. Very much a family operation (two brothers—Peter and Steven Stremmel—run it), the firm holds auctions approximately twice a month.

Stremmel began in 1970 with on-site auctions, and in 1978 acquired its own facility in Sparks. Exhibitions of items to be auctioned take place not only in Sparks but also in Reno, at Peter Stremmel's art gallery, 1400 South Virginia Street, which sells American paintings, bronzes, and the like. Viewing is 4 days before the sale, 8 A.M.–6 P.M.

The enthusiastic Stremmels catalogue most sales. The catalogues are available gratis at the auction. Sales are announced in the local press and through mailings (to get on the mailing list, just write). Most sales are held midweek nights, and offer roughly 200 lots. All goods are sold "as is," but buyers do have the opportunity to return goods that prove to be not as catalogued. State and local taxes: 3.5 percent.

There is no buyer's premium. Bidding is with numbered cards. Stremmel accepts MasterCard and Visa. Accounts should be settled immediately after the auction. The minimum value for a consignment is $50. The commission structure is: for lots sold between $50 and $100, 33⅓ percent; $101–$500, 25 percent; $501–$1,000, 20 percent; above $1,000, 15 percent. Most lots sell for less than $175. Consignors are not charged insurance, but are charged for warehousing. Commissions are negotiable, depending on the situation. Reserves are accepted. The charge for buy-ins is 5 percent of the reserve price.

Stremmel also buys and sells on its own behalf.

119. Philip Swedler & Son
850 Grand Avenue   Tel. (203) 624-2202/562-5065
New Haven, CT 06511

Swedler's reports that "we will auction anything" and it would seem that they have, from the furnishings of New Haven's Hotel Taft to the contents of CBS labs. Although primarily industrial liquidators, Swedler's from time to time holds house and estate sales that involve the decorative or fine arts. Liquidations, such as in the case of the Taft, include FURNITURE. They have an extensive mailing list "divided into several categories, depending on the type of auction certain people are interested in." To get on this mailing list, send Swedler's a postcard with your name and address and your interests; mark it: "Attention: Janet."
There is no buyer's premium. Viewing is usually 24 hours before the sale. Accounts must be settled within 2 days after the sale. Norman Swedler reports that "at furniture auctions we are sometimes agreeable to accepting MasterCard and Visa." No guarantees of authenticity are offered, nor is the opportunity to return goods that do not prove as catalogued. State sales tax: 7.5 percent.
The standard consignor's commission varies between 10 and 30 percent, depending on the situation and the value of the merchandise to be auctioned. Goods consigned are usually sold within 30 days. Settlement is made within a week to 10 days after the auction.

120. Tepper Galleries
110 East 25th Street   Tel. (212) 677-5300/1/2
New York, NY 10010

Auctions, uncatalogued, are held alternate Saturdays at 11 A.M. Exhibition is the preceding Friday, 9 A.M.–7 P.M. Sales are usually mixed lots. Tepper will execute order bids from bidders who are known to it or have established credit.
There is no buyer's premium. Settlement is within 1 week, "unless specifically arranged." According to its advertisements, "Ample Meter Parking is Available." Among the items Tepper emphasizes are FURNITURE, JEWELRY, and RUGS. Tepper advertises in such newspapers as the *New York Times*.
Consignor's commission, usually 20 percent, "is flexible, depending on the situation," states auctioneer Max Drazen. Goods are usually sold within 2 weeks. Settlement is within 30 days. State and local sales tax: 8 percent.
Tepper does buy and sell on its own behalf: "We do buy items from owners or estates and do offer them for sale in our auctions." The firm belongs to the Auctioneers Association of America and the Appraisers Association of America.

121. Trend Galleries, Inc.
2784 Merrick Road   Tel. (516) 221-5588
Bellmore, NY 11710

Sales are held every other Friday night at this gallery, which is located in
Nassau County on the south shore of Long Island, not far from the New York
City line.

Directed by Ruth and Eugene Weiss, Trend Galleries regularly advertises
its sales in daily newspapers, such as the *New York Times* and *Newsday*.
Catalogues are available the day before the sale at the gallery; they are not
obtainable by subscription.

Specialties of the firm, whose turnover is approximately 10,000 lots annually, include ART DECO, ART NOUVEAU, CLOCKS AND WATCHES, FURNITURE, and
GLASS. Viewing is the Thursday before the sale, 5–9 P.M.

There is no buyer's premium. Buyers have 1 week after the sale to settle
their accounts. Packing and shipping services are not offered. As for returns:
"We are a small business, responsible both to our customers and for our
word." Minimum value for acceptance of a consignment is $20. Goods are
sold within 2 weeks of being consigned. Settlement is made 10 days after the
sale. State and local taxes: 7 percent.

The firm does buy and sell on its own behalf: "We are always prepared to
purchase merchandise, which we sell unreserved on our own behalf."

122. Valle-McLeod Gallery
3303 Kirby Drive   Tel. (713) 523-8309/8310
Houston, TX 77098

A general-purpose auction operation which holds 6 sales annually, Valle-
McLeod is also a retail operation. Hours are 10 A.M.–6 P.M., Monday–
Saturday.

There is no buyer's premium. Credit cards are accepted: American Express,
MasterCard, Visa. Settlement must be made within 24 hours after the sale.
Viewing is for 2 days prior to the sale, 10 A.M.–6 P.M.

Auctions are held on the premises, and in addition, Valle-McLeod conducts
house sales. Catalogues are not available by subscription or mail, but can be
obtained in person prior to the sale. State and local sales tax: 6 percent.

The consignor's commission, which is negotiable, is 20 percent for nondealers, less for dealers. Reserves are accepted. Consignors are charged for
insurance on consigned property. Goods are usually sold within 8–10 weeks;
settlement is made 21 days after the sale.

Valle-McLeod belongs to the National Auctioneers Association and the
Texas Antique Dealers Association.

The gallery buys and sells on its own behalf.

123. The Watnot Auction
Box 78   Tel. (518) 672-7576
Mellenville, NY 12544

Richard Tanne and his wife hold sales as necessary. These are usually mixed lots, whether held at the Tannes' usual venue—the firehouse in Churchtown, New York—or on the consignor's premises. Sales are advertised regularly in the local press (the area north of Poughkeepsie, New York, and west of Springfield, Massachusetts) and in specialty periodicals, such as *Antiques and the Arts Weekly*.

The sales are not catalogued. There is no buyer's premium. The usual viewing procedure is exhibition 2 hours before the sale and during it. Consignor's commission normally is 20 percent, but it is negotiable. Buyers must settle immediately; settlement with consignors is after 7 days. State and local sales taxes: 6 percent.

There are no reserves and no charge for buy-ins: "Everything we get on consignment is sold. This is an auction, not a retail store." The Tannes do buy and sell on their own behalf; sometimes "we buy out whole households and small lots so we can sell them at the auction, no holds barred."

124. Adam A. Wechsler & Son
905-9 E Street NW   Tel. (202) 628-1281
Washington, DC 20004

Wechsler's has been operated by the same family since its establishment in the 1890s. A general-purpose auction house, Wechsler's holds uncatalogued sales every Tuesday, featuring mixed lots of general household merchandise. In addition, 4 times a year, usually in September, December, February, and May, catalogued estate sales are held. The goods sold at these estate sales include FURNITURE (18th & 19th c. American & Continental), GLASS, PAINTINGS, PORCELAIN, and SILVER, as well as CHINESE and JAPANESE WORKS OF ART and RUGS.

Each catalogue costs $15; a subscription to all 4 is $50. Post-sale price lists are available for an additional $2 each. These catalogued sales are advertised in the local press, as well as in specialty periodicals, such as *Antiques Monthly*. The house will also put you on their mailing list free of charge; just write. The uncatalogued sales are advertised in the local press only.

Viewing for the weekly sales is Monday, 9 A.M.–5 P.M.; for the catalogue sales, 4 days before the sale, Friday, Saturday, Monday, 10 A.M.–5 P.M., Sunday, noon–5 P.M. Since September 1979, there has been a buyer's premium of 10 percent. Buyers must settle by noon of the following day for the weekly sales, and 3 days after the final day of sale for the catalogued auctions. Absentee bids are accepted. The house does not offer packing and shipping services. Local sales tax: 5 percent.

"Consignments can be refused at discretion of appraisers if of very insignificant value; no set minimum, however." Commission: 10 percent on items fetching over $500; 15 percent on items fetching up to and including $500.

Reserves are accepted; buy-ins are 10 percent of high bid, but if property is "left with no reserve, it will be sold." Settlement is 30 days after auction. In catalogue sales, consignor is charged $35 per black-and-white photo in catalogue, $185 for color. Consignor is also charged insurance on basis of 20¢ per $100 valuation per month for a maximum of 3 months.

Wechsler's belongs to the American Society of Appraisers.

125. White Plains Auction Rooms
572 North Broadway   Tel. (914) 428-2255
White Plains, NY 10603

Mixed-lot general-purpose sales, held monthly by this firm, offer such items as AMERICANA, CLOCKS AND WATCHES, JUDAICA, PAINTINGS, RUGS, SILVER.

Sales are held on the premises and occasionally on location at private homes, etc. They are advertised in the regional press, in the *New York Times,* and through mailings. Catalogues are not available by subscription, but can be obtained for individual sales: write, telephone, or come in during exhibitions.

Since the beginning of 1980, there has been a 10 percent buyer's premium. Mail order bids are accepted. Packing and shipping services are available, at the buyer's expense. Goods that prove to be not as catalogued may be returned. The usual viewing procedure is 3–4 days before a sale, 10 A.M.–5 P.M., and some evenings. Buyers must settle accounts immediately. Credit cards are accepted: MasterCard, Visa. The sales tax is 7 percent.

The standard consignor's commission is "20 percent below $500/10 percent over." It is negotiable, depending upon the situation. Reserves are not accepted. There is no minimum value necessary for a consignment. Consigned goods are sold within 4–6 weeks. Settlement is 14 days after the sale. Consignors are not charged insurance or storage (prior to sale).

126. The Wilson Galleries
P.O. Box 102   Tel. (703) 885-4292
Fort Defiance, VA 24437

Located on U.S. Route 11 in picturesque Verona, right by Fort Defiance and just north of Staunton, and within easy distance of Charlottesville, the Wilson Galleries hold Saturday sales toward the end of the months of January, March, May, July, September, and November.

The auctions, which usually comprise 300–350 lots, are a mixture of objects, but according to Mark Wilson the following items are included in every catalogued auction: AMERICANA, CLOCKS AND WATCHES, FURNITURE, PAINTINGS (Old Master, 19th c. European, pre-20th c. American, Impressionist), PORCELAIN, RUGS, SILVER.

Viewing is always the Friday before the sale, as well as one or two other days in the week preceding. Catalogues are available for $5 at the house, or $6 through the mail; a subscription to all catalogues costs $36 (the mail order price includes post-sale price lists).

There is no buyer's premium. Absentee bids are accepted. No guarantees of authenticity are offered. Packing and shipping services are offered, at the buyer's expense. Settlement is on the same day for buyers present, and upon receipt of invoice for all others. State and local taxes: 4 percent.

Consignor's commission is 20 percent on any lot grossing less than $300; and 17.5 percent on any lot grossing $300 or more. Consignors are not charged for catalogue illustrations, insurance, packing or shipping, warehousing. Reserves are not accepted. There is no charge for buy-ins.

The Wilson Galleries estimates its annual turnover as $1 million. The Wilsons, husband and wife, also maintain a small retail operation, which operates "by appointment only."

127. Helen Winter Associates

355 Farmington Avenue   Tel. (203) 747-0714/677-0848
Plainville, CT 06062

This firm holds auctions every 2 weeks, on Monday evenings. Its specialties include AMERICANA, DOLLS, FURNITURE, PAINTINGS (pre-20th c. American), PORCELAIN, RUGS, and SILVER. Sales are held at the auction house and at the premises of the consignor.

Announcements of sales are available upon request; you can be placed upon the mailing list at no charge. Catalogues are not available by subscription, but can be had for single sales. There has been a buyer's premium of 10 percent since October 1979. Sales tax must be paid where bidder is not exempt. "We accept mail order bids from buyers who are known to us. We pack and ship at buyer's expense. We stand behind our merchandise and will accept the return of any goods which are incorrectly advertised. Inspection time, one to two hours before the auction or by appointment." Credit is available to buyers known to the management. Helen Winter Associates accepts MasterCard and Visa. State sales tax: 7.5 percent.

Consignor's goods are sold "at the first appropriate auction." Settlement is made within 2 weeks of the auction. Reserves are accepted. There is no buy-in charge, "unless a reserve has been stipulated, then 10 percent of the price reached in the bidding is charged." Consignor's commission is 10 percent on lots that sell for over $500, and 20 percent for those that sell for less. The consignor commission is negotiable for dealers and for large consignments, such as entire estates. The house buys and sells on its own behalf "rarely," but it does "work in close cooperation with Helen Winter's Grist Mill Antique Gallery" in Farmington.

128. Richard Withington, Inc.

Hillsboro, NH 03244   Tel. (603) 464-3232

Since the late 1940s, Richard Withington has been an auctioneer and appraiser. Incorporation came only in 1964. He holds 40–50 sales a year, at least one each summer month at his home in southern New Hampshire, at least one each winter at the Sheraton Rolling Green Inn at Andover, Massachusetts, and all over New England on site for estate and house sales.

Sales are advertised in the local and regional press, as well as in specialty periodicals, such as *Maine Antique Digest.* Announcements of forthcoming sales are sent out regularly; you can be placed on the mailing list by request at no cost.

Catalogues are not available by subscription, and Withington reports that "we rarely produce catalogues except for monthly doll auctions." These cost $5.

Most sales are of mixed lots, which include AMERICANA, CLOCKS AND WATCHES, FURNITURE, PAINTINGS, PEWTER, PORCELAIN, RUGS, SILVER and TOYS. DOLLS are a Withington specialty, for which the firm is well known. There is no buyer's premium. The usual viewing procedure is exhibition 2 hours prior to the sale, although doll auctions have a preview. Buyers must settle accounts immediately after the sale. Withington does not guarantee authenticity, does not offer buyers the opportunity to return goods that prove to be not as catalogued, and does not execute absentee bids, but it will assist buyers to obtain packing and shipping services.

The consignor's commission is "20 percent flat, with no deviation." Goods are sold within 90 days, and settlement with consignors is made after 48 hours. Reserves are not accepted; "everything is sold with no reservations." Withington will only "on rare occasions" accept consignments from dealers.

Richard Withington, Inc., does "occasionally" buy and sell on its own behalf.

129. Richard Wolffers, Inc.

127 Kearny Street   Tel. (415) 781-5127
San Francisco, CA 94108

STAMPS and related subjects, such as PHILATELIC BOOKS, are auctioned by this firm at approximately 6-week intervals. The auctions are usually held Wednesday, Thursday, and Friday evenings at 6:30 P.M., and occasionally on Saturday afternoons as well. The auction room in San Francisco is on the second floor, 133 Kearny Street, but venues outside San Francisco and the U.S. are occasionally used.

Sales are announced in specialty stamp periodicals, both in the United States and overseas. An annual subscription for catalogues (including prices realized) is $15 U.S. and $30 elsewhere (sent by airmail).

Since April 1979, there has been a buyer's premium of 10 percent. The firm will execute mail order bids; indeed, "over 1,000 people send mail bids per auction." All lots are on display at Wolffers' offices for 1 week prior to the sale, Monday–Friday, 9 A.M.–6 P.M., and by appointment. "Out-of-town clients can request postal viewing of small-size lots up to 2 weeks prior to the dates of sale. Lots must be returned within 24 hours of receipt and postage; registration and insurance must be paid by client both ways."

The firm offers packing and shipping services, at the buyer's expense. Authenticity is guaranteed, as is the right to return goods that prove to be not as catalogued; according to a company vice-president, "buyers have 30 days from auction to return if not genuine or misdescribed." Dealers have 30 days after sale to settle; others have 10 days. Credit cards are accepted: MasterCard, Visa. State and local sales tax: 6.5 percent.

Consignor's commission, which is negotiable, is as follows: Lots selling for $1–100, 15 percent; $101–500, 10 percent; $501–1,000, 9 percent; $1,001–2,000, 8 percent; $2,001–3,000, 7 percent; $3,001 and up, 5 percent. Consignors do not pay for catalogue illustrations, insurance, packing and shipping, or warehousing. Minimum value for acceptance: "Total consignment must expect to gross $750; lots average $200 plus." Consigned goods are sold within 10–16 weeks. Settlement is 45th day after sale "or when cleared by purchaser." Reserves are accepted "very rarely."

Richard Wolffers, Inc., does buy and sell on its own behalf: "House may own 20–30 percent of material in auctions. We may also bid on any lot."

The firm estimates its annual turnover to be in excess of $4 million.

Appraisal service is available: the cost is 2.5 percent of the appraised value, plus expenses. Minimum charge in the store is $25; outside the store, $50.

For the convenience of customers in Great Britain, West Germany, and Switzerland, the firm maintains local currency accounts in each country, to which payment may be made at the prevailing rate of exchange.

130. Samuel Yudkin and Associates

1125 King Street   Tel. (703) 549-9330
Alexandria, VA 22314

Yudkin specializes in BOOKS, PRINTS, and STAMPS, and holds sales once a month, directed at both absentee bidders and those in the room. There are usually 50–75 people at each auction; about 2,000 catalogues have been sent out throughout the United States and overseas.

Catalogues are $1; with prices realized, another $1. Catalogues are also available by subscription. (Book and print catalogues are $15; with prices realized, $25. Stamp and first day cover catalogues are $2; with prices realized, $5.)

The buyer's premium is 10 percent. Credit cards are accepted: MasterCard and Visa. Bidding is in 10 percent increments over $50. Floor bidders are expected to pay a $5 deposit. Payment is required within 5 days of the sale, "or notification in the case of absent bidders." A refund of the purchase price is made "only if a definite error in catalogue description has been made, and only if the bidder has had the chance to examine the lot." State and local sales tax: 4 percent.

Consignor's commission is 15 percent (with a minimum of $3) and "an entry fee of $2.50 each auction is charged consignors." Goods are usually sold 30–60 days from receipt, and settlement is 30–60 days from auction date.

The house does buy and sell on its own behalf: "Most lots are from consignors. We have a general used and rare book shop. Some lots are used to fill in if we are short in a category (e.g., cookbooks, etc.)."

United Kingdom
and Eire

The auction market for fine arts and chattel goods (such as furniture) in the United Kingdom and Eire is a richly varied one. (Let no one be offended by the inclusion of Eire here, for with certain exceptions, such as taxes and export regulations, its system is generally the same as the British one and a number of its auctioneers belong to the British professional groups.) This auction market includes the establishment London houses and their satellites in the metropolitan area and in various regions; the provincial and second-rank auction firms, whose sales include everything from antiques to pure junk; and the country auctions, with their idiosyncratic atmosphere and diversified wares, at the lower end of the price spectrum.

In the following listings, you will find discussed more than 200 auction venues, at which you can bid, consign, or simply observe the passing show. Whatever the bidding range in the saleroom, wherever it is located, however it is decorated, each of these venues has certain features in common with the others. For our purposes, the most important of these common features is that most operate on a two-tier basis.

On one level are the general-purpose mixed-lot sales (usually described as "general furniture and effects"), at which almost anything may turn up, and usually does. Think of the most outlandish object that you can, and chances are it has turned up at such a sale. These general sales are usually held on a regular basis—weekly or biweekly on the same day of the week—and the cataloguing is minimal or non-existent. Just about every auction firm in the U.K. and Eire holds such sales. Christie's and Sotheby's do not, but their satellites do. The sales of "furniture, carpets, and objects of art" at Christie's South Kensington are much beloved by bargain hunters.

On another level are the specialist sales, which are usually held less frequently. Such sales are the staple of the multinational firms, but the vast majority of auction houses in the U.K. and Eire group their better consignments to hold such sales every two weeks or monthly or quarterly, or whenever they get enough good stuff to hold one. Such sales are described as "antique furniture and collectors' items," or less narrowly as "furniture, porcelain, silver, and other antique items," or more specifically as, say, "silver and plate." The spread of such sales in recent years, as well as the firms' increasingly active advertising of them, has meant, to use the words of one newspaper saleroom correspondent, that there is "good business to be done without taking antiques to London." The cataloguing for such sales varies with the ambitions of the house; often it is just list-like, in octavo or somewhat larger format, with minimal descriptions. The estimate sheets are laid in and have to be requested separately. Price lists must also be requested separately, if indeed they are published at all.

There are two very useful weekly publications which can serve as guides to the constantly changing auction scene. *Antiques Trade Gazette* [116 Long Acre, London WC2E 9PA, tel. (01) 836-0323] each week presents relatively extensive reports on various sales and publishes a reasonably thorough auction calendar. *Art & Antiques Weekly* [Bridge House, 181 Queen Victoria Street, London EC4V 4DD, tel. (01) 236-6626], distributed by Argus Distribution Ltd. [12–18 Paul Street, London EC2A 4JS, tel. (01) 247-8233], is more gossipy and juicier, glossier, but less extensive in its listing of forthcoming sales or its saleroom coverage. The *Gazette* sales reports, moreover, have the added advantage of indicating whether the auctioneer charges a buyer's premium, and if so, how much. The London papers, which are national in scope, also carry both reports and advertising about auctions. The *Daily Telegraph* Monday edition and the Tuesday *Times* are well known for their auction ads and well worth a perusal.

The buyer's premium has been a bone of contention ever since it was introduced to the U.K. by Christie's and Sotheby's in 1975. In recent years, it has spread extensively and it is now being charged by a multitude of auction houses on most goods, the exceptions being coins, stamps, and wines. The trade resents the premium and has challenged it strenuously, the most notable effort being the case brought against Sotheby's and Christie's by a number of leading antiques and fine arts dealers who hope to have the practice declared illegal. At this writing, the case is pending.

As a buyer, you should be aware of practices and restrictions which may affect your bidding. Many auction firms, if they do not know you or your financial situation, may ask for a cash deposit of up to half your winning bid right after you have made it. You may sometimes have your bid placed by a saleroom porter (you can't attend, you must leave the auction, etc.) in the absence of a more formal absentee bidding arrangement; it is customary to tip the porter if his bid takes the lot for you. It is true, as B. P. Bearne, the head of the Sotheby's operation in Torquay, has pointed out, that "the success of auction sales is dependent to a great extent upon support by the antiques trade." And for all the disharmony between the dealers and the auction houses, the latter do recognize Bearne's point and make certain concessions to the trade, such as the extension of credit and the organization of exhibition hours for the trade only. But the number of private buyers is constantly increasing and no longer do 90–95 percent of all sales go to dealers. On the contrary, in many instances as much as half of a sale will go to persons outside the trade.

From time to time, successful bidders may have other considerations to take into account. A lot may prove not to be as catalogued or even if viewed may prove to be something else than was suggested. Many auctioneers allow for some kind of reasonable return policy within a stated limited time; others are less amenable to such arrangements. In the U.K., the Misrepresentation Act of 1967 has led to a tightening of descriptions by auctioneers and means that should you wish to pursue a legal recourse, you stand a better chance than you did before the passage of this act. However, most auction house employees are reasonable people and usually something can be worked out. In Eire, the general policy is "no returns," but in that country also, auctioneers are reasonable if a bit less flexible.

More difficult is the problem that arises when you buy something in the U.K. that needs an export license. Under the restrictions currently in effect, such a license is needed for any of the following:

- a work of art that is over 50 years old and worth more than £8,000
- any archaeological item, document, manuscript, or archive over 50 years old
- any photograph over 60 years old and having a value of more than £200

Given inflation, you may run into this problem sooner than you think. But on the whole the authorities are reasonable, and the major houses can and will assist you in dealing with the bureaucracy involved. However, with really important objects, the reviewing committee may balk. The granting of an export license will be delayed for a set, limited period of time so that a U.K. institution which has expressed interest in the object may have the opportunity to raise funds (publicly or privately) in order to buy the object at the bidder's successful price.

The consignment of goods is usually quite a simple matter in the U.K. and Eire. Many catalogues contain an entry form. You describe the goods to be consigned and in due course the firm notifies you as to when it can accept delivery. Many firms simply announce the date of their next sale and the date when consignments will be accepted. Relatively few auctioneers in the U.K. and Eire will just accept delivery of goods any old time, even after an inspection.

In Eire, insurance if desired is usually arranged for by the consignor. In the U.K., a consignor can arrange for it, but the more usual practice is for the auctioneer to charge insurance on goods stored pending sale at a fixed fee. This fee is normally 50p per £100 of the value realized at auction. Many houses have a minimum fee of 10p.

It is worthwhile repeating here that generally you should pay nothing for warehousing prior to the sale. If the goods are unsold and you do not reclaim them within a set period of time, you will be charged warehousing; the cost generally is fixed.

Remember that many auctioneers in the U.K. have a minimum lot charge. If the sale commission on your property is higher than the minimum lot charge, then you need give the matter no further thought. But if not, you pay the minimum lot charge and the auctioneer gains at your expense.

The consignor's commission varies. There are standard charges, but as you will see in detail in the following listings, most firms in the U.K. and Eire are willing to negotiate the consignor's commission, "depending upon the situation." In negotiating this commission, be reasonable and use your common sense. The quality and quantity of the proposed consignment have much to do with the auctioneer's response: the person with three rooms of prime Chippendale is certainly in a stronger bargaining position than the potential consignor of a houseful of ordinary furniture. If you think that your position is one of strength, however, don't hesitate to bargain, for the staff members at every type of auction house in the U.K. and Eire know that getting quality property is far more difficult than selling it.

Value Added Tax: In the U.K., VAT is charged to both consignors and buyers. Foreign consignors who reside outside the U.K. and not in an EEC country and who are not registered for VAT purposes in the U.K. do not pay VAT. All other consignors must pay VAT at the standard rate—currently 15 percent—on all fees normally charged by the auctioneers, including the consignor's commission as well as charges for the auctioneer's other services, such as catalogue illustration, insurance, cartage, and so on. VAT is shown as a separate item on the statement sent to all consignors after a sale.

All consignors whose goods can be classed as assets of their business or who are registered for VAT purposes as dealers in antiques, works of art, and/or general chattels are required by law to enter their VAT registration number on the sales entry form when placing items with auctioneers for sale at auction. Such consignors are asked to indicate which of these items may be exempt from VAT under the special scheme set out in H.M. Customs and Excise Number 712.

Buyers at auction do not pay VAT unless the item has been entered in the sale by a vendor who is registered for VAT purposes and whose items may be classed as assets of his business, or by a consignor who is registered for VAT purposes as a dealer in antiques, works of art, and/or general chattels. Buyers are not, however, required to pay VAT on items entered in a sale by such a consignor if the items fall into one of the following categories:

- paintings, drawings, and pastels executed by hand
- original engravings, prints, and lithographs
- original sculptures and statuary, in any material
- antiques of any age exceeding 100 years, except loose pearls and loose gemstones
- collections and collectors' pieces of zoological, botanical, mineralogical, anatomical, historical, archaeological, paleontological, or ethnographic interest

At a fair number of auction firms, items on which a buyer is required to pay VAT (and such items are always clearly marked with an asterisk or some other symbol in the catalogues of all firms) are sold VAT inclusive: the buyer pays VAT on the premium only as would be the case in any event. Those buyers who are registered for VAT purposes as dealers in antiques, works of art, and/or general chattels can if they so desire have their invoice broken down to show the details of the amount of VAT charged inclusive in the bid.

All buyers must pay VAT on the buyer's premium at the standard rate of 15 percent.

In Eire, there is 10 percent VAT on the buyer's premium and on the commission charged the consignor by the auction house.

There is also a 10 percent VAT on goods imported into Ireland for sale at auction.

British telephone codes (STD codes) in the following section are given in parentheses, and are not normally required if you are dialing from the town or city itself. For instance, the prefix for London—(01)—is not necessary if you are calling from anywhere in the London area.

FRICS in the following entries stands for Fellow of the Royal Institution of Chartered Surveyors; ARICS is Associate of the same. FSVA stands for the Fellow of the Society of Valuers and Appraisers.

England and Wales

131. Edward Bailey & Son
17 Northgate   Tel. (0636) 703 141 (7 lines)
Newark, Nottinghamshire NG24 1EX

An old-line firm, established in 1866, Edward Bailey & Son has various offices in Nottinghamshire. The auctioneers' offices and salerooms are in Newark, at Northgate, away from the center of the town and not far from the river Trent.

General furniture sales are held every Thursday, general antiques sales once a month. These monthly sales may include just about everything listed below or only some such items. Over 350 lots are sold at each sale. Most sales begin at 11 A.M.

The catalogue descriptions are fair but minimal. Although as of this writing the catalogues were not available by subscription, this situation may change during 1981, and thus if you are interested you should check with Ms. M. Smith, the secretary.

Contact person: M. A. H. Hopewell, FRICS

Days/hours of operation: Mon.–Fri. 9 A.M.–5:30 P.M.

Areas in which general auctions and special sales are held:

Arms and Armor	Paintings
Art Deco	Old Master
Art Nouveau	17th c. British
Clocks and Watches	18th c. British
Drawings	19th c. European
Engravings	Pewter
Etchings	Porcelain
Furniture	Prints
Glass	Rugs
Jewelry	Silver
Maps	Toys
Musical Instruments	

Sales are advertised in the local press and in specialty periodicals, such as *Art & Antiques Weekly* and *Antiques Trade Gazette.* Announcements are also available from Bailey; write to be put on the mailing list.

Individual catalogues, at 30p, are available approximately 4 days before a sale.

Usual viewing procedure: Exhibition is 2–5 P.M. the day before the sale, and 9–11 A.M. the morning of the sale.

Bidder Information

Most sales are held on the premises, but house and estate sales are also conducted from time to time.

The buyer's premium is 5 percent. Accounts must be settled within 24 hours or by "arrangement with the auctioneer." You may be asked to pay a 25 percent deposit immediately on any items your bid wins.

There are no guarantees of authenticity; all statements in the catalogue "are statements of opinion, and are not to be taken as, or as implying, statements or representations of fact." Absentee bids are not executed. Packing and shipping services are not provided. Goods may not be returned if they prove to be not as catalogued.

Consignor Information

Those wishing to consign property should contact the saleroom, either in writing or by phone. Minimum value accepted is at "auctioneer's discretion."

Consignor's commission is "between 10 and 12.5 percent on antique items, 15 percent on general furniture." Commissions are negotiable, depending on the situation.

Consignors do not pay for catalogue illustrations, insurance, warehousing, or packing and shipping.

Reserves are accepted; the buy-in charge is 5 percent.

Goods are usually sold within 2–3 weeks; settlement is made within 3 days of the sale.

Appraisal service is available. There is no charge if the goods are sold at auction by Edward Bailey & Son. Otherwise, the charge is £10 per hour plus VAT.

132. Bonhams Montpelier Galleries

Montpelier Street	Tel. (01) 584-9161 (10 lines)/589-4577
Knightsbridge	Telex: 916477
London SW7 1HH	Cable: BONHAMS LONDON SW7

133. Bonhams Chelsea

65–69 Lots Road, King's Road	Tel. furniture (01) 352-0466
London SW10 ORN	pictures (01) 351-1380

This family-owned and -managed firm is a good middle-rank auction house that labors in the shadow of its giant London competitors and deserves to be better known. It offers its clients a good range of services. Bonhams holds as many as 12 auctions a week (the average is 7). Consigned goods are advertised widely, if necessary, and sold fast—usually in less than 8 weeks and sometimes in 3. Settlement is 21 days after the sale. The firm has been innovative and smart in its handling of sales and in attracting merchandise. The annual turnover is in excess of £8 million—4 times what it was at the beginning of the 1970s, which even with the rampant English inflation is a healthy jump upward.

The firm began in 1793 as a partnership between William Charles Bonham and George Jones, and for the next 150 years or so had a checkered history. In some decades it did well, and in some it did not. The current corporate title— W. and F. C. Bonham and Sons Limited—was formalized in the 1870s. Bonhams had a variety of quarters in the next three quarters of a century, finally settling on Montpelier Street in the mid-1950s. These attractive quarters are just across the Brompton Road from Harrods. At the end of the 1950s, Bonhams acquired a secondary saleroom in Chelsea; the next to the last of such venues, the Old Chelsea Galleries (as they were known) were located at 75–81 Burnaby Street. These galleries became a warehouse and furniture store on the opening of the more spacious New Chelsea Galleries, just across the King's Road, at the end of the 1970s. This venue is now known as Bonhams Chelsea.

The auction schedule of Bonhams gives some idea of the diversity of the sales held. The schedule at Montpelier Street is as follows:

Tuesday:	Silver and Plate	fortnightly
	Wines and Spirits	monthly
Wednesday:	Watercolors and Drawings	monthly
	Prints	every 6 weeks
	20th c. Paintings and Graphics	periodically
	Books and Manuscripts	periodically
	Arms	periodically

Thursday:	Antique Furniture	weekly
	European Oil Paintings	weekly
	Oriental Carpets	periodically
Friday:	Ceramics and Works of Art	weekly
	Jewels and Objects of Virtu	monthly
	Clocks and Watches	periodically
	Stamps	bimonthly

The schedule at Bonhams Chelsea is:

Monday:	Pictures, Bric-a-brac and Miscellanea	fortnightly
Tuesday:	Modern and Reproduction	
	Furniture and Effects	weekly
	Carpets and Rugs	weekly

Nick Bonham, formerly the managing director, has been a driving force in the expansion of the firm's operations, but he also knows when to pause and regroup. He was among the first to acknowledge publicly the effects of stagflation on the English auction market in 1980 and Bonhams reduced its "peripheral activities," closing for the moment its textiles and bygones departments, with the anticipation of reviving them in the future when conditions improve.

The catalogue descriptions are sparse but more than adequate, even if they do not have all the detail that one might like. The saleroom atmosphere is pleasant. Refreshments can be obtained at the Montpelier Street galleries at a buffet open Monday–Friday, 10 A.M.–4 P.M. There is evening viewing to 7 P.M. at Montpelier Street on Tuesdays; and at Bonhams Chelsea on Mondays.

Bonhams describes itself as "auctioneers and valuers," and carries out many valuations, mostly for insurance purposes. The valuations office is located just steps away from the Montpelier Street Galleries, at 23 Cheval Place, London SW7 1EW, tel. (01) 589-4072. It is energetically directed by Andrew Acquier; the business has been boosted with advertisements that showed a photo of a ransacked premises captioned "Can you afford to be burgled tonight?"

Contact person: Nicholas Bonham

Days/hours of operation: Mon., Wed.–Fri. 9 A.M.–5:30 P.M.; Tues. 9 A.M.–
                           7 P.M.

Areas in which general auctions and special sales are held:

Arms and Armor	Drawings
Art Deco	Engravings
Art Nouveau	Etchings
Books	Furniture
Ceramics	Jewelry
Chinese Works of Art	Manuscripts
Clocks and Watches	
Coins	
Dolls	

Paintings   Rugs
    Old Master   Scientific Instruments
    19th c. European   Silver
    Modern Art   Stamps
Porcelain   Wine
Prints

Sales are advertised regularly in the London press (*Daily Telegraph, Times*) and in specialty publications, such as *Antiques Trade Gazette.*

Catalogues are available singly for each sale at the salerooms and by post; the price varies. Catalogues are also available by subscription. The annual subscription is available by category (there are over 20) and the price varies considerably, ranging from a few pounds to £45–£50. For information write to Catalogue Dept., Bonhams, 1–3 Cheval Place, Knightsbridge, London SW7 1EW.

Usual viewing procedure: Exhibition is normally 2 days prior to sale. In addition, silver and jewelry are on view the morning of the sale, and paintings are on view for 3 days.

Bidder Information

Not all sales are on premises; Bonhams also holds house and estate sales.

The buyer's premium is 10 percent of the hammer price, excluding wines, coins, and medals. Absentee bids are executed. Telephone bids must be confirmed by letter, telex, or telegram. Settlement is by the end of the first working day following the sale, unless the purchaser has an account. Credit terms are available; contact Mr. Bonham—although in 1980 no new accounts were being accepted.

Packing and shipping services are not available from the firm.

No guarantees of authenticity are offered, but buyer may return (within 1 year of sale) goods that prove to be not as described, provided that the lot purchased is a forgery, and that term is defined by Bonhams to mean "an imitation intended by the maker to deceive."

Consignor Information

Persons interested in consigning goods should get in touch with the London offices of the firm or their nearest representative. There is no minimum value for consignment.

The standard consignor's commission is 5 percent for the trade and museums and 10 percent for others; the commission is negotiable, depending upon the situation.

Consignors pay insurance (50p per £100 of realized value, with a minimum charge of 20p). Should a cataloguer believe that an item might benefit from being illustrated, there may be a cost to the consignor (black-and-white photos range from £15 to £50; color is more expensive). Bonhams can arrange for goods to be removed to the saleroom by an independent contractor; the consignor bears the cost.

Consigned goods are sold within 3–8 weeks generally, but "special items are kept back for special sales."

Settlement is 21 days after the sale.

Reserves are accepted. There is a minimum lot charge of £4 at Montpelier Street and £2 at Bonhams Chelsea. Stamps are sold at a commission charge of £5 per lot. The buy-in charge is £4 per lot if reserve is agreed to by Bonhams, 3 percent of the reserve price if not agreed to by Bonhams.

Appraisal service is available. Valuations for insurance: 1.5 percent up to £10,000; 1 percent on the next £40,000; and 0.5 percent on the balance. Valuations for probate, capital transfer tax, etc.: 2 percent up to £5,000; 1 percent on the next £20,000; and 0.5 percent thereafter. There is a minimum fee of £25, and travel and out-of-pocket expenses are charged for valuations outside of London. If any of the items included in valuations is sold at Bonhams within 1 year of the date of the valuation, the fee will be reduced.

You can take items to Bonhams for a free inspection and valuation with reference to possible consignment. Bonhams, at the discretion of its specialists, will undertake inspections of a possible consignment within Greater London free of charge. Elsewhere, a fee is charged, plus out-of-pocket and traveling expenses; if the property is consigned to Bonhams within 3 months of the inspection, the fee, excluding expenses, will be refunded.

Bonhams is a member of the Society of Fine Art Auctioneers.

Bonhams

REGIONAL REPRESENTATIVES

These representatives are primarily concerned with the solicitation of goods, either for sale at Bonhams salerooms in London, or via a house or estate sale on location. The representative will also assist bidders by providing catalogues and by placing bids.

SCOTLAND: Major Alistair Hewat   Tel. (083 57) 358
           Alerigg
           Lilliesleaf, Melrose, Roxburghshire TD6 9EJ

ENGLAND: Tim Barclay   Tel. (0553) 84 02 03
           Middleton Tower
           King's Lynn, Norfolk PE23 1EE

           Lt. Col. Digby Willoughby, M.C.   Tel. (0297) 329 65
           Coaxdon Hall
           Axminster, Devon EX13 7LP

           Kim North   Tel. (099 382) 2535
           The Ampney Cottage
           Ampney St. Mary
           Cirencester, Gloucestershire

134. Christie's

8 King Street, St. James's   Tel. (01) 839-9060
London SW1Y 6QT   Telex: 916429
                                      Cable: CHRISTIART

Christie, Manson & Woods Ltd., to give the firm its full corporate title in the U.K., has a well-deserved and long-standing reputation as a distinguished auction house. A successful establishment-oriented firm, Christie's was for much of its long history the premier auction house in the world. The firm lost some of its gloss during the kaleidoscopic changes that revolutionized the auction scene everywhere during the 1960s and 1970s. But in recent years, under the energetic day-to-day direction of Paul Whitfield, the firm has demonstrated that it understands quite well not only how to deal with its traditional English country house and ducal home clientele but also how to market its services much more broadly to a younger, economically less rarefied public. One result has been an annual U.K. turnover in excess of £80 million—a figure less than Sotheby's but more than double the total sales domestically *and* internationally of Christie's other main rival. While here we are concerned with the U.K., it is not out of place to note that the total annual turnover of the Christie's group (including U.K., U.S., etc.) is in excess of one third of a billion dollars—again less than Sotheby's, but over 400 percent more than the turnover of its next nearest rival.

There can be no doubt whatsoever that such figures were not even a gleam in James Christie's eye when he began the firm in 1766. Although Christie's today advertises itself as "fine arts auctioneers since 1766," James Christie's first catalogue offered few works of art of any kind, but did present such household goods and effects as chamber pots, brass candlesticks, sheets, pillow rigs, flatirons, and a lady's sedan chair. It took Christie, who had been involved in auctions prior to 1766, some time to build up the fine arts aspects of his business, but build it up he did, as did his successors (including his son). Although well into the 19th century the firm sold real estate and other such unaesthetic properties, fine arts had become the mainstay of the firm by 1823, when it moved to King Street (where it has maintained offices ever since, except for a hiatus caused during the Second World War by a direct bomb hit on Christie's). In the early 1830s, the well-known bookseller William Manson was taken on as a partner and lent his name to the firm—as did the legendary auctioneer Thomas Woods at the end of the 1850s, when he became a partner while still a young man. The last member of the Christie family active in the firm retired in 1889, and Woods retired in 1903. The firm became a public company in the early 1970s, but tradition still plays a strong role and various members of the firm (including at least one of the directors) are the second and third generation of their family to be employed by Christie's.

The firm's major emphasis is still on the fine arts, and its experts in this area are many, first-rate, and hardworking. But Christie's also auctions with distinction a wide variety of lots in other areas, as can be seen from how the sales week is divided up. A day of the week is allotted to a particular specialty, although areas in which sales are less frequent are allotted fewer days during the year:

Monday:	Porcelain
Tuesday:	Objects of art and virtu, prints, drawings, watercolors, coins, antiquities, musical instruments, glass
Wednesday:	Silver and jewelry alternately, books, arms and armor, modern sporting guns
Thursday:	Furniture, wine
Friday:	Pictures

These sales usually begin at 10:30 or 11 A.M.; periodically there may be an afternoon session, which normally begins at 2:30. In the case of unusual or special collections, sales are held in the evening, as with the Chanel collection of costume jewelry, and wine from the private cellar of Château La Mission Haut Brion. Christie's has also had considerable success with its house and estate sales. The catalogues for all sales have continued to be intelligent, thorough, and relatively free from hyperbole; estimates are included, usually at the end of the catalogue.

Additionally, Christie's offers its clients a valuation service, be it for the purpose of insurance, probate, or whatever. An advisory tax service is also available under the direction of a twenty-year veteran of the Inland Revenue. Naturally, there is a fee for these services. But the traditional front counter service is free: at King Street, a valuation and an oral expert opinion will be given on any art you bring to the reception desk. This advice is given without obligation, but the firm estimates that in any one year "approximately 200,000 pictures and works of art are examined in this way and received for sale."

Tradition has remained a hallmark of Christie's. But this observance of tradition (which does have its drawbacks) has not stifled initiative at the firm. Much of Christie's operational functions are being computerized. The highly successful establishment of Christie's South Kensington (see next entry) has allowed the firm to respond intelligently and profitably to new kinds of collecting interests and to sell lower-priced properties. The addition of a subsidiary saleroom in Glasgow has also bolstered the firm's fortunes.

Contact person:	Any of the experts mentioned below or John Herbert in the Press Dept.
Valuation:	Charles Allsopp
Taxation:	Christopher Ponter
Days/hours of operation:	Mon.–Fri. 9:30 A.M.–5 P.M.

Areas in which general auctions and special sales are held (incl. some contact people):

Arms and Armor (Peter Hawkins)	Art Nouveau (Rachel Russell)
Art Deco (Rachel Russell)	Autographs
	Books (William Spowers)

Chinese Works of Art
(James Spencer)
Clocks and Watches
(Richard Garnier)
Coins
(Raymond Sancroft-Baker)
Drawings (Noël Annesley)
Engravings
Etchings
Ethnographica
(Hermione Waterfield)
Furniture (Hugh Roberts)
Glass (Rachel Russell)
Icons (Mrs. Elvira Cooper)
Islamic Art
(Philippa Vaughan)
Japanese Works of Art
(Sir John Figgess)
Jewelry (Albert Middlemiss)
Manuscripts
Maps
Medals
(Raymond Sancroft-Baker)
Medieval Works of Art
Musical Instruments
(Frances Gillham)

Paintings
Old Master
(Patrick Lindsay)
17th c. British
18th c. British
19th c. British
(Simon Dickinson)
19th c. European
Pre-20th c. American
Impressionist (John Lumley)
Modern Art (John Lumley)
Contemporary Art
(John Lumley)
Modern British
(Frances Farmer)
Pewter
Porcelain
(Hugo Morley-Fletcher)
Prints (James Rowndell)
Rugs (Anthony Thompson)
Russian Works of Art
(Mary Fielden)
Silver (Tom Milnes Gaskell)
Steam Models
Wine (Michael Broadbent)

Sales are advertised regularly in the local, regional, national, and international press, as well as in a broad variety of specialty publications, ranging from *Antiques Trade Gazette* to *Coin World*. A monthly illustrated preview of Christie's sales worldwide is available by subscription [£10 in the U.K.: write to Christie's Subscription Dept., c/o White Brothers (Printers), Prima Road, London SW9 ONA; $36 in the U.S.: write to Christie's Subscription Dept., 502 Park Avenue, New York, NY 10022].

Catalogues for each sale are available at the house and by order, as well as at most Christie's offices. The price varies. Annual subscriptions are offered to all the King Street catalogues or to a particular group. A subscription to all the catalogues costs £635/$2,570 (a 10 percent reduction on buying the catalogues individually). A particular group of catalogues can cost anywhere from £39/$158 (for Old Master Paintings) to £8/$32 (for Modern Sporting Guns and Vintage Firearms). To order, see addresses above.

Usual viewing procedure: Exhibition is usually at least 2 days preceding sale, and often more, during regular business hours.

Bidder Information

Not all sales are held on the premises. Christie's in the U.K. holds house and estate sales, special sales at various venues such as hotels, and specialized sales in suitable venues [e.g., steam models, locomotives and other models; historical machinery and tools, 2 or 3 times a year at the Brighton and Hove Engineerium, off Nevill Road, Hove, East Sussex BN3 7QA, tel. (0273) 55 95 83].

There is a buyer's premium of 10 percent on the hammer price, except for wine, coins, and medals, on which there is no buyer's premium. Accounts must be settled within 7 days after the sale. Credit is available "to the trade only subject to satisfactory references." Absentee bids are executed "subject to satisfactory references." Phone bids must be confirmed in writing.

Packing and shipping is available at the buyer's expense.

Buyers have the right to return goods that prove to be not as catalogued, provided that Christie's is notified in writing within 21 days of the sale and that within 14 days thereafter, the lot is returned to the auction house. The buyer must demonstrate that the "lot is a deliberate forgery"—"a lot made or substantially made with an intention to deceive, when considered in the light of the entry in the catalogue, and which at the date of the sale had a value materially less than it would have had if it had been in accordance with that description." The restrictions are harsher in print than in practice, one is told.

Consignor Information

Persons wishing to consign property to Christie's should contact the firm or the relevant department or their nearest Christie's saleroom or representative.

The standard consignor's commission is 6 percent of the hammer price for the trade and 10 percent for everyone else, except in the case of wine, coins, and medals, for which the commission is 15 percent. The consignor's commission is negotiable, depending upon the situation.

Consignors may pay for catalogue illustrations (the house has discretion to spend up to £35 for a photograph unless the consignor indicates that such an expenditure is not wished). Consignors pay 50p per £100 insurance, and for cartage to the saleroom, unless other arrangements are made. Consignors do not pay for warehousing prior to sale.

There is no minimum value for a consignment, although common sense dictates that you should not try to consign Aunt Fanny's old galoshes.

Consigned goods are usually a minimum of 8 weeks at the house before being put up for sale, and it may take longer, depending upon the type and quality of the consignment. Settlement is 1 month after the sale, provided "that Christie's have by then been paid the purchase price in full by the Buyer."

Reserves are accepted. The buy-in charge is 5 percent of the final bid, if the reserve is not mutually agreed upon.

Appraisal service is available. The cost is as follows: "for supplying valuations with detailed inventories for probate, insurance, or family divison," the charge is 1.5 percent up to a value of £20,000 and thereafter by negotiation. There is a minimum fee of £25 in London and £50 elsewhere in the country. "Out of pocket expenses are calculated at £5 per day plus traveling expenses." Christie's is always prepared to call and advise with a view to sale of properties at auction in the firm's salerooms. There is a small fee plus expenses charged for such an inspection. If within a year from the inspection the properties evaluated are sent to Christie's for sale, the fee will be refunded, "provided that the sale total exceeds £2,000."

Christie's

REGIONAL REPRESENTATIVES

The firm has for the moment decided on a course with regard to the provinces that is summed up by its advertising slogan: "You don't have to come to London to come to Christie's." The firm has representatives in various areas of England, Scotland, Northern Ireland, and Eire. These representatives advise and assist bidders and consignors. Indeed, as the firm points out in its advertising, "the cost of carriage to our London rooms for consignments selected by our representatives will be paid for by Christie's." These representatives are:

SCOTLAND:

Sir Ilay Campbell, Bt.   Tel. (04995) 286
Cumlodden Estate Office
Furnace by Inverary, Argyll

Michael Clayton   Tel. (031) 225-4757
5 Wemyss Place
Edinburgh, Lothian

Jack Buchanan   Tel. (0463) 34603
111 Church Street
Inverness
Highlands

ENGLAND:

Aidan Cuthbert   Tel. (043471) 31 81
Eastfield House, Main Street
Corbridge, Northumberland

Victor Gubbins   Tel. (0768) 667 66
St. Andrew's Place
Penrith, Cumbria

Nicholas Brooksbank   Tel. (0904) 309 11
46 Bootham
York, North Yorkshire

Michael Thompson   Tel. (07462) 618 91
Stanley Hall
Bridgnorth, Salop

Sir Andrew Duff
  Gordon, Bt.   Tel. (0242) 518999
Downtown House
New Radnor
Presteigne, Powys

Henry Bowring   Tel. (0603) 614546
26 Prince's Street
Norwich, East Anglia

Philip Leatham   Tel. (0242) 51 89 99
(Rupert de Zoete, consultant)
111 The Promenade
Cheltenham, Gloucestershire

Denys Wrey   Tel. (0264) 37 50
The Common, Smannell
Andover, Hants.

Richard de Pelet   Tel. (0963) 705 18
Monmouth Lodge
Yenston, Templecombe, Somerset

Nigel Thimbleby   Tel. (0305) 687 48
Wolfeton House
Dorchester, Dorset

Christopher Petherick   Tel. (0726) 646 72
Tredeague
Porthpean, St. Austell, Cornwall

NORTHERN IRELAND: John Lewis-Crosby   Tel. (0396) 83 05 74
Marybrook House, Raleagh Road
Crossgar, Downpatrick, Co. Down

ISLE OF MAN: Quentin Agnew-
  Somerville   Tel. (0624) 81 37 24
Mount Auldyn House
Ramsey, Isle of Man

CHANNEL ISLANDS: Richard de La Hey   Tel. (0534) 775 82
8 David Place
St. Helier, Jersey

EIRE: Desmond Fitz-Gerald,
  The Knight of Glin   Tel. (0001) 69 39 25
Glin Castle
Glin, Co. Limerick

135. Christie's South Kensington

85 Old Brompton Road   Tel. (01) 581-2231
London SW7 3JS   Cable: VIEWING

This division of Christie's was opened in 1975, and must be classed as that firm's "great leap forward" of the mid-1970s if not the decade. South Ken has proved to be an exciting, profitable, and innovative auction operation. To establish South Ken, Christie's bought out the firm of Debenham and Coe, a successful firm of auctioneers who sold goods mostly at the lower end of the price spectrum. Christie's took over Debenham and Coe's premises (which were spruced up) and its managing director (Bill Brooks, an engaging, exciting auctioneer who is now managing director of South Ken). The new subsidiary was christened Christie's South Kensington, but quickly became known among staff, buyers, and consignors as South Ken—a name-shortening which typifies the easy informality that has marked operations there since the beginning.

Christie's had essentially two goals in opening South Ken: firstly "to deal ... with the growing volume of general works of art in the lower price ranges on the basis of rapid turnaround and payment; and secondly to allow for the development of some of the new specialist collectors' fields in markets which have grown up in the last few years." Both these goals have been met handily.

Properties that are consigned at South Ken do not take months to be inventoried, catalogued, and sold. For the vast majority of goods, the elapsed time from consignment to sale is 4 weeks, and settlement is made with the consignor within 14 days after the sale. That may not seem very fast, but it is extraordinarily speedy compared, let us say, to the Great Rooms at King Street. And remember that this timetable includes cataloguing. The South Ken catalogues are not so fancy as those produced for the Christie's sales at its main quarters, but there is a catalogue for each South Ken sale (and there are about 15 a week, 5 a day), and some of these catalogues are illustrated.

South Ken, moreover, offers not only speed but also an exciting range of traditional and innovative specializations, ranging from costume and less expensive kinds of silver, which were moved from the main salerooms, to dolls, toys, games, and children's books. South Ken with its lower overhead, indeed, has made it possible for Christie's quite profitably to sell objects that otherwise the firm would not handle at all—for example, less expensive goods that it may have had to take along with something an expert really wanted. Conversely, quite often better-quality goods that are consigned at South Ken find their way to the main salerooms, with the consignor's consent, of course. However one approaches the South Ken operation, there is no gainsaying that it has grown quickly in a very short time. During the auction year 1975–1976, the turnover was approximately £2.2 million; it has now grown to more than 6 times that amount.

Much of the success of South Ken can be attributed to sound planning, good management, etc. But a large role has also been played by the staff—mostly young, eager, bright, much like a group of superintelligent children let loose in a playground away for the moment from their parents (i.e., the heads of departments across town). And the staff, given a bit of freedom, has done well without being irresponsible or breaking loose. There is an attractive hurly-burly atmosphere to the goings on at South Ken, which certainly contributes to its success. That South Ken does not charge a buyer's premium also contributes heavily to its success.

Contact person: Bill Brooks

Days/hours of operation: Mon.–Fri. 9 A.M.–5 P.M.

Areas in which general auctions and special sales are held (incl. some contact people):

Art Deco	Paintings
Art Nouveau	Photographica
Books (Anthony Payne)	(David Allison)
Ceramics	Photographic
Chinese Works of Art	Instruments (David
Clocks and Watches	Allison)
Dolls	Porcelain
Drawings	Postcards
Engravings	Posters
Etchings	Prints
Furniture	Railwayana
Glass	Rugs
Islamic Art	Scientific Instruments
Japanese Works of Art	Silver
Jewelry	Textiles and Costume
Mechanical Musical and Scientific	(Susan Mayor)
Instruments (Christopher Proudfoot)	Toys (Debbie Ohlman
Militaria (Christopher Lennox-Boyd)	or Richard Lane)
	Wine

Sales are advertised regularly in the local and national press, as well as in various specialty publications. Sales are also listed in the monthly illustrated preview of Christie's sales (see Christie's entry, above).

Catalogues for each sale are available at South Ken and by order. The price varies. Catalogues are also obtainable by subscription on an annual basis. A subscription to all the catalogues costs £382/$1,541 (these sums represent a 10 percent reduction on buying the catalogues individually). A particular group of catalogues can cost anywhere from £48/$194 (for Furniture, Objects, Clocks, Rugs, and Carpets at South Kensington) to £5/$20 (for Cigarette Cards, Postcards, Baxter Prints, and Ephemera). In the U.K., catalogue subscriptions should be ordered from Christie's Subscription Dept., c/o White Brothers (Printers), Prima Road, London SW9 ONA; in the U.S., write to Christie's Subscription Dept., 502 Park Avenue, New York, NY 10022.

Usual viewing procedure: Viewing varies from sale to sale, but is usually at least 1 day prior to auction, sometime between 9:30 A.M. and 4:30 P.M. Late viewing for some sales takes place on Mondays to 7 P.M.

Bidder and Consignor Information

With the following exceptions, the conditions of sale and acceptance are the same as at the main salerooms at Christie's (see above).

Bidder:

There is no buyer's premium at South Ken.

Buyers must settle accounts within 2 days after sale.

Buyers can return goods that are a "deliberate forgery," provided that South Ken is notified in writing within 7 days of the sale and that the goods are returned within another 7 days. Check the conditions of sale, since each category may have its own restrictions as well; thus the return policy does not apply in various cases with regard to books sold at auction, including lots sold for £50 or less.

Consignor:

Property is usually sold within 4 weeks of consignment.

The standard consignor's commission is 10 percent to the trade and 15 percent to all others.

Settlement is within 14 days of sale, "provided payment has been received from the buyer."

Insurance is £1 per £100, with a minimum charge of £1.

For all other details which for all practical purposes are the same as the Christie's main saleroom, see the Christie's entry.

Appraisal service is available. See the Christie's entry for details.

136. Lawrence Fine Art of Crewkerne

19b Market Street   Tel. (0460) 730 41
Crewkerne, Somerset TA18 7JU

Crewkerne, a small, attractive market town, is the home of a manifold auction operation which has grown substantially in recent years and become a multi-million-dollar operation. The quality of the lots put up for sale is such that many of the buyers are foreigners. They have come not for bargains but for the goods available, which one correspondent, describing a sale there, has defined as the wares that make the U.K. "the antique storeroom of Europe."

Lawrence Fine Art of Crewkerne holds its sales in its newly refurbished saleroom on South Street. This saleroom is within walking distance of the train station, roughly three quarters of a mile, and is not far from the Market Street offices (about 500 yards). Light refreshments are available in the Horseshoe Cafeteria, in the same building as the saleroom, open on sale days from 10 A.M. until the last lot is sold. There is usually a lunch break if the sale begins in the morning. Periodically Lawrence holds sales of more than one day.

Contact person: Simon Lawrence

Days/hours of operation: Mon.–Fri. 9 A.M.–5:30 P.M.

Areas in which general auctions and special sales are held (incl. some contact people):

Arms and Armor (Stephen Meadowcroft)	Japanese Works of Art
	Jewelry (Phillip Rouse)
Art Deco	Maps (Richard Watkins)
Art Nouveau	Medals (Richard Watkins)
Books (Richard Watkins)	Musical Instruments
Chinese Works of Art	(Stephen Meadowcroft)
Clocks and Watches	Paintings (Peter Brooks)
(Ken Wills)	Pewter
Coins (Robert Light)	Porcelain (Kay Kleinfeldt)
Dolls	Prints (Stephen Meadowcroft)
Drawings	Rugs (Peggy Hannam)
Furniture	Scientific Instruments (Ken Wills)
(Martin Bartlett)	Silver (Philip Rouse)
Glass	Stamps (Ted Jenkins)

Sales are advertised in the regional press (e.g., *Somerset County Gazette*), the national press (e.g., *Daily Telegraph*), and in specialty publications, such as *Antiques Trade Gazette*.

Catalogues for each sale are available at the firm's offices and in the saleroom, as well as through the mail; the prices vary with the sale, but range upward from £1. For further information and details, contact Ms. Jane Lewis in the Catalogue Subscription Dept. Catalogues are also available on an annual basis, either by category, such as Furniture and Metalwork (£10) or Musical Instruments (£4), or on a total basis, £30 per annum, a considerable saving. Anyone wanting catalogues airmailed on a subscription basis outside the U.K. should be prepared to pay twice as much because of postage and handling costs.

Usual viewing procedure: Up to 2 days' viewing before each sale.

Bidder Information

Most sales are held on the premises, but there are some house and estate sales.

The buyer's premium is 10 percent of the hammer price. All lots must be cleared by noon the day after the sale, and all accounts should be settled within 7 days of the sale. Absentee bids are executed; all telephone bids must be confirmed in writing before the sale.

Packing and shipping services are available.

Each lot is sold "with all faults and defects therein," but if within 7 days the purchaser notifies the house in writing that the lot as sold is a forgery and within 14 days thereafter returns the lot and demonstrates that the item in question is a "deliberate forgery," the firm will rescind the sale.

Consignor Information

Persons wishing to consign property should contact the house in writing or by phone. In the case of a large possible consignment, request a visit from a Lawrence representative. There is no minimum value for a consignment.

The standard consignor's commission is 10 percent and is negotiable, depending upon the situation.

Consignors pay for catalogue illustrations, insurance, and packing and shipping if the consignor requests that the firm arrange for consignments to be removed to the saleroom. The scale of charges for insurance is: £1 per consignor's statement over £50 and up to £300; £2 over £300; £5 over £500; £7.50 over £1,000; £10 over £2,000; £15 over £5,000; and £20 over £10,000. There is a minimum lot charge of £6.

Consigned goods are sold "within 3–9 weeks according to specialty." Settlement is made with the consignor 14 days after the sale.

Reserves are accepted, but "no reserve price under £30 will be accepted." Unless the firm is instructed to the contrary, "a 10 percent discretion will be used on all reserves." The buy-in charge is 5 percent of the reserve price.

Consignments are not accepted from dealers.

Appraisal service is available. Mr. Lawrence reports that there are "no costs where goods are genuinely bought to us with a view to possible sale." For detailed information about costs of valuations for insurance and other purposes, contact Mr. Lawrence.

Lawrence Fine Art of Crewkerne is a member of the Society of Fine Art Auctioneers.

Associated with this firm are the following operations:

137. Lawrence Saleroom Two

South Street   Tel. (0460) 730 41 (ext. 35)
Crewkerne

Located cheek by jowl with its more elegant associate, Lawrence Saleroom Two holds "regular fortnightly" general-purpose mixed-lot sales of what is described as "Good Victorian and Edwardian Furniture, Ornamental China and Glass, Pictures, Books, Small Silver and Plated Items, Copper and Brass and Interesting Collectors' Items together with Good Modern Furnishings and Outside Effects."

About 600–800 lots are sold at each session, which begins at 9:30 A.M.; viewing is usually the day before the sale, 10 A.M.–4 P.M.. Conditions of sale and of consignment are generally similar to those at Lawrence Fine Art. Jim Hooper is Lawrence Saleroom Two manager.

138. Priory Saleroom

Winchester Street
Taunton, Somerset

Lawrence Fine Art of Crewkerne is in association with Greenslade and Company, a firm of chartered surveyors with offices in Taunton and elsewhere in the area. A. Keith Amor, FRICS, a partner in Greenslade, is a director of

Lawrence Fine Art as well, and is responsible for coordinating activities between the two firms. He can be reached at 2–13 Hammet Street, Taunton, Somerset TA1 1RN, tel. (0823) 771 21.

Regular monthly sales at the Priory Saleroom offer mainly general-purpose mixed lots consisting of such items as furniture, silver, china, pictures, copper, and brass.

The reason for the association is that higher-quality items that might not do as well at the Priory Saleroom or that might otherwise go elsewhere will be consigned to Lawrence Fine Art of Crewkerne. Items consigned through the Priory Saleroom must be "suitable" for Lawrence Fine Art.

139. Messenger May Baverstock
93 High Street   Tel. (048 68) 72 22
Godalming, Surrey GU7 1AL

Surrey is essentially a commuter county, and Godalming is a typical pretty shopping center for such a "house and garden" shire—stretches of which periodically get swallowed up by emigrants from Greater London. The Godalming office oversees this firm's fine arts saleroom, at which auctions are held every 2 weeks or so. A veteran, old-line firm, whose roots were planted in 1882, this firm of art auctioneers, valuers, and chartered surveyors has over the decades developed into a multibranch operation with 10 offices in the area.

The firm holds general auctions and "regular specialist sales." Some of the pieces handled are quite valuable and sell for well over a thousand pounds sterling, but the bulk falls below that price. Specialized sales are sometimes 2-day multisession events, at which over 700 lots are sold. The catalogue descriptions are fair, useful, but minimal (e.g., "a child's elm stick back Windsor chair").

Contact person: H. C. Thompson

Days/hours of operation: Mon.–Fri. 9 A.M.–5:30 P.M.

Areas in which general auctions and special sales are held:

Arms and Armor	Glass	Pewter
Clocks and Watches	Jewelry	Porcelain
Coins	Maps	Prints
Drawings	Medals	Rugs
Embroidery	Paintings	Silver
Furniture		

Sales are advertised in the local and national press, as well as in specialty publications. Announcements of forthcoming sales are available; write to be placed on the mailing list.

Catalogues are available for a specific sale; the cost is 30p–95p. Catalogues are also available by subscription; all catalogues are £9.50 per annum.

Usual viewing procedure: Exhibition 3 or 4 days before sale, 10 A.M.–4 P.M.

Bidder Information

Most sales are on premises, but there are occasional house or estate sales.
The buyer's premium is 10 percent. Accounts must be settled within 7 days
after sale takes place. Credit is "not normally available."
Absentee bids are accepted. Packing and shipping services are available, at the
buyer's expense.
No guarantees of authenticity or warranties are offered, but if within 21 days
after the sale goods prove to be not as described, they may be returned,
provided that this is done within the next 14 days. The burden of proof
is on the purchaser.

Consignor Information

Those wishing to consign property should contact the firm.
Consignor's commission is 7.5 percent of the hammer price, and is negotiable,
depending on the situation.
The firm will not accept consignments from dealers.
Consignors are not charged for catalogue illustrations, but must pay insurance
(50p per £100). Consignors are not charged warehousing, but must pay
cartage of goods to saleroom, and storage if unsold.
Reserves are accepted, and the buy-in charge is "nil," avers Mr. Thompson,
"if reserve agreed with us."
Consigned goods are sold within 6 weeks maximum, and settlement is made
14 days after the sale.

Appraisal service is available; contact the firm.

The firm's annual turnover is estimated at over £1 million.

Messenger May Baverstock belongs to the Society of Fine Art Auctioneers.

140. Neales of Nottingham
192 Mansfield Road   Tel. (0602) 62 41 41
Nottingham, Nottinghamshire NG1 3HX

Nottingham is a city of legend, known for its folk heroes—Robin Hood and
the Luddites, among others. A generation after the Luddites had failed to halt
the industrial revolution, Neales of Nottingham was established. Since 1840
the firm has flourished, and its Nottingham salerooms are now among the
largest in the U.K. outside London. In recent years, the firm, which also has
an active property department (which manages, sells, and rents commercial
and residential properties), has established itself as an important auction
center.
   Neales holds weekly uncatalogued sales of "General Furniture and Shipping Goods" on Tuesdays, at each of which about 800 lots are sold. More
specialized, catalogued sales are held regularly, often 3–4 times a month. At
these sales, about 550–650 lots are sold, at the rate of roughly 100 an hour.
The catalogue listings are not overly detailed but are more than adequate.

"Discovery Days" are held throughout the Midlands: a team of Neales experts gives owners a free oral valuation of property brought in for inspection at various locations, and often these items are left for inclusion in the firm's auction sales. Occasional house and estate sales are held.

Contact person: B. V. Fearn, FRICS

Days/hours of operation: Mon.–Fri. 9 A.M.–5:30 P.M.; Sat. 9 A.M.–12:30 P.M.

Areas in which general auctions and specialized sales are held (incl. some contact persons):

Books (Tom Reid)	Musical Instruments (M. Chellingworth)
Ceramics (M. Swain)	Paintings (Tom Reid)
Coins (T. Vennett-Smith)	Porcelain
Dolls	Postcards
Drawings (Tom Reid)	Prints
Furniture (B. V. Fearn)	Silver (M. Swain)
Jewelry (M. Swain)	Stamps (T. Vennett-Smith)
Medals (T. Vennett-Smith)	Toys (Jeremy Wood)

Sales are advertised in the local press, the national newspapers (e.g., *Daily Telegraph*), and specialty publications, such as *Antiques Trade Gazette*. Annual sales calendar can be obtained free of charge; to be placed on the mailing list, write Neales.

Except for the weekly sales, catalogues are available. Single catalogues are £1 at the firm's office and the saleroom, £1.20 by post. An annual subscription (excluding stamp, coin, and medal sales) is £17.

Usual viewing procedure: Morning of the sale for uncatalogued sales; Tuesday prior to sale days for other sales (10 A.M.–8 P.M.).

Bidder Information

Most auctions are held on the premises.

The buyer's premium is 10 percent. Accounts must be settled immediately after the sale. Credit cards are not accepted. Checks are not accepted from persons unknown to the auctioneers unless a banker's reference has been received. Absentee bids are executed.

Credit terms are available "by negotiation."

Packing and shipping services are available, at buyer's expense, "only for specialist sales."

No guarantees of authenticity are offered. Goods are sold subject to all faults.

Consignor Information

Persons interested in consigning properties should write or phone Neales before bringing such property in quantity to the firm. There is no stated minimum value for a consignment to be accepted.

The standard consignor's commission is 7.5 percent and is negotiable, depending upon the situation. There is a separate rate for dealers "by negotiation."

Consignors pay for catalogue illustrations, insurance (50p per £100), and
packing and shipping. There is no charge for warehousing.
Reserves are accepted. The buy-in charge is 4 percent of the reserve price.
There is a minimum charge of £1 for catalogued sales and 25p for
uncatalogued sales.
Consigned goods are sold within 1–6 weeks. Settlement is made approximately
10 days after the sale.

Appraisal service is available. The cost varies. Contact Mr. Fearn.

141. Phillips Blenstock House
7 Blenheim Street, New Bond Street   Tel. (01) 629-6602
London W1Y OAS   Telex: 298855

142. Phillips West 2
10 Salem Road   Tel. (01) 221-5303
London W2 4BU

143. Phillips Marylebone
Hayes Place, Lisson Grove   Tel. (01) 723-2647
London NW1 6UA

This firm has a long, honorable history which began when James Christie's
chief clerk decided to go into business for himself. In 1796, Harry Phillips, at
age 30, began to hold sales on his own and quickly proved successful—so
much so that when Queen Victoria decided to redecorate part of Buckingham
Palace in the mid-1830s, it was Phillips (in the only recorded auction to have
taken place there) who handled the sale of the unwanted furnishings. In 1840,
William Augustus Phillips took over the firm on the death of his father. For-
ty-two years later, he took into partnership his son-in-law, giving the firm the
name (Phillips, Son & Neale) by which it was known formally in the U.K.
until the early 1970s and which is still utilized by some non-U.K. subsidiaries.
The firm's fortunes declined during the latter part of the 19th century and the
first third of the 20th. The upswing began, slowly, when the Lisson Grove
auctioneer Hawkings bought the firm in 1937. Two years later, it moved into
the basement and main floor of Blenstock House. An indication of the slow
improvement in the fortunes of the firm is the fact that not until the middle
1960s did it take another floor in Blenstock House. Dramatic changes, however, followed the appointment of Christopher Weston as chairman in 1972.
Phillips as we know it today, for both good and bad, is very much the product
of Weston's energy and vision. (He is of course helped by the fact that Phillips
is privately held and not subject to the various regulations that government
has properly enacted in order to protect the shareholders in a public company,
but that have had the unfortunate side effect of stifling entrepreneurship.)
Appointed at the relatively young age of 35, Weston has had impact on just
about every aspect of Phillips' operations since 1972.
In less than a decade, Phillips became a multinational concern, very much

"the international auction people," to use one of the company's advertising catch phrases. The firm is much smaller than its multinational rivals and of course the annual turnover is much less, but it has grown apace every year. Both internationally and in the U.K., the firm has introduced new fields for sales and expanded old ones. In the U.K. during the mid and later 1970s, it spread across the land, creating subsidiary operations, mostly by taking over established provincial auction houses. There is now a Phillips saleroom to be found at every point of the compass in the U.K.

Yet for all its expansion, in terms of both the number of salesrooms and the type of sales held, the firm runs a lean operation, which depends to a considerable extent on the expertise to be found at Phillips' London headquarters. None of the provincial houses employs more than 25 people and most employ less than a dozen. New employees are informed that "our specialists are always happy to share their knowledge if this can assist any other company in the group. . . . A list of London specialists is available and please contact them if you feel they can help."

The company has also inaugurated a traveling appraisal service which plies the highways and byways of the U.K. A local room is rented (in a hotel or some other easily accessible, well-known place); the area is blitzed with publicity urging all and sundry to bring their heirlooms, bric-a-brac, and what have you, "for inspection and free valuation without any obligation to sell." However, should someone decide that the object should be sold, and the specialist considers it worthwhile, the "object is immediately transported to a Phillips saleroom, free of charge, and included in a suitable sale." Phillips now even goes on the road to fairs, exhibitions, and other events with a special vehicle which "incorporates a large display area and a separate section for the discussion of confidential matters."

141. Blenstock House

Phillips operates out of cramped quarters here, though the firm has spread out some in recent years. The Valuation Department is at 22 Woodstock Street, a few steps away from Blenstock House. Some offices are in 4–8 Haunch of Venison Yard, a small cul-de-sac off Brook Street, just behind Blenstock House. These offices can be reached by walking through from one of the upper floors of Blenstock House. At 7 Haunch of Venison Yard, which can also be reached through Blenstock House, is the new Collectors Centre, which houses the departments handling stamps, banknotes, railwayana, books, and manuscripts, as well as such collectibles as toy soldiers, dolls, pot lids, and Staffordshire ware. Phillips has expanded its auction market in such collectibles considerably during the past few years and is constantly adding new categories to the field of collectibles, a recent one being firemarks.

Blenstock House itself, once you penetrate beyond the pleasantly decorated front desk, is a refurbished rabbit warren of fascinating and seemingly endless corridors, niches, and dead-end passages. About 10–12 sales a week are held there, in approximately 40 different categories. There are ten salesrooms of various sizes in the building. The catalogues for these sales are sparse in some instances, attractive in others, and generally more than adequate in almost all cases; but Phillips normally makes no attempt to create reference works. For most specialized sales, estimates are printed, and "often result sheets." The Blenstock House salerooms usually auction the better-quality goods consigned to Phillips.

Some idea of the range of goods auctioned at Blenstock House may be gleaned from the program of weekly sales:

Monday:	Antique furniture, rugs, china, glass, and objects of art; also watercolors, oils, prints
Tuesday:	Antique English and Continental furniture, Eastern carpets and rugs, bronzes and works of art
Wednesday:	Antique porcelain, pottery, and glass, alternating with Oriental ceramics and works of art
Friday:	Antique silver and old Sheffield plate

Collectors' sales of such goods as pot lids, dolls, postcards, toys, models, automobilia, and sporting items are held on Wednesdays.

Specialized sales are held on specific days; thus pewter is sold approximately 7 times a year on Tuesdays, arms and armor is sold 5 times a year on Wednesdays, art nouveau is sold approximately once a month on Thursdays, etc.

Auctions are held all year round at Blenstock House; there is no hiatus during the summer months; bank holiday periods are the only time that the pace slackens. Phillips also has Saturday viewing (8:30 A.M.-noon) every week for at least 3 forthcoming auctions, a convenient service not to be found at many other English auction houses. The Blenstock House auctions very much exemplify the attic-to-basement attitude typical of Phillips at most of its salerooms. If you have something to sell, they will accept it on consignment; they are not interested only in fine pieces.

Contact person: Andrew Clayton-Payne

Days/hours of operation: Mon.-Fri. 8:30 A.M.-5 P.M.; Sat. 8:30 A.M.-noon, except before bank holidays

Areas in which general auctions and special sales are held (incl. some contact people):

Arms and Armor	Chinese Works of Art
Art Deco (Keith Baker)	Clocks and Watches
Art Nouveau (Keith Baker)	Costume
Automobilia	(Anne Marie Benson)
(Andrew Hilton)	Cricketana
Baxter Prints	(Marcus Halliwell)
(Andrew Hilton)	Dolls (Anna Marrett)
Books (James Smith)	Drawings

Embroidery
Engravings
Etchings
Firemarks
Furniture
  (Christopher Hawkings)
Glass
Icons (James Dick)
Islamic Art
Japanese Works of Art
Jewelry (Peter Beaumont)
Maps
Musical Instruments (Edward Stollar)
Paintings
  Old Master
  17th c. British (Nicholas Wadham)
  18th c. British (Nicholas Wadham)
  19th c. European
  Impressionist (Elizabeth Harvey-Lee)
  Modern Art (Elizabeth Harvey-Lee)
  Contemporary Art

Pewter
Photographica (Susan Arthur)
Photographic Instruments
Porcelain
Postcards (Susan Arthur)
Posters
Pot Lids (Andrew Hilton)
Pre-Columbian Art
Prints
Railwayana (David Borthwick)
Rugs
Scientific Instruments
  (Christopher Hawkings)
Silver (Eric Smith)
Sporting Items
Stamps (David Boyd)
Toy Soldiers (David Borthwick)
Toys (David Borthwick)

Sales are advertised regularly in the regional and national press (e.g., *Daily Telegraph*), as well as in relevant specialty publications (such as *Antiques Trade Gazette* or *Stamps*). A quarterly illustrated glossy quarto-size brochure, *Phillips Preview*, is available on an annual subscription basis; the cost is £3 U.K., £4 Europe, £5.50 U.S., £6.50 Australia (includes airmail charges where necessary). Write Catalogue Subscription Dept., Blenstock House, 7 Blenheim Street, New Bond Street, London W1Y OAS.

Single catalogues are available at Phillips offices, at Blenstock House, and through the mail. The cost varies. Write as above. Annual subscriptions are also available. The price varies, from firemarks catalogues, the cheapest (£1.50 U.K., £2 Europe, £3 U.S., £3.50 Australia), to all the silver catalogues (£40 U.K., £49 Europe, £73 U.S., £77 Australia). There are some combinations, such as all the Monday and Tuesday furniture sales catalogues or all the oil painting sales catalogues, where there is some small saving in subscribing to a group of catalogues. For subscription information, write as above. Catalogues are available 2–3 weeks before the sale.

Usual viewing procedure: Varies from sale to sale, but is usually at least 1 day prior (9 A.M.–5 P.M.) and for some sales includes Saturday viewing and/or the morning of the sale (the latter is true of the Wednesday Collectors' Sales).

Bidder Information

Not all sales are held on the premises; house and estate sales are conducted. The buyer's premium is 10 percent of the hammer price. Accounts must be settled by "the end of the second working day after the sale." Credit is available "by arrangement."

Phillips offers packing and shipping services "through recommended agents" at the buyer's expense.

Guarantees of authenticity are not offered, but goods that prove to be not as catalogued may be returned, provided that notice in writing is given by the buyer to Phillips within 14 days after the sale and the property is returned within 21 days after such notification. The catalogue states the "burden of proof to be upon the buyer," who must satisfy "Phillips that considered in the light of the entry in the catalogue the lot is a deliberate forgery." The sale will then be rescinded and the purchase price refunded.

Consignor Information

Persons wishing to consign property should contact any Phillips office, either by phone or in writing. There is no minimum value for a consignment.

The standard consignor's commission is 10 percent, "but negotiable to a lower figure for important consignments." There is a separate rate structure for dealers and institutions. There is a minimum charge of £4 per lot.

Consignors pay for catalogue illustrations, insurance (50p per £100 of realized value), and cartage to the saleroom. There is no charge for storage prior to sale.

Consigned goods are sold between 2 weeks and 2 months, depending upon the item.

Settlement is 14 days after the sale.

Reserves are accepted. The buy-in charge is 2.5 percent of the reserve if the firm agreed to the reserve, 5 percent if it did not.

Appraisal service is available. The fee for "all types of valuations" is 1.5 percent up to value of £10,000, 1 percent on the next £90,000, and 0.5 percent thereafter. A small charge will be made for visiting "intending vendors" and inspecting goods. This charge will be refunded if the goods are sold within 6 months for a minimum value of £1,000. Travel expenses are charged in addition.

Phillips belongs to the Society of Fine Art Auctioneers.

142. West 2

Opened in 1976, this building was a warehouse until redone by Phillips, at considerable expense and with some style.

Every Thursday at 10 A.M., antique and modern furniture, porcelain, and works of art are sold, as are "effects." List-like catalogues are available singly for each sale and by annual subscription (£23 U.K., £28 Europe). Viewing is on the Wednesday preceding the sale, 9 A.M.–7 P.M.

Bidder and Consignor Information

For all practical purposes, the details of buying and consigning at West 2 are the same as at Blenstock House (see above).

Each of the salerooms at West 2 is about 4,000 square feet and has its own loading bay for easy access.

143. Marylebone Auction Rooms

Lisson Grove was Eliza Doolittle's native habitat. Today there are few Elizas to be found in this area, but there are shops selling all kinds of things— including antiques of both questionable and real value. The auction rooms were established on their present site in 1800, the original buildings rebuilt in 1957. Phillips sells antique and modern furniture, ceramics and objects every Friday at 10 A.M. at this location. Pictures are sold every other Friday at 12:30 P.M. These are general-purpose mixed-lot sales at which anything that might bring cash is sold. Much of the material is household effects. Viewing is on the day before the sale, 9 A.M.–5 P.M.

List-like catalogues are available singly for each sale, and by annual subscription (£22 U.K., £27 Europe). The catalogues are not available by subscription elsewhere.

The premises contain 3 auction rooms of varying size. There is off-street loading and unloading. The Marylebone Underground station is close by.

Bidder and Consignor Information

For all practical purposes, the details of buying and consigning at the Marylebone Auction Rooms are the same as at Blenstock House (see above).

Phillips

REGIONAL REPRESENTATIVES

These representatives offer advice to both consignors and bidders. The representatives will accept consignments, and they will place bids. Catalogues for all Phillips offices are available from the representatives.

ENGLAND:	Mrs. C. Owen 16 College Avenue Formby, Merseyside L37 3JL	Tel. (07048) 74654
	Mr. S. Kaye 3 Opie Street Norwich, Norfolk NR1 3DP	Tel. (0603) 61 64 26
EIRE:	Major George Malone 75 Frankfort Ave. Rathgar, Dublin 6	Tel. (0001) 97 96 84

144. Phillips & Husseys
Alphin Brook Road   Tel. (0392) 390 25/390 26
Exeter, Devon EX2 8TH

Husseys is an old-line firm established in the 1770s; it still has a flourishing
agricultural and estate practice, which it operates from offices nearby. A great
deal of refurbishment has been undertaken on these premises and this Phillips
branch has modern salerooms and cataloguing facilities at its disposal. Sales
are held about twice a month, but Phillips has expressed the intent "to expand
greatly" that frequency and the branch's coverage of the West of England.
The staff is small, numbering only 4, and it employs "technical assistance"
from the Phillips branch at Bath.

Contact person: R. E. Campbell Connolly

Days/hours of operation: Mon.–Fri. 9 A.M.–5 P.M.

Areas in which general auctions and special sales are held:

Books	Jewelry	Rugs
Clocks and Watches	Paintings	Silver
Furniture	Porcelain	Victoriana
Glass	Prints	

Sales are advertised regularly in the local and regional press. They are also
    announced in the quarterly *Phillips Preview;* for subscription informa-
    tion, see Phillips' Blenstock House entry.
Catalogues are available singly and by subscription. For information, write to
    the branch manager, R. E. Campbell Connolly.
Usual viewing procedure: Exhibition is the day before the sale, 9 A.M.–5
    P.M., and the morning of the sale, 9–10:30.

Bidder and Consignor Information

For all practical purposes, the details of buying and consigning at Phillips &
    Husseys are the same as at Blenstock House in London (see above).

Appraisal service is available. Contact Mr. Campbell Connolly.

Phillips & Jollys Auction Rooms of Bath
145. 1 Old King Street   Tel. (0225) 31 06 09/31 07 09
Bath, Avon BA1 1DD

146. Old Malthouse Saleroom   Tel. (0225) 31 06 09/31 07 09
Comfortable Place, Upper Bristol Road
Bath, Avon BA1 1DL

Located in the center of the city, the Old King Street rooms are the scene of
sales almost every Monday and some Fridays. There are monthly antique furniture sales, bimonthly sales of pictures (including paintings, prints, drawings,

and watercolors), and quarterly sales of books, as well as special sales of collector's items (e.g., toys) and sporting guns.

More general mixed-lot sales are held at fortnightly intervals at the Old Malthouse Saleroom. This secondary saleroom has proved to be quite popular. Phillips personnel believe that Jollys, which was taken over in 1976, has been holding furniture auctions at one venue or another in Bath since not long after the turn of the century.

This branch of Phillips is completely independent of the retail store named Jolly's. There is Saturday viewing at the Phillips & Jollys rooms and it has elicited much favorable response—people have voted with their feet and the auction rooms are usually full on Saturday mornings.

Contact person: Christopher Overton

Days/hours of operation: Mon.–Thurs. 8:30 A.M.–5 P.M.; Fri. 8:30 A.M.–6 P.M.; Sat. 9 A.M.–noon

Areas in which general auctions and special sales are held (at Old King St.):

Books	Glass	Prints
Ceramics	Jewelry	Rugs
Clocks and Watches	Musical Instruments	Silver
Costume	Paintings	Textiles
Drawings	Pewter	Toys
Furniture		

Sales are advertised in the local and regional press, as well as in specialty publications, such as *Antiques Trade Gazette.* They are also announced in the quarterly *Phillips Preview;* for subscription information, see Phillips' Blenstock House entry.

Single catalogues are available at Phillips & Jollys, at other Phillips offices, or through the mail. Annual subscriptions are also available. All catalogues except that for general furniture will be sent for £18 per annum, or they can be subscribed to by category (e.g., the book catalogues cost £1.50 per annum). Subscription to the general furniture catalogues costs £4.50 per annum.

Usual viewing procedure: For Monday sales, exhibition is the preceding Friday (10 A.M.–6 P.M.) and Saturday (10 A.M.–noon). For Friday sales, exhibition is Thursday, 10 A.M.–5 P.M.

Bidder and Consignor Information

For all practical purposes, the details of buying and consigning at Phillips & Jollys are the same as at Blenstock House in London (see above).

Appraisal service is available. Contact Mr. Overton.

147. Phillips at Hepper House
17a East Parade   Tel. (0532) 44 8011
Leeds, West Yorkshire LS1 2BU

Hepper is a well-known and respected name in Yorkshire. Hepper, Watson & Son, a firm of chartered surveyors, estate agents, etc., with various offices in the area, was established in 1820. Heppers of Leeds was one of the leading Yorkshire auctioneers when Phillips took it over in 1976. Hepper House is located in the center of Leeds, an easy walk from this erstwhile mill town's train station. The Phillips salerooms are located in a splendid Victorian Gothic building, restored by the firm, which has been the site of auction sales since the early part of the last century.

Phillips at Hepper House prides itself on "being one of the only Auction Houses in the north to hold sales by speciality," maintaining that "higher prices are thus generated." Sales are usually held on Wednesdays. Antique and Victorian furniture, bronzes, and objets d'art are usually sold on the last Wednesday of the month. Other specialties are scattered throughout the year. Occasional house and estate sales are also held.

Contact person: John R. Walsh

Days/hours of operation: Mon.–Fri. 9 A.M.–5 P.M.; Sat. 9 A.M.–noon

Areas in which general auctions and special sales are held:

Arms and Armor	Japanese Works of Art
Art Deco	Jewelry
Art Nouveau	Maps
Books	Militaria
Ceramics	Musical Instruments
Chinese Works of Art	Paintings
Cigarette Cards	Photographica
Clocks and Watches	Postcards
Coins	Prints
Dolls	Rugs
Drawings	Scientific Instruments
Furniture	Silver
Glass	Toys

Sales are advertised regularly in the local and regional press and in specialty publications, such as *Antiques Trade Gazette*.
Single catalogues are available at Hepper House, at other Phillips offices, and through the mail. The price varies. Catalogues are also obtainable by subscription, either in individual categories, such as Scientific Instruments, or as a group. A subscription to all sales (including country houses) is £20 per annum.
Usual viewing procedure: Day prior 10 A.M.–4 P.M. or by arrangement.

Bidder and Consignor Information

For all practical purposes, the details of buying and consigning at Hepper House are the same as at Blenstock House in London (see above).

Appraisal service is available. Contact General Manager John Walsh or Nicholas J. B. Merchant.

148. Phillips in Knowle

The Old House   Tel. (056-45) 61 51
Station Road
Knowle, Solihull, West Midlands

This branch of Phillips is just about smack dab in the center of England. The main building, which is featured in all the advertising, dates from the middle of the 17th century; there are also more modern salerooms.

Sales are normally held on Wednesdays at 11 A.M., sometimes on Fridays as well. This branch of Phillips has Saturday-morning viewing.

Contact person: J. B. Haycraft

Days/hours of operation: Mon.–Fri. 9 A.M.–5 P.M.; Sat. 9 A.M.–noon

Areas in which general auctions and special sales are held:

Art Deco	Drawings	Pewter
Art Nouveau	Furniture	Porcelain
Books	Japanese Works of Art	Pot Lids
Chinese Works of Art	Jewelry	Prints
Clocks and Watches	Medals	Silver
Coins	Paintings	Toys
Dolls		

Sales are advertised regularly in the local press, the regional press (incl. the Birmingham *Post*), and in specialty publications, such as *Art & Antiques Weekly*. Sales are also announced in the quarterly *Phillips Preview*; for subscription information, see Phillips' Blenstock House entry.

Single catalogues are available at The Old House, at other Phillips offices, and through the mail. The price varies. Subscriptions are obtainable by category (the price varies between 70p and £8 the half year). A subscription to all Phillips in Knowle catalogues costs £15 for a half year; this represents a slight saving over subscribing by category.

Usual viewing procedure: Exhibition is normally the Saturday, Monday, and Tuesday before the sale, during regular business hours.

Bidder and Consignor Information

For all practical purposes, the details of buying and consigning at Phillips in Knowle are the same as at Blenstock House in London (see above).

Appraisal service is available. Contact either Mr. J. B. Haycraft or Mr. M. J. Welch.

149. Phillips, Incorporating Brooks, Fine Art Auctioneers

39 Park End Street   Tel. (0865) 72 35 24
Oxford, Oxfordshire OX1 1JD

This branch came into being in June 1979, when the fine arts division of E. J. Brooks of Oxford (a respected old-line firm of chartered surveyors, etc.) joined the Phillips group. The linkup resulted in an interesting series of shifts within the Phillips organization. Robert Gowland, who had been very active in the running of this saleroom while it was still part of Brooks, within months left for the U.S. to run the Phillips operation there. Paul Viney, who had been active in the U.S. operation, was chosen to head up the Oxford branch. These appointments promoted able men.

The Oxford salerooms are well located, just a few steps from the train station, and down the street from a good-size car park. Sales take place 2–3 times a month on Tuesdays or Fridays. About every 2 weeks, there is a sale of furniture, ceramics, and household items. These sales alternate with more specialized sales. Occasional house and estate sales are also held.

Contact person: Paul Viney

Days/hours of operation: Mon.–Fri. 9 A.M.–5 P.M.; Sat. 9 A.M.–noon

Areas in which general auctions and special sales are held:

Clocks and Watches	Jewelry	Prints
Furniture	Paintings	Rugs
Glass	Porcelain	Silver

Sales are advertised in the local and regional press, as well as in specialty publications, such as *Antiques Trade Gazette*. Sales are also announced in the quarterly *Phillips Preview*; for subscription information, see Phillips' Blenstock House entry.

Single catalogues are available at the branch office, at other Phillips offices, and through the mail. Subscriptions are also available. You can subscribe either by category or for all the catalogues (£21 per annum). To subscribe, write either to the Oxford branch or to the main Phillips office in London.

Usual viewing procedure: Exhibition is 1 or 2 days prior to the sale, during regular business hours, and the morning of the sale.

Bidder and Consignor Information

For all practical purposes, the details of buying and consigning at Phillips in Oxford are the same as at Blenstock House in London (see above).

Appraisal service is available. Contact Paul Viney.

Sotheby's

150. 34–35 New Bond Street   Tel. (01) 493-8080
London WIA 2AA   Telex: 24454
                                                Cable: ABINITIO LONDON

151.   Aeolian Hall
Grosvenor Hill, Bond Street
London WIA 2AA

151a.   Conduit Street Gallery
26 Conduit Street
London, W1A 2AA

There is no escaping Sotheby's pervasive influence on the auction world. The firm's innovations, its extensive public relations campaigns, its dramatic and highly successful name sales, all have meant that the impact of Sotheby's is felt almost everywhere that fine arts auction sales are held.

Here, however, we are concerned with the U.K. operations of the firm, specifically at its London salerooms, and these operations are impressive indeed. Sotheby's will inspect, evaluate, and auction (as well as sell by private treaty if necessary). If you are a consignor, the firm will help you deal with a need for restoration prior to sale, currency fluctuations, and the various and often confusing regulations laid down by the Inland Revenue. If you are a purchaser, the firm will help you with shipping your purchase (inland or out), with arranging for insurance, with framing, and if necessary with handling the export restrictions that may have to be faced if you have bought a "national treasure."

The firm doesn't yet offer cradle-to-grave service, but as far as concerns the buying and selling at auction of various kinds of property, Sotheby's services can be said to extend beyond the grave. Thus the Probate Department is designed "to meet the special requirements of solicitors, Bank trustee departments, and other clients involved in the executorship and administration of Estates."

The firm came into being during the 1730s, founded by Samuel Baker, a bookseller and publisher. The first recorded auction took place in 1744, when Baker offered his own as well as other people's books for sale at auction. No Sotheby was connected with the firm until 1778, when after Baker's death his nephew John Sotheby was taken into partnership. No Sotheby has been connected with the firm since 1861, when Samuel Leigh Sotheby—the third generation of his family to be associated with the business—died. By then the firm had developed sales in other areas, although books remained its chief stock in trade. Throughout the 19th century, sales were held not just of books, but of pictures, jewelry, coins, wine, and furniture. The firm moved to Bond Street during World War I and grew during the interwar years. After World War II, developments were limited until the mid 1950s, when the British government removed some currency restrictions and allowed Sotheby's once again to pay the proceeds of auction sales in the consignor's own currency. Since then the firm has expanded dramatically, in considerable part due to the direction of Peter Wilson (who retired as chairman in 1980 after a 22-year tenure).

Among the significant developments that took place during Wilson's directorship were the introduction of completely specialized sales, the purchase of Parke-Bernet, the internationalization of the fine arts auction market, and the organization of the U.K. regional network (which has resulted in the establishment of a series of salerooms and representative offices in England and Scotland to service particular areas). The firm did not just march from triumph to triumph; there were also setbacks. The first World Ephemera Congress, scheduled for September 1980 and sponsored by Sotheby's, never took place—in large part because of a lack of public interest. A superb account of Sotheby's history is Frank Herrmann's *Sotheby's* (Chatto & Windus, 1980).

During 1981, further developments were scheduled that should certainly be of interest to consignors, bidders, and auction buffs—the most important being the movement of some departments from their traditional New Bond Street locations to Aeolian Hall, which is almost directly opposite the main London premises. Sotheby's acquired an 81-year leasehold interest in Aeolian Hall in March 1979. Built at the turn of the century, the hall—probably best known in recent years as a BBC recording studio—has been refurbished; the auditorium has been turned into a pleasant saleroom; the Books and Manuscripts, Jewelry, and Coins departments have been relocated in the hall. Also in 1981 Sotheby's began holding weekly sales at Conduit Street, offering properties that normally did not exceed £1,000 in value (with an average price below £200). This saleroom aimed for speed and convenience, offered pocket-sized "simplified" catalogues, and alternated offerings with one week being given over to the decorative arts and another to the fine arts.

In January 1980, Sotheby's Veteran Vintage and Special Interest Vehicle Department was moved to Glaspant Manor, Capel Iwan, Newcastle Emlyn, Dyfed, Tel. (0559) 37 00 24. Contact Michael Worthington-Williams in this South Wales town. The sales are held all over the U.K.

Contact person: The expert in your area of interest or the press office

Days/hours of operation: Mon.–Fri. 9:30 A.M.–4:30 P.M.

Areas in which general auctions and special sales are held (incl. some contact people):

Arms and Armor	Engravings
(D. Jeffcoat)	Furniture (G. J. T. Child)
Autographs (R. L. Davids)	Glass (P. W. Wood)
Books (J. F. R. Collins)	Icons (J. I. Stuart)
Chinese Works of Art	Islamic Art (F. Nicholson)
(C. J. D. Mackay)	Japanese Works of Art
Clocks and Watches	(N. K. Davey)
(E. J. W. Vaughan)	Jewelry (P. J. Hinks)
Coins (M. R. Naxton)	Judaica
Drawings	Manuscript
(P. M. R. Pouncey)	(C. F. R. de Hamel)

Maps
Medals (M. R. Naxton)
Medieval Works of Art
Musical Instruments
  (G. W. H. Wells)
Netsuke
Paintings
  Old Master (D. E. Johns)
  17th c. British
  (A. T. Festing)
  18th c. British
  (P. Bowring)
  19th c. European
  (A. P. Apsis)
  Pre-20th c. American
  Impressionist
  (M. J. Strauss)
  Modern Art
  Contemporary Art
  (L. Pellegrini)

Pewter
Porcelain (T. H. Clarke)
Pre-Columbian Art
  (R. J. Bleakley)
Prints
  Old Master (N. Bialler)
  Japanese (A. O. Shann)
  British (I. J. McKenzie)
  20th c. (L. Howie)
Rugs (J. Franses)
Russian Works of Art
  (H. von Spreti)
Scientific Instruments
  (T. Millar)
Silver (R. M. Camber)
Stamps (J. N. Michael)
Wine (P. R. Grubb)

Sales are advertised regularly in the local, regional, and international press, as
    well as in a variety of specialty publications, both domestic and inter-
    national—the extent of the advertising depending upon the quality
    and style of the sale in question. Also available is *Preview,* an attrac-
    tive glossy illustrated foretaste of sales to come, and news of world-
    wide developments and sales among the Sotheby group. An annual
    subscription costs: £10 U.K., £12 Europe, £14 rest of the world.
Catalogues for each sale are available at varying prices at Sotheby offices or
    by post; write to Catalogue Subscriptions Department, 34–35 New
    Bond Street, London W1A 2AA, or telephone (01) 493-8080. Cata-
    logues are normally available 3–4 weeks before the sale; they are de-
    tailed, frequently illustrated, and often live up to the firm's boastful
    description of them as "valuable works of reference in their own
    right." Subscriptions are available to all the catalogues for a given
    specialty, such as Old Master Drawings or Books; a subscription to
    all the catalogues on an annual basis can result in significant savings
    over buying them piecemeal. The cost including *Preview* is £783
    U.K., £889 Europe, £1,381 rest of the world (includes airmail post-
    age). These prices should be valid until September 1981. For annual
    catalogue subscriptions, write to the Catalogue Subscriptions
    Department.
Usual viewing procedure: Exhibition is usually a "minimum of 4 days before
    the sale" during regular business hours.

Bidder Information

Not all sales take place on the premises. House and estate sales are held, as are special sales—often in conjunction with an institution, a charity, or some other firm—in various parts of the U.K., at diverse locations including hotels and museums.

There is a buyer's premium of 10 percent on all lots except wine, coins, and medals, on which the commission is 15 percent. Absentee bids are executed, but telephone bids must be confirmed in writing. Accounts must be settled immediately, unless credit terms have been arranged.

The firm offers packing and shipping services, at the buyer's expense, through a subsidiary: James Bourlet & Sons Ltd., 3 Space Waye, Pier Road, Feltham, Middlesex, tel. (01) 751-1155.

Guarantees of authenticity are offered, but these are limited, depending upon the sale; it is important that you read thoroughly the conditions of sale in the catalogue. Buyers have the right to return goods that prove to be not as described within 21 days to 5 years, depending on the type of object involved (e.g., with regard to books, the purchaser must notify the firm in writing within 21 days; if the artist of a picture proves to be different from the catalogue attribution, the purchaser has up to 5 years to notify the firm and have the sale rescinded).

Consignor Information

Those wishing to consign goods should contact, either in writing or via the telephone, the nearest Sotheby's saleroom or representative, or should get in touch with the relevant expert.

The standard consignor's commission is 6 percent to the trade and 10 percent to all others. These commissions are negotiable, depending upon the quality and the quantity of the proposed consignment.

Consignors pay for catalogue illustrations (£6–£30), insurance (50p per £100), and for cartage to the saleroom if the firm has to remove the goods. There is no charge for warehousing prior to the sale. If unsold goods are left beyond a reasonable stay, the consignor is charged storage.

Consigned goods are sold as soon as possible, but the minimum is 2 months.

Reserves are accepted; the buy-in charge is 2 percent to the trade and 4 percent to other vendors.

The firm states that "Sotheby's shall remit 'sale proceeds' to the seller not later than one month (or in the case of numismatic items, 14 days) after the auction, but if by that date Sotheby's has not the 'total amount due' from the buyer then Sotheby's will remit the 'sale proceeds' within five working days after the day on which the 'total amount due' is received from the buyer."

Appraisal services are available. The firm states that indeed "the provision of valuations is an essential part of our service." The fee for usual probate and insurance valuations: 1.5 percent up to £10,000; 1 percent from £10,000 to £100,000; 0.5 percent thereafter. The fees for other kinds of valuations vary and are established by negotiation. Saleroom estimates are provided free of charge: bring the item to a Sotheby office. Experts from the firm can also visit you, and for an oral opinion you are charged out-of-pocket expenses; the fee will be refunded if within the year you consign the property for sale.

152. Sotheby's Belgravia
19 Motcomb Street   Tel. (01) 235-4311
London SW1X 8LB   Telex: 24454
                                     Cable: GAVEL LONDON

Opened in 1971, this division of Sotheby's (often described as a "secondary saleroom") has become an unqualified success in terms of sales. Between 1975 and 1980, the annual turnover more than kept pace with inflation, tripling to approximately £10 million during the auction year. This turnover is derived principally from the sale of material limited to the century 1830–1930 (and the main salerooms now direct most categories of such material to the Belgravia operation). Much of what Belgravia sells—be it furniture, paintings, silver, objects of virtu—can be described by the term "Victoriana." Sotheby's Belgravia has also carved out for itself an impressive niche as auctioneer of photographica and of diverse collectibles, such as working models of steam engines and children's games.

The Motcomb Street building was erected in the early 1830s and over the years has been used for both retail and auction selling. Located on a side street of fancy galleries, shops, and restaurants in a posh section of town, this division of Sotheby's is smack dab in the middle of the bedrooms of London's transient new rich (oilmen, Arabs, property developers, media people, inflation-proof diplomats, and their families). The large saleroom on the main floor is light, airy, often crowded, and conducive to the more informal atmosphere that can be found at the sales here. Bidding is with numbered paddles. The catalogues are thoroughly illustrated, if sometimes a bit less detailed than those issued across town. Lots bought can be paid for and then removed during a sale; a buyer can come just for a particular part of an auction, complete his or her business, and leave; there is no need to wait for a sale to be completed.

The atmosphere, the kind of goods available, the location—all without any question play a role in the fact that private buyers take many more lots at Sotheby's Belgravia than at the firm's other London salerooms, where the trade is much more prominent and often still captures 85–90 percent of the lots at any given sale.

The variety of goods offered for sale at Sotheby's Belgravia is remarkable. Sales are usually held every day but Monday. On Fridays, collectibles of various kinds (including railwayana, automobilia, photographica, musical machines, posters, ephemera, etc.) are sold. Tuesday sales are often given over to the auctioning of Victorian paintings, drawings, and watercolors. However, the auction calendar is quite flexible and you should check to see what is selling on any particular day.

Contact person: Derek Chapman

Days/hours of operation: Mon.–Fri. 9:30 A.M.–4:30 P.M.

Areas in which general auctions and special sales are held (incl. some contact people):

Art Deco	Paintings
Art Nouveau	19th c. British (P. J. Nahun)
Chinese Works of Art	Photographica (P. D. Garner)
Clocks and Watches	Porcelain
Drawings (19th, 20th c.)	Postcards
(D. A. Battie)	Posters
Furniture (C. M. Payne)	Railwayana
Glass (Sarah Battie)	Rugs
Japanese Works of Art	Scientific Instruments
Mechanical Musical Instruments	Silver (John Culme)
	Steam Models
	Toys (Hilary Kay)

Sales are advertised regularly in the London press and in a variety of domestic and international specialty publications. Sotheby's Belgravia sales are also announced in *Preview* (see Sotheby's main entry, above).

Catalogues are available singly at varying prices for each sale. They are also available by subscription annually, either by specialty (e.g., Victorian Paintings, Drawings, and Watercolors, or Musical Boxes) or in toto. The cost for an annual subscription to all the Sotheby's Belgravia catalogues is £274 U.K., £366 Europe, £463 rest of the world (includes airmail postage). For information about ordering catalogues, see Sotheby's entry, above.

Usual viewing procedure: Exhibition is at least 3 days before the sale, during regular business hours.

Bidder and Consignor Information

For all practical purposes, there are almost no distinctions drawn between the formal practices of Sotheby's Belgravia and the company's other London salerooms. For details, see Sotheby's entry, above.

Appraisal service is available. See Sotheby's entry, above.

Sotheby's

REGIONAL REPRESENTATIVES

The firm has various representatives in different parts of the U.K., who provide a point of contact with Sotheby's for both consignors and purchasers. The local representative can facilitate consignments and can place bids for absentee bidders. The workings of the auction market are explained. And so on. Exhibitions of goods to be sold at various Sotheby salerooms are occasionally held in the offices at Edinburgh, Harrogate, and Bournemouth. These offices

are usually open to the public 9:30 A.M.–1 P.M. and 2–5 P.M. The offices and
the representatives are:

SCOTLAND: John Robertson   Tel. (031) 226 7201
            112 George Street   Cable: ABINITIO EDINBURGH
            Edinburgh EH2 4LH

            Anthony Weld-Forrester   Tel. (041) 221 4817
            146 West Regent Street
            Glasgow G2 2RQ

ENGLAND: Mrs. FitzRoy Clayton   Tel. (0202) 29 44 25/6
            44 Holdenhurst Road
            Bournemouth, Dorset BH8 8AF

            Lady Victoria Leatham   Tel. (0223) 676 24/5
            Sidney House, Sussex Street
            Cambridge, Cambridgeshire CB1 1PA

            John Harvey   Tel. (0242) 51 05 00
            18 Imperial Square
            Cheltenham, Gloucestershire GL50 1Q2

            Mrs. J. H. N. Towers   Tel. (0423) 50 14 66
            8–12 Montpellier Parade
            Harrogate, North Yorkshire HG1 2TJ

            Sir Michael Salt, Bt.   Tel. (0823) 884 41
            Sotheby Humberts
            Magdalene House, Magdalene Street
            Taunton, Somerset TA1 1SB

EIRE: Nicholas Nicholson   Tel. Drogheda 24401
            Slane Castle
            Slane, Navan
            Co. Meath
               Consultants: Tel. (0001) 32 31 10/32 20 21
               Mrs. Gertrude Hunt
               Mrs. Mary Boydell

153. Sotheby Bearne
Rainbow, Avenue Road   Tel. (0803) 262 77
Torquay, Devon TQ2 5TC   Telex: 426611

The Bearne in Sotheby Bearne is Brian Bearne, now a member of Sotheby's
board of directors and in 1977 the head of the Torquay firm of Bearne and
Waycott, who agreed to its becoming a division of Sotheby's. A good provincial auction house whose business had been gradually but very well built up
since the end of the Second World War, this firm was the first member of
what became Sotheby's regional network. As a division, this auction operation

has continued to prosper; the annual turnover is now well in excess of £2 million. Incidentally, the tie with Waycott (a respected Devon firm of chartered surveyors, valuers, auctioneers, residential and commercial property agents) lingers on in that Sotheby Bearne continues to hold some of its sales at The Waycotts Rooms, 228 Union Street. Sotheby Bearne also holds sales outside its premises, at The Bearnes Rooms, 3 Warren Road. Both these locations are within relatively easy walking distance from the train station and have parking nearby. The same holds true for Rainbow, an attractive, marvelously restored Victorian home which is set in its own spacious grounds and which serves Sotheby Bearne as headquarters and frequent saleroom. Rainbow, without any doubt, must number among the most attractive salerooms in auctiondom. Sales are usually held there on Wednesdays. And the marvelous climate (this is a popular resort area) makes the Rainbow garden refreshment room a pleasant stop even on days when neither exhibitions nor sales are in progress. Occasional house and estate sales are also held.

Contact person: Bill Simpson

Days/hours of operation: Mon.–Fri. 9:30 A.M.–1 P.M., 2:15–5:30 P.M.

Areas in which general auctions and specialized sales are held (incl. some contact people):

Ceramics	Paintings (Robin Barlow)
Clocks and Watches (Alan Bennett)	17th c. British
Dolls	18th c. British
Drawings	19th c. British
Furniture (Gillan Westfall)	19th c. European
Glass	Prints
Jewelry (Jethro Marles)	Rugs (A. M. R. Gilchrist)
	Scientific Instruments
	Silver (Neal Heasman)
	Toys

Sales are advertised regularly in the local and regional press, as well as in specialty publications, such as *Antiques Trade Gazette*.

Single catalogues for each sale are available at the firm's offices, the saleroom, and through the mail (the price varies from £1 up, but does include postage). For annual subscription rates, write to Rainbow.

Usual viewing procedure: Exhibition is at least 1 full day before the sale and sometimes 2; for viewing at Rainbow, the hours are the regular business hours; at the other salerooms the hours are 10:30 A.M.–4:30 P.M.

Bidder and Consignor Information

For all practical purposes, there are almost no distinctions drawn between the formal practices of Sotheby Bearne and Sotheby's main London salerooms. For details, see Sotheby's entry above.

Appraisal service is available. See Sotheby's entry above.

154. Sotheby Beresford Adams

Booth Mansion Tel. (0244) 31 55 31
28–30 Watergate Street Telex: 61577
Chester, Cheshire CH1 2NA

This division of Sotheby's is another link in the company's regional network. Beresford Adams & Son, Sotheby's partner in this venture—which was announced in the fall of 1978 and held its first auctions in July 1980—is an important old-line (est. 1889) firm of estate agents and chartered surveyors, with various offices in the region handling property sales and management, insurance, and valuation. A fourth generation of the Beresford Adams family is active in the firm.

Sotheby Beresford Adams has two salerooms in Chester. The Booth Mansion, built in 1700 and used as a private home, a club, a school, and local government offices, then abandoned, was extensively restored and now is utilized for offices, exhibitions, and cultural events, as well as for more specialized better-quality sales of paintings, silver, ceramics, furniture, Victorian works of art, and objects of local interest. The Duke Street saleroom is used for more general mixed-lot sales and for what it is hoped will result in Sotheby Beresford Adams becoming a major book auction center. Though the salerooms are within the still-standing walls of the city (which has been described as "the best-preserved walled city in England"), both have parking nearby. By train, Chester is 2½ hours from London.

The director of the new auction house is Philip Wadsworth, an energetic young man who had been in charge of Sotheby's valuation department in London. He was a most understandable choice, for apart from his many other qualities, he was expected to make use of Sotheby's London-based experts. Although the resident staff of Sotheby Beresford Adams included trained specialists in a variety of areas, the new house also intended to "call upon the more specialist knowledge in particular fields available to us from New Bond Street and Belgravia." With its inaugural sales in 1980, the new house made a most auspicious start in the auction business.

Contact person: Philip Wadsworth

Days/hours of operation: Mon.–Fri. 9 A.M.–5:30 P.M.

Areas in which general auctions and special sales are held:

Books	Manuscripts
Ceramics	Maps
Chinese Works of Art	Paintings
Clocks and Watches	Pewter
Furniture	Prints
Glass	Rugs
Japanese Works of Art	Scientific Instruments
Jewelry	Silver

Sales are advertised regularly in the regional press, the national press, and specialty publications, such as *Antiques Trade Gazette*.

Single catalogues for each sale are available at Sotheby offices, in the salerooms of Sotheby Beresford Adams, and through the mail; prices vary. Annual subscriptions are also obtainable: these are grouped by category (e.g., "Books, Maps, and Manuscripts" or "All Ceramics, Glass and Oriental Works of Art"). The cost of each group is £15 U.K., £18 Europe, £25 rest of the world (includes airmail postage). Write to Sotheby Beresford Adams at Booth Mansion for further information. Usual viewing procedure: Exhibition is at least 2 days before a sale (weekdays, 9:30 A.M.–4:30 P.M.; Sat., 9:30 A.M.–12:30 P.M.).

Bidder and Consignor Information

For all practical purposes, there are almost no distinctions drawn between the formal practices of Sotheby Beresford Adams and Sotheby's main London salerooms. For details, see Sotheby's entry, above.

Appraisal service is available. See Sotheby's entry, above.

155. Sotheby King and Chasemore

Station Road   Tel. (07982) 38 31
Pulborough, West Sussex RH20 1AJ

King and Chasemore as well as Humberts were firms of chartered surveyors and estate agents who conducted fine arts auctions jointly in Taunton. Indeed, Humbert King and Chasemore was a member of the Society of Fine Art Auctioneers, as was King and Chasemore, which held sales on its own in Pulborough. In July 1979, Sotheby's bought the fine arts auction division of these firms' businesses and the Pulborough auction operation became a division of Sotheby's as part of its regional network.

The town of Pulborough is noted for the fine fishing available nearby, but it is only just over an hour from London's Victoria train station. The main saleroom is approximately 50 yards from the Pulborough railroad station, and the Station Saleroom, where all book auctions and certain furniture and other sales are held, is directly opposite the station exit. There is parking available behind both salerooms, and this space should be utilized, because as is the rule in most small towns where the main street is also a main road, no parking is allowed there.

Sotheby King and Chasemore continues its association with the estate agency to which the auction operation once belonged, and Sotheby's chairman believes that this link "will lead to a considerable flow of business." No doubt a help in achieving this business is the fact that the catalogues are intelligently put together, are illustrated, and offer estimates that are reasonable. In addition to occasional house and estate sales, Sotheby King and Chasemore offers auction sales of military vehicles at the Warnham War Museum and of equestrian paintings at Goodwood House. Sales are held in Pulborough weekly, sometimes extending over 2 days.

Contact person: Richard Quilter

Days/hours of operation: Mon.–Fri. 9 A.M.–1 P.M., 2–5 P.M.

Areas in which general auctions and special sales are held (incl. some contact people):

Arms and Armor (Gordon Gardiner)	Musical Instruments
Art Deco	Paintings (Dendy Easton)
Art Nouveau	18th c. British
Books (Roger Griffiths)	19th c. British
Chinese Works of Art (Mark Grant)	19th c. European
Clocks and Watches	Pewter
Coins (Alistair Morris)	Porcelain (Gordon Lang)
Dolls	Postcards
Furniture (Anthony Rogers)	Prints (Dendy Easton)
Glass (Gordon Lang)	Rugs (Philip Hedger)
Japanese Works of Art (Mark Grant)	Silver (John Downes Hall)
Jewelry (Peter Pawson)	Stamps (Jeremy Rye)
Maps	Toys (Alistair Morris)
Medals	

Sales are advertised regularly in the regional press, the national press (e.g., *Daily Telegraph*), and specialty publications, such as *Antiques Trade Gazette*. A forthcoming sales list is available free; just write the firm.

Single catalogues are available from the firm, from other Sotheby offices, and through the mail, at £1, plus 40p for postage. Annual subscriptions are available. Contact Rhona Gorringe.

Usual viewing procedure: All sales can be viewed the Saturday (9 A.M.–noon) and Monday (10 A.M.–4 P.M.) prior to the sale. Limited viewing is possible the morning of the sale.

Bidder and Consignor Information

For all practical purposes, there are almost no distinctions drawn between the formal practices of Sotheby King and Chasemore and Sotheby's main London salerooms. For details, see Sotheby's entry, above.

The one important distinction is that consigned goods are sold much faster at Sotheby King and Chasemore; the time can be reckoned in terms of weeks instead of months. There is a minimum value of £30 for a consignment.

Appraisal service is available. See Sotheby's entry, above.

156. Weller & Dufty Ltd.

141 Bromsgrove Street   Tel. (021) 692-1414/5
Birmingham, West Midlands B5 6RQ   Telex: 338024
Cable: FINEART, BIRMINGHAM

Self-advertised as "Europe's Largest Arms Auctioneers," this venerable firm (established in 1835, during the reign of William IV) holds sales every 5 weeks or so. These 2-day multisession sales feature more than 1,300 lots (some of which are bunches) including shotguns, sporting rifles, antique long-arms, machine guns, rim-fire and pin-fire weapons, Lugers, automatic pistols, pepperboxes, blunderbusses, matchlocks, flintlocks, and wheel locks. The firm also handles more traditional goods, such as paintings, manuscripts, jewelry, and coins, provided they are "of a military nature" or are concerned with arms and armor. This includes Nazi material.

The catalogues for these sales are candid as concerns condition and working order, thorough (at times almost encyclopedic), well-written, and generously illustrated. It is understandable that they are kept by collectors as reference works, and Weller & Dufty sells a binder fitted with steel rods, which easily holds a year's worth of catalogues (£2 including postage).

The selling of weapons of any kind is a highly regulated affair, and bidders at Weller & Dufty must be prepared to face certain bureaucratic restrictions. U.K. purchasers of various items must hold either a Firearms Certificate, a Registered Firearm Dealer's Registration, or a Shotgun Certificate. Non-U.K. bidders cannot take possession of their purchases in the U.K.; all weapons are either forwarded in the mail or delivered to a registered English weapons dealer, who will handle the matter from then on. American purchasers should familiarize themselves with the restrictions on the importation of firearms into the U.S., restrictions which often necessitate the use of a registered American dealer. The firm cannot dispatch ammunition; thus absentee bids for ammunition will be accepted only if "the Bidder indicates on the Bidding Form that he is able to collect" in person.

Weller & Dufty is conveniently located at the rim of Birmingham's downtown area, a healthy but not overlong walk from the main train station. There are some items that sell for hundreds of pounds sterling, but at any given sale the vast bulk of the offerings will sell for less than £100, and many will go for less than £50. At an average selling rate of 100 lots an hour, the sales are long. Fortunately, hot and cold refreshments are available from an in-house snack bar during the sale.

Contact persons: H. A. Otten/P. E. C. Dufty

Days/hours of operation: Mon.–Fri. 9 A.M.–5:30 P.M.

Areas in which general auctions and specialized sales are held:

     Arms and Armor
     Militaria

Sales are advertised in the national press, in trade publications, such as *Antiques Trade Gazette,* and "internationally."

Catalogues are available for each sale and by subscription. Single catalogues are £2.50 plus postage. Annual subscriptions for approximately 10 sales cost as follows (including airmail postage where necessary): £15 U.K., £22.50 Europe, £25 Africa, Middle East, and America, £27.50 Australia and Far East.

Usual viewing procedure: Exhibition is the Tuesday before the sale during regular business hours, and the morning of the sale, 9–11.

Bidder Information

All sales are held on premises.

There is a buyer's premium of 5 percent. According to H. A. Otten, buyers "when present at sale must settle accounts immediately; when postal bidders, within 28 days." Absentee bids are executed. Clients unknown to the firm or who do not have an account with it must deposit 20 percent of the bid(s). Telephone bids must be confirmed in writing before the auction commences.

No guarantees of authenticity are offered, but buyers may return goods that prove to be not as catalogued; Mr. Otten says the procedure is "unreserved."

Bidders who have not paid fully for previous purchases will not be allowed to bid.

Packing and shipping services are available, at the buyer's expense.

Consignor Information

Persons wishing to consign goods should write with as full details as possible.

Standard consignor commission rates are: firearms/shotguns—trade 12.5 percent; private 15 percent. All other items—trade 10 percent; private 12 percent.

There is a minimum commission of £1 per lot.

According to Mr. Dufty, commissions are negotiable.

Reserves are accepted; the buy-in charge to the trade is 1 percent of the reserve price, with a minimum charge of £1 per lot; to private consignors, 2.5 percent of the reserve price, with a minimum charge of £1 per lot.

Consignors are charged 40p per £100 for insurance, with a minimum charge of 40p.

Consignors are charged for catalogue illustrations (£10 per full page, "with a pro rata reduction for smaller illustrations").

Consigned goods are sold within 4–7 weeks; settlement is 2–4 weeks after the sale.

For weapons that need proving, a charge will be leveled (£1–£2).

Appraisal service is available, "but only in a limited area." The cost is subject to negotiation. Contact Mr. D. A. Nie.

The firm estimates its annual turnover as well in excess of £600,000.

157. Woolley & Wallis
The Castle Auction Mart   Tel. (0722) 274 05
Castle Street
Salisbury, Wiltshire SP1 3SU

Every 2 weeks or so, this firm, which has a general estate and property management practice apart from its auction activities, holds what it calls "shutter sales." These include "good quality household furniture and effects, kitchen and garden equipment, domestic appliances, and bygones." Approximately twice a month, the firm also conducts specialized sales of such items as books, jewelry, rugs, and silver. A staple of these specialized sales is "antique furniture," some of which sells for very healthy prices. The firm reports that "our policy of specialized sales is an undoubted success and will be continued and expanded."

The saleroom is pleasantly located, set back from the street and reached by walking through a passageway formed by the firm's offices. The catalogues include the train schedule to and from Waterloo Station in London. The firm has followed a very aggressive and ambitious policy these last few years and has had considerable success in increasing the quality and quantity of its turnover. Woolley & Wallis is a first-rate example of a progressive provincial auction house.

Contact person: J. Timothy Woolley

Days/hours of operation: Mon.–Fri. 9:30 A.M.–5:30 P.M.

Areas in which general auctions and specialized sales are held:

Books	Manuscripts
Chinese Works of Art	Maps
Clocks and Watches	Paintings
Furniture	Porcelain
Glass	Prints
Japanese Works of Art	Rugs
Jewelry	Silver

Sales are advertised in the local press, occasionally in the national press, and from time to time in specialty publications, such as *Antiques Trade Gazette,* or in the case of books, *Antiquarian Book Monthly Review.* A twice-yearly sales calendar is available free of charge. To be placed on the mailing list, write or telephone the saleroom office.

Catalogues are available for single sales, either at the firm's offices or through the post; subscriptions are also offered. Prices vary with the number and category of sales. Write the saleroom office for information on catalogue rates and availability.

Usual viewing procedure: Exhibition is day prior to sale, 10 A.M.–4:30 P.M., and morning of sale.

Bidder Information

All auctions are held on the premises, except in the case of house sales, which are held in situ.

There is no buyer's premium. Absentee bids are executed, but for bidders unknown to the house, either a deposit or bank references is required.

Packing and shipping services are not available from the firm.

Accounts must be settled immediately after the sale.

Within the limits prescribed by law, buyers may return goods which do not prove to be as described in the catalogue.

Consignor Information

Persons interested in consigning goods should write or telephone the saleroom office to learn the date of the next suitable sale; in the case of all larger items, such as furniture, space must be booked in advance.

Book expert Diana Berry reports that "there is no minimum value for the household and effects (shutter) sales; for all specialized sales, the experts concerned must consider the items to be of sufficient standard to be included (e.g., £10 for book sales, £50 for picture sales)."

The standard consignor's commission is: £100 and under, 15 percent; £100–£500, 12.5 percent; over £500, 10 percent.

Consignors pay for catalogue illustrations (£15) and for insurance (35p per £100). Reserves are accepted; the buy-in charge is "at the discretion of the auctioneers."

Consigned goods are sold within 2–6 weeks; settlement is made 2–3 weeks after the sale.

The firm estimates its auction sales turnover to be in excess of £1 million.

Woolley & Wallis is a member of the Society of Fine Art Auctioneers.

Scotland

158. Christie's & Edmiston's Glasgow
164–66 Bath Street   Tel. (041) 332-8134/7
Glasgow, Strathclyde G2 4TC   Telex: 779901

During the 1970s, some of the larger U.K. auction houses gobbled up their provincial competitors. Phillips especially has followed an aggressive policy in this regard, and it was toward the end of this decade that Sotheby's began to build its regional network. With one exception, Christie's has stood aloof from the scramble. That exception was what became this division of the firm.

Edmiston's was an old-line Glasgow auction house, established in 1856, with premises in the center of the city, in easy walking distance of both railroad stations. In late 1978, Christie's announced that it had bought the firm and that "extensive rebuilding, redecoration and extensions" of the premises were to take place. Paul Whitfield, Christie's managing director, denied that this purchase represented a change in company policy: "this operation . . . is intended to deal with middle to low range goods. It would not make sense to transport those some 400 miles across the country at today's freight costs."

Christie's & Edmiston's, which began operations in the fall of 1979, has concentrated on rapid, efficient service for buyer and consignor with regard to items in the lower price range and lots that might have a Scottish tint. The firm announced that "anything of exceptional interest or value may be sent for sale in London or elsewhere when considered appropriate."

In the main, this subsidiary company has intelligently followed these policies and in its first year managed an annual turnover of over £2 million. Sales are usually held on Tuesdays, Wednesdays, and Thursdays, beginning at 11 A.M. The catalogues are list-like but adequate. In keeping with the intent for quick turnaround, no buyer's premium is charged and consignors' goods are sold relatively speedily (usually within 4 weeks); settlement is made within 14 days of the sale.

Contact person: Mathew Garse

Days/hours of operation: Mon.– Fri. 9:30 A.M.–5:30 P.M.

Areas in which general auctions and special sales are held (incl. some contact people):

Arms and Armor (Michael Clayton)	Paintings (William Hardie)
Books (Charles Douglas)	19th c. British
Clocks and Watches	Modern Scottish
Furniture (Joseph Mullen)	Pewter
Glass	Porcelain (Barry Beck)
Japanese Works of Art	Prints
Jewelry	Rugs
	Silver (Arthur McRae)
	Stamps (Charles Douglas)

Sales are advertised regularly in the local and regional press, and in specialty publications, such as *Antiques Trade Gazette*. Sales are also announced in the monthly illustrated preview of Christie's sales (to subscribe, see the Christie's entry, above).

Catalogues for each sale are available at varying prices at the Glasgow office, other Christie's offices, and through the mail (be sure to include postage). Write the firm for the cost of annual subscriptions.

Usual viewing procedure: Exhibition is the day prior to the sale, 10 A.M.– 4 P.M.

Bidder Information

Not all sales are on the premises; occasional house and estate sales are held.

There is no buyer's premium. Accounts must be settled within 2 days after the sale. Absentee bids are executed. Subject to references, the firm will give 7 days credit.

Packing and shipping services are available, at the buyer's expense.

No guarantees of authenticity are offered, but buyers can return goods if a lot proves to be a "deliberate forgery," provided that the firm is notified in writing within 7 days of the sale and the property in question is returned to the firm within another 7 days.

Consignor Information

Persons wishing to consign should get in touch with Christie's & Edmiston's or with a local Christie representative, either in writing or by phone. There is no minimum value for a consignment, but as Mr. Garse points out: "we reserve the right to refuse anything which we deem to be unsalable and to consign to secondary auctioneers goods which we do not feel suitable for sale by ourselves."

The standard consignor's commission is 10 percent of the hammer price for the trade, 15 percent for everyone else. The commission is negotiable, depending upon the situation.

Consignors pay for insurance (50p per £100 of realized value), and for cartage if they do not transport goods to the saleroom. There is no charge for warehousing prior to sale.

Reserves are accepted, but if the consignor does not indicate a desire for a reserve, the goods will be offered at the auctioneer's discretion. "Clients are advised that property unsold against reserve will automatically be reoffered without reserve in the next available sale." The buy-in charge is 5 percent of the highest bid if the firm did not agree to the reserve; "if unsold on an agreed reserve, no charge."

Settlement is made 14 days after the sale.

Appraisal service is available. For all practical purposes, the costs are the same as those charged in Christie's main London salerooms. For details, see the Christie's entry.

Phillips in Scotland

159. 65 George Street   Tel. (031) 225-2266
         Edinburgh, Lothian EH2 2JL

160. 98 Sauchiehall Street   Tel. (041) 332-3386
         Glasgow, Strathclyde G2 3DQ

Dowell's was established in Edinburgh in 1830; Morrison, McChlery & Co. was established in Glasgow in 1844. Both have recently been incorporated into Phillips, the Glasgow operation in 1979 and the Edinburgh operation a few years earlier.

Edinburgh:

The five spacious salerooms on George Street are within easy walking distance of the train and bus stations, and are located in a quite pleasant section of town on a street lined with Georgian buildings. Not far away are two elegant squares, the National Gallery of Scotland, and parking.

Phillips in Edinburgh is basically a two-tier operation, holding specialized catalogued sales mostly on Fridays, and in addition holding weekly sales on Thursdays of "good furniture, china, and household effects." The normal plan for the specialized sales is pictures on the first Friday of the month, porcelain on the second, silver on the penultimate, and antiques on the last. The firm finds that "there is a strong demand here for ... objects with a Scottish flavour."

Contact person: Frank Haston

Days/hours of operation: Mon.–Fri. 9 A.M.–5 P.M.; Sat. 9 A.M.–noon

Areas in which general auctions and special sales are held (incl. some contact people):

Books (Eddie MacLachlan)	Militaria (Tom Scott)
Ceramics (Caroline Currie)	Paintings
Chinese Works of Art (Caroline Currie)	Prints
Coins (Derek Graham)	Railwayana
Furniture (Paul Roberts)	Rugs (Paul Roberts)
Japanese Works of Art	Silver (Derek Graham)
Jewelry (Angus Lauder)	Toy Soldiers (Tom Scott)
Maps (Eddie MacLachlan)	Toys (Tom Scott)
Medals	

Glasgow:
This operation, smaller in terms of sales and staff than Edinburgh, draws on the other Phillips Scottish branch for specialist advice. The salerooms are located in downtown Glasgow, a longish walk from the city's various train and bus stations. The director, Michael McChlery, is a descendant of the family that founded the operation.

Catalogued specialized sales of modern furniture and carpets, as well as antique furniture and objets d'art, are held on successive Thursdays in the middle of the month. Jewelry, art deco/art nouveau, and silver sales are held on Thursdays at 2- or 3-month intervals. Books are sold periodically on Wednesdays. Like Edinburgh, this branch is a two-tier operation, with lesser-quality goods ("household furniture and effects, electrical and other goods, etc.") sold weekly on Tuesdays at 10 A.M.

Contact person: Michael McChlery

Days/hours of operation: Mon.–Fri. 9 A.M.–5 P.M.; Sat. 9 A.M.–noon

Areas in which general auctions and special sales are held (incl. some contact people):

Art Deco (Graeme McLeish)	Jewelry (Glen Collins)
Art Nouveau (Graeme McLeish)	Paintings
Books (Peter Nelson)	Photographica (Peter Nelson)
Cigarette Cards (David Hall)	Postcards (Peter Nelson)
Coins (Lynn Douglas)	Prints
Dolls	Rugs (Peter Nelson)
Drawings	Silver (Lynn Douglas)
Furniture (Peter Nelson)	Stamps
Glass (Graeme McLeish)	

Auctions in both the Glasgow and the Edinburgh salerooms are advertised in the Glasgow *Herald* on Mondays and in the *Scotsman* on Saturdays, as well as in specialty publications as necessary.

Catalogues are available for all the specialized sales; the price varies. Annual subscriptions are obtainable for particular categories at one house or the other (i.e., all jewelry sales in Edinburgh or all stamp sales in Glasgow); also for all Edinburgh sales (£40) or all Glasgow sales (£22); the price represents a small saving over ordering the catalogues individually or by category. In addition, you can subscribe to all Scottish sales (£60, which represents a slightly bigger saving). Write to the Edinburgh, Glasgow, or main London office of Phillips.

Usual viewing procedure: Normally, at least the day before the sale, during regular business hours.

Bidder and Consignor Information

Except for the following, the details of bidding and consigning are the same for Phillips in Scotland as for Phillips at Blenstock House in London (which see).

The exceptions are that at Phillips in Scotland, the minimum charge per lot for selling is £2 instead of £4; and at stamp and coin sales, no buyer's premium is charged. Conversely, the standard consignor's commission, which is negotiable, is 16 percent instead of 10 percent.

Appraisal service is available. For insurance valuations, the fee is 1 percent up to £10,000, 0.75 percent from £10,000 to £100,000, and 0.5 percent thereafter. For other purposes, such as family division or inventories, the fee is negotiable, subject to a minimum of £60 per day plus travel and out-of-pocket expenses outside a 10-mile radius from Edinburgh or Glasgow. Inspections of items considered for consignment will be made for a small charge, which is refundable if the goods are sold within 3 months for a minimum of £1,000. Travel and out-of-pocket expenses are also charged.

Both Edinburgh and Glasgow branches advertise that "a professional meeting can be resolved more amicably in a neutral environment and we have offices and rooms available for such meetings at modest charges."

United Kingdom and Eire: also worthy of note

England and Wales

161. Aldridges—The Auction Galleries
130–132 Walcot Street   Tel. (0225) 628 30/39
Bath, Avon BA1 6AC

The tag line on the catalogue covers is "auctioneers since 1740," but the original Aldridges was long gone when British Car Auctions bought the name in the mid-1970s for a few hundred pounds sterling. That company revived Aldridges first in a remote part of Somerset and then in 1976, less than a year later, relocated it in Bath. The galleries are in a lovely location along the river, in a delightful building that was once a school and more recently housed a failed mail order business. British Car Auctions sold Aldridges to a Swiss company at the end of the 1970s.

Aldridges has done well since its rebirth. The firm holds general-purpose mixed-lot sales, as well as specialist sales, usually on Tuesdays. Among the lots sold at these sales are BOOKS, FURNITURE, PAINTINGS, and PORCELAIN. The efficient manager is John Street, who was for many years at Jollys before the takeover of that Bath firm by Phillips.

There is no buyer's premium. Viewing is at least 1 day before the sale (10 A.M.–5 P.M.) and the morning of the sale. Buyers, states the catalogue, "purchase all lots as viewed with all faults, imperfections, and errors of description." Settlement must be made within 2 working days of the sale.

The consignor's commission is negotiable and depends on the quality and quantity of the consignment. There is a separate commission structure for the trade. Consigned goods are sold within 1–3 months. Settlement is within 21 days after the sale.

162. Alonzo Dawes & Hoddell
Six Ways   Tel. (0272) 87 60 11
Clevedon, Avon BS21 7NT

Sales are held monthly by this firm in what is locally known as the "Clevedon Salerooms." This auction operation is part of a larger business, which has "six other estate agents offices in Avon." The partner in charge of the auction operation is John Hawkings, FRICS; saleroom manager is Marc Burridge.

Sales are advertised in the local press and in specialty periodicals, such as *Antiques Trade Gazette*. Broadsheets detailing the sales are available for £2 per annum; just write the saleroom office. General-purpose mixed-lot sales are the rule, such items as FURNITURE being sold. Occasional sales are held at private residences.

Minimal catalogues are available on viewing and sale days. Viewing is usually a day prior to the sale (10 A.M.–5 P.M.) or by appointment, as well as on the day of the sale. There is no buyer's premium. Packing and shipping services are available, at the buyer's expense. Buyers are offered the opportunity to return goods that are not as described. Buyer must settle accounts within 48 hours of the sale.

The standard consignor's commission on single lots is: over £200, 12.5 percent; between £100 and £200, 15 percent; under £100, 17 percent. Commissions are negotiable, depending on the situation. Consigned goods are usually sold within a month; settlement is 1–2 weeks after the sale. The firm does not accept consignments from dealers. Minimum value for a single lot to be accepted is "about £10." Consignors are not charged for insurance or warehousing, but they must pay "removal charges to saleroom," which are "deducted from sale proceeds where appropriate." Reserves are accepted; the firm retains the option to "charge half commission when vendor's reserve is not reached."

Trade Association memberships include the Royal Institute of Chartered Surveyors and the Institute of Valuers and Appraisers.

163. Ambrose & Son
149 High Road   Tel. (01) 508- 2121/3
Loughton, Essex IG10 4L7

This firm holds a sale on the premises every month, but "occasionally when a large house has been sold the contents are sold from the property (sometimes other items are added)." Generally, the sales are of mixed lots and can include CLOCKS AND WATCHES, FURNITURE, JEWELRY, and SILVER.

Sales are advertised in the local press and in specialty trade periodicals, such as *Antiques Trade Gazette*.

Listings, which usually are not illustrated, are available for each sale (32p) and by subscription (£3.50 per annum). Write to Mr. K. Lawrence, the saleroom manager.

There is no buyer's premium. The firm does not execute absentee bids or offer packing and shipping services. It does give buyers the opportunity to return goods that do not prove to be as described, but no guarantees of authenticity are offered. Settlement is within "24 hours if possible." Viewing is the day before the sale, 9 A.M.–7 P.M.

The consignor's commission rate is 15 percent, but it is negotiable, depending on the situation. The minimum value of a lot for consignment is £30. Reserves are accepted; the buy-in charge is £2. There is no charge for insurance or warehousing. Mr. A. C. Gilbert, a partner, reports that "arrangements for collection of items are made and paid for by the consignor." These goods usually come into the saleroom the first week of the month and are sold in the last week of the month. Settlement is made approximately 10 days after the sale.

Ambrose & Son estimate their annual turnover as approximately £200,000.

164. Ashby-de-la-Zouch Auction Sales
58 Market Street   Tel. (053 04) 27 66
Ashby-de-la-Zouch, Leicestershire LE6 5BD

The town owes its unusual name to the La Zouch family from Brittany, who came to this town during the early Middle Ages. Ivanhoe, Sir Walter Scott's legendary hero, fought in a tournament staged here. Stevenson and Barratt, a firm of chartered surveyors with a general practice, are the principals in Ashby-de-la-Zouch Auction Sales.

General-purpose mixed-lot sales are held monthly, in which objects sold include FURNITURE and CERAMICS. Occasional house and estate sales are held. Announcements of forthcoming sales are available; write to Mrs. S. Loomes.

Catalogues, which are list-like, are available singly for each sale and by subscription (the cost per annum is £4.85 plus postage).

There is no buyer's premium. Packing and shipping services are not available from the firm. No guarantees of authenticity are offered. Viewing is the day before the sale, 10 A.M.–4 P.M. and 7–8 P.M. Buyers must settle their accounts within 24 hours.

The standard consignor's commission is 15 percent for goods valued under £100, and 12.5 percent thereafter; commission is negotiable, depending upon the situation. Consignors are charged for insurance (there is a minimum charge of 10p), and for packing and shipping if the firm has to undertake removal of goods to the saleroom. Consigned goods are sold within 1–2 months and settlement is 14 days after the sale. Reserves are accepted; the buy-in charge is 3 percent of the reserve price. There is a minimum value of £10 necessary for consignment.

Appraisal service is available. Contact either S. R. Easton, FRICS, or R. M. Fallowell, FRICS, who are the directors of Stevenson and Barratt.

165. Baitson's

194 Anlaby Road   Tel. (0482) 22 33 55
Hull, North Humberside HU1 7IG   after hours:
                                        (04302) 24 98 or (0482) 64521

Baitson's, "The Edwardian Auction Galleries," holds sales every Wednesday. These are advertised in the local and regional press, as well as in specialty periodicals. Sales are sometimes held on site at houses, warehouses, factories, shops, etc.

Most of Baitson's sales are of mixed lots, including ART DECO, ART NOU-VEAU, CLOCKS AND WATCHES, FURNITURE, JEWELRY, MEDALS, PORCELAIN, RUGS, and SILVER. Viewing is the Tuesday before the sale, 9 A.M.–8 P.M. List-like catalogues are not available by subscription, but can be obtained on request.

There is no buyer's premium. Absentee bids are accepted. Packing and shipping is available, at the buyer's expense. There are no guarantees of authenticity, but the firm will accept return of goods that prove to be not as described. Buyer must normally settle accounts within 2 days of the sale.

The standard consignor commission rates are: dealers, 12.5 percent; private individuals, 17.5 percent. Consignors are not charged for insurance, warehousing, or packing and shipping. Goods are sold within 7 days, and settlement made after a week. Reserves are accepted and there is a fee for buy-ins. The consignor's commission is negotiable, depending on the situation. There is no minimum value for acceptance.

Appraisal service is available. The costs are "based on valuation and dependent upon whether items are eventually sold through saleroom." Contact Gilbert Baitson.

166. Michael G. Baker
4 Latimer Street   Tel. (0794) 51 33 31
Romsey, Hampshire S05 8DG

This firm holds auctions twice weekly in its Romsey auction rooms (86 The Hundred), usually general-purpose mixed-lot sales that include among other items FURNITURE and SILVER. The sales are advertised in the regional press and in specialty periodicals. The firm publishes a free annual calendar of sales; just write and request one.

Catalogues for each sale are available by mail and at the firm's various offices. Catalogues are also available by subscription at £5 per annum. There is no buyer's premium. Viewing is the day prior to the auction (noon–7:30 P.M.) and the next morning until the sale. Absentee bids are executed. Guarantees of authenticity are not offered. Packing and shipping is available, at the buyer's expense, for "local delivery." Goods that prove to be not as described may be returned. Buyers must settle accounts within 48 hours of the sale. Credit terms are available: "Payment may be delayed for a few days by arrangement."

The standard consignor's commission is as follows: institutions (by negotiation), 7.5–10 percent; dealers, 12.5 percent; all others, 15 percent. Commissions are negotiable. There is no minimum value for acceptance of consigned goods. Goods are sold within 2–4 weeks; settlement is made after 21 days. Reserves are accepted, but there is no buy-in charge ("no sale, no charge"). Consignors are not charged for insurance, warehousing, or packing and shipping.

Appraisal service is available: "fee by agreement." Contact Michael G. Baker, FSVA.

167. Richard Baker & Thomson
9 Hamilton Street   Tel. (051) 647 9104
Birkenhead, Merseyside L41 6DL

Located just off Hamilton Square, which is noted for its Victorian architecture, this firm holds sales fortnightly. A sale may be either of FURNITURE or of mixed lots embracing ARMS AND ARMOR, BOOKS, CLOCKS AND WATCHES, DRAWINGS, GLASS, JEWELRY, MEDALS, PAINTINGS, PEWTER, PORCELAIN, PRINTS, RUGS, and SILVER. The Thomson in the name refers to the Thomson family, which has an interest in Thomson, Roddick & Laurie (see entry below) and which bought an interest in this firm during the summer of 1980; formerly Richard Baker had been a family firm. Richard Baker & Thomson is a typical general-purpose auction house.

Sales are advertised in the Saturday issue of the Liverpool *Daily Post,* as well as in specialty periodicals, such as *Antiques Trade Gazette.* Sales are usually held in the ground-floor auction salerooms, but occasionally house and estate sales are held on site. Catalogues are available by subscription: Fine Arts Sales, £4.20 per annum; Furniture Sales, £7.20 per annum. Catalogues are also available singly for specific sales. To obtain catalogues or to be put on the mailing list, write to Mrs. A. Stern.

Since April 1, 1978, there has been a 5 percent buyer's premium. The firm will execute absentee bids. Guarantees of authenticity are not offered. Packing and shipping services are not available. Buyers may return goods that are not as described. Viewing is usually Friday and Saturday before the sale on Monday (Friday, 9 A.M.–5 P.M.; Saturday, 9 A.M.–12:30 P.M.). Buyer must settle accounts within 2 days after the sale.

The standard consignor's commission rate is 15 percent. Normally the rate is not negotiable, but depending on the situation, adjustments can be made. Baker's does not accept consignments from dealers. There is no minimum value for acceptance, but, reports Maurice H. Baker, "goods are vetted for acceptance." Consignors are not charged for warehousing or for packing and shipping, but must pay insurance on any consignment that totals above £7,000 in value. Consigned goods are usually sold within a month. Settlement is made after 10 days. Reserves are accepted, but for not less than £30; the buy-in charge is 7.5 percent of the reserve price.

Insurance appraisal service is available. The cost is 1 percent of the total value, with a minimum fee of £10. Contact Maurice Baker.

Richard Baker & Thomson estimates its annual turnover at £200,000.

168. Baldwin & Partners
26 Railway Street　　　　　　　　　　Tel. (0634) 40 01 21
Chatham, Kent ME4 4JT

This firm specializes in bankruptcy and liquidation sales, which are held on premises once a month at their Medway Auction Rooms or on site if necessary. As might be expected, these sales include a wide variety of items, including FURNITURE.

Sales are advertised regularly in the local and regional press, as well as in specialty periodicals, such as *Antiques Trade Gazette*. Announcements of forthcoming sales are available from Baldwin & Partners for £3.50 per annum; write to Mr. W. G. Miskimmin. List-like catalogues for each sale may be obtained by writing to the firm.

There is no buyer's premium. Viewing is 10 A.M.–4 P.M. on Saturday prior to sale, and 10 A.M.–7 P.M. on Tuesday prior to sale. Absentee bids are executed. Packing and shipping services are available, at buyer's expense. Goods that prove not to be as described may be returned. Buyer must settle accounts "by 1:00 P.M. day following sale."

The standard consignor's commission is 10 percent to the trade and 15 percent to all others, but the commission is negotiable, depending on the situation. The minimum value for acceptance of a consignment is £10. Consignors are charged "at cost" for insurance and for packing and shipping. Consignors are not charged for warehousing. Goods are usually sold within 4 weeks. Settlement is made 7 days after the sale. Reserves are accepted; buy-in charge is 5 percent ("2.5 percent if reserve is based on our appraisal," reports senior partner C. W. Baldwin).

Appraisal services are available. The charges are "variable." Contact C. W. Baldwin, Sr.

169. Barnsley and Co.
The Saleroom, Cattle Market   Tel. (0432) 668 94
Hereford, Hereford and Worcester HR4 2PS

Sales are held by Barnsley and Co. every 3–4 weeks on Tuesdays in this venerable cathedral city. "Occasional sales are held on clients' property," reports principal E. G. Powell. Sales are advertised in the Hereford *Times*.

The general-purpose mixed-lot sales include diverse items such as FURNITURE. Neither announcements nor catalogues are available. The firm does not charge a buyer's premium; no absentee bidding is possible; there are no guarantees of authenticity; packing and shipping services are not available. Buyers must settle accounts immediately, unless other arrangements have been made.

Barnsley and Co. does not accept consignments from dealers and institutions. The standard consignor commission is 15 percent and is not negotiable. Reserves are accepted; the buy-in charge is a "nominal charge only." Goods are sold within 3–4 weeks. Settlement is made after 7 days. Consignors are charged only for packing and shipping.

The Bearnes Rooms: see Sotheby Bearne (Torquay, Devon)

170. Bermondsey Auctions Ltd.
MacNeills Warehouse, Newhams Row   Tel. (01) 403 2065
175 Bermondsey Street
London SE1 3UW

Self-styled "the International Auction Centre," Bermondsey holds sales twice monthly of various kinds of properties, including FURNITURE and RUGS, and quarterly of better properties, including JEWELRY and SILVER. Most sales are held at Bermondsey's saleroom, not far from Tower Bridge, but occasionally house or estate sales are held on site.

Sales are advertised in the regional press and in specialty periodicals, such as *Antiques Trade Gazette*. An annual calendar of sale dates is available free on application to the firm. Catalogues are available for specific sales from the auctioneers (50p plus postage); a subscription is £5 per annum. Viewing is usually the day preceding the sale and on sale day.

There is no buyer's premium. Absentee bids are executed. Packing and shipping is available, at the buyer's expense. Goods may be returned "without limitation" if not as described, according to A. D. Robinson, the manager. Settlement is on the day of the sale, "except by prior arrangement with 'known' clients."

The standard consignor commission rates are "15 percent with 3 percent reduction to bona fide dealers and 10 percent on individual lots with an estimated value in excess of £1,500." These rates are negotiable, depending on the situation.

Consignors are not charged for warehousing. "Packing and carriage are not charged for within a 30-mile radius of London; thereafter we will arrange carriage by agreement with vendor," reports Mr. Robinson. Reserves are accepted; there is no buy-in charge. Goods are sold within one month of consignment, "except when consigned for quarterly sales." Settlement is after 7 working days. The minimum value for a consignment is £10.

Appraisal service is available. "Valuation for sale is made free of charge where goods are consigned for sale within 3 months." Valuation for probate and insurance is charged at a rate of 0.5 percent on the total estimated value of the goods.

The firm normally does not buy and sell on its own behalf; "However, small estates or deceased individual's effects may be purchased by agreement with executor" and later put up for auction.

Biddle & Webb
171. Icknield Square, Ladywood   Tel. (021) 455 8042
Middleway, Birmingham B16 OPP

172.
Enfield Hall, Islington Row   Tel. (021) 643 4380
Edgbaston, Birmingham B15 1QA

Biddle & Webb, started after the end of World War II, is a relative newcomer to the Birmingham auction scene. The firm has evolved quite successfully into a two-tier operation, with an annual turnover estimated to be well in excess of £1 million.

The Icknield Square salerooms, under the direction of Mr. Biddle, one of the founders of the firm, now in his sixties, hold weekly sales on Tuesdays and Wednesdays of general merchandise—mostly mixed lots of lesser value. The Icknield Square operation, which began in the 1970s, is housed in what was once a factory.

The Enfield Hall salerooms are managed by Mr. George Eames, a recent addition to the firm. In his thirties, Eames has helped to build up sales of better properties, which are auctioned off on Fridays 3 times a month. These Enfield Hall sales have been enhanced by the addition to the galleries of a saleroom designed for the presentation of paintings and the like. The usual succession of sales is paintings one Friday, antiques the next, then jewelry and silver.

Icknield Square

Mixed-lot sales at this location include FURNITURE, GLASS, and RUGS. Sales are advertised in the local press and in specialty periodicals. A list-like catalogue is available at the saleroom. Viewing is the day prior to the sale.

There is no buyer's premium. Accounts must be settled within 48 hours. Absentee bids are executed. There are no guarantees of authenticity. Packing and shipping services are available, at the buyer's expense.

The standard consignor's commission is 15 percent, but it is negotiable, depending on the situation. Consignors are charged for shipping and packing, but not for warehousing or insurance. Goods usually are sold within 1 week. Settlement is made within 1 week. Reserves are accepted. The buy-in charge is 7.5 percent of the last bid obtained. No reserve; no buy-in charge.

Enfield Hall

General auctions and special sales are held in such areas as CLOCKS AND WATCHES, DRAWINGS, FURNITURE, JEWELRY, NETSUKE, PAINTINGS, and SILVER. Sales are advertised regularly in the local and regional press, as well as in specialty periodicals, such as *Antiques Trade Gazette*. Illustrated brochures are sent out to a mailing list; just ask to be put on.

Catalogues for each sale are available at the house or by mail order. Catalogues are also available by subscription: the cost is £5 per annum for each Friday sale; £15 for all sales. Exhibition is 4 days before the sale, during regular business hours.

All sales are held on premises. There is no buyer's premium. Accounts must be settled within 48 hours of the sale. Absentee bids are executed. Packing and shipping services are available, at the buyer's expense. No guarantees of authenticity are offered, but goods that prove to be not as catalogued may be returned within 7 days of purchase.

If interested in consigning goods, write or phone. There is no minimum value for acceptance of goods. Standard commission structure is 12.5 percent on lots to £100; 10 percent on lots over £100. The commission is negotiable, depending upon the situation. There is a separate commission rate of 10 percent for dealers and institutions. Consignors pay for shipping and packing, but not for insurance and warehousing. Reserves are accepted. The buy-in charge is nil if there was no reserve on the lot, but otherwise the charge is 5 percent of the last bid obtained. Goods are usually sold within 3–4 weeks. Settlement is 3–4 weeks after the sale.

A free valuation service is held on Thursday mornings at Enfield Hall.

173. Blinkhorn and Company
41–43 High Street   Tel. (038 685) 24 56/7
Broadway, Hereford and Worcester WR12 7DP

This well-established firm of chartered surveyors, estate agents, valuers, and auctioneers has offices also in Evesham, Stow-on-the-Wold, Pershore, and Moreton-in-Marsh, but it holds its auctions "as required" in Broadway at Lifford Hall and the Lygon Arms. House and estate sales are also held from time to time. Sales are advertised in the local press and in specialty periodicals such as *Antiques Trade Gazette*.

Mostly the firm holds general-purpose mixed-lot sales of items such as FUR-NITURE, JEWELRY, and SILVER. Catalogues are available individually and by subscription; just write to the Broadway office.

There is no buyer's premium. Absentee bids are executed. Packing and shipping services are offered, at the buyer's expense. There are no guarantees of authenticity, and if goods prove inadvertently to be not as described, the firm will not accept their return. The usual viewing procedure "varies according to sale but mostly is morning of sale," according to Michael Blinkhorn. Buyer must settle accounts forthwith; credit is not given unless by arrangement, and then for 7 days.

The standard consignor's commission rates are 12.5 percent up to £100 per item and 10 percent over £100. The commission is negotiable, depending on the situation. Consignors pay for insurance and for packing and shipping. Consignors do not pay for warehousing. Goods are usually sold within 8 weeks. Settlement is made after 14 days. Reserves are accepted. Buy-in charge is up to 5 percent of reserve—no reserve, no charge.

Appraisal service is available. Contact M. L. Blinkhorn at the Broadway office.

174. Boardman, Fine Art Auctioneers
Station Road Corner   Tel. (0440) 37 84
Haverhill, Suffolk CB9 0EY

Boardman's has its office in one picturesque town and holds its sales every 5 or 6 weeks in another. Auctions are held at the town hall, Clare, Sudbury, Suffolk, about 10 miles from Haverhill as the crow flies and a bit longer by road.

Sales are advertised "throughout Great Britain, France, Belgium, Holland, and Germany. Occasionally U.S.A." Postcard announcements of forthcoming auctions are sent on request. Write Neil Lanham, FRICS, at Boardman's. Catalogues are available for each sale (80p plus postage); a subscription for the whole year is £6.

Among the items auctioned are CLOCKS AND WATCHES, FURNITURE, PAINT-INGS (Old Master, 17th & 18th c. British, 19th c. European), PEWTER, and RUGS. The firm prides itself on the oak furniture it sells, and claims a world record for a piece of oak furniture sold at auction: £33,000.

There is no buyer's premium. Absentee bids are executed. No guarantees of authenticity are offered. Packing and shipping services are available, at the buyer's expense. Settlement of accounts must take place "on day of sale or within a week." Credit is available, but "only by special arrangement." Viewing is usually on day preceding sale (2–7 P.M.) and morning of sale (8–10).

Standard consignor commission rates are: "Private vendors—individual items up to £500 in value, 15 percent; above £500 in value, 10 percent. Trade vendors—individual items up to £500 in value, 12 percent; above £500, 8 percent. For all parties, over £1,500 by arrangement." Commissions are negotiable, depending on situation. Consignors are not charged for insurance, packing and shipping, or warehousing. Consigned goods are sold in the next sale—that is, within 6 weeks. Settlement is within 3 weeks. Reserves are accepted. There is no buy-in charge if the reserve was agreed upon with the auctioneer. Minimum value for a consignment is £200.

175. Bonsor Penningtons
Warwick Lodge, 82 Eden Street   Tel. (01) 546 0022
Kingston-upon-Thames KT1 1DF

An old-line firm located at the outer edges of Greater London, Bonsor Penningtons has offices in Surrey too. Chartered surveyors, valuers, and estate agents as well as auctioneers, they also conduct house and estate sales.

Sales are held approximately twice a month, most of them mixed-lot auctions, including such items as FURNITURE, PAINTINGS, and RUGS. Prices fall well within the £500 range, and a lot that sells over £1,000 is unusual. Sales are advertised in the regional press.

There is no buyer's premium. Viewing is Tuesday 2–8 P.M. and Wednesday 9 A.M.–4 P.M. before the sale, which begins Thursday morning at 10 A.M. Shipping and packing services are available, at the buyer's expense. Absentee bids are executed. List-like catalogues are available. No guarantees of authenticity are offered. Settlement is right after the sale.

The standard consignor's commission is 17.5 percent. It is negotiable, depending on the situation. Reserves are accepted; "items not reaching a reserve price will be charged at 8.75 percent on highest bid." Removals can be arranged at owner's expense. There is no charge for warehousing of auctionable property, which should be sold within 3–4 weeks. Settlement is usually after 28 days.

Appraisal service is available: insurance valuations are 1.5 percent on total valuation, with a minimum charge of £10. Probate valuations are 5.5 percent on first £700 of valuation, 2.5 percent on residue.

176. Borough Auctions
6–8 Park Street, Borough Market   Tel. (01) 407-9577
London SE1

Off Stoney Street, not far from London Bridge, in rather inelegant premises, Borough Auctions holds sales every Sunday, beginning at 2:30 P.M. About 400 lots are sold at each auction, including FURNITURE, JEWELRY, PAINTINGS, PORCELAIN, PRINTS, SILVER, and assorted bric-a-brac.

There is no buyer's premium. Packing and shipping are not available from the firm. Settlement is immediate. Viewing is Friday (10 A.M.–2 P.M.), Saturday (10 A.M.–4 P.M.), and the morning of the sale.

The standard consignor's commission is 12 percent, but it is negotiable, depending upon the situation. There is no charge for unsold lots. Goods received by Tuesday will be sold on Sunday. Settlement is the Thursday after the sale.

177. Boulton & Cooper, Ltd.

St. Michael's House   Tel. (0653) 21 51/4
Malton, North Yorkshire YO17 0LR

Located in St. Michael's House in the attractive town of Malton (known for its livestock market) is this branch of a firm of chartered surveyors, estate agents, etc., which holds catalogued special sales approximately once a month. Among the items auctioned at the Milton Rooms are CLOCKS AND WATCHES, FURNITURE, GLASS, JEWELRY, SILVER, and RUGS. House and estate sales are held occasionally on site, and more regularly, there are sales for the disposition of general merchandise.

The catalogued sales are advertised in the local and national press, as well as in specialty periodicals. Announcements are available at no charge; to be placed on the mailing list, just write to the Secretary, Fine Arts Division. Catalogues are available singly for each such sale (approximately £1.50), either at the firm or through the mail. A subscription to all catalogued special sales costs approximately £10 per annum.

At the catalogued sales there is a buyer's premium of 10 percent. Viewing is 2 days before the sale, which may be a multisession event taking more than 1 day: exhibition is Monday (1–6 P.M.) and Tuesday (9 A.M.–4 P.M.). Absentee bids are executed, provided that they are received in writing 24 hours before the sale commences. Packing and shipping services are available, at the buyer's expense. Goods inadvertently miscatalogued may be returned, provided that the firm is notified within 14 days and the goods are returned within an additional 7 days. Buyer must settle account within 2 weeks after the sale. Credit cards are accepted: American Express, Barclaycard.

The standard consignor's commission is 15 percent, but it is negotiable, depending on the situation. Consignments of property are not accepted from dealers for the catalogued sales. Consignors are charged £5 for each catalogue illustration and 1 percent of value for insurance. There is no charge for warehousing. Consigned goods are sold within 3 months. Settlement is made after 4 weeks.

Appraisal service is available. Insurance is 1.5 percent on the gross valuation. W. L. Cooper, chairman and managing director, points out that there is "no charge if the article is ultimately put up for sale."

Boulton & Cooper belongs to the Society of Fine Art Auctioneers. The firm's estimated annual turnover is in excess of £500,000.

178. Brocklehursts

11 King Edward Street   Tel. (0625) 275 55 (4 lines)
Macclesfield, Cheshire SK10 1AL

Brocklehursts, established in the 1890s, holds weekly sales, usually on Wednesday, of mixed-lots which include mainly FURNITURE. Occasional house and estate sales are also held.

These sales are advertised in the local and regional press, as well as in specialty periodicals. The usual viewing time is the day before and morning of the sale. Announcements are sent out; write to be placed on the mailing list. Listings are not available by subscription, but can be obtained for each sale.

There is no buyer's premium—at least, "not yet," according to partner M. J. Pickwell, FRICS. Absentee bids are not accepted. Packing and shipping services are available, at the buyer's expense. The auctioneer, according to the notice to prospective buyers, "will accept no responsibility or liability . . . and buyers must rely on their own judgment and take full responsibility for their purchases." Settlement must be immediately after the sale. Credit cards are accepted: Barclaycard, Access.

Consignors are not charged for warehousing, but are charged for insurance if they want it. The standard consignor commission is 17.5 percent on items over £100, and 15 percent on items sold for £100 or below. The commission is negotiable, depending on the situation. There is a separate rate for dealers (12.5 percent). Consigned goods are sold within 3–4 weeks. Reserves are accepted. Unsold goods normally cost the consignor nothing.

William H. Brown
179. Westgate   Tel. (0476) 688 61/663 63
Grantham, Lincolnshire NG31 6QF

180. Northgate House   Tel. (0529) 30 30 40
Northgate
Sleaford, Lincolnshire NG34 7BZ

William H. Brown was a successful old-line (est. 1897) firm of appraisers, chartered surveyors, etc. who over the years had successfully developed a multi-branch structure covering Lincolnshire, Nottinghamshire, Cambridgeshire, Leicestershire, and Norfolk. In 1980 it merged with Stanilands, keeping its salerooms under its own name, and adding another as Stanilands William H. Brown (see entry below).

Sales are held as necessary at both Northgate and Westgate. Goods for sale include FURNITURE, PAINTINGS, and SILVER. Occasional house and estate sales are also held.

These sales are advertised in the local and regional press, as well as in specialty publications, such as *Antiques Trade Gazette*. Announcements of forthcoming sales are available; write to Ian Ward at 31 St. Peters Hill, Grantham, Lincs. NG31 6QF. Single catalogues cost approximately 40p; an annual subscription, £5.

There is no buyer's premium. Absentee bids are executed, but "banker's references are required," reports Mr. Ward, director of the saleroom operation. Packing and shipping services are not available from the firm. No guarantees of authenticity are offered. The usual viewing procedure is the day before the sale, noon–5 P.M. Buyer must settle accounts "immediately if demanded."

The standard consignor's commission is 12.5 percent. It is negotiable, depending upon the situation; the minimum commission is 10 percent. Consignments from dealers are not accepted. Consignors are not charged for catalogue illustrations, insurance, or warehousing, and are charged only "minimum costs" for packing and shipping. Reserves are accepted. There is no charge on unsold goods on which there was no reserve, "unless items are to be packed for return." Consigned goods are sold, "maximum one month." Settlement is approximately 10 days after the sale. There is no minimum value necessary for acceptance of consignments.

Appraisal service is available, at "no cost if items are to be sold through auction" at the firm. Contact Mr. Ward.

181. Buckell & Ballard
49 Parsons Street   Tel. (0295) 531 97
Banbury, Oxfordshire OX16 8PF

This veteran firm (est. 1887) of chartered surveyors, auctioneers, and estate agents has headquarters in Oxford and offices elsewhere. The Banbury branch oversees regular auction sales of FURNITURE and other effects, such as BOOKS, PAINTINGS, and SILVER. The saleroom is centrally located in this pleasant old town, right by a multistory parking garage which makes attendance at the twice-monthly auctions that much easier. Sales are held off premises when an estate or house contents are auctioned off.

Auctions are advertised in the regional press and in specialty periodicals, such as *Antiques Trade Gazette.* Catalogues (75p) are available for specific sales, either at the house or by mail (add postage); by subscription, catalogues are £10 per annum.

There is no buyer's premium. Viewing is the day prior to the sale, 10 A.M.–6 P.M., as well as the morning of the sale. It is also possible to arrange for private viewing by appointment. Absentee bids are executed, "by telephone if necessary." Packing and shipping services are available, at the buyer's expense. No guarantees of authenticity are offered. If goods wrongly described are returned within 7 days, the sale is rescinded.

The standard consignor's commission rate is 10 percent on articles selling for £500 or more, 12.5 percent on articles selling for between £200 and £500, 15 percent on articles selling for under £200. "An additional standard charge of 1 percent per lot is charged whether the lot is sold or unsold." The commission rate is negotiable, depending on the situation. Reserves are accepted, but not for less than £5. There is a buy-in charge of 5 percent, except where the reserve has been left to the discretion of the auctioneer, in which case the "standard charge" is £1 per lot.

"Small articles and selected antiques are stored and insured free of charge. Larger articles are stored in first-class warehousing at reasonable rates." Removal, according to a firm brochure, is at "reasonable rates." Consigned goods are usually sold within 3–4 weeks. Settlement is made after 2 weeks. There is no minimum value for acceptance of consignment.

Appraisal service is available. Articles intended for sale are valued free of charge. Insurance valuations are 1–2.5 percent, "depending upon the work involved." Probate valuations are 2.5 percent. Contact T. J. Holloway, FRICS, at the Banbury office.

182. Bucksey & Hosmer Coin Auctions

8 The Cattle Market, Great Knolly's Street   Tel. (734) 59 51 42
Reading, Berkshire RG1 7HU

Bucksey & Hosmer holds auctions of COINS and coin-related material the last
Thursday evening of every month at the Bell Hotel in downtown Reading.

Sales are advertised in coin collectors' magazines. There is no charge for
the list-like catalogue. About 300 lots are sold at a sale. There is no buyer's
premium. Absentee bids are executed. Floor bidders must settle accounts immediately. Absentee bidders, according to Mr. Bucksey, are sent goods "on
approval against cash, which is returnable if sale is rescinded" because of
disagreement over catalogue description.

Prospective consignors should get in touch with the firm either in writing or
by phone. Coins are valued on grades. The standard consignor's commission is
10 percent. Consignors are not charged for shipping and packing, warehousing, or insurance. Consigned goods are sold at the first available sale, usually
within a month. Settlement is made after 2 weeks. Reserves are accepted.
There is no buy-in charge except the cost of returning goods.

183. Burrows & Day

39/41 Bank Street   Tel. (0233) 243 21
Ashford, Kent TN23 1DJ

Established shortly after the battle of Waterloo, this firm of chartered surveyors holds auctions of various kinds. There are the occasional house or estate
sales; there are the quarterly specialized sales, usually at the Kempton Manor
Hotel in nearby Hothfield, about 4 miles west of Ashford; and approximately
12 times a year, sales, usually of less valuable properties, are held at the Victoria Crescent saleroom in Ashford.

Announcements of these sales are to be found in the regional press and in
specialty periodicals, such as *Art & Antiques Weekly*. Catalogues for each
sale are available at the firm, at the saleroom, or by post. A subscription to all
catalogues costs £6 per annum; to the Victoria Crescent sales, £3.50; and to
the quarterly sales and any house sales, £2.50.

Whatever the value of the properties, the conditions of sale are roughly the
same. There is no buyer's premium. Absentee bids will be executed, provided
that they are in hand by 5 P.M. the day before the sale and that adequate bank
references are provided by parties not known to the firm. No guarantees of
authenticity are provided; "no redress can be made for any items subsequently
found faulty." Viewing is the day prior to the sale, 10 A.M.–4 P.M. Settlement
is day of sale or the day following.

Sales, even of higher-value properties, are mixed lots and include, as did
one recently, BOOKS, CLOCKS AND WATCHES, FURNITURE, GLASS, JEWELRY,
RUGS, and SILVER. Approximately 100 lots are sold per hour, and a sale beginning at 10 A.M. will usually last well into the afternoon, with a half-hour
luncheon break.

The standard commission rate for consignors is 12.5 percent on all single items £50 and over; 15 percent of the realization price for items fetching less than £50. There is a minimum charge of 50p per lot to cover expenses. Consignors pay for catalogue illustrations (£10 per illustration), packing and shipping, and insurance (0.5 percent of the realization price). The firm does attempt to keep charges to a minimum. Consigned goods are sold within 1–3 months. Settlement is made within 1–3 weeks. Reserves are accepted. The buy-in charge is 7.5 percent of the reserve price.

184. Burtenshaw Walker
66 High Street   Tel. (079 16) 42 25
Lewes, East Sussex BN7 1XB

A well-established firm with branches elsewhere in Sussex, Burtenshaw Walker holds "periodical sales of antique and modern FURNITURE, carpets, SILVER, plate, etc., at the Lewes Auction Rooms," on Garden Street, a short walk from the firm's High Street offices. Burtenshaw Walker also holds "auction sales of all classes of property," including "live and dead farming stock." The periodic sales at the Lewes Auction Rooms are held Thursdays approximately every 6 weeks, and are catalogued. The firm also conducts weekly sales of less valuable "household furniture and effects" every Monday at approximately 12:30 P.M. at the Lewes Market.

The catalogued sales are announced in the regional press and in specialty trade periodicals, such as *Art & Antiques Weekly*. Catalogues, illustrated though list-like, are available for each sale at 25p (plus postage). A subscription is £3 per annum; contact J. C. Dawson at the High Street address.

There is no buyer's premium. Absentee bids are executed. There are no guarantees of authenticity, and shipping and packing services are not available. The firm, except as required by law, will not take back goods that do not prove to be as catalogued. Viewing is usually the previous day, 9:30 A.M.–7:30 P.M., and the preceding Saturday, 9:30 A.M.–1 P.M. Accounts must be settled immediately. Buyers not known to the firm will have their checks accepted only with proper references.

The standard consignor's commission is 15 percent on the first £500 and 12.5 percent on the residue. The commission is negotiable, depending on the situation. For dealers, the commission is 12.5 percent throughout. Consigned goods are usually sold within 3–6 weeks; settlement is made after 8 days. Reserves are accepted; the buy-in charge is 5 percent unless the auctioneer has agreed to the reserve, in which case the charge is nil.

Consignors are not charged for catalogue illustrations, shipping and packing, warehousing, or insurance.

Appraisal service is available. There is no charge if goods are subsequently sold at auction by Burtenshaw Walker. Otherwise, the cost is 1 percent for insurance, and for probate the cost is 5.5 percent on the first £700, 2.5 percent on the residue.

The minimum value for consignments is £20 for small lots, £30 for furniture.

185. Capes, Dunn & Company
38 Charles Street   Tel. (061) 273 6060
Manchester M1 7DB

Sales are held fortnightly by this firm, with extra sales as necessary. A variety of goods is offered, ranging from FURNITURE to PORCELAIN, and including among other things MUSICAL INSTRUMENTS, PAINTINGS (18th c. British, 19th c. European), and SILVER.

Sales are announced in the *Guardian* and in the specialty press, such as *Antiques Trade Gazette*. Catalogues are available for individual sales, either through the post or at the firm's offices; subscriptions are £12 per annum.

There is no buyer's premium. Absentee bids are accepted. Packing and shipping services are not available. No guarantees of authenticity are offered. Goods that prove to be not as catalogued may be returned within a set time limit. Viewing is usually Monday, the day prior to the sale (10 A.M.–4 P.M.), and where possible, the morning of the sale. Accounts must be settled by Thursday noon following the sale.

The standard consignor's commission, according to Mr. M. W. Perry, FSVA, is "on any one lot 17.5 percent on the first £200 and 12.5 percent on the residue." The commission is negotiable, depending on the situation. Reserves are accepted. The buy-in cost is 2.5 percent of the reserve. Consigned goods are usually sold within 2 weeks. Settlement is normally made 7 days after the sale.

Appraisal services are available. Contact Mr. Perry.

The estimated annual turnover is £500,000.

186. Chapel & Chapel
453 London Road   Tel. (0702) 437 34
Westcliff-on-Sea, Essex SS0 9LG

This well-established firm, with offices elsewhere in the area, holds mixed-lot general-purpose auction sales every 2 weeks, which include such items as FURNITURE and SILVER. Occasional house and estate sales are also conducted.

Sales are advertised in the local press and in specialty periodicals, such as *Antiques Trade Gazette*. List-like catalogues for each sale are available "by application"; an annual subscription is £5.

There is no buyer's premium. Absentee bids are not accepted. Packing and shipping services are not available. No guarantees of authenticity are offered. The usual viewing procedure is "4 hours prior to sale," according to D. J. Burrage, FRICS. Settlement is within 48 hours of the end of the sale.

The standard consignor's commission is 15 percent. It is negotiable, depending on the situation. There is no minimum value necessary for acceptance of a lot as consignment. Consignors are not charged for insurance or warehousing. Consignors must pay packing and shipping to the saleroom and removal of goods if unsold. Goods are usually sold within 4 weeks. Reserves are accepted. The buy-in charge is 7.5 percent. Settlement is 1 week after the sale.

Appraisal service is available. Contact Mr. Burrage.

187. Chapman, Moore, & Mugford

9 High Street   Tel. (0747) 24 00
Shaftesbury, Dorset SP7 8JB

This firm of chartered surveyors also holds fortnightly auctions, which include FURNITURE and effects, and are advertised in the local press. List-like catalogues are available for each sale. There is no buyer's premium. Absentee bids are not accepted. Packing and shipping services are not available. No guarantees of authenticity are offered. Viewing is the day prior to the sale, 10 A.M.–4 P.M. Settlement is expected "immediately on the fall of the hammer."

The standard consignor's commission is 10 percent of the sale price. Consignors are not charged for insurance, but are charged for shipping and handling and storage. Consigned goods are usually sold within 2 weeks. Settlement is made "within 24 hours." Reserves are accepted; the buy-in charge is 5 percent of the reserve price.

188. Churchman's Auction Galleries

Station Road, off Church Street   Tel. (0903) 81 38 15
Steyning, West Sussex BN4 3LA

These galleries are part of the operations of the old-line firm of Churchman Burt, Auctioneers and Valuers, with branches elsewhere in the area. The administrative offices for the galleries are at 53 High Street, Steyning, a hop, skip, and jump from the galleries, where sales are held the first Saturday and the following Monday of each month. A typical sale will include CLOCKS AND WATCHES, FURNITURE, GLASS, JEWELRY, PAINTINGS, SCIENTIFIC INSTRUMENTS, and SILVER. The catalogue for the March 1980 sessions included that rarest of lots, "objects of virtue." About 1,000 lots are sold during the 2-day sessions. Occasional house and estate sales are held.

Sales are advertised in the local and national press, as well as in specialty publications, such as *Antiques Trade Gazette*. An announcement is sent out in advance; to be placed on the mailing list, contact Mrs. G. M. Boyle. Catalogues for each sale are available at the firm or the galleries or by post (70p; postage extra). Catalogues are available by subscription in the U.K. at £7 per annum.

There is a buyer's premium of 10 percent. Absentee bids are executed. The firm guarantees that it "will undertake to reimburse in full the purchase price, including the premium, of any lot that can be shown by the purchaser to be incorrectly described as to age and attribution (that is to say, place of manufacture, period, style, artist, etc.) provided that the article is returned to the auctioneers within 10 days of the date of the sale, in the same condition as at the time of the sale." Packing and shipping services are available, at the buyer's expense. Viewing is the Friday before the sale, 10 A.M.–8 P.M. All accounts must be settled day of sale, except for postal bids, which have 7 days.

The standard consignor's commission, according to saleroom manager Mark Poncia, is "10 percent, private vendors; trade, by arrangement." There is no charge for catalogue illustrations or for warehousing. Consignors are charged 20p insurance on each lot, and "a transport charge is deducted from proceeds and paid to the carrier." Consigned goods are usually sold within 1 month. Settlement is made within 10–14 days after the sale. Reserves are accepted. According to Mr. Poncia, "no unsold charge as such is made; however, a minimum commission of £1 per lot is charged whether the lot is sold or not."

Incidentally, local legend has it that the town of Steyning was founded in the 8th century after St. Cuthbert, having suffered a breakdown of his wheelbarrow during an attempt to wheel his invalid mother north, stopped here and decided to erect a church.

189. Coates Auctions

15 South Loading Road   Tel. (7017) 894 18
Gosport, Hampshire

This firm holds auction sales once a month of such items as FURNITURE, JEWELRY, POSTCARDS, and SILVER. Most auctions are held on premises, but occasional estate and house sales are held. List-like catalogues are available for 30p, either at the firm or through the mail (add postage).

Sales are announced in the local press and in specialty periodicals. There is no buyer's premium. Absentee bids will be executed. Packing and shipping services are not available. There are no guarantees of authenticity or the right beyond the requirements of the law to return goods that prove not as catalogued. Viewing is 2 days prior to sale, 9 A.M.–7 P.M. Accounts must be settled within 48 hours after the sale.

The consignor's commission, as R. J. Coates points out, is "negotiable between 10 and 20 percent." Minimum value for acceptance of a consignment is £10. Consignors are not charged for warehousing, insurance, or shipping and packing. Reserves are accepted; there is no buy-in charge. Consigned goods are sold within a month. Settlement is made within 8 days.

Coates Auctions does buy and sell on its own behalf.

190. Percy Collett & Son

111–113 Elm Grove, Southsea   Tel. (0705) 207 01
Portsmouth, Hampshire PO5 1JT

This old-line firm with branch offices elsewhere in the area has its main office in Southsea, an integral part of the historic city of Portsmouth and described as "an unashamedly noisy English seaside holiday resort with four miles of beaches." Maybe it's the noise, maybe it's the beaches, or maybe it's the firm's style, but Percy Collett & Son hold "mainly house sales"—of general household goods including FURNITURE—and quite successful ones. These are advertised in the local and regional press, and also via mailed announcements. To be put on the mailing list, write the firm. Catalogues are available for specific sales, but not by subscription.

There is no buyer's premium. Absentee bids are executed. Viewing is the day prior to the sale. Packing and shipping services are not available. Settlement is within 24 hours, unless previous arrangements have been made. The consignor's commission varies between 10 and 15 percent. Reserves are accepted. Consignor's costs vis-à-vis insurance, etc., "depend upon goods and value." Settlement is made 1 month after the sale. Consignor's costs for lots that do not sell are "out-of-pocket expenses."

191. Geoffrey Collings & Co.
13 High Street   Tel. (0406) 36 20 98
Long Sutton, Lincolnshire P12 9DB

This firm, which has offices elsewhere, holds sales approximately every 8 weeks. Among other places, these sales occur at the Victory Hall, in Gedney, a small village a few miles from Long Sutton. Occasional house and estate sales are also held. Among the items auctioned by Collings are ARMS AND ARMOR (esp. sporting guns), CLOCKS AND WATCHES, FURNITURE, PORCELAIN, and SILVER.

Sales are advertised in the regional press and in specialty periodicals; also via mailed announcements. If you wish to be placed on the mailing list, write to Geoffrey Collings & Co., 17 Blackfriars Street, King's Lynn, Norfolk. Catalogues are available singly but not by subscription. There is no buyer's premium. Absentee bids are executed. Packing and shipping services are available, at buyer's expense. No guarantees of authenticity are offered. Viewing is day prior to sale. Buyer must settle within 7 days after the sale.

The consignor's commission is 15 percent. Consignments are not accepted from dealers or institutions. Consignors are charged for catalogue illustrations (£2 per illustration), and for cost of transportation to get consignment to saleroom. Consignors are not charged insurance or warehousing. Minimum value for a consignment is £10. Consigned goods, according to David D. Wilson, ARICS, are sold within "a maximum of 6 months." Settlement is "variable, but maximum of 4 weeks."

Reserves are accepted. The buy-in charge is 5 percent of the reserve.

192. Jose Collins & Harris
29 Coinagehall Street   Tel. (03265) 33 55
Helston, Cornwall

Every other month or so, this firm holds specialist sales, including GLASS, JEWELRY, and SILVER; in between, more general sales are held. Both kinds of sales include that staple of U.K. auction houses, FURNITURE. Occasional house and estate sales are also held.

Jose Collins & Harris is an old-line firm (est. 1869) which advertises its sales locally and in specialty publications, such as *Antiques Trade Gazette*. Catalogues are available for some sales (20p–30p at the office or in the saleroom; add postage of 15p for mail delivery). There is a buyer's premium of 5 percent. Absentee bids are executed. Packing and shipping services are offered. At most sales, the buyer has 1 week to settle accounts, but occasionally it is "cash and clearance at close of sale," depending on the venue. Viewing is at least the morning of the sale.

The consignor's commission is negotiable. Consignments are not accepted from dealers or institutions. Consignors are charged insurance. Consignments are usually sold within 1–2 months. Settlement is made 10 days after the sale. Reserves are accepted.

Appraisal service is available. For details and cost, contact the firm.

193. George Comins & Son
3 Chequer Lane   Tel. (0353) 22 65
Ely, Cambridgeshire CB7 4NT

This firm of auctioneers and valuers holds sales approximately 5 times a year. These sales, which are not held on the premises, are usually of mixed lots and include FURNITURE and SILVER. Occasional house and estate sales are conducted. Sales are advertised in the local press and in specialty periodicals, such as *Art & Antiques Weekly*. Postcard announcements are sent out prior to each sale. To be placed on the mailing list, just write to the firm. Catalogues are available only at time of viewing and cannot be obtained by subscription.

There is no buyer's premium. Absentee bids are executed. No guarantees of authenticity are offered. There are no packing and shipping services. Viewing is 5–7 P.M. on the day preceding sale "and from 9 A.M. onward on sale day and throughout sale." Buyer must settle accounts immediately, unless other arrangements have been made.

The standard consignor's commission is 15 percent. It is negotiable. There is no minimum value for acceptance of a consignment. Consignors are not charged for warehousing and insurance; they are charged "time spent packing and transport from consignor to store or saleroom." Goods will be sold within 2–3 months. Settlement is made "about 10 days" after sale. Reserves are accepted; buy-in charge is 5 percent.

Appraisal service is available; there is no cost if the goods are sold by the firm. Contact Mr. E. S. Legge.

194. S. W. Cottee & Son
The Market, East Street   Tel. (092 95) 28 26
Wareham, Dorset BH20 4AF

This firm holds biweekly FURNITURE auctions and monthly COIN sales, advertised in local newspapers. Announcements of sale dates are sent out at the beginning of the year; to be put on the mailing list, write to Cottee.

Catalogues are available singly for each sale. Subscriptions are available only for the coin catalogues, which are a bit more detailed than the furniture listings, since all coins are graded. Viewing is the day prior to the sale, 2–5 P.M., 6–8 P.M.

There is no buyer's premium. Absentee bids are executed for coin sales only. No guarantees of authenticity are offered. Packing and shipping services are not available. Coins that prove to be not as catalogued may be returned. Buyer must "generally" settle on day of sale.

The consignor's commission, usually 12.5 percent, is negotiable, depending on the situation. Consignors are not charged for shipping and packing, insurance, or warehousing. Consigned goods are generally sold within 2–3 weeks. Settlement is made 10 days after sale. Reserves are accepted. The buy-in charge is "variable." S. W. Cottee & Son will not accept consignments from dealers.

Croydon Auction Rooms: see Rosan & Co. (Croydon, Surrey)

195. Dacre, Son & Hartley

1–5 The Grove   Tel. (0943) 60 06 55
Ilkley, West Yorkshire LS29 9HS

This firm of "Chartered Valuation Surveyors and Estate Agents, Auctioneers and Land Agents" has offices throughout the Yorkshire region. At Ilkley, on the edge of the moors, in a town that was once an inland resort, Dacre, Son & Hartley holds mixed-lot general-purpose auction sales every other Wednesday. Sales include FURNITURE and PAINTINGS. Occasional house and estate sales are presented.

These sales are advertised in the regional press, such as the Yorkshire *Post,* and in specialty periodicals, such as *Antiques Trade Gazette.* Announcements of forthcoming sales are available, as are catalogues, singly or by subscription (£3 per annum); write to Andrew D. Hartley at the Ilkley office.

There is no buyer's premium. Packing and shipping services are not available. Absentee bids are executed; "postal bids received no later than 24 hours prior to auction can be accepted." Guarantees of authenticity are not offered, but goods "may be returned within 7 days of sale, if not as catalogued." There is a minimum of 2 days viewing prior to sale, "plus some time on the sale day itself." Other arrangements can be made. Buyer must settle accounts within 48 hours.

Consignments are not accepted from dealers. The standard consignor's commission is 15 percent on items sold for £1,000 or less, 10 percent on items sold over £1,000. Commissions are negotiable, depending on the situation. Consignors are not charged insurance or warehousing. Cost of transporting consignments to and from the saleroom is "charged at cost." Consigned goods are usually sold within 1–2 months. Settlement is made within 7 days after sale. Reserves are accepted. There is no buy-in charge.

Appraisal service is available. The cost is free if items are later sold at auction through Dacre, Son & Hartley. Contact Andrew D. Hartley, FRICS, or Sally Watson.

196. Dee & Atkinson

The Exchange   Tel. (0377) 431 51
Driffield, North Humberside YO25 7LB

This firm, which has additional offices in the area, holds monthly auctions at the Exchange saleroom. Some of these are 2-day affairs. Merchandise for sale includes FURNITURE, GLASS, JEWELRY, PORCELAIN, and SILVER. Occasional house and estate sales are held.

Sales are advertised in the local press and in specialty periodicals, such as *Antiques Trade Gazette*. Announcements are sent out in advance of sales; write to be placed on the mailing list. Catalogues are available singly for each sale (70p, including postage) and by subscription (£5 per annum).

There is no buyer's premium. Absentee bids are executed. Viewing is 2 days prior to the sale, 11 A.M.–4 P.M. Packing and shipping services are available, at the buyer's expense. No guarantees of authenticity are offered, but goods that prove to be not as described in the catalogue may be returned and the sale rescinded. Settlement is "before removal."

The standard consignor's commission varies between 10 and 15 percent. There are separate rates for dealers. Consignors are not charged for shipping, packing, insurance, or warehousing. Consigned goods are sold within 1 month. Settlement is 10 days after the sale. Reserves are accepted. The buy-in charge can go up to 5 percent. The minimum value for a consignment is £20.

Devon and Exeter Auction Galleries: see Whitten and Laing (Exeter, Devon)

197. Diamond, Mills & Co.

117 Hamilton Road   Tel. (039 42) 22 81 (2 lines)
Felixstowe, Suffolk IP11 7BL

This veteran firm (est. 1906) holds 3 sales weekly, in Orwell Hall on Orwell Road. These are mixed-lot sales that include FURNITURE. Occasionally a house or an estate sale is held.

The sales are advertised in the local press. Listings for each sale are available for 15p (plus postage).

There is no buyer's premium. Absentee bids are executed. Neither guarantees of authenticity nor packing and shipping services are available. Goods that prove to be not as described may be returned within the time limit allowed by law. Viewing is the day before the sale, 10 A.M.–4 P.M. Accounts must be settled the same day.

The standard consignor's commission is 15 percent, and it is negotiable. Consignments from dealers are "not normally" accepted. Consignors are not charged insurance, but are charged shipping and packing, as well as warehousing. Consigned goods are sold within 3–6 weeks. Settlement is 1 week after the sale.

Mr. G. W. Mills, FSVA, reports that credit cards are accepted.

198. Robert Dove & Partners
Dover House, Wolsey Street   Tel. (0473) 551 37 (6 lines)
Ipswich, Suffolk IP1 1UD

Self-advertised as "East Anglia's Auction Centre," Robert Dove & Partners holds monthly sales. These sales are mixed lots that can include, as did one recently, ARMS AND ARMOR, CLOCKS AND WATCHES, DRAWINGS, FURNITURE, GLASS, PAINTINGS, PEWTER, PORCELAIN, and SILVER (or as it was put in one advertisement, "200 interesting table lots of high quality").

List-like illustrated catalogues are available for each sale, at the saleroom or via the mail (50p, plus postage). Catalogues are also available by subscription (£6 per annum). Sales are advertised regularly in the local press, in the national press (*Daily Telegraph*), and in specialty periodicals.

There is no buyer's premium. Absentee bids are executed. Packing and shipping services are available, at the buyer's expense. The usual viewing procedure is the day preceding and the morning of the sale. Goods that do not prove to be as catalogued may be returned within 14 days. The firm reports that "everything is arranged for the convenience of purchase." Settlement is within 24 hours of sale.

The consignor's commission varies between 12.5 and 15 percent. There is a separate structure for dealers. Consignors are not charged for catalogue illustrations, for insurance, or for warehousing. They are charged for packing and shipping of consigned property to saleroom. Consigned goods are sold "quickly" and settlement is made 7 days after the sale. Reserves are accepted; the buy-in charge is "negotiable."

Appraisal service is available. Contact the firm.

199. Dreweatt, Watson & Barton
22 Market Place   Tel. (0635) 460 00
Newbury, Berkshire RG14 5AZ   Telex: 848580

This firm is not as old as the town of Newbury—the remains of the house where "Jack of Newbury" baptized John Smallwood and entertained Henry VII still stand—but Dreweatt, Watson & Barton can trace its establishment back to 1759. This firm of chartered surveyors and estate agents also holds auctions, occasionally at private houses and on a regular basis at the saleroom, off Northcroft Lane in Newbury. Sales are also held in the Donnington priory, about a mile from the firm's Newbury offices.

The firm holds weekly sales of items of lesser value and in addition offers specialized sales of BOOKS, JEWELRY, PAINTINGS, and SILVER. The staple of the weekly sales is FURNITURE. Other items sold include CLOCKS AND WATCHES and PORCELAIN. Catalogues are available singly for each sale and cost approximately 60p (plus postage for mail orders). Catalogue subscriptions are also available on the following basis: Antique Sales and Private House Sales, £4.50 per annum; Ordinary Collective Furniture Sales, £3.40 per annum; Special Sales of Silver and Jewelry, £2 per annum; Special Sales of Pictures and Books, £2 per annum. Sales are also announced regularly in the local press and in specialty periodicals, such as *Antiques Trade Gazette*. There is no buyer's premium. Absentee bids are not executed. Packing and shipping services are not available. No guarantees of authenticity are offered, but as partner R. W. Barton points out, "if a lot is returned within a reasonable period and is shown not to be as catalogued, the purchase price will be refunded in full." Viewing is usually 2 days prior to the sale, 9:30 A.M.–3:30 P.M., and special arrangements can be made. Buyer must settle accounts within 1 week of the sale. Bidders unknown to the firm may be asked to put a deposit of 50 percent on each lot bought, prior to final payment.

The consignor's commission is negotiable, depending on the situation, but the standard rates are: individual lots realizing less than £100, 15 percent; individual lots realizing between £100 and £500, 12.5 percent; individual lots realizing more than £500, 10 percent. Consignors do not pay for catalogue illustrations or for warehousing, but do pay for insurance (35p per £100 realized) and are responsible for transport to the salerooms. Consigned goods are usually sold within 4–5 weeks. Settlement is 10 days after the sale. Reserves are accepted. There is no buy-in charge as such, but consignor must pay for transportation of unsold property from the saleroom.

Dreweatt, Watson & Barton is a member of the Society of Fine Art Auctioneers.

200. Hy. Duke & Son
40 South Street   Tel. (0305) 44 26
Dorchester, Dorset DT1 1DG

This firm of "Chartered Surveyors, Chartered Auctioneers and Estate Agents, Valuers" has 3 other branches. The Dorchester office, in addition to its other functions, conducts auctions approximately every 6 weeks at Hy. Duke & Son's salerooms on Weymouth Avenue—tel. (0305) 50 80—across the street from the British Rail South Station and the Eldridge Pope & Co. Brewery (producers of one of the world's strongest beers, which to reach full strength should be kept on the shelf for a few years).

The items sold at auction by Hy. Duke & Son include CHINESE WORKS OF ART, CLOCKS AND WATCHES, DOLLS, DRAWINGS, ENGRAVINGS, ETCHINGS, JAPANESE WORKS OF ART, JEWELRY, MAPS, PAINTINGS, PEWTER, PORCELAIN, PRINTS, RUGS, SILVER, and as the firm reports, "our general sales always include FURNITURE." House and estate sales are held occasionally.

Sales are advertised in the local and regional press, as well as in specialty periodicals. Catalogues are available singly (50p) and by subscription (£5.50 per annum). Write Mrs. G. Brooks or Mr. R. H. Stent.

Since December 1978, there has been a buyer's premium of 10 percent. Absentee bids are executed. Phone bids must be reconfirmed by a letter received before the sale. No guarantees of authenticity are offered, but if a work proves to be not as described and is returned within 14 days of the sale, the purchase price will be refunded. Viewing is 2 days prior to the sale, 9:30 A.M.–5 P.M. Settlement must be made within 7 days. Sales—comprising about 900–1,000 lots—often are morning and afternoon sessions over 2 days.

The standard consignor's commission is 10 percent, but it is negotiable. For dealers who are known to the firm the commission is 6.5 percent; for other dealers it is 8 percent. Minimum value for a consignment is £20. Consignors are charged for catalogue illustrations (e.g., £8 per full page). Consignors are charged for insurance (0.5 percent of the sale price). Consignors are charged for packing and shipping. Warehousing costs vary "with time and person." Consigned goods are usually sold within 6 weeks. Settlement is after 2 weeks. Reserves are accepted. The buy-in charge is 5 percent unless the firm has agreed to the reserve as not being too high.

Appraisal service is available. The cost is refunded if items are subsequently sold at auction by Hy. Duke & Son.

The firm is a member of the Society of Fine Art Auctioneers and various partners are Fellows of the Royal Institution of Chartered Surveyors.

201. Earl & Lawrence

55 Northgate   Tel. (0529) 30 29 46
Sleaford, Lincolnshire NG34 7AB

This branch, one of several in the region, holds auction sales on its premises every 2 weeks, and "where necessary on premises of owner." These mostly mixed-lot general-purpose auctions include FURNITURE, PAINTINGS, and RUGS.

Sales are advertised regularly in the local press and in specialty periodicals. There is a "computer list" for catalogues. Ask to be put on it; write to one of the partners, J. J. C. Daykin, FRICS.

There is a buyer's premium of 5 percent. Absentee bids are executed. Packing and shipping services are not available. Guarantees of authenticity are not offered, but goods that prove to be not as described may be returned and the sale rescinded. Usual viewing procedure is day prior to sale or "as advertised." Settlement is day of sale.

The standard consignor's commission is 15 percent; it is negotiable; dealers are offered a lower rate. There is no minimum value for acceptance of a consignment. Consignors must pay packing and shipping charges, but not warehousing or insurance. Consigned goods are sold within 1 month "maximum." Settlement is within 2–3 weeks after the sale. Reserves are accepted. The buy-in charge is 5 percent of the reserve price. Appraisal service is available. If items are consigned to sale, the service is free.

202. Eddisons

4–6 High Street   Tel. (0484) 331 51
Huddersfield, West Yorkshire HD1 2LS

An old-line firm (est. 1844) of chartered surveyors with a wide practice and offices elsewhere in the region, Eddisons holds general-purpose mixed-lot auction sales every 3–4 weeks. The quality of these sales varies, and periodically the firm conducts a "special catalogue sale," which includes items such as FURNITURE, JEWELRY, PAINTINGS, and SILVER of better quality. Occasional house and estate sales are also offered.

Announcements of forthcoming sales are available; contact R. Butterworth to be placed on the mailing list. Sales are regularly advertised in what the firm describes as "the appropriate newspapers and magazines," including *Antiques Trade Gazette.* Catalogues are available singly for most sales (50p, plus postage), but not by subscription.

There is no buyer's premium. Absentee bids are executed. Packing and shipping services are not available from the firm. No guarantees of authenticity are offered. The usual viewing procedure is 1 day before the sale, 10 A.M.–4 P.M. Settlement is expected immediately.

The consignor's commission varies between 7.5 and 20 percent. It is negotiable. There is a separate rate structure for dealers and institutions: "depends on situation." Consignors are not charged for insurance or for warehousing, but must pay transport costs to the saleroom if they do not remove goods themselves. Consigned goods are sold in the next sale. Settlement is 14 days after the sale. Reserves are accepted.

Appraisal service is available. Contact the firm.

203. Edwards, Bigwood, & Bewlay

The Old School   Tel. (0789) 694 15
Tiddington
Stratford-upon-Avon, Warwickshire CV37 7AW

On Fridays, approximately 30 times a year, the firm holds auction sales in this small town a few miles from Stratford-upon-Avon. Like so many of its peers, the firm, in effect, serves as a dispose-all for vendors and a bargain mart for purchasers, offering FURNITURE, GLASS, PORCELAIN, and the like. Occasional house and estate sales are also held.

These sales are advertised in the local press and in specialty publications. List-like catalogues are available for each sale, and can be obtained by subscription (£15–£20 per annum).

There is no buyer's premium. Absentee bids are executed. Packing and shipping services are available. Viewing is 2–3 days before the sale. Buyer must settle accounts "immediately."

The consignor's commission is negotiable, depending upon the situation. Consignors are charged for insurance, shipping and packing, and warehousing. Consigned goods are usually sold within 2 months. Settlement is made 7 days after the sale. Reserves are accepted. No minimum value is necessary for a consignment.

204. Peter J. Eley

100 High Street   Tel. (039 55) 25 52
Sidmouth, Devon EX10 8AJ

Because of its Regency architecture, Sidmouth has been called "the Brighton of the southwest of England." Here Peter J. Eley holds monthly auctions. A recent one was described as offering such mixed-lot general-purpose goods as "antique FURNITURE and effects, SILVER, and collector's items." Such mixed-lot general-purpose goods comprise the bulk of the auctions conducted by Eley. These sales take place at the East Street Auction Rooms, not far from Eley's office and a sizable car park. Occasional house and estate sales are also held.

Sales are announced regularly in the local press and in specialty periodicals. A catalogue, really a listing, is available for the price of a stamped, self-addressed envelope sent to Stephen Eley at the above address.

There is no buyer's premium. Absentee bids are not accepted. Packing and shipping services are available, at the buyer's expense. Guarantees of authenticity are not offered. Viewing is the day prior to the sale. Buyers must settle accounts the day of the sale.

The standard consignor's commission is 15 percent and is not negotiable. Consignments are not accepted from dealers. There is no charge to consignors for insurance or warehousing. But consignors must pay "normal carrier's charges" for transportation of consigned goods to Eley. Reserves are accepted. Consigned goods are sold within 4 weeks. Settlement is made within 1 week.

205. Ekins, Dilley & Handley

Centenary House, Castle Moat Road   Tel. (0480) 561 71
Huntingdon, Cambridgeshire PE18 6PQ

The Huntingdon office is but one of several for this firm, which holds sales every other Tuesday at its auction rooms in nearby (about 7 miles away) St. Ives. These sales are mainly mixed-lot auctions, which include a mighty array of differing items, such as FURNITURE, GLASS, PAINTINGS, RUGS, and SILVER, as well as such objects as two Aladdin oil stoves and a Futura perambulator. About 500–600 lots are sold at these sales, which are all-day affairs with a short break for lunch.

Sales are advertised in local and national newspapers, as well as in specialty periodicals. Announcements of forthcoming sales are available; to be placed on the mailing list, write the firm. Catalogues for each sale are available singly (10p) either at the firm's offices or through the mail the Friday before the sale. Subscription to all catalogues is £10 per annum; contact J. H. Johnson.

There is no buyer's premium. Absentee bids are executed. Guarantees of authenticity are not offered. Packing and shipping services are not offered. The conditions of sale in the catalogue note that "all statements in the catalogue . . . are statements of opinion, and are not to be relied on as statements or representations of fact and intending purchasers must satisfy themselves by inspection or otherwise as to all matters related to the lot." Viewing is usually Saturday morning and all day Monday. Buyers must settle accounts right after the sale.

The consignor's commission is 15 percent; for some dealers it is 12–12.5 percent. Consignors are not charged for catalogue illustrations, insurance, packing and shipping, or warehousing. Consigned goods are sold within 14–28 days. Settlement is made with the consignor the day after the sale. Reserves are accepted. There is no minimum value for acceptance of a consignment for sale.

206. Elliott & Green
40 High Street   Tel. (0590) 772 22
Lymington, Hampshire SO4 9ZE

Lymington is a departure point for ferries to the Isle of Wight, a yachting center, and the location of the Emsworth Road auction salerooms of the firm of Elliott & Green, which has various offices in the area. Auctioneers, estate agents, surveyors, and valuers, Elliott & Green hold two kinds of sales. Those held every other Thursday are of less valuable properties and include everything from a Flymo Professional Rotary Mower to a Victorian pink opaque glass vase some 12 inches high. More valuable properties are sold quarterly and include FURNITURE, GLASS, and the usual.

Catalogues in the form of complete lists are provided. The quarterly catalogues include illustrations. Occasional house and estate sales are also held. Sales are announced in the local press. Catalogues are available singly or by subscription (£8.50 per annum, including postage in the U.K.).

There is no buyer's premium. Absentee bids are executed. Packing and shipping services are not available. No guarantees of authenticity are offered. Viewing is the day preceding the sale, noon–4:30 P.M., and the morning of the sale from 9 until the sale commences (usually at 11).

The consignor's commission is as follows: for dealers and institutions, 12.5 percent; for others, 15 percent on all lots sold for less than £100; 12.5 percent on lots sold for £100 or more. Reserves are accepted. The buy-in charge is 5 percent. Consignors are not charged for catalogue illustrations, warehousing, or insurance. Consignors must pay for packing and shipping. Goods consigned to biweekly sales are sold within 2–4 weeks; goods consigned to quarterly sales are sold within 3 months. Settlement is usually 14 days after the sale.

Appraisal service is available. Contact M. E. D. Peckham, FSVA.

E. Tegid Evans & Co.
207. Mrwog Street   Tel. (08242) 22 76
Ruthin, Clwyd LL15 1LB

208. Clwyd Street
Ruthin, Clwyd LL15 1HN

This firm of auctioneers, valuers, and estate agents holds sales fortnightly on Thursday, either in its Mrwog Street saleroom, known as the Furniture Mart Auction Galleries, or in the Star Salerooms, not too far away. These are mostly mixed-lot general-purpose sales, uncatalogued, and as might be expected, they include FURNITURE. Occasional house and estate sales are also held.

Sales are advertised in the local and regional press. There is no buyer's premium. Absentee bids are not accepted. Packing and shipping services are not available from the firm. No guarantees of authenticity are offered. Viewing is the day preceding and the morning of the sale. Buyer must settle accounts within 3 days.

The standard consignor's commission is 20 percent of the hammer price.

Consignors are not charged for catalogue illustrations, insurance, or warehousing. Nor are they charged for packing and shipping of consigned property. The consignor's commission is negotiable, and there is a different rate structure for the trade and for institutions. Consigned goods are sold within 1 month. Settlement is made 10 days after the sale.

209. Morgan Evans & Co. Ltd.
27 Church Street   Tel. (0248) 72 33 03 (3 lines)
Llangefeni, Gwynedd LL77 7DU

Evans & Co., "Auctioneers, Valuers, Land and Estate Agents," with offices elsewhere on the isle of Anglesey, hold sales monthly. These are basically mixed-lot general-purpose sales which include FURNITURE and SILVER. Occasional house and estate sales are also held.

The sales are announced in the local and regional press. List-like catalogues are available (17p, plus postage) for single sales but not by subscription. There is no buyer's premium. Absentee bids are executed. Packing and shipping services are not available from the firm. No guarantees of authenticity are offered. The usual viewing procedure is the evening before and the morning of the sale. Buyers must settle accounts on the day of the sale. Credit is available "for well-known and regular buyers."

The standard consignor's commission is 17.5 percent. The commission is negotiable, depending upon the situation. There is a separate rate structure for dealers. Consignors are not charged for catalogue illustrations, insurance, or storage prior to the sale. The firm reports that after the sale, "property must be removed or will be burned in 2 days, condition of acceptance." Settlement is made 3 days after the sale.

210. Frank H. Fellows & Son
Bedford House, 88 Hagley Road   Tel. (021) 454 1261/1219
Edgbaston, Birmingham B16 8LU

Fellows & Son holds sales, at least once a month and often more frequently, of COINS, FURNITURE, JEWELRY, and SILVER, among other items. The sales are advertised in the local press and in specialty periodicals, such as *Antiques Trade Gazette*. A yearly sales schedule is available free of charge; write to Miss Milnes at the above address. Catalogues can be obtained for each sale (£1), either at the house or through the post (include postage); an annual subscription costs approximately £12 plus postage.

There is no buyer's premium. Absentee bids are executed. No guarantees of authenticity are offered. Packing and shipping services are not available. Goods that prove to be not as catalogued may be returned. Settlement must be made within 7 days after the sale. Viewing is as follows: jewelry and silver, 3 days prior to the sale, 10 A.M.–4 P.M.; furniture, 3 days prior to the sale, 10 A.M.–8 P.M.

The standard consignor's commission is 15 percent, private, and 12.5 percent, trade. The commissions are negotiable, depending on the situation. Consignors are not charged shipping and packing, insurance, or warehousing. Consigned goods are sold as follows: jewelry and silver, maximum 1 month; furniture, maximum 2 months. Settlement is made as follows: jewelry and silver, 24 hours after the sale; furniture, 7 days after the sale.

211. Forrest & Co.

79–85 Cobbold Road   Tel. (01) 534-2931
Leytonstone, London E11 3NS

Forrest holds 2 kinds of sales: general ones, advertised only in the local press, and "antiques & objets d'art," which are also advertised in national organs, such as the *Daily Telegraph*.

Sales are held fortnightly. Most auctions take place on the premises, but occasionally there is a house or an estate sale. A typical "antiques" sale will include FURNITURE, JEWELRY, PAINTINGS, and SILVER, as well as "miscellaneous," which in one instance meant "Garden Ornaments, Inn Signs, Brass Telescopes, etc."

List-like catalogues are available singly, either at the firm or through the post, and also by subscription (general sales: £4.50 per annum; antiques sales: £1.50 per annum). Viewing is the day prior to the sale.

There is no buyer's premium. Absentee bids are not executed. Packing and shipping services are not available. The catalogue asserts that "as public view is given to all lots previous to sale, no allowance under any circumstances will be made for any faults, defects, deficiencies, or otherwise." Buyers must settle accounts by the end of the day after the sale. Unknown bidders must put down a 25 percent deposit on each bid won.

The standard consignor's commission, which Mr. Forrest says is not negotiable, is 15 percent. Consignors pay for insurance only in special cases. They do not pay for warehousing. Reserves are accepted. The buy-in charge is 5 percent. Consigned goods are sold within 2–6 weeks. Settlement is 2 weeks after the sale. Minimum value for a consignment is £15.

212. Fox & Sons

5–7 Salisbury Street   Tel. (0425) 521 21
Fordingbridge, Hampshire SP6 1AD

The firm of Fox & Sons—Chartered Surveyors, Auctioneers, Estate Agents, Valuers—was established in 1765. In the two centuries since then, the firm has evolved a policy of holding monthly sales of mixed lots, including FURNITURE and SILVER, at the Auction Mart, Roundhill, in Fordingbridge, which is near Whitsbury. Sales are advertised in the local press, such as the Fordingbridge *Journal*. Catalogues are available singly upon application to the Auctioneer's Clerk, and by subscription for £3 per annum.

There is no buyer's premium. Absentee bids are executed. No guarantees of authenticity are offered. Packing and shipping services are not available.

Viewing is 9 A.M.–5 P.M. the day before the sale. Settlement is expected immediately.

Michael Carpenter, FRICS, reports that consignments are not accepted from dealers. The standard consignor's commission rate is 15 percent, explained as follows: "7.5 percent sale commission plus 7.5 percent contribution to advertising, cataloguing, porterage, etc." The commission is negotiable, depending on the situation. Consignors are charged for insurance "in certain circumstances." Mr. Carpenter also reports that "we pass on shipper's charges, storage, and warehousing charges. We do not charge . . . ourselves." Consigned goods are sold within 1 month. Settlement is 14 days after the sale. Reserves are accepted. There is no buy-in charge, provided that the property is "removed quickly."

Appraisal service is available: "Cost of appraisal services is difficult to generalize, but 0.5–2.5 percent of value."

213. John Francis, Thomas Jones & Sons
Queen Street   Tel. (0267) 331 11
Carmarthen, Dyfed SA31 1JT

This town is among the oldest in South Wales, its roots reaching back to Roman times. The firm, while well established, is not quite that old, having been organized only in the 1870s. It has various offices in the region and an extensive practice in property management, etc., in addition to holding mixed-lot general-purpose sales of such items as FURNITURE, PEWTER, and TOYS. Annually, a special sale is devoted to BOOKS. "Antique sales" are held approximately once a month on Tuesdays; "white elephant sales" of less valuable but similar items are held somewhat less frequently, also on Tuesdays. Sales take place in the King Street salerooms. Occasional house and estate sales are also conducted.

These sales are advertised in all Welsh papers, some of the Anglophone local and regional press, occasionally in the national dailies, and in specialty publications, such as *Antiques Trade Gazette*. Illustrated list-like catalogues are available singly for each sale (60p, plus postage) and by subscription (£6 per annum, including postage).

There is no buyer's premium. Absentee bids are executed. Packing and shipping services are available, at the buyer's expense. No guarantees of authenticity are offered, but the firm does give buyers the opportunity to return goods that prove to be not as catalogued if, as partner R. G. Francis points out, "obvious mistakes have been made, such as misprints, etc." Viewing is usually the day prior to the sale, 3–6 P.M., and the morning of the sale, 9:30–10:15. All lots "shall be paid for by the end of the second working day following the sale."

The standard consignor's commission is 12 percent in the antique sales, 17 percent in the white elephant sales. If the total consignment sells for £20,000 or more, the commission is 10 percent. There is a minimum value of £5 for a consignment. Consignors are not charged for catalogue illustrations, insurance, or warehousing. If consignors have the firm remove goods to the saleroom, carriage and packing is charged. Reserves are accepted. The buy-in charge is £1 per £100. Consigned goods are usually sold within 1 month. Settlement is 10 days after the sale.

Appraisal service is available. The rates vary, but if the appraisal is made for consignment, there is no charge.

John Francis, Thomas Jones & Sons is a member of the Society of Fine Art Auctioneers.

214. Freckeltons

1 Leicester Road   Tel. (0509) 21 45 64
Loughborough, Leicestershire LE11 3EU

Once a month, on Tuesdays, Freckeltons holds mixed-lot general-purpose sales, featuring such goods as CLOCKS AND WATCHES, COINS, FURNITURE ("all periods of English Furniture"), PORCELAIN, and SILVER. Most auctions are held on the premises. There is an occasional house or estate sale.

Sales are advertised in the local press, such as the Loughborough *Echo* and the Leicester *Mercury*. Announcements of sales are sent out; to be placed on the mailing list free of charge, write to Mr. M. Freckelton.

Catalogues (which are in effect listings) are available singly for each sale and by subscription. There is no buyer's premium. Absentee bids are executed. Packing and shipping services ("through a recognized firm") are available, at buyer's expense. No guarantees of authenticity are offered. Viewing is the Saturday and Monday prior to sale (9:30 A.M.–1 P.M., 2–5 P.M.). Buyers must settle accounts "at the end of the sale unless by prior arrangement."

The standard consignor's commission is 15 percent. Consignors are charged packing and shipping as well as warehousing, and insurance "if applicable." Consigned goods are sold within 6–8 weeks. Settlement is made 3 days after the sale. Reserves are not accepted.

Appraisal service is available. Contact Mr. S. J. Freckelton.

Furniture Mart Auction Galleries: see E. Tegid Evans & Co. (Ruthin, Clwyd)

215. Geering & Colyer

Highgate   Tel. (058 05) 31 81
Hawkhurst, Kent TN18 4AD

This firm has offices scattered through Kent, Sussex, and Surrey, but its auction operations in the fine arts are directed from Hawkhurst, and sales are held in the still sylvan surroundings of the Spa Hotel, Royal Tunbridge Wells, about a dozen miles away as the crow flies or the hawk swoops. Sales are held every 2 months and are advertised in the national press (*Daily Telegraph*), the local press, specialty periodicals, such as *Antiques Trade Gazette,* and "other antiques journals when appropriate." Occasional house and estate sales are held.

Catalogues for each sale are available at the firm's offices, the saleroom, and by application through the mail. Catalogue subscriptions are £5 per annum for the U.K., including postage, £10 per annum for elsewhere in the world, including airmail postage. Sales as in most English auction operations run the gamut and include FURNITURE and SILVER.

There is no buyer's premium. Absentee bids are executed. Packing and shipping services are available, at the buyer's expense. No guarantees of authenticity are usually offered, but goods that prove to be not as catalogued may be returned. Viewing is usually the day prior to the sale, 11 A.M.–5 P.M. Buyers must settle within 2 days, unless special arrangements have been made.

The standard consignor's commission is 15 percent, but it is negotiable, depending on the situation. Consignors are not charged for catalogue illustrations or insurance, but according to Mr. M. F. P. Carey, warehousing is "subject to negotiation." Packing and shipping charges are billed direct by the removal firm dealing with the consignor. Consigned goods are sold within 3 months. Settlement is within 2 weeks after the sale, "subject to our being paid by the purchasers." Reserves are accepted; the buy-in charge is subject to negotiation.

216. Stanley Gibbons Auctions Ltd.

Drury House, Russell Street
London WC2B 5HD

Tel. (01) 836-8444
Telex: 28883
Cable: PHILATORS

Gibbons is a well-known dealer in stamps and philatelic accessories; the company began operations in the middle of the last century and has achieved renown for its catalogues and its sales. In the 1950s and 1960s, first in conjunction with another company and then on its own, Gibbons began to hold stamp auctions. In the 1970s, especially as the firm diversified and began selling such nonphilatelic items as bond and stock certificates and banknotes, it expanded its range of auction sales. During the 1970s, Gibbons was taken over by Letraset, which had various plans for its new acquisition. Some of these, such as the book department, proved abortive. Yet Gibbons remains a giant in its field, and the auction division continues to hold interesting sales of ANTIQUE MAPS, AUTOGRAPHS, BOND AND STOCK CERTIFICATES, PAPER MONEY, PLAYING CARDS, POSTAL HISTORY DOCUMENTS, PRINTS, and of course, STAMPS.

Sales are held with some regularity and are advertised in the local press and in specialty publications. Catalogues with reasonable estimates are available for each sale, either at the firm's offices (£1) or through the mail (add postage). Subscription prices vary with each set of catalogues; the catalogues for the quarterly collectibles sales cost £3 per annum in the U.K., £4 outside. The list of prices realized costs 20p in the U.K., 40p (including airmail postage) elsewhere.

Floor bidders obtain a numbered bidding card when registering for the sale. Absentee bids must be accompanied by a 20 percent deposit unless the bidder is known to Gibbons. There is a buyer's premium of 10 percent on the ham-

mer price. Viewing is always at least the day before the sale (10 A.M.–4 P.M.)
and the morning of the sale (10 A.M.–noon). Settlement is as follows: "each lot
shall be paid for in full . . . by a purchaser in the United Kingdom within 7
days from the date of the sale and by a purchaser overseas within 14 days of
the sale." Gibbons gives guarantees of genuineness for lots comprising less
than 4 items, as well as lots of larger size: material that proves to be not as
described may be returned within 30 days. The ability to return books, atlases,
maps, prints, and "like material" is much more circumscribed, to the point
that bunches of books, "unnamed in lots, may not be returned for any reason."

The consignor's commission varies and is negotiable, depending upon the
situation. Reserves are accepted. Settlement is usually made 1 month from the
date of the sale. Consignors do not pay for catalogue illustrations, but are
responsible for getting material to the saleroom.

217. Glendining & Co.

    7 Blenheim Street, New Bond Street   Tel. (01) 493-2445
    London W1Y 9LD

The specialties of this firm are the sale and valuation of COINS and MEDALS.
About 25 auctions are conducted each year, usually on Wednesdays, but generally not during January or August. The annual turnover is in excess of £1
million.

Glendining & Co., a veteran company of coin auctioneers and valuers, became part of the Phillips organization in 1946, maintaining offices and saleroom in a nook of Blenstock House, while continuing to run quite separately.
Phillips recommends to its branches that "details of coins" be "referred to
Glendining's and its staff if local expertise is not available."

Conditions of sale and consignment at Glendining's are the same as at Phillips, except that there is no buyer's premium and the consignor commission is
10 percent. For details, see the Phillips Blenstock House entry.

218. Arthur G. Griffiths & Sons

    57 Foregate Street   Tel. (0905) 264 64
    Worcester, Hereford and Worcester WR1 1DZ

This firm, with a branch at Evesham (91 High Street, tel. [0386]2981), holds
monthly mixed-lot auctions. Sales are held in local halls in Worcestershire,
and occasional house and estate sales are conducted. Sales are advertised in
the local press. Among the items auctioned are DRAWINGS, FURNITURE, PEW-
TER, PORCELAIN, and SILVER.

Catalogues are not available by subscription, but listings can be had for
each sale, at approximately 50p. There is no buyer's premium. The usual
viewing procedure is the day prior to the sale. Buyer must settle account on
day of sale if, as partner Calvin Chapman, FRICS, points out, "not known to
us."

Consignments are not accepted from dealers. There is no minimum value
for acceptance. Reserves are accepted. There is no buy-in charge. Goods con-

signed are sold within 1 month. Settlement is made within 30 days after the sale.

219. Hall, Wateridge & Owen
Welsh Bridge   Tel. (0743) 570 74 (10 lines)
Shrewsbury, Salop SY1 14L

A well-established firm with offices elsewhere in the Salop area (including Ellesmere, Owestry, and Wrexham), Hall, Wateridge & Owen holds mixed-lot auction sales every week on Fridays at the Welsh Bridge saleroom. Friday has been a traditional market day in this old Roman town. J. D. Williams, FRICS, reports that the firm holds "country house sales when convenient."

These sales are advertised regularly in the local press and in specialty periodicals, such as *Antiques Trade Gazette*. The firm has also built up a sizable subscription list for its catalogues (really listings), which cost only £3 per annum. Catalogues are also available singly. Among the goods auctioned recently have been ART DECO, ART NOUVEAU, CLOCKS AND WATCHES, DRAWINGS, FURNITURE, GLASS, JEWELRY, PAINTINGS (18th c. British, 19th c. European), PEWTER, PORCELAIN, POSTCARDS, PRINTS, RUGS, and SILVER.

There is no buyer's premium. Viewing is the day prior to the sale, the morning of the sale to 10:30 (sale begins at 11), and by appointment. Absentee bids are accepted. Packing and shipping services are available, at the buyer's expense. Guarantees of authenticity are not offered, but buyers can, within the time constraints imposed by law, return goods that prove to be not as catalogued. Buyers must settle accounts on the day of the sale.

The standard consignor's commission is 15 percent. There is an allowance of 2.5 percent for recognized dealers. Consignors are not charged for packing and shipping, insurance, or warehousing. Consigned goods are sold within 6 weeks. Settlement is made after 1 week. Reserves are accepted. The buy-in fee is by arrangement. Consignments of property are not accepted from dealers.

Mr. Williams estimates the annual turnover of the saleroom to be about £500,000.

220. Hanbury Williams
34 Church Street   Tel. (0263) 51 32 47
Cromer, Norfolk NR27 90S

This firm of chartered surveyors, estate agents, valuers, and auctioneers has branch offices scattered throughout Norfolk. The Cromer branch, in the heart of some very attractive scenery, is responsible for the auction sales, held every 3 weeks. These take place mainly at the Olympia saleroom, Garden Street, Cromer, but occasional sales are held in Norwich, Great Yarmouth, and Ipswich. There are also occasional house and estate sales.

Sales are advertised regularly in the local press and in specialty periodicals, such as *Art & Antiques Weekly,* and from time to time in the national press. Mostly mixed-lot auction sales are held, including FURNITURE, PAINTINGS,

PORCELAIN, and SILVER. A single printed sheet giving date and time of sale and containing details of major items is available free of charge from the firm; write to Mrs. M. B. Watling at the Cromer office. Catalogues for each sale are available either at one of the firm's offices or through the mail (contact Mrs. Watling).

There is no buyer's premium. Absentee bids are executed. Guarantees of authenticity are not offered. Packing and shipping services are available, at the buyer's expense. Goods that prove to be not as catalogued may be returned. Viewing at the Olympia saleroom is the afternoon prior to the sale. Settlement is as follows, according to K. G. Hammond of the Cromer office: "persons unknown to us—immediately; persons known to us—within 28 days."

The standard commission for consignors is 15 percent, but it is negotiable, depending upon the situation. Goods are not accepted from dealers. "Rates for institutions negotiable according to the value of the consignment and the number of lots." Consignors are charged for catalogue illustrations; "consignor either arranges own insurance, packing and shipping, or we will arrange and charge the amount charged to us by independent contractors." Consigned goods are sold within 4 weeks. Settlement is made within a maximum of 4 weeks after the sale. Reserves are accepted "only if those reserves are considered to be realistic by our experts." The buy-in charge is negotiable, but the maximum is 2.5 percent of the reserve price.

Appraisal services are available. The fee is negotiable, but is a maximum of 5.5 percent on the first £7,000 and 2.5 percent on the remainder of the amount of the valuation.

221. Harmer's of London Stamp Auctioneers Ltd.

41 New Bond Street   Tel. (01) 629-0218/9 and 0377
London W1A 4EH   Telex: 268312 (prefixed WESCON G/
                                        Attn: PHISTAMSEL)
                                        Cable: PHISTAMSEL

Henry R. Harmer became involved with the buying and selling of stamps in 1887, and in 1918, just before the end of the First World War, he held his first auction on his own in London. Since then, Harmer's has become a tricontinent operation (see U.S. and Australia listings). Harmer's remains a family firm, though the seat of control is now with the family in New York. Leading personnel in the U.K. are no longer members of the Harmer family but are veteran professionals who have been with the firm for many years. The managing director is Ian J. Glasborow.

Harmer's in London as elsewhere primarily auctions STAMPS, but it also sells MAPS and POSTCARDS. Sales of 2–3 days duration are held every 2 weeks from mid-September to mid-July. They are advertised in the national press and in national and international philatelic journals. All sales are held on premises. Catalogues are available singly for each sale and by annual subscription (£20 U.K., £24 Europe, £35 rest of the world).

There is no buyer's premium. Packing and shipping services are available at buyer's expense. Guarantees of authenticity are offered. Buyers may return goods that prove to be not as catalogued. Usual viewing procedure is several days in advance of sale, 10 A.M.–4 P.M. Buyer must settle at auction or upon receipt of invoice. Credit terms are available to "credit-established clients."

The standard consignor commission is as follows: properties realizing £1,000 and over, 15 percent; under £1,000, 20 percent; however, individual lots realizing £500 and over, 12.5 percent. Commissions are negotiable, depending on the situation. Consignor arranges and pays for shipping, but does not pay for catalogue illustrations, insurance, or warehousing. Reserves are accepted; the unsold charge is £2 per lot, but where vendors' reserves have not been agreed to by Harmer's, the cost is the commission on the bought-in price. Consigned goods are usually sold within 3 months; settlement is 35 days after sale.

Appraisal service is available. Fees range from 1–2.5 percent of value; travel costs, etc., are additional. Where goods are put up for sale within 2 years of valuation, fees are refunded.

222. R. Harper & Son
70 Main Street   Tel. (0587) 202 93
Sedbergh, Cumbria LA10 5AD

Sales are held monthly by this firm, at the Guldrey Auction Mart in Sedbergh and on vendors' premises. Lots sold include FURNITURE and SILVER.

Harper advertises regularly in the local press. Announcements of forthcoming sales are available; write to the firm. Catalogues are not available by subscription, but can be obtained from the firm, either at its offices or through the post.

There is no buyer's premium. Absentee bids are not executed. Buyers are not offered packing and shipping services or guarantees of authenticity. There is no opportunity to return goods that prove to be not as described. Viewing is "variable." Settlement is "cash."

The standard consignor's commission is 15 percent, but it is negotiable. Consignments from dealers are not accepted. Consignors are charged for packing and shipping, insurance, and warehousing. Settlement is made approximately 1 week after the sale.

223. Harrods Auction Galleries
Arundel Terrace   Tel. (01) 748-2739
Barnes, London SW13

The Harrods Estate Offices—a division of the marvelous department store—run these galleries and have been holding auction sales since the early 1920s. Harrods had salerooms at various locations in London, then settled into their present site in the late 1960s. South of the river and close by the Hammersmith Bridge, the galleries are located in a vast, imposing red-brick building that serves Harrods for a variety of other purposes as well. There is parking for some 200 cars.

Harrods Auction Galleries hold diverse sales. The schedule gives some indication of what is sold:

Wednesday: morning—carpets and RUGS; afternoon—antique and modern FURNITURE

Thursday: morning and afternoon—specialist sales of BOOKS, COSTUME, JEWELRY, SILVER, TOYS, etc.

The more general sales are held fortnightly, the specialist sales both fortnightly and bimonthly.

Catalogues are available singly for each sale (approximately 60p) and by subscription (for details and costs, write to the above address).

Sales are advertised in the local press and in specialty publications, such as *Art & Antiques Weekly.* There is no buyer's premium. Absentee bids may be executed for you by a porter. Settlement is within 24 hours after the sale. Viewing is usually 2 days before the sale, 9 A.M.–5 P.M. Packing and shipping is available.

The consignor's commission varies between 12.5 and 15 percent. It is negotiable, depending upon the situation. There is a separate rate structure for dealers; the announced one is 10 percent. Catalogue illustrations are charged to the consignor, as is insurance. Consigned goods are usually sold within 2 weeks. Settlement is after 14 days. Reserves are accepted. The buy-in charge is 2.5 percent of the reserve price if the auctioneer agreed to the reserve; otherwise, it is 5 percent. Settlement is usually 14 days after the sale.

Appraisal service is available. Contact Harrods Estate Office at the above address for information as to cost.

224. Harvey's Auctions Ltd.

22–23 Long Acre   Tel. (01) 240 1464/5/6/7
London WC2E 9LD

Located not far from the recently upgraded Covent Garden area in a street full of small and interesting shops and businesses, Harvey's holds auctions every Wednesday. These are mostly mixed-lot general-purpose sales and include BOOKS, CLOCKS AND WATCHES, FURNITURE, MUSICAL INSTRUMENTS, PAINTINGS, PRINTS, and SILVER. Occasional house and estate sales are held, but only if valued over £10,000.

Sales are announced in the *Daily Telegraph* (Monday auction page) and in specialty periodicals, such as *Antiques Trade Gazette.* The cataloguing for these sales is minimal but adequate. Catalogues are available singly (approximately 35p) and by subscription. A nice touch is the metric conversion table in the back of each catalogue.

There is a buyer's premium of 10 percent. Viewing is the day before the sale, 9:30 A.M.–3:30 P.M., and sometimes also the morning of the sale. Absentee bids are accepted. Packing and shipping services are available at the buyer's expense. Harvey's reports that "goods wrongly described or fakes intended to deceive can be returned, but not damaged goods." Buyer must settle accounts within 3 days of the sale.

The standard consignor's commission is 10 percent, but commissions are negotiable ("valuable consignments are always negotiable"). Consignors pay for delivery to Harvey's, "of course," Consignors also pay insurance, at £1 per £100. Consignors do not pay for warehousing. Reserves are accepted. The buy-in charge is 2.5 percent of the reserve, subject to a minimum of £2 per lot. Consigned goods are usually sold within 2–3 weeks; settlement is made 2–3 weeks after the sale.

Appraisal service is available. There is no cost if appraisal is done with a view toward auction. Otherwise, valuation and probate insurance fees are within the usual range of the Institution of Chartered Surveyors fees.

Harvey's estimates its annual turnover as being well over £650,000.

225. C. Wesley Haslam & Son
St. Helens Place, High Street   Tel. (0745) 44 67 / 8
Rhyl, Clwyd LL18 1TR

This firm, which has other offices in the area, holds auctions in this Welsh beach town at its North Wales Auction Galleries on High Street. Sales of what partner F. E. Redfearn describes as "ordinary furnishings" are held fortnightly; approximately 6 times per annum, there are "special Antique Auctions." Among the items offered are ARMS AND ARMOR, CLOCKS AND WATCHES, FURNITURE, GLASS, JEWELRY, PAINTINGS, PEWTER, PRINTS, and SILVER. Occasional house and estate sales are also held.

Sales are advertised in the local and regional press, and in the case of the special auctions, in publications such as *Antiques Trade Gazette*. The firm also sends out announcements of the sales, and Mr. Redfearn indicates that "upon request names are added to the list of dealers and private buyers wishing to become notified of future sales, and a circular is sent out prior to the auction." Catalogues are available singly, but not by subscription; apply to the firm.

There is no buyer's premium. Absentee bids are accepted, "provided they [the bidders] have already inspected the goods themselves." Packing and shipping services are available, at the buyer's expense. Viewing is the day prior, 9 A.M.–5 P.M., for antique sales, the afternoon prior for ordinary household sales. Mr. Redfearn reports: "we prefer accounts to be paid on the day of the sale, but all must be settled within 7 days; banker's reference required for cheques."

The standard consignor's commission is 20 percent. Consignors do not pay for catalogue illustrations, insurance, packing and shipping, or warehousing. Consigned goods are offered at the first available sale after receipt of the property. Settlement is approximately 10 days after the sale. There is no minimum value necessary for a consignment. Goods are not accepted from dealers or institutions.

Appraisal service is available. Contact Mr. Redfearn.

226. Hatch & Fielding
The Albany Galleries   Tel. (0704) 346 78
341 Lord Street
Southport, Merseyside PR8 1NL

This firm holds general-purpose mixed-lot sales approximately every second week, which include items such as FURNITURE. The firm reports that the "majority" of sales are "at our premises," but there are a "few at clients' premises."

Sales are advertised locally. Announcements of the sales can be obtained from the firm. There are no catalogues. There is no buyer's premium. Absentee bids are not accepted. Packing and shipping services are available "through independent shippers," at the buyer's expense. The firm does not offer guarantees of authenticity. Viewing is the day prior to the sale. Buyer must settle account within 7 days.

The standard commission for consignors is 17 percent. Consignors are not charged for warehousing and insurance, but must pay packing and shipping. Reserves are accepted. There is no buy-in charge. Consigned goods are sold within "a few weeks." Settlement is made 14 days after the sale.

227. Charles Head & Son
113 Fore Street   Tel. (0548) 23 52
Kingsbridge, Devon TQ7 1BG

This firm, a partnership with a sole principal, holds auctions monthly, mixed-lot general-purpose sales that include FURNITURE. Sales are advertised in the local press, such as *Western Morning News*. There are occasional house or estate sales, but most of Head's auctions are held at the Market Hall in Fore Street.

To be placed on the mailing list free of charge, just write Mr. C. W. A. Head, FRICS. House sales are catalogued, but not those held at Market Hall. There is no buyer's premium. Absentee bids are accepted. Viewing is the day before the sale, 9 A.M.–6:30 P.M., and the morning of the sale, 9–10:30. No guarantees or warranties are offered. Packing and shipping services are not available. Buyer must settle account on day of sale.

The standard consignor's commission is 15 percent on items sold up to £200, 10 percent on items sold over £200. Consignors are not charged for insurance. Items are delivered at consignor's expense. Mr. Head reports: "We have a store; if it is not possible for removals to be made direct to Market Hall because of date difficulty, then storage can be arranged for short periods between delivery and entry in Market Hall." Goods are sold within 1 week usually; settlement is made 6 days after sale. Reserves are accepted. There is no buy-in charge except if a lot is not sold by reason of the reserve, in which case 5 percent of reserve is charged.

228. Duncan Heins & Son

Imperial Chambers, 24 Widemarsh Street Tel. (0432) 581 67
Hereford, Hereford & Worcester   and 24 13

This firm holds sales every second week or so at the Portland Street saleroom in Hereford, which is near the Hereford Market. The sales are of FURNITURE, GLASS, and the like. About 250 lots are sold, at the rate of roughly 100 lots an hour. The firm's offices are a short walk (maybe 10 minutes) from the saleroom. Occasional house and estate sales are also held.

Sales are advertised in the local and "occasionally" the national press. Not every sale is catalogued; indeed, most are not—only the better-quality sales held every now and then are accompanied by a list-like catalogue. In any event, catalogues are not available by subscription.

There is no buyer's premium. Packing and shipping services are not available from the firm. No guarantees of authenticity are offered, but Nicholas Heins, auctioneer and partner, reports: "if potential buyers are able to show that the goods are not as described . . . then they have the opportunity to return the goods within 48 hours." The usual viewing procedure is Saturday, 9 A.M.–noon, and the morning of the sale. Buyer must usually settle account within 48 hours, unless prior arrangements have been made.

The standard consignor's commission is: "period pieces or large consignments, 10 percent; small quantities of low value, 15–17.5 percent." Consignors are not charged insurance or warehousing. Mr. Heins says that "if we are required to arrange packing and collection of consignment . . . cost is deducted from proceeds of sale." Consigned goods are usually sold within 4–6 weeks, usually less. Settlement is "1 week unless consignment is split over 2 sales."

Appraisal service is available. The cost is "5.5 percent on first £700, 2.5 percent on the residue. Minimum fee is £10." Contact Mr. Heins or Stephen Hughes.

229. Highgate Auctions

Warehouse No. 8, Camden Goods Depot Tel. (01) 267 2124
Chalk Farm Road
London NW1 2RL

London is an exciting city, but on Sundays it can be a bit dull—there is not all that much to do. If you want a bit of excitement and the chance for the occasional bargain, go to the mixed-lot general-purpose auctions held every Sunday at 2:30 P.M. by Highgate. In addition to everything else, the sales of such goods as FURNITURE, RUGS, and SILVER are fun. And the first Tuesday of each month at 7 P.M., Highgate holds a picture sale which generally includes some fascinating if not very valuable PAINTINGS.

Sales are advertised in the local press and in specialty periodicals, such as *Antiques Trade Gazette*. Announcements are available; write to the firm. Catalogues are available for each sale but not by subscription.

There is a buyer's premium of 10 percent. Absentee bids are executed. Packing and shipping services are available, at buyer's expense. Goods that prove to be not as catalogued may be returned. Viewing is Saturdays, 10 A.M.–6 P.M., and Sundays, 10:30 A.M.–sale time, for the Sunday sales. Viewing for the picture sales is the day of the sale, 10 A.M.–sale time. Settlement is within 4 days after the sale.

The standard consignor's commission is 10 percent, "subject to a minimum charge of £2 per lot," according to partner C. W. Cussins. The commission is negotiable, depending on the situation. There is a minimum value of £20 necessary for a consignment. Consignors are not charged packing and shipping or insurance. Highgate charges warehousing only if consignor fails to pick up unsold lots and, as Mr. Cussins put it, "We feel that we are being used as a warehouse." Consigned goods are sold within 1 week. Settlement is made 9 days after the sale.

Appraisal service is available. The charge is 1.5 percent, subject to a £10 minimum charge—"refundable if the same goods are subsequently entered for auction."

230. Cooper Hirst

Goldlay House, Parkway   Tel. (0245) 581 41
Chelmsford, Essex CM2 7PR

This firm holds weekly uncatalogued sales at Chelmsford Market every Friday and auction sales of FURNITURE and other effects at Chancellor Hall in Chelmsford approximately every 6 weeks. Occasional estate and house sales are also conducted. These sales are advertised in the local press and in specialty periodicals, such as *Antiques Trade Gazette*. Announcements of sales are sent out; to be placed on the mailing list, phone or write the office.

Catalogues are available for each sale: singly the cost is 40p, which includes postage; a subscription is £4 per annum. Write to Mrs. E. C. Hirst. There is no buyer's premium. Absentee bids are accepted. Packing and shipping services are available, at the buyer's expense. Goods that do not prove to be as described may be returned within 7 days and the sale rescinded, but no warranties or guarantees are given. Viewing is the evening prior to sale day (Mr. Hirst says "strictly 4:30–8:30 P.M.") and the morning of the sale (9–10:30). Buyer must settle accounts "immediately."

The standard consignor's commission is 12.5 percent up to £1,000, and 10 percent over £1,000. Commission is negotiable, depending on the situation. Consignors pay for insurance and warehousing, and to get goods to Hirst. Reserves are accepted. Buy-in charge is 2 percent and any cartage costs. Goods are sold within 6 weeks maximum and settlement is "cash on sale day or cheques sent on day following sale."

Appraisal service is available. Cost is variable, according to R. L. C. Hirst, FRICS, "depending on value of items and time spent—but approximately 0.5–1 percent."

231. Hobbs and Chambers

"At the Sign of the Bell"   Tel. (0285) 47 36
Market Place
Cirencester, Gloucestershire GL7 1QQ

The firm's offices are located on the spacious marketplace opposite the splendid church of St. John the Baptist. The monthly auctions are held at the Bingham Hall, some 800 meters away on King Street. This building serves many functions; it is, for example, also the local theater. The auction sales held by Hobbs and Chambers in Cirencester are mixed-lot general-purpose sales and include such items as might be found at any local or regional sale, such as GLASS or SILVER. The occasional house or estate sale is also held.

Sales are advertised in the local press. Announcements are sent through the post; to be placed on the mailing list free of charge, just write. Minimal catalogues are available for each sale at between 30p and 50p. There is no buyer's premium. Absentee bids are not executed. Packing and shipping services are not available. No guarantees of authenticity are offered. Viewing is the day prior to the sale, 10 A.M.–8 P.M., and the morning of the sale. Buyers must settle account the day of the sale.

The consignor's commission is "basically 15 percent, subject to variations depending on vendor's circumstances," reports Fraser R. Glennie, FRICS. Consignors are not charged insurance, but must pay for packing and shipping, as well as warehousing. Goods are sold usually in 6–8 weeks. Settlement is made 2 weeks after the sale. Reserves are accepted. Consignor's costs for a buy-in vary.

Appraisal service is available. Arrangements may be made with Mr. Glennie.

232. John Hogbin & Son

53 High Street   Tel. (058 06) 22 41
Tenterden, Kent TN30 6BG

A full-service firm which is involved in everything from the selling of deadstock to planning appeals, John Hogbin & Son holds auctions 2–3 times a month, usually on Wednesdays. The firm, which has other offices in the area, auctions a wide variety of goods, including DRAWINGS, FURNITURE, PAINTINGS, and PORCELAIN. Occasional house and estate sales are also held.

These sales are advertised in the local and national press (*Daily Telegraph*), as well as in specialty periodicals. Catalogues for each sale are available at the firm's offices, the saleroom, and via the mail; cost varies between 20p and 30p.

There is no buyer's premium. Absentee bids are executed, provided that "bidders have made proper financial arrangements." Packing and shipping services are not available. Goods that prove to be not as catalogued may be returned within 14 days for refund. Viewing is 1 or 2 days before the sale. Buyer must settle accounts immediately.

Consignors have to pay for insurance in certain cases, where item's value is over £500. Consignors are charged packing and shipping only on items that have to be returned to them; they are responsible for getting items to the saleroom. Warehousing is charged only on items that are not collected after failing to sell. Consigned goods are sold "when appropriate sale arises." Settlement is made 14 days after sale. Reserves accepted.

Honiton Galleries: see Laurence and Martin Taylor (Honiton, Devon)

233. Edgar Horn
47 Cornfield Road   Tel. (0323) 228 01/2/3
Eastbourne, East Sussex BN21 4QJ

This firm holds approximately 10 sales annually, at roughly 5-week intervals, in the Auction Mart, 46–50 South Street, just around the corner from the firm's offices. Most of these are mixed-lot general-purpose sales, often multisession 2- or 3-day affairs. Among the items put up for sale are FURNITURE, GLASS, PAINTINGS, PORCELAIN, RUGS, and SILVER. Occasional house and estate sales are also held.

Sales are advertised regularly in the local press and in specialty periodicals. List-like catalogues are available approximately 1 week before each sale (30p, plus postage). Catalogues are also available by subscription (£3 per annum, plus postage).

There is no buyer's premium. Absentee bids are executed. Packing and shipping services are not available. No guarantees of authenticity are offered, but goods that prove to be not as catalogued may be returned. Viewing is generally Saturday, 9 A.M.–1 P.M., and Monday, 10 A.M.–1 P.M., 2–4 P.M.; sales begin on Tuesday. Settlement must be effected by Tuesday following.

The standard consignor's commission is 17.5 percent. Dealers' goods are not accepted. The commission is negotiable, depending on the situation. Consignors must pay for transporting goods to saleroom, but do not pay for insurance or warehousing. Consigned goods are usually sold within 4–5 weeks. Settlement is made 2 weeks after the sale. Reserves are accepted. There is no buy-in charge.

Appraisal service is available. Contact the firm.

234. Howkins & Harrison
12 Albert Street   Tel. (0788) 783 81
Rugby, Warwickshire CV21 2RX

This firm holds auctions "as arranged." These sales, advertised in the regional press and in specialty periodicals, are "at house where FURNITURE stands." Catalogues are not available by subscription, but are obtainable for each sale; "contact the Rugby office." The firm does have offices elsewhere in the area.

There is no buyer's premium. Absentee bids are not accepted. Packing and shipping services are not available. No guarantees of authenticity are offered.

Viewing is 2 days prior to the sale, 10 A.M.–4 P.M. Accounts must be settled on day of sale.

Consignor's commissions are not negotiable. Settlement is 3–4 weeks after the sale. There is no charge if consigned property does not sell.

235. Edward Jackson
22 Church Street   Tel. (0695) 760 61/4
Ormskirk, Lancashire L39 3AN

Some 20 miles south of Liverpool lies the town of Ormskirk, and smack in the middle of the town are the offices of Edward Jackson (which has other offices in the area). Sales of FURNITURE and the like are held every 4 weeks—Tuesday seems to be the favorite day. Occasional house and estate sales are also held.

The sales are advertised in the local and regional press. Only those sales with a better quality of merchandise are catalogued. The list-like catalogue is for sale on view days and at the auction.

There is no buyer's premium. Absentee bids are executed. Viewing is the day before the sale, 2–5 P.M., and the morning of the sale. Packing and shipping services are available, at the buyer's expense. Goods that prove to be not as described may be returned. Accounts must be settled within 7 days after the auction.

The standard consignor's commission varies between 12.5 and 17.5 percent, "according to client," states partner Edward Abbott, FRICS. The commission rate is different for dealers. Reserves are accepted. Consignors are not charged for warehousing or insurance, but are charged for "carriage of goods to saleroom." Goods consigned are sold within 3–4 weeks. Settlement is "within 28 days."

Jackson & Associates
236. 9 Castle Street   Tel. (0624) 84 20 71
Peel, Isle of Man

237. The Old Drill Hall
High Street   Tel. (0487) 81 23 61
Ramsey, Cambridgeshire

This family business is in 2 very disparate locations. The Isle of Man is not less than 3 hours by ferry from Belfast, Dublin, or Liverpool. Ramsey is a small town not far from Cambridge on the east coast of England. Jackson's holds approximately 2 sales a month in each location, on premises and in "local halls." Most sales are of FURNITURE and effects, such as "an assortment of costume jewelry, a Victorian photograph album, and a Royal Doulton toby jug." Occasional house and estate sales are held. Mr. Jackson estimates that his firm sells 8,000–10,000 items annually.

These sales are advertised in the local press, on the local radio, and in specialty publications, such as *Art & Antiques Weekly*. List-like catalogues are available for each sale; an annual subscription to the catalogues at one location is £5 per annum. There is no buyer's premium. Absentee bids are executed. Packing and shipping services are available, at the buyer's expense. Mr. Jackson comments on the possibility of returning goods as follows: "we do not accept any goods liable to bring discredit upon us, likewise we cannot be responsible for people who 'change their mind'... because we have paid out cash within 3 days of sale." Viewing is day previous to sale, 9 A.M.–8 P.M., and morning of sale. Buyer, must settle accounts "as soon as possible."

The standard consignor's commission is 10 percent and is negotiable, depending on the situation. Consignors are not charged for insurance or for warehousing. Consignor must get goods to Jackson's. There is no minimum value necessary for a consignment. Consigned goods are sold within 14 days. Settlement is made 3 days after the sale, "as a rule."

238. Jackson-Stops & Staff
Market House, High Street   Tel. (0386) 84 02 24
Chipping Campden, Gloucestershire GL55 6AJ

"Chipping" is Old English for market or trading center. This small town is no longer such a center, but it is where Jackson-Stops & Staff holds "regular sales of antique and reproduction FURNITURE, ornamental items, POTTERY and PORCELAIN, GLASS, SILVER, copper and brassware, pictures, BOOKS, JEWELRY, and WINE." The firm, which has offices elsewhere, including York, London, and Ireland, also holds "auction sales of ... contents of private homes." Auction sales are but a small portion of this firm's activities, which include "property management, valuations, estate management, town planning, and advice on and sales of leisure developments."

Sales are advertised in the local press, the national press, and specialty publications. Catalogues are available for a single sale (75p) and by subscription (approximately £5 per annum). For information about announcements, the mailing list, and catalogues, contact Gordon Patrick, Chattel Valuer, at the London office: 14 Curzon Street, London W1Y 7FH, tel. (01) 499-6291.

There is no buyer's premium. Mr. Patrick reports that "postal bids are accepted for all our sales." Packing and shipping services are not available from the firm. No guarantees of authenticity are offered. Viewing is usually 2 days before the sale, 10 A.M.–4 P.M. Settlement is by 1 P.M. the day following the sale.

The standard consignor's commission is 15 percent, but it is negotiable, depending upon the situation. Consignors pay for catalogue illustrations, insurance, packing and shipping, and warehousing, or as Mr. Patrick puts it, "vendor pays all expenses." Consignments are not accepted from dealers. Reserves are accepted. Settlement is usually 4 weeks after the sale.

Appraisal service is available.

239. Jacobs & Hunt

Lavant Street   Tel. (0730) 27 44/5
Petersfield, Hampshire GU32 3EF

This firm of estate agents and valuers holds general-purpose mixed-lot auctions of FURNITURE and effects every 6–8 weeks. These sales are advertised in the local press and in specialty publications. List-like catalogues are available for each sale; a subscription costs £1.80 per annum.
There is no buyer's premium. Absentee bids are executed. Packing and shipping services are available "by arrangement," at the buyer's expense. No guarantees of authenticity are offered. Viewing is the day prior to the sale, 10 A.M.–4 P.M. Buyers must settle accounts within 1 week.
The consignor's commission is 10–15 percent of the hammer price. Consignments are not accepted from dealers. Consignors are charged insurance but not warehousing. Consignors who fail to bring their property to the saleroom will be charged for cartage if the firm undertakes the transport. Consigned goods are sold within 8 weeks. Settlement is made 2 weeks after the sale. Reserves are accepted. The buy-in charge is 2.5 percent of the reserve price.

240. James Norwich Auctions Ltd.

33 Timberhill   Tel. (0603) 248 17
Norwich, Norfolk NR1 3LA   Telex: 975247

James Norwich Auctions has much the character of a movable feast. During one 3-month period recently, sales were held in London, Norwich, Ipswich, and Cambridge. Although the emphasis in these sales was on STAMPS, also sold were POSTCARDS, MEDALS, COINS, SILVER, PORCELAIN, BOOKS, FURNITURE, SCIENTIFIC INSTRUMENTS, and GLASS. Altogether, the firm holds about 30 auctions a year, in London hotels, Norwich hotels, and elsewhere in the U.K. The firm established itself as "International Philatelic and Numismatic Auctioneers," and has branched out.
Sales are advertised in the national and local press and in specialty periodicals (including collectors' magazines). Announcements of forthcoming sales are available free of charge; to be put on the mailing list, write Mr. James Glennie. Catalogues for all sales are available singly, either at the firm's offices, during viewing wherever exhibition may be, or by mail (the cost varies from 50p to £3). Catalogues are also available by subscription: Postage Stamps—£6.50 U.K., £7 Europe, £11 elsewhere (includes airmail postage). Coins, Medals, Banknotes—£2.20 U.K., £2.40 Europe, £3.60 elsewhere (includes airmail postage). Maps, Prints, Books, Cigarette Cards, Photos—£2.20 U.K., £2.40 Europe, £3.60 elsewhere (includes airmail postage). Postal History, Postcards—£2.20 U.K., £2.40 Europe, £3.60 elsewhere (includes airmail postage). All 4 sets of catalogues: £12 U.K., £13 Europe, £19.50 elsewhere (includes airmail postage).
There is no buyer's premium. Absentee bids are executed. Packing and shipping services are available, at the buyer's expense. The catalogue states

that "each lot is believed to be genuine (unless otherwise stated) . . . but should any lot prove to be a forgery, or reprint or . . . defective or wrongly described in the catalogue, the purchaser is at liberty to reject the lot by giving written notice within 7 days (or in the case of an overseas buyer within a reasonable amount of time of the date of the sale)." Viewing is normally a minimum of 1 day before and the morning of the sale day, and frequently is several days, including evening viewing. Accounts must be settled within 21 days of auction for absentee bidders, within less time by floor bidders.

The standard consignor's commission is 15 percent, but it is negotiable, "depending on value and saleability of goods." Consignors are not charged for catalogue illustrations. Consignors are charged for insurance and for warehousing. Consigned goods are sold within 6–12 weeks. Settlement is 35 days after sale. Reserves are accepted. The buy-in charge is £2 per lot or 5 percent of the reserve set by the vendor, "whichever is the greater." Unsold lots are carried over into the next auction and are offered at a lower price; if the vendor does not wish the auctioneer to do this, he must be notified.

Mr. Glennie, the auction manager, estimates the annual turnover of the firm to be well in excess of £100,000.

241. Kelly Poster Auction Rooms, Inc. Dennis Taylor
5 Falcon Grove   Tel. (01) 228-1375
Clapham Junction, London SW11

This business is a partnership, and the two partners, J. Kelly and M. Poster, run and supervise every aspect of the business. Dennis Taylor used to hold about 6 auctions a year at the premises of 5 Falcon Grove, which were taken over by the partnership when Taylor's was acquired by Kelly Poster in 1978. Frequency of auctions has since increased to 1 every 2 weeks on alternate Wednesdays, with some success. These auctions are held in what once was a church hall. One of the auctioneers—unusual for the male-dominated salerooms of the U.K.—is a woman, Mrs. J. Kelly (a.k.a. Kelly McEvoy). She has had considerable experience in the antiques trade, exporting various kinds of items to Southern Ireland. Poster was active in the furniture trade. Sales are held on site as well.

Kelly Poster sells a wide range of goods: a typical sale will include FURNITURE, JEWELRY, and what is engagingly described as "miscellania" and includes RUGS, PORCELAIN, BOOKS, and the occasional crash helmet or brass cannon. List-like catalogues are available for each sale at the saleroom, at 30p each. An annual subscription costs £3.60 (postage included within the U.K.). Sales are advertised regularly in the London press, *Time Out*, and trade periodicals, such as *Antiques Trade Gazette*.

There is no buyer's premium. Absentee bids are accepted from persons "known to us," reports the firm. Packing and shipping services are available, at the buyer's expense. No guarantees of authenticity are offered, but goods that prove to be not as described may be returned within 48 hours. Viewing is Sunday, Monday, Tuesday prior to the sale, 10 A.M.–4 P.M., and 9–10 the morning of the sale. Settlement must be within 48 hours of the sale "or storage charges are enforced." Credit cards are accepted: Access, American Express.

The standard consignor's commission is 15 percent. It is negotiable, depending on the situation. There is, "if requested," a separate rate structure for dealers (10–12.5 percent). The minimum value for a consignment is £3. Consignors pay for catalogue illustrations, insurance, packing and shipping, and warehousing. Consigned goods are usually sold within 10 days. Settlement is made 1 day after sale "if so requested." Reserves are accepted, but there is "a disposal charge."

Appraisal service is available. "The fee depends on value of the goods valued."

242. G. A. Key

8 Market Place   Tel. (026 373) 31 95
Aylsham, Norfolk NR11 6EH

This firm of auctioneers, surveyors, valuers, and estate agents has other offices elsewhere, but holds auctions in the Aylsham salerooms. Ample parking facilities are available. What D. J. Lines, who handles antiques and fine arts sales for G. A. Key, describes as "inferior items" are sold weekly in what are in effect uncatalogued sales. Every third Tuesday or so, Key holds an "antique sale," at which a variety of items are sold, including CLOCKS AND WATCHES, FURNITURE, PORCELAIN, SCIENTIFIC INSTRUMENTS, and SILVER, as well as other effects, such as Prattware pot lids, carriage lamps, and mounted butterflies. Every two months, on the second Friday of the month, there is a "picture sale," at which DRAWINGS, ENGRAVINGS, ETCHINGS, PAINTINGS, and PRINTS are sold. There are occasional house and estate sales.

The catalogued sales are advertised regularly in the local and national press (e.g., *Daily Telegraph*), as well as in specialty periodicals. A yearly date list of catalogued sales is available free of charge; write to Mr. Lines and ask to be placed on the mailing list. Catalogues are available singly for each sale (30p–75p) and may be obtained at the firm's offices, in the saleroom, or via mail (add postage). Catalogues are also available by subscription: antique sales, £7; picture sales, £2.50; both sets, £9.

There is no buyer's premium. Absentee bids are executed. Packing and shipping services are available at buyer's expense. Guarantees of authenticity are not offered, but as Mr. Lines points out, "We will within 48 hours of sale accept any item back that proves to be not as described." The usual viewing procedure for the Tuesday and Friday sales is the day prior to the sale, 2:30–8:30 P.M. The other sales, which are usually held on Mondays, are on view Saturday morning and the morning of the sale, 9–10:30. Settlement is expected within a reasonable period of time, "i.e., 14 days."

The standard consignor's commission is 15 percent, but it is negotiable. Consignors do not pay for catalogue illustrations, for insurance, or for warehousing, but do pay "for removal to saleroom." Should an item go unsold, there is also a charge for delivery from saleroom. Reserves are accepted. Consigned goods are sold within 2–6 weeks. Settlement is 21 days after the sale. There is no set minimum value for acceptance of a consignment.

Appraisal service is available. The cost is nil if items are sold through G. A. Key.

The firm estimates its annual turnover to be in the neighborhood of £1 million.

Kittows

243. 16 Old Town Street   Tel. (0752) 648 41 and 630 46
Plymouth, Devon PL 12 6BA

244. 58 Fore Street   Tel. (075 55) 3768/2355
Saltash, Cornwall PL 12 6JP

245. 41 Fore Street   Tel. (057 93) 3585/6
Callington, Cornwall PL 17 7AR

246. 5 Barras Street   Tel. (0579) 433 27
Liskeard, Cornwall PL 14 6AD

An old-line (est. 1850) firm of estate agents, auctioneers, surveyors, and valuers, Kittows—according to Eric Distin, FRICS—has monthly sales conducted by each of the offices above. Other offices do not hold auctions. Not all sales are held on premises; there are occasional house and estate sales. In Callington, use is made of the Panner Market, and in Liskeard, the Auction Room. Specialties of the firm include FURNITURE, COINS and STAMPS.

Sales are advertised regularly in the local press, such as the *Western Morning News.* Catalogues are not available by subscription but are available singly for each sale; phone or write.

There is no buyer's premium. Absentee bids are accepted. Packing and shipping services are available, at the buyer's expense. Guarantees of authenticity are not offered, but goods that prove to be not as described may be returned for a refund within a limited period of time. The usual viewing procedure is the afternoon and morning prior to a sale. Buyer must settle accounts within 1 week.

The standard consignor's commission is 15 percent; it is negotiable, depending on the situation. There is no minimum value necessary for acceptance of consignments. Consignors are not charged for insurance or for warehousing. Mr. Distin reports that "collection of items is carried out by private carriers and so a charge is made." Reserves are accepted. Settlement is made 14 days after the sale.

Appraisal service is available; no charge if the items are put up for sale by Kittows. Contact Mr. Distin.

247. G. Knight & Son
West Street   Tel. (073 081) 24 56/7/8
Midhurst, West Sussex GU29 9NG

Every 6–8 weeks, G. Knight & Son—Auctioneers, Valuers, Estate Agents, and Surveyors—holds a mixed-lot general-purpose auction sale which includes items running the gamut from FURNITURE to SILVER. Occasional house or estate sales are conducted.

Sales are advertised in the local press and in specialty periodicals. Announcements of forthcoming sales are sent out; to be placed on the mailing list, just write the firm. List-like catalogues are available singly for each sale, and by subscription (£2 per annum).

There is no buyer's premium. Absentee bids are not accepted. Guarantees of authenticity are not offered, but goods that prove to be not as described may be returned within 14 days of the sale. Packing and shipping services are not available. Viewing is the day prior to the sale. Buyer must settle accounts within 7 days of the sale.

The standard consignor's commission is 15 percent; it is negotiable. Consignors are not charged for insurance, packing and shipping, or warehousing. Consigned goods are sold within 2–3 months. Settlement is made within 2 weeks of the sale. Reserves are accepted. The buy-in charge is 2.5 percent of the reserve. There is no minimum value necessary for consignment.

Appraisal service is available.

248. Laidlaws
Crown Court, Wood Street   Tel. (0924) 753 01
Wakefield, West Yorkshire WF1 2SU

Laidlaws holds about 6 sales per annum, "collective sales of antiques, etc.," including BOOKS, CLOCKS AND WATCHES, FURNITURE, GLASS, PAINTINGS, PORCELAIN, POTTERY, RUGS, and SILVER. There are also occasional house and estate sales.

Sales are advertised in the local press, as well as in specialty periodicals. List-like catalogues are available "by written application" for each sale, but not by subscription. There is no buyer's premium. Absentee bids are not executed. Guarantees of authenticity are not offered. Packing and shipping services are available, at buyer's expense. Harry K. Thornton, FRICS, reports that "if an item is not as catalogued it may be returned within 7 days." The usual viewing procedure is: Friday, 9 A.M.–5 P.M. (trade only); Saturday and Monday, 10 A.M.–4 P.M. Sales normally begin on Tuesday. Buyer must settle as soon as possible after auction.

The standard consignor's commission is 15 percent. It is negotiable, depending on the situation. Consignments are accepted from dealers "with reservations." Dealer's commission is 10 percent. Consignors are not charged insurance or warehousing, but must pay for carriage to saleroom. Goods are usually sold within 6–8 weeks. Settlement is made 2 weeks after sale. Reserves are accepted; buy-in charge varies.

W. H. Lane

249. Morrab Road   Tel. (0736) 22 86
Penzance, Cornwall TR18 2QT

250. Trelawney Lane   Tel. (0752) 206 67/8
Plymouth, Devon PL4 6QG

W. H. Lane is the fine arts division of Taylor, Lane & Creber (see entry below). Originally established in the 1930s, the firm has met with some success in recent years, branching out from Penzance to Plymouth. Its annual turnover in 1979–80 was estimated as comfortably in excess of £1 million. Much of its success is due to the energy of partner Michael Newman, FRICS, and in 1980 he negotiated the merger which resulted in Lane's new status.

Among the more interesting sales held by Lane are those, every few years, that deal with sunken treasure. The catalogues for these are fascinating, since they not only list the items for sale, but also offer some history of the wreck from which the items have been taken, as well as information about its discovery and salvage. Each lot is accompanied by a Certificate of Origin, stating from which wreck the lot emanated.

Other auctions are held about twice a month in each location, usually in the middle of the week; these are all-day affairs and sometimes they run for 2 days. About 100 lots an hour are sold, in such areas as BOOKS, COINS, FURNITURE, MAPS, MEDALS, PRINTS, RUGS, SCIENTIFIC INSTRUMENTS, and SILVER. Occasional house and estate sales are held.

Sales are advertised regularly in the local and regional press, as well as in specialty periodicals, such as *Antiques Trade Gazette*. A sales calendar is available free of charge; write to Jill Chesterman in Penzance. Catalogues for each sale are available at the firm's offices or by mail order. Prices vary between 50p and £2.50. Catalogues are also available by subscription.

Most sales are held on the premises, in either Penzance or Plymouth. There is a buyer's premium of 7.5 percent. Absentee bids are executed; settlement must be right after sale. Packing and shipping services are available, at buyer's expense. No guarantees of authenticity are offered, but if goods prove to be not as described, they may be returned within 21 days after the sale. Viewing takes place the day preceding a sale, during business hours.

Prospective consignors should contact the firm by phone or in writing, detailing what goods they wish to consign. There is no minimum value for consignments, which are not accepted from dealers. Standard consignor's commission is: antiques and pictures, 12.5 percent to £250, 10 percent over £250; books, postcards, stamps, medals, 12.5 percent; household effects, 15 percent. Commissions are negotiable, depending on the situation. Consignors do not pay for catalogue illustrations or warehousing; they do pay for carriage to the saleroom and for insurance at 0.5 percent.

Reserves are accepted; the buy-in charge is 5 percent on reserves fixed by the vendor and 2.5 percent on reserves suggested by the auctioneers.

Goods are usually sold within 4–6 weeks; settlement is 21 days after sale.

The firm belongs to the Society of Fine Art Auctioneers.

251. J. G. Lear & Son

46 Foregate Street   Tel. (0905) 251 84/94
Worcester, Hereford and Worcester WR1 1EE

This firm, whose history as chartered surveyors, valuers, and estate agents dates back to the time of the American Revolution, has 4 other offices in the region and branches elsewhere in the country. It holds monthly antiques and bimonthly fine arts auction sales at the Star Hotel in Worcester and in local halls, as well as in situ for house and estate sales. Among the various items sold are FURNITURE and, as might be expected, ROYAL WORCESTER PORCELAIN.

These sales are advertised in the local and national press as well as in such specialty publications as *Antiques Trade Gazette*. Calendars of the season's sales are available free of charge; write to the Fine Art and Chattels Dept. Catalogues are available for each sale; an annual subscription costs £7.50 (including postage).

There is no buyer's premium. Absentee bids are executed. Packing and shipping services are not available from the firm. No guarantees of authenticity are offered. Viewing is at least the morning of the sale. Settlement is "immediately unless auctioneers otherwise agreed."

The consignor's commission is "a sliding scale dependent on valuation." There is a separate rate for dealers and institutions. A minimum for consignments depends on the sale. Consignors are charged for catalogue illustrations, packing and shipping, and warehousing, but not for insurance. Goods are sold "in first convenient sale." Settlement is within 28 days after the sale. Reserves are accepted, but only "in conjunction with auctioneers."

252. Lefevre & Partners

152 Brompton Road   Tel. (01) 584-5516
London SW3 1HX   Cable: PERCADIST

This firm, known and esteemed worldwide, is the Mercedes-Benz of carpet, tapestry, and rug dealers. Five times a year, Lefevre & Partners holds specialist auctions of TEXTILES, RUGS, and some ISLAMIC WORKS OF ART. All auctions are held on the premises.

Sales are advertised in the national press and in specialty publications. To be placed on the mailing list for advance notice of sales, write Penny Oakley. Catalogues with estimates are available before each sale (£4). Annual subscription rates are as follows: £14 U.K., £16 Europe (airmail), £25 other countries (airmail).

There is no buyer's premium. Absentee bids are executed. Packing and shipping services are available, at the buyer's expense. The catalogue notes that "the utmost care is taken to ensure that information given as to origin, date, provenance and condition is reliable and accurate. It must be understood that nomenclature remains a debatable subject and that names cannot be construed as definite information but reflect only generally accepted contemporary knowledge. The identification of periods and dates can only be treated as considered opinion rather than proven knowledge." Buyers may return goods only "if they can prove a reasonable complaint." Viewing days are Monday–Friday, 9:30 A.M.–6:30 P.M., as well as Saturday, 10 A.M.–4 P.M. Settlement is "as soon as possible."

The standard consignor's commission is 20 percent, but it is negotiable, depending on the situation. Though there is no minimum value for acceptance, the firm "will accept items only if they are of suitable quality." Parties interested in consigning property should write or telephone. The firm recommends that photographs be sent before an item is shipped. Consignors are charged for insurance, packing and shipping, and catalogue illustrations, but not for warehousing. Reserves are accepted. "Entries withdrawn or remaining unsold will not be subject to any commission, but charges not included in the standard commission will remain payable. The auctioneers may undertake to sell an unsold entry by private treaty subject to standard rate of commission charged on the offer obtained and accepted by the owner."

Appraisal service is available. There is no charge for valuation with view to sale. Contact Jean Lefevre.

253. Leigh Auction Rooms
86-90 Pall Mall   Tel. (0702) 775 01
Leigh-on-Sea, Essex SS9 1RG

These rooms are located in a once independent fishing village which has now become part of Southend-on-Sea ("the day tripper's delight"). Leigh Auction Rooms holds general-purpose mixed-lot sales of "FURNITURE and effects" once a month on Tuesdays.

Sales are advertised in the local press and in trade magazines. List-like catalogues are available singly for each sale and by subscription. Apply to the office for copies and rates.

There is no buyer's premium. Absentee bids are executed. Packing and shipping services are available, at the buyer's expense. Viewing is usually the Saturday and Monday preceding sale, 10 A.M.–6 P.M. Buyer must settle account within 24 hours.

The standard consignor's commission is 15 percent. It is negotiable, depending upon the situation. No minimum value is necessary for a consignment. Consignors are charged insurance and warehousing. Consignors who do not bring their goods to the auction rooms will be charged cartage. Goods are normally sold within 1 month. Settlement is 14 days after the sale. Reserves are accepted. The buy-in charge is 5 percent of the reserve price.

254. R. L. Lowery and Partners
Woolpack House, 24 Bridge Street   Tel. (0604) 215 61 (10 lines)
Northampton, Northamptonshire NH1 1NT

Lowery is located at the edge of a Pedestrians Only area in downtown Northampton, an agreeable city and the center of what was once known as the "county of spires and squires." Lowery sales, every 8–9 weeks, are "usually on owners' premises or in village halls." A typical sale offers "Antique and Modern Furniture and Household Effects including Clocks, Silver and Plate, Oriental Porcelain, China, Oil Paintings, Victorian and Modern Jewelry, Cut Glass, Carpets, Rugs, etc."

The sales are advertised in the local press and in specialty periodicals, such as *Art & Antiques Weekly*. Announcements of forthcoming sales are available; write to be placed on the mailing list. Catalogues are available singly for each sale (40p) and by subscription (£2.50 per annum). Write to Mr. W. E. Picton.

There is no buyer's premium. Absentee bids are accepted. Packing and shipping services are not available. No guarantees or warranties are made, but goods that prove to be not as described may be returned within a limited period of time and the sale rescinded. Viewing is the preceding day, 10 A.M.–4 P.M. Settlement is "same day or following day."

The standard consignor's commission is 10 percent, but it is negotiable, depending on the situation. Dealer's rate is 5 percent. Consignors are charged for catalogue illustrations and for insurance, but not for warehousing. Consigned goods are usually sold within 2 months. Settlement is usually made 2 weeks after the sale. Reserves are accepted. The buy-in charge is "nominal."

255. McCartney, Morris & Barker
25 Corve Street   Tel. (0584) 26 36
Ludlow, Salop SY8 1DA

This firm holds sales every 3–4 weeks in the Portcullis salerooms, usually of a mixed-lot general-purpose character and including BOOKS, COINS, FURNITURE, JEWELRY, PORCELAIN, and SILVER. Occasional house and estate sales are also held. Advertisements appear in the regional press and in specialty publications, such as *Art & Antiques Weekly*. An annual calendar of sales is available free; just write. Catalogues, really listings of what is up for auction, can be obtained singly for each sale or by subscription (£10 per annum).

There is no buyer's premium. Absentee bids are not executed. Packing and shipping services are not available. No guarantees of authenticity are offered, but if a work does not prove to be as catalogued and is returned within 7 days, the sale is rescinded and the money refunded. Viewing is the Saturday (10 A.M.–4 P.M.) and the Monday (10 A.M.–7 P.M.) prior to the sale, as well as the same morning (9–10:30). Accounts must be settled within 7 days.

The standard consignor's commission is 15 percent. It is negotiable, depending on the situation. Consignors are not charged for catalogue illustrations or warehousing. Insurance is charged at 7p per £100 of value. Consignor must arrange to get property to the saleroom. Consigned goods are sold within 3–4 weeks maximum. Settlement is 7–10 days after the sale. Reserves are accepted. The buy-in charge is 4 percent.

McCartney, Morris & Barker is a member of the Society of Fine Art Auctioneers.

Mallams
256. 24 St. Michael's Street   Tel. (0865) 414 66/413 58
          Oxford, Oxfordshire OX1 2DS

257. 26 Grosvenor Street   Tel. (0242) 357 12
          Cheltenham, Gloucestershire GL50 1HZ

Established in 1788, much to its pride, Mallams "hold monthly auction sales in each of our salerooms in Oxford and Cheltenham, of Antique, Victorian and Edwardian furniture, clocks, porcelain and pottery, metalware, glass, and works of art. Selected sales are held every two months of silver and jewelry, Oriental carpets and rugs, oil paintings, watercolors and prints, and antiquarian books." Occasional house and estate sales are held.

Sales are advertised in the local press, the national press (*Daily Telegraph*), and in specialty periodicals, such as *Antiques Trade Gazette*. Announcements of forthcoming sales are available. To be placed on the mailing list, contact B. J. Lloyd at the Oxford office. Catalogues for each sale are available (£1–£1.50) either at the firm's office or by post. A subscription is £20 per annum for all sales.

There is no buyer's premium. Absentee bids are accepted. Packing and shipping services are available at the buyer's expense. No guarantees of authenticity are offered and goods that prove to be not as described may not be returned. The usual viewing procedure is 2 days prior to the sale, 9 A.M.–5 P.M. Settlement must be made immediately. The firm requires a 50 percent deposit at the time of a winning bid from purchasers unknown to Mallams.

The standard consignor's commission is "basically 15 percent." Consignments are not accepted from dealers. There is no minimum value for acceptance of a consignment. There is no charge for catalogue illustrations. Consignors pay 0.5 percent for insurance, and for cartage to the place of sale. There is no charge for warehousing. There is a cataloguing charge of £2 per lot for furniture, and £1 for other items. Consigned goods are sold within 1–3 weeks. Settlement is made within 7–10 days after the sale. Reserves are accepted.

Appraisal service is available. The fee is 1.5 percent of the amount of the valuation; minimum charge is £10. There is no charge for "intending vendors."

258. Frank R. Marshall & Co
         Marshall House, Church Hill   Tel. (0565) 534 61 (6 lines)
         Knutsford, Cheshire WA16 6DH

No more than King Canute (for whom this charming town is named) could stay the tides can one stay the auctions held by Marshall twice a month. Nor would one want to do so. Lots for sale include the usual mixture of FURNITURE and effects, much of it quite interesting. Occasional house and estate sales are held as well.

Sales are advertised in the local and regional press and in specialty publications, such as *Antiques Trade Gazette*. List-like catalogues are available for each sale (50p), and an annual subscription costs £7.50. There is no buyer's premium. Absentee bids are not accepted, and packing and shipping services are not available. Buyers can return goods that prove to be not as catalogued, "in accordance with British conditions of sale." Viewing is the day prior to sale, 2–7 P.M. Buyers must settle accounts by end of day after sale.

The standard consignor's commission is, according to D. R. Dyson, auctioneer, "15 percent first £100, 10 percent £101–£500, then 6 percent thereafter, collected per lot." There is no charge to consignors for catalogue illustrations, insurance, or warehousing. There is a charge for packing and shipping to get consignment to Marshall. Reserves are accepted. Buy-in charge is £1.50 per lot or 2.5 percent of the reserve, whichever is greater. Consigned goods are usually sold within 3–5 weeks. Settlement is made after 10 days.

Appraisal service is available. Appraisal for sale, no charge. Appraisal for insurance, etc., 7.5 percent of first £1,000, then 1 percent "plus out-of-pocket expenses and travel."

Marylebone Auction Rooms: see Phillips (London)

259. Martin & Pole
5a & 7 Broad Street   Tel. (0734) 78 07 77
Wokingham, Berkshire RG11 1AY

Once a silk trade center, Wokingham today is primarily a bedroom community for folks who work elsewhere in the region. Martin & Pole, with associated offices in the area, serves that community. Every 3 weeks or so, the firm holds mixed-lot general-purpose auction sales at its salerooms on Milton Road, close to the town center. Offered for sale are FURNITURE and effects, including PAINTINGS, SILVER, and such items as "a reproduction china bowl of fruit." House and estate sales are held "when the opportunity arises."

These sales are advertised in the local press. Catalogues, on the order of listings, are available singly for each sale (20p). For an annual subscription (£7.50), apply to the office. There is no buyer's premium. Absentee bids are not accepted. Packing and shipping services are not available. No guarantees of authenticity are offered, and the firm reports that goods that prove to be not as catalogued will not be accepted back. The usual viewing procedure is Saturday mornings and Mondays and Tuesdays prior to the sale, on Wednesday. Buyer must settle accounts within 48 hours of the sale.

The standard consignor's commission is 15 percent, but it is negotiable, depending on the situation. There is no minimum value for a consignment. Consignors are not charged for insurance or for catalogue illustrations; they may have to pay for packing and shipping and for warehousing, depending on circumstances. Goods are sold at "the next available auction date." Settlement is 7 days after the sale. Reserves are accepted. The buy-in charge is 2.5 percent ("where goods are not sold or had not reached reserve").

260. Martin & Stratford
70 High Street   Tel. (0420) 844 02
Alton, Hampshire GU34 1EX

This firm, which has other offices in the region, holds sales twice a month at the Auction Mart at Market Square, close by the High Street offices. Sales, advertised in the local press, are usually of FURNITURE and effects, which can range from SILVER to what have you. Announcements of forthcoming sales are available at no cost; telephone or write.

List-like catalogues for each sale are available (30p) either at the firm's offices, at the saleroom, or through the post; an annual subscription is £7.20. There is no buyer's premium. Absentee bids are not accepted. Packing and shipping services are not available. No guarantees of authenticity are offered. Goods that prove to be not as described may not be returned. Viewing is the evening before the sale (5–6 P.M.) and the morning of the sale. Settlement must be made on the day of the sale.

The standard consignor's commission is 15 percent. Consignors are not charged for insurance or warehousing. Consignors are not charged for delivery of goods to the saleroom or for return if necessary. Consigned goods are sold within 6 weeks. Settlement is 7 days after the sale. Reserves are accepted. The buy-in charge varies.

261. Matthews & Sons
51–53 Church Road   Tel. (021) 476 1171
Northfield, Birmingham B31 2LB

This old-line firm (est. 1865) holds sales regularly every 3–4 weeks and advertises them in the local press. List-like catalogues are available singly for each sale but not by subscription. Among the items sold by Matthews & Sons are STAMPS and COINS.

There is no buyer's premium. Absentee bids are not accepted. Packing and shipping services are not available. No guarantees of authenticity are offered. Partner I. R. Matthews, FRICS, reports that goods that prove to be not as described may not be returned. Viewing is the day before, 9 A.M.–5 P.M. Settlement is immediately.

The consignor's commission is 15 percent on prices realized. It is negotiable, depending on the situation. There is a separate rate structure for dealers and institutions. Consignors pay for packing and shipping and for insurance, but not for warehousing. Consigned goods are sold within 2 months. Settlement is usually made 7 days after the sale. Reserves are accepted. The buy-in charge is 2.5 percent.

Appraisal service is available, at varying cost; contact Mr. Matthews.

262. Thomas Mawer & Son
63 Monks Road   Tel. (0522) 249 84
Lincoln, Lincolnshire LN2 5HP

Established in 1864, this firm is now part of the Earl & Lawrence group (which see). Sales, held on the premises every other week, include FURNITURE, SILVER, and effects, which can range, as was the case in one sale, from a 6-tread stepladder to a set of Avery scales. Occasional house and estate sales are also presented.

Sales are advertised in the regional press, and announcements are sent out; write to be put on the mailing list. Catalogues are available for each sale (30p; 40p postpaid) and by subscription (£5 per annum). There is a buyer's premium of 5 percent. Absentee bids are accepted. Packing and shipping services are available, at buyer's expense. Goods that prove to be not as described may be returned "subject to notification immediately after the sale." Viewing is 2 days prior to the sale, 9:30 A.M.–4:30 P.M. Settlement is same day for floor bidders and upon receipt of invoice for postal bidders. Credit cards are accepted: Visa, Barclaycard.

The consignor's commission is 15 percent to £1,000, and 12.5 percent thereafter. The commission is negotiable, depending on the situation. The commission rate for dealers is 10 percent. Consignors are not charged for insurance or warehousing, but must pay for cartage to the saleroom and for return packaging and cartage if not sold. Reserves are accepted. The buy-in charge is 5 percent, unless the firm fixed the reserve.

263 May, Whetter & Grose
Cornubia Hall   Tel. (072 681) 22 71
Par, Cornwall PL24 2AQ

Specialized sales are held by this branch of May, Whetter & Grose every month but August. One month features "specialist sales," which include ARMS AND ARMOR, BRASS, CLOCKS AND WATCHES, FURNITURE, PAINTINGS, RUGS, SILVER, and the like. The next month offers "collector's sales," which present BOOKS, CIGARETTE CARDS, COINS, MEDALS, POSTCARDS, STAMPS, and TOYS. Occasional house and estate sales are also held. General mixed-lot furniture and effects sales are held every Thursday most of the year. All these sales are advertised regularly in the regional press and in specialty periodicals, such as *Antiques Trade Gazette*. Announcements of sales are available at no cost; write to R. G. Tappin. Catalogues are available singly for each sale (25p), either at the firm's offices or through the post (admission to the "specialist sales" is by catalogue only). A subscription to either set of catalogues costs £4.

A buyer's premium has existed since the firm was founded, before World War II. Absentee bids are accepted. Packing and shipping services are available, at the buyer's expense. Mr. Tappin, the saleroom manager, reports that "we will refund purchase price if we agree that goods are wrongly catalogued." Viewing is the day prior to the auction, 10 A.M.–8 P.M., for the specialized sales. For the general weekly sale, viewing is morning of the sale, from 9 to sale time.

The consignor's commission varies between 12.5 and 15 percent. It is negotiable, depending on the situation. There is a separate rate for dealers. Consignors do not pay for insurance, packing and shipping, warehousing, or catalogue illustrations. Reserves are accepted. Mr. Tappin reports that "if the reserve is agreed with us," there is no buy-in charge. Consigned goods are sold within 2 months. Settlement is made 2 weeks after the sale.

"Appraisal with view to sale is free."

264. Meads of Brighton
St. Nicholas Road   Tel. (0273) 20 29 97/8
Brighton, East Sussex BN1 3LP

This firm of "Auctioneers of Art and Antiques, Valuers for Insurance and Probate" holds sales monthly on Thursdays at its quarters just a few blocks from the train station. Mostly these are mixed-lot sales and a typical one will include BOOKS, FURNITURE, and whatever else the auctioneers are offered that seems likely to sell.

Sales are advertised regularly in the local press and in specialty publications, such as *Art & Antiques Weekly*. Announcements of forthcoming sales are sent out; to be placed on the mailing list, write or call Miss Jones. List-like catalogues are available for each sale and by subscription (£6 per annum).

There is a buyer's premium of 10 percent, which was put into effect in January 1979. Absentee bids are executed, but banker's references must accompany the bid. Packing and shipping services are not available. Goods that prove to be not as described may be returned within 14 days of the sale. The usual viewing procedure is Tuesday, 10 A.M.–8 P.M., and Wednesday, 10 A.M.–4 P.M., before the sale. The trade can also view by arrangement. Settlement should be as soon as possible, but at a maximum, 7 days after the sale.

The consignor's commission varies from 5 to 10 percent, and it is negotiable, depending upon the situation. There is a different rate structure for dealers. Consignors pay for catalogue illustrations (£5) and for insurance (10p per lot). They do not pay for warehousing. Consigned goods are usually sold within 4 weeks. Settlement is made 2 weeks after the sale. The minimum value for a consignment is £20.

Appraisal service is available at fees up to 2 percent. Contact Mr. J. M. Hawes.

265. Mid-Devon Auctions
11 St. James Street   Tel. (0837) 25 94
Okehampton, Devon

Geoff Combes took over Mid-Devon Auctions in 1974, and he has built up a good country operation. This general-purpose auction house offers mixed lots for sale once a month at the Old Market Hall on Market Street. Two lines taken at random from a recent advertisement indicate the broad range of goods for sale: "Mahogany Hallstand, Carved Oak Hallstand, Pedestal Drop Leaf Table, Set Victorian Beer Engines, Cork Puller, McCulloch Chainsaw, Pair Hedge Anchors."

Sales are announced regularly in the local press. A calendar of sales can be obtained at no cost; write to Mr. or Mrs. Combes. "We do not issue catalogues," reports Mr. Combes; "the goods arrive for sale (approx. 1,500 lots). We sell by the goods. The auctioneer moves around the hall." There is no buyer's premium; Mr. Combes considers it "immoral." If goods prove to be not as described, the purchaser "has 48 hours to prove us wrong" and price will be refunded. Viewing is half a day prior to sale and an hour and a half before it. Settlement is at the close of the sale. Credit is available if prior arrangements have been made.

The standard consignor's commission is 15 percent, and it is negotiable, depending on the situation. Goods are sold within 4 weeks, and settlement is 7 days after the sale.

The firm does buy and sell on its own behalf, "very occasionally but only as a last resort."

266. Thomas Moore—Auctioneers

143 Lewisham Way   Tel. (01) 692-1970
New Cross, London SE 14

FURNITURE and effects are sold weekly in general-purpose mixed-lot sales held on Thursdays at 11 A.M. Periodically the firm holds specialized sales, and occasional sales are held "at private residences." Sales are announced in the London press and in specialty periodicals. Catalogues are available singly and by subscription ("rates available on application").

There is no buyer's premium. Absentee bids are acceptable: "A letter to the above address is sufficient for a postal bid," reports Mr. Chris Gibson. Packing and shipping services are not available. No guarantees of authenticity are offered and goods that prove to be not as described may not be returned. For the general sales, viewing is Wednesday, 2–8 P.M., and Thursday, 9 A.M.–sale time. For the specialized sales, the viewing is "8 hours prior to the auction." Settlement is expected within 3 days after the sale.

The standard consignor's commission is 15 percent. It is negotiable, depending on the situation. There is a separate rate, 12 percent, for dealers and institutions. Consignors are charged for catalogue illustrations, insurance, and warehousing: £12 is charged per inserted photograph; insurance is 2 percent of the value of the item; warehousing is charged if the property is unsold and not removed. Consigned goods are sold within 14 days to 3 months. Settlement is made approximately 5 days after the sale. Reserves are accepted.

Appraisal service is available; contact Mr. Moore. The cost is nil if the goods are to be auctioned; otherwise, the cost is 1.5 percent on the first £10,000, 1 percent on the next £40,000, and 0.5 percent on the balance.

267. Morphets

4 and 6 Albert Street   Tel. (0423) 50 22 82/5
Harrogate, North Yorkshire HG1 1JL   Cable: MORPHETS AUCTIONEERS

This firm of auctioneers, valuers, etc., is located in downtown Harrogate, a charming city which has successfully made the transition from spa to conference center without losing the greenery and gardens for which it is justly well known. With regard to auctions, Morphets is a two-tier operation. Almost every Thursday, the firm holds general-purpose mixed-lot uncatalogued auctions of FURNITURE and effects. Interspersed with these auctions are 10–12 catalogued sales (not always held on Thursdays), which offer better-quality goods, including BOOKS, CLOCKS AND WATCHES, FURNITURE, JEWELRY, PAINT-INGS, PORCELAIN, and RUGS. Occasional house and estate sales are held.

All sales are advertised regularly in the local and regional press, as well as in specialty publications, such as *Antiques Trade Gazette*. For certain sales, catalogues are available, approximately 10 days before; the cost is 50–80p, including postage. An annual subscription is £6. The catalogues provide reasonable estimates, a useful touch.

There is no buyer's premium. Absentee bids are accepted, "subject to proved financial status." Packing and shipping services are not available. Guarantees of authenticity are not offered. Buyers may return goods that prove to be not as catalogued, but "only on a goodwill basis if error genuinely misleads and returned within 7 days." Viewing for the public is usually Wednesday prior to sale, 10 A.M.–4 P.M., and for the trade only, Tuesday, 2–4:30 P.M. Buyers must settle accounts immediately, unless prior arrangements have been made.

The standard consignor's commission is as follows: 15 percent on lots realizing £3–£99; 12.5 percent from £100 to £499; 10 percent over £500. There is no minimum value for consignments. The commission is negotiable, depending upon the situation. There is a separate rate structure for dealers: "selective Trade concessions of 12.5 percent and 10 percent over £100." Consignors are charged for catalogue illustrations (£15 full page; £10 half page), and for insurance (50p per £100). Consignors are not charged warehousing. Goods consigned to the catalogued sales are usually sold within 4–6 weeks; goods for the more general sales are sold faster. Settlement is 10 days after the sale. Reserves are accepted and if unsold are subject to a buy-in charge.

Various Morphets partners are members of the Royal Institution of Chartered Surveyors.

268. Neal Sons & Fletcher

26 Church Street   Tel. (03943) 22 63 (3 lines)
Woodbridge, Suffolk IP12 1DP

Neal Sons & Fletcher was previously known as Dennis H. B. Neal. Both Neal and E. N. Fletcher are Fellows of the Royal Institution of Chartered Surveyors, and in this office and their Framingham one, they are concerned with many activities besides the holding of auctions. This firm holds general lesser-quality sales once a month and a specialized higher-quality sale approximately every 3 months. The special sales do reasonably well; Mr. Neal averages the turnover at about £50,000. Occasional house and estate sales are also held.

These sales are advertised in the local press, the London press (*Daily Telegraph*), and the specialty press, such as *Antiques Trade Gazette*. Announcements of sales are sent out; to be placed on the mailing list, write the firm. List-like catalogues are available for each sale and a subscription for all catalogues is available at £4 per annum. Sales include, as might be expected, FURNITURE as well as JEWELRY, SILVER, and RUGS.

There is no buyer's premium. Absentee bids are executed. Packing and shipping services are not available. No guarantees of authenticity are offered. Viewing is the day and evening prior to the sale (11 A.M.–4:30 P.M., 6:30–8 P.M.). Accounts should be settled immediately after the sale.

The standard consignor's commission for the special sales is 12.5 percent, and it is negotiable, depending on the situation. The rate is higher for the more general sales. There is no minimum value for acceptance of a consignment. Reserves are accepted. "Normally," according to Mr. Neal, there is no charge to consignors for catalogue illustrations, insurance, or warehousing. Consignors must get (or pay for getting) consignment to Neal Sons & Fletcher. Consigned goods are sold within 1–3 months. Settlement is usually within 3 weeks after the sale.

Appraisal service is available. Fees as appropriate. Contact the firm.

269 Nelson and Wycherley
Church Buildings   Tel. (044 84) 23 01/2
Grange-over-Sands, Cumbria LA11 6BB

This firm is located in a town that has been called "the Torquay of the North," because of its year-round mild climate. Nelson and Wycherley holds sales approximately every 6 weeks, except in July and August. The firm sells "all types of good quality antiques and items of interest," including FURNITURE and SILVER. Sales are also held in the Village Hall in Cartmel, a few miles away. Occasional house and estate sales are also offered.

Sales are advertised in the local press, and announcements are available from the office. List-like catalogues for each sale can be obtained from the firm.

There is no buyer's premium. Packing and shipping services "can be arranged," at the buyer's expense. No guarantees of authenticity are offered and goods that prove to be not as catalogued cannot be returned. Viewing is the day prior; the "hours vary." Buyer must settle accounts "at time of sale."

The consignor's commission, which is negotiable, is 10 percent plus expenses (advertising). Consignors must deliver goods to saleroom. Consignors are charged warehousing but not insurance. Reserves are not accepted. According to W. H. C. Wycherley, settlement is made "within 14 days."

270. Nicholas

13 Bridge Street   Tel. (0734) 47 96 65/6/7
Caversham, Berkshire RG4 8AA   Telex: 849322

Nicholas, with offices in Reading and elsewhere in the region, is a full-service firm that handles property sales, structural surveys, valuations, and project management. In addition to occasional house and estate sales, there are auction sales, approximately every 5 weeks, at the village hall, Goring, approximately 10 miles from Reading and 18 miles from Oxford.

The mixed-lot general-purpose sales of "Antique Furniture and other high quality household effects," include such items as JEWELRY, SILVER, and a copper teakettle. About 500–600 lots are sold at an auction. There is usually a luncheon interval, at which light refreshments are available.

Sales are advertised in the local and regional press and in specialized publications, such as *Art & Antiques Weekly*. Catalogues, available for each sale, can be obtained from the office at Caversham. Subscriptions are approximately £6 per annum.

There is no buyer's premium. Absentee bids are accepted and executed. Packing and shipping services are not available. No guarantees of authenticity are offered, but as the firm points out, "we believe in fair play and will consider any disputes with cataloguing, etc. on their merits." Viewing is the day prior to the sale, 3–6:30 P.M., and the morning of the sale, 9–10:45. Buyers unknown to Nicholas may be asked to pay a deposit of 25 percent on each of their winning bids.

The consignor's commission is "a flat 15 percent to include insurance." Consignors are not charged for catalogue illustrations or for warehousing prior to sale. Consignor is charged for shipping and packing only if Nicholas has to collect goods. Consigned goods are usually sold within 2 months, and settlement is "within two weeks, allowing for poor postal system." Reserves are accepted.

Appraisal service is available; fees vary. Contact L. J. Rose, FSVA, or S. A. Jones.

271. Nock, Deighton & Son

10 Broad Street   Tel. (0584) 23 64/37 60
Ludlow, Salop SY8 1PP

This firm, which has several branches in the area, holds Wednesday auction sqles every 6 weeks at 1 Mill Street, Ludlow, which is close by the firm's offices in that pleasant small town. Sold at auction are a wide range of items, including FURNITURE, GLASS, JEWELRY, RUGS, SILVER, and some more unusual lots, such as "Two pairs of Antlers." Occasional house and estate sales are also held.

Sales are advertised in the local and regional press, as well as in the usual specialty publications. Announcements of forthcoming sales can be obtained by writing to one of the firm's offices. List-like catalogues at £1 each are available at any Nock, Deighton office; postage is extra. A subscription is £5 per annum; write to the Ludlow office.

There is no buyer's premium. Absentee bids are executed. Packing and shipping services are not available. Authenticity is guaranteed "to the extent of our own knowledge," reports the firm; "goods returned if fake or otherwise defective and not announced at the sale within 2 weeks." Viewing is the Sunday (3–6 P.M.), Monday (10 A.M.–5 P.M., 7–9 P.M.), and Tuesday (10 A.M.–5 P.M.) before the sale. Buyer must settle accounts as follows: "1 week if commission bid, otherwise day of sale."

The standard consignor's commission is 15 percent, but it is negotiable. Consignors are not charged for catalogue illustrations or for warehousing. Consignors pay insurance of 50p per £100 value. Consignments are not accepted from dealers. Consigned goods are sold within 1–6 weeks. Settlement is made 1 week after the sale. Reserves are accepted; there is no charge on unsold items, provided that the reserve has been agreed upon with the auctioneers.

Appraisal service is available; fees vary. Contact any branch.

272. Norris & Duvall
106 Fore Street   Tel. (032) 522 49
Hertford, Hertfordshire SG14 1AH

This firm specializes in agricultural matters, and runs the Hertford Cattle Market. But every 5 weeks or so, on a Thursday, it puts its expertise to use in another area and holds auction sales of antique FURNITURE and effects, such as a Victorian nightdress or a set of Royal Doulton plates. Occasional specialized and house/estate sales are also held.

The sales, advertised in the local and regional press and in specialty publications, such as *Art & Antiques Weekly*, are held in the Castle Hall—"a large modern building situated in the grounds of Hertford Castle." Elizabeth I apparently spent many happy days in the castle as a child; the local council meets there today. List-like catalogues are 40p (postpaid) and can be obtained from the firm. A subscription for the year costs £3.

There is no buyer's premium. Absentee bids are executed "if required." Packing and shipping services are "not usually" available. No guarantees of authenticity are offered, but buyers may return goods that are not as described, "under certain circumstances." Viewing is on Wednesday before the sale, noon–7 P.M. Settlement must be made by "evening of sale day."

The standard consignor's commission is 15 percent, but it is negotiable, depending on the situation. Consignors are asked to pay for catalogue illustrations, insurance, packing and shipping, reports the firm, "only if we incur expense." Norris & Duvall does ask consignors to pay a nominal handling charge with regard to storage. Settlement is usually 3 days after the sale. Reserves are accepted, but the firm reports "we reserve the right to charge a nominal amount" if goods are not sold.

Appraisal service is available "under normal circumstances." Write or phone the firm.

273. Northampton Auction Galleries

33-35 Sheep Street   Tel. (0604) 37 263/4
Northampton, Northamptonshire NN1 2LU

This firm holds weekly sales of lesser-quality merchandise and periodic "arts and antiques" sales. FURNITURE, BOOKS, and GLASS are but some of the items featured. Occasional house and estate sales are also held.

Sales are advertised in the local and regional press and in specialty publications, such as *Antiques Trade Gazette.* Individual catalogues are 30p, and you cannot gain admittance to the periodic sales without one. A subscription to either the weekly catalogues or the Arts and Antiques catalogues is £5 per annum; a subscription to both is only £7 per annum. These list-like catalogues usually number between 500 and 600 lots.

There is no buyer's premium. Absentee bids are executed. Packing and shipping services are available, at buyer's expense. Payment should be made immediately. Buyers not known to Northampton Galleries will have to wait 2 days for checks to clear before picking up purchases. Viewing is 9 A.M.–4 P.M. day preceding sale, and morning of sale. No guarantees of authenticity are offered; the firm's conditions of sale point out that "the Misrepresentation Act of 1967 has substantially reduced the protection formerly given to vendors by the usual caveat emptor clause in auction conditions of sale, and that in some circumstances a vendor may be liable to a purchaser in respect of an incorrect description of . . . goods in a catalogue even though such description has been composed innocently and in good faith."

The standard consignor's commission is 15 percent for goods valued at £100 or more, 20 percent for goods sold at less than £100. There is a minimum lot charge of £1. The consignor's commission includes "auctioneer's selling fees, cataloguing, advertising, storage pending sale, and insurance (all goods are fully insured whilst on our premises)." Collection and transport will have to be paid for by the consignor if the firm removes the goods to the saleroom. Reserves are accepted, with a buy-in charge of 5 percent of the reserve. Settlement is usually 8 days after the sale.

Partner Nicholas C. Penn estimates the firm's annual turnover as in excess of £700,000.

Appraisal service is available. Contact Mr. Penn or Brian C. Cross for details and costs.

Nottingham Auction Mart: see Walker Walton Hanson (Nottingham, Nottinghamshire)

274. Osmond, Tricks & Son

7-8 Queen Square   Tel. (0272) 29 31 71 (10 lines)
Bristol, Avon BS1 4JG

Osmond, Tricks & Son is a multifaceted firm of estate agents, chartered surveyors, and valuers, with a successful auction operation in addition (according to M. Harvey Kitto, ARICS, its director, the turnover rose by 300 percent between 1977 and 1980). The auction operation is based in the firm's Regent Street salerooms, located in the pleasant Bristol suburb of Clifton (tel. 372 01/308 10), not too far from the zoo. Occasional house and estate sales are also held.

The salerooms are kept busy with a variety of sales: quarterly sales of antiques and objets d'art, which include PEWTER, CERAMICS, GLASS, SILVER, PAINTINGS, PRINTS, JEWELRY, CLOCKS, RUGS, and MUSICAL INSTRUMENTS among other items; fortnightly "collective sales of household furniture, furnishings & effects"; twice-yearly sales of WINE ("including corkscrews and related material") and of pictures and prints; special sales as necessary, including liquidations and varied items, such as STAMPS, as consignments are made.

Sales are advertised in the local press, national newspapers (such as the *Daily Telegraph*), and specialty publications (such as *Antiques Trade Gazette*, or in the case of wine sales, *The Decanter*). An auction calendar is distributed each year; write to Mr. Kitto. Catalogues are available singly for each sale, costing as follows: Antiques and Objets d'Art, 45p, 60p by post; Household Furniture, Furnishings, and Effects, 20p, 35p by post; Pictures and Prints, 50p, 65p by post; Wine, 45p, 60p by post. A subscription to all sales costs £13 per annum; Antique sales only, £2.50; Household sales, £8; Pictures and Prints, £1.50; Wine, £1.20.

There is no buyer's premium. Absentee bids are executed. Packing and shipping services are available, at the buyer's expense. No guarantees of authenticity are offered, but goods that prove to be not as described may be returned within 14 days and the sale will be rescinded. The viewing procedure varies with each sale, but "is never less than one full day," and usually includes the morning of the sale. Accounts must be settled promptly ("within 24 hours"), and to ensure that end, the firm has computerized its accounts system. Credit is available, but "only under exceptional circumstances."

The consignor's commission scale varies with the kind of object being sold, as follows: Antiques and household effects, 17 percent on individual lots up to and including £100; 15 percent to £500; 12.5 percent to £1,000; 10 percent to £2,500; 7 percent on individual lots thereafter. Pictures and prints, 10 percent on individual lots up to and including £2,500; 7 percent on individual lots thereafter. Wine, etc., 10 percent on individual lots, with no limits.

Consignors are not charged for catalogue illustrations, insurance, warehousing. Reserves are accepted. The buy-in charge is 5 percent of the reserve price or estimated value. Consigned goods are never held longer than 4 or 5 months. Settlement is 10–14 days after the sale. There is no minimum value for consignment.

Appraisal service is available. "No charge is made in respect of an appraisal of items entered for sale." Contact Mr. Kitto.

275. Outhwaite & Litherland

Fontenoy Street   Tel. (051) 236-6561/3
Liverpool, Merseyside L3 2BE

This firm's offices and salerooms are located a few blocks from the main train station, and across the street from the Walker Art Gallery, in the heart of downtown Liverpool. Notwithstanding its central location, parking facilities are available for those doughty enough to brave the traffic. Fine art sales are held monthly on Wednesdays, specialist sales fortnightly, also on Wednesdays; Victorian, Edwardian, and modern furnishings sales are held weekly on Tuesdays. There are occasional house and estate sales.

At one time or another, Outhwaite & Litherland sell any or all of the following: ARMS AND ARMOR, ART DECO, ART NOUVEAU, BOOKS, CLOCKS AND WATCHES, COINS, DRAWINGS, EMBROIDERY, FURNITURE, GLASS, JEWELRY, MAPS, MEDALS, MUSICAL INSTRUMENTS, PAINTINGS, PEWTER, PORCELAIN, RUGS, SCIENTIFIC INSTRUMENTS, SILVER, and STAMPS. Sales are advertised in the local press, in the national press (e.g., *Daily Telegraph*) and in specialty publications, such as *Art & Antiques Weekly*.

Catalogues are available singly for each sale; the price varies. Annual subscriptions are also obtainable; for prices, apply to the firm: in 1979–80, the cost was £10.

There is a buyer's premium of 5 percent on the hammer price. Absentee bids are executed (Mr. Litherland reports that "postal bids are to be received 24 hours before sale and to include name, address, lot no., bid, bank reference"; there is a mail bidding slip in each catalogue). Packing and shipping services "can be arranged," at the buyer's expense. Goods that prove to be not as catalogued may be returned: "Buyers have 21 days from date of sale to return goods and to prove mistake." Viewing is Mondays for the Tuesday sales, and Mondays and Tuesdays for the Wednesday sales (9:30 A.M.–4:45 P.M.). Settlement must be made within 48 hours.

The consignor's commission is "negotiable from 15 percent down." Consignments are accepted only "occasionally from dealers." There is no minimum value for consignment. Consignors are not charged for catalogue illustrations, insurance, or warehousing. Cost of collection of consignment is payable by vendor. Consigned goods are sold in approximately 4–6 weeks. Settlement is made 28 days after the sale. Reserves are accepted. Buy-in charge is 5 percent of the reserve price, but none if auctioneer withdraws lot at his discretion.

Appraisal service is available at varying cost; it is free if objects are consigned for sale.

Outhwaite & Litherland is a member of the Society of Fine Art Auctioneers.

276. Parsons, Welch & Cowell

129 High Street   Tel. (0732) 512 11/4
Sevenoaks, Kent TN13 1UU

This firm of chartered surveyors, auctioneers, and estate agents holds 2-day multisession sales every 5–6 weeks. One such auction of close to 1,000 lots offered the following (in the order of sale): dolls, toys, games; musical instruments, photographs, postcards, etc.; Oriental works of art; militaria; cigarette cards; scientific instruments; pottery and porcelain; glass; bronzes, pewter; clocks and watches; rugs and textiles; furniture; silver; jewelry; objects of virtu; coins and medals; stamps; oil paintings; prints and maps; books. These sales are held in the Argyle salerooms, the Drill Hall, Argyle Road. The train station is within walking distance and parking is close by. Occasional house and estate sales are also held.

Sales are advertised in the local and national press and in specialty publications, such as *Antiques Trade Gazette*. Announcements of forthcoming sales are available, as is an auction calendar for the year, both free of charge. Catalogues are available singly for each sale (70p) as well as by subscription (£7 per annum).

Since 1979, there has been a buyer's premium of 10 percent. Absentee bids are accepted, "but personal viewing of items is always recommended." Viewing is usually the day immediately prior to the sale, 11 A.M.–4:30 P.M., and the hour before the sale begins. Settlement: "immediately preferred, but certainly within one week."

The standard consignor's commission is 10 percent. Consignors are not charged separately for catalogue illustrations, insurance, and warehousing, but must pay packing and shipping. Goods are sold, reports partner D. W. Sanders, FRICS, within "maximum period of one month." Settlement is made 2 weeks after the sale. Reserves are accepted: the buy-in charge is 5 percent of the reserve price.

Parsons, Welch & Cowell belongs to the Society of Fine Art Auctioneers. Appraisal service is available. The cost is 1.5 percent of the total valuation.

277. Robert Patterson & Son
8–10 Orchard Street   Tel. (041 889) 24 35
Paisley, Strathclyde

Paisley lies cheek by jowl with Glasgow, and like that Scottish city, has seen better days in its past—a fact that may work to the advantage of this firm, which holds auctions usually every 2 weeks, and sometimes every week. These are mostly mixed-lot general-purpose sales. Occasional house and estate sales are also held.

Sales are advertised in the local press (e.g., the Glasgow *Herald*). Catalogues are not offered by subscription but are available for single sales. Contact Andrew Patterson.

There is no buyer's premium. Absentee bids are executed. Packing and shipping services are available, at the buyer's expense. No guarantees of authenticity are offered. The usual viewing procedure is the day before the sale, 9 A.M.–5 P.M. Buyer must settle account within 2 days after the sale.

The consignor's commission varies and is negotiable, depending upon the situation. There is a separate rate structure for dealers. Consignors are not charged for catalogue illustrations or for insurance, but if the firm has to remove the goods, the consignor pays for packing and shipping. Consigned goods are sold within 2 weeks. Settlement is made 1 week after the sale.

Appraisal service is available. Contact Mr. Patterson.

278. Peacock
58 St. Loyes Street   Tel. (0234) 508 12
Bedford, Bedfordshire MK40 1HD

A firm of chartered surveyors, estate agents, valuers, and auctioneers, Peacock holds weekly auctions of lesser-quality goods and monthly auctions of "antiques." The firm, which has offices elsewhere in the area as well, offers mixed-lot general-purpose sales which of course include FURNITURE. The firm also from time to time auctions "trade stocks, building materials, automobiles, plants, trees, shrubs, eggs, etc." Occasional house and estate sales are also held.

Sales are advertised in the local press, and in specialty publications "when appropriate." Announcements are available free of charge; to be placed on the mailing list, write Mark Baker. Catalogues are available singly and by subscription; the cost varies. There is no buyer's premium. Absentee bids are accepted. Packing and shipping services are not available. No guarantees of authenticity are offered; goods that prove to be not as catalogued may be returned "in certain circumstances." The usual viewing procedure is the day prior to and the morning of the sale. Buyers must settle "within 24 hours unless special arrangements are made."

The consignor's commission "is charged at the rate of 15 percent on the net proceeds of the sale subject to minimum commissions, the maximum of which is £5 per lot." The commission is negotiable, depending on the situation. There is no charge for insurance or warehousing. Packing and shipping are handled by the consignor. Goods are sold within 1 month. Settlement is made after 7 days.

Appraisal service is available. Cost depends upon service. Contact Mr. F. G. M. Peacock.

279. John E. Pinder and Son
Stone-Bridge   Tel. (077 478) 22 82/39 93
Longridge, Preston, Lancashire

Located in a small town about 20 miles inland from the popular seaside resort of Blackpool, this firm holds sales twice a week, Saturday and Thursday. These are general-purpose mixed-lot sales, most of which are not catalogued. Among the items sold are EMBROIDERY, CLOCKS AND WATCHES, and RUGS.

Sales are advertised regularly in the local and regional press. There is no buyer's premium. Absentee bids are accepted. Packing and shipping services are not available. No guarantees of authenticity are offered, but "goods may be returned if damaged items are not specified at the time of sale." Viewing is the day prior to the sale, 9 A.M.–5:30 P.M. Buyer must settle within 3 days after the sale.

The standard consignor's commission, which is negotiable, is "20 percent; single items of £100 charged at 10 percent; minimum commission is £2.50." Consigned goods are usually sold in 7–10 days. Settlement is made within 4–7 days. Reserves may be accepted, but must be negotiated.

Appraisal service is available: "no charge if goods are to be sold within auction room." Contact Mr. K. J. L. Pinder.

280. E. Reeves Ltd.

Reeves Corner, Church Street   Tel. (01) 688-3136 (3 lines)
Croydon, Surrey CR9 1QS

The Reeves auction rooms are the site of sales of FURNITURE and effects every Monday barring public holidays. E. Reeves Ltd. also holds COIN and MEDAL auctions the first Friday of every month in the church hall opposite the auction rooms. "Very occasionally," house and estate sales are held.

Sales are advertised in the local press; the coin sales are also advertised in specialist publications. List-like catalogues are available for each sale at 18p–40p, plus postage, and are also obtainable by subscription (annual cost, including postage: Furniture, £15; Coins and Medals, £4 U.K., £8 Europe, £12 outside Europe).

There is no buyer's premium. Absentee bids are executed. Packing and shipping services are available only for coin/medal auctions. No guarantees of authenticity are offered. Goods that prove to be not as described in the coin/medal auctions may be returned "within a reasonable time." Viewing is as follows: furniture—Friday, 2:15–5 P.M., and Saturday, 9 A.M.–5 P.M.; coins/medals—day prior to sale, 10 A.M.–3 P.M. Buyer must settle accounts immediately.

The consignor's commission is: "individual lots over £100, 17.5 percent; individual lots below £100, 20 percent; trade commission rate is 2.5 percent less." Reserves are accepted. Buy-in charge is 2.5 percent of reserve price. There is a minimum charge of £2 per account, 50p per lot. Consignors are not charged for catalogue illustrations, insurance, or warehousing. Consigned goods are sold within 1–2 months. Settlement is made with chattel consignors in approximately 1 week; with coin and medal consignors in approximately 4 weeks.

The firm does buy and sell on its own behalf: "goods sold on behalf of retail furniture division of E. Reeves Ltd."

Appraisal service is available. Contact Mr. M. W. Reeves.

281. Renton & Renton

16 Albert Street   Tel. (0423) 615 31
Harrogate, North Yorkshire HG1 1JP

This firm, which has other offices in the area, holds auctions weekly of FURNITURE and effects. These are advertised regularly in the local press. List-like catalogues are available for each sale; a subscription is £2.50 per annum.

286   AUCTION HOUSES

There is no buyer's premium. Absentee bids are not accepted. Packing and shipping services are not available. No guarantees of authenticity are offered. Viewing is usually the day before the auction, 10 A.M.–4 P.M. Settlement must be made by noon the day following the sale.

The consignor's commission, according to director H. C. Bigg, ARICS, is "10–17.5 percent, depending on type of sale, status of vendor, and type of goods." Consignors are charged for catalogue illustrations and insurance, and are responsible for bringing consignments to saleroom or must pay for transport. Consignors are not charged warehousing. Consigned goods are usually sold within 7 days. Settlement is within 7 days after the sale. Reserves are accepted. The buy-in charge is negotiable.

282. Riddetts of Bournemouth

26 Richmond Hill, The Square   Tel. (0202) 256 86 (4 lines)
Bournemouth, Dorset BH2 6EJ

In 1979, Riddetts celebrated the centenary of its founding by shedding its property division and taking a 999-year lease on its auction galleries, its auction operations having proved quite successful in recent years. Occasional house and estate sales are also held.

The firm holds multisession 2–4-day sales of FURNITURE and other effects approximately twice a month. And 6–8 times a year, the firm holds "collective sales of fine general antiques, SILVER, JEWELRY, RUGS, PAINTINGS, etc.—specially selected." Altogether, the firm offers 26 sales a year, advertising them in the national press (e.g., *Daily Telegraph*), the local and regional press, and specialty publications. An auction calendar is available free of charge; contact the firm.

Catalogues are available for each sale, which is usually well over 1,400 lots. These catalogues are 30p unillustrated, and 50p illustrated; postage is extra. An annual subscription in 1980 cost £15, including postage, for all 26 catalogues.

There is no buyer's premium. Absentee bids are executed, but "not without prior arrangement," says senior partner Stacey Adams, FRICS. Packing and shipping services are available, at the buyer's expense. No guarantees of authenticity are offered, but buyers may return goods that prove to be not as described ("the time limit is 7 days from the fall of the hammer"). The usual viewing procedure is 10 A.M.–4 P.M. on the day prior to first day's sale. Buyers not known to the firm may be asked to put down a 25 percent deposit immediately after their winning bid. Settlement must be by 11:30 A.M. on Saturday after the sale, in cash or certified check.

The standard consignor's commission is "15 percent for private consignors, 12.5–10 percent for specially good items." The commission is negotiable. Consignors are not usually charged for catalogue illustrations. Consignors are responsible for getting their goods to the saleroom; they are not normally charged for warehousing. The firm insures only against "loss arising from fire, storm, tempest, flood, burglary, or robbery. Any additional coverage (e.g., breakage, petty larceny, and 'all risks') must be covered by consignor." Consigned goods are usually sold within 3–4 weeks. Settlement is 3 weeks after the sale. Reserves are accepted. The buy-in charge is 5 percent of the reserve. Appraisal service is available. "No charge at the galleries. Personal calls will be quoted for on application, depending on type, time and distance."

Riddetts of Bournemouth estimates its annual turnover as being over £1.5 million. The firm is a member of the Society of Fine Art Auctioneers.

Robson Lowe Ltd.

283. 50 Pall Mall   Tel. (01) 839-4034
London SW1Y 5JZ   Telex: 915410
Cable: STAMPSLONDON

284. 39 Poole Hill   Tel. (0202) 232 35/99
Bournemouth, Dorset BH2 5PX

This firm has made the auctioneering of STAMPS, artifacts of POSTAL HISTORY, and PHILATELIC LITERATURE a highly profitable and well-run business. Since its first auction in the mid-1930s, it has held hundreds. The Bournemouth branch is the result of Robson Lowe's purchase of Bournemouth Stamp Auctioneers in the late 1940s. At the end of the 1960s, Lowe began a mutually advantageous association with Christie's which in 1980 resulted in the firm's formally becoming a part of Christie's International Ltd. Robson Lowe's annual turnover is in excess of £7 million.

Robson Lowe Ltd., which also publishes various respected philatelic journals and standard philatelic reference works, holds auctions in the U.K. approximately 4–5 times a month. The more specialized sales, such as the auction of a particular collection, are held in the pleasant functional saleroom in London; what are described as "general sales" are held in Bournemouth. Much of the bidding in these sales, as in most stamp auctions, comes from mail order bids, and Robson Lowe, like its counterparts, has a "postal viewing" system. Clients interested in making use of this should send references well in advance.

Sales are advertised in "all important general and specialized publications." Catalogues are available singly for each sale and by subscription. Most catalogues cost £1. The annual subscription rate depends on what you wish to subscribe to and from where you are subscribing. For example: catalogues for all sales (London, Bournemouth, and overseas) cost £30 U.K., £45 Europe, £55 Middle East, £65 U.S. and Africa, £75 Australia and Japan; catalogues going outside the U.K. and Europe are sent 2nd-class airmail. Prices are correspondingly less if you subscribe to only some sales, such as postal history, or British Empire specialized.

There is no buyer's premium. Absentee bids are executed (there are postal bid forms in all catalogues). Guarantees of authenticity are offered. Packing and shipping services are available, at the buyer's expense. "Any item not as described can be returned for re-examination and credited if accepted." The usual viewing procedure is "in respective auction rooms usually the week prior to the sale; postal viewing is at our discretion to known buyers." Settlement is maximum 7 days for bidders in the U.K., and "immediately on the receipt of invoice for overseas buyers." All purchases made by "residents in the dollar area must be paid for in dollars at the controlled rate of exchange or by Sterling Draft."

The consignor's commission is negotiable, depending upon the situation. No single consignment should value less than £35. Consignors pay for transport of goods to Robson Lowe offices, and pay for return packing and shipping if goods go unsold. There is no charge for warehousing. Consigned goods are sold on the average in 5 months. Settlement is 4–5 weeks after the sale. Reserves are accepted. The buy-in charge "depends upon type of property and if reserved by owner; lowest is £2 per lot."

Appraisal service is available. The cost "depends upon the result of the appraisal—varies from 2 percent to 1 percent. No charge if we sell."

Robson Lowe also has a "Busy Buyers Service," which will send catalogues and "cuttings" in specialized areas to subscribers. You should fill out the information sheet and application form before subscribing. Write to Mrs. L. Gullivar in Bournemouth.

285. Rosan & Co.

144–150 London Road   Tel. (01) 688-1123/4/5
Croydon, Surrey CR0 2TD

Every Saturday at 10 A.M., Rosan & Co. holds auction sales at what used to be the Croydon Auction Rooms and often are still so described. These sales, of which many lots have been entered by the bailiffs and by H.M. Customs and Excise as well as by various liquidators, cover a wide range of territory. Sale No. 551 (August 4, 1979) offered among other items furniture, stamps, a jerry can, 2 electric blankets, a Lynx toilet cistern, and an onyx chess set and board. Sharing the same address is the Croydon Car Mart, "for quality used cars." Liquidation sales on site as well as occasional house and estate sales are held.

Sales are advertised in the local press and in specialty publications. List-like catalogues for each sale are available at the firm's offices and at the saleroom, and an annual subscription can be had for £16 per annum. There is no buyer's premium. No guarantees of authenticity are offered. Buyers may return goods "only in the event of misrepresentation," reports auctioneer I. G. Morris, FSVA. Viewing is Fridays, 9:30 A.M.–5 P.M., and the morning of the sale. Settlement is same day.

The standard consignor's commission is 20 percent private, 17.5 percent trade. The minimum charge per lot is £1. Consigned goods are sold within 14 days. Settlement is 10 days after the sale. Reserves are accepted. The buy-in charge is 2.5 percent of the reserve, but keep in mind the minimum charge. There is a minimum value of £5 for a consignment.

Rugby Salerooms: see Seaman of Rugby (Rugby, Warwickshire)

Rye Auction Galleries: see Vidler & Co. (Rye, East Sussex)

286. Lacy Scott and Sons
3 Hatter Street   Tel. (0284) 635 31 (10 lines)
Bury St. Edmunds, Suffolk IP33 1NB

The fine art auction department of this firm holds 2-day sales each quarter at the Angel Hotel and its neighbor on Angel Hill, the Athenaeum. Both sites are well known to Charles Dickens fans. It was while staying at the Angel that Mr. Pickwick learned to his horror that Mrs. Bardwell was bringing a breach-of-promise action against him. And it was at the Athenaeum that Charles Dickens, who also stayed at the Angel Hotel, gave readings from his works just a few years before Lacy Scott was founded in 1869. The firm, which has branch offices that handle estate and commercial matters, also holds house and estate sales from time to time, as well as wine sales.

About 1,600–1,700 lots are sold at these sales, at the rate of some 100 lots an hour. The pace is fast and there is no luncheon interval. Among the items sold are CLOCKS AND WATCHES, COINS, FURNITURE, GLASS, JEWELRY, MAPS, PAINTINGS, PORCELAIN, PRINTS, RUGS, and SILVER. Twice a year, the sales include WORKING STEAM AND SCALE MODELS.

These sales are advertised in the local and national press, as well as in specialty periodicals, such as *Antiques Trade Gazette* and *Art & Antiques Weekly*. A sales calendar is available free of charge from the firm. List-like catalogues (without estimates) are available singly for each sale from the firm, at the saleroom, and through the post for 50p. An annual subscription costs £3.

There is no buyer's premium. Packing and shipping services are available, at the buyer's expense. The usual viewing procedure is: Angel Hotel, a few hours before beginning of the auction; Athenaeum, 4–8 P.M. the day before the sale. The sale is generally divided up between these 2 venues, in various rooms. In the catalogue, a special condition of sale states: "Each lot . . . is sold with all faults, imperfections, and errors of description. . . . Purchasers are deemed to have satisfied themselves by inspection or otherwise. . . . Neither the vendor nor the auctioneers make or give . . . any representation or warranty." But the firm will within the limits of the law rescind any sale where the catalogue has erred. Buyer must settle within 14 days, and certainly before removal of goods.

The standard consignor's commission is 12.5 percent, but it is negotiable, depending on the situation. The firm does not accept consignments from dealers. Consignors pay for catalogue illustrations, insurance, packing and shipping, and warehousing. Reserves are accepted. The buy-in costs are removal, warehousing, and 2.5 percent of reserve price. Goods are sold within 3 months. Settlement is usually 8 days after the sale.

Appraisal service is available, free of charge for items that are subsequently consigned for auction. Contact Peter Chrichton, ARICS.

Various members of the firm are members of the Royal Institution of Chartered Surveyors.

287. Seaman of Rugby

Auction House, 20 Little Church Street   Tel. (0788) 2367
Rugby, Warwickshire CV21 3AW

Located within walking distance of the famous school, this family business of auctioneers and valuers holds weekly Monday-morning sales and an "Antique and Collectors' Auction" every 2–3 months. The latter sales are catalogued. Occasional house and estate sales are also held.

Sales are advertised in the local and national press. For announcements of forthcoming sales, write to be put on the mailing list. Catalogues are available at the firm's offices and through the post; a subscription is £1 per annum.

Since 1979, there has been a buyer's premium of 10 percent. Absentee bids are executed "if we know the client," reports M. G. Seaman. Packing and shipping services are available, at the buyer's expense. Guarantees of authenticity are not given: "we ask the client to view and give our opinion." Settlement is expected by the end of the day following the sale.

The consignor's commission "depends on the value per single item." Consignors are not charged for catalogue illustrations, insurance, or warehousing. Consignors are expected to get their goods to the saleroom. Settlement is made 10 days after sale. Reserves are accepted. The buy-in charge is 5 percent of the reserve price.

288. Simons and Company

32 Roman Bank   Tel. (0754) 660 61
Skegness, Lincolnshire PE25 2SL

This firm, which has offices elsewhere in the area, holds monthly general-purpose mixed-lot sales in its own saleroom. They are advertised in the local and regional press. List-like catalogues are available 10 days prior to the sale; write to R. J. Turner. Catalogues are not available by subscription.

There is a buyer's premium of 5 percent. Absentee bids are not accepted. Packing and shipping services are available, at the buyer's expense. No guarantees of authenticity are offered. Viewing is the day before the sale. Buyers must settle accounts within 48 hours, unless other arrangements have been made.

There is a standard consignor's commission of 12.5 percent; it is negotiable. Consignments are not accepted from dealers. Consignors are charged for insurance and warehousing, but packing and shipping is the consignors' responsibility, and there is a charge only if the firm has to undertake the cartage of goods to the saleroom. Consigned goods are sold within 3 months. Settlement is made 1 month after the sale. Reserves are accepted, but as partner J. D.

Turner, FRICS, reports, the buy-in charge is "10 percent if subject to reserves; nil otherwise."

Appraisal service is available. Contact either Mr. Turner.

289. Smythe Son & Walker

174 Victoria Road West   Tel. (0253) 85 21 84 / 85 40 84
Cleveleys, Lancashire

This firm holds sales on Tuesdays throughout the year in this small town some miles north of Blackpool. Lots auctioned include FURNITURE and JEWELRY, as well as plants and shrubs in season. Occasional house and estate sales are held.

Sales are advertised in the local and regional press. List-like catalogues are available for each sale (but not by subscription); write the firm. There is no buyer's premium. Absentee bids are not executed. Packing and shipping services are not available from the firm. No guarantees of authenticity are offered. Viewing is the day prior to the sale, 9:30 A.M.–4:30 P.M. Settlement must be made within 7 days after the sale.

The standard consignor's commission is 20 percent. It is negotiable, depending upon the situation. There is a separate rate for dealers: 10–20 percent. Consignors are not charged insurance, warehousing, or packing and shipping (if goods have to be returned). Consigned goods are sold within 1 week; settlement is 7 days after the sale. Reserves are accepted. There is no minimum value necessary for a consignment.

Appraisal service is available. The fees vary. Contact Patrick J. D. Smythe, FSVA.

290. Southam & Sons

Corn Exchange   Tel. (08012) 24 09
Thrapston, Nr. Kettering
Northamptonshire NN14 4LJ

Thrapston is located 11 miles northwest of Huntingdon and 19 miles southwest of Peterborough. The Corn Exchange saleroom is located in the center of town, and there Southam & Sons conducts a variety of auction sales during the year: monthly antique sales, monthly general sales, and twice-yearly ARMS sales, which include lots of MILITARIA. There is "ample free parking." Occasional house and estate sales are also held.

Sales are advertised regularly in the local press and in specialty publications of various kinds. List-like catalogues at 30p are available for each sale, and can be obtained at the firm's offices, at the sale, or through the post. An annual subscription to all catalogues costs £3 per annum in the U.K.

There is no buyer's premium. Absentee bids are executed. Packing and shipping services are not available. No guarantees of authenticity are offered. The usual viewing procedure is: antique sales, preceding day, 9:30 A.M.–8 P.M., and morning of sale; general sales, morning of sale; gun sales, afternoon of sale (usually held in early evening). Settlement is "immediately unless by special arrangement with auctioneers."

The standard consignor's commission is 15 percent, but it is negotiable, depending on the situation. Minimum value for a consignment is £5. Consignors are not charged for catalogue illustrations, insurance, or warehousing. Reserves are accepted. The buy-in charge is £1 per lot.

291. Robert Spark and Company
Olde Englishe Road   Tel. (0629) 24 51
Matlock, Derbyshire DE4 3LT

This firm holds sales once or twice a month of FURNITURE, PORCELAIN, SILVER, etc., at its saleroom by Dale Road, off Olde Englishe Road. Spark, a firm of chartered surveyors, auctioneers, valuers, and estate agents, runs a two-tier operation—sales of lesser-quality furniture and effects, and of better-quality goods, which are sold in a general antiques sale. Occasional house and estate sales are also held.

Sales are advertised in the local and regional press (e.g., the Matlock *Mercury* and the Derbyshire *Times*). List-like catalogues are available for each sale "on request" and by subscription (£5 per annum). Mr. Spark points out that "for overseas visitors a subscription would not be effective and it would be better to contact our office for catalogues for individual sales when in this country."

There is no buyer's premium. Absentee bids are not executed. Packing and shipping services are not available from the firm. No guarantees of authenticity are offered, but goods that prove to be not as catalogued may be returned: "there is no time limit," reports Mr. Spark; "purchasers are protected under the Trades Descriptions Act and whilst every care is taken in describing goods in our catalogues, we are responsible for our own descriptions and will refund purchase money if a mistake has been made." Viewing is 2 days prior for sales of general antiques and 1 day prior for sales of household furniture and effects (all 10 A.M.–4 P.M.). "Buyers are expected to settle on the day of the sale or the day following, but exceptions can be made."

The consignor's commission is "generally 15 percent," and it is negotiable, depending upon the situation. Consignors who are dealers are charged a different rate: 10–12.5 percent. Consignors are not charged for catalogue illustrations or for warehousing prior to sale; they are charged for insurance and for cost of cartage to saleroom. Goods are generally sold within 1 month. Settlement is usually 14 days after the sale. Reserves are accepted; the buy-in charge is 3 percent of the reserve price (with a minimum charge of £1).

Appraisal service is available. Fees vary. Contact Mr. Spark.

292. Henry Spencer & Sons
20 The Square   Tel. (0777) 70 67 67
Retford, Nottinghamshire DN22 6DJ

This firm of auctioneers, valuers, land and estate agents has flourished since its founding in 1840. At present, there are offices at 10 other locations in the area, handling a variety of tasks. At Retford, once described as "a brisk market town," the firm has established its Fine Arts Centre, in whose pleasant functional salerooms Henry Spencer & Sons holds specialized sales on Wednesdays and Thursdays during most of the auction season. The catalogues for these sales are well put together, and though sometimes sparse in detail, are a good guide to the lots being sold.

Catalogues are sold in groups, and these give a good indication of what is sold by the firm: Clocks, Watches and Scientific Instruments; Antique Furniture and Works of Art; Victorian and Later Furniture, etc.; Silver and Jewelry; Porcelain and Glass; Pictures; Coins, Medals and Stamps; Books; Oriental Ceramics, Furniture and Works of Art; Country House Sales. Catalogues, 85p each, are available at the firm's offices and the salerooms, as well as by mail (£1, including postage). Subscription prices vary with sale and with location of subscriber; write to the address above for details.

These sales are advertised in the local press, the national press (e.g., *Daily Telegraph* and *Financial Times*), and specialty publications, such as *Antiques Trade Gazette* and *Art & Antiques Weekly*. Each catalogue lists forthcoming sales for the next 6 weeks or so.

Since 1978, there has been a buyer's premium of 10 percent. Absentee bids are accepted (each catalogue contains a postal bidding form). Packing and shipping services are available, but only "on a small scale within the United Kingdom" and at buyer's expense. No guarantees of authenticity are offered, but buyers may return goods that are not as described, and any "deliberate forgery," if they notify the firm within 14 days and return the goods within the subsequent 7 days. The usual viewing procedure is 1 or 2 days prior to the sale, 10 A.M.–3 P.M., and the morning of the sale. Settlement must be made within 7 days after the sale.

The standard consignor's commission (except in specialist coin sales) is 10 percent of the hammer price, and it is negotiable, depending upon the situation. The minimum charge per lot is £2. The consignor's commission for the coin sales is: 20 percent of the price realized for each lot sold up to £99.99; 15 percent from £100 to £999.99; 12.5 percent at £1,000 or more. The minimum charge is 50p per lot.

There is no minimum value necessary for consignment. Consignors are charged for catalogue illustrations (up to £10) and for insurance (75p per £100). Consignors are also charged for cartage if the firm has to bring the goods to the saleroom. There is no charge for warehousing. Consigned goods are sold "depending on sale schedule in approximately 3–8 weeks." Settlement is approximately 15 days after the sale. Reserves are accepted. There is a buy-in charge of 5 percent of the reserve price (with a minimum charge of £2 per lot), but if the reserve was advised and agreed upon by the auctioneers, the charge is £2.

Appraisal service is available. It is free if given on the premises; otherwise, the cost varies, depending on the type of valuation and the location of the property. Contact John Causton.

Henry Spencer & Sons belongs to the Society of Fine Art Auctioneers.

293. Spurgeon & Company
57 Station Road   Tel. (0255) 218 71/2
Clacton-on-Sea, Essex CO15 1RT

The resort of Clacton-on-Sea has a reputation for being noisy but friendly, and so too do the Central Auction Rooms on Hayes Road, just a hop, skip, and jump from the administrative offices of the firm, which holds auction sales at 6–8-week intervals, as well as occasional house and estate sales.

Sales are advertised in the local press. List-like catalogues are available for each sale on viewing and on sale day; by subscription, the price per annum is £5. Write to I. H. Gilchrist, FRICS.

There is no buyer's premium. Absentee bids are executed. Packing and shipping services are not available from the firm. No guarantees of authenticity are offered, but buyers have the opportunity to return goods that are not as described ("each case is treated on merit"). The usual viewing procedure is day prior to sale, 11 A.M.–4 P.M., and morning of sale, 9–10. Settlement must be made by 4:30 P.M. on day after sale.

The standard consignor's commission is 17 percent, but it is negotiable, depending upon the situation. Consignors pay for illustrations "where used" and for insurance (50p per £100). Consignors pay cartage if they do not bring goods to saleroom. Consignors do pay for warehousing. Reserves are accepted. Buy-in charge is "percentage calculation on reserve price fixed by consignor." Settlement is made 1 week after sale. How long before goods consigned are sold? "Indefinite."

Appraisal service is available. "Charges are according to situation." Contact Mr. Gilchrist.

294. Stanilands William H. Brown
28 Nether Hall Road   Tel. (0302) 677 66
Doncaster, South Yorkshire DN1 2PW

Stanilands was an active firm of surveyors, valuers, auctioneers, and estate agents who during the 1960s and 1970s dramatically expanded their activities in Yorkshire. William H. Brown was a successful old-line firm (see entry above). The two merged in 1980, to "provide a service second to none." Under the direction of Peter Young, Stanilands William H. Brown holds at the Nether Hall auction rooms "auction sales of miscellanea fortnightly" and periodically holds "specialized sales of Antiques and Works of Art." Goods sold include CLOCKS AND WATCHES, FURNITURE, JEWELRY, PAINTINGS, PORCELAIN, POSTCARDS, SCIENTIFIC INSTRUMENTS, and SILVER. Occasional house and estate sales are also held.

Catalogues are available singly for each sale and by subscription for the better-quality periodic sales (£3 per annum). Contact Miss A. L. Ingram. Sales are advertised in the local and national press as well as in specialty publications.

There is no buyer's premium. Absentee bids are executed. Packing and shipping services are available, at the buyer's expense. No guarantees of authenticity are offered, but goods that do not prove to be as described may be returned if the purchaser notifies the firm within 14 days and returns them within the next 7 days. The usual viewing procedure for the better-quality Thursday sales is Monday 2:30–8 P.M. and Tuesday 10 A.M.–4 P.M.; for the fortnightly Tuesday sales: Saturday 9:30–11:30 A.M. and Monday 10 A.M.–4 P.M. Settlement is immediately after the sale.

The standard consignor's commission is 15 percent, but it is negotiable, depending on the situation. There is a separate rate for dealers and institutions, although according to Mr. Young, consignments are "not generally accepted" from dealers. There is no charge for catalogue illustrations, insurance, or warehousing. Consigned goods are sold mostly within 2 weeks. Settlement is made 10 days after the sale. Reserves are accepted.

Appraisal service is available; "free of charge" if made at office, "small charge if journey is made." Contact Mr. Young.

Star Salerooms: see E. Tegid Evans & Co. (Ruthin, Clwyd)

295. Stride & Son
Southdown House, St. John's Street   Tel. (0243) 78 26 26
Chichester, West Sussex PO19 1XQ

This firm of chartered surveyors, livestock auctioneers, and real estate agents also holds auctions of FURNITURE and works of art. Sales of furniture and effects are offered the last Friday of every month, and more specialized sales of items including JEWELRY and SILVER are scheduled as necessary. Occasional house and estate sales are also held.

These sales are advertised in the local press and in specialty publications, such as *Antiques Trade Gazette*. List-like catalogues for each sale are available at the firm's offices; or write to Mark Hewitt. An annual subscription costs £5 per annum.

There is no buyer's premium. Absentee bids are executed. Packing and shipping services are available, at the buyer's expense. Buyers may return goods that prove to be not as described; the firm reports that "under English law we sell subject to Trades Description Act and Misrepresentation Act. If it can be proved that we have miscatalogued we will refund purchase price within one month." Viewing for trade buyers during office hours; for private buyers, day before the sale, 10 A.M.–4 P.M. Buyers must settle accounts within 7 days.

Standard consignor's commission for those not in the trade is 15 percent. The commission is negotiable, depending on the situation. There is a separate 12.5 percent rate for dealers. Consignors are not charged for insurance or warehousing, or for packing and shipping if they bring goods to the saleroom. Goods are sold within 1 month. Settlement is made 10 days after the sale. Reserves are accepted; the buy-in charge is "nil if reserve agreed to."

Appraisal service is available. Contact Mr. Hewitt.

296. The Sunderland Auction Rooms
Chippendale House, Mary Street   Tel. (0783) 560 20
Sunderland, Tyne & Wear

Sales, held fortnightly, are advertised in the local press. The firm also holds occasional house sales. Catalogues are available for the house sales only.

There is a buyer's premium of 5 percent. Absentee bids are not accepted. Packing and shipping services are not available from the firm. No guarantees of authenticity are offered. The usual viewing procedure is 2 days before the sale. Settlement is "immediately unless regular client."

The consignor's commission is "negotiable." Consignors are charged for insurance but not for warehousing. Consigned goods are sold within 2–4 weeks. Settlement is one week after the sale. There is a minimum value of £20 for a consignment. Reserves are accepted. The buy-in charge is 5 percent plus the cartage cost of returning the goods to the consignor or hauling them away.

297. G. E. Sworder & Sons
Chequers, 19 North Street   Tel. (0279) 524 41 (10 lines)
Bishop's Stortford, Hertfordshire CM23 2LF

Sworder (est. 1782) is a venerable firm whose many activities include the holding of mixed-lot auction sales on Tuesdays at approximately 2-week intervals. The following is the firm's advertising description of the contents of one such sale (May 13, 1980): "Approx. 500 lots to include 1963 Rolls-Royce Silver Cloud III. Furniture to include fine set 6 William IV mahogany dining chairs. Regency mahogany cylinder top bureau bookcase; Georgian oak bureau; 2 Edwardian bureau bookcases; antique oak settle; Victorian 3 pc. parlor suite and several Victorian arm chairs; Victorian walnut credenza. Other interesting lots include rare 16″ Oriental weight driven wall timepiece, antique netsuke, 19th century maps, silver, plate, and pictures." Occasional house and estate sales are also held.

Sales are advertised in the local press and in specialty publications, such as *Antiques Trade Gazette.* Catalogues are available singly for each sale and by subscription; contact Mrs. Sheppard for information.

There is no buyer's premium. Absentee bids are not accepted. Packing and shipping services are not available from the firm. No guarantees of authenticity are offered. Goods that prove to be not as described may be returned (the firm states "unconditional refund of miscatalogued lots"). Viewing is Saturday, 9 A.M.–12:30 P.M., Monday, 9 A.M.–4:30 P.M., and the morning of the sale. Settlement is within 2 weeks of the sale.

The consignor's commission is 15 percent up to £100; 12.5 percent £100–£500; 10 percent £500 and up. The commission is negotiable, depending on the situation. Consignors are not charged for insurance or warehousing (provided that unsold goods are collected within 2 weeks). Consignors must pay cartage if the firm delivers goods to the saleroom. Consigned goods will be sold within 6 weeks. Settlement is 1 week after the sale (provided purchaser has paid). Reserves are accepted; the buy-in charge is "by arrangement prior to sale." There is no minimum value necessary for a consignment.

Appraisal service is available. Contact D. S. Fletcher.

298. Laurence and Martin Taylor
63 High Street   Tel. (0404) 2404/5
Honiton, Devon EX14 8PW

The pleasant town of Honiton has a long High Street lined with Georgian-style buildings, one of which houses the local office of the Taylors—estate agents, auctioneers, surveyors, and valuers. Not too far away, at 205 High Street, is a more modern building with its own parking area: their saleroom, the Honiton Galleries, at which the Taylors hold sales approximately twice a month, usually on Fridays. These are mixed-lot sales generally, of 2 basic types: PAINTINGS, DRAWINGS, and PRINTS; and antique FURNITURE, PORCELAIN, SILVER, etc. At Christmas time the sale includes TOYS. At other times the Taylors sell BOOKS and garden machinery.

Sales are advertised in the local and national press, such as the *Daily Telegraph,* as well as in specialty periodicals, such as *Antiques Trade Gazette.* Catalogues for each sale are available singly (50p) at the firm's offices, the galleries, and through the post. A subscription within the U.K. is £7 per annum. For rates outside the U.K., write to Mrs. S. H. White at 63 High Street.

There is no buyer's premium. Absentee bids are executed. Packing and shipping services are available, at the buyer's expense. Guarantees of authenticity are offered within clearly defined limits at the picture sales. Goods that prove to be not as described may be returned within 14 days. Viewing is 9 A.M.–5 P.M. on day preceding sale, and morning of sale. Buyer must settle account immediately unless otherwise arranged. Credit references are necessary for any purchase paid for by a check for over £50.

The standard consignor's commission is 15 percent for individual lots up to £100; 12.5 percent between £100 and £300; 10 percent over £301. According to M. J. Taylor, FRICS, consignors are "sometimes" charged for catalogue illustrations and for warehousing; they are charged for packing and shipping, but not for insurance. Consigned goods are sold within 4 weeks to 3 months. Settlement is made 14 days after the sale. There is no minimum value necessary for a consignment to be accepted. Reserves are accepted. The buy-in charge is 5 percent ("not always enforced"). There is a minimum charge of £1 per lot, whether it is sold, unsold, or withdrawn. Mr. Taylor also reports that "although we do not encourage too many trade lots we do, in certain circumstances, offer 2.5 percent discount to a minimum of 10 percent to the trade."

Appraisal service is available. The cost is "by negotiation." Contact Mr. Taylor.

299. Louis Taylor & Son

Percy St. Hanley   Tel. (0782) 26 02 22 (10 lines)
Stoke-on-Trent, Staffordshire ST1 1NF

A veteran firm (est. 1877) which has offices elsewhere in the area and is involved with property management, etc., Taylor & Son holds weekly mixed-lot general-purpose auction sales and special "fine art" sales from time to time on Mondays and/or Tuesdays. Goods sold include FURNITURE, PORCELAIN, SILVER, and STAFFORDSHIRE POTTERY. P. H. Taylor has been involved with this firm's fine art sales for over 40 years. Occasional house and estate sales are held.

List-like catalogues, which are not obtainable by subscription, are normally available about a week prior to the sale. Absentee bids are accepted. Viewing is the Wednesday, Thursday, and Friday prior to sale. There is no buyer's premium. Payment is expected as soon as possible.

The consignor's commission is 15 percent to private individuals and 10 percent to the trade. No other charges are made to consignors. About 1 month elapses between consignment and sale of goods. Settlement is within 14 days after the sale. Reserves are accepted and are fixed by discussion.

300. Taylor, Lane & Creber

24 Queen Ann Terrace, North Hill   Tel. (0752) 26 62 95
Plymouth, Devon PL4 8EQ

This firm is the result of a 1980 merger between Taylor, Son & Creber, and W. H. Lane and Son. W. H. Lane serves as the firm's fine arts auction branch (see entry). Taylor, Lane & Creber, which has many other activities in the property and appraisal field, also continues to hold weekly mixed lot auction sales of what are described as "household effects" and "shipping goods." These sales are held in the Western Auction Rooms, 38 North Hill, only a long jump from the firm's main offices. House and estate sales are held occasionally.

Sales are advertised in the local press (e.g., *Western Morning News*). List-like catalogues are not available by subscription, but can be obtained singly for each sale; contact the main office. There is no buyer's premium. Absentee bids are accepted. Packing and shipping services are available, at the buyer's expense. No guarantees of authenticity are offered. Viewing is as advertised. Settlement must be made within 7 days after the sale.

The standard consignor's commission is 15 percent. Consignments are not

accepted from dealers. Consignors do not pay for catalogue illustrations, insurance, or warehousing. Consigned goods are sold within 1 month, and settlement is made within 1 month after the sale. Reserves are accepted. The buy-in charge is "to be agreed upon."
Appraisal service is available. Contact the main office.

301. James Thompson
64 Main Street   Tel. (0468) 7 15 55
Kirkby Londsdale, Cumbria LA6 2AJ

This firm, which has other offices in the area, holds 2-day auction sales generally once a month, on Wednesdays and Thursdays. Specialties of the firm are Georgian and Victorian FURNITURE, 19th-century British PAINTINGS, and SILVER. Other kinds of goods are also sold at its auctions, which can include as many as 1,500 lots.

Sales are advertised in the local press and in specialty publications, such as *Art & Antiques Weekly.* Announcements of forthcoming sales are available at no cost; write the firm to be put on the mailing list. Catalogues are not available for the sales; there are, however, detailed lists, which can be obtained by writing to the firm.

There is no buyer's premium. Absentee bids are not accepted. Packing and shipping services are not available from the firm. No guarantees of authenticity are offered. Goods that prove to be not as described may be returned, but that is "guaranteed only if specifically stated." Viewing is usually the Tuesday before the sale. Accounts are to be settled "immediately."

The consignor's commission is 15 percent of the selling price. The only negotiable rates are for sales held on the vendor's premises. Consignors are not charged for warehousing, or for packing and shipping if they deliver goods, but are charged for insurance (25p per £100). Goods are normally sold within 4–8 weeks. Settlement is approximately 14 days after sale. Reserves are accepted.

Appraisal service is available: "Normally 1 percent of valuation. Free if items are entered for sale."

Thomson, Roddick & Laurie
302. 24 Lowther Street   Tel. (0228) 289 39
Carlisle, Cumbria

303. 60 Whitesands   Tel. (0387) 53 66
Dumfries, Dumfries and Galloway

This firm of "Auctioneers and Estate Agents in Cumbria and South West Scotland" has its more important offices in Carlisle (a reasonably prosperous border city 'twixt Scotland and England) and in Dumfries (often referred to as Scotland's "Queen of the South," the market center for a rich and large area). The firm holds auctions in these 2 towns and in others in the area, including Wigton, which is in England, and Annan, which is in Scotland. Sales in Carlisle are held in the Crown and Mitre Hotel, without any doubt the best hotel in town and within walking distance of the train station. Sales in Dumfries are held in the Loreburn Hall, in the center of town and also not a long walk from the train station. Both locations have parking close by.

Thomson, Roddick & Laurie holds monthly general sales of FURNITURE and effects at Wigton and Annan; regular catalogue sales of antiques and Victoriana, sometimes at Wigton and more often at Dumfries; and occasional specialist collectors' sales, particularly of antiquarian BOOKS and related items, SILVER, COINS, MEDALS, etc., mostly at Carlisle. Occasional house and estate sales are also held. These sales are advertised in the local and regional press, and in the case of the better-quality sales, in specialty publications, such as *Antiques Trade Gazette*.

Only the better-quality sales are catalogued. A single catalogue costs 50p (plus postage if ordered by mail). A subscription is £5 per annum. Write to the Carlisle office.

There is no buyer's premium. Mail order bids are executed. Packing and shipping services are available, at the buyer's expense. No guarantees of authenticity are offered; indeed, in one catalogue it is stated that "a number of items are damaged or defective; purchasers must therefore satisfy themselves as to the authenticity and condition of all articles." Viewing is generally the morning of the sale and the day before, 11 A.M.–7 P.M. Settlement is "immediately except by special arrangement."

The standard consignor's commission is 15 percent, but it is negotiable, depending upon the situation. According to J. D. M. Thomson, ARICS, consignments are "not generally" accepted from dealers. Consignors do not pay for catalogue illustrations, insurance, or warehousing. They do pay for cartage of goods to the saleroom. Consigned goods are sold "minimum of 3 weeks, maximum 3 months." Settlement is made 2 weeks after the sale.

Appraisal service is available; "it is free if goods are for sale, otherwise fee is by arrangement."

304. Turner & Sons
28–36 Roscoe Street   Tel. (051) 709 4005
Liverpool, Merseyside L 1 9DW

This firm holds mixed-lot general-purpose auctions weekly on Thursdays, FURNITURE being among the goods for sale. Occasional house and estate sales are also held. The sales are advertised in the local press (e.g., Liverpool *Daily Echo*). Catalogues are not available by subscription, but these list-like rundowns of what's for sale are obtainable singly for each auction. Contact A. F. Gilmore.

There is no buyer's premium. Absentee bids are executed. Packing and shipping services are available, at the buyer's expense. Viewing is the previous day. Settlement must be completed within 48 hours. The consignor's commission is variable (10–22.5 percent) and negotiable. Consignments are not accepted from dealers. Consignors are not charged insurance. Consignors must pay cartage if they do not deliver goods to saleroom. Reserves are accepted; the buy-in charge "depends upon reserve." Consigned goods are sold within 2 weeks. Settlement is made approximately 10 days after the sale. Appraisal service is available. Contact Mr. Gilmore.

305. Turner, Rudge & Turner
29 High Street Tel. (0342) 241 01/3; 242 28
East Grinstead, West Sussex RH19 3AJ

Every Thursday at noon, this firm (which has other offices in the area) holds mixed-lot general-purpose auction sales, mostly uncatalogued offerings of FURNITURE and effects. Approximately once a month, a sale is catalogued; a subscription for the year to these listings is only £1. Sales are advertised in the local press and in specialty periodicals.

There is no buyer's premium. Absentee bids are not executed. Packing and shipping services are not available. No guarantees of authenticity are offered. The firm reports that "mis-catalogued goods may be returned and purchase price refunded in most cases." Viewing is the day previous to sale, 2–7 P.M., and the morning of the sale, 9 A.M. to sale time. Settlement is immediately.

The standard consignor commission is as follows: catalogued sales, 15 percent; uncatalogued sales, 12.5 percent. Consignors must arrange to get goods to saleroom; they are not charged for insurance or warehousing. Settlement is made 1 week after sale. Reserves are not encouraged but are accepted; the buy-in charge is 5 percent of the reserve price. There is no minimum value for acceptance of consigned goods.

Appraisal service is available. There is no charge for goods placed for sale at auction. Contact P. D. Wood, FRICS.

306. Vergettes
38 St. Mary's Street Tel. (0780) 521 36
Stamford, Lincolnshire PE9 2DF

Stamford is a town of many churches; 6 of them stand within a 1-mile-square area. In that same area are to be found the offices of Vergettes, which has branches elsewhere in the region, but which holds its mixed-lot general-purpose auction sales in Stamford. These sales, often of "FURNITURE and effects," are normally held every third week. Occasional house and estate sales are conducted.

Vergettes runs a two-tier operation, and its better-quality sales are catalogued and are advertised more extensively (e.g., in specialty publications). But all sales are advertised in the local press. Catalogues are not available, in any event, by subscription. To find out what sales are catalogued and to get a copy of these list-like catalogues, apply to the Stamford offices.

Vergettes reports that it does not have a buyer's premium as such, "but by old established custom buyers pay 5 percent commission in addition to hammer price." Absentee bids are accepted "only if bidder [is] known to us," reports the firm. Packing and shipping services are not available from the firm. No guarantees of authenticity are offered. The usual viewing procedure is the day before the sale. Buyer must settle accounts immediately.

The commission structure differs for the trade and private individuals. Apply to the firm for the rates. Consignors do not pay for insurance or warehousing, but must pay cartage charges if they have not removed goods to the saleroom. Consigned goods are sold within 4–6 weeks. Settlement is made within 2 weeks. Reserves are accepted, "but subject to conditions." There is no minimum value necessary for consignment.

Appraisal service is available. Contact the Stamford office.

307. Vidler & Co.

Cinque Ports Street   Tel. (079 73) 21 24/5; 33 45
Rye, East Sussex TN31 7AL

Vidler & Co. are not only chartered surveyors, valuers, estate agents, and auctioneers, but also the sole proprietor of the Rye Auction Galleries, located at the rear of the firm's offices. These galleries, which are devoted "entirely and exclusively to Sales of Furniture and Effects by Auction," are also the site for quarterly evening sales of fine art. The regular sales are held the first Friday of every month throughout the year. The galleries report that "Broken and Rubbish items will not be accepted," nor will they accept "brass-and-iron beds, old radios, nondescript pictures and books, and Kilner Jars." The gallery premises include "special facilities . . . for testing electrical appliances (to enable purchasers to see if they are in working order)."

Sales are advertised in the local and regional press, and in specialty publications. Catalogues are available singly for each sale and by subscription (£5 per annum). There is no buyer's premium. Absentee bids are executed. Packing and shipping services are not available from the firm. No guarantees of authenticity are offered. Viewing is the afternoon prior to the sale day and "pre-sale time" on sale day. Buyers should settle their accounts immediately.

The standard consignor's commission is: "items realizing over £1,000 per lot, 10 percent; all other items, 15 percent; minimum charge, 50p per lot."

L. Holden Stutely, FRICS, reports that the commission is negotiable and that there are separate rates for dealers. Consignors are responsible for cartage to (and if necessary from) the saleroom, and for insurance of their property. Consigned goods are normally sold within 4–6 weeks. Settlement is 8 days after the sale. Reserves are accepted. The buy-in charge is 10 percent of the reserve price.

Mr. Stutely estimates that the annual turnover of the Rye Auction Galleries is over £200,000.

308. Walker, Singleton and Company
18-20 Rawson Street   Tel. (0422) 643 11
Halifax, West Yorkshire HX1 1NH

Walker, Singleton has dubbed its offices at Rawson Street "the commercial centre," and the firm, which has other offices in the region, also has a "property centre" and an "auction centre" in Halifax. It is at the "auction centre" on Saddleworth Road, West Vale, Halifax, that the firm holds mixed-lot general-purpose sales "at least monthly." Occasional house and estate sales are also held.

These sales are advertised in the local press (e.g., the *Yorkshire Post*). Announcements of forthcoming sales are sent out free of charge; to be placed on the mailing list, write Karen Somerfield. Catalogues are not available for single sales or by subscription. There is no buyer's premium. Absentee bids are executed. Packing and shipping services are available, at the buyer's expense. No guarantees of authenticity are offered. The usual viewing procedure is exhibition the day before the sale, 10 A.M.–4 P.M. Accounts must be settled within 7 days of the sale.

The consignor's commission is negotiable, but the minimum is 10 percent. Consignors are not charged insurance or warehousing. Consigned goods are sold within 7 weeks. Settlement is made after 2 weeks. Reserves are accepted. The buy-in charge is "nominal." There is no minimum value necessary for a consignment.

309. Walker Walton Hanson
Byard Lane, Bridlesmith Gate   Tel. (0602) 542 72
Nottingham, Nottinghamshire NG1 2GL

This is a veteran firm (est. 1841) which has various divisions and offices, one of which holds mixed-lot general-purpose auction sales in its saleroom, the Nottingham Auction Mart. A typical auction sale of "collective antiques" will include FURNITURE, GLASS, JEWELRY, PAINTINGS, SILVER, and such items as a set of commemorative Wedgwood china, an old magic lantern, and a 19th-century sword stick with ivory handle. These sales are usually held on Wednesdays, their frequency varying. Contact F. G. Tomlinson to find out the dates. Occasional house and estate sales are also held.

Sales are advertised in the local press and in specialty publications, such as *Antiques Trade Gazette*. Announcements of forthcoming sales are sent out; to be placed on the mailing list, write to the firm. Catalogues are available singly for each sale (50p, plus postage). A subscription is £7 per annum, including postage.

There is no buyer's premium. Absentee bids are not accepted. Packing and shipping services are available "by arrangement," at the buyer's expense. No guarantees of authenticity are offered. Viewing is the Monday (9 A.M.–5 P.M.) and Tuesday (9 A.M.–4 P.M.) prior to a Wednesday sale. Buyer must settle accounts within 48 hours. Firm can ask for 25 percent deposit immediately after the hammer has fallen.

The standard consignor's commission is 15 percent. K. B. Stone, the company's secretary, reports that "under certain restrictive circumstances certain expenses may be added to this sum." Consignors are charged for catalogue illustrations (£10 per photograph) and for insurance (50p per £100). Consignors who deliver their goods to the saleroom are not charged cartage. Consignors are not charged warehousing. Goods are usually sold in a maximum of 2 months, normally within 3 weeks. Settlement is usually within 10–14 days. Reserves are accepted. The buy-in charge is usually nil, but "the company reserves the right to charge up to 50 percent of the reserve price."

Appraisal service is available. Contact Mr. Tomlinson or any partner of Walker Walton Hanson.

310. Warner, Sheppard & Wade
16–18 Halford Street   Tel. (0533) 216 13
Leicester, Leicestershire LE1 1JB

At its saleroom in what might be described as the heart of downtown Leicester, this long-established firm, founded in 1846, and active in various aspects of management, sales and valuations, holds general antiques sales every 3 weeks, household-effects sales weekly, and specialist sales when necessary. A typical sale can include FURNITURE, GLASS, SILVER, and what have you, such as "pomade pot lids" and an old flintlock pistol ("damaged"). Traffic is difficult in this burgeoning city, but there is a multistory public car park within steps of the salerooms. Occasional house and estate sales are also held.

Sales are advertised in the local press; better-quality sales are also advertised in the national press and in specialty publications, such as *Antiques Trade Gazette*. A "printed sheet of main general sales through the year" is available free of charge; write to be placed on the mailing list. List-like catalogues are available singly for each sale (25p–60p, plus postage) and by subscription (£7.50 per annum).

There is no buyer's premium. Mail order bids are executed. Packing and shipping services are not available from the firm. No guarantees of authenticity are offered. Viewing is at least 1 day prior, 9 A.M.–5 P.M. Buyers should settle accounts as soon as possible because, as partner R. A. Young, ARICS, explains, "the quicker they pay, the sooner the vendor is paid."

The consignor's commission is 15 percent, plus 1 percent insurance, of the hammer price. Consignors pay for the cost of any catalogue illustrations. They do not have to pay for warehousing prior to sale. Consignors who deliver goods to the saleroom do not pay cartage. Consigned goods for a "general" sale are sold within 2–3 weeks; a "specialist" sale could take several months to put together. Settlement is "within 2 weeks (often less)." Reserves are accepted; the buy-in charge is 5 percent of the reserve price.

Appraisal service is available. Mr. Young reports that "advice is given freely regarding goods in sales."

311. Warwick & Warwick Ltd.

3 High Street   Tel. (0926) 49 99 90 and 443 33/4
Warwick, Warwickshire CV34 4AP

STAMPS are auctioned by this firm, which also deals in various aspects of philately and has shops in a number of locations. In Warwick, it has established what is called the National Philatelic Centre, which in addition to a stamp shop, houses a rare stamp room and a philatelic library.

Sales, advertised in philatelic journals, are held twice monthly, one on the premises at Warwick, the other at various locations. Catalogues are available for each sale and by subscription. A sample catalogue can always be had on request. The annual subscription price for catalogues varies with the location of the subscriber: £6 U.K., £8 Europe, £10 other countries.

There is no buyer's premium. Absentee bids—an important part of stamp auctions—are executed. Warwick & Warwick have added a nice touch to the proceedings with what they describe as their "Green Card bidding." Clients who have provided satisfactory references are issued cards which entitle them to purchase the lots through postal bidding sent in advance of payment. Guarantees of authenticity are offered, and buyers may return lots that prove to be not as catalogued. The viewing procedure varies, but lots are always on view for a day or two preceding the sale. Some lots may also be on view at Warwick & Warwick's stand in the Strand Stamp Centre, London. There is also the possibility of "postal viewing" for clients known to the firm, and it recently instituted a photocopy service for postal bidders. Settlement is within 7 days for floor bidders and on receipt of invoice for postal bidders. Credit terms are available "by arrangement," according to partner Graham Warwick.

The consignor's commission is 15 percent. Consignors pay for catalogue illustrations, as well as for transport of goods to the auction house. Reserves are accepted; there is a buy-in charge of 7.5 percent, but not on unreserved lots. Consigned goods are sold within 3–4 months. Settlement is made 30 days after the sale. The minimum value for a consignment is approximately £50.

The house does buy and sell on its own behalf; there is a separate retail department.

Appraisal service is available. Contact the auction manager.

The Waycotts Rooms: see Sotheby Bearne (Torquay, Devon)

312. Weller Eggar

74 Castle Street   Tel. (0252) 71 62 21 (5 lines)
Farnham, Surrey GU9 7CP

Farnham, the westernmost town in Surrey, is a very pretty place indeed. Castle Street, where Weller Eggar's offices and showrooms are located, has some very attractive medieval buildings with Georgian facades. Weller Eggar is a full-service firm of chartered surveyors, estate agents, etc., which conducts sales of "selected antique FURNITURE and effects" monthly and specialized sales as necessary. Occasional house and estate sales are also held. These sales are advertised in the local and regional press and in specialty publications, such as *Antiques Trade Gazette.* Announcements of forthcoming sales are available; to be placed on the mailing list, write to Mr. R. Kay, saleroom manager. List-like catalogues are available singly for each sale (50p; 65p by post) and by subscription. For cost, write to the house. Since 1978, the firm has had a buyer's premium of 10 percent. Absentee bids are executed. Packing and shipping services are available at the buyer's expense. No guarantees of authenticity are offered, but goods that do not prove to be as catalogued may be returned. The usual viewing procedure is 3 days prior to the sale, 9 A.M.–4 P.M. Settlement is "immediately, with the exception of certain trade credit arrangements."

The standard consignor's commission is 7.5 percent, but it is negotiable, depending upon the situation. There is a separate rate structure for dealers and institutions. Consignors are charged for catalogue illustrations (£8) and for insurance (50p per £1,000). Consignors are not charged packing and shipping if they transport goods to saleroom, and are not charged for warehousing. Goods are sold within the month, and settlement is 10 days after the sale. Reserves are accepted. There is no minimum value for a consignment.

Appraisal service is available. Contact Mr. Kay.

313. Wentworth Auction Galleries
Station Approach   Tel. (099 04) 37 11
Virginia Water, Surrey GU25 4DL

In the heart of what has been referred to as "the stockbroker belt," Wentworth Auction Galleries, a company within J. Alexander Gunn Ltd., holds auction sales several times a month. There is no set schedule; A. G. Richards, the managing director, reports that "we decide the date of the next sale at the time of cataloguing the previous one." The galleries hold mixed-lot general-purpose sales of "Antiques and Quality Furniture," each sale usually exceeding 700 lots.

Catalogues are available singly for each sale (the firm "will always send a complimentary catalogue for a single sale"). An annual subscription is £3 in the U.K., £5 overseas (including airmail postage). Sales are advertised regularly in specialty publications, such as *Antiques Trade Gazette.* Since 1978, there has been a 10 percent buyer's premium. Absentee bids are not accepted. Packing and shipping services are available at the buyer's expense. The firm will "reimburse for any goods which are not as catalogued providing they are returned within 24 hours of purchase." Viewing is always the day before the sale, 9 A.M.–8 P.M. Buyer must settle account within 24 hours.

The standard consignor's commission is as follows: Antiques and quality items totaling £100 or more, 10 percent; under £100, 15 percent. There is a separate rate for dealers: "a flat 10 percent on any quantity submitted." There is a minimum charge of 50p per lot and "all press advertising, lotting, cataloguing, and portering charges are included in a nominal £2 account charge."

Reserves are accepted. There is a buy-in charge of 2.5 percent of the reserve price: "we rarely charge if item does not reach reserve, providing such a reserve is sensible." Goods are sold within 4 weeks; settlement is made 7–10 days after the sale. No minimum value is necessary for a consignment.

314. West London Auctions

Sandringham Mews, High Street   Tel. (01) 567 6215/7096
Ealing, London W5

Ealing, the locale of the movie studio that gave us such films as *Passport to Pimlico* and *The Man in the White Suit,* is the home of West London Auctions, a source of slightly different delights. The firm holds auctions of "general FURNITURE and effects" every other Saturday, and more specialized sales 1 or 2 Wednesdays a month. These specialized sales are so organized that one can come at a given time for the selling of JEWELRY or an hour later or earlier for SILVER or CERAMICS.

West London Auctions is well situated in a building with more than one saleroom, and car parking close by. All auctions are held on the premises. These sales are advertised in the local press and in specialty publications, such as *Antiques Trade Gazette.* List-like catalogues are available for each sale and by subscription. For price, etc., contact director Bill Boyd or Tony Sullivan. The firm also offers sales of office furniture and equipment.

There is a buyer's premium of 10 percent. Absentee bids are executed. Packing and shipping services are not available from the firm. No guarantees of authenticity are offered. Buyers may return goods that are not as described, "depending on the circumstances," according to Mr. Sullivan. Viewing is the day prior to and the morning of the sale. Settlement of accounts should be undertaken within 48 hours. The standard consignor's commission is 12 percent. It is negotiable, depending upon the situation. There is a separate rate for dealers and for institutions. Consignors are charged for catalogue illustrations, insurance, and packing and shipping (if the firm arranges for transport of consigned goods). Consignors are not charged for warehousing unless unsold goods are not picked up. Consigned goods are sold usually within 2 weeks. Settlement is 2 weeks after the sale. Reserves are accepted; the buy-in charge is 6.5 percent.

Appraisal service is available. Contact Mr. Boyd or Mr. Sullivan.

West London Auctions periodically holds free valuation sessions ("Bring Your Treasure and Increase Your Knowledge"). There is no obligation to consign items, but the firm's staff is on hand "and will advise concerning sale."

Western Auction Rooms: see Taylor, Lane & Creber (Plymouth, Devon)

315. Whitten and Laing
20 Queen Street   Tel. (0392) 593 95
Exeter, Devon EX4 3SN

This firm's offices are in the shadow of the magnificent cathedral of St. Peter and St. Mary. Its auction rooms are about a 25-minute walk away, across the river Exe: Devon and Exeter Auction Galleries, 32 Okehampton Street, Exeter EX4 1DY, tel. (0392) 526 21. Whitten and Laing, like so many firms in the U.K. that hold auction sales of antiques, has a general practice in property management, etc.

Sales are held twice weekly; periodic specialized sales are also conducted. The firm auctions the gamut of goods, ranging from BOOKS to FURNITURE and including, among other things, RUGS and SILVER. List-like catalogues are available. A subscription to the catalogues for the specialized sales costs £4 per annum. Occasional house and estate sales are held. Auctions are advertised regularly in the local press and occasionally in specialty publications.

There is no buyer's premium. Absentee bids are not executed. Packing and shipping services are not available from the firm. No guarantees of authenticity are offered. Buyers may return goods that prove to be not as catalogued; as partner J. W. Whitten, FRICS, puts it: "law requires this." Viewing is the day before. Buyer must settle accounts within 14 days.

The consignor's commission varies from 5 to 15 percent, depending on the goods. There is a separate rate structure for dealers. Consignors do not pay for insurance or warehousing, but must pay for cartage if the firm picks up the consignment. Consigned goods are sold within 1–6 weeks. Settlement is made 14 days after the sale. Reserves are accepted. There is no minimum value necessary for consignment.

316. Frank G. Whitworth
32–34 Wood Street   Tel. (0484) 274 67 (5 lines)
Huddersfield, West Yorkshire HD1 1DL

Whitworth specializes in industrial auctions, but every 3 weeks or so holds mixed-lot general-purpose sales which include such items as FURNITURE. Catalogues are not available by subscription but they are available individually on application to the Auction Department. Occasional house and estate sales are also held.

Sales are advertised in the local and regional press, and on occasion elsewhere. There is no buyer's premium. Absentee bids are not accepted. Viewing is usually for 3 days before the sale. Buyer must settle accounts within 3 days of the sale.

The standard consignor's commission is 15 percent. It is negotiable, depending upon the situation. Consigned goods are sold within 3 weeks. Settlement is 7 days after the sale. Reserves are accepted. The buy-in charge is 5 percent of the reserve price.

Appraisal service is available. Contact Mr. Whitworth.

317. Peter Wilson & Company
Fine Arts Department   Tel. (0270) 638 78/9
Victoria Gallery, Market Street
Nantwich, Cheshire CW5 5RL

This division of a firm that has an extensive estate agency practice offers general-purpose mixed-lot sales of lesser-quality goods usually once a week. More specialized, 2-day "fine arts and antiques" sales are held approximately 6–9 times a year, in which the "emphasis is on decorative arts 1870–1940." Items sold include BOOKS, COSTUME, FURNITURE, GLASS, JAPANESE WORKS OF ART, MUSICAL INSTRUMENTS, RUGS, and SILVER. Occasional house and estate sales are also held.

Sales are advertised in the local and national press, as well as in specialty publications, such as *Antiques Trade Gazette*. Announcements of forthcoming sales are available; to be placed on the mailing list, contact Mrs. Russell. Catalogues for the specialized sales unfortunately do not include estimates, but they are well done and the descriptions, though not overly detailed, are more than adequate.

Since 1979, there has been a buyer's premium of 10 percent. Absentee bids are accepted; telephone bids must be confirmed in writing. Mark Marshall, the saleroom manager, maintains that buyers should "only mail bids if they have actually seen the goods." Packing and shipping services are available, at the buyer's expense. Goods that prove to be not as described may be returned within 14 days after the sale, provided that Peter Wilson has been notified in writing within 7 days. Viewing for the specialized sales is usually Sunday, 2–4 P.M., Monday and Tuesday, 10:30 A.M.–4 P.M. Settlement is expected "immediately."

The standard consignor's commission is 10 percent, but it is negotiable. There is a separate rate structure for dealers and for institutions. Consignors are not charged for catalogue illustrations or for insurance. Consignors who do not transport their goods to the saleroom pay for removal at the rate of £9 per hour. There are no charges for warehousing prior to auction, and none if unsold goods are removed in timely fashion. Sale of consigned goods is as follows: "general goods in 6 days maximum; fine arts 5 weeks maximum." Settlement: "General goods, one week; fine arts, 15 days." Reserves are accepted. The buy-in charge is 5 percent of the reserve price.

Appraisal service is available. The cost varies. Valuation with a view to selling at auction is free. Valuation for insurance purposes is 1.5 percent on the first £10,000 and 1 percent thereafter. Valuation for probate purposes is 2 percent on the first £10,000 and 1.5 percent thereafter.

318. P. F. Windibank
18-20 Reigate Road   Tel. (0306) 88 45 56
Dorking, Surrey RH4 1SQ

Windibank holds monthly Saturday sales of "FURNITURE and effects." Periodic BOOK sales are offered, as well as occasional house and estate sales.

Sales are advertised in the local and regional press, as well as in specialty publications, such as *Antiques Trade Gazette*. List-like catalogues are available for specific sales and by subscription. To find out current costs, write or phone J. E. C. Wood.

A buyer's premium of 10 percent on the hammer price has been in effect since 1978. Absentee bids are executed. Packing and shipping services are available "to some extent," at the buyer's expense. No guarantees of authenticity are offered, but the opportunity to return goods that are not as described is available within limits. Viewing is the day before, 10 A.M.–5 P.M., and the morning of the sale. Settlement is "within 7 days."

The consignor's commission is 7.5 percent, but it is negotiable, depending upon the situation. Consignors are charged for catalogue illustrations and for packing and shipping of consigned property if the firm has to remove it to the saleroom. Consignors are not charged for insurance or for warehousing prior to sale. Consigned goods are sold within 2–4 weeks; settlement is 14 days after the sale. Reserves are accepted; "unsold lots or lots bought in under a reserve are charged at the following rates: 5 percent up to £50; 2.5 percent up to £100; and 1.75 percent over £100."

Appraisal service is available. Contact Mr. Wood.

319. Wingett & Son
24-25 Chester Street   Tel. (0978) 535 53/552 45
Wrexham, Clwyd LL 18 8BP

This firm, which has a general practice away from the auction field, holds monthly sales of "all types of antiques and works of art." The firm's premises are located not far from the train station in this commercial and industrial center of northern Wales, and parking is available nearby. Occasional house and estate sales are also held.

These sales are advertised in the local press, and in specialty publications, such as *Antiques Trade Gazette*. Catalogues for each sale are available by mail or in the firm's offices; subscriptions are obtainable at £10 per annum. Since September 1979, there has been a 10 percent buyer's premium. Absentee bids are executed if the bidders are known to the firm. Packing and shipping services "can be arranged," at the buyer's expense. Sales normally take place on a Wednesday and viewing is the previous Sunday, 10:30 A.M.–4 P.M., and Monday, 9 A.M.–4 P.M., as well as by appointment. Buyer must settle on day of sale.

The standard consignor's commission is 10 percent. It is negotiable, depending upon the situation. Consignors are not charged for catalogue illustrations, warehousing, or insurance. But "cartage is charged on owner's items if they cannot deliver to saleroom themselves." Consigned goods are usually sold within 1 month. Settlement is "within 14 days." Reserves are accepted. The buy-in charge is 10 percent of the reserve price.

320. Worsfolds
40 Station Road West   Tel. (0227) 689 84
Canterbury, Kent CT1 2TP

Located but a short walk from one of this cathedral city's train stations, Worsfolds, which has other offices in the area and a wide-ranging general practice as a chartered surveyor, holds auction sales monthly, mostly of "FURNITURE and effects." These are advertised in the local press and in specialty publications, such as *Antiques Trade Gazette*. List-like catalogues are available singly for each sale and by subscription (the cost is £5 per annum; "overseas by arrangement").

There is no buyer's premium. Absentee bids are accepted. Packing and shipping services are not available from the firm. No guarantees of authenticity are offered, but buyers can return goods that prove to be not as described. The usual viewing procedure is the day prior to the sale, 9:30 A.M.–4:30 P.M., and the morning of the sale. Settlement is as soon as possible.

The standard consignor's commission is 15 percent for private individuals, 12 percent for dealers; these terms are negotiable. Consignors pay for catalogue illustrations (£12 each) and insurance (1 percent of the value as established by the hammer price). Consignors also pay for removal of goods to the saleroom, unless they undertake that task themselves. Consignors do not pay for warehousing prior to sale; nor after if they remove unsold goods in timely fashion. Consigned goods are sold within 6 weeks; settlement is 1 month after the sale. Reserves are accepted. The buy-in charge, which is negotiable, ranges between 2.5 percent and 5 percent. There is no minimum value for a consignment, but, points out M. L. Lawrence, FRICS, "no household goods."

321. Norman Wright & Hodgkinson
2-6 Priestgate   Tel. (0733) 63921/7
Peterborough, Cambridgeshire PE1 1JQ

This firm, which has branches elsewhere, holds auctions as necessary—mostly mixed-lot general-purpose sales—in the shadow of a splendid cathedral. If you don't want to visit Peterborough for the sales, go to see the cathedral. Occasional house and estate sales are held.

Sales are advertised in the local press and in specialty publications. List-like catalogues are available for each sale, but not by subscription. There is no buyer's premium. Absentee bids are executed. Packing and shipping services are not available. Viewing is the day prior to the sale. Settlement is within 7 days after the sale.

The standard consignor's commission is 15 percent, but it is negotiable, depending upon the situation. Consignors are not charged for insurance or warehousing. Reserves are accepted. S. G. Collins, FRICS, reports that settlement is 7 days after the sale.

Wyatt & Son (in conjunction with Whiteheads)

322. Baffins Hall   Tel. (0243) 78 75 48
Baffins Lane
Chichester, West Sussex

323. St. Martin's Hall
St. Martin's Square
Chichester, West Sussex

Main Office: 59 East Street   Tel. (0243) 78 65 81
Chichester, West Sussex PO19 1HN

Auction sales by this firm are held in two locations: Baffins Hall and St. Martin's Hall, both within easy walking distance of each other and of the firm's main office (it has other offices in the area). Wyatt & Son, like Whiteheads, are chartered surveyors, estate agents, and valuers with a wide field of general and specialized practice.

Sales of household FURNITURE and effects are held monthly on Tuesdays in St. Martin's Hall. Sales of antiques and reproduction FURNITURE, CLOCKS, PAINTINGS, Persian and other RUGS are held monthly on Thursdays at Baffins Hall. From time to time, on the Wednesday before the Thursday sale, there is an auction of "PORCELAIN, POTTERY, GLASS, SILVER, JEWELRY, and Bric-a-brac." Occasional house and estate sales are also held.

These sales are advertised in the local and regional press, and in some instances in specialty publications, such as *Antiques Trade Gazette*. An auction calendar is available free of charge; write to be placed on the mailing list. Catalogues are available singly and by subscription. The sparse listings for the Tuesday sales are 10p each, and cost £2.85 per annum (including postage). List-like catalogues for the other sales cost £5.45 per annum (including postage). A combined subscription costs £8 per annum (including postage). These are U.K. prices; other arrangements have to be made for outside the U.K.

There is no buyer's premium. Absentee bids are executed. Packing and shipping services are available, at the buyer's expense. Goods not as described may be returned within a limited time period. Viewing is usually the day before the sale. Buyers must settle accounts within 7 days.

The consignor's commission varies, depending on the situation. According to John Haywood, saleroom manager, consignments are not accepted from dealers and the minimum value for a consignment to Baffins Hall is £50. Consignors are not charged for catalogue illustrations, insurance, or warehousing. Consigned goods are sold within 4 weeks. Settlement is 10–14 days after the sale.

Appraisal service is available. Contact Mr. Haywood.

Scotland

324. Thomas R. Callan

9 Old Bridge Street   Tel. (0292) 676 81/2
Ayr, Strathclyde KA7 1QA

Ayr is a medium-sized Scottish town, probably best known for its connection with Robert Burns, who described the Auld Brig as a "poor, narrow footpath of a street,/Where twa wheelbarrows tremble when they meet."

Not far from this firm's head office on Old Bridge Street are the salerooms, at 108 High Street. There, in the words of David Callan, the firm sells "everything from a needle to an anchor." Occasional house and estate sales are also held.

Sales are advertised in the local press. They are held "always at least one per fortnight and on occasions once per week." They are not catalogued.

There is no buyer's premium. Absentee bids are not accepted. Packing and shipping services are available at the buyer's expense. No guarantees of authenticity are offered. Buyers may return goods that are not as described; "the purchaser has 5 days in which to complain." Mr. Callan reports that the "auction rooms are always open to the public, although main view days are Wednesdays, with sales on Thursdays." Immediate settlement is required.

The consignor's commission is 15 percent and negotiable, depending upon the situation. There is a separate rate structure for dealers. Consignors are not charged for insurance or for storage, but if the firm has to collect the goods, "a charge is made for collecting." Consigned goods are sold within a fortnight. Settlement is made 1 week after the sqle.

Thomas R. Callan belongs to the Scottish Association of Auctioneers.

325. Robert Dowie

Station Road   Tel. (0333) 234 38
Leven, Fife KY8 4QU

Located directly across the Firth of Forth from Edinburgh, this firm holds sales weekly. The sole partner, Vernon J. Pragnell-O'Neill, specializes in antique FURNITURE, JEWELRY, and SILVER. Occasional house and estate sales are also held.

Sales are advertised in the local and regional press, such as *The Scotsman* and the *St. Andrew's Citizen*. Catalogues are not available by subscription, but can be obtained singly by writing or phoning the firm or attending the exhibition.

There is no buyer's premium. Mail order bids are executed. Packing and shipping services are available, at the buyer's expense. No guarantees of authenticity are offered and as concerns returning goods that do not prove as catalogued, Mr. Pragnell-O'Neill indicates that "we are always pleased to discuss this eventuality." The usual viewing procedure is the day before the sale, 10 A.M.–5 P.M. Buyer must settle account at conclusion of sale.

The standard consignor's commission is 15 percent, and it is negotiable, depending upon the situation. There is a separate rate of 10 percent for the trade and for institutions. Reserves are accepted. Consignors are not charged for catalogue illustrations, insurance, or storage. The firm does charge for packing and collecting goods for auction. Settlement depends on the kind of goods, but is generally within 2 weeks of the sale. Consigned goods are normally sold within 1 month.

326. Kirkwall Auction Mart Ltd.
44 Junction Road   Tel. (0856) 25 20
Kirkwall, Orkney

The Orkney Islands are far to the north, but not too far for auctiongoers. Kirkwall, the capital of the Orkneys—a busy port of graystone two- and three-story houses—has a thriving auction mart. A cooperative limited company, the firm deals much in real estate and livestock, but it also holds mixed-lot sales weekly which include BOOKS and FURNITURE. Not all sales are held on the premises; some are held at "farms, etc."

Sales are advertised in the local press (*The Orcadian*). They are not catalogued. There is no buyer's premium. Absentee bids are executed. Packing and shipping services are available, at the buyer's expense. Buyers may return goods that do not prove to be as described—in effect, "any goods which prove to be reproductions if stated as authentic at sale," according to Michael Corsie. The usual viewing procedure is the day prior to the sale. Buyers must settle accounts immediately after the sale.

The consignor's commission "varies depending on articles for sale." Consignors are not charged insurance (that is done on livestock only) or warehousing. Packing and shipping are charged to the consignor if the firm removes the property to the saleroom. Consigned goods are sold within 1 month. Settlement is made 1 week after the sale.

Appraisal service is available. The cost "varies depending on what is being appraised." Contact Gordon Muir.

327. Thomas Love & Sons Ltd.
12 St. Johns Place   Tel. (0738) 241 11
Perth, Tayside PH1 5TB   Cable: LOVES

An old-line firm of auctioneers and valuers (est. 1869), Thomas Love & Sons hold regular sales at 52 Canal Street. These galleries are but a few blocks from the firm's offices and an easy walk from the train and bus stations. The firm holds a variety of general and more specialized sales, which include such objects as FURNITURE, PORCELAIN, and SILVER. These are advertised in the local press and in specialty publications, such as *Art & Antiques Weekly*.

Not all sales are catalogued. For information and details about sales catalogues, contact the firm. There is no buyer's premium. Viewing varies, but is at least the morning of the sale. Settlement is immediately.

The consignor's commission is 10 percent, but it is negotiable, depending upon the situation. Insurance is charged on property consigned. Consigned goods are sold within 1–2 months. Settlement is within the month after the sale. Appraisal service is available. For details and costs, contact Lindsay Burns.

328. John Milne
9-11 North Silver Street Tel. (0224) 503 36/7
Aberdeen, Grampian AB1 1RJ

The capital of the North Sea oil boom, referred to as the Houston of Scotland, Aberdeen is a flourishing city which can well support a firm of Fine Art Auctioneers and Valuators such as Milne. Established in 1867, the firm is now being run by the fourth generation of the family. John Milne's premises are but a short walk from the central train station. However, many auctions are held on the vendors' own premises. Milne, on its premises, holds a sale of household goods weekly, an antiques sale weekly, specialist fine arts sales approximately 4 times a year, and book sales 3–4 times a year. Frances Milne reports that "our specialist catalogue sales include fine PAINTINGS, antique FURNITURE, SILVER, CERAMICS, ARMS AND ARMOR, RUGS, etc. We also specialize in BOOK sales."

The weekly sales are advertised in the local press, the other sales in the Scottish national press and in various specialty publications. Single fine arts catalogues cost £1.25 (including postage) and a subscription for a year costs about £3.75. Single book sale catalogues cost 75p and a subscription is about £2.25 per annum.

There is no buyer's premium. Absentee bids are executed. Packing and shipping services are available. No guarantees of authenticity are offered and all goods are sold as is. Notwithstanding these caveats, in some instances, as with books, goods that prove to be not as described may be returned within 10 days of the sale. Check the conditions of sale at each auction held by the house. The usual exhibition procedure varies with the type of sale, but there is always at least 1 full day of viewing, plus viewing on sale day, 8–10 A.M. Settlement must be made within 2 working days after the sale. Credit may be extended "in exceptional cases to well-known/old customers only."

The consignor's commission varies with the sale: household goods, 20 percent; antiques sale, 18 percent; specialist sales, 15 percent. Commissions are negotiable, depending upon the situation. There is a separate rate structure for dealers. Consignors are charged for catalogue illustrations (£10 per photograph). They are not charged for insurance or for warehousing (at least until after the sale). How long before consigned goods are sold "depends on type of goods and forthcoming sales." Settlement is 3 days after weekly sales, and 3 weeks after specialized sales. Reserves are accepted. The buy-in charge is 5 percent of the reserve price. There is no cost if there was not a reserve price. There is no minimum value necessary for a consignment, but "our minimum commission is £3, which effectively eliminates unsalable items."

Appraisal service is available. The cost varies. The firm does run "a free valuation service" on Fridays (2:30–4:30 P.M.). Contact Messrs. Graham Lumsden, Sandy Milne, or Edward Mearns.

329. L. S. Smellie & Sons Ltd.
5 Church Street   Tel. (0698) 28 20 07 (3 lines)
Hamilton, Strathclyde

This firm holds auction sales on a two-tier basis: weekly sales of FURNITURE and effects, and more specialized quarterly sales, which include DRAWINGS, PAINTINGS, PRINTS, and SILVER. The weekly sales are held at the Furniture Mart on Lower Auchingramont Road, a short walk from the firm's Church Street offices and a somewhat longer walk from the train station. There is parking nearby. Occasional house and estate sales are also held.

These sales are advertised regularly and announced in the local and regional Scottish press, as well as in specialty publications, such as *Art & Antiques Weekly*. Catalogues cannot be obtained by subscription, but they are available for the weekly sales and for special sales. For either, contact Robert Smellie or James Strachan.

There is no buyer's premium. Mail order bids are not accepted. Packing and shipping services are available, at the buyer's expense, with local carriers and packers. No guarantees of authenticity are offered. Viewing is every Saturday, 9–11 A.M., preceding the weekly Monday sale. There is a full day of viewing before the quarterly sale. Buyer must settle accounts immediately after the sale. Credit terms are available, "subject to negotiation."

The scale of consignor's commission varies and is subject to negotiation. There is a separate rate structure for dealers. There is no minimum value for a consignment. Consignors are "sometimes" charged for catalogue illustrations, but not for insurance or warehousing (at least prior to sale). Consigned goods are sold as follows: "weekly sale, 7 days; quarterly sale, 12 weeks." Settlement is day of sale or the following day.

L. S. Smellie & Sons Ltd. belongs to the Scottish Association of Auctioneers.

Thomson, Roddick & Laurie (Dumfries, Dumfries and Galloway): see entry in English section

Northern Ireland

330. Seamus Coyle & Co. Ltd.
Handel House, English Street   Tel. (0861) 52 46 46
Armagh, Armagh BT 61 7LA

A firm of "Auctioneers, Valuers, Estate Agents and Insurance Brokers," Coyle holds mixed-lot general-purpose auction sales of various kinds of properties from time to time. Occasional house and estate sales are also conducted. Sales are advertised in the local and regional press. Catalogues are not available by subscription. There is no buyer's premium. Absentee bids are not accepted. Packing and shipping services are not available from the firm. Buyers may return "within 3 days of receipt" goods that do not prove to be as described. Viewing is the previous day. Buyers must settle accounts within 1 week.

The standard consignor's commission is 10 percent, but it is negotiable, depending upon the situation. Consignors are charged for catalogue illustrations and for insurance. Consigned goods are sold within 2–3 weeks. Settlement is made within 2 weeks. There is no minimum value necessary for consignments.

331. Frank Donaghy Auctions
Main Street   Tel. (05047) 414 35
Dungiven, Derry

In a small town some 25 miles from Londonderry, Frank Donaghy holds weekly auctions of livestock, land, and chattels. These are advertised in the local press. Occasional house and estate sales are also held.

Catalogues are not available by subscription. There is no buyer's premium. Mail order bids are not executed. Packing and shipping services are available, at the buyer's expense. No guarantees of authenticity are offered. Viewing is the day of the sale. Buyer must settle accounts immediately.

The consignor's commission varies, and it is negotiable, depending upon the situation. Consignor's costs vary with the kind of goods put up for sale.

332. F. J. McCartney & Crawford
28-30 Thomas Street   Tel. (0266) 22 72/68 89
Ballymena, Antrim

Located in a Northern Irish town at the edge of the foothills that become the mountains of Antrim, F. J. McCartney & Crawford, a firm of estate agents, holds occasional mixed-lot general-purpose auctions, as well as house and estate sales. These are advertised in the local press.

Sales are uncatalogued. There is no buyer's premium. Absentee bids are executed. Packing and shipping services are not available from the firm. Viewing is the day before the sale, settlement the day of the auction.

The consignor's commission varies, depending upon the situation. Consignors are expected to share the cost of advertising the sale; they are not charged insurance or warehousing. Goods are sold as soon as possible. Settlement is the day after the sale.

333. Osborne, King & Megran
14 Montgomery Street   Tel. (0232) 202 33
Belfast, Antrim BT1 4NZ

This firm of estate agents, auctioneers, and valuers, established in 1930, has offices elsewhere in Northern Ireland and in Eire and England. The firm does not have a saleroom in Belfast but holds on-site auctions about once a month, at which are sold the contents of a house—which invariably include FURNITURE, RUGS, and SILVER, as well as such curiosities as "a William IV Mahogany Sarcophagus shape Garde de Vin."

These sales are advertised regularly in the local press and in specialty publications, such as *Antiques Trade Gazette*. There is a mailing list; write Alison Vance. Catalogues are not available by subscription, but are obtainable singly for each sale (the usual cost is about £2).

There is no buyer's premium, but it is "customary for purchasers in the North of Ireland to pay a 5 percent commission." Absentee bids are accepted. Packing and shipping services are not available from the firm. No guarantees of authenticity are offered. Viewing is usually 2 days prior to the sale, 10 A.M.–4:30 P.M. Buyer must settle accounts immediately at the end of the sale.

The standard consignor's commission is 7.5 percent. Consignors may have to pay the cost of advertising the sale, plus "(when necessary) charge for hire of a marquee, loos, etc." Consignors are charged for catalogue illustrations. The commission is negotiable. Consignments are not accepted from dealers. Reserves are accepted.

334. R. Thompson & Son
12–14 William Street   Tel. (07622) 222 46
Lurgan, Armagh

It has been some years since Thompson held auctions on its own premises, but it still holds, "irregularly," house and estate sales. These are advertised in the local press. Catalogues may be obtained from the firm's offices or at the sale premises.

There is no buyer's premium. Viewing is 2 days before the sale, 10 A.M.–4 P.M. Buyer must settle accounts within 2 working days after the sale. The consignor's commission varies. Generally, consignors pay "expenses—catalogue printing costs, advertising, etc., plus a 5 percent commission on selling price." Settlement is made 7 days after the sale.

B. T. Thompson reports that the firm is now concerned with "estate agency work mostly."

335. James Wilson & Son
79 Main Street   Tel. (039 674) 212
Castlewellan, Down BT31 9DQ

This firm of auctioneers, valuers, and estate agents, with a branch in Newcastle in County Down, "is a small family business which has occasional auctions of antique FURNITURE, mostly in private houses." Off-site auctions are usually held in a local hall.

Sales are advertised in the local press. Catalogues are usually available. There is a buyer's premium of 5 percent. Mail order bids will be executed, "provided that they are accompanied by a guaranteed cheque for 25 percent of the value." Packing and shipping services are not available from the firm. No guarantees of authenticity are offered. Viewing is usually the day prior to the sale. Settlement must be made within 24 hours of the sale.

The consignor's commission varies; "all charges are negotiable." Consigned goods are usually sold within 4 weeks. Settlement is 7–10 days after the sale.

Eire

336. James Adam & Sons
26 St. Stephen's Green North   Tel. Dublin 76 02 61
Dublin 2

This is an old-line firm (est. 1887) with a wide property and estate practice, of which fine arts auctions are only one aspect. Sales are held every 5–6 weeks, and they are advertised in the Irish press. Among the items sold at the fine arts sales are antique FURNITURE, GLASS, JEWELRY, RUGS, and PAINTINGS. Occasional house and estate sales are also held.

Like many other property and estate agents, Adam & Sons runs a two-tier operation. At their Kildare Street salerooms, just a short walk from the main saleroom, antiques are not the order of the day. There, general-purpose mixed-lot sales are held at 2–3-week intervals. Lots sold include Victorian and modern furniture, silver, glass, china, etc.

A buyer's premium has been in effect most of this century. Absentee bids are executed. Packing and shipping services are not available from the firm. No guarantees of authenticity are offered. Each bid advances at least 5 percent over the previous bid. Bidders make a minimal deposit of 25 percent on their purchases. Settlement must be within 24 hours. Viewing is usually 2 full days before the sale.

Catalogues are available singly for each of the fine arts sales. The cost is approximately Ir£1.25 each, plus postage. Catalogues are also available by subscription—the price is Ir£12 per annum.

The standard consignor's commission if 10 percent. Consignors do not pay for catalogue illustrations, but must keep their own insurance in force on consigned property. Consignors are also responsible for arranging transport of goods to saleroom. Consigned goods are usually sold in 4–6 weeks. Settlement is made 2 weeks after the sale. Reserves are accepted on items valued over £50. The buy-in price is 7.5 percent. There is a minimum lot charge of Ir£10.

Appraisal service is available. Contact Brien Coyle.

337. Buckley Galleries
27-28 Sandycove Road   Tel. Dun Laoghaire 80 54 08/80 39 88
Dun Laoghaire, Co. Dublin

One of the partners reports that "our specialty is that we claim to sell any-thing that fits through our doors"—among them, FURNITURE and SILVER. These mostly general-purpose mixed-lot sales are held every Thursday. They are advertised in the *Irish Times*.

Catalogues are not available. There is a buyer's premium of 5 percent. Packing and shipping services are offered: "we will arrange delivery of goods nationwide." Absentee bids are executed: "porters will bid on buyer's behalf." No guarantees of authenticity are offered, and there is no opportunity to re-turn goods that prove to be not as described. Viewing is the Wednesday before the sale, 9:30 A.M.–5:30 P.M., and the morning of the sale. Buyers must settle accounts before 1 P.M. on the following Saturday. Credit is generally not avail-able to private individuals but is extended for 6 weeks to recognized members of the trade.

Consignors are not charged for insurance. There is a nominal charge if Buckley makes the collection of the goods. There is no charge for warehousing prior to sale. The standard consignor's commission is 10 percent of the ham-mer price. Consigned goods are usually sold within 4 days. Settlement is with-in 6 days after the sale. Reserves are accepted.

Appraisal service is available. For details and costs, contact the firm.

338. Liam Lynch Auctions
Sarsfield Street   Tel. Kilmallock 133/178
Kilmallock, Co. Limerick

Lynch has what he describes as "general clearance auctions" the second Wednesday of each month in the People's Hall in Kilmallock. Three times a year, Lynch holds "Antique and Fine Art Auctions," two of these at the Deer-park Hotel in Charleville, Co. Cork, and the other at the Old Ground Hotel in Ennis, Co. Clare. Occasional house and estate sales are also held.

Sales are advertised in the national and local Irish press. Catalogues, which are list-like, are available; those for the fine art sales cost Ir£1 each or Ir£3 per annum by subscription. There is a buyer's premium of 5 percent. Absentee bids are executed. No guarantees of authenticity are offered. Neil Lynch states that "all goods must be examined by the buyer before purchase. If not viewed don't buy. No returns in this country." Usual viewing procedure is day of sale. Buyer must settle account on day of auction or day after.

The consignor's commission is 12.5 percent on antiques and 3 percent on property. Consignors are not charged for catalogue illustrations. Insurance is left up to the consignor. Packing and shipping are charged to consignors who do not bring goods to Lynch. "We are slow to accept reserves." The buy-in charge is 10 percent. Consigned goods are sold in approximately 8–12 weeks if consigned to the fine art auctions, and within 4 weeks if consigned to the general clearance sales. Settlement is "usually" 3 weeks.

The firm does undertake appraisals. Contact the firm for details and costs. The firm buys and sells on its own behalf, but "very little."

339. O'Reilly's Auction Rooms
25-26 Merchants Quay   Tel. Dublin 77 20 77
Dublin

This firm sells at auction everything from antique and modern JEWELRY to what managing director Michael Jordan describes as "secondhand goods, i.e., radios, cameras, etc." The firm holds periodic fine arts auctions, and twice a week, on Mondays and Thursdays at 7 P.M., holds "the usual auctions of pawnbrokers' unredeemed jewelry, silver, etc." Sales are advertised every Saturday in the *Irish Independent*. Occasional house and estate sales are also held.

List-like catalogues are available for each sale (about 10p each) and by annual subscription (Ir£5 per annum). Since October 1977, there has been a buyer's premium of 5 percent. Absentee bids are executed. Packing and shipping services are not available from the firm, but "we can help." Viewing is usually the day of the sale, which takes place at 2:30 P.M. Buyers must settle accounts immediately.

The consignor's commission is negotiable, "usually 10–12.5 percent." There is a separate rate for dealers. Consigned goods are sold within 2–6 weeks depending upon the consignment. Settlement is 10 days after the sale. Consignors pay for catalogue illustrations, insurance, and packing and shipping, but all "are negotiable and we may undertake some of the expenses." Reserves are accepted.

Appraisal service is available. For details and costs, contact Mr. Jordan.

Royal Auctioneers Ltd.
340. The Steeple Buildings, High Street   Tel. Trim 315 25
Trim, Co. Meath

341. 2 Main Street   Tel. Blanchardstown 21 23 11
Blanchardstown, Dublin

This firm, which has offices in Blanchardstown, a suburb of Dublin, and in Trim, about 25 miles farther north, deals mostly in commercial and residential property, but every 2 weeks it holds auctions of FURNITURE and other chattels. Maurice Harlin, the sales manager, reports that "we generally have a bit of everything on offer." Sales are usually held in a local town hall. There are occasional estate and house sales. The sales are advertised in the local press and in the national *Irish Independent*.

Mr. Harlin indicates that "catalogues are only used when time permits or when a specialized auction is on the go, e.g., a liquidation sale." Absentee bids are not accepted. The firm does not offer packing or shipping services. Buyer can return certain types of goods if they prove not as described or faulty—

"depends on the situation." Viewing is usually 1 day before the auction. Settlement must be made as soon as possible and certainly before the article is taken away. There is a buyer's premium of 5 percent.

The standard consignor's commission is 10 percent, but it is negotiable, depending upon the situation. When there is a catalogue, the firm does not charge for illustrations, nor does it charge for insurance. Storage is charged only if an unsold item is not retrieved by the consignor. Goods are usually sold within a limited period of time, but it "depends on how sellable an article is for selling." Settlement is generally a week after the sale. Reserves are accepted. There is no minimum value for a consignment.

Argentina

Even banks can be regular auctioneers of antiques and fine arts in Argentina. Buyers at auction here should know that there is a 16 percent value added tax on auction commissions and a 10 percent sumptuary tax on gold, crystal, ivory, silver, and the like. Consignors of goods may also be liable for tax; check before consigning.

342. Banco de la Ciudad de Buenos Aires
Departamento de Ventas
Esmeralda 660   Tel. 392-4511/392-1694/392-9531/392-8144
1015 Buenos Aires   Telex: 122365 BANMU

The daily auctions held by this bank include sales of antiques, household goods, land, automobiles, boats, livestock, and what have you. They are advertised in the national newspapers, and important sales may be advertised in the foreign press as well. Announcements of forthcoming sales are available from Rodolfo Perriere, and catalogues for individual sales are obtainable for the price of postage. Mail order bids are accepted under certain circumstances; write Sr. Perriere for details. Packing and shipping services are not offered, but there are many shipping agents in Buenos Aires. Accounts must be settled within 3 days, and there are no credit terms. There is a 10 percent buyer's premium on all objects except fixed properties, on which the rate is 3 percent. Sales tax must be paid where applicable.

The minimum value necessary for acceptance of a consignment is the equivalent of £10 or $20. The commission rate is 5 percent of the sale price plus applicable taxes. Charges are also made for insurance and for freighting and warehousing if applicable. It takes 30 days for consigned goods to be sold, and settlement is 5 days after that. Reserves are not accepted, and there is a fee for unsold property. If you have jewels, carpets, or real estate to sell, write to Primo Luzzi.

Appraisal service is available at a cost of approximately 5 percent of value. Write Sr. Perriere.

343. Christie's International Ltd.

Libertad 1269   Tel. (01) 41 16 16/42 20 46
1012 Buenos Aires

The Christie's consultant in Argentina is Cesar Feldman.

344. Guerrico Remates S.R.L.

Capital 1011   Tel. 393-2025/393-3618/393-2476
1231 Posadas

Every week Guerrico holds auctions, which are advertised in *La Nacion* and *La Prensa*. The specialties of this house are ARMS AND ARMOR, FURNITURE, and PAINTINGS. All sales are held on the premises, and catalogues are available for specific sales. Write to the firm to receive them. Viewing is allowed during the 3 days preceding the sales, and mail order bids are accepted. Guerrico does not offer packing and shipping services, nor does it accept returns. Buyers pay no premium, but must pay applicable taxes and must settle accounts within 48 hours.

The consignment rate is 20 percent, and usually is not negotiable. There is also a 2 percent insurance fee. The elapsed time from consignment to sales varies, and settlement is made 15 days after a sale. Reserves are accepted, and there are no charges on unsold lots. Write to Santiago Tavella Madariaga for details about consigning.

345. Sotheby's—Kerteux Antiques

Libertad 846   Tel. (041) 393-0831
1012 Buenos Aires   Cable: ANTIKER-BAIRES

Sotheby's man in Argentina is William R. Edbrooke, who, as a representative of the firm, helps bidders and solicits consignments.

Australia and New Zealand

In auction terms, Australia and New Zealand are the Southern Hemisphere's answer to Canada. Nationalism reveals itself in art collecting Down Under: Australians collect Australian art; New Zealanders collect New Zealand art. This even applies to such art commodities as stamps. The market in Australia and New Zealand is national, not international. There are auctioneers who import containers of furniture and antiques from England for sale at auction, but that's the "forebears" market. Most auction houses in Australia hold general rather than specialist sales, and many of these are cash-and-carry operations. You may find some surprisingly good pieces at the furniture sales that are held as adjuncts to sales of real estate.

Some auctioneers here charge a buyer's premium, but most do not (even Christie's doesn't). Be certain to check the conditions of sale before setting your bidding limits. Sales tax will be charged if you buy new goods at auction in Australia. By and large, though, Australia and New Zealand are a blessed relief from the regulations surrounding auction in such countries as France. Here, there are regulations and standards which the auctioneers must meet, but the buyer and seller are blissfully free from most entanglements with the law. If you like Australian and New Zealand art and artifacts, then you will find the relaxed auction scene rewarding and very pleasant.

Australia

346. A.S.A. Stamps Co. Pty. Ltd.

138-140 Rundle Mall   Tel. 223-2951
National Bank Building
Adelaide, South Australia 5001

A.S.A. holds monthly "mart" sales and 3 catalogued sales of stamps each
year, which are advertised in the *Australian Stamp Monthly*. The firm specializes in Australia & Territories, New Zealand & Dependencies stamps and
collections, and "from time to time better Great Britain." All auctions are
held on the premises, and you can write to be put on the mailing list for
announcements. Viewing is 3 days prior to a sale or by appointment. Mail
order bids are accepted, and packing and shipping services are offered. The
policy here on returns and guarantees of authenticity is "as per GB Standard
Terms & Conditions for Philatelic Auctions." Buyers must settle accounts on
the day of sale or, for mail bidders, by return mail.

Consignors should write A.S.A. to see if the property is suitable and acceptable. The commission structure is 15 percent, but negotiable above $A5,000.
Dealers enjoy a separate rate structure. The minimum value per lot is $A100.
It takes up to 4 months for consigned stamps to be sold, and settlement is 3
weeks after a sale. Reserves are accepted, but unsold lots with reserves will be
charged 5 percent of the reserve.

Appraisal services are available for 2 percent of the valuation figure under
$A5,000, and above by negotiation.

347. Associated Auctioneers Pty. Ltd.

800-810 Parramatta Road   Tel. 560-5899
Lewisham, New South Wales 2049

In the 16 years it has been in business, Associated has become a large firm
with 20,000 square feet of auctioning space and an average of 3 sales per
week. Many are general-purpose mixed-lot auctions, but Associated's specialties include CLOCKS AND WATCHES, AUSTRALIAN COLONIAL FURNITURE, GLASS,
JEWELRY, BRITISH 19TH-CENTURY PAINTINGS, PHOTOGRAPHIC INSTRUMENTS,
PORCELAIN, RUGS, and SILVER. Catalogues are not available by subscription,
but a note to Rodney Hyman stating your interests will get you on the mailing
list. Viewing is usually 8:45 A.M.–4:30 P.M. on the day before a sale and 8:30
A.M.–sale time. Postal bids will be accepted with payment of 10 percent deposit. Any goods found to be misdescribed "prior to payment made to our vendors
will get immediate refund. Otherwise we will make representations on their
behalf." There is a buyer's premium of 1 percent on all purchases. Packing
and shipping are available.

Commission rates at Associated are 17.5 percent of gross sale proceeds plus
4 percent for insurance, advertising, and other out-of-pocket expenses. Sales
held on site have a commission rate of 12.5 percent of the gross sale proceeds

plus out-of-pocket expenses. A separate rate schedule applies to sales on behalf of liquidators, receivers, insurance companies, and insurance loss adjusters. Consigned goods are sold within 28 days and sometimes within 10 days. Settlement is made with the consignor 10 days after the sale. Reserves are accepted, and there is no charge for buy-ins. Contact Rodney Hyman for fine arts, Anthony Hyman for general goods.

Appraisal is a large part of Associated's business. One of their brochures shows a safety pin and an airplane and states: "You Name It . . . We'll Value It! Then Auction It!" On-site evaluations cost $A45 per hour plus expenses, while valuations carried out in Associated's rooms cost $A35 per hour. Verbal appraisals are given free. "50% of all Valuation fees will be rebated against our commission on any 'on-site' Auction Sale following upon such Valuation (within 6 months) and consisting of substantially the whole of the goods valued."

348. G. J. Brain Auctioneers Pty. Ltd.

122 Harrington Street   Tel. 271701
Sydney, New South Wales 2000

Geoff Brain's two specialties are MODERN FURNITURE and EARTHMOVING AND MINING EQUIPMENT. Most of his weekly sales are of the general-purpose mixed-lot variety. They may be held in the rooms or on site, and are announced in the Sydney *Morning Herald*. Catalogues are available singly for a specific sale but not by subscription. Viewing is the day prior to the auction, and mail order bids are accepted. Brain offers no guarantees or shipping services, and "unknown buyers must have a letter of credit or some other means of establishing their ability to meet commitments." Buyers must settle their accounts "prior to delivery, which is generally within 2 days after sale."

Goods consigned for sale on the premises are charged a 17.5 percent commission; for on-site sales the fee is 7.5 percent plus expenses, which include the expense of producing a catalogue. There are no other charges unless illustrations are required. Reserves are accepted, and the only costs for unsold property are advertising and cartage, if any.

Appraisal service is available. "Costs vary according to the type of work and the time involved."

349. Bright Slater Pty. Ltd.

Box 205 G.P.O.   Tel. 312415
Lower Ground Floor
Brisbane Club Building, Isles Lane
Brisbane, Queensland 4000

A member of the Benchmark Real Estate Group, Bright Slater can also be reached through its branch offices at Ashgrove, Clayfield, Coorparoo, Kenmore, Southport, and Surfer's Paradise. The head office is open 8:30 A.M.–5 P.M. weekdays, and the suburban branches are open 7 days a week. Bright

Slater's specialty is, of course, property auctions, but sales of furniture, household effects, machinery, and livestock are arranged as they are available. Sales are advertised in regional newspapers and on radio, occasionally even on television. Announcements are sent to those whose names are on the mailing list. Catalogues are not available by subscription, but single catalogues are available for some sales. Viewing is the day of the sale. There are no mail order bids, no returns, and no packing or shipping services. Payment must be made on sale day.

Consignors pay 12.5 percent plus advertising costs and illustration or warehousing costs if applicable. Commissions may be negotiable in some circumstances. Settlement is usually on sale day. Reserves are accepted, and the charges for unsold lots are negotiated beforehand.

Bright Slater belongs to the Australian Institute of Valuers and will do appraisals on a graduated scale. Write R. L. Hancock for details.

350. Christie, Manson & Woods (Australia) Ltd.
298 New South Head Road, Double Bay   Tel. 326-1422
Sydney, New South Wales 2028   Telex: AA26343
                                      Cable: CHRISTIART SYDNEY

When Christie's launched their Australian operation some time back, they hoped to create an international auction center there. As it happened, their most interesting sales in Australia were of books, such as the collection of Dr. Clifford Craig, sold by Christie's in 1975 in Launceston, Tasmania. Now Christie's in Australia limits itself to 2 sales a year, of BOOKS, MAPS, TOPOGRAPHICAL PRINTS relating to Australasia, and similar material.

Their expert and representative in Australia is Sue Hewitt, a remarkable woman who once held a nonstop 14-hour session in order to complete a sale in a single day. The semiannual auctions are held in hired premises in Sydney or Melbourne and they are advertised locally and in Christie's international publications.

Catalogues are available singly or by subscription (roughly $A10; apply to Christie's in Australia or to the London or New York offices). Viewing is for 3 days preceding each sale, at hours announced in the catalogue, and buyers must settle their accounts within 1 week after the sale, unless special arrangements have been made in advance. Sale conditions are those of Christie's worldwide as concerns the return of goods that prove to be not as catalogued. Mail order bids are accepted, and packing and shipping services are available. There is no buyer's premium.

Consignors pay 17.5 percent commission, and the trade pays 15 percent, as do institutions. And there are separate fees for illustrations, insurance, and packing and shipping. Goods are placed in the next auction, and settlement is 1 month after the sale, "provided we have been paid." Reserves are accepted. Should an item go unsold, there is a buy-in commission, "only if we disagree on the reserve."

Miss Hewitt will appraise Australian paintings, prints, and drawings, as well as books, maps, and topographical prints and manuscripts relating to Australia. Write or call her for the cost of such service.

351. William S. Ellenden Pty. Ltd.
67-73 Wentworth Avenue   Tel. 211-4035/211-4477
Sydney, New South Wales 2000

Mixed-lot general sales are the meat and potatoes of Bill Ellenden's business. These are advertised in the Sydney *Morning Herald,* and they take place on alternate Thursdays in Ellenden's saleroom or, in the case of a house sale, on site. Announcements are sent only for important sales, and catalogues normally are available at viewing times, which usually are 2 days prior to a sale. House bids are accepted at all sales. As for returns, if there is "a genuine error in cataloguing, the matter would be put to rights." Buyers are urged to settle accounts within 24 hours.

Bill Ellenden has been in the auction business for nearly 30 years, and he has expert consultants on tap for almost any field. A telephone call will suffice to get the consigning process under way. The commission is 17.5 percent for everything except paintings and jewels, which are charged at 15 percent. Dealers get a trade discount of 2.5 percent, "usually more for charitable institutions." There are no other fees, and consigned goods usually come up for sale within 2 weeks. Settlement is made within 2 weeks after the sale. Reserves are accepted, "but only for good-quality effects." The consignor pays nothing for unsold property, "unless special advertising requested."

For details of the appraisal services available, write or call Bill Ellenden.

352. Bruce Granger Auctions
10 Hopetoun Street   Tel. 559-4767
Hurlstone Park, New South Wales 2193

The specialties of this firm are ORIENTAL RUGS, PERSIAN RUGS, and antique SILVER. Sales, both general and specialized, are held about twice monthly at various venues in various cities. Each sale is advertised in the leading morning newspaper of the city in which it is held. A mail or phone request will bring the potential buyer announcements of forthcoming sales or catalogues. Bidders from outside Australia can receive catalogues for a nominal mailing cost.

Mail order bids are accepted, but such bidders should furnish credit references "or some evidence of capacity to honor bids if successful." Guarantees of authenticity are available, as are packing and shipping services. Goods that prove to be not as catalogued can be returned. Unless other arrangements have been made in advance, the buyer must settle immediately after the sale. Viewing is 2–3 hours before the sale or by appointment. Credit terms are available "through any major Australian lending/finance organization. Bona fides required before sale if this is intention."

The basic commission is 30 percent of the sale price, but this is negotiable for specific consignments. There is a separate rate for dealers but not for institutions. No other fees are charged, but the consignor is expected to bear the expenses of shipping. If the vendor "requires immediate settlement, goods can be purchased at sale valuation, less 10 percent."

Mr. Granger conducts appraisals, with charges on an individual basis. There is no charge for the appraisal of goods subsequently offered for auction sale.

353. Hamilton & Miller Pty. Ltd.
130 Parramatta Road   Tel. 519-2922/519-6317
Camberdown, New South Wales 2050

A general-purpose auction house, Hamilton & Miller sell the usual range of goods, including FURNITURE, AUSTRALIAN PAINTINGS, SILVER, and TOYS. The auctions are usually held on the premises, although occasionally house or estate sales are held.

The weekly sales are announced in the local press. List-like catalogues are available, but only at the sale. There is no buyer's premium. Absentee bids are not accepted. Packing and shipping services are not available. There are no guarantees of authenticity and the opportunity to return goods is not available. Buyer must settle account within 2 days of the sale.

Prospective consignors should write the firm; it "will advise if goods are saleable." Consignors are charged for catalogue illustrations, insurance, and packing and shipping. Goods are usually sold relatively quickly. Settlement is within 14 days. The consignor's commission is according to the scales set by the Australian Valuers Association and is not negotiable. Reserves are accepted "by agreement."

Appraisal service is available. Contact the firm for fees.

354. Harmer's of Sydney Pty. Ltd.
Philas House   Tel. 235-8685
17-19 Brisbane Street   Cable: HARMSTAMPS SYDNEY
Sydney, New South Wales 2010

Mailing Address:
P.O. Box 577
Darlinghurst, New South Wales 2010

About 5,000 lots in 6 to 8 sales are sold by this part of the Harmer's stamp network. STAMPS, with a minor emphasis on MAPS, AUTOGRAPHS, and POST-CARDS, are their business. Catalogues for these sales are available within Australia for $A14, in New Zealand and the Pacific islands by airmail for $A16, and in the rest of the world by airmail for $A20; single catalogues also are available free at Harmer's office, or by mail for $A2. All auctions are held on the premises, and lots are on view 10 A.M.–4 P.M. for 10 days prior to any sale. "Time and postal services permitting, lots of convenient size can be sent by post for private inspection upon application." Postal bids are quite usual here; they are executed free of charge, subject to the conditions of sale in the catalogue. The usual guarantees and shipping services are available. Harmer's does have a 10 percent buyer's premium. Buyers should pay at the auction or by return mail on shipped goods, but "credit-established clients" have 30 days to pay.

Would-be consignors should begin by writing for the free booklet "Philatelic Selling," which details facilities and procedures. The minimum value necessary for acceptance is $A250. The commission is 10 percent on the total selling price, with a separate structure for dealers. Where reserve prices have been agreed or where no satisfactory bid is obtained, the buy-in charge is $A2 per lot, but when a reserve has not been agreed, Harmer's charges an 18 percent commission on the highest bid. Lots withdrawn from the sale will also be charged an 18 percent commission based on the estimate. Payment normally is made within 30 days after an auction, and can be made in a variety of currencies. Interim payments in the form of presale advances are available; write for details. Insurance is free, unless "no instructions have been received within 3 months of receipt of the property," in which case there will be a charge.

Valuations made at Harmer's offices are at a fee of 1.5–2.5 percent of the market value, according to the time and the amount of research involved. The minimum charge is $A10. For on-site examinations, expenses are charged as well. Valuation fees are refunded in full "when such properties are sold in their entirety through our auction house within 2 years of the valuation."

Harmer's also will arrange sales by private treaty to other clients or occasionally to themselves, but only when a consignor will not sell at auction or when a quick cash sale is essential.

355. Kenneth Hince (Book Auctions)
138-140 Greville Street
Prahran, Victoria 3181

BOOKS, MANUSCRIPTS, MAPS, AUTOGRAPHS, and AUSTRALIAN COLONIAL PAINTINGS AND PRINTS are the specialties of Kenneth Hince (Book Auctions). Auctions are held regularly each 6 months, with special auctions as appropriate. Hince's sales are advertised in the Melbourne, Sydney, and Adelaide press, and catalogues (and price lists) are available on an annual basis for $A10.

Hince offers mail order bid service, packing and shipping, and guarantees of authenticity. "We refund if books found imperfect, not as described, not as catalogued—with some reservations if defects are only of condition. But our cataloguing standards are scrupulous and exhaustive." Hince usually holds its sales on Tuesdays. Viewing is offered Sunday afternoon, Monday all day, and Monday evening to the trade only. Buyers pay immediately after the sale, though members of the trade have 30 days to pay. Credit terms are available "to our own retail customers at their discretion."

Hince aims at a minimum value of about $A100, but a great many exceptions are made. The commission rate is 17.5 percent (12.5 to the trade), with no other charges. When goods are sold is subject to the closure of the regular semiannual catalogue, and settlement is within 30 days after the sale. Reserves are accepted, and the charge for unsold lots is "2.5 percent, not always applied."

Hince's parent firm, Kenneth Hince (Old and Fine Books), will appraise collections at $A25 per hour including traveling time, rebated in case of sale or auction contract.

356. Leonard Joel
17 McKillop Street   Tel. 672893/672014
Melbourne 3000

Art Department:
1195 High Street
Armadale, Victoria

This firm holds weekly sales in various places, including vendors' homes and the Malvern Town Hall in Victoria. Many of these are general-purpose mixed-lot sales, but Joel's does specialize in DOLLS, ENGRAVINGS AND ETCHINGS, 18TH AND 19TH CENTURY FURNITURE, JEWELRY, AUSTRALIAN PAINTINGS, PORCELAIN, RUGS, and SILVER. Sales are advertised in the Melbourne press, and announcements are available to those who write and ask to be put on the mailing list. Bidding by mail is accepted, and packing and shipping services are available. Goods that prove to be not as catalogued may be returned, but no guarantees of authenticity are offered. Buyers are asked to settle their accounts immediately after the sale, and credit terms are not available.

Consignors should write or phone the auction rooms or the art department, depending on what they have to sell. Names to know are Graham Joel (managing director) and Paul Dwyer. The commission rate is 16.5 percent, but it is negotiable, and the dealers' rate is 12.5–14 percent. The elapsed time from consignment to sale is "variable," and settlement is 7 days to 4 weeks, "depending on type of sale." Reserves are accepted, but there is no charge for unsold lots. Consignors will also be charged for catalogue illustrations and for packing and shipping if arranged through Joel's.

For information about appraisal service, write Graham Joel.

357. Johnson Bros. Auctioneers & Real Estate Agents
328 Main Road   Tel. 725166/492909 (after hours)
Glenorchy, Tasmania 7011

Weekly on Saturdays (except Christmas to mid-January), Johnson Bros. holds auction sales of all kinds. About twice a month, these are antique and collector sales, and occasionally specialist sales are held of CLOCKS AND WATCHES, COINS, DOLLS, ENGLISH AND AUSTRALIAN FURNITURE, JEWELRY, MEDALS, PEWTER, PHOTOGRAPHICA, PORCELAIN, POSTCARDS, POSTERS, SILVER, and AUSTRALIAN STAMPS. The Saturday sales are at Johnson Bros.' rooms, but the firm also holds country sales, house sales, government sales, etc. Catalogues are available singly for specific sales on request; enclose a self-addressed envelope. Sales are advertised in the local newspaper, the *Mercury*. Viewing for the regular sales is 9 A.M.–5 P.M. Friday and prior to the start of the sale on Saturday. Bidding by mail, and packing and shipping services, are available, but Johnson Bros. offers no guarantees or returns. Settlement is the day of sale or by prior arrangement, and credit terms are not available.

Consignors should contact D. J. Shields. The commission is negotiable, and dealers have a separate rate. Charges are made for illustrations, for insurance on consigned property that is worth more than $A1,000, for packing and shipping, and for warehousing, depending on the labor involved and the value of the goods. Consigned goods are sold within 14 days, and settlement costs are 5 days after the sale or on the completion of the sale of all goods consigned. Reserves are accepted, and the consignor is charged for unsold lots.

For appraisal service, please write D. J. Shields or C. V. Johnson.

358. James A. Johnson & Co.
92 Boronia Road   Tel. 877-2754/874-3632
Vermont, Victoria 3133

Johnson's sales are not held on a regular basis; one has to keep an eye on the Melbourne *Age* to find out when one is about to take place. About once a month, the searching eye is rewarded with news of a forthcoming sale on the premises or, in the case of estate sales, in a home. Catalogues are available at the viewings, which are held during the 2 days prior to an auction, and to regular clients only without cost. Mail order bids are not accepted, and no guarantees are offered. Packing and shipping "may be arranged if sufficient notification is given." Buyers must settle within a week, and checks from unknown buyers must clear before the goods will be released.

The minimum value for consignment here is $A50 per item. Those who wish to consign goods should write or call Mr. Johnson. The commission rate, which sometimes is negotiable, is 15 percent, and that goes for dealers too. Depending on the value of a consigned item, there may be charges for insurance, illustration, shipping, and warehousing. Consigned goods are sold within a month, and settlement is a month after the sale. Reserves are accepted, and there is a fee of at least $A10 per unsold item. Johnson does sell on its own behalf; in fact, "some sales or part sales are imported directly by us from the U.K."

James Johnson is also available to conduct appraisals, at a negotiated fee.

359. Jolly Barry Pty. Ltd.
212 Glenmore Road   Tel. 357-4494
Paddington, New South Wales 2021

This firm holds general-purpose mixed-lot sales on its premises every week. The sales are advertised in the Sydney *Morning Herald,* and announcements and single catalogues are available from the firm. A lay-by plan is available for buyers, who also may pay with American Express, Diners Club, Bankcard, and MasterCard. Consignors pay 33⅓ percent commission. Goods are sold and settlement is made "as soon as possible." There is a separate rate structure for dealers, but all rates are "varying." Appraisal services are not available.

Jolly Barry is a member of the Professional Picture Framers Association.

360. James R. Lawson Pty. Ltd.

236 Castlereagh Street	Tel. 266408
Sydney, New South Wales	Cable: LAWSONS SYDNEY

The Sydney *Morning Herald* is the place to look for Lawson's weekly sales announcements. Most of the weekly sales are held on the premises, but Lawson's holds house sales and sales of commercial and industrial equipment as well. Announcements of forthcoming sales are available, as are catalogues, either singly or by subscription. Buyers can enjoy the opportunity to bid by mail or to have their purchases packed and shipped at cost, but there are no returns and no guarantees of authenticity here. Viewing is 10 A.M.–8 P.M. on the 2 days preceding a sale, and the successful bidder must pay up within 24 hours.

The percentage paid for commission by consignors varies, but is above the 15 percent paid by dealers. The insurance fee is 0.5 percent of the hammer price, and packing and shipping will be done at cost. Sale takes place 1–4 weeks after the goods are consigned, and settlement is made 7–14 days after the sale. Reserves are accepted, and the costs for unsold items are nil to 2.5 percent.

Lawson's will appraise at a fee of 1 percent of value.

361. Mason Greene & Associates

91–101 Leveson Street	Tel. 329-9911
North Melbourne, Victoria 3051	Telex: MCCOM AA33991
	Cable: REGENT MELBOURNE

With 6 auction rooms at its Leveson Street premises, Mason Greene holds 2 auctions per week plus 1 or 2 on vendors' premises. Most of these are general-purpose mixed-lot sales, but some feature light and heavy machinery. Sales are announced in the Melbourne *Age,* and brochures and other descriptive literature about sales are available to those who phone or write. Catalogues are not available by subscription, though. Viewing is the day prior to the sale, and mail order bids are accepted. No returns, guarantees, or packing and shipping services are offered. Accounts must be settled within 24 hours.

J. N. Mason (managing director), G. A. Roberts (director), and J. R. Nankervis (general manager) are the people to contact if you want to consign goods here. The average commission is 15 percent, but sometimes it is negotiable. No special terms for dealers or institutions. Usually, consigned goods are sold within 4 weeks, with settlement 10 working days after the sale. Reserves are accepted, and there are no other charges unless a lot is unsold, in which case cartage may be charged for its return to the consignor.

Appraisal is a major activity of Mason Greene, and it is done at no cost if the appraisal results in an auction.

362. Mercantile Art Auctions

317 Pacific Highway   Tel. 922-3610/922-3608
North Sydney, New South Wales 2060   Cable: ANTIQUES SYDNEY

Through its partners, Mercantile Art Auctions is interrelated with Aronson Antiques and Frank's Persian Bazaar (Oriental Carpets) Pty. Ltd. Auctions are infrequent, news of them being carried in the Sydney *Morning Herald* and by announcement to people on Mercantile's mailing list. Write to the manager to be put on the list or to place a mail order bid. Mercantile assumes legal responsibilities for catalogue descriptions and will accept returns of goods that prove to be not as catalogued. Viewing takes place during the normal trading hours of 9 A.M.–4:45 P.M. for 2 days before each sale. Buyers must pay within 24 hours, and Bankcard is accepted.

Consignors with Oriental carpets should write or phone Mr. J. Frank, while those with antiques or fine arts should seek out N. or C. Aronson. The commission rate is negotiable and is lower for dealers and institutions. Additional charges will be made for illustrations, insurance, and packing and shipping. The length of time before goods consigned are sold is "dependent upon individual arrangements," and settlement is made "usually within 14 days" of the sale. Reserves are accepted, and consignors' costs for unsold lots are negotiable.

The Aronsons and Mr. Frank will do appraisals for $A30 per hour. Contact them for details.

363. James R. Newall Auctions Pty. Ltd.

164 Military Road   Tel. 903023/902587 (Sydney exchange)
Neutral Bay, New South Wales 2089

Every Friday, Newall's of Neutral Bay holds an auction. Some of these are general, but the firm does emphasize CLOCKS AND WATCHES, COINS, ENGRAVINGS, ETCHINGS, Georgian, Victorian, and Edwardian FURNITURE, GLASS, JEWELRY, AUSTRALIAN PAINTINGS, PORCELAIN, POSTCARDS, SILVER, and STAMPS. Sales are advertised in the Sydney *Morning Herald* each Thursday and sometimes on Saturday. Except for house sales, all auctions are held on the premises.

Announcements and single catalogues are available; write to Newall's. Neither mail order bids nor packing and shipping services are offered, but buyers can return goods if they are "found to be contrary to the way in which we describe or catalogue any article or a fault not announced at time of sale is found," says managing director John S. Strahan. Viewing is 2:30–4:30 P.M., 6:30–8 P.M. each Thursday and 8 A.M. to sale time (10:30 A.M.) on Friday.

Buyers must pay within 3 days of the sale, and no credit terms are available. The house buys and sells on its own behalf "only if a potential consignor has exceptional circumstances or reasons for not selling by auction sale."

The firm receives goods for auction sale each Monday, Tuesday, and Wednesday, and transport can be arranged. The commission is 20 percent and there is no separate rate for dealers or institutions. There are no other charges. Reserves are accepted, and the consignor pays nothing if a lot is bought in.

Newall's of Neutral Bay conducts appraisals for 1 percent of the total value or a minimum of $A30, whichever is greater. There is no cost if the goods are consigned for auction.

364. P. L. Pickles & Co. Pty. Ltd.
655 Pacific Highway   Tel. 498-8069/498-2775
Killara, New South Wales 2071

These specialists in MARINE PAINTINGS, PRINTS, AND MUSICAL INSTRUMENTS hold 2 or 3 general sales each month. Other Pickles specialties are AUSTRALIAN ART, VICTORIAN AND GEORGIAN FURNITURE, GLASS, JEWELRY, and MAPS. Catalogues for individual sales are mailed on request, and the cost varies; catalogues are not available by subscription. Regular announcements of forthcoming sales appear in the Sydney *Morning Herald* and the *Australian,* along with information about whether the sale is to be held in Pickles' rooms or on site. Goods may be viewed for 3 days preceding a sale, and bids by mail are accepted for all catalogue sales. Items that prove to be not as catalogued may be returned within 6 days of the sale. Packing and shipping services are available at cost. Settlement of accounts is to be made within 3 days of the sale.

The commission rate on consignments of furniture and books is 20 percent; for paintings, silver, china, and such, it is 17.5 percent. Dealers get a 15 percent rate, which drops to 12.5 percent for items in excess of $A20,000. Insurance is 1 percent on gross sale, and packing and shipping is done at cost. There is a warehousing charge only on furniture that is unsold and uncollected after 6 months. At Pickles, it takes from 2 weeks to 2 months for goods to be sold, and settlement is made 7 days after the sale. Reserves are accepted, and in case of unsold items, the consignor is charged return packing and post or storage of $A1 per item per month after 6 months.

Peter L. Pickles will appraise at a rate of $A50 for the first hour of inspection or research, $A30 thereafter.

365. Sotheby Parke Bernet Group Ltd.
115 Collins Street   Tel. (03) 63 39 00
Melbourne, Victoria 3000

The auction house is represented in Australia by Bruce Rutherford. This SPB representative will help interested parties to bid and to consign.

366. H. E. Wells & Sons
326 Rokeby Road   Tel. 3819448/3819040
Subiaco, West Australia

"Wells Sells Well" is the motto of this firm, and they sell often as well—every week, in fact. Almost all their sales are general ones, for "due to the size and isolation of Perth, hence the relative scarcity of specialist collectors, it is not practical to really specialize in particular categories." Both the on-premises and on-site sales are advertised in such papers as the *West Australian*. Catalogues are prepared only for special auctions; such catalogues are available at the viewing and by mail on request. Mail order bids are accepted. Guarantees and returns are available only if the vendor personally wishes to make the guarantee or accept the return. Packing and shipping are available, at the buyer's expense. Terms are cash on "fall of the hammer" unless other arrangements have been made.

The commission fees are 15 percent for auctions held on premises, except for motor vehicles, for which the charge is 7.5 percent plus advertising costs. There is a minimum commission of $A6 on any consignment. All outside auctions have a commission rate of 7.5 percent, plus advertising and expenses. General goods are insured without cost, but consignors may wish to pay for additional insurance on valuable articles. For general goods, the elapsed time from consignment to sale is a maximum of 1 week; special items are held for appropriate sales. Settlement is 1–2 weeks, "sooner upon request." Reserves are accepted, "providing it's realistic and then only on valuable or worthwhile items."

Appraisal fees are 2.5 percent up to $A4,000 and 1.5 percent thereafter, with a minimum fee of $A25.

367. Young Family Estates Pty. Ltd.
229 Camberwell Road   Tel. 821433
East Hawthorn, Melbourne 2123

This firm, known as Young's Antiques/Auctions, holds auctions every Friday. Most of these are general-purpose mixed-lot sales, though the Youngs are most interested in EARLY VICTORIAN AND EDWARDIAN FURNITURE and JEWELRY. Announcements are made in the Melbourne press, but neither announcements nor catalogues are available from the firm. Young's also holds house sales from time to time. Viewing hours for the regular sales are Tuesday–Thursday, 9 A.M.–5:30 P.M. Buyers may bid by mail, and Young's offers packing and shipping services, as well as accepting returns of goods that prove to be not as catalogued. Accounts must be settled within 24 hours.

Consignors pay 17 percent for all goods sold, and there are no other fees unless the consignor wishes Young's to handle the matter of cartage. Goods are sold within 3 weeks, and settlement is made the Monday after the sale, "providing all goods are sold." Reserves are accepted if the house agrees that they are sensible, and there is no charge for unsold lots. A finder's fee of 5 percent of all goods sold is paid to anybody who successfully brings a collection in to Young's.

W. J. Young will see to the appraisal of goods for a fee of 2 percent on the first $A4,000 and 1 percent thereafter.

New Zealand

368. Devereaux & Culley Ltd.
200 Dominion Road   Tel. 687429/687112
Mt. Eden, Auckland

General-purpose mixed-lot auctions are held every week by Devereaux & Culley, usually on the premises, though "house sales" and real estate sales are specialties of the firm. Specialized sales as such are rarely held, yet many of the catalogues are divided into sections by type of object—paintings, silver, or whatever. By writing to the firm, one can get catalogues for specific sales, or for the whole year at an approximate cost of NZ$10. Viewing is 2–3 days prior to sale. Absentee bids are accepted, and any dispute about goods not being as catalogued must be registered within 7 days. Freight services can be arranged at cost. Credit terms are not available, and buyers are expected to settle their accounts immediately after a sale.

The commission rate for consignors is 20 percent, plus insurance and freight charges if applicable. Commissions may be negotiable, and there is a separate rate for dealers with a high volume of consigned goods. The usual time to sale is 2–3 weeks, with settlement 2 weeks after sale. Reserves are accepted, but there is no charge for unsold lots unless the lot has been specially advertised. Would-be consignors should contact Mr. Devereaux if they have furniture, paintings, silver, or real estate to sell, and Mr. J. Cullen if they have jewelry, stamps, coins, or clocks and watches.

Appraisal service is available. Write to the firm for details.

369. Alex Harris Ltd.
P.O. Box 510   Tel. 773955/740703
377 Princes Street
Dunedin

189 George Street
Dunedin

Nobody quite knows why there is a carved stone American bald eagle atop the building that has served as Harris's headquarters since its establishment in 1903. Dunedin, by the way, is the home of Otago University, and its name is the ancient name of Edinburgh. Harris is now run by A. R. Harris, the son of the firm's founder, and weekly sales are held here, with very occasional sales of PAINTINGS, SILVER, and PERIOD FURNITURE (Regency, Victorian, Edwardian). Only the special sales are catalogued; ordinary sales are simply advertised in the local papers. Mail order bids will be accepted reluctantly; "we prefer that buyers see the property before they leave a bid." Packing and shipping arrangements can be made on request. Viewing is the day before the sale; and accounts are to be settled immediately after the sale.

The normal commission is 20 percent across the board, but on occasion the commission is negotiable. Ordinary goods take a week or two to come up for sale, but it takes longer to arrange a special sale. Settlement is made within a week of the auction. Reserves are accepted, and the charge for unsold lots is "generally nil unless furniture is stored for some length of time."

Appraisal services are available at 2.5–5 percent, depending on the type of goods.

370. Roger Moat Ltd.
College Hill and Beaumont Street   Tel. 371588/371686/371595
Auckland

Once a week in its own rooms, and from time to time at houses, factories, and government buildings, Moat holds sales of anything and everything. These are not catalogued sales, but they are advertised in the *New Zealand Herald*. This is a cash-and-carry operation, with no mail order bids, no guarantees, no returns, and no shipping services. Viewing is 9 A.M.–3 P.M. on the day preceding the sale.

Consignors are told to "bring goods to rooms, collect consignment receipt, and await check." The commission rate here (dealers too) is 20 percent, sometimes negotiable; for outside clearance sales, the commission is 15 percent up to NZ$20,000 and 5 percent thereafter. There are no other fees. All goods are sold without reserves. Consigned goods are sold in 1 week, and settlement is made 10 days after the sale.

Appraisal service is available at a fee of 2.5 percent of the appraised value, but the fee is waived if the goods are for auction. Write for details.

371. New Zealand Stamp Auctions
P.O. Box 3496   Tel. 375490/375498
Queen and Wyndham Streets   Cable: AUCKSTAMPS, AUCKLAND
Auckland

STAMPS are the sole specialty of this firm, which holds 3–4 auctions a year on its premises. Readers of philatelic journals will see these sales advertised; others can write for a sample catalogue or an annual subscription (NZ$3). NZSA holds postal auctions only. In addition to stating a maximum bid on each lot, "if you wish you may bid on all lots of interest to you but still control your total purchases by writing on the bid form 'Limit of Purchase $ . . .' Once this total is reached, all bids on further lots are canceled." If two bids are for the same amount, the earlier wins. NZSA also accepts "Buy Bids," but "only on the condition that the Auctioneer's discretion is absolute, and his decision, in case of dispute, final." Bids from minors will be accepted only when accompanied by full cash deposit or a suitable guarantee. Any lot found to be incorrectly described may be returned, provided that the return is made within 48 hours of receipt. NZSA will arrange for old and new clients who send a full cash deposit to view lots by postal inspection when such lots are not too large or too bulky. The would-be bidder must pay the registration and insurance for this service. All accounts must be paid within 48 hours of receipt.

The consignor's commission at NZSA is 20 percent flat rate; large holdings will be negotiated. Minimum value for a lot is NZ$20. Consigned stamps will be sold within 6 months for certain, and sometimes within 2 months; settlement is 4 weeks after the auction. Reserves are accepted; and the consignor's cost for unsold lots is NZ$2 per lot. NZSA does not buy on its own account, but its parent company, Auckland City Stamps, does.

A free appraisal service is available on the premises.

372. Alistair Robb Coin Auctions
La Aitken Street, Box 3705   Tel. 727-141
Wellington

Alistair Robb is one of the world's great originals, and his coin auctions, which take place once or twice a year, sometimes coincide with the race meetings at Trentham, where "some of N.Z.'s finest horses will be running." Sales have been held in the St. George Hotel in Wellington, with viewing the day before. Some lots can be viewed earlier by special arrangement.

Buyers who arrive in Wellington by airplane can arrange with Robb to be met at the airport. In his catalogues, Robb does not use certain designations: "Good and Very Good are never used, as they are not good describers of coins." All lots are sold for cash, due on the day of sale unless prior arrangements have been made. Postal bidders will be expected to pay within a few days of receipt of the invoice and to pay the registered and insured mail fees when the coins are sent to them. Postal bidders have the right to reject any lot within 3 days of receipt of the lot, and saleroom bidders can reject any lot within 7 days of the sale should it "prove to be a forgery, restrike or inadvertently falsely listed."

Would-be consignors should write to Mr. Robb for information. And coin collectors in general might wish to know more about the numbering system for Australian and New Zealand private bank note issues prior to 1934 devised by Mr. Robb and Tony Grant.

373. Dunbar Sloane Ltd.
32 Waring Taylor Street   Tel. 721-367
Wellington

Dunbar Sloane is particularly well known for its annual national art sale of NEW ZEALAND PAINTINGS. Other specialties here are ARMS, SOUTH PACIFIC

PRIMITIVE ART, NEW ZEALAND ARTIFACTS, and other colonial art. Sales are held weekly (including estate, customs, and machinery sales, held on premises), special sales about once a month. Both radio and newspapers are used to advertise, and everybody whose name is in the firm's mail order book receives announcements of the specialist auctions. To get in the book, write Dunbar Sloane. Each announcement contains an application form for the catalogue. Buying orders by mail are accepted, and goods are received back if proved to be not as catalogued. "Arrangements can be made with a very reputable carrier to send goods anywhere." Viewing is 2 days prior to the sale, 9 A.M.–5 P.M., and the evening before the sale, 5–8. Unless special arrangements are made, the buyer must pay immediately after the sale.

Consignors should contact either Dunbar Sloane or Paul Neal. The commission is negotiable. No charge is made for insurance, but illustrations and costs of packing and shipping will be billed to the consignor. Goods are sold within 2 months, and settlement is made 3 weeks after the sale. Reserves are accepted, and no charge is made if the lot fails to sell. The house does buy and sell on its own behalf: "We import containers from England."

Appraisal services are available free if the items are received for auction. Otherwise, "a reasonable fee to cover time and expenses is charged."

374. Thornton Auctions Ltd.
89 Albert Street   Tel. 30888 (3 lines)
Auckland 1

Both general sales and special sales of art and antiques are held by Thornton's. The *New Zealand Herald* carries notices of its weekly sales, and if you write to Terry Thornton, you will receive free announcements. Catalogues of individual art sales are available by post, but subscriptions are not available. Viewing takes place during the 2 days preceding a sale, and buyers must settle their accounts immediately after the sale. Mail order bids will be taken; packing and shipping services are available; objects found to be not as catalogued may be returned.

Consignors of antiques or fine art properties should write or phone Terry Thornton. The commission rate, which may be negotiable, is 20 percent, and there is a minimal insurance charge as well. General goods are sold within a week, and antiques within a month. Settlement is 14 days after the sale. Reserves are accepted, and Thornton's makes no charge for lots that do not sell. The house does buy and sell on its own behalf.

Appraisal services are available.

375. Daniel J. Visser
109 and 90 Worchester Street   Tel. 68853/67297
Christchurch

Mr. Visser's FURNITURE and household effects auctions are an offshoot of his real estate business. His uncatalogued occasional sales are held either in his firm's auction rooms or "on demand anywhere." Check the newspapers or write to be informed. Viewing procedures and the amount of time for settlement of accounts also are advertised.

Consignors must have a total value of NZ$5,000 to sell, and the terms of commission are available from Mr. Visser. He also does appraisals.

376. Peter Webb Galleries Ltd.

T & G Building, Wellesley and Elliot Streets   Tel. 373090/374404
Auckland

Mailing Address:
P.O. Box 7008
Auckland

Fine Art Auctioneers & Appraisers, Contemporary Art Dealers, and Publishers for The Print Club—such are the activities of Peter Webb Galleries. They hold monthly sales of general antiques and art and occasional specialized sales of such categories as NEW ZEALAND PAINTINGS, SILVER, JEWELRY, RUGS, and 18th and 19th century EUROPEAN FURNITURE. Sales are advertised in the national press, and catalogues will be sent at a rate of NZ$8 per 5 catalogues, plus overseas postage. Auctions are held on the premises or at vendors' houses. Viewing for 4 days before a sale is the usual routine, and mail order bids are accepted. Guarantees are offered, and buyers may return goods that prove to be not as catalogued. Packing and shipping service is available, at the buyer's expense. Credit terms are negotiable, but the buyer must pay 10 percent of the purchase price on the fall of the hammer; otherwise, the lot may be resold immediately.

The consignment fees here are 20 percent on items of small value, 15 percent on larger items. Rates for dealers and institutions are negotiable. Reserves are accepted, and the consignor must be responsible for removal costs on unsold lots. There is an optional 1 percent insurance fee. Consigned goods will be sold in 4–6 weeks, with settlement 14 days after the sale.

Appraisal services are available. Write to Peter Webb or Peter Downey for details.

Austria

The Dorotheum dominates the Austrian auction market. There are other houses, but none that compare to it. The market is thin in part because of the relative closeness of established markets in West Germany and Switzerland, which offer for sale, at less cost to the buyer, high-quality merchandise of the kind that is of interest to Austrians.

Not only the commission structure is expensive. VAT can be charged at 8 percent, 18 percent, or 30 percent of the hammer price—determined by the kind of item. VAT is not payable on lots sold to residents of foreign countries if payment is made in a foreign currency and if an export certificate is obtained. Most auction houses will accept their forwarding of the goods to a non-Austrian destination as sufficient proof of export. You may not need to get an official export certificate, but check, for not all auctioneers are so accommodating.

377. Christie's
Ziehrerplatz 4/22   Tel. (0222) 73 26 44
A-1030 Vienna

The Christie's agent in Austria is Vincent Windisch-Graetz, and he functions as do the representatives of the multinational firms in other countries. He solicits consignments, helps bidders, and otherwise assists interested parties.

378. Kunstauktionshaus Friedrich Deutsch
Dorotheergasse 13   Tel. (0222) 52 23 71
A-1010 Vienna

This auction house exists in the very shadow of the auction giant the Dorotheum. In addition to holding auctions from time to time, Deutsch is a dealer; in both capacities he handles FURNITURE, PAINTINGS, PORCELAIN, and SCULPTURE. Sales are advertised in the local press.

Catalogues may be available. The conditions of sale vary, so it is best to check with the house at the time of the sale.

The standard consignor's commission is 12 percent. The firm does buy and sell on its own behalf.

In the past, Deutsch took some pride in the catalogues produced, offering birth and death dates for many of the artists being sold, and noting in the front that the catalogue was a work of lasting worth because it included dates not to be found in the usual sources.

379. Dorotheum

Dorotheergasse 17   Tel. (0222) 52 85 60
A-1010 Vienna   Cable: DOROTHEUM VIENNA

In 1707, less than a generation after the Turks knocked on the gates of Vienna, the Dorotheum was founded. It was originally called the Versatz-und Frag-Ambt, and takes its present name from the abandoned church to which it moved in the mid-1780s. Since then, the Dorotheum has admirably fulfilled a dual function—as a pawnshop providing funds at reasonable cost to the needy who pawn their possessions, and as an auction forum selling a variety of goods to those with funds. Currently it is estimated that less than a quarter of the goods auctioned represent items pawned.

The Dorotheum, which now includes a bank as well, is located in a section of Vienna that is replete with antique shops, book dealers, art galleries, and curio sellers. For much of its history the Dorotheum could at best have been described as of local importance. It still is, of course, but in recent years it has become an auction operation that has international significance as well, having reached an annual turnover of approximately $25 million in the mid-1970s.

More than 2,500 auction sales are held annually by the Dorotheum in its various salerooms at its headquarters and at 16 other sites in Vienna (the Dorotheum blankets Vienna and Austria with some 24 branches). Obviously, many of the sales that are held are of little significance and offer items that the *New York Times* correctly described as "humble," such as "tennis balls, pipes, pepper grinders, a crocodile medical bag, and a feathered fan suitable for the Merry Widow." But the Dorotheum also offers a wide variety of items that are not just a slice of everyday life.

Both in Vienna and in provincial cities such as Graz and Salzburg, the Dorotheum offers specialized auctions of BOOKS, JEWELRY, PAINTINGS, PORCELAIN, RUGS, SILVER, STAMPS, and such other items as VINTAGE MOTOR VEHICLES. These auctions are held in addition to the more general sales, which take place, as in the case of FURNITURE, about 3 times a week, or as in the case of BOOKS, twice a month. The Dorotheum is very much a two-tier operation.

It is also a multifaceted one. The organization offers an interesting array of services; these include the summer care of furs, rug storage and cleaning, evaluations of domestic and business property, and the safekeeping of valuable art objects. The fine arts division occupies a separate building (Dorotheergasse 11), as does the bank (Dorotheergasse 20). On the ground floor in the main building are to be found for sale the more valuable items; less valuable objects are usually sold on the next floor. Given the array and number of sales, it is not surprising to find more than one sale taking place at the same time. The fine arts division of the Dorotheum has an official foreign representative: L. C. B. Treuhand AG, Aeschenvorstadt 15, Basel, Switzerland, tel. (061) 23 26 25/48. This representative will bid for you and thus ensure that you are not charged Austrian VAT, and will charge 3 percent of the hammer price for so doing. This representative will also, for an additional charge, undertake transport, insurance, and customs formalities.

The Dorotheum is open for business Monday–Friday, 7:30 A.M.–6 P.M., but sales and exhibitions take place on Saturdays as well. Sales are mostly advertised in the Austrian and South German press, but more specialized auctions are also advertised in specialty publications. There is a house newsletter, which is available on a subscription basis; for details and costs, contact the subscription department.

Catalogues are available singly and by subscription. The quality varies with the kind of sale. Some are just listings, others detailed descriptions, heavily illustrated. The price of the single catalogues varies from S10 to S95 and the price of the annual subscription ranges from S100 to S600, depending on the kind and number involved.

There is a buyer's premium, which varies with the kind of sale. It ranges from 8 to 12 percent. There are some instances, as the catalogue points out, in which "the successful bidder's fee is a standard 20 percent," but that includes VAT. The Dorotheum advises prospective bidders to open an account before the auction and to bid using the account number; this will mitigate the necessity of immediate cash payment. Prices listed in the catalogues are usually the starting prices. Bidders who intend to export lots will not be charged storage fees until 2 months after the auction. Absentee bids are executed. Packing and shipping services are available. Bidding is usually raised by 10 percent each time. Viewing is 5–8 days before the sale, and in the case of the specialized auctions, generally includes Saturday viewing. Accounts must be settled in cash at the time of the sale, but up to 8 days will be allowed floor bidders if they put up at least 50 percent of the winning bid and fees. Kurt Hrstka, the director, reports that credit cards are not accepted "at the moment."

The standard consignor's commission is 15 percent in most instances and 10 percent for motor vehicles and motorcycles. There is not a special rate structure for dealers, but Mr. Hrstka does indicate that there are special rates "in some special cases for dealers." Consignors are not charged for catalogue illustrations, insurance, or storage (prior to sale); nor are they charged packing and shipping if they remove consignments to the saleroom. Reserves are accepted. The buy-in charge is 2.3 percent of the starting price. Settlement is quick; "the consignor can get the net yield from the third day after the auction."

The Dorotheum pays a finder's fee of 2 percent of the highest bid.

Appraisal service is available. The cost is 1 percent of the appraised value (with a minimum fee of at least S100), plus VAT reckoned at 18 percent.

The Dorotheum estimates its annual turnover as at least S500 million. The branch establishments of the Dorotheum are:

VIENNA

380. Taborstrasse 24a
A-1020 Vienna   Tel. (0222) 24 94 03

381. Landstrasse Hauptstrasse 67
A-1030 Vienna   Tel. (0222) 72 63 95

382. Viktor Christ-Gasse 19
A-1050 Vienna   Tel. (0222) 55 31 79

383. Schadekgasse 5
A-1060 Vienna   Tel. (0222) 56 42 42

384. Kaiserstrasse 1
A-1070 Vienna   Tel. (0222) 91 71 83

385. Feldgasse 6-8
A-1080 Vienna   Tel. (0222) 42 16 01

386. Währingerstrasse 2-4
A-1090 Vienna   Tel. (0222) 34 21 86

387. Wielandgasse 6-8
A-1100 Vienna   Tel. (0222) 64 13 71

388. Tanbruckgasse 3
A-1120 Vienna   Tel. (0222) 83 95 68

389. Hietzinger Hauptstrasse 3
A-1130 Vienna   Tel. (0222) 82 25 84

390. Schanzstrasse 14
A-1150 Vienna   Tel. (0222) 92 56 03

391. Friedrich Kaiser-Gasse 36-38
A-1160 Vienna   Tel. (0222) 46 22 94

392. Kalvarienberggasse 27
A-1170 Vienna   Tel. (0222) 43 41 40

393. Gentzgasse 8
A-1180 Vienna   Tel. (0222) 34 54 21

394. Wallensteinstrasse 57
A-1200 Vienna   Tel. (0222) 33 71 78

395. Pitkagasse 4
A-1210 Vienna   Tel. (0222) 38 13 04

OUTSIDE VIENNA

396. Jakominiplatz 7-9
A-8010 Graz   Tel. (03122) 79 480

397. Adamgasse 7a A-6020 Innsbruck	Tel. (05222) 20 937
398. Villacherstrasse 8 A-9010 Klagenfurt	Tel. (04222) 8 23 48
399. Fabrikstrasse 26 A-4020 Linz	Tel. (07222) 7 31 32
400. Schrannengasse 7 A-5027 Salzburg	Tel. (06222) 7 16 71
401. Rathausplatz 3-4 A-3100 St. Pölten	Tel. (02742) 34 25
402. Bahnhofplatz 2 A-2700 Wr. Neustadt	Tel. (02622) 24 67
403. Dr. Koss-Strasse 8 A-4600 Wels	Tel. (07242) 22 061

404. Wolfdietrich Hassfurther
Hohenstaufengasse 7   Tel. (0222) 63 41 74
A-1010 Vienna

Hassfurther presides over a gallery and an antiques establishment, as well as running approximately 2 auctions a year, spring and fall. The quality of these auctions varies. Among the items for sale are AUTOGRAPHS, BOOKS, PAINTINGS, POSTERS, and PRINTS. In 1979–80, Hassfurther held 2 interesting sales of Austrian art, 1880–1945. These sales are advertised in the Austrian and German press, and in specialty publications. Catalogues are available singly for each sale: S100 Austria, S120 Europe, S200 elsewhere (prices include postage, airmail overseas).

There is a buyer's premium of 12 percent for the trade and 15 percent for all others. The catalogue prices, which are estimated to be roughly one third of the market value, are the starting prices and bids are raised 10 percent each time. Packing and shipping services are available. Absentee bids are executed. Buyers have the opportunity to return goods that prove to be not as catalogued, but all claims must be made within 1 week of receipt of the lot.

Consignor's conditions vary and you should check with the firm if you are interested in consigning goods to it. The house does buy and sell on its own behalf.

Belgium

Auctions in Belgium are usually of quite good quality, for they are expensive to mount, and prices paid are high. VAT here is 16 percent, so be certain to make careful arrangements for export. Many houses collect 20–30 percent on top of the hammer price for taxes and their own expenses. If you are exporting your purchases, be certain to find out in advance whether you have to pay the whole buyer's premium and then wait for a refund if all taxes do not apply to you.

405. Maurice Baeten & Co. S.A.
7 Rue Dumidi   Tel. (02) 512-6455
B-1000 Brussels

STAMPS are the specialty of this firm, which also auctions AUTOGRAPHS and MAPS. Sales are held 3 times a year in the Hotel des Colonies in downtown Brussels. As with most stamp auction houses, mail order bids are probably more important than floor bids and the firm's conditions of sale and advertising are keyed to absentee bidders.

Sales are advertised in specialized publications. Catalogues are available for each sale. Usually the illustrations are bound separately from the catalogue listing the lots for sale. The catalogue for each sale costs Bfr75, plus postage. Regular clients receive the catalogues free.

There is no buyer's premium, but there is a surcharge of 25 percent for Belgian bidders and 10 percent for non-Belgians, to cover various costs. Absentee bids are executed. Packing and shipping services are available. Goods that prove to be not as described may be returned within 21 days after the auction ("with a certificate signed by the expert" that the lot is not bona fide; in the case of a need for more than 21 days, the firm may grant an extension of time). The usual viewing period is for 10 days before the sale, 10 A.M.– noon, 2–6 P.M. Floor bidders must pay immediately; others unknown to the house, before delivery; those known to the house, upon receipt of the goods.

The standard consignor's commission is 20 percent. The minimum value for a consignment should be Bfr10,000, or Bfr1,000 for a lot. Consignors do not pay for catalogue illustrations, or for insurance. Consigned goods are sold

within 3–4 months. Settlement is 6 weeks after the sale. Reserves are accepted "exceptionally and must have our agreement," reports the firm.
Appraisal service is available. Contact Ms. Solange Baeten. The firm does buy and sell on its own behalf.

406. Campo Gallery
Meir 47–55   Tel. (031) 32 12 24/25
B-2000 Antwerp

Nineteenth-century and contemporary BELGIAN ART are the specialties of this firm, which holds auctions 4 times a year (usually in April, May, October, and December). These sales are advertised in the Belgian press and in European newspapers.
Catalogues are available singly for each sale and by subscription. An annual subscription costs (including postage) Bfr1,200 Europe, Bfr1,500 U.S. There is a buyer's premium, and according to the firm, there has been one "since always." The premium is 30 percent (which includes all taxes). Absentee bids are executed. Packing and shipping services are available. The firm does not offer buyers a chance to return goods that prove to be not as catalogued. Viewing is 10 days before the auction. Settlement is cash immediately.
The standard consignor's commission is 15 percent, and it is negotiable, depending upon the situation. Reserves are accepted. Consignors are not charged for insurance or for catalogue illustrations. Consigned goods are usually sold within 6 months. Settlement is made within 1 month after the sale.
Appraisal service is available. Contact the gallery for costs and details.
Compo Gallery is a member of the Chambre des Antiquariat de Belgique.
The firm estimates its annual turnover as more than Bfr110 million.

407. Christie, Manson & Woods (Belgium) Ltd.
33 Boulevard de Waterloo   Tel. (02) 512-8765/512-8830
B-1000 Brussels   Telex: 62042

This is a representative office and the Christie's agents here are Janine Duesberg and Richard Stern (who is also active at Christie's Geneva).

Galerie Moderne
408. 3–7 Rue du Parnasse   Tel. (02) 513-9010
B-1040 Brussels

409. 31 Rue Caroly
B-1040 Brussels

410. 6 Rue du Grand Cerf
B-1000 Brussels

Sales are held monthly by this firm, usually for 2 days. Mostly these are general-purpose mixed-lot sales and include a wide range of objects, including

FURNITURE, GLASS, MUSICAL INSTRUMENTS, PAINTINGS, PORCELAIN, PRINTS, and much else. There are also specialized auctions.

Sales are advertised in the Belgian press. Catalogues are available singly for each sale (Bfr250–Bfr300), and by annual subscription (Bfr2,000, plus Bfr600 for the estimates and price results). Postage is extra in both cases.

There is no buyer's premium, and dealers as well as foreign buyers who are exporting goods can get back the VAT charged. Absentee bids are executed. Packing and shipping services are available. Guarantees of authenticity are not offered. The usual viewing procedure is Friday 6:30–9 P.M., Saturday 10 A.M.–noon, 2–6 P.M., Sunday 10 A.M.– noon, 2–6 P.M., and Monday 9 A.M. to just before sale time. Settlement is within 2 days after the sale.

The standard consignor's commission is 10 percent of the hammer price. Consignors are not charged for catalogue illustrations, insurance, or storage (prior to the sale); they are responsible for the cost of removal to the saleroom. Consigned goods are sold within 1 month for the general sales; Mr. Coosemans, the manager, reports that it "takes longer for special auctions." Settlement is made 10 days after the sale. Reserves may be accepted; it depends on the situation. The buy-in charge is 10 percent.

Appraisal service is available. Contact Mr. Coosemans.

Galerie Moderne belongs to the Chambre Syndicale des Salles de Vente.

411. Kunstgalerij De Vuyst

Kerkstraat 24-52   Tel. (091) 48 54 40
B-9100 Lokern

At least 3 times a year in this Flanders town, De Vuyst holds auction sales which include COINS, FURNITURE, ICONS, PAINTINGS, and PRINTS. These are advertised in the Belgian press as well as in other European newspapers; they are also advertised in specialty publications, such as *Antiques Trade Gazette*. The firm also sends out announcements of forthcoming sales; to be placed on the mailing list, write to De Vuyst.

Catalogues are available singly for each sale and by annual subscription. The cost for a single catalogue is Bfr200–Bfr300 in Belgium and Bfr250–Bfr350 elsewhere, including postage. An annual subscription is Bfr1,100–Bfr1,250 for non-Belgians, including postage.

There is no buyer's premium, but there is a surcharge for taxes, etc. Absentee bids are executed, but they must be in writing. Packing and shipping services are not available from the firm. Guarantees of authenticity are offered: De Vuyst states that "authenticity is guaranteed by seller and he has to take it back if proved not to be as he delivered it." Viewing is Thursday to Thursday before the auction, 10 A.M.–noon, 2–7 P.M. Buyer must settle account within 3 days of the sale.

The standard consignor's commission is 15 percent. There is no minimum value necessary for acceptance of a consignment, but De Vuyst points out that "quality is necessary." Consignors are not charged for insurance, but must pay for catalogue illustrations (Bfr1,000 for black and white, Bfr5,000 for color). Consigned goods are usually sold within 2 months. Settlement is 2 weeks after the sale. Reserves are accepted. Appraisal service is available. Contact the gallery.

412. Kunstveilingen De Vos
Keizer Karelstraat 75   Tel. (091) 25 63 68/24 00 13
B-9000 Ghent

Every month, Kunstveilingen De Vos holds sales of fine art objects such as DRAWINGS, PAINTINGS, PORCELAIN, SCULPTURE, and SILVER. The firm also holds house and estate sales, especially in East Flanders. To be placed on the mailing list for announcements, write the firm.

Sales are advertised in Belgian newspapers, in the Western European press, and in specialty publications in the U.K., France, Belgium, and West Germany. Catalogues are available singly for each sale and by subscription (Bfr1,500 per annum).

Absentee bids are executed. Packing and shipping services are not available from the firm. Sales are usually on Monday and Tuesday at 7:30 P.M. Viewing is Friday and Saturday 2–7 P.M., and Sunday 10 A.M.–noon, 2–6 P.M., before the sale. Settlement is 1 day after the last day of the sale.

The standard consignor's commission is 15 percent and it is negotiable, depending on the situation. There is a separate rate structure for dealers, beginning at 10 percent. If a consignor wants a lot illustrated, the cost is Bfr1,000. Consignors are not charged for insurance. Consigned goods are usually sold within 4–6 weeks, "depending upon the situation," reports Jean Pierre De Bruyn. Settlement is made with the consignor 10 days after the sale. Reserves are accepted.

Dr. De Bruyn reports that Kunstveilingen De Vos does buy and sell on its own behalf.

Kunstveilingen De Vos is a member of the Syndicale Kamer der Veilingzalen van Belgie.

413. Roepzaal Marnix
Terninckstraat 1   Tel. 32 48 18
2000 Antwerp

Once every 2 weeks, Roepzaal Marnix holds a sale of such goods as CHINESE AND JAPANESE WORKS OF ART, CLOCKS AND WATCHES, FURNITURE, JEWELRY, PAINTINGS, RUGS, and SILVER. Check the newspaper for advertisements, or write to manager Jan B. Lambrechts for details of catalogue subscription costs. Sales are held Monday, with viewing on Saturday, 2–5 P.M., and Sunday, 10 A.M.–1 P.M. Packing and shipping services are available, but the house does not accept mail order bids. Buyers may not return goods bought here. Successful bidders pay 20 percent over the hammer price for a combination of tax and surcharge. Accounts must be settled 2 days after the sale, but credit terms are available and some credit cards are accepted—check with Mr. Lambrechts.

Consignors pay a 10 percent commission, and there may be insurance or illustration charges on some lots. Goods are sold in 2 weeks, and settlement is 3 days after the sale. Reserves are accepted, and there is no cost to the consignor for unsold lots.

414. Service des Ventes Publiques de la Société des Expositions du Palais des Beaux-Arts

Rue Royale 10   Tel. 512 18 94/512 85 78
1000 Brussels

Once a month, except for July and August, a sale of antiques and modern art is held at the Palais des Beaux-Arts. Catalogues for these sales are available at a cost of Bfr2,600 in Europe and Bfr3,000 if sent to America, Africa, or Asia. Payment must be made by bank transfer in Belgian funds; foreign checks are not accepted. Write to the director, Cecile de Mul, for details.

Viewing commences 3 days before a sale, and mail order bids are accepted. Packing and shipping services are not offered, and lots are sold "as is." Accounts must be settled within 5 days and in Belgian funds; otherwise, objects may be resold. Anyone who is exempt from VAT must give his number at the time of sale. There is a total surcharge of 30 percent here, and a *droit de suite* payable on works of living makers or those who have died within the past 60 years; this is charged at a rate of 2 percent to Bfr10,000, 3 percent to Bfr20,000, 4 percent to Bfr50,000, and 6 percent thereafter.

For consignors there is a basic charge of 12 percent for the mounting of the sale. For each object or lot that sells for less than Bfr5,000, there is a further 15 percent charge. Non-agreed reserves for lots that fail to sell result in a 10 percent charge, which is subject to VAT; there is no charge for lots with agreed reserves that fail to sell. Unsold lots must be removed from the premises within 15 days to avoid warehousing charges.

Appraisal services are available. Contact Cecile de Mul for details.

415. Sobelar S.P.R.L.

Rue Van Elewijck 111   Tel. 267 6755
B-1820 Grimbergen, Brussels   Telex: 24077 BENETR B

Twice a year, Sobelar holds auctions of COINS and MEDALS in hotels. These sales are advertised in Belgian newspapers, and catalogues can be obtained by writing the firm. Neither announcements nor subscriptions are available. Viewing is held 2 days before an auction. Mail order bids and shipping services are available, as are guarantees of authenticity. Buyers can return goods that prove not to be as catalogued. There is a 20 percent buyer's premium, and VAT if applicable. Accounts must be settled within a week of sale.

The minimum value for acceptance of a coin or medal is Bfr1,000. The commission rate is 15 percent for everybody, but it is negotiable in some situations. Illustrations are charged at a rate of Bfr100 per coin. Consigned goods are sold in the next auction, and settlement is 1 month after sale. Reserves are accepted, and there is no charge for unsold lots.

Appraisal service is available at a cost of 5 percent of value, but without cost if the coins are left for auction. Write Mr. Youroukov for details.

416. Sotheby Parke Bernet Belgium
Rue de l'Abbaye 32   Tel. 343 50 07
1050 Brussels

This is a representative office under the direction of Count Henry de Limburg Stirum. No sales are held here at this time.

417. Verkoopzaal Leys N.V.
Kipdorpvest 46   Tel. 32 69 69/31 63 61
B-2000 Antwerp

Leys holds about 12 auctions a year, and its calendar is available to anyone who writes requesting one. Specialties include WINE, PORCELAIN, JEWELRY, and ORIENTAL RUGS. Not all sales are catalogued, though that for the wine sale always is. Sales are advertised in the Belgian newspapers, in the *Telegraaf* in Holland, and in other foreign publications, such as *Apollo* and *Antiques Trade Gazette*. Sales are held on Monday and Tuesday from 7:30 P.M., and viewing is the Saturday and Sunday preceding the sale, 10 A.M.–6 P.M. The buyer's premium is "20% inclusive of all local and other taxes (VAT included 16%)." Bids by mail are accepted, and packing and shipping services are available. The house offers a guarantee of origin on carpets and rugs and a descriptive certificate for contemporary jewels. Buyers must settle accounts within 3 days, and no credit terms are available.

Would-be consignors should call or write to the office, which will make certain that the proper expert is notified. Consignors pay 15 percent of the hammer price, negotiable in exceptional circumstances, with no costs for unsold goods. Reserves are accepted. There are no charges for illustrations, insurance, or warehousing. The time to sale is 15 days to 2 months, and settlement is 8 days after the sale.

Appraisal fees are 2 percent of the estimated value, with a minimum of Bfr1,000 plus 16 percent VAT, and will be "paid back pro rata on items put in auction."

Canada

In terms of auction, Canada has very much in common with Australia. Both use the English system of auction, and both are very much local markets. By and large, the best buys for the auctiongoer in Canada are Eskimo art and artifacts and Canadiana. French Canada is not rich in auction venues; in fact, Montreal has seen one auction house move to Toronto and another close in the past 2 years. In time, the Canadian auction market may become an international market, but for now it reflects the history of Canada very strongly indeed.

418. A-1 Auctioneer Evaluation Services Ltd.

P.O. Box 926 Tel. (506) 762-0559 (office)/
Saint John, N.B. E2L 4C3 762-8749 (hall)

With hours of operation from 9 A.M. to 10 P.M., A-1 manages to hold more than 80 sales a year, with specialization in FURNITURE, DOLLS, GLASS, JEWELRY, and PAINTINGS. They also do heavy equipment and farm auctions on site.

Sales are advertised in all major eastern Canadian newspapers and by announcement. Write to Miss Henderson or Mr. Charles Polk. Photo listings will be sent to special buyers, but usually no formal catalogue is produced. There is no buyer's premium, and one may bid by mail, obtain packing and shipping services, and return goods that prove to be not as catalogued. However, there is no guarantee of authenticity. Viewing is the evening before and the morning of the sale. In the case of an evening sale, there is a 2-hour viewing period. Buyers must settle accounts immediately by cash, approved check, or Chargex and Visa cards.

Consignors "must phone at least 2 weeks previous to the auction date. If we know the person and can trust his judgement we take his description; if not, we go to see the goods and use our own description." Tax matters are taken care of for the consignor by the house, and there is no charge for illustration, insurance, or warehousing. The consignor must pay all transportation and packing charges. Goods are usually sold within 2 weeks, and settlement is within the week following the sale. The commission structure ranges from 25 to 15 percent, depending on value, and reserves are discouraged but not forbidden. The people to contact are Gordon Jennings for art, Charles Polk for furniture, and Miss Henderson for glass, china, etc. The house rewards detective work: "We pay 33⅓ percent of the net profit to the person responsible for getting us a sale." Appraisal services are available at C$25 per hour.

419. Appleton Auctioneers Ltd.
1238 Seymour Street   Tel. (604) 685-1715
Vancouver, B.C. V6B 3N9

Eskimo INUIT CARVINGS AND SCULPTURE are the prime specialties of this firm, which also sells CHINESE AND JAPANESE WORKS OF ART, NETSUKE, RUGS, and PRINTS. Appleton Galleries, as it is known, is open weekday mornings, and it holds 2 or 3 auctions a month in the ballrooms of such hotels as the Four Seasons in Vancouver and the Sheraton and Canadian Pacific in Edmonton, Calgary, Victoria, and Toronto. House sales are also conducted.

Sales are advertised in local and regional newspapers, and list-like catalogues are available at the previews or the sales. To receive announcements of forthcoming sales, write Ronald Appleton. Viewing is from noon on sale day to sale time. There is no buyer's premium and no credit terms are available. Mail order bids are not accepted. According to Mr. Appleton, "If requested, we offer a packing and shipping service with no additional charge except for shipping expenses. We stand behind all goods sold, and if there is a valid reason we will refund or put up the item for resale."

Consignors should write to Mr. Appleton. It takes approximately 6 months before goods are sold, but settlement usually is made within a week after the sale, and there is no buy-in charge. Reserves are accepted "only in very specific circumstances."

Appraisal service is available, "dependent upon items involved and their location." Once again, write to Mr. Appleton.

420. Ashton Auction Service
P.O. Box 500   Tel. (613) 257-1575
Ashton, Ontario K0A 1B0

Ashton claims "our service does not cost—it pays!" Open from 9 A.M. to 5 P.M. on weekdays, and sometimes on weekends as well, Ashton holds sales "as advertised" in the Ottawa *Citizen* and Ottawa *Journal,* usually in the Thursday editions. Catalogues are not available by subscription, but Mrs. L. Laflame can see that you get them if you write or call. Auctions are held at various sites, for Ashton does a fair amount of liquidation and bankruptcy selling. Mail order bids are accepted, and returns, packing and shipping, and guarantees are useful services offered. Viewing is the afternoon of the day preceding each sale and 1 hour before the sale. Payment must be made immediately unless other arrangements have been made, and both MasterCard and Chargex are accepted. There is no buyer's premium, but local taxes are charged if required.

Consignors should make an appointment with Gerald W. Lepage at least 3 weeks before a sale is scheduled. Commission rates vary and should be discussed with Mr. Lepage. The only other charges are for packing and shipping. Reserves are accepted, but there is a 5 percent charge on buy-ins. Settlement is 2 weeks after the sale.

Appraisal services are available, but the cost varies; again, Mr. Lepage is the man to consult.

421. Canada Book Auctions

35 Front Street East   Tel. (416) 368-4326
Toronto, Ontario M5E 1B3   Cable: BOOKAUC TORONTO

The successor to Bernard Amtmann's Montreal Book Auctions Ltd., Canada Book Auctions was formed in 1979 by a group that includes both Americans and Canadians. The new firm is holding 6–8 sales a year of BOOKS, MANUSCRIPTS, AUTOGRAPHS, MAPS, and PRINTS at their Front Street offices or at St. Lawrence Hall, 157 King Street East.

Sales are advertised in the Toronto *Star* and the Toronto *Globe and Mail,* and in such trade journals as *AB Bookman's Weekly.* A catalogue subscription is C$28 Canada and U.S., C$38 for airmail to the rest of the world; this includes price lists, which are inserted in the following catalogue. Viewing is usually from 8 days before the sale through the day before the sale.

There is a buyer's premium of 10 percent, and buyers' accounts must be settled within a week after the sale. Absentee bids are executed. New buyers may be asked to pay 50 percent of the purchase price immediately. Maps may be subject to provincial sales tax.

The standard consignor commission rates are 15 percent for everybody, although these are negotiable, depending on the situation. Consignors are not charged for warehousing or for illustrations, according to Canada Book's president, Craig Fraser, but there is a 1 percent insurance fee and charges for packing and shipping if such are required. Reserves are frowned upon but sometimes accepted. Then "the reserve can be obtained by inquiry. When a lot fails to make the reserve, it will be so announced during the auction." There is a buy-in charge of 10 percent. Goods are sold within 60 days of consignment, and settlement is made after 30 days. The minimum value for a consignment is C$50.

Appraisal service is available at a fee of 2 percent with a minimum of traveling expenses, which will be remitted on property subsequently sold through Canada Book. The firm does not buy and sell on its own behalf.

422. Christie's International Ltd.

Suite 2002, 1055 West Georgia Street   Tel. (604) 685-2126
Vancouver, B.C. V6E 3P3   Telex: 04-507838

Murray MacKay serves as a consultant to Christie's in this part of the world. He solicits consignments, assists bidders, and generally makes himself useful to interested parties.

423. Robert Deveau Galleries

297-299 Queen Street East   Tel. (416) 364-6271
Toronto, Ontario MSA 157

RDG, as it is known, is a division of International Fine Art Galleries, Ltd., and the firm's particular specialties are CHINESE WORKS OF ART, BRONZES, and RUGS. Auctions are held on the premises and in major cities across Canada and are advertised in local newspapers and some magazines. Sales are held every 6–8 weeks, and a detailed invitation is sent to everybody who has asked to be on the mailing list. Catalogues normally are ready 1 week before each sale, and viewing arrangements vary.

There is no buyer's premium. Absentee bids are not executed, nor are packing and shipping services offered. All lots are sold "as is," but RDG indicates that under some circumstances returns may be accepted. Buyers may pay by Visa or MasterCard, as well as by check with ID, and accounts are due immediately.

Standard consignor commission rates are 25 percent up to C$2,500 (no reserves under C$500 per lot); 20 percent from C$2,501 to C$5,000; 15 percent from C$5,001 to C$15,000; and 12.5 percent "or by mutual agreement" for C$15,¢1 and over. A minimum commission of C$25 is charged for each lot sold, and there is a buy-in charge, which varies depending on the value of the item. Rates for dealers usually are 5 percent less than those for private individuals. There are no charges for illustrations, insurance, or warehousing of consigned property.

Appraisal service is available at a charge of 1.5 percent up to the value of C$50,000 and 1 percent on any amount in excess. "A flat fee can be arranged in certain circumstances." A partial rebate will be made on property consigned to RDG within a year.

424. Gallery Sixtyeight Auctions

3 Southvale Drive   Tel. (416) 421-7614/421-7573
Toronto, Ontario M4G 1G1

This firm holds sales 7–9 times a year. Items auctioned are mostly in the furnishings line, as might be expected from an operation owned by Home Culture Ltd., and include FURNITURE, GLASS, PEWTER, PORCELAIN, and POSTERS. The gallery also auctions JEWELRY and PAINTINGS. All sales are on the premises, and are advertised in the Canadian press, the *New York Times,* and various trade newspapers and journals. Catalogues are not available by subscription but announcements are sent to a mailing list; to be placed on that list just write. Illustrated catalogues usually cost about C$4. Hours of business are 9:30 A.M.–6 P.M., Monday–Friday.

The house does have a buyer's premium of 10 percent which was instituted in 1980. Buyers have to pay a 7 percent provincial sales tax if they are not dealers. The trade is exempt. Absentee bids are executed. Packing and shipping services are available at the buyer's expense. Viewing is usually from noon–7:30 P.M. the day preceding the sale, and from noon until the auction begins on sale days. Buyers must settle accounts immediately after the sale.

The commission structure for consignors varies between 10–25 percent depending upon the value of the property. The commission is negotiable depending upon the situation. Consigned goods are usually sold at "the next auction sale." Settlement is made 14–21 days after the sale. Consignors do not pay for catalogue illustrations, or for insurance. Reserves are accepted.

Appraisal service is available; contact Mr. E. Voxner.

425. Maynards Industries

1233 West Georgia Street   Tel. (604) 685-7378
Vancouver, B.C. V7S 2L6

REPRESENTATIVE OFFICES

111 Richmond Street West
Toronto, Ontario

824 Fort Street
Victoria, B.C.

According to Miss N. L. Young of the firm's art and antiques department, Maynards holds home furnishings auctions 2–3 times a month and antiques sales 2–3 times a year. Each of the antiques sales lasts 3 or 4 days and includes a variety of goods. Sales are advertised in newspapers in Canada and in the U.S. Pacific Northwest. The firm publishes a pictorial brochure before each antiques sale, which also tells when catalogues are available and at what charge. Write to Miss Young to be put on the mailing list.

Potential buyers will be pleased to note that there is no buyer's premium at Maynards, although there is a 4 percent provincial sales tax, except on books and furs. There are no guarantees of authenticity, no packing and shipping services, and no returns. Settlement is "immediately." Viewing is usually 2–3 days before the first session of the auction; in special instances, private arrangements may be made for viewing on the day of the sale.

The commission structure for consignors is on a per item basis as follows: 25 percent up to C$50; 20 percent from C$51 to C$1,250; 15 percent from C$1,251 to C$2,500; and 12.5 percent for C$2,501 and over. Individual lots over C$10,000 may receive a lower rate. Dealers whose total consignment is in excess of C$10,000 will be charged 2–3 percent lower than private consignors. Reserves are accepted only if agreeable to the auction house. Consignors should write to Miss Young or to B. W. Scott, who can arrange for cartage service to be deducted from the consignor's check. Note that "we are not in the habit of accepting articles like 78 rpm records, postcards, Wild West souvenirs, etc., as there isn't a demand for that type of article here yet." There is no buy-in charge in most cases, but consignors must remove the goods promptly unless Maynards agrees to hold them over for another sale. Settlement is approximately 14 days after the last session of an auction, and there are no charges for illustrations, insurance, or warehousing.

Appraisal service is available either on a percentage fee of 1.5 percent up to C$25,000 and 1 percent over that amount, or on a negotiated hourly flat rate. Out-of-town traveling expenses would be charged to the customer.

426. Miller & Johnson Auctioneers Ltd.
2882 Gottingen Street   Tel. (902) 425-3366 / 425-3606
Halifax, Nova Scotia B3K 3E2

Weekly on Wednesday, Miller & Johnson holds an auction of general household goods or antiques. Some of these are bankruptcy sales, held on site, and all are announced in the local press. One can subscribe or get catalogues singly by writing to Miller & Johnson, and one can bid by mail. Packing and shipping are available. Viewing is 1 day prior to sale. Purchases may be charged on Chargex or MasterCard. Otherwise, buyers pay within 2 days after a sale.

There is a minimum value for lots consigned, but it is "not in dollars but quality." The commission varies between 20 and 25 percent, and goods are usually sold within 2 weeks, with payment made "when entire consignment sold," often a week after the sale. Charges are made for packing and shipping and when Miller & Johnson "warehouse over 1 week." Commissions may be negotiable, but there is no separate rate for dealers. No reserves may be set; accordingly, there is no charge for unsold lots.

G. H. Miller will appraise properties at a rate of C$50 per hour.

427. Phillips Ward-Price Ltd.
76 Davenport Road   Tel. (416) 923-9876
Toronto, Ontario M5R 1H3   Cable: AUCTIONS TORONTO

The well-known Toronto firm of Ward-Price now is part of the Phillips network and is holding weekly auctions, which are advertised in the local newspapers. The founding family are represented by fifth- and sixth-generation descendants of Walter Ward-Price, who founded the firm in 1912. Subscriptions for catalogues of all sales including country houses are available for C$180. Potential buyers also may subscribe (C$12 to C$48) to catalogues in the specialties listed below. Write to Margaret Browne or Ina Sweeney.

Buyers at Phillips Ward-Price can view goods for 2 days prior to a sale, 10 A.M.–9 P.M. There is a buyer's premium of 10 percent and an Ontario sales tax of 7 percent on total purchase price unless the buyer is a registered dealer or can provide proof of export from Ontario. Guarantees of authenticity are not provided, but Phillips Ward-Price accepts mail order bids, provides packing and shipping services, and takes back goods that are not as catalogued within the framework of their conditions of sale. Payment is immediately, and no credit terms are available. The house emphatically does not buy or sell on its own behalf.

Would-be consignors should write or call the following specialists:

Art Nouveau and Deco, Art Glass	(Anthony Barkworth)
Books, Manuscripts, Prints	(Graham Garrett)
Canadiana, Eskimo and Indian Art	(David Tyrer)
Canadian Paintings	(Jack Kerr-Wilson)
Collector's Items, Toys	(David Tyrer)
Ethnographic Art and Antiquities	(Jack Kerr-Wilson)

European and Canadian Silver	(Robert Parks)
European Ceramics and Glass	(Anthony Barkworth)
Furniture, Clocks, Decorations	(Anthony Barkworth)
Guns, Weapons, Militaria	(Kent Browne)
Jewelry, Watches, Objects of Virtu	(Debra Fraleigh)
Models, Lead Soldiers, Memorabilia	(David Tyrer)
Oriental Carpets and Rugs	(Anthony Barkworth)
Oriental Ceramics and Art	(Jack Kerr-Wilson)
Paintings	(Christopher Edmondson)
Photographica	(David Tyrer; Penelope Dixon)

The commission structure for consignors is 10 percent for catalogue sales and 25 percent for household effects sales. It takes about 8 weeks for consigned goods to be sold, and settlement is about 2 weeks after the sale. Charges for illustrations range from C$12.50 for a quarter page to C$50 for a full page, and there are charges for insurance and for packing and shipping. On unsold lots, the fee is 2.5 percent of an agreed reserve or of the best bid at "auctioneer's discretion," and 5 percent of a non-agreed reserve (that is, if the consignor insists on a reserve which the auction house thinks the object will not make). Charges to consignors may be negotiable in some situations.

The director of appraisals, Richard Price-Browne, will arrange any sort of appraisal for 1 percent of the total value up to C$50,000 and 0.5 percent thereafter. Out-of-town expenses are additional. If appraised goods are consigned within 1 year, all or part of the fee will be refunded.

OTTAWA REPRESENTATIVE

Mrs. J. Belyea
345 Island Park Drive   Tel. (613) 722-0882
Ottawa, Ontario K1Y OA6

As with most representative offices, this one helps prospective bidders, solicits consignments, and otherwise aids anyone interested in consigning to or buying at the Toronto saleroom of Phillips Ward-Price Ltd.

428. Sotheby Parke Bernet (Canada), Inc.
156 Front Street   Tel. (416) 596-0300
Toronto, Ontario M5J 2L6

Union Station and the Royal York Hotel are Sotheby's immediate neighbors in Toronto. Auctions are held in the Sotheby building's saleroom just about once a month. Write the Customer Service Dept. for announcements, but be certain to specify your area of interest. Specialties here are CHINESE WORKS OF ART, ENGRAVINGS, ETCHINGS, FURNITURE, GLASS, JEWELRY, 18TH AND 19TH CENTURY U.S., CANADIAN, AND BRITISH PAINTINGS, PORCELAIN, PRINTS, RUGS, and SILVER.

Sales are advertised in newspapers, magazines, and the SPB newsletter. Catalogues are available by subscription; write Linda M. Poulin. Mail order bids are accepted and the house offers packing and shipping services. There is a 10 percent buyer's premium and 7 percent tax. Though no guarantees of authenticity are offered, buyers may return goods that are not as catalogued. Settlement is within 24 hours, though credit terms are available to the trade.

The minimum value of a consignment should be C$1,000, and the minimum commission is C$35 per lot. The commission is 15 percent on lots worth C$500 or less, and 10 percent on lots that sell for more than C$500. Consignors are charged for illustrations (C$50 half page, C$70 full page, C$600 color plate); insurance (minimum C$5, and C$5 per thousand realized on premises; C$7 per thousand including transit); and packing and shipping ("as applicable"). Commissions may be negotiable, and dealers may be given trade terms. From consignment to sale takes "several months" and settlement is made "on or about 35 days after the sale." Reserves are accepted, and the buy-in charge is 5 percent of the reserve.

Appraisal service is available at a rate of 1.5 percent of the total value. Inspection visits cost C$50 within the Toronto area and C$100 outside Toronto, plus expenses. The fee is refundable if the goods are consigned to Sotheby Canada within 6 months. Call or write John Phillips.

REPRESENTATIVE
David Brown
2321 Granville Street   Tel. (604) 736-6363
Vancouver, B.C. V6H 3G4

This man represents Sotheby Parke Bernet in the western part of Canada, and helps prospective bidders and consignors.

429. Waddington, McLean & Co. Ltd.
189 Queen Street East   Tel. (416) 362-1678 (sale) / 362-2083
Toronto, Ontario   (valuation)

Although they sell a great variety of goods, Waddington's most interesting specialties are CANADIANA and ESKIMO GRAPHICS AND CARVINGS. They hold sales twice a week, on Wednesday and Saturday, and their premises are open from 8:30 A.M. to 5:30 P.M. on weekdays and from 8:30 A.M. to 3 P.M. on Saturdays. Waddington's quarterly fine art sales in particular are advertised in local newspapers and in trade magazines. To get on their mailing list, write or call Mrs. V. Brown.

Waddington's has instituted a 10 percent buyer's premium on their catalogued fine arts sales, and there is also a 7 percent Ontario sales tax. Mail bidding, packing and shipping, guarantees of authenticity, and return of goods that prove to be not as catalogued are all provided. Viewing varies according to the sale. No credit terms are available except by special arrangement; accounts should be settled within 48 hours of the sale.

For consignors, there are 2 commission structures: regular sales, 25 percent up to C$200 per lot, 20 percent from C$201 to C$2,500, and 15 percent from there on up; catalogued sales, 10 percent up to C$5,000, 7.5 percent from C$5,001 to C$10,000, and 5 percent from there on up. Dealers with desirable material may consign at a 6 percent rate.

Consigned goods may take 1–3 months to sell, and settlement is 21 days after the sale. The only charges to the consignor are the commission and packing and shipping if done by Waddington's. If you have Canadian or European paintings to sell, contact Ronald McLean or Eric Peters; for Inuit art and ethnographical artifacts, Duncan McLean; for antique furniture and silver and such, Alastair McLean and Bill Kine; and for books, Robert Russell. Scouts will be delighted to learn that Waddington's pays a finder's fee of 2 percent of gross.

Appraisal services are available at 1 percent of the total value below C$25,000 and 0.5 percent above C$25,000. These fees are waived if the appraised objects are sold at Waddington's.

Denmark

There is an auction market in this country, but its VAT structure helps keep it from being of much importance internationally.

Denmark has a hefty VAT, which is now over 22 percent and has to be paid on the total amount of the auction purchase (i.e., hammer price plus buyer's premium). Purchased lots sent outside Denmark are exempted from the VAT when shipped through a forwarding agent.

If you buy at auction in Denmark and wish to take your purchase with you outside the country, what happens depends on where you live. Buyers with a permanent address in another EEC country can take along their purchases if they have been paid for in full and if the VAT amount has been deposited with the auction house. The house will refund the VAT as soon as it receives its invoice with a note of official importation from the customs authorities of the EEC country in which the buyer lives. Buyers with a permanent address outside the EEC area, with the exception of Sweden and Finland, can only export works of art of gold or silver (except coins) and gold or silver jewelry including watches, provided that the lots have been paid for in full and that the VAT has been deposited with the auction house. Then the buyer must go before the Danish customs authorities at the time of departure from Denmark and deal with the requisite form. Export Form A29 must be returned to the auction house with the Danish customs certification of export. The auction house will then refund the VAT. (NOTE: All other lots will be exempted from Danish VAT only when shipped through a forwarding agent.)

430. Kunsthallens Kunstauktioner A/S

Købmagergade 11   Tel. (01) 13 85 69
DK 1150 Copenhagen

Approximately 4 times a year, at the Odd Fellow Palaeet, Bredgade 28, Copenhagen, this firm holds sales of PAINTINGS "old and new," to use the phrase of Jens Thygesen.

These sales are advertised in the Danish press. Catalogues are available. Cost is roughly Kr15 plus postage.

There is a buyer's premium of 12.5 percent. Absentee bids are executed. Packing and shipping services are available. And Mr. Thygesen states that "we vouch for the goods we sell." Viewing is 3 days before the sale. Settlement is at once, but "trustworthy buyers are granted weeks respite."

The standard consignor's commission is 15 percent. Consignors are not charged for anything else. Goods are usually sold within 3 weeks to 4 months. Settlement is "inside of 2 weeks." Reserves are accepted.

Appraisal service is available. Contact Paul Jacobsen.

431. Nellemann & Thomsen

Neilgade 45   Tel. (06) 12 06 66 / 12 00 02
DK-8000 Aarhus

Art Division:
Kunstsalonerne
Christiansgade 24
DK-8000 Aarhus

This firm holds 8–10 art and antique sales a year. Most of these are held on the premises, but a number are held on site, at castles or at manor houses. The firm also makes use of hotels. Specialties here are CHINESE WORKS OF ART, COINS, DRAWINGS, FURNITURE, GLASS, JAPANESE WORKS OF ART, JEWELRY, DANISH PAINTINGS, PORCELAIN, and RUGS.

These sales are advertised regularly in the Danish press.

Catalogues are available singly for each sale and by subscription. An annual subscription costs about Kr100. Write to Vita Thorsoe for specific information.

There is no buyer's premium. Absentee bids are executed. Packing and shipping services are available. And as for returning goods that prove to be not as catalogued, "it does not happen," says manager C. Walther Thomsen. Viewing is 1 or 2 days before the auction. Settlement is the same day, but credit is available for up to 3 weeks "if a bank guarantee is shown."

About 1/7 of the hammer price goes to the consignor's commission. The rate is negotiable, depending upon the situation. There are no other charges unless the consignor wants Nellemann & Thomsen to arrange for the goods to be shipped. Consigned goods may be sold 1–3 months after consignment. Settlement is usually 5 weeks after the sale. Reserves are accepted. There is a small charge for unsold lots.

Appraisal service is available; "the cost depends on many factors." Write to Mr. Thomsen for particulars.

432. Arne Bruun Rasmussen Kunstauktioner I/S

Bregade 33   Tel. (01) 13 69 11
DK-1260 Copenhagen

Sales, held on the average once a month except July, are often multisession auctions that last for several days, sometimes even spanning a week. The categories of catalogues indicate what the house offers: PAINTINGS AND WORKS OF ART, MODERN ART, COINS AND MEDALS, BOOKS AND MANUSCRIPTS.

These catalogues are available singly for each sale and by subscription, the subscription price being determined by whether or not the catalogues have to be airmailed outside of Europe. Each catalogue includes estimates. The prices vary: Books and Manuscripts (1 catalogue), Kr25 Europe, Kr50 airmailed elsewhere; Paintings and Works of Art (10–12 catalogues), Kr250 Europe, Kr400 airmailed elsewhere. Prices fetched at a sale are printed "in one of the next catalogues of the same category."

Sales are advertised in the Danish press. The firm's "international auctions" are also advertised in various European specialty publications, such as *Weltkunst* and *Antiques Trade Gazette.*

There is a 12.5 percent buyer's premium. Absentee bids are executed. Packing and shipping services are available. Viewing is usually 3 days before the sale. No guarantees of authenticity are offered. Buyers have the opportunity to return goods that prove to be not as catalogued within 14 days after the sale. Accounts are due immediately after the purchase of a lot, but "trustworthy buyers who contact us before the auction may expect 3 weeks of interest-free respite against satisfactory security for the amount due."

Consignors pay a 15 percent commission, whether they be private individuals or dealers. Consigned goods are sold within 1–2 months and settlement is approximately 1 month after the sale. There is no minimum value necessary for a consignment. Reserves are permitted. There is no charge to consignors for insurance, catalogue illustrations, or warehousing (prior to the sale).

Appraisal service is available. The costs are generally 1 percent of the total amount of the appraised effects. Contact Per H. Limkilde, Jens Hermann, or Jesper Bruun Rasmussen.

433. Vejle Sagførerauktioner Lrs. Børge-Nielsen

Lrs. Børge-Nielsen (office)   Tel. (05) 82 77 22
Torvegade 20
DK-7100 Vejle

Vejle Sagførerauktioner (auction house)
Flegmade 13
DK-7100 Vejle

Børge-Nielsen holds monthly sales of such objects as FURNITURE, PAINTINGS, RUGS, and SILVER at the auction house on Thursdays. The goods are usually of medium-range quality. Occasional house and estate sales are also conducted, as are sales "on location" at a hotel (the latter usually offer a "better" range of goods).

These sales are advertised in the local Danish press. Catalogues are available a week before the sale. These list-like catalogues are available singly or by subscription (Kr50 per annum, plus postage). Contact Ms. Hanne Kristensen.

There is an auctioneer's fee of 15 percent, which is negotiable. Mail order bids are accepted, but cash must accompany them. Packing and shipping services are not available from the firm. Goods that prove to be not as catalogued "can be returned within a fortnight," according to auction manager Lars Fuglsang-Madsen. Viewing is the day before the sale, 4–7 P.M., and the morning of the sale, 9 A.M.–noon. Settlement must be within 14 days after the sale.

The standard consignor's commission is 15 percent and it is negotiable, depending upon the situation. The goods must be in hand 14 days before the sale. Forty percent of the estimates can be paid in advance or the consignor will receive payment 3 weeks after the sale. Consignors do not pay for insurance. Reserves are accepted.

Appraisal service is available. For details contact Mr. Fuglsang-Madsen.

France

In France, the auction system is a strange, complex structure which is dominated by the firms, called *études,* that make up the Compagnie des Commissaires-Priseurs de Paris. This tight little body, with a current membership of 78, has enjoyed a monopoly in Paris since the 18th century. Although each of the *études* has its own office, it must rent a saleroom in the Hotel Drouot in order to hold an auction in Paris. Some 600 catalogues a year are issued by these firms, but they do not prepare the catalogues. A body of government-certified experts is responsible for the catalogues and for the accuracy of the descriptions. The guarantee of authenticity on works of art in France extends for 30 years, and to complicate things further, the expert is often more important than the *étude* holding the sale.

Auctions were held here and there in Paris (the first catalogued auction took place in 1741) until 1851, when the architects Levasseur and Pallard built the Hotel Drouot on the street of that name in the 9th Arrondissement. After serving the Compagnie well for about 30 years, the Hotel Drouot began a decline, and finally, after many years during which alternative auction sites were often used, it became so outmoded, uncomfortable, and generally disgusting that the Commissaires-Priseurs decided there was nothing for it but to tear the whole thing down, and construct a superb new Hotel Drouot. This happened in 1976. During the 4 years of construction, sales were held at "Drouot Rive Gauche" in the old Gare d'Orsay, now known as the Palais d'Orsay, where 18 salerooms were created. The exile certainly didn't hurt business, and some of the auctioneers were reluctant to leave the art and antiques center of the Left Bank. At this writing, some sales are still held at the Palais d'Orsay, but it soon will become a museum of the 19th century.

The architects of the Nouveau Drouot, Andre Biro and Jean-

Jacques Fernier, saw their first plan for the new building rejected. They were required by the Ministry of Culture to make the building blend with the Haussmann structures around it. The result is a building whose facade appeals greatly to some and strikes others as conscious parody, but whose interiors are undeniably modern and rational, with 24-hour parking for 400 cars, huge storage spaces, automatic temperature control, freight elevators which can handle a herd of statuary, a floor plan whereby the salerooms are reached from a central foyer on each of the 3 selling floors, and storage rooms behind each large saleroom. There are few worries about security in the building, for in addition to having guards, it contains a police station—perhaps because the other partners in the venture are the City of Paris and the Banque Nationale de Paris. On the evening of May 13, 1980, the Nouveau Drouot was ceremoniously inaugurated by the mayor of Paris, Jacques Chirac, who praised the decision to rebuild in a somewhat unfashionable quarter.

On May 14–17, the general public was invited to the Nouveau Drouot to see two exhibitions on the first floor, one displaying the cream of the objects to be auctioned in May and June, and the other tracing the history of public auctions in France. Sales began on May 20, and one of the first was held by the fine firm of Ader, Picard, Tajan, and offered the Francis Kettaneh collection of books and manuscripts. The expert was the world-renowned Claude Guerin, and the sale included a fine 15th-century book of hours illuminated by the "Boucicaut Master," which went for Fr3.8 million, and a First Folio of Shakespeare, which brought Fr2.6 million.

Nonetheless, Ader, Picard, Tajan questioned the way fees were being charged at the Nouveau Drouot and complained that they would have to use the Hotel George V for some important sales because the new facility has only 16 salerooms. Indeed, with some 600,000 objects passing through Drouot every year, many of them being sold by court order, time and space can be a problem. And the fees system, whereby half the auctioneers' fees are held in common by the Compagnie and divided equally at year's end among the members, means that the large *études* like Ader, Picard, Tajan are in effect subsidizing the smaller, sometimes less efficient ones. Furthermore, most smaller firms have mixed-lot sales, which tend to sell first what is on the walls, then objects usually kept in cabinets (glass, porcelain, silver, and the like), then furniture, then rugs, and then light fixtures. Many of these sales are uncatalogued. Moreover, the members of the Compagnie are not allowed to advertise except to tell of forthcoming sales.

Not just anybody can become a Commissaire-Priseur. You have to be French, serve an apprenticeship, have some legal training, pass an examination, and be co-opted by the group if and when a *charge* or practice becomes vacant. Then you have to pay anywhere from Fr400,000 to Fr4,000,000 to buy the practice, depending on how good a business your predecessor had. After that you are certified by the Ministry of Justice.

The system of Commissaire-Priseurs obviously does not lend itself to radical change. But cracks in the structure are beginning to show. Within the Compagnie, the *étude* of Loudmer, Poulain defiantly built its own saleroom in the Rue Faubourg St. Honoré and is conducting sales there. The lower courts have ruled their action illegal, but sales are still being held at the new site pending an appeal, and the final settlement of the case will be of considerable importance to the future of Nouveau Drouot. A potentially more serious challenge is being made by Jean Pannier, a jurist and numismatic dealer, who has formed the Association du Mesnil Marigny and is working to end the monopoly of the Compagnie des Commissaires-Priseurs de Paris.

At the same time, the Ministry of Justice has made various proposals in the hope of helping the Compagnie compete in the international market. These include allowing auctioneers to negotiate the choice of experts; take in an outside financial or management partner (but not Sotheby's or Christie's); have guaranteed reserves; and renegotiate the state tax of 7 percent which is built into the buyer's premium and the 3 percent of hammer price *droit de suite* which must be paid a modern artist each time his picture is sold. At this writing, the proposals are still proposals, but if they become law, great changes will take place in auctioneering in France.

Right now, consigning at auction in Paris costs between 10 and 15 percent, depending on whether catalogues are issued. An expert usually gets between 3 and 6 percent of that fee, the house gets 5 percent, and the catalogue charges are 5 percent. Five percent also is the normal charge on an unsold lot. When a government institution like the Bibliothèque Nationale or the Louvre preempts an item for the hammer price, the would-be buyer doesn't get the object and the seller gets paid when the wheels of government grind out his request for payment—it can take years. The successful bidder at auction pays a buyer's premium of 9 percent, with taxes on top of that, so that the total is 16 percent up to Fr6,000, 11 percent from Fr6,001 to Fr20,000, and 10 percent from Fr20,001 on up. For modern art there may be the additional 3 percent *droit de suite.*

The best way to find out what sales are coming up is to consult the weekly *Gazette de l'Hôtel Drouot* or the thrice-weekly *Moniteur des Ventes.* If you are in Paris, you can consult or buy these publications at the ground-floor library of the Nouveau Drouot (enter at 9, rue Drouot), Monday–Saturday between 11 A.M. and 6 P.M., the exhibition hours. Or you can write to 99, rue de Richelieu, Paris 75002, to subscribe. Many *études* do not issue price lists, and the *Gazette* may be the only place where results are listed.

Because of the baroque structure of the Paris auction world and the stringent export regulations in France, we do not recommend that the amateur buy there. By all means read the *Gazette* and the *Moniteur,* and by all means go to the Nouveau Drouot when you are in Paris, but by all means bid only through a reliable dealer with a full grasp of French export restrictions.

The following lists the members of the Compagnie and gives you an overview of their specialties, insofar as these exist in the French system and as they indicated them. We do not describe the *études* one by one for obvious reasons—although an *étude* like Ader, Picard, Tajan may hold book sales as a specialty, the book sales of expert Pierre Beres may be held at more than one *étude.*

434. Ader, Picard, Tajan

12, rue Favart   Tel. 261.80.07
75002 Paris

Arms and Armor	Islamic Art	Porcelain
Art Deco	Japanese	Postcards
Art Nouveau	Works of Art	Posters
Autographs	Manuscripts	Pre-Columbian
Chinese	Medals	Art
Works of Art	Medieval	Prints
Clocks and Watches	Works of Art	Rugs
Dolls	Netsuke	Scientific
Drawings	Paintings	Instruments
Engravings	French 17 and 18 c.	Silver
Etchings	Paintings	Stamps
Furniture	Pewter	

435. Artus
15, rue de la Grange-Batelière   Tel. 523.12.03
75009 Paris

436. Audap
32, rue Drouot   Tel. 742.78.01
75009 Paris

437. Binoche
5, rue La Boétie   Tel. 742.78.01
75008 Paris

438. le Blanc
32, avenue de l'Opéra   Tel. 266.24.48
75002 Paris

Art Deco	Furniture
Art Nouveau	Jewelry
Clocks and Watches	Silver

439. Boisgirard
2, rue de Provence   Tel. 770.81.36
75009 Paris

440. Bondu
17, rue Drouot   Tel. 770.36.16
75009 Paris

441. Boscher, Gossart
3, rue d'Amboise   Tel. 260.87.87
75009 Paris

Arms and Armor	Etchings	Photographic
Art Deco	Furniture	Instruments
Art Nouveau	Jewelry	Postcards
Chinese Works	Paintings	Rugs
of Art	Photographica	Silver
Engravings		Stamps

442. Briest
15, rue Drouot   Tel. 770.66.29
75009 Paris

443. de Cagny
4, rue Drouot   Tel. 246.00.07
75009 Paris

444. Cardinet
14, quai de la Mégisserie   Tel. 236.89.12
75001 Paris

445. Chambelland
1, rue Rossini   Tel. 770.94.16
75009 Paris

446. Charbonneaux
134, rue du Faubourg Saint-Honoré   Tel. 359.66.57
75008 Paris

Art Deco	Dolls	Jewelry
Art Nouveau	Drawings	Paintings
Chinese Works of Art	Furniture	Toys

447. Chayette
10, rue Rossini   Tel. 770.38.89
75009 Paris

Chinese Works of Art	Jewelry	Posters
Furniture	Paintings	Wines

448. Chochon
15, rue de la Grange-Batelière   Tel. 770.38.37
75009 Paris

449. Cornette de Saint-Cyr
24, avenue George-V   Tel. 723.47.42
75008 Paris

450. Courtier, de Nicolay
51, rue de Bellechasse   Tel. 555.85.44
75007 Paris

451. Daussy
46, rue de la Victoire   Tel. 874.38.93
75009 Paris

452. Delaporte, Rieunier
159, rue Montmartre   Tel. 508.41.83
75002 Paris

453. Delorme
3, rue de Penthièvre   Tel. 265.57.63
75008 Paris

454. Deurbergue
19, boulevard Montmartre   Tel. 261.36.50
75002 Paris

455. Dumont
22, rue Drouot   Tel. 523.39.66
75009 Paris

456. Ferri
53, rue Vivienne
75002 Paris
Tel. 233.11.24

457. Gluck-Mercier
14, rue Favart
75002 Paris
Tel. 297.43.54

458. Godeau
32, rue Drouot
75009 Paris
Tel. 770.67.68

459. Grandin
18, rue Mazarine
75006 Paris
Tel. 634.01.50

460. Gridel, Boscher
25, rue Le Peletier
75009 Paris
Tel. 523.34.59

Art Deco	Orientalia	Scientific Instruments
Art Nouveau	Paintings	Silver
Autographs	Rugs	Vintage Cars
Furniture		

461. Gros
22, rue Drouot
75009 Paris
Tel. 770.83.04

Art Deco	Coins	Porcelain
Art Nouveau	Drawings	Postcards
Autographs	Furniture	Posters
Chinese Works	Musical	Rugs
of Art	Instruments	Scientific
Clocks and Watches	Paintings	Instruments

462. de Heeckeren
2, rue de Provence
75009 Paris
Tel. 770.81.36

463. Hoebanx
10, rue Chauchat
75009 Paris
Tel. 770.82.67

464. Jozon
4, rue Rossini
75009 Paris
Tel. 770.34.91

Arms and Armor	Chinese Works	Coins
Art Deco	of Art	Dolls
Art Nouveau	Clocks and Watches	Drawings

Engravings	Musical	Postcards
Furniture	Instruments	Posters
Glass	Netsuke	Pre-Columbian Art
Islamic Art	Paintings	Prints
Jewelry	Pewter	Rugs
Judaica	Photographica	Silver
Maps	Porcelain	Toys
Medals		

465. Labat
10, rue de la Grange-Batelière   Tel. 824.70.18
75009 Paris

466. Langlade
12, rue Descombes   Tel. 227.00.91
75017 Paris

467. Laurin, Guilloux, Buffetaud, Tailleur
12, rue Drouot   Tel. 770.72.48
75009 Paris

468. Libert, Castor
3, rue Rossini   Tel. 824.51.20
75009 Paris

469. Loudmer, Poulain
73, rue du Faubourg Saint-Honoré   Tel. 266.90.01
75008 Paris

"Ranges from Primitive Art to Vintage Cars" and includes Arms and Armor, Drawings, Furniture, Jewelry, Netsuke, Paintings, Photographica, Posters, Rugs, and Toys.

470. Maignan
6, rue de la Michodière   Tel. 742.71.52
75002 Paris

471. Maringe
16, rue de Provence   Tel. 770.61.15
75009 Paris

472. Marlio
7, rue Ernest-Renan   Tel. 734.81.13
75015 Paris

473. Mathias
54, rue Taitbout   Tel. 874.84.44
75009 Paris

474. Millon
14, rue Drouot
75009 Paris
Tel. 770.00.45

475. Morand
7, rue Ernest-Renan
75015 Paris
Tel. 734.81.13

476. Morelle
50, rue Sainte-Anne
75002 Paris
Tel. 296.69.22

477. le Mouel
22, rue Chauchat
75009 Paris
Tel. 770.86.36

478. Neret-Minet, scp
31, rue Le Peletier
75009 Paris
Tel. 770.07.79

      Coins   Furniture   Medals

479. Offret
4, rue Saint-Lazare
75009 Paris
Tel. 280.13.29

480. Oger
22, rue Drouot
75009 Paris
Tel. 523.39.66

481. Pechon, Delavenne, Lafarge
12, rue de la Grange-Batelière
75009 Paris
Tel. 824.71.60

482. Pescheteau, Pescheteau-Badin
16, rue de la Grange-Batelière
75009 Paris
Tel. 770.88.38

483. Renaud
6, rue de la Grange-Batelière
75009 Paris
Tel. 770.48.95

484. Ribault-Menetiere, Lenormand
12, rue Hippolyte-Lebas
75009 Paris
Tel. 878.13.93

485. Ribeyre
5, rue de Provence
75009 Paris
Tel. 770.87.05

486. Robert
5, avenue d'Eylau   Tel. 727.95.34
75016 Paris

487. Rogeon
16, rue Milton   Tel. 878.81.06
75009 Paris

488. Rostand
30 bis, rue Bergère   Tel. 770.50.11
75009 Paris

489. le Roux
18, rue de la Grange-Batelière   Tel. 770.83.00
75009 Paris

490. Solanet
32, rue Drouot   Tel. 523.17.33
75009 Paris

491. Sourmais
8, rue Drouot   Tel. 770.95.36
75009 Paris

492. Tilorier
32, avenue Paul-Doumer   Tel. 520.38.24
75016 Paris

Drawings

493. Vincent
14, rue de la Grange-Batelière   Tel. 770.84.03
75009 Paris

494. Wapler
16, place des Vosges   Tel. 278.57.10
75004 Paris

If you are traveling through France, you may wish to visit one or more of the following auction houses located outside Paris, some of which hold sales of international importance. Sales are advertised in the *Gazette de l'Hôtel Drouot* and *Moniteur des Ventes*.

BERGERAC

495. Hotel des Ventes Mobilieres
Gerard Feydy, Commissaire-Priseur
13, Place Gambetta   Tel. 57.38.16
24100 Bergerac

Sale once a week

Arms and Armor	Furniture	Scientific
Chinese Works	Pewter	Instruments
of Art	Porcelain	Silver
Clocks and Watches	Rugs	Stamps

CHARTRES

496. Galerie de Chartres
Jean et Jean Pierre Lelievre, Commissaires-Priseurs
1 bis, Place du General de Gaulle   Tel. 36.04.33
28000 Chartres   Telex: CHAMCO CHARTRES 760 830

Sales 2–3 times a week

Antique Tools	Jewelry	Photographica
Arms and Armor	Mechanical	Porcelain
Art Deco	Music Instruments	Postcards
Art Nouveau	Paintings	Silver
Dolls	French 17 and 18th c.	Toys
Furniture	Painting	

GRENOBLE

497. Maitre Pierre Blache
Étude et Hôtel des Ventes
15, rue de Bonne   Tel. 46.73.66
38000 Grenoble

Sales twice a week; specialized sales 10–12 times a year

LYON

498. Genin, Griffe, Leseuil
Hotel du Vente des Tuiliers
Xavier Genin, Commissaire-Priseur
Didier Griffe, Commissaire-Priseur
Bernard Leseuil, Commissaire-Priseur
31, rue des Tuliers   Tel. 858.24.56
69008 Lyon   Telex: 340753 CEDSLEX LYON

Sales several times a week

Arms and Armor	Chinese Works	Coins
Art Deco	of Art	Dolls
Art Nouveau	Clocks and Watches	Furniture

Jewelry	Netsuke	Rugs
Medieval Works	Paintings	Silver
of Art	Porcelain	Stamps
Musical	Postcards	Toys
Instruments	Prints	Vintage Cars

MAYENNE

499. Hôtel des Ventes ("Reche")
32, General Leclerc   Tel. 04.13.74
Mayenne

Sales twice a week

Arms and Armor	Engravings	Musical	Porcelain
Art Deco	Etchings	Instruments	Postcards
Art Nouveau	Furniture	Netsuke	Posters
Coins	Glass	Orientalia	Prints
Dolls	Jewelry	Paintings	Rugs
Drawings	Judaica	Pewter	Silver
Embroidery		Photographica	Stamps

ORLEANS

500. Galerie des Ventes d'Orleans
Louis Savot, Commissaire-Priseur   Tel. 62.67.84 / 53.80.93
2, impasse Notre-Dame du Chemin
Orleans

Frequent small sales, 24 major specialized sales per year; closed in August

| Arms and Armor | Ceramics | Furniture | Paintings |
| Books | Coins | Medals | Postcards |

VERSAILLES

501. Blache—Hôtel Rameau
Georges Blache, Commissaire-Priseur
5, rue Rameau   Tel. 950.55.06 / 951.23.95
78000 Versailles

Sale once a week

Arms and Armor	Furniture	Netsuke
Art Deco	Glass	Paintings
Art Nouveau	Japanese Works	Porcelain
Chinese Works	of Art	Rugs
of Art	Jewelry	Scientific
Clocks and Watches	Judaica	Instruments
Coins	Maps	Silver
Drawings	Medals	Stamps

502. Paul Martin & Jacques Martin
3, impasse des Chevau-Legers   Tel. 950.58.08
78000 Versailles

Sales at least once a week

A number of non-French auction houses have representatives in that country.

503. Bonhams
Baron Foran, Duc de Saint-Bar   Tel. (1) 637-1329
2, rue Bellanger
92200 Neuilly sur Seine

504. Christie's
Princess Jeanne-Marie de Broglie   Tel. (331) 261-1247
17, rue de Lille   Telex: 213468
75007 Paris

505. Sotheby's
Rear Admiral J. A. Templeton-Cotill, C. B.   Tel. (1) 266-4060
3, rue de Miromesnil   Telex: 640084
75008 Paris   Cable: ABINITIO FRANCE

Hong Kong

A more natural setting for auctions can hardly be imagined. Goods pour into Hong Kong from everywhere in the Pacific, and so do potential buyers.

506. Sotheby Parke Bernet (Hong Kong) Ltd.

P.O. Box 83
705 Lane Crawford House
64–70 Queen's Road Central
Hong Kong

Tel. 22-5454
Telex: 75486 LANE HX
Cable: ABINITIO HONG KONG

Sotheby's representative on the scene here is Mamie Howe. Sotheby's began to use Hong Kong for important porcelain auctions some time back, when the firm decided to take the goods to the market rather than hope that buyers would come to the London, New York, and Los Angeles sales of Chinese porcelain. The Hong Kong sales become stronger every year. They are held in association with Lane Crawford Holdings Ltd., usually at the Mandarin Hotel. Conditions of sale are basically like those of Sotheby's in London, including the 10 percent buyer's premium. Individual catalogues are available at a cost of HK$65 (about £6/US$13), and subscription information may be obtained from Ms. Howe.

507. Victoria Auctioneers Rooms

A-1 Ho Le Commercial Building
38–44 d'Aguilar Street
Hong Kong

Tel. 5-247611/5-247905
Cable: KAMCHOW HONG KONG

This firm of auctioneers, real estate agents, valuers, and jewelry and antique merchants is under the able direction of Kamuel S. L. Chow. Sales are held irregularly, but are well advertised in the leading local newspapers, both Chinese and English. PORCELAIN and VINTAGE CARS lead the specialties here, some of the others being CHINESE WORKS OF ART and EMBROIDERY. Catalogues are available for specific sales, many of which are held in leading local hotels. Mail order bids are not accepted, and Victoria neither offers nor permits return of goods that prove not to be as catalogued. Shipping is available. Viewing is 2–3 days before a sale, and buyers are to settle accounts immediately on the fall of the hammer.

Consignment is a matter to be negotiated with Mr. Chow, as are the rates of commission. There are charges for illustrations, insurance, warehousing, and packing and shipping. The length of time before consigned goods are sold "varies" and settlement is within 3 days after the sale. Reserves are accepted, and there is a 2 percent charge based on value for unsold lots.

Victoria will appraise fixed properties for a fee of 0.5 percent and works of art for 0.5–2 percent. Write Miss Eleanor Chan for details.

India

508. S. M. G. Beaty Private Ltd.
9-D Connaught Place
New Delhi 110001

Tel. 353294/353696
Cable: BEATY LTD.

In addition to being government auctioneers, Balak Ram, Shivraj Singh Garg, and Sudhir Gupta are commission agents and furnishers, "stockists" for Modi rayons and silk fabrics and for Kalco's shoes. The Beaty firm holds 5–10 auctions per month, which are advertised in newspapers and by means of handbills. Some of these take place on the premises, a fair number on site. Specialties here are FURNITURE, MUSICAL INSTRUMENTS, PHOTOGRAPHIC INSTRUMENTS, and RUGS, as well as such desirable electrical equipment as refrigerators, gas cooking ranges, typewriters, and washing machines. Write to get on the mailing list, for catalogues are available only on a sale-by-sale basis. Goods are sold on an "as is where is" basis, and viewing is usually restricted to a half hour before the sale. In the case of machinery, a couple of days are allowed. Payment is cash and carry, except for machinery, which must be paid for within a week. Sales tax must be paid when applicable.

Consignors pay 2–5 percent for on-site sales, plus expenses like catalogue illustration; premises sales have a commission rate of 10 percent. Goods are sold within 2 weeks, and settlement is made the next working day. Reserves are accepted, and there is no charge for unsold lots.

Italy

Two laws, No. 1089 of 1939 and No. 487 of 1972, along with a host of other export regulations, make Italy a difficult place for auctiongoers. If you *must* bid at an Italian auction, find a dealer who has a firm grip on the export regulations. Another nasty surprise for foreign buyers and sellers is that they have to pay a VAT of 14 percent on auction commissions. Sotheby's and Christie's hold some fascinating sales here, and their offices in Italy and in other countries will assist the would-be buyer in cutting through the thicket of regulations. But even the multinationals are sometimes stymied. Both Christie's and Sotheby's have prepared to hold sales on occasion, have issued the catalogues and accepted mail order bids, only to have the government authorities come in and "enchain" (*vincolare*) the sale.

If you must buy or sell in Italy, here is a list of possible venues. But we really don't recommend playing the auction game here.

509. Christie's (International) S.A.

Palazzo Massimo Lancellotti   Tel. 6541217
Piazza Navona 114   Telex: ROME 62524
00186 Rome

Christie's men on the spot are Maurizio Lodi-Fé and Dr. Paolo del Pennino. Consultant is d. ssa. Luisa Vertova Nicolson.

510. Christie's (Italy) S.R.1.

9 Via Borgogna   Tel. 794712
20144 Milan

The company's agents here are Edoarda Sanna and Giorgina Venosta.

511. Finarte S.P.A.
Piazzetta Bossi 4   Tel. 877041
20121 Milan

512. Finarte S.P.A.
Via delle Quattro Fontane 20   Tel. 463564
Rome

513. Palazzo Internationale delle Aste ed Esposizioni, S.P.A.
Palazzo Corsini   Tel. 293000
Il Prato 56
Florence

514. Sotheby Parke Bernet Italia
26 Via Gino Capponi   Tel. 571410
50121 Florence

In charge here is Count Alvise di Robilant. Consultant is Carmen Gronau, an
art expert of distinction, who after years of service in London (including a
long stint as Sotheby's only woman director) retired to Italy.

515. Sotheby Parke Bernet Italia
Via Montenapoleone 3   Tel. 783907
20121 Milan

The Sotheby's representative is Yolanda Galli Zugaro.

516. Sotheby Parke Bernet Italia
Palazzo Taverna   Tel. 6561670/6547400
Via di Monte Giordano 36
00186 Rome

The Sotheby's representative is Jonathan Mennell.

Japan

Auctions by their very nature invite and involve public competition. And in the auction rooms of the West, the Japanese have proved to be tigerish competitors, whether for jewelry in Geneva or for Impressionist paintings in London. But the Japanese believe in free access to the marketplace only outside their national boundaries. The Japanese economy is marked by state-enforced controls which are designed to keep foreign and sometimes even domestic competition at bay. At a 1980 Conference on U.S. Competitiveness, Ezra Vogel, author of *Japan as Number One,* characterized the Japanese marketplace as "not easy for outsiders to enter, and Japanese businessmen and government officials at times still add to the difficulties of foreign businessmen."

The fine arts market in Japan is not immune to government regulation, although not always for economic reasons. The desire to protect national treasures runs strong. The Japanese know well what it feels like to see their cultural heritage carted off in the steamer trunks and suitcases of Western visitors and understandably wish to avoid situations like the one that developed in regard to samurai swords. After the Meiji Restoration in 1868, when the samurai lost the privilege of carrying two swords, so many swords were bought by foreigners that Japanese dealers must now go abroad to obtain them, and must then register them with a government agency.

By the mid-1880s, the sale of valuable artworks to Western museums and collectors had already generated efforts to curb the export of such works. Restraints of one sort or another were imposed over the years until, in the 1950s, an export code of rigorous formal procedures was established, and a cultural affairs agency was assigned to keep tabs on all Japanese works of art of any consequence. The result has been what one Western museum curator describes as "enlightened registry." No work of art—be it scroll, ceramic, painting, drawing, sculpture—can be exported legally from Japan if the government considers it of cultural importance. Government approval is required for the export of most lesser Japanese works of art, but it is fairly easy to obtain. (This registration and approval system can have an unhappy effect upon the seller, because it provides a handy guide for the tax collector.)

As might be expected, public auctions do not flourish in this regulatory climate. Individuals are much more likely to turn to dealers for the transfer of art properties, in the hope that they may remain anonymous. They tend also to use dealers because of "face." It is one thing for a wealthy and powerful Japanese to lose out in the bidding for a necklace in a Geneva jewelry auction, but quite another to lose out on home ground. It is, therefore, safer and easier to have a dealer handle the matter.

Fine arts auctions do exist in Japan, but almost none are open to the general public, and most of them bear little resemblance to their counterparts in the United States or Great Britain. They are dealer-only auctions, and with a vengeance. Indeed, some sales are open only to those dealers who are members of the association conducting that specific auction. The dealer-only auctions are referred to in Japanese as *kokankai* (exchange meeting) or *shijo* (market), and almost daily *kokankai* are held by the Tokyo Art Dealers Association—which, with over 400 members, is among the largest organizations of its kind in that city. Membership in the association—necessary if one is to participate in the *kokankai*—does not come easily. An applicant is required to have at least 5 years experience as a recognized art dealer and the sponsorship of at least 4 members of the association.

As for the hundreds of Tokyo art dealers (some estimates run as high as 3,000) who are not members of the Tokyo Art Dealers Association, their need for a venue is filled by the smaller but more numerous *shijo*, which, depending on location, are held on either a daily or a weekly basis. The *shijo* are designed to meet the needs of the less prosperous, less established dealers, and most *shijo* admit almost any certified art dealer.

Generally speaking, there are two kinds of art dealers in Japan: the *miseshi*, who own their own shops, and the *hatashi*, who do not. Many of the latter are little more than "runners" who collect items from various individuals or shops and then sell them at a *shijo*. The *miseshi* supplement their stock at such *shijo* or use them to dump unwanted items.

Whether at a *shijo* or at a *kokankai*, prices are carefully regulated—which is one reason dealers have supported the "closed auction" system. Prices, which are not made public, are not allowed to find their own level at these sales. Whether the pace be hectic or not, bidding is halted by the auctioneer when it reaches a certain price level, and the buyer is then determined by drawing lots. In 1979, Kazuo Fujii, then head of the Tokyo Art Dealers Association, expressed his belief that "the participation of amateurs in auctions pulls up bidding prices unnecessarily."

This sort of control makes for what one American museum official has described with some disgust as "a *very* orderly market." Yet it is true that the closed auction system has its advantages, and not for dealers only. It ensures the smooth operation of sales between professionals, who are unlikely to renege on a deal. Prices are kept relatively low—on what might be called a wholesale level—and collectors can benefit to a degree if they are buying. (To sell into such a system through a dealer seems disadvantageous in the extreme.) Moreover, because of the nature of the sale and the participants, the guarantees of authenticity are not limited to weeks or months. In Japan, a refund can be obtained years after a sale if a lot turns out to be not as catalogued.

Among opponents of the closed auction system are private collectors unhappy with the dealers and younger dealers who have felt that the insiders among their competitors had an unfair advantage. These critics would have welcomed change, but change has not been forthcoming until recently. Efforts by both Christie's and Sotheby's in the late 1960s and early 1970s to hold public auctions in Tokyo proved abortive, even though that was a boom period in the fine arts market in Japan.

One result of the Christie and Sotheby efforts, however, was the setting up in 1971 of **(517)** the Japan Art Auction Company (Nihon Bijitsuhin Kyobai Kaubushiki Kaisha, 6-3-2 Ginza, Chou-Ku, Tokyo, tel. 574-6543), organized to hold open auctions, called *okushyon*. Even here "open" is a relative term, for bidders have to be members of the company, albeit membership is relatively cheap, costing only Y10,000 (less than $75/£35). These auctions are little advertised;

word of mouth seems to be the main source of information for non-members. Sales are held 6 times a year: February, April, June, September, November, and December. Catalogues are in Japanese and English, and the works for sale tend to offer various kinds of Japanese art (ranging from tea-ceremony utensils to quite good examples of *sumi-e*, or ink-and-brush painting), with occasional minor works by such Western artists as Chagall and Munch.

The sales themselves are what are known in the West as "silent" auctions. All bidding is done in writing, and bids are tendered during the 2- or 3-day exhibition period prior to the auction. The catalogue lists suggested prices, and bidding normally is based on the catalogue estimate. A bidder can make one bid only, and identical high bids are resolved by drawing lots. In 1979, the president of the Japan Art Auction Company outlined the rationale behind the use of the written bid system, saying that the company favored it "because it is very difficult for an amateur to compete with a professional in voice bidding. Plus there is always the danger of an amateur being tricked by a false bidder who merely bids to push up the price." It is true, however, that prices at the Japan Art Auction Company *okushyon* usually are not much higher than those at the closed auctions.

During the past decade, the Japan Art Auction Company has held more than 40 sales, with many lots in the Y10,000–Y15,000 range. Among the highest prices fetched was Y30 million for a Picasso. Non-Japanese who wish to participate may do so through a member (tourists can make arrangements to contact one through their hotels), and on viewing days nonmembers can have a look and then place a bid through a member. The member will often suggest how much to bid, and quite frequently the suggested bid turns out to be the appropriate one. Traditionally, a Japanese dealer acting for a client has earned his fee from the 10 percent discount offered by the auctioneer on the knockdown price. But this system is under review and changes may be in the offing. In Japan, as elsewhere, it would benefit anyone making use of a dealer at auction to review fee arrangements before the sale takes place.

Auction aficionados may also enjoy participating secondhand in the occasional sales at the Bijutsu Club (**518.** Nihon Bijutsu Keyokai, 1-2 Ueno Koen, Daito-Ku, Tokyo, tel. 833-4191), which is located in a quaint Japanese-style house, with a lovely garden in the courtyard. The Bijutsu Club is an art dealers' group whose premises are available for exhibitions, and much of the art put up for sale is by Japanese artists painting in the Western manner. Bidding is possible for dealers only at the club, which, in effect, has closed auctions. But on viewing days, a nondealer can have a look and then place a bid through one of the many dealers who are willing to act as agents and help to arrange for export of the purchase. Here, too, tourists can make arrangements through their hotels, and fees should be negotiated in advance.

The Osaka equivalent of the Tokyo arts club group holds similar sales a couple of times a year (**519.** Osaka Minambijutukaikan, 2-45 Niponbashisuji, Minamiku, Osaka), but according to one Western dealer and collector long resident in Japan and familiar with them, "just how it is all managed is a mystery I don't think even they can fathom."

The most serious and strongest challenge to the closed auction system was made by Christie's when they held, at the fashionable Hotel Okura in Tokyo on February 14–16, 1980, a 6-session public sale complete with voice bidding. According to a spokesman, Christie's undertook the enormous effort necessary to organize such a public auction because Japan was the only country in the developed non-Communist world where no public auctions existed. The officers of Christie's well appreciated the fact (to use the words of a successful Japanese art dealer) that "although Japan's market for luxury items has diminished since the oil crisis in 1973, the art and antique market has been the least severely damaged of the luxury markets. The prices have been able to remain fairly constant in contrast to most other luxury items."

The arranging of the Christie's sale required both steel and finesse. Whereas Christie's had previously worked in tandem with a Japanese dealers' association, the auction firm now decided to strike out on its own. Obtaining the necessary authorizations took more than 2 years of unrelenting effort, mostly on the part of Sir John Figgess. An Oriental ceramics expert and a Christie's director since 1973, Sir John had spent much of his distinguished diplomatic career in post–World War II Japan and had a thorough knowledge of the workings of Japanese governmental bodies and their personnel. Nevertheless, despite his best efforts, in the end Christie's was forced to agree that only those people who held invitations to the auction would be admitted to participate as bidders. True, almost anyone who could provide the proper bank references could wangle an invitation and Christie's even placed advertisements in the press explaining how to obtain admission to the sale. But form had to be observed, and the public could not just drop in and bid, as in London or New York. Japanese police regulations concerning the sale of secondhand goods (no more or less outrageous than the California requirement that antiquarian book dealers be fingerprinted) meant, as *World Business Weekly* put it, that Christie's "had to send the list of its 1,000 invited guests to the police for approval." Licensee for the auction was Dodwell and Company, an old-line Far Eastern trading company with offices in Japan competent to provide administrative support.

Each session at the Christie's sale opened with an explanation of auction procedures (e.g., reserves, buyer's premium, etc.), and the auctioning of two dummy lots in order to demonstrate typical public auction techniques, including voice bidding. Sir John Figgess, speaking Japanese, conducted most of the sessions, which totaled 850 lots. The highlight of the 3-day sale was the portion devoted to Oriental ceramics. They were of high quality and they did exceedingly well. In addition, a Chagall attained a price of Y78 million (approximately $320,000), setting what was then a world record for the work of any living painter sold at auction. (Overall, however, the quality of the pictures put up for sale was uneven, and it was estimated that about 80 percent of them were bought in.) During the course of the 3 days, 71 percent of the lots were sold, for a total of Y1,550,000,000 ($6,348,360/£2,741,000). The sale, which was regarded as a historic occasion in Japan, received enormous attention there, including extensive television coverage of the sessions themselves. Christie's, of course, did its part to promote the event before, during, and afterward: an *Australian Financial Review* correspondent received a telex on the auction and its results which was a staggering 42 paragraphs long.

Whatever the bottom-line figures for this 3-day push, whether profit or loss for Christie's, the auction house can be pleased with the results. Sir John Figgess, like Commodore Perry more than a century earlier, opened a new market in bringing public auctions to Japan. And Christie's has decided to service that market and to hold at least one set of major public auction sessions annually in Tokyo. They hold these sales in mid-February (as in 1981), and should the demand warrant another set of sessions, these would be held at the end of September or the beginning of October. Dodwell and Company will continue to serve as licensee, providing the administrative infrastructure. Christie's man on the spot is Toshi Hatanaka (**520.** c/o Dodwell Marketing Consultants,

No. 1 Kowa Bldg, 11-41 Akasaka, 1-chome, Minato-Ku, Tokyo 107, tel. 584-2351), a high-powered Japanese in his early thirties, who is already a Christie's veteran, having spent almost a decade with the auction house in London and New York.

Unlike Christie's, Sotheby's has elected an indirect approach to the Japanese market and has decided for the moment not to try to hold public auctions but to give increased exposure to art properties scheduled for sale elsewhere, especially in Hong Kong. In September 1979, a contract was signed between Sotheby vice-chairman Peter Spira and Yoshiaki Sakakura, the head of the Seibu Department Stores Ltd., a Japanese company which for some time has been involved with the fine arts in Japan both commercially and as a patron.

The contract calls for Sotheby's to be provided with prime exhibition space in Seibu's Ikebukuro store, one of the largest and most important in Japan—on one floor of which is a department devoted to selling Western art, books, and music. Sotheby's now exhibits there and at the Tokyo Prince Hotel (managed by the Seibu group), and the exhibitions include both original works of art and photographs of other works, all of which will be coming up for sale at the company's various auction rooms throughout the world. Catalogues are available in English or in the language of the country in which the sale is to be held. Seibu prepares Japanese-language catalogues of the exhibition items, and the exhibition counters are manned by Seibu personnel, who provide interested Japanese and others with information, place bids, and handle all matters concerning payment, customs, and transportation. For these services Seibu charges individuals 10 percent and the trade 8 percent. Obviously, Sotheby's hopes through such exhibitions to reach a significant portion of Japan's affluent middle and upper classes and eventually to find art properties that can be sold in its auction rooms elsewhere. The Sotheby's representative in Japan and liaison person with Seibu is a hardworking young woman, Kazuko Shiomi (521. Pisa Counter, Tokyo Prince Hotel, 3-3-1 Shibakoen, Minatou-ju, Tokyo, tel. 437-1916/434-4411, ext. 2507).

Sotheby's would seem to have chosen an ideal partner in this attempt to broaden the Japanese base of interest in public auctions. The Seibu Group is an aggressive organization, a self-described "multichannel retailing organization" with close ties to such non-Japanese companies as Sears, Roebuck, Knoll International, and Van Cleef & Arpels. Among the Seibu group's member companies are Rive Gauche

Seibu and Dunkin' Donuts of Japan. Their pioneering Seibu Museum of Art, established in the mid-1970s on a floor of the Ikebukuro store, although limited in scope has become an important force in the Tokyo art scene.

Malaysia: see Singapore and Malaysia

Monaco

We first became aware of the auction market in Monaco in November 1975, when we received the catalogue of the Diaghilev-Lifar Library from something called Sotheby Parke Bernet Monaco S.A. This firm, through the offices of the Monagasque auctioneer J. J. Marquet, was holding the sale, which was organized with the collaboration of the Societe des Bains de Mer, at the "Sporting d'Hiver," Place du Casino. At that time the conditions of sale weren't even printed in the catalogue; our guess is that they were of sufficient complexity that they weren't ready in time for inclusion in the catalogue. Thus the note that they "will be available." From the start, Dr. S. N. Cristea headed the Monaco office at 57 Rue Grimaldi.

Now Monte Carlo is an established venue for Sotheby's. The catalogues contain 4 pages of conditions of sale, and another member of the Marquet family, M.-Th. Escaut Marquet, is now the Monagasque auctioneer. (By law at the Monte Carlo sales, the Monagasque auctioneer must bring the hammer down. It is a strange sensation indeed to watch Peter Wilson complete the bidding on a lot and then give a little nudge to the auctioneer so that she knows when to bring the hammer down.)

As an auction market, Monte Carlo is the unwitting creation of the Compagnie des Commissaires-Priseurs de Paris. The sorts of books and furniture, for instance, which appeal to the French do not sell well in London. The obvious next choice was Paris, but the Compagnie has a stranglehold on auction there. Thus the logical choice became Monte Carlo—French in most ways and no water to cross to get there. In June 1979, the fabled Wildenstein family collection of 18th-century French furniture, which would have been sold in Monaco in 1977 except that it had been bought en bloc a few weeks before the scheduled sale by Akram Ojjeh for $15 million, sold to a saleroom filled with

393

leading collectors and dealers for $13 million, with pieces such as a Louis XV ormolu-mounted marquetry encoignure going for prices like Fr7,600,000 (£835,165/$1,712,088).

Should Paris become an open market, then it is likely that Monaco will lose its desirability as a venue. In the meantime, it has one other spur to development: Peter Wilson has a home on the Riviera, and since his retirement as chairman of the Sotheby Parke Bernet Group, this supercharged auction man has had a bit more free time. Look for the Wilson mark in Monaco in the coming seasons.

522. Sotheby Parke Bernet Group

P. O. Box 45 Sporting d'Hiver
Place du Casino, Monte Carlo

Tel. (93) 30 88 80

The Netherlands

The world's first book auctions were held in Leiden, and the Netherlands remains a center for antiquarian book sales and similar intellectual specialties. VAT is charged on the auctioneer's commission and on the buyer's premium here at 4 or 18 percent, unless the goods are exported. So-called Dutch auctions, which start at a high price with the bid going lower until a buyer cries out that he will take it, seem to be unknown in the Netherlands.

523. J. L. Beijers B.V.

Achter Sint Pieter 14	Tel. 310958
3512 HT Utrecht	Cable: BOOKBEE UTRECHT

BOOKS, PRINTS, and MANUSCRIPTS are auctioned by Beijers 3–4 times every year. The catalogues are wonderful productions, with French books described in French, English books in English, and so on. Subscriptions cost fl30 per year, fl50 if sent abroad; if you have bought books at a Beijers auction in the preceding 12 months, you may subtract a percentage of the subscription price.

Sales usually begin on a Tuesday, and the viewing days are the Friday and Saturday preceding, 10 A.M.–6 P.M., Monday 9 A.M.–1 P.M. Mail order bids are accepted, and books can be sent by post or freight anywhere. "If goods do not conform to catalogue descriptions, they can be returned within a fortnight of receipt, but notice must be given promptly." There is a buyer's premium of 16 percent of the hammer price plus 10 Dutch cents per item. According to Edgar Franco, "The 10 cent charge in Holland used to be a gratuity to the porters moving the books from shelf to auctioneer's desk at the moment of auctioning and putting them back after they had been sold (these were usually casual labourers, mostly aged people who earned an occasional extra in this way)." Buyers must settle accounts within 2 weeks. Credit terms are sometimes available, "depending on who the buyer is and what the goods are and what our agreement as to payment is with the consignor."

The minimum value for consignment at Beijers is fl800–fl1,000, depending on the items. Write or telephone the learned and helpful Mr. Franco. The commission rate is 24 percent of the hammer price, sometimes negotiable.

Dealers pay 20 percent. Reserves are accepted, and there is no charge for unsold lots. The time to sale varies, and settlement is about 3 months after the sale.

For appraisal service, contact H. L. Gumbert, Mrs. N. A. Franco-Schinkel, or Mr. Franco. Rates are 5 percent up to fl5,000; 3.5 percent from fl5,001 to fl10,000; and 2.5 percent above that.

Beijers also has a retail operation, which sells antiquarian books.

524. Christie, Manson & Woods Ltd.

Rokin 91   Tel. (020) 23 15 05
1012 KL Amsterdam   Telex: 15758
                                                      Cable: CHRISTIART

In the Netherlands, Christie's is represented by Andries Bart and Harts Nystad. They help interested parties to consign and to bid at various Christie's auctions, and periodically fall and spring hold multisession sales of works of art including COINS, MEDALS, PAINTINGS, and SILVER as well as works of Dutch interest. In recent years most of these sales have been held at the Singer Museum in Laren.

525. Sotheby Mak Van Waay B.V.

102 Rokin   Tel. 24 6215
1012 KZ Amsterdam   Telex: 13267 MAKSO
                                                      Cable: ABINITIO AMSTERDAM

Sotheby's takeover of "Mak," as it is known, has been something of a bumpy ride, for the Dutch market did not "internationalize" as easily as the London firm had hoped. Such traditional interests as DUTCH PAINTING, FURNITURE, and PORCELAIN are still among the strongest specialties here. Sales are held monthly at Mak and are advertised in newspapers and magazines. Write the Catalogue Subscription Dept. for announcements of forthcoming sales, single catalogues, or subscriptions (fl135 locally for all catalogues). Mail order bids are accepted, and all the other usual Sotheby services and guarantees are offered. Viewing is 10 A.M.–4 P.M. for 3 days before a sale. Accounts must be settled immediately after a sale unless other arrangements have been made in advance of the sale. There is a 16 percent buyer's premium.

Prospective sellers should contact Miss Zwarteveen, who will see that the proper expert advises them. The commission rate is 15 percent; 10 percent for paintings. The rate for dealers is 10 percent across the board. There are no charges for illustrations, insurance, or warehousing. It takes about 6 weeks for consigned goods to be sold, and settlement is 1 month after the last sale day. Reserves are accepted, and there is no charge for unsold lots.

Appraisal services are available. The fee "depends on value, purpose, and distance."

526. Van Dieten Stamp Auctions B.V.

2 Tournooiveld   Tel. 70-464312/70-648658
2511 CX The Hague   Cable: VADIFIL THE HAGUE

Quarterly auctions of STAMPS, unreserved auctions at that, have won Van Dieten an international reputation. The sales are advertised in the philatelic press,
and single catalogues are available for fl10. After one has bought 4 catalogues, the next is sent without cost. Viewing is for 1 week before a sale, and
buyers have 2 weeks after a sale to settle accounts. Credit arrangements sometimes can be made at a rate of 1 percent per month. Mail order bids are
accepted, and packing and shipping is a relatively simple matter. Guarantees
are available, and bona fide returns are accepted for 14 days after a sale. The
buyer's premium at Van Dieten is 15 percent plus 50 Dutch cents per lot.
    A consignment should have a value of at least fl1,000. The commission rate
is 12.5 percent inland, and 15 percent for collections from abroad. There is no
separate rate for dealers or institutions. As "everything will be sold," there is
no charge for unsold lots. Consigned goods are sold within 4 months, and
settlement is 4 weeks after the sale. Other than VAT on the commission, when
applicable, there are no other charges to consignors.
    Appraisal services are available. Write the firm for details.

527. A. L. Van Gendt & Co. B.V.

Keizersgracht 96-98   Tel. 234107
1015 CV Amsterdam   Cable: RIGHTBOOK

Several times a year, Van Gendt holds auctions of BOOKS, MANUSCRIPTS, and
PRINTS. The catalogues are well documented, and each lot is described in the
language of the author (books in Latin and Greek seem to be described in the
language of the most likely buyer). Catalogues, which usually are priced at
around fl6, are available on application to the firm. Viewing is usually 10
A.M.–4 P.M. for 3 days before the first session of a sale. A mail order bidding
form is provided with each catalogue. Lots are sold under guarantee, with
certain exceptions which are described in the conditions of sale (e.g., framed
prints which cannot be inspected without damage to the frame). There is a 20
percent buyer's premium plus 10 Dutch cents payable on each lot bought.
Settlement is immediate, or on receipt of the goods to mail order bidders.
Tardy payers will be charged interest after 1 month at a rate of 1.5 percent
per month or part of a month.
    Consignor commissions are 25 percent for each lot knocked down at less
than fl300 and 15 percent for lots knocked down at fl300 or over. Time from
consignment to sale and from sale to settlement varies.
    Appraisals are undertaken for fees of 1.5 percent up to fl50,000; 1 percent
from fl50,000 to fl500,000; and 0.5 percent thereafter. If the goods are consigned for auction within 3 months, the fee will be refunded. Expenses are
charged for off-premises evaluations, in addition to the usual fees.

B.V. Vendu Notarishuis
528. Haringvliet 96   Tel. 010-122330
3011 TH Rotterdam

529. Plein Eendragt 11   Tel. 010-269651
Schiedam

This house holds sales 3 times a year at its Rotterdam venue and every month at Schiedam. The Rotterdam sales are more specialized groupings of artworks and antiques. Announcements are sent to those who ask to be on the mailing list, and catalogues can be purchased individually or by subscription. Mail order bids are accepted, and goods that prove to be not as catalogued can be returned. Packing and shipping services are available at cost. There is a buyer's premium of 20 percent plus fl1. Settlement is within 1 week, and credit cards are accepted. Viewing hours before a sale vary; one recent sale had 3 days of viewing, 10 A.M.–4 P.M.

Consignors pay varying rates of commission, and sometimes are charged for illustrations, insurance, and warehousing. The time from consignment to sale varies, and settlement is usually a month after the sale. Reserves are accepted, and the charge for unsold lots is "sometimes 7.5 percent, sometimes nothing."

Appraisal services are available at varying rates. Write J. E. C. Koks for details.

New Zealand: see Australia and New Zealand

Rhodesia: see Zimbabwe

Singapore and Malaysia

Little mystery attends the auctioning of goods in Singapore. Buyers, however, should check current export regulations before bidding at auction.

530. Victor & Morris Pte. Ltd.

39 Talok Ayer Street
Republic of Singapore

Tel. 94844
Telex: RS 22169
Cable: MENVICT SINGAPORE

Suite 335, Ampang Shopping Complex
Jln. Ampang
Kuala Lumpur, Malaysia

Victor & Morris is open 9–5 every day except Sunday, and it holds auctions once a week on its own premises, as well as at hotels and warehouses. The specialties here are ORIENTAL ANTIQUES, RUGS, FURNITURE, machinery and real estate. Viewing is the day before the sale, and there is no buyer's premium. Mail order bids are accepted, as are returns of goods not as catalogued. Packing and shipping services are available. Guarantees of authenticity are not offered. Buyers must settle their accounts immediately after the sale and must remove their purchases within a week. Diners Club and American Express cards are acceptable methods of payment.

The hardworking managing director, Victor Wu, will see that consigned goods are auctioned off within 2 weeks, with settlement a week after the sale. The commission is 10 percent, with additional charges if illustrations, insurance, packing and shipping, or warehousing is required. Reserves are accepted, with a 5 percent charge if the property consigned is not sold. In some situations, the commission rate is negotiable.

Victor & Morris is a member of the Singapore Institute of Valuers and will appraise property at a rate of 0.75 percent of the value.

South Africa

Auctions in South Africa follow a pattern that is quite familiar to British and American buyers and consignors. Do remember, though, that there is a general sales tax of 4 percent here. Exemptions are buyers registered as vendors with the Department of Inland Revenue and holding a valid certificate of registration issued in terms of the Sales Tax Act, 1978. Also exempt are purchasers making payment from and taking delivery outside the Republic of South Africa.

531. Ashbey's Galleries
43-47 Church Street   Tel. 22-7527
Cape Town 8001

Every Thursday on the premises, and sometimes elsewhere on other days, Ashbey's holds general-purpose mixed-lot sales of everything from gold rings to guitars. Sales are advertised in the local press, and catalogues are available by annual subscription for about R6 domestically and about $10 abroad. Viewing hours are 8:30 A.M.–noon on Saturday and 8:30 A.M.–5 P.M. Monday to Wednesday. Mail order bids are accepted from known buyers only, and goods that prove to be not as catalogued may be returned. No guarantees of authenticity are offered, nor are packing and shipping services. Settlement for buyers is within 3 days, unless other arrangements are made.

Insurance is considered the "seller's affair unless requested, although we carry our own insurance." Illustrations are rare in Ashbey's catalogues, but if requested they would cost about $15 per picture. Private consignors pay 17.5 percent as commission, the trade pays 15 percent, and charitable institutions often are charged nothing at all. Ashbey's also sells on its own behalf, stating frankly that "we carry a stock which we use to 'fill in' depleted catalogues." Reserves are accepted, and there is no charge for unsold lots with an agreed reserve. However, the unsold lot charge is 5 percent if a "seller insists on a reserve which we consider too high." Consigned goods are sold in 1–4 weeks, and settlement is made within 7 days after the auction.

Should appraisal services be required, phone or write B. Robinson or J. D. Thompson, who will charge 0.5 percent of total value plus traveling expenses.

532. Claremart Auction Centre
47 Main Road   Tel. 66-8826/66-8804
Claremont, Cape Town 7700

If you need a Volkswagen Beetle or a lapis lazuli pendant, Claremart may be the place to buy. In addition to MOTORCARS and JEWELRY, the specialties of the house are COINS, FURNITURE, MUSICAL INSTRUMENTS, RUGS, SILVER, STAMPS and WINES. Claremart holds at least 2 sales per week, some of these being "house sales" or sales in hotels. All are advertised in the *Cape Times* and the *Argus*. List-like catalogues and announcements are free of charge; write to the Administrative Office or phone 8:30 A.M.–5 P.M. on weekdays and 8:30 A.M.–noon on Saturdays. Mail order bids are accepted; guarantees of authenticity are offered; goods that prove to be not as catalogued are returnable, and packing and shipping services are available at cost. Viewing is the day preceding and day of the sale. Unless previous arrangements have been made, goods must be paid for immediately after the sale.

Auctioneer David Dorfman will be glad to hear from would-be consignors of jewelry, gold, coins, medals, and such, while D. M. Heller awaits news of antiques, silver, carpets, and objets d'art. The commission is negotiable, 17.5 percent being the maximum. There are no charges for insurance or warehousing, and illustration charges are on an individual basis. Reserves are accepted; should a lot fail to meet the reserve, the buy-in charge is negotiable, usually nil. Claremart usually shepherds consigned goods to sale within 2 weeks, and settlement is usually within 2 days of the sale.

533. Ford & Van Niekerk Pty. Ltd.
156 Main Road   Tel. 71-3384
P.O. Box 8
Plumstead, Cape Town

Fixed properties situated in the southern suburbs of Cape Town are the staple of Ford & Van Niekerk's business. Their auctions of household furniture and effects take place only in conjunction with sales of buildings, and the vast majority are held on site. One must check the *Cape Times* or the *Argus* for the real estate sales and then inquire about effects. Viewing is by appointment. No mail bids, guarantees, returns, or certificates of authenticity.

Consignors must give Ford & Van Niekerk a sole agency agreement to dispose of immovable property for a period of 2–3 months. The real estate commission structure is 5 percent on the first R20,000 and 3.5 percent on the balance. Commission on goods is negotiated.

534. Sotheby Parke Bernet South Africa Pty. Ltd.

Total House, Smit and Rissik Streets   Tel. 39-3726
P.O. Box 310010   Telex: 4-22261 SA
Braamfontein 2017   Cable: ABINITIO JOHANNESBURG

LIVE GAME is the most exotic specialty of Sotheby's in South Africa, which also features other sorts of AFRICANA. At a recent general sale, the lots ranged from a Wedgwood Fairyland Lustre Dish to a 140cm Penny Farthing bicycle, c.1880. Sales are held biweekly and are advertised in the local press and sometimes in the *Burlington Magazine*. Some sales are held on site. Not just anybody can buy the live game offered here; you have to be a zoo or an estate or a licensed commercial hunter or breeding farm. But anybody can subscribe to and buy from the catalogues for the specialized sales of BOOKS (including maps and prints), COINS AND MEDALS, STAMPS, SILVER, JEWELRY, WATCHES and objects of virtu, PAINTINGS, watercolors, and DRAWINGS, FIREARMS and EDGED WEAPONS, ceramics, works of art, clocks, rugs and carpets.

Announcements of forthcoming sales are available free. Remember that this Sotheby's unit is blissfully free of the buyer's premium. Viewing hours are 9:30 A.M.–5 P.M. for 2 or 3 days preceding a sale. Mail order bids are accepted (in the event of identical bids, the earliest wins), and packing and shipping services are available. All lots are sold with a 5-year guarantee against forgery. Unless special credit terms have been arranged, the buyer has 5 working days to settle accounts and remove purchases after a sale. Buyers unknown to the house may be asked for bank references or for an immediate 50 percent deposit.

No minimum value is necessary for consignment, and reserves are accepted. Rates of commission are 17.5 percent on pictures, silver, and works of art; 20 percent on books, coins, and stamps. Other rates on application. All rates are reduced by ⅕ for dealers. Insurance costs are 60¢ on R100 hammer price; packing and shipping are actual costs; and the average illustration cost is R80. It takes about 3 months for consigned goods to be sold. Settlement is 30 days after the sale "or, if by that date we have not yet received the said proceeds, within three business days after actually receiving the same in full." Five percent of the final bid is charged on unsold lots.

Finder's fees are 20 percent of the commission realized.

Charges for appraisal service are 1.5 percent of the appraised value.

535. Volks Auctioneers Sales Company

224 Schubart Street   Tel. 48-5066 (several lines)
Pretoria 0002

Mailing address:
Box 2144
Pretoria 0001

Two to three sales a month is the average for Volks, which is open for business Monday–Friday 8 A.M.–5 P.M. and Saturday 8 A.M.–noon. Specialties here are

AFRICANA, ART DECO, BOOKS, FURNITURE, and PORCELAIN. Smaller sales and house sales are advertised locally; larger sales, nationally. Write to Mrs. Ryll Hartdegen to receive announcements of sales and information about catalogue subscriptions. Mail order bids, guarantees of authenticity, packing and shipping services, and return of goods not as catalogued are all offered by Volks. Two days of viewing before a sale is the rule here, and settlement time for the buyer is usually the day of sale.

Volks is a flexible firm, and "it depends" is very often the response to questions about consignment. One begins by contacting Edward or Romano Bernardi. In the "depends" category are commission structure; charges for insurance, shipping, and warehousing; negotiability of commissions; whether or not reserves are accepted, length of time before sale (usually 4 to 8 weeks), and length of time to settlement (usually 2 weeks, but 4 for book auctions). Black-and-white catalogue illustrations cost R25 each, and unsold lots are charged at 1 percent of the reserve.

Appraisal service "again, depends, but usually 1 percent of value." Contact Mrs. Hartdegen or Mrs. M. Raubenheimer.

Spain

For years the reign in Spain sent auction down the drain. Now we can expect to see more auction activity.

536. Juan R. Cayon

41 Fuencarral Tel. 221 08 32/221 43 72/222 95 98
Madrid Telex: 42498 CAYN-E

4 Augusto Figueroa
Madrid

Cayon's occasional auctions are of COINS AND STAMPS, and BOOKS related to those two fields. All auctions are held on the premises, and free catalogues are available for specific sales by writing Sr. Cayon. Lots may be viewed for 5 days before a sale. Mail order bids are accepted, packing and shipping services are available, and goods that prove to be not as catalogued may be returned. Accounts must be settled within 25 days.

The minimum value for an acceptable lot is 1,000 Pts ($15/£7). The commission rate for everybody is 15 percent, and there are additional charges for catalogue illustrations and insurance, but these are minimal. Reserves are accepted, and there is no charge for unsold lots. Consigned goods are sold within 60 days, with settlement 35 days after the sale.

Appraisal services are available at a fee of 2 percent of value.

537. Christie's International Ltd.

Casado del Alisal 5 Tel. (01) 228-9300
Madrid 14 Telex: 43889
Cable: CHRISTIART MADRID

Christie's is well represented in Spain, by Casilda Fz-Villaverde de Eraso, Carlos Porras, and Edificio Propac.

538. Sotheby Parke Bernet & Co. Scursal de Espana
Calle del Prado 18   Tel. 232-6488/232-6572
Madrid 14

Edmund Peel is the person to speak to at this representative office.

Sweden

For auction buyers in Sweden, the sticking point is a decree passed in May 1927 which forbids the export of certain cultural property produced before 1860. The decree bears foremost on furniture, mirrors, clocks and clock cases, household utensils of wood, and parts of interior fittings. Exemption from this regulation may be granted. For any object to which the decree is applicable, buyers must apply for an export license to the Central Office of National Antiquities (Riksantikvarieämbetet), which is the decision-making authority, with the Nordiska Museet as advisory body. The license must accompany the object at the point of exportation for customs purposes. In many instances, the Nordiska Museet inspects the objects in an auction sale, and the auction house will either list the numbers of the lots which cannot be exported or place an asterisk next to the lot number in the catalogue.

If you are not a resident Swede, you also should be very careful indeed about trying to consign goods from abroad into Sweden.

539. W. Bolin Auktions Aktiebolag

Sturegatan 12
S-11436 Stockholm

Tel. (08) 60 66 22/33
Cable: NILOB

When W. Bolin, the Court Jewelers of Sweden, established a subsidiary auction company in 1966, the market level was at a "pitiful low," according to Hans Bolin. Today there is a very good market indeed, with buyers coming from a number of countries. Bolin holds auctions twice a year, usually in March and October. These are advertised in Swedish publications only. If you live outside Sweden, write to Jacqueline Bolin so that you can receive announcements of forthcoming sales. The current catalogue cost is Kr30 per year, plus postage (about $13). Note that catalogues are in Swedish only, but they are fairly well illustrated. Viewing is 3 days prior to the auction and is on the premises at Sturegatan 12. The auctions are held across the street at the

Hotel Anglais. Mail order bids are accepted, but the successful bidder must accept delivery C.O.D. Mr. Bolin points out: "We guarantee lots to be as described in the catalogue. We do not, however, guarantee for wear or such defects as may emanate from wear." Buyers have 8 days to settle their accounts.

Bolin "cannot accept goods from other countries than Sweden—our current laws make this impossible." If your jewels happen to be in Sweden, you can consign them at Bolin for a fee of 16 percent if you are a private individual or an institution (but not a dealer). There are no further fees unless packing and shipping are arranged through Bolin. Goods must reach Bolin 3 months before the auction, and settlement is a month afterward. For lots exceeding Kr 100,000, the commission is reduced. Reserves are accepted, and there is a 6 percent of value charge for unsold lots.

Bolin will appraise jewelry for no charge if it is left for auction.

540. Ab H. Bukowskis Houkonsthandel
Wahrendorffsgatan 8   Tel. (08) 28 41 65
S-111 47 Stockholm

Four times a year, the auctioning arm of this firm, known as Aktiebolaget Bukowski-Auktioner, or Bukowskis, holds multisession sales of 1,500 lots or more. Write to Mrs. D. Pudeck for announcements of sales schedules and information about subscription costs for the art and antiques catalogues and the modern art catalogue. Viewing is for a week before a sale, and mail order bids are accepted. Packing and shipping services are available, and buyers can return goods that prove to be not as catalogued. Buyers must settle accounts within 8 days of the sale. Note, however, that credit is given to private buyers "from a credit institute. Maximum US$10,000. Repayment in five years."

The minimum value for acceptance of a consignment is the equivalent of $400. The commission, which is not negotiable, is 15 percent of the final price. Reserves are accepted, and buy-in costs are 10 percent for a returned item, dropping down to 6 percent if the item is valued at over the equivalent of $1,200. Consignors are billed for catalogue illustrations, but not for insurance. The elapsed time from consignment to sale is variable, and settlement is made 1 month after the sale.

Bukowskis offers no-cost appraisals at the firm's reception desks.

541. Christie's International Ltd.
Hildingavägen 19   Tel. (08) 755-1092
S-182 62 Djursholm   Telex: 12916

The Christie's agent in Sweden is Lillemor Malmström, whose functions are the same as those of Christie's agents elsewhere: help consignors and bidders.

542. Göteborgs Auktionsverk AB

Tredje Langgatan 7-9   Tel. (031) 12 44 30/ 14 47 39/ 24 58 05/
S-413 03 Göteborg   24 58 56/ 12 16 10

Every week, except during July, Göteborgs Auktionsverk holds a sale. Many of these are general sales of antiquities and artworks, but there are also specialized sales of BOOKS, for instance. Viewing usually takes place during the 3 days preceding a sale, and catalogues are available singly at about Kr35 per catalogue or by subscription. Write Ingrid Johansson. Buyers should pay for and take away their purchases within 8 days of a sale. Mail order bids are accepted; goods that prove to be not as catalogued may be returnable, and packing and shipping services are available.

Would-be consignors should write to the Göteborgs Auktionsverk for details on rates and procedures. Roughly speaking, the commission ranges between 14 and 10 percent, with a 5-7 percent charge for unsold lots. Reserves are accepted. One week or 3 months may pass before goods are sold, depending on what is consigned; settlement is 14-30 days after the sale.

543. Gösta Mellquist Auktioner Ab

Fleninge Gästgifworegard   Tel. (042) 20 54 50/ 20 46 91
Stjörnan, Ödakra

This firm holds general-purpose mixed-lot sales about once a month, and these are advertised in the local newspapers. Single catalogues are available by phone or at the viewing, several hours before the sale. Phone and mail bids are accepted; authenticity is guaranteed; export shipping can be arranged; and goods that prove to be not as catalogued may be returned. The buyer must settle accounts within 8 days of a sale unless special credit terms have been arranged. "All the usual" credit cards are accepted.

Consigned goods must have a value of at least Kr50. The commission rate is 20 percent up to Kr1,000, and 10 percent above that. The elapsed time to sale "depends on the time before the next auction and how much is already left to be sold." Settlement is about 3 weeks after a sale. Reserves are accepted, and there is no charge for unsold lots if reserves have been agreed upon in advance.

Annual turnover is estimated to be about Kr900,000. The firm buys and sells on its own behalf.

Appraisal services are available. Write for details.

544. Sotheby Parke Bernet

Arsenalsgatan 4   Tel. (08) 10 14 78/9
S-111 47 Stockholm   Telex: 17380

Rolf Larson is the SPB representative in Sweden and he is expected to deal with all Scandinavia, soliciting consignments, assisting bidders, and keeping in touch with interested parties.

545. Ab Stockholms Auktionsverk

Jakobsgatan 10   Tel. (08) 14 24 40
S-103 25 Stockholm

Mailing address:
Box 16256
S-103 25 Stockholm

Every day, Monday through Friday, there is an auction at the Auktionsverk, which is a corporation owned by the city of Stockholm. There are a number of specialized sales which can stretch over a number of days: 2 Kvalitetsauktions (Quality Auctions) per year, usually in April and November, of antique silver, furniture, paintings, and the like, which are advertised in such foreign periodicals as *Apollo, Connoisseur,* and *Weltkunst;* 2 prints and drawings auctions per year, 2 sales of antique and collectors books, 30–40 ordinary book sales, and 20 sales of stamps and coins.

Catalogues for the specialized sales are available singly or by subscription; for details write to Hans Sundblom or Claes Göran Rasmusson. Viewing procedures vary, but 4 days before a Kvalitetsauktion is usual. Mail order bids are accepted; goods that prove to be not as catalogued may be returnable; and packing and shipping services are available within Sweden. Accounts should be settled within 6 days of a sale; in some cases, arrangements can be made with credit institutions for sums up to Kr50,000. Since August 1, 1980, there is a buyer's premium of 10 percent up to Kr6,000 and 5 percent thereafter. MasterCard is accepted for payment.

Consignors should write to the Auktionsverk for information about what can be consigned, the minimum value for any lot being Kr25. Write to the following experts by category:

Autographs, Engravings, Japanese and Chinese Works of Art, Prints	(Claes Göran Rasmusson)
Furniture, Bronzes, Mirrors, Clocks, Old Paintings	(Hans Sundblom)
Glass, China, Porcelain, Jewelry, Embroidery, Netsuke, Rugs, Toys	(Elsebeth Welander)
Manuscripts, Books, Maps	(Erik Falk)
Medals, Stamps	(Lars Jonsson)
Silver, Pewter	(Ursula Sjöberg)
Swedish 20th-c. Art, Arms	(Anders Lundström)

The consignor pays Kr5 per object and 10 percent of the selling price up to Kr6,000, dropping to 5 percent thereafter. There are no charges for illustrations, insurance, or warehousing. Reserves are accepted, but the charge for an unsold lot is the same as if it were sold. Dealers and institutions do not get separate rates, and no finder's fees are offered. Settlement is 20 days after a regular auction, 30 days after a specialized sale. Goods placed in regular sales are auctioned in 2 weeks to a month; for the quality sales, the elapsed time is longer and variable.

Appraisal service is available. Write for details.

Switzerland

The undisputed auction center of this country is Zurich. In many ways (some of them quite admirable), Zurich retains a small-town bourgeois atmosphere. But it must also rank among the financial and fine art centers of the world. The money and the expertise are there, and in recent years—especially as the Swiss franc has gone from strength to strength—Zurich has carved out an enviable reputation. Moreover, this city is the headquarters for Galerie Koller, the Swiss auction firm which during the last decade has made a strenuous effort to reach out transatlantic for a worldwide clientele.

There are other important auction houses in Switzerland, but Koller—which like many of its peers also functions as a dealer—must rank among the most important. Its efforts beyond Switzerland have not met with unqualified success, however. Some of its sales have done very well, but the disposal of the Ernest Brummer Collection (of Greek, Roman, Middle East, Medieval, and Renaissance works of art) in 1979 in conjunction with an English firm proved disappointing, especially compared with the projections made prior to the sale.

Koller has not completely broken away from the traditional Swiss pattern of holding 1 or 2 massive sales a year. These last for several days, with each session often given over to a specialty. You need not worry about missing a sale while attending another, since the Swiss auction houses are careful to avoid schedule conflicts. Mostly, these sales are held in the spring and fall. There are firms that hold sales in the winter and more than twice a year, but sales such as these are frequently not multisession. The summer is generally very quiet on the Swiss auction front.

Switzerland is a favorite venue of the multinational firms, all of which have offices there. Sotheby and Christie's, as well as Phillips to a lesser extent, follow the same pattern as the Swiss and group their sales into multi-lot sessions in fall and spring. These are diversified in what they offer, but the focus of the lots gives a very good idea of the strength and weakness of the Swiss auction market. The multinational firms focus on fine jewelry, antique silver, and gold objects—those portable "stones and metals" that have been correctly described by one auction correspondent as "the closest the art market comes to commodities." These firms and their indigenous counterparts also offer Swiss art, but the market for that art is limited. It appeals to few non-Swiss buyers, and the Swiss market is limited (there are fewer people living in Switzerland than in New York City).

The catalogues prepared by the Swiss houses (and their multinational counterparts) are first-rate, profusely illustrated, intelligently put together with full descriptions. Quite often for the more important sales the catalogue descriptions are multilingual (usually German and English, occasionally French as well as or in place of English; in the French-speaking part of Switzerland, the situation is reversed). In many cases, these catalogues can be used as reference works. Note that an increasing number of Swiss auction houses charge a fee (normally 5 percent of the hammer price) for executing order bids. Before you telex, telephone, or mail your bid to a Swiss auction house, check to see if the firm charges for executing that service and try to negotiate the fee. The Swiss houses on the whole seem very flexible in their fee structure, which is quite high. Even the Swiss press has noted that there are "strong variations" between the houses, and commissions are generally negotiable, depending upon the situation. But be reasonable in your approach: remember a Sfr500 bid does not extend much leverage for negotiation, nor does the possibility of a Sfr1,000 consignment.

Given Switzerland's central location in Europe, the wealth the country attracts as a center for flight capital, and the attractive portable objects presented at auction, the Swiss first-rank auction houses should continue to be of importance on the international auction scene. It is doubtful if Zurich will ever rival London, New York, or Paris, but that Swiss city should certainly continue to rank among the top ten auction venues in the world.

Taxes: In Switzerland there is a turnover tax known in German as *Warenumsatzsteuer*, or familiarly as WUST. The current rate is 6 percent of the hammer price, and it is generally included in the buyer's surcharge. However, various kinds of buyers can obtain rebates for WUST paid: for example, buyers residing outside Switzerland will receive a refund upon presentation to the auction house of an official Swiss Export Declaration for the objects purchased, duly stamped by Swiss customs; or registered wholesalers—foreign or Swiss—who qualify under the Swiss Sales Tax Law can obtain a rebate upon producing their registration card, known as a *carte de grossiste* or a *Grossistenkarte*. Not all houses rebate the full amount of the tax, so it is necessary to check carefully.

There are also circumstances under which consignors must pay WUST, as when nonregistered foreign consignors consign objects that are sold to a private customer. Be sure to go over the ground rules thoroughly with the auction house before you consign goods. WUST for the consignor is charged at a slightly different rate than WUST for the buyer.

546. Daniel Beney

Avenue des Mousquines 2   Tel. (021) 22 28 64
CH-1005 Lausanne

This auctioneer and valuer has offices in a pleasant section of town, and holds sales from time to time. These are mostly general-purpose mixed-lot sales. Check the local press to see what he is doing: there is no set schedule to his operations.

547. Blanc

Arcade Hotel Beau-Rivage, Box 84   Tel. (021) 27 32 55/26 86 20
CH-1001 Lausanne

This auctioneer holds approximately 10 sales a year at various venues, as well as estate and house sales. All are advertised in the local press.

The sales are usually not catalogued, but they include a wide variety of items, among them FURNITURE, PRINTS, and SILVER. There is no buyer's premium. No guarantees of authenticity are offered. Packing and shipping services are not available from the firm. The usual viewing procedure is 2 hours before the auction. Settlement is in cash and immediately.

The standard consignor's commission is negotiable and varies downward from a high of 25 percent of the hammer price. Dealers have a separate rate. Settlement is made 1 week after the sale. Reserves are not accepted.

Christie's (International) S.A.

548. 8 Place de la Taconnerie   Tel. (022) 28 25 44
CH-1204 Geneva   Telex: 423634
Cable: CHRISAUCTION GENEVA

549. Steinwiesplatz   Tel. (01) 69 05 05
CH-8032 Zurich   Telex: 56093

As is usually the case with the multinational auction houses, the Christie's
offices are located in elegant sections of Geneva and Zurich.

Ms. Maria Reinshagen, the representative in Zurich, accepts and solicits
consignments and bids. She is available to assist Christie's clients with their
auction problems.

The Geneva operation holds sales (of usually a week's duration) in the fall
and spring at the posh and fancy Hotel Richemond. These sales, which include a variety of objects ranging from silver and jewelry (probably the most
important jewelry sales in the world) to wines and art deco, are carefully
timed to take place either before or after the sales held by Sotheby's in
Zurich.

Dr. Geza von Hapsburg, Christie's man in Geneva, has over the years built
up a loyal following and the sales there are of more than just passing interest.
The conditions of sale and of consignment are similar to those of the other
Swiss auction houses. For details, consult the nearest Christie's office or write
to the Geneva office.

550. Auktionshaus Dobiaschofsky AG.
Monbijoustrasse 28/30   Tel. (031) 25 23 72/73/74
CH-3001 Berne   Cable: GALDOB BERNE

This firm deals in artworks of various kinds, and twice a year—usually in
May and November—holds multisession sales that normally stretch over 4
days. Among the items sold at these sales are CHINESE WORKS OF ART, DRAW-
INGS, MAPS, PAINTINGS, PORCELAIN, POSTERS, and SILVER.

Founded in 1923 and holding auctions since 1955, Dobiaschofsky does not
show its age in any way, and is quite dynamic in its approach. A Polaroid
picture of any lot not illustrated in the catalogue is available for a small fee
(Sfr8, plus postage), and it is also possible to obtain a blow-up of any lot
depicted in the catalogue (Sfr12, plus postage).

Sales are advertised regularly in the Swiss press and in national and international specialty publications, such as *Weltkunst*. Catalogues are available
for each sale (Sfr20, plus postage). Announcements of forthcoming sales are
sent out; to be placed on the mailing list, write the firm.

There is a buyer's premium, which varies because of taxes. It is 20 percent
on objects bought up to Sfr4,999, and 15 percent thereafter. For most foreign
and domestic dealers the premium is 15 percent. Absentee bids are executed.
Packing and shipping services are available. Guarantees of authenticity are
offered for only "certain items," but goods that prove to be not as catalogued
may be returned within 3 weeks of the sale, insofar as "our contract with
consignor allows to return such items before settlement is made." All goods
are sold "as is." Settlement is as soon as possible. Viewing is 12–14 days
before sale. Credit is available "to regular customers by previous agreement
only."

The standard consignor's commission is 20 percent for items of low value (e.g., graphics) and 16 percent for items of higher value (e.g., paintings). The commission is negotiable, depending upon the situation. Consignors are charged for catalogue illustrations. Insurance is included in the commission. The firm will collect consigned goods and then bill the consignor costs such as freight, taxes, etc. Goods are usually sold within 3–6 months. Reserves are accepted. If goods are unsold, the minimum charge is 1 percent for insurance (based on reserve price). Settlement is 4–6 weeks after the sale. There is a minimum value necessary for consignment: paintings, etc., Sfr500; prints, etc., Sfr200.

Dobiaschofsky does buy and sell on its own behalf.

Appraisal service is available. Contact Mr. H. Dobiaschofsky.

Auktionshaus Dobiaschofsky belongs to Verbandes Schweizerischer Auktionatoren von Kunst und Kulturgut.

551. Galerie Fischer

Haldenstrasse 19   Tel. (041) 22 57 72/73
CH-6006 Lucerne

This firm, which also sells retail, holds auctions twice yearly at its premises in a picturesque portion of this very tourist-oriented town. Objects sold by the firm include PAINTINGS (Old Master, modern art) and PRINTS. Sales are advertised in the Swiss press and specialty publications.

Catalogues are available for each sale, at Sfr20, plus postage, and can be obtained by writing. There is a buyer's premium. Absentee bids are executed. Settlement is as soon as possible after the sale.

The standard consignor's commission is negotiable, depending upon the situation. There is a separate rate structure for dealers. Reserves are accepted.

Appraisal service is not available.

552. Germann Auktionshaus

Zeltweg 67   Tel. (01) 32 83 58/32 01 12
CH-8032 Zurich   Telex: 54551
                                                    Cable: ERGON ZURICH

Since 1979, Germann has been holding its semiannual auctions not, as of old, at hotels in downtown Zurich, but in its own quarters in a modern building just a bit away from the hustle and bustle—and the spiraling costs—of central Zurich. Germann is now located on the other side of the Limmat River from the main train station—a healthy walk or short trolley ride. Items for sale include DRAWINGS, ENGRAVINGS, ETCHINGS, MAPS, PAINTINGS, and SCULPTURE.

Sales are advertised in the local press, the European press, and in specialty publications, such as *Weltkunst*. Illustrated catalogues are available singly for each sale; two catalogues cost Sfr35, plus postage.

There is a buyer's premium of 15 percent on the hammer price, reduced to

10 percent for dealers from Switzerland and the principality of Liechtenstein if they are registered as wholesalers. The premium is also reduced to 10 percent for foreign dealers who provide an export declaration.

Absentee bids are executed. Packing and shipping services are available. Guarantees of authenticity are offered in some instances; paintings, for example, may be returned by the original buyer up to 5 years after the sale, provided that certain conditions are met: "the object cannot be returned if the description in the catalogue was made in keeping with the level of research or according to the opinion of the majority of experts at the time when the catalogue was being compiled." Most other items are sold "as is," without any guarantees of any kind.

Settlement is to be made within 10 days after the sale. Viewing is at least 5 days before the sale with at least one late night to 8 P.M.

The usual consignor's commission is 15 percent for Swiss property and 10 percent for property from abroad. There is no minimum value necessary for acceptance of a consignment. The commission is negotiable, depending upon the situation. Consignors are expected to pay for catalogue illustrations, insurance, and packing and shipping (if the firm has to remove consigned goods to the saleroom). Settlement is made 30 days after the sale. Reserves are accepted.

Germann Auktionshaus is a member of Verbandes Schweizerischer Auktionatoren von Kunst und Kulturgut.

553. Haus der Bücher AG

Baumleingasse 18   Tel. (061) 23 30 88
CH-4051 Basel

This firm of booksellers holds a major auction of books, autographs, and manuscripts once or twice a year. The usual sale is quite large and will include well over 1,500 lots.

Alain Moirandat, a principal in the firm, writes that "we prefer to give more detailed informations only to the interested consignor."

554. Adolph Hess AG

Haldenstrasse 5   Tel. (041) 22 43 92 / 22 45 35
CH-6006 Lucerne

COINS and MEDALS are the specialties of this firm, which holds 1 or 2 auctions annually, usually in a local hotel, which may last more than a day.

Sales are advertised in the Swiss press and in specialty publications, such as coin magazines all over the world. Profusely illustrated catalogues are available for each sale (Sfr20). There is a buyer's premium of 10 percent. If silver and copper coins are delivered in Switzerland, the premium is 16 percent because of taxes.

"The authenticity of the pieces is unconditionally guaranteed," states the catalogue; but complaints can be made only within 8 days of receipt of the merchandise. The lots to be sold are on view in the firm's offices during regular business hours (9 A.M.–noon, 2–5 P.M.) for some time prior to the sale. Absentee bids are executed. Packing and shipping services are available. Accounts must be settled within 1 week of the sale.

The minimum value for a consignment to be accepted is Sfr500. Consignors do not pay for catalogue illustrations, insurance, or storage prior to sale. Settlement is made with consignors 1 month after the sale. Reserves are accepted.

Appraisal service is available. The cost varies. For Greek and Roman coins, get in touch with Mr. Dürr; for modern coins, Mr. Hollesberger.

Adolph Hess AG does buy and sell on its own behalf.

555. Auktionshaus Peter Ineichen

C.F. Meyerstrasse 14
CH-8002 Zurich

Tel. (01) 201-3017
Telex: 58097
Cable: INAUKTION

ARMS AND ARMOR, CLOCKS AND WATCHES, DOLLS, HELVETICA JEWELRY, SCIENTIFIC INSTRUMENTS, and TOYS are among the specialties of this firm. It holds 5–10 auction sales annually, usually in spring and fall. The firm's quarters are located in the Enge section of Zurich, not far from the commuter Bahnhof Enge, and public parking is close by.

Sales are advertised regularly in the Swiss and international press, as well as in specialty publications. Profusely illustrated catalogues, with intelligent, useful, and full descriptions, are available for each sale; the usual price is Sfr30, plus postage.

There is a buyer's premium of 20 percent. For Swiss dealers registered as wholesalers, the commission is 12 percent. Swiss and foreign dealers not registered as wholesalers pay 18 percent commission. Nonregistered purchasers who return an export declaration duly stamped by Swiss customs are given a 5 percent rebate.

Absentee bids are executed; telephone bids must be confirmed in writing. Packing and shipping services are not available from the firm. Guarantees of authenticity are not offered and goods are sold as is, but "should a purchaser be able to bring proof in writing by a recognized expert within 20 days of the sale . . . that a purchase is a forgery . . . the auction house will rescind the sale and restitute the sale price on the condition that the object is returned within 14 days of receipt of said proof." The usual viewing procedure is 4 days before the sale, 11:30 A.M.–7:30 P.M. Settlement must be made within 10 days.

The standard consignor's commission varies between 16 and 20 percent and is negotiable, depending upon the situation. Consignors pay for catalogue illustrations, insurance, and packing and shipping (if the consignor does not remove goods to the saleroom). The firm maintains that "the charges cover only a part of the costs."

Goods must be entered in the sale 2 months before the auction takes place. Settlement is made in 30 days. There is no minimum value necessary for a consignment. Reserves are accepted. There is a buy-in charge based on the costs of photos, insurance, etc.

Appraisal service is not available.

The firm estimates its annual turnover at 7–9 million Swiss francs.

Auktionshaus Peter Ineichen is a member of Verbandes Schweizerischer Antiquare und Kunsthändler and Verbandes Schweizerischer Auktionatoren von Kunst und Kulturgut.

556. Galerie Koller AG

Ramistrasse 8	Tel. (01) 47 50 40
CH-8001 Zurich	Telex: 58500

557. Koller St. Gallen

St. Gallen	Tel. (071) 23 42 40

Koller is an important multifaceted operation with a secondary saleroom in St. Gallen, where sales of varying kinds of lesser-quality goods are held monthly.

The main branch, in Zurich, holds 2 massive sales a year; these are multisession sales that last several days, and a wide variety of objects is offered, including: ARMS AND ARMOR, BOOKS, CHINESE WORKS OF ART, CLOCKS AND WATCHES, DRAWINGS, FURNITURE, GLASS, ISLAMIC ART, JAPANESE WORKS OF ART, JEWELRY, MAPS, MEDIEVAL WORKS OF ART, MUSICAL INSTRUMENTS, NETSUKE, PAINTINGS (Old Master, 19th c. European, Impressionist, modern art, contemporary art, Swiss masters), PEWTER, PORCELAIN, PRE-COLUMBIAN ART, PRINTS, RUGS, SCIENTIFIC INSTRUMENTS, and TOYS.

Announcements of forthcoming sales are available gratis. To be placed on the mailing list, please write to the Zurich office. Catalogues are available singly for each sale and by subscription (prices realized are included); 2 catalogues per year in the various specialties cost Sfr40–Sfr50, plus postage.

Sales are advertised in most important international art magazines, international newspapers, the Swiss press, and specialty publications.

The buyer's premium varies, from 8 to 18 percent. Absentee bids are executed. Packing and shipping services are available. Some items are sold as is and others are guaranteed for up to 5 years within certain restrictions. Viewing (10 A.M.–10 P.M.) is usually for 2 weeks before the sales commence. Buyers must settle accounts within 12 days after the sale.

The consignor's commission varies between 10 and 18 percent, in accordance with "objects, quantity, and circumstances." There is no minimum value necessary for a consignment. Consignors pay for catalogue illustrations (up to Sfr 200 for a quarter page), insurance (at 0.5 percent of realized value), and packing and shipping (if the consignor does not bring items to the saleroom). Consigned goods are sold within 1½–4 months. Settlement is made with the consignor "at the latest, 6 weeks after the sale." Reserves are accepted; the buy-in charge is 3 percent of the reserve price.

Appraisal service is available: "depends on the individual case; contact the main office."

Galerie Koller does buy and sell on its own behalf, both at auction sales and at the several retail outlets that it owns.

The firm has a New York office, which solicits consignments and assists bidders:

> Galerie Koller, New York Office, Inc.
> 575 Madison Avenue, Suite 1006   Tel. (212) 486-1484
> New York, NY 10022   Telex: 237699

558. Kornfeld & Co.
Laupenstrasse 49   Tel. (031) 25 46 73
CH-3008 Berne   Cable: ARTUS

Successor to the elegant and well-respected firm of Kornfeld and Klipstein, this equally posh and worthy firm holds sales once a year, usually in June. These are multisession sales of a large array of lots in an auction that lasts at least 2 days. Sales take place in a charming venue which is a healthy but not impossible walk from the train station. Items offered for sale include BOOKS, DRAWINGS, ENGRAVINGS, ETCHINGS, PAINTINGS (19th c. European, Impressionist, modern art), POSTERS, and PRINTS.

Sales are advertised regularly in the Swiss press, the international press, and in specialty publications, such as *Weltkunst*. Announcements are sent on written request. Catalogues are available; for cost and availability, please write to E. W. Kornfeld. There is a buyer's premium of 15 percent for private individuals and 10 percent for registered dealers. Absentee bids are executed. Packing and shipping services are available. Guarantees of authenticity are offered, but "claims can be considered only within 3 days from receipt of the objects and only if proved that descriptions in the catalogue are incorrect." No claims will be considered 4 weeks after the sale. Settlement is immediately. Viewing is 5–6 days in advance (10 A.M.–noon, 2–6 P.M.).

The consignor's commission is negotiable, depending upon the situation. The standard charges are: 15 percent for paintings, graphic works, drawings, sculptures, and illustrated books; lots that require "extensive research work" and do not sell for over Sfr500 are charged a seller's commission of 20 percent; lots that sell for Sfr30,000 or over are charged 10 percent.

Consignors are not charged for catalogue illustrations, insurance, or storage prior to sale. They are responsible for getting their goods to Berne; the firm will advise and assist, but transport charges are borne by the consignor. There is no minimum value for a consignment. Reserves are accepted. If the house agrees to the reserve, there is no buy-in charge; otherwise, the cost to the consignor is 5 percent of the reserve price, should the lot not sell. A condition of consignment is that "items entrusted to us for sale can no longer be withdrawn." Settlement is made "so far as is possible, about a fortnight after auction; payment of balance become due 60 days after auction."

Appraisal service is available "only in relation with auction sale offers."

Kornfeld & Co. is a member of Verbandes Schweizerischer Auktionatoren von Kunst und Kulturgut.

559. Phillips Son & Neale SA

6 Rue de la Cité   Tel. (022) 28 68 28
CH-1204 Geneva   Telex: 22985

The Geneva operation was the first overseas branch established by Phillips and was an important step in its development as a multinational company. These ground-floor premises, opened in the late fall of 1977, are in the heart of Geneva, where, as a Phillips PR release has it, "the old town meets the shopping and financial centres."

Sales, often in the evening, are held twice yearly, fall and spring, at the prestigious Hotel des Bergues. Objects sold are usually clocks and watches, jewelry, and silver.

The conditions of sale and of consignment follow the usual Swiss model. For details, contact your nearest Phillips office or Geneva.

560. Christian Rosset

Salle des Ventes, 29 Rue du Rhone   Tel. (022) 28 96 33/34
CH-1204 Geneva

The Salle des Ventes has been in existence since 1971. Rosset holds about 10 auctions a year there, monthly except for July and August. Rosset auctions a variety of objects, including CHINESE WORKS OF ART, DRAWINGS, FURNITURE, JAPANESE WORKS OF ART, PAINTINGS, PORCELAIN, PRINTS, and SILVER. Occasional house and estate sales are also held.

Sales are advertised in the Swiss press and in the *Gazette Drouot*, Paris. Illustrated catalogues are available prior to most sales; they are free in Europe; write to M. Christian Rosset.

Buyers pay a surcharge of 15 percent. Absentee bids are executed, but the house would like references or financial bona fides from unknown bidders. Guarantees of authenticity are generally not offered. Packing and shipping services are available. Goods that prove to be not as catalogued may be returned by bidders within 10 days of receipt of goods. The usual viewing procedure is 1 or 2 days before the auction, 3–8 P.M. Buyer must settle accounts immediately, reports M. Rosset, "if he is not known to us." Time is available for foreign buyers who must "send money from their own country."

The standard consignor's commission of 15 percent is negotiable, depending upon the situation. Items to be sold must be brought to the office at least 6 weeks before the auction. There is no minimum value necessary for a consignment. Consignors do not pay for catalogue illustrations, insurance, or storage prior to sale. Consignors pay shipping and packing if they do not remove goods to the saleroom by themselves. Settlement is made within 1 month of the sale. Reserves are accepted. The buy-in charge is 3 percent of the reserve price.

561. **Schweizerische Gesellschaft der Freunde von Kunstauktionen**
11 Werdmühlestrasse   Tel. (01) 211-4789
CH-8001 Zurich   Cable: MAXBOLLAG ZURICH

This is an auction club over 2 decades old, open to anyone, which claims over 1,000 members all over the world. Auctions are held monthly except August. The only kinds of objects sold at these auctions are ENGRAVINGS, ETCHINGS, and PAINTINGS of 19th-century European artists, as well as Impressionist, modern, and contemporary art. For sale is the occasional Picasso and Van Velde, but many of the artists offered are less familiar names, such as Steinlen, Isnard, and Schmidmeister.

The director of this operation is Max G. Bollag, who has established a gallery on a side street not far from the train station. In this gallery can be viewed the works put up for sale. The fee for the list-like, unillustrated catalogue issued each month is Sfr5 per annum. The works to be auctioned are chosen through the preview; if there is a bid on them, the membership is informed through the catalogue that these works are up for auction. Bids can be made by mail or in person. Goods may not be returned if they prove to be not as described. Packing and shipping services are available. The usual viewing procedure is 3 weeks before the sale. Settlement is usually within 3 days after the sale, but can be extended to 3 weeks for mail order customers. The buyer's premium is 10 percent.

The standard consignor's commission is 20 percent, but it is negotiable, depending upon the situation. Consignors must pay for insurance and for packing and shipping to get goods to the saleroom. Reserves are accepted. Settlement is made within 2 weeks after payment. There is no specific monetary minimum value necessary for consignment, but the club, according to Mr. Bollag, is interested "only in objects of quality."

The club does not buy and sell on its own behalf at auctions.

Sotheby Parke Bernet AG
562. 20 Bleicherweg   Tel. (01) 202-0011
CH-8022 Zurich   Telex: 52380
Cable: ABINITIO ZURICH

563. 24 Rue de la Cité   Tel. (022) 21 33 77
CH-1024 Geneva   Telex: 2890098
Cable: ABINITIO GENEVA

The Sotheby representative in Geneva is Nicholas Rayner; the firm's man on the spot in Zurich is Dr. J. G. Wille, "in partnership with Aldred Schwarzenbach." The Zurich office runs sales.

Both offices are located in posh sections of their respective home communities. Twice a year, fall and spring, in Zurich, Sotheby's holds sales, in deluxe hotels or equivalent locations, of BOOKS, JEWELRY, and SILVER, as well as other objects. During the winter for the past few years, Sotheby's has also held a sale in St. Moritz of jewelry.

The fall and spring sales tend to be carefully timed to take place either just before or just after Christie's holds its sales in Geneva.

Generally, the conditions of sale and of consignment are much the same as at the other Swiss auction houses. For details, contact your nearest Sotheby's office or the Zurich office of the firm.

564. Dr. Erich Steinfels, Auktionen
Rämistrasse 6   Tel. (01) 34 12 33 (fine art and antiques)
CH-8001 Zurich   (01) 252-1233 (wine)

This auction operation is part of a multifaceted firm, Steinfels & Partners AG, which buys and sells industrial machinery, real estate, and factories. Dr. Steinfels holds auctions of wine as well as of fine art and antiques, including such objects as PAINTINGS, RUGS, SCIENTIFIC INSTRUMENTS, and SILVER. Sales are held at various hotels and other locations in Zurich. A recent venue was the Haus "Zur Kaufleuten," in the heart of the city. The wine auctions are held 6 times a year in Zurich and in West Germany. Dr. Steinfels asserts: "we are the largest wine auctioneer of continental Europe."

Sales are advertised in the Swiss press, the international press when relevant, and in specialty publications. Catalogues are available singly for each sale; the usual price is Sfr5–Sfr6 for the wine sales and Sfr25–Sfr30 for the art and antiques sales. There is a buyer's premium of 10 percent. Absentee bids are executed; telephone bids must be confirmed in writing. Packing and shipping services are available. All goods are sold "as is," yet if within 30 days of the sale the buyer can prove that goods are not as catalogued, the sale will be rescinded. Usual viewing procedure is 5–8 days before the sale. Settlement is within 10 days of the sale.

The standard consignor's commission is 10 percent, but it is negotiable, depending upon the situation. Consignors pay for catalogue illustrations (Sfr40 per picture), insurance, packing and shipping (if the firm has to transport the consigned goods), and storage if an object remains unsold and is not picked up. Settlement is made 8 weeks after the sale. Reserves are accepted; the buy-in charge is 3 percent of the reserve price. Reserves are not accepted on many wines. There is no minimum value for a consignment.

Contact persons are Mr. Gilg for the arts and Mr. Wermuth for wine.

Appraisal service is available. Contact Dr. Steinfels.

565. Frank Sternberg
Bahnhofstrasse 84   Tel. (01) 211-7980
CH-8001 Zurich

COINS are the specialty of this dealer, who conducts auctions 1–2 times a year. These sales, normally held in the Hotel Bellerive au Lac, are advertised in the international numismatic press, as well as in the Swiss press. Catalogues are available for each sale; the cost is Sfr20 prior to the auction and Sfr30 after the auction (includes list of prices realized).

There is a buyer's premium: the trade pays 5 percent; others, 10 percent. In addition, for silver and copper coins there is a 6 percent turnover tax that has to be paid by the purchaser unless the merchandise is officially exported from Switzerland. Absentee bids are executed, but there is a charge of 5 percent in some sales. Packing and shipping services are available. Guarantees of authenticity are offered: "our catalogues are prepared with great care and accuracy." All claims must be made within 8 days of receipt of the lot. Viewing is 2 days prior to the sale, 10 A.M.–noon, 3–6 P.M. Settlement is within 4 weeks after the sale.

The standard consignor's commission, which is negotiable, is 15 percent of the hammer price. Minimum value for a consignment should be Sfr1,000 per lot and Sfr 100,000 per consignment as a total. Consignors are not charged for catalogue illustrations, insurance, or storage prior to sale. They are also not charged for shipping or packing. Consigned goods are sold within "6 months or more." Reserves are accepted "only in exceptional cases."

The firm does buy and sell on its own behalf, "from time to time."

566. Jürg Stucker Gallery Ltd.
Alter Aargauerstalden 30   Tel. (031) 44 00 44
CH-3006 Berne   Cable: STUKERGALERIE

The gallery is set in very picturesque sylvan surroundings on the far side of the Nydegg Bridge, not far from where the river Aar loops around the old city. A multisession sale which lasts several days is held every fall, usually in November. This sale is advertised in the Swiss press, the international press, and in specialty publications, such as *Weltkunst, Connaissance des Arts*, etc. The impressive range includes CLOCKS AND WATCHES, COINS, DRAWINGS, GLASS, HELVETICA, MUSICAL INSTRUMENTS, PAINTINGS, PORCELAIN, RUGS, SILVER, and TOYS.

A catalogue, available for Sfr30, contains "everything we offer at our sales." There is a buyer's premium, which is 20 percent of the hammer price for private buyers, 15 percent for the trade. Absentee bids in writing are executed. Packing and shipping services are not offered by the firm. Though there are no guarantees of authenticity, director U. C. Haldi points out that "we are always prepared to discuss any problems which might occur." The usual viewing procedure is a fortnight before the sale, 8 A.M.–noon, 2–6:30 P.M.; closed on Mondays and open Sunday afternoon by appointment. Settlement is expected within 2–4 weeks.

The standard consignor's commission "for all" is 20 percent. It is negotiable, depending upon the situation. Persons wishing to consign goods should get in touch with the house and enclose photos. Consignors are not charged for catalogue illustrations or for insurance, but must pay packing and shipping fees if the house undertakes to collect the consigned property. Consigned goods are sold within 8–10 weeks of delivery to Stucker. Reserves are accepted. Settlement is 6 weeks after the end of the sale. There is a minimum value for consignment of Sfr100.

Appraisal service is available; contact Mr. Haldi.

Jürg Stucker, which also has a retail operation and which buys and sells on its own behalf, is a member of Verbandes Schweizerischer Antiquare und Kunsthändler.

567. Uto Auktions AG

Lavaterstrasse 11	Tel. (01) 202-9444
CH-8027 Zurich	Telex: 52783
	Cable: UTOAUKTION

This firm is located in the area of Zurich known as Enge, not far from Bahnhof Enge and right by the Hotel Ascot—a section of Zurich once considered suburban but now almost swallowed up and part of the metropolitan area. Among Uto Auktions' specialties are CLOCKS AND WATCHES and SCIENTIFIC INSTRUMENTS. Sales, held twice a year, are advertised in the Swiss press, as well as in specialty publications worldwide.

The well-illustrated and intelligently put together catalogues are often bilingual. They are available for each sale, at Sfr20. There is a buyer's premium of 18 percent, which includes local taxes; foreign dealers who have filed for and received a stamped export declaration pay only 12 percent. Each bid must be at least 5 percent over the previous bid. Absentee bids are executed. Packing and shipping services are available. Buyers are offered the opportunity to return goods that prove to be not as catalogued if within 3 weeks the house is notified in writing and if within an additional 2 weeks the item is returned. The usual viewing procedure is 10 days before the sale, 10 A.M.–8 P.M., including Saturdays and Sundays. Settlement must usually be made within 21 days after the sale. Credit is available if "the buyer is very well known to the auction house."

The standard commission for consignors is 18 percent to private individuals and 12 percent to the trade. These commissions are negotiable, depending upon the situation. There is no minimum value necessary for consignment. Consignors pay for catalogue illustrations, insurance (5 percent of the price realized), packing and shipping (if Uto Auktions has to remove the consignment to the saleroom), and storage (starting 1 month after the auction if an object goes unsold). Goods are usually sold within 4 months of consignment. Settlement is made 30 days after the sale. Reserves are accepted; the buy-in charge is 3 percent of the reserve price. Even if there is no reserve and an object goes unsold, Uto is entitled to 3 percent of "the minimum prices fixed."

Appraisal service is available. Contact Mrs. A. Dauko.

Uto Auktions does buy and sell on its own behalf: "only very exceptional pieces."

Uruguay

The auction market in Uruguay is a national one. Both buyers and sellers should be aware that there is an 18 percent value added tax on commissions.

568. Eugenio Bavastro S.A.
Trienta y tres 1325 Tel. 90-73-47/90-00-68
Misiones 1366-70

Everything from URUGUAYAN PAINTINGS to real estate is sold at weekly auctions in uncatalogued sales. Check the newspapers for announcements. Sales are on the premises or on site, depending on what is being sold. Viewing is Tuesdays and Wednesdays. No mail bids are accepted, and no freighting services are offered. Buyers must settle within 6 days. There is a 10 percent buyer's premium.

Consignors pay a commission rate of 12 percent. The experts to contact are Hector Bavastro for furniture and real estate; Antonio De Fazio Bavastro for antiques; and Hector Bavastro, Jr., for cattle. There are no charges for insurance or storage, and goods are sold within 2 weeks. Settlement is 6 days after the sale. Reserves are accepted, and there is no charge for unsold lots.

Appraisal service is available, at a cost of 3 percent of value.

West Germany

The cultural and commercial centers of West Germany are also its auction centers. Most of the more important auction houses are to be found in Cologne, Frankfurt, Hamburg, Munich, etc. But there are auction houses the length and breadth of the country, most of them also dealers, or tied intimately to a retail organization. Indeed, many houses not only sell properties on consignment but also sell on their own behalf—within, of course, the restrictions outlined by West German law.

The bulk of the more important houses hold only a few sales (4–6) each year, usually in fall and spring. Almost never do the auctions overlap, and for days one can go from auction to auction and see many of the same faces. Usually these are 2- or 3-day affairs, with morning and afternoon sessions. Occasionally, for more important or expensive items, an evening session is scheduled. The sessions are run like clockwork, with the auctioneer carefully regulating the pace. If a catalogue indicates that a particular lot will be offered within a given time period, you can be reasonably sure that will be the case.

Unless a special sale is scheduled (e.g., Expressionist art or photographica), these auctions—whether held by a large house or a smaller one—offer a striking array of properties. It is not unusual for the bigger houses to offer over 3,000 lots, and from time to time a gargantuan sale of over 5,000 lots is held. Keep an eye on the rostrum: if there is a vase with red roses, in some houses you can be sure that whenever a bidder takes a property with what is a new record price, the auctioneer will present him with a rose.

The West German auction houses are strenuous competitors, both on the domestic scene and internationally. They are in business to do business; they are in the marketplace to sell the property they offer at auction at the highest bid possible and will take great care to woo bidders. Such wooing is not limited to the awarding of red roses, and ranges from attractive, thorough catalogues to snappy advertising, from making hotel reservations for prospective known bidders to offering credit (for 30, 60, 90 days, etc.) to bidders known to be big spenders—influential dealers, well-known collectors—even though the house may state that credit is not available.

The more important bidders are assured reserved seats in the auction rooms, though the rooms are open to anyone who wishes to bid. Bidding and sitting are not always the same thing. Indeed, the auction houses welcome prospective bidders, but understandably the West German houses—like their counterparts elsewhere in the world—nurture those bidders likely to spend big sums. In West Germany, bidding is generally done with a numbered card, which is assigned upon registration before the sale. This system assures the house of some control over the auction process, and weeds out known cranks, phonies, and deadbeats. It also facilitates speedy auctions in crowded salerooms, as the auctioneer need only deal with a bidder's number and not consider whether a mumble or the scratching of an eyebrow is a bid.

Should you be interested in submitting mail order bids to those houses which execute them, note that a significant number of West German auction houses will not accept what they consider excessively low bids. Check the order bid form for the limitation, which does vary in range between the houses. Some indicate that they will not accept an order bid two thirds below the catalogue estimate for a given lot; others will not accept a bid 50 percent below the estimate.

For years after the end of World War II, the tendency was for goods to be taken out of West Germany, especially to the United States. There never will be (indeed, there probably never can be) an accurate count of the number of cuckoo clocks, Meissen plates, and 19th-century prints that found their way across the Atlantic. This process is currently being reversed as a consequence of the relative strengths of the German and American economies and currencies. The strength of the deutsche mark and the weakening of the dollar have driven many American bidders from the West German auction rooms. Properties are still being shipped across the Atlantic, but the traffic flow is in the other direction as these goods are put up for auction in West Germany. Consignors include private parties as well as dealers.

In the main, the West German auction market is fair and responsive. Most West German auction houses are vital, efficient, free of bureaucratic excess, and receptive to trends—some of which, of course, they innovate. A West German auction sale is well worth the visit.

Taxes: *Mehrwertsteuer* (Value Added Tax) is charged on the invoice price (i.e., the knockdown price plus the buyer's premium plus shipping costs, if any). MwSt. in most instances is charged at the reduced rate of 6.5 percent of the invoice price, but some few objects are taxed at the full rate of 13 percent. All exports, with the exception of those to EEC countries, having a total invoice value of less than DM457 are exempt from MwSt. Foreign buyers who take possession of property after a sale and export it themselves will be refunded the MwSt., which is collected by the auction house, provided that within a reasonable time they present export documents. In the case of the EEC countries, the buyer must show import documents. No MwSt. is charged on lots exported through the auction house, except exports to EEC countries with a total invoice value of less than DM457.

569. Galerie Gerda Bassenge

Erdener Strasses 5a   Tel. (030) 892 19 32/891 29 09
D-1000 West Berlin 33   Cable: GALBAS BERLIN

Located in the pleasant, leafy Grunewald area of West Berlin, this auction house usually holds sales 4 times a year. Its catalogues are sophisticated in their descriptions of lots, profusely illustrated, and thoroughly indexed—they make bidding easy and a joy. The list of authorities cited is formidable. Emphasis in most sales is on books.

Although each sale includes some items of considerable worth, the average knockdown price per lot is less than DM1,000. In most recent sales, only about 15 percent of the lots sold fetched more than DM999. The house claims an annual turnover of approximately DM2.5 million.

Lots that go unsold at a given sale may be purchased by interested parties; the price is negotiable. The house does buy and sell on its own behalf, "but only according to the few exceptions German law entitles you to."

Contact persons: Gerda Bassenge/Tilman Bassenge

Days/hours of operation: Mon.–Fri. 9 A.M.–6 P.M.

Areas in which general auctions and special sales are held:

Autographs	Paintings
Books	Old Masters
Drawings	19th c. European
Engravings	Modern Art
Etchings	Photographica
	Prints

Sales are advertised in the German daily press and in specialty magazines, such as *Weltkunst*. Forthcoming auctions are listed in each catalogue. Catalogues for each sale are available singly at the house and by order: DM20 West Germany; DM30 elsewhere in Europe; $15 U.S.

Usual viewing procedure: Exhibition begins 2 weeks before the sale. Lots are available for viewing daily 10 A.M.–6 P.M., but some days are for non-Berliners only.

Bidder Information

All auctions are held on premises.

The buyer's premium is 12 percent for recognized dealers and 15 percent for all others. It is not negotiable. Mail order bids are acceptable. Accounts must be settled within 3 weeks after the sale. Non-Germans can pay in their own currency valued at the current exchange rate.

The house does not offer guarantees of authenticity but does accept return of goods that are not as catalogued.

Packing and shipping services are available at a fee.

Consignor Information

Prospective consignors should write or call the house. Minimum value for property accepted (either 1 item or a collection) is DM400.

Commissions are generally 15 percent for dealers, 20 percent for others. The commission is negotiable, "depending on the situation."

Consignors do not pay for insurance on consigned property or for its warehousing. There is no charge for illustrations in the catalogue.

There is no buy-in fee for property that does not sell.

Settlement is made 4–5 weeks after the auction.

Reserves are accepted subject to mutual agreement.

Finder's fees are paid, up to 5 percent of the knockdown price of property sold at auction.

Galerie Gerda Bassenge belongs to Bundesverband Deutscher Versteigerer and to the International League of Antiquarian Booksellers, as well as to Verband Deutscher Antiquare.

570. Kunstauktionen Waltraud Boltz

Bahnhof Strasse 25-27   Tel. (0921) 206 16
D-8580 Bayreuth

Boltz, one of West Germany's newer houses, holds auctions up to 10 times a year. It offers a wide variety of objects, ranging from decorative ironwork to the holdings of an antiques dealer. The house is the outgrowth of a retail operation.

In November 1979, Waltraud Boltz held *"Die 1. Nachttopfauktion der Welt." Nachttöpfe* are chamber pots, an unusual area of collecting, to say the least. The catalogue for this sale, typically for Waltraud Boltz, was splendidly illustrated (in this case more thoroughly illustrated perhaps than one might wish). The catalogue had a fascinating introduction on the "role of the chamber pot in cultural history," which drew on such diverse sources as an 1819 French history of the Venetian Republic, a Wagner opera, and the memoirs of Casanova.

Waltraud Boltz, which is named for its enterprising owner/director, bids fair to do well; it is a growing operation which held 6 auctions in spring 1980 alone.

Contact person: Waltraud Boltz

Days/hours of operation: Mon.–Fri. 9 A.M.–noon, 3–6 P.M.

Areas in which general auctions and special sales are held:

Antique ironwork (such as keys and signs)	Embroidery
Antique textiles	Engravings
Drawings (17th–19th c. Continental)	Etchings
	Toys

Sales are advertised regularly in the German press and in both German and non-German magazines, such as *Weltkunst* and *Apollo*. Catalogues list forthcoming sales.

Catalogues are available singly for each sale at the house and by order, the average price being DM20. Subscription to a fall or spring season set of sales catalogues costs: DM100 West Germany, DM120 elsewhere.

Usual viewing procedure: Exhibition, beginning approximately 3 weeks prior to sale, is daily (including Saturday and Sunday the weekend before the sale), 10 A.M.–noon, 2–6 P.M.

Bidder Information

All auctions are held on the premises.

The buyer's premium is 12 percent for recognized dealers, 15 percent for all others. Accounts must be settled within 10 days of the sale. Mail order bids are acceptable.

The house offers neither guarantees of authenticity nor shipping and packing services. It does offer buyers the right to return within a limited period of time goods that do not prove to be as catalogued.

Consignor Information

Persons wishing to consign property should contact the house. No minimum value is stated, but the goods must be of "good quality." Commissions are 10–12 percent for dealers and institutions, 15 percent for all others.

Reserves are accepted.

Consignors are not charged for warehousing or insurance on their property. They are charged for illustrations in the catalogue.

Consignors are not charged if property goes unsold.

Settlement is made 3–4 weeks after the sale.

The house buys and sells on its own behalf as well.

571. Brandes

Wolfenbütteler Strasse 12   Tel. (0531) 737 32
D-3300 Braunschweig 1   Cable: BUCHBRANDES

Like many of its West German counterparts, Brandes is a retail operation that
also holds auctions. Presented twice yearly (fall and spring), these multisession sales include hundreds of lots.

Located in downtown Braunschweig, a mini-hike from the train station,
Brandes is situated across from a pleasant park, in a cheerfully gabled 3-story
19th-century-style house.

Brandes auctions concentrate on books and decorative graphics. The vast
bulk of the lots offered for sale have estimates of less than DM500.

The owner of Brandes is Ulrich Schneider, a man of energy and varied
interests.

Contact person: Ulrich Schneider

Days/hours of operation: Mon.–Fri. 8 A.M.–5 P.M.

Areas in which general auctions and special sales are held:

Books	Maps
Engravings	Prints
Etchings	

Sales are advertised regularly in the German press. Future sales are announced in the catalogue.

Catalogues are available singly for each sale at the house and by order. Cost is
DM10 West Germany, $7.50 U.S. (including airmail postage).

Usual viewing procedure: Exhibition, during business hours, begins 1 week
before auction; 1 day is solely for foreigners.

Bidder Information

All auctions are held on the premises.

The buyer's premium is 15 percent. It is not negotiable. Accounts must be
settled either right after the auction or on receipt of invoice. Credit
terms are available "only to well-known customers." Credit cards are
not accepted. Mail order bids are acceptable.

Any claims with regard to lots not being as catalogued have to be made within
7 days of receipt of the property. Brandes will not honor any claims
with regard to runs of periodicals, series, bundles, or multipart works.

Packing and shipping services are offered at buyer's expense.

Consignor Information

Prospective consignors should send as detailed a list of property as possible.
The minimum value of a consignment is DM100.

Commission rate is 15–25 percent for private parties, and 15–20 percent for
dealers, the exact charge depending on the quality and quantity of the
material. The commission is negotiable.

Consignors do not pay for warehousing or insurance of consigned property, nor for catalogue illustrations, but they do pay for packing and shipping.

Settlement is made 5 weeks after the sale takes place.

Reserves are accepted.

Appraisal service is available, the cost 3–5 percent of estimated value of the property in question.

The house pays finder's fees, the exact amount depending on the situation.

The house does buy and sell on its own behalf.

Brandes is a member of Verband Deutscher Antiquare and Bundesverband Deutscher Kunstversteigerer.

572. Gernot Dorau

Johann-Georg Strasse 2   Tel. (030) 892 61 98
D-1000 Berlin 31

This firm deals in various aspects of numismatics (including coins and bank notes of various eras, as well as new and antiquarian books about the subject), and in medals. Auctions are held twice yearly, in venues such as the fashionable Hotel Kempinski.

Contact person: Gernot Dorau

Days/hours of operation: Mon.–Fri. 10 A.M.–noon, 4–6 P.M.

Areas in which auctions are held:

     Coins   Medals

Sales are advertised in various international numismatic publications, such as *Money Trend* and *Münzen Revue*.

Catalogues are available singly for each sale; the cost is DM10.

Usual viewing procedure: Exhibition before the sale by appointment and during regular business hours.

Bidder Information

Auctions are held off premises.

The buyer's premium for Germans is 18 percent, which includes the various taxes; for lots taken by foreigners who are shipping the properties out of West Germany, the commission is 15 percent.

Accounts must be settled immediately after the auction, or in the case of mail order bids, which are accepted upon arrangement, upon receipt of an invoice.

The house offers guarantees of authenticity, but will not accept return of lots that are not as catalogued. However, for certain kinds of defects, such as unnoticed chips on a coin, etc., the house will provide a refund if it is claimed within 8 days of receipt.

The house offers shipping and packing services, for which the buyer pays.

Consignor Information

Prospective consignors should write with details. Minimum value for a consignment, of either a series of lots or one, should be DM2,000.
The consignor's commission is 20 percent, but it is negotiable.
Consignors do not pay for catalogue illustrations, insurance, or warehousing.
Goods are usually sold within 3 months of receipt, and settlement is made roughly 6 weeks after sale.
Consigned property that is bought in costs the consignor nothing.
Reserves are accepted upon mutual agreement.

Gernot Dorau buys and sells on its own behalf.

573. F. Dörling

Neuer Wall 40-41   Tel. (040) 36 46 70/36 52 82
D-2000 Hamburg 36   Cable: DOERLINGANT

Buch-und Kunstantiquariat F. Dörling (to use its full name) has been in existence since 1797, a fact ceaselessly mentioned in the firm's literature and advertising. The current owner of this reputable, well-established dealer is Wolfgang K. Goerigk, who is aggressively publicizing the firm's auctions outside West Germany, with some success.

Dörling's auctions, held 3 times a year, are truly gargantuan affairs, even for West Germany, where lots for each auction can run into the thousands. The June 1980 Dörling auction included over 5,700 lots (a goodly number of which were bunches), and the sale ran for 3 days, morning and afternoon. Lots for sale at this auction, typical of the firm's offerings, ranged from the usual art books and 19th-century Continental graphics to a 7-minute 16mm color film of Hamburg as it looked right after the devastating fire bombing of the city by the British in 1943.

The catalogues are remarkably thorough, with first-rate descriptions of the lots for sale, illustrations of the more valuable properties, and an exhaustive index. Interestingly enough, given the worth of some of the lots for sale, there are a significant number of relatively inexpensive items offered. In the June 1980 sale, roughly 10 percent of the items had estimates of less than DM300.

Contact person: Wolfgang Goerigk

Days/hours of operation: Mon.–Fri. 9 A.M.–6 P.M.

Areas in which general auctions and special sales are held:

Art Deco	Glass
Art Nouveau	Islamic Art
Autographs	Japanese Works of Art
Books	Jewelry
Chinese Works of Art	Judaica
Drawings (15th–20th c.)	Manuscripts
Engravings	Maps
Etchings	Nautica

Paintings   Photographica
  Old Master   Postcards
  17th–18th c. British   Posters
  19th c. European   Prints (15th–20th c.)
  Impressionist   Scientific Instruments
  Modern Art   Silver
  Contemporary Art

Sales are advertised in the German press and in international journals and
  yearbooks, such as *American Book Prices Current, Apollo, Connoisseur, Mercato dell'Arte, Weltkunst,* etc. Forthcoming sales are also
  announced in the catalogue.
Catalogues are available singly for each sale and by subscription from the
  house. The annual cost is approximately DM50 for the 3 sales.
Usual viewing procedure: Exhibition begins 2 days prior to the sale, 9 A.M.–6
  P.M. or by appointment.

Bidder Information

Most auctions are held on the premises, but sales can be held elsewhere if
  required.
The buyer's premium is as follows: 15 percent, private individuals; 12 percent,
  dealers; 10 percent, auctioneers. It is not negotiable. Payment is expected immediately upon receipt of invoice for mail order bids; otherwise, accounts must be settled at once. However, credit terms are
  available, upon individual arrangement.
Bids by phone are acceptable if confirmed by prior arrangement in writing.
The house offers for a fee packing and shipping services. Goods that prove to
  be not as catalogued may be returned up to 3 days after receipt, but
  not more than 3 weeks after the sale.

Consignor Information

Persons wishing to consign property should write and send details and if necessary photographs. Minimum value for goods to be accepted for consignment is DM100.
The commission structure for consignors who are not dealers is 10–20 percent,
  depending on the value of the property. The commission structure for
  dealers is 10–12 percent. Commissions are negotiable, and the final
  figure depends upon the situation.
Consignors do not pay for insurance or warehousing, but are charged for catalogue illustrations.
Consigned property is usually sold within 3–4 months of receipt and settlement is approximately 2 months after the auction.
Reserves are accepted.
There is no charge if goods consigned are bought in.

Appraisal service is available. The cost varies and application should be made
  to the house.

The house does pay a finder's fee, but the figure depends on the value and
situation.

F. Dörling belongs to Bundesverband Deutscher Kunstversteigerer, and
Chambre Syndicale de l'Estampe, du Dessin et du Tableau.

The house buys and sells on its own behalf.

574. Roland A. Exner Kunsthandel-Auktionen

Am Ihmeufer   Tel. (0511) 44 44 84
D-3000 Hannover 91

Also a dealer, Exner holds auctions approximately 4 times a year, more if
necessary. As with most West German auction houses, these sales are massive
and wide-ranging: the more than 250-page catalogue for a June 1980 2-day
sale enumerated over 2,000 lots in such areas as books, ceramics, furniture,
glass, graphics, jewelry, and oil paintings.

A good example of the multifaceted auction houses that are to be found
scattered throughout West Germany and are the backbone of the country's
fine arts auction market, Exner is intelligently run, staffed with a number of
in-house experts, fair in its dealings, and energetic in seeking consignments.
The house announced an annual turnover of DM5 million for 1979.

Contact person: Roland A. Exner

Days/hours of operation: Mon.–Fri. 9 A.M.–1 P.M., 3–6 P.M.

Areas in which general auctions and special sales are held:

Art Deco	Paintings
Art Nouveau	Old Master
Books	17th c. British
Ceramics (European)	18th c. British
Chinese Works of Art	19th c. European
Clocks and Watches	Impressionist
Drawings	Modern Art
Engravings	Contemporary Art
Etchings	Pewter
Furniture	Porcelain
Glass	Rugs
Japanese Works of Art	Silver

Sales are advertised regularly in daily newspapers and in magazines such as
Weltkunst.

Catalogues for each sale are available singly at the house and by order. Subscriptions to a season's catalogues cost: DM70 West Germany, DM90
Western Europe, DM110 elsewhere (including airmail postage).

Usual viewing procedure: Exhibition usually begins a week prior to sale: weekdays 10 A.M.–8 P.M.; weekends 2–8 P.M.

Bidder Information

All auctions are held on premises.

The buyer's premium is 12 percent for registered dealers, 17 percent for all others. The buyer's premium includes Value Added Tax. Accounts must be settled within 10 days of the auction, except that overseas bidders have up to 3 weeks. Credit cards are not accepted. Mail order bids are acceptable.

The house offers buyers packing and shipping services for a fee.

The house offers guarantees of authenticity and will accept return of goods that are not as catalogued.

Consignor Information

Those wishing to consign property should make contact by telephone or in writing; if the latter, a photograph or description of the property to be consigned should be included. There is no stated minimum value for property to be accepted, but it must be "good quality."

Commissions are 12 percent for dealers, 17 percent for all others. Commissions are not negotiable.

Consignors pay for illustrations in the catalogue (DM75 per picture) and for insurance (depending on value, but usually 5 percent). The consignor is not charged for warehousing or for packing and shipping of consigned property.

Settlement is made 4–8 weeks after the property is auctioned.

Consigned property is usually sold 8–10 weeks after being received by the house.

Reserves are accepted, depending on the property.

Appraisal service is available, and there is no charge if the house is consigned the property for auction. Otherwise, the fee is negotiable.

Roland A. Exner Kunsthandel-Auktionen is a member of Bundesverband Deutscher Kunst-und Antiquitätenhändel.

575. Hartung & Karl

Karolinenplatz 5a   Tel. (089) 28 40 34
D-8000 Munich 2   Cable: BUCHAUKTION MÜNCHEN

Hartung & Karl, a well-run, specialized auction house, has a small retail operation, but concentrates on its 2 annual sales. The house was established relatively recently—its first auction sale was in 1972—but the Hartung family has been active in the German fine arts auction market since well before World War II, the older Hartung having handled autographs, books, and manuscripts for Karl & Faber, a veteran Munich auction house (which see).

And thereby hangs a tale. The Karl in both houses is the same, active in the day-to-day management of the family-owned Karl & Faber, and a limited "sleeping partner" in Hartung & Karl. The two firms cooperate to the extent that each refers prospective consignors to the other if the goods in question would be better sold there. Annual turnover is approximately DM5 million.

Respected by the trade, Hartung & Karl auctions properties within a wide range of prices, but despite the occasional stellar attraction, the bulk of the lots at most sales falls within the DM100–DM800 range. The catalogues, which are a joy to read, are indexed and almost encyclopedic in content. Sales are held twice annually (usually May and November).

Contact person: Felix Hartung

Days/hours of operation: Mon.–Fri. 9 A.M.–1 P.M., 3–6 P.M.

Areas in which sales are held:

Autographs	Manuscripts	Prints
Books	Maps	

Sales are advertised regularly in German newspapers and trade journals. Future sale dates are announced in the back of the catalogue.

Catalogues for each sale are available singly at the house and by order (DM12–DM20 West Germany, DM35–40 elsewhere, including airmail postage).

Usual viewing procedure: Exhibition begins 1 week prior to sale, daily 9 A.M.–1 P.M., 3–6 P.M. One day is given over to prospective buyers from out of town.

Bidder Information

All auctions are held on premises.

The buyer's premium is 12 percent for registered dealers, 15 percent for all others. Accounts must be settled immediately after the auction. Mail order bids are accepted. Credit cards are not accepted.

During an auction, bids will be raised approximately 10 percent, or at least DM5, to DM500; DM10 to DM1,000, etc.

The house offers packing and shipping services, cost to be billed to the buyer.

The house does not offer guarantees of authenticity, but will accept return of goods that are not as catalogued; such claims must be made 3 days after receipt of shipment (the right to return lapses 3 weeks after the end of the sale).

Consignor Information

Those wishing to consign property should contact the house in writing and list items to be consigned (for books, information should include author, title, year of publication) and minimum prices accepted. Minimum value for a consignment is DM500.

Commission structure is 25 percent for objects knocked down below DM500, 20 percent for those knocked down for DM500 and above.

If a property is consigned without reserve, the consignor pays nothing but shipping costs; if there is a reserve and the goods remain unsold, the consignor has to pay 5 percent of the reserve fixed.

Settlement is made 4–8 weeks after the auction takes place.

Reserves are accepted, but only on items the house estimates to be worth at least DM500.

Finder's fees are paid: usually 5 percent of the hammer price of consigned property.

Hartung & Karl is a member of Bundesverband Deutscher Kunstversteigerer and the International League of Antiquarian Booksellers.

576. Hauswedell & Nolte
Pöseldorfer Weg 1   Tel. (040) 44 83 66
D-2000 Hamburg 13   Cable: HAUSNOLTE

One of West Germany's more important auction houses, Hauswedell & Nolte was founded in 1927 by the learned and shrewd Dr. Ernst Hauswedell, one of the more important and engaging personalities on the German auction scene. The firm, which held its first auction in 1930, is also an important and respected antiquarian book and fine arts dealer. Ernst Nolte, who was not even born when the business was founded, became a partner in the 1960s, and in 1976 assumed the sole proprietorship of the firm. The venerable Dr. Hauswedell, however, did not retire entirely but continued many of his activities, including the annual publication of *Jahrbuch des Auktionspreise für Bücher, Manuskripte und Autographien.* A German counterpart to *American Book Prices Current* and equally useful, *Jahrbuch* covers the prices realized at auction in the German-speaking world of books, autographs, and manuscripts.

Hauswedell & Nolte has continued to thrive under Nolte's astute direction. Sales are usually held 3 times a year. There are 2 sales (normally in the spring and fall) of books, autographs, and manuscripts, as well as various aspects of non-European art. The most important sale, that of important works of art, which attracts bidders from all over the world, takes place "regularly at the beginning of June." Most of the firm's sales are held in Hauswedell & Nolte's pleasant quarters in an attractive house in one of the city's more fashionable neighborhoods.

As with many German auctions, each sale is massive, numbering hundreds of lots and taking place over a 2- or 3-day period with morning and afternoon sessions. At the June fine arts auction, lots on the average fetch well over DM1,000. At the other auctions, the average lot is sold for considerably less. Annual turnover, it is estimated, is over DM15 million.

Contact persons: Ernst Nolte, Klaus Hänel, Gabriele Braun

Days/hours of operation: Mon–Fri. 9 A.M.–5 P.M., Sat. 9 A.M. –1 P.M.

Areas in which general auctions and special sales are held:

Art Deco	Maps
Art Nouveau	Netsuke
Autographs	Paintings
Books	Old Master
Chinese Works of Art	19th c. European
Drawings (19th–20th c.)	Modern Art
Engravings	Contemporary Art
Etchings	Pre-Columbian Art
Japanese Works of Art	Prints (19th–20th c.)
Manuscripts	

Sales are advertised through mailings, advertisements in the German as well as the European press, and in specialized magazines, such as *Weltkunst*. Catalogues also announce forthcoming sales.

Catalogues for each sale are available singly at the house and by order; the price varies, depending on the size of the catalogue: the fall 1979 catalogue cost DM20 Germany, Fr40 France, £5 U.K., $15 U.S. (including airmail postage).

Usual viewing procedure: One week before the sale takes place, during regular business hours. Normally 1 or 2 days of the exhibition are given over to non-Germans.

Bidder Information

Auctions are generally held on premises.

There is a buyer's premium, which is as follows: 10 percent to auctioneers, 12 percent to dealers, 15 percent to all others. Accounts must be settled within 3 weeks after the auction. Credit terms are available, subject to mutual agreement.

Mail order bids are accepted.

Packing and shipping services are available, but are charged to the buyer. Buyers are offered the opportunity to return goods that prove to be not as catalogued, but only up to 3 days after receipt of the goods and in any case no later than 3 weeks after the auction. The house does not guarantee the completeness of serial runs, multivolume series, bundles of papers, and will not accept returns of these.

Consignor Information

Those wishing to consign property should write or telephone, providing as much detail as possible.

The commission structure depends on the quality of the consignment and ranges from 10 to 15 percent. The commission is negotiable, depending on the situation, and differs for private individuals, dealers, and institutions.

Consignors do not pay for catalogue illustrations, nor for warehousing or insurance with regard to consigned property.

Reserves are accepted.

There is no charge if goods are unsold.

Settlement is made 6 weeks after the auction.

Appraisal service is available at 2 percent of the estimated value of the property.

The house pays finder's fees, subject to negotiation.

Trade association memberships include Bundesverband Deutscher Kunstversteigerer, Verband Deutscher Antiquare, and the International League of Antiquarian Booksellers.

577. Karl & Faber
Amiraplatz 3 (Luitpoldblock)   Tel. (089) 22 18 65/66
D-8000 Munich 2   Cable: KARLANTI

Karl & Faber, well known as an established dealer, also holds auctions twice
yearly, fall and spring. The house held its first auction in May 1927: a sale of
German Baroque literature. The May 1980 sales included Old Masters, modern art, posters, and decorative arts.

Head of house Louis Karl also holds a proprietary interest in Hartung &
Karl (which see), but is not active in its operations. However, the two houses
do cooperate and avoid selling the same kind of consignment (thus books generally are sold by Hartung & Karl, Old Masters by Karl & Faber, etc.).

While each sale does include expensive items—a 1979 sale, for example,
included a Kirchner oil that went for over DM150,000—the average lot sells
for less than DM2,000. Occasionally the house will mount a specialized theme
sale, as was the case with sale 150 (November 1979), composed of German
19th-century drawings and aquarelles, predominantly from the Romantic
period.

Contact persons: Louis Karl/Klaus Dietz

Days/hours of operation: Mon.–Fri. 9 A.M.–1 P.M., 3–6 P.M.

Areas in which sales are held (incl. contact people):

Drawings (18th–19th c. Continental)	(Mr. Karl)
Maps	(Mrs. Gutzeit)
Paintings	
18th–19th c. European	(Mr. Schlottke)
Impressionist	(Mr. Dietz)
Modern Art	(Mr. Dietz)
Prints (18th–19th c. Continental)	(Messrs. Dietz and Karl)

Sales are advertised regularly in the German press and in various magazines,
in Germany and elsewhere in Europe.

Catalogues for each sale are available singly at the house and by order at
DM20. Subscriptions to a season's catalogues cost: DM70 West Germany and Western Europe; $35 U.S. (including airmail postage).

Usual viewing procedure: All items are exhibited on premises beginning 2
weeks prior to sale—weekdays, 9 A.M.–1 P.M., 3–6 P.M., except
Wednesday, 9 A.M.–1 P.M.; Sunday 10 A.M.–1 P.M.

Bidder Information

All sales are held on premises.

The buyer's premium is 15 percent of the knockdown price. Accounts must be
settled within 3 weeks of the auction. Credit cards are not accepted.

Mail order bids are executed.

Bidding is in the following increments: 10 percent or at least DM1 to DM500,
at least DM5 to DM1,000, at least DM10 to DM10,000, etc.

The house offers buyers packing and shipping services.

The house works on the assumption that each buyer who attends has had the chance to view the objects, and therefore it will accept return of goods not as catalogued from those who have put in mail order bids, the time limits being 3 days after receipt of the goods and no later than 3 weeks after the auction.

Consignor Information

Those wishing to consign property should contact the house by telephone or in writing, being prepared to give price ranges expected, if any. Writers should enclose photographs of items difficult to identify from description.

Commissions are 20 percent per item to value of DM1,000 and 15 percent thereafter. The commission is not negotiable and the house assures that there is no separate rate structure for dealers or institutions.

Consignors are not charged for insurance or for warehousing consigned property.

Minimum value is DM300 per item or DM500 for a variety of items.

Deadline for delivery of consigned goods is 2 months before sale; settlement is made 6–8 weeks after the sale.

Reserves are accepted only on property valued over DM1,000.

There is no charge for consigned property not sold unless a reserve was in effect, in which case a mutually agreed upon fee is charged.

Appraisal service is available. There is no fee if goods are put up for auction. Otherwise, charges are according to value: up to DM5,000, the charge is 5 percent, with a minimum of DM50; DM5,000–DM30,000, 3 percent, minimum DM200; over DM30,000, the charge is by mutual agreement.

The house pays a finder's fee of 2 percent of the knockdown price.

The house buys and sells on its own behalf.

Karl & Faber is a member of Bundesverband Deutscher Kunstversteigerer and Verband Deutscher Antiquare.

578. Graf Klenau Ohg Nachf

Maximilian Strasse 32   Tel. (089) 22 22 81/82
D-8000 Munich 1   Cable: KLENAUKTION

Fascinating objects are auctioned by Graf Klenau as a result of its specializing in certain areas. Recent sales have included medals and decorations from Napoleonic France, the 1914 Ukraine, and present-day Mexico; medieval and Renaissance weapons, such as crossbows, halberds, and rapiers; and under the heading "Militaria," a pair of slippers belonging to Emperor Franz Joseph of Austria, late-19th-century French officers' dress hats, a copy of the *Daily Mail* commemorating the coronation of Elizabeth II of Great Britain, and Nazi impedimenta such as Hitler drawings given to Albert Speer, elegant photos of an opulent picnic basket given to Hermann Göring, and various ideological tomes and picture books from the days of the Third Reich.

Graf Klenau is basically a dealer, and the saleroom is in its pleasant museum-like quarters on a main street of the city. Most lots sell quite reasonably; at a 1980 sale of antique weapons the average lot went for less than DM1,250 (exclusive of buyer's premium) and the most expensive object (DM36,000) was a signed late-16th-century rapier with a proved provenance. The directors of Graf Klenau are Ernst Blass and Wolfgang Hermann, who also handle the auctions; they have written various standard works on their areas of specialty (Hermann on militaria and Blass on Prussian decorations). Auctions are held 14–16 times a year.

Contact persons: Ernst Blass/Wolfgang Hermann

Days/hours of operation: Mon.–Fri. 9 A.M.–noon, 2–5 P.M.

Areas in which general auctions and special sales are held:

Arms and Armor	Militaria
Autographs	Pre-Columbian Art
Ethnologica	Primitive Money
Medals	

Sales are advertised regularly in the German press, such as *Süddeutsche Zeitung,* and in specialty magazines, such as *Weltkunst.*

Catalogues for specific sales are available by mail order or at Graf Klenau. A year's subscription to all catalogues costs DM80 in West Germany, $55 U.S. (includes airmail postage). Individuals can subscribe to catalogues just for sales in Orders and Decorations (DM30; $20), Militaria and Arms (DM30; $20), and Primitive Money and Ethnologica (DM20; $15).

Usual viewing procedure: Exhibition begins 1 week prior to sale, Mon.–Fri. 10 A.M.–1 P.M., 3–6 P.M.; Sat. 10 A.M.–2 P.M.

Bidder Information

All auctions are held on premises.

The buyer's premium is 15 percent and negotiable. Credit cards are not accepted. Mail order bids will be executed. Accounts must be settled in cash immediately after the sale (checks are accepted only if prior arrangements have been made); mail bidders have 10 days from receipt of invoice to settle.

The house offers guarantees of authenticity, the opportunity to return goods that prove not as catalogued, and packing and shipping services (at the buyer's cost).

Consignor Information

Those wishing to consign property should write enclosing a description and/or a photo of property to be consigned. Minimum value is DM500 for property to be accepted.

Commissions charged to consignors are on a sliding scale of 20 percent, 15 percent, and 10 percent, the cost depending on the price a lot fetches. The commission is negotiable, "depending on situation." The commission charged dealers is 10 percent.

Consignors do not pay for illustrations in catalogue, insurance on consigned property, packing and shipping of consigned property, or warehousing.

Goods are usually sold 2 months after consignment.

Settlement is made 6–8 weeks after property is auctioned.

There are no fees if an item does not sell.

Reserves are accepted.

Consignments are accepted from institutions, dealers, and private individuals.

Graf Klenau pays finder's fees.

Appraisal service is available; the fee is negotiable.

579. Numismatik Lanz München

Promenadeplatz 9   Tel. (089) 29 90 70
D-8000 Munich 2   Telex: 05-22844

Dr. Hubert Lanz is an important numismatic dealer. Twice yearly he holds auctions which feature a wide array of ancient and medieval coins, coins and medals of the Holy Roman Empire and Austria-Hungary, and coins and medals of West Germany and the surrounding countries. Sales are held off the premises in the posh Bayrischer Hof hotel, which is right by Lanz's premises.

Contact person: Dr. Hubert Lanz

Days/hours of operation: Mon.–Fri. 9 A.M.–1 P.M. and by appt.

Sales are advertised in the important numismatics newspapers and magazines of various countries, and "cards are sent to about 10,000 customers asking if they want to receive the next catalogue."

Catalogues are available singly for each sale: DM20 Western Europe; $10 U.S. (including airmail postage).

Usual viewing procedure: During regular business hours 6 weeks before the sale, and at special exhibition the day before the sale.

Bidder Information

All auctions are held off premises (see above).

The buyer's premium is 12 percent. Accounts must be settled immediately, except for bids executed by the house, which must be settled within 8 days of the sale. Mail order bids are acceptable.

The house offers successful bidders packing and shipping services; the house will accept return of goods that are not as catalogued.

Consignor Information

Potential consignors should write to Dr. Lanz. The minimum value for a collection to be accepted is DM300; the minimum value for an individual piece is DM1,000. "The average consignment should have a value of DM500, at least."

The normal commission rate is 20 percent for nondealers, 15 percent for recognized dealers and institutions, although in all instances the rate depends on the material consigned.

Consignors do not pay for catalogue illustrations, or for warehousing, packing, shipping, or insurance of consigned property.

Settlement is made 45 days after the auction; there is no fee if goods go unsold.

Reserves are not accepted.

The house pays finder's fees, the fee depending on the material consigned.

Appraisal service is available, the fee negotiable.

The house belongs to Verband der Deutschen Münzenhändler.

580. Kunsthaus Lempertz

Neumarkt 3   Tel. (0221) 21 02 51/52
D-5000 Cologne 1   Cable: LEMPARTE

The history of Lempertz and its direct predecessors (firms incorporated through either merger or acquisition) stretches back into the early 19th century. The modern history of the firm begins with the assumption of control by the Hanstein family, who since the turn of the century have built up and maintained the fortunes of the business. For visitors to Cologne, whether the Kaiser in days of yore or multinational business executives today, Lempertz always has been worth a visit.

Henrik Rolf Hanstein, the fourth generation of his family to assume direction of Lempertz, did so in his twenties because of tragic circumstances: his father died in an automobile accident while still relatively young. The latest Hanstein, though barely 30, has proved himself. He embodies the family attributes of energy, ambition, and imagination. Lempertz under his direction remains a vital, innovative firm, among the very first rank of West German auction houses.

Lempertz, which has over 40 employees, is located in somewhat cramped but adequate quarters which were built in downtown Cologne after World War II. The house holds 2–3 auctions each fall and spring. They number hundreds of lots and usually extend over 2–3 days of morning and afternoon sessions. The fare for these sales is varied. A 3-day June 1980 auction of *Alte Kunst* included paintings, icons, sculpture, porcelain, glass, silver, furniture, rugs, tapestries, and Egyptian artifacts from over 2,000 years ago. Lempertz was among the first West German auction houses to hold photographica sales. The catalogues are straightforward and to the point, like the house, without frills. The house does buy and sell on its own behalf.

Located on the premises is a gallery, Lempertz Contempora, which mounts various exhibits during the year, sells a variety of modern art, and represents some of the more important West German artists, such as Gerhard Marcks. A Hanstein was active in the organization of the Bundesverband Deutscher

Kunstversteigerer, and an officer of the house (Dr. Schütte) is currently its president.

Prices at Lempertz vary dramatically with the quality of the objects put up for sale. The June 1980 *Alte Kunst* auction had few lots estimated for less than DM1,000, and a significant number fetched much higher prices. On the other hand, at the sale of East Asian art objects a week earlier, few lots were estimated at more than DM500 and many sold for much less.

Lempertz has an American representative: Ernest M. Werner, 17 East 96th Street, New York, NY 10028, tel. (212) 289-5666. Mr. Werner, who is an art dealer with his own gallery, helps interested parties to place bids or consign properties, advises about German auction procedures, etc.

Contact person: H. R. Hanstein

Days/hours of operation: Mon.–Fri. 9 A.M.–1 P.M., 2–5 P.M.; Sat. 9 A.M.–1 P.M.

Areas in which general auctions and special sales are held:

Art Deco	Paintings
Art Nouveau	Old Master
Books	17th–18th c. British
Chinese Works of Art	19th c. European
Clocks and Watches	Pre-20th c. U.S.
Drawings (19th–20th c.)	Impressionist
Embroidery	Modern Art
Engravings	Contemporary Art
Etchings	Pewter
Furniture (to beg. of 19th c.)	Photographica
Glass	Porcelain
Islamic Art	Posters
Japanese Works of Art	Prints (modern)
Jewelry	Rugs
Medieval Works of Art	Scientific Instruments
Netsuke	Silver

Sales are advertised in German newspapers and the international press, such as the *New York Times,* and in various magazines, such as *Weltkunst.* Future sales are announced in catalogues.

Catalogues for each sale are available singly at the house and by order, usually for DM20. Catalogues are also available for spring/fall sales in a given area, at some saving (e.g., Modern Art in 1980 cost DM35 West Germany; £10 U.K.; $30 U.S., including airmail postage; Fr95 France).

Usual viewing procedure: Exhibition is 1 week before sale; viewing is during regular business hours.

Bidder Information

All sales are held on premises.

The buyer's premium is 12 percent for dealers, 15 percent for private parties.

Mail order bids are acceptable. Bidders attending the sale in person must settle accounts at once unless other arrangements have been made. Other bidders must pay on receipt of invoice.

The house makes no guarantees of authenticity and will not accept return of goods that are not as catalogued, although it "is prepared to forward justified complaints made by the buyer within the statutory warranty period to the seller who entered the respective item or items, provided that the auctioneer is in a position to do so." Shipment of goods purchased is at the expense and risk of the buyer.

Consignor Information

Those wishing to consign property should either write in detail or request special forms.

Commissions are 10–15 percent of the hammer price, depending on the consignor, the value of the lot, and prior arrangements.

Consignors pay for illustration of property in the catalogue and for shipping and packing of consignment; consignors do not pay for warehousing or for insurance of consigned property.

Consignor's cost for a buy-in depends on arrangements made at time of consignment.

Reserves are accepted.

Settlement is made within 4 weeks maximum.

Lempertz pays finder's fees, the fee subject to special arrangement.

Appraisal service is available, the cost dependent on negotiation and on whether the goods are put up for auction by Lempertz.

Lempertz belongs to Bundesverband Deutscher Kunstversteigerer.

581. Stuttgarter Kunstauktionshaus Dr. Fritz Nagel

Mörikestrasse 17-19　　　　　　　Tel. (0711) 61 33 87/77
D-7000 Stuttgart 1

Nagel is best known for the two first-rate rug and tapestry auctions it conducts annually, which are of international interest. In addition, the house holds more general auctions 4 times a year, where the quality of lots also generally is quite high.

Nagel was organized in 1924 and has held over 280 auctions; the more general ones are multisession sales which offer hundreds of lots. The house is located in pleasant quarters just outside the center of the city. Nagel also deals in many of the kinds of objects that it handles on consignment for auction.

The quality of the cataloguing is very high. Catalogues for the rug sales are models of their kind, prepared with great intelligence and much scholarship.

Contact person:　　　　　　　Fritz Nagel

Days/hours of operation:　　　Mon.–Fri. 8:30 A.M.–6 P.M.

Areas in which general auctions and special sales are held (incl. contact people):

Furniture	Paintings
(Mr. Nagel, Jr.)	Old Master (Dr. Zargermann)
Glass	19th c. European, esp. S. Ger.
Japanese Works of Art	(Dr. Zargermann)
Jewelry (Miss Lauche)	Pewter (Mr. Nagel, Jr.)
Netsuke	Porcelain (Mr. Nagel, Jr.)
	Rugs (Mrs. Eder)

Sales are advertised in German newspapers and in German and international art journals. Future sales are announced in catalogues. A "preview letter" is available without cost to those who request to be put on the mailing list.

Catalogues for each sale are available singly at the house and by order. Subscriptions for the 4 regular sales are DM50, plus airmail charges where necessary; for the 2 rug sales, DM30, plus airmail charges where necessary.

Usual viewing procedure: Exhibition begins 3 days in advance of the sale, usually during regular business hours.

Bidder Information

All sales are held on premises.

The buyer's premium is 12 percent. It is not negotiable. Credit terms are available by mutual agreement. Accounts must be settled within 8 days of the sale. Mail order bids are accepted.

Guarantees of authenticity are offered "in special cases."

The house offers packing and shipping services, at the buyer's expense; goods that prove to be not as catalogued may be returned within the short time period allowed.

Consignor Information

Those wishing to consign property should send in a detailed list of the objects, if possible with photos and estimate prices. There is no minimum value for acceptance.

Commissions are 12 percent for dealers and institutions, 15 percent for private parties. Commissions are negotiable.

Consignors are not charged for warehousing or for packing and shipping. Consignors are charged for insurance (4 percent of the estimate) and for catalogue illustrations (full page DM160, half page DM80).

Reserves are accepted.

Goods are usually sold 6–8 weeks after receipt; settlement is 3–4 weeks after auction.

Appraisal service is available. The cost is 1–3 percent of the value of the item(s) being appraised.

Nagel pays a finder's fee of 1–3 percent, "in special cases, 5 percent."

The house is a member of Bundesverband Deutscher Kunstversteigerer and Bundesverband Deutscher Kunst-und Antiquitätenhändel.

582. Neumeister Münchener Kunstauktionshaus KG

Barer Strasse 37   Tel. (089) 28 30 11
D-8000 Munich 40   Cable: KUNSTMITTLER

A correspondent for the authoritative *Frankfurter Allgemeine Zeitung* has estimated that Neumeister's annual turnover of approximately DM25 million represents almost 10 percent of the total yearly gross of that country's fine arts auction houses. Presiding over the company's vigorous, intelligent policies is the energetic Rudolf Neumeister, who assumed control of the auction house in 1958, some twenty-four years after its founding.

The house regularly schedules 6 annual sales (totaling approximately 12,000 lots) and holds special sales as necessary. Such was the 1979 auction of the notable Oertel Collection, built around medieval and Renaissance wooden and ceramic sculptures, which realized over DM4 million in less than 75 minutes of spirited bidding. Actually, the house estimates that the average lot sells for a bid in the neighborhood of DM1,000.

Some 40 employees (including a number of recognized fine arts historians), an inviting saleroom, and offices are located in a pleasant blend of landmark and modern architecture in central Munich. Indeed, the modern addition won a design prize in the late 1970s for blending harmoniously with the much older original building.

Contact person: Rudolf Neumeister

Days/hours of operation: Mon.–Fri. 9 A.M.–1 P.M., 3–5:45 P.M.

Areas in which general auctions and special sales are held:

Arms and Armor	Netsuke
Art Deco	Paintings
Art Nouveau	Old Master
Chinese Works of Art	19th c. European
Clocks and Watches	Impressionist
Dolls	Modern Art
Drawings (16th–20th c.)	Contemporary Art
Embroidery	South German School (19th c.)
Engravings	Pewter
Etchings	Porcelain
Furniture (17th–20th c.)	Postcards
Glass	Pre-Columbian Art
Islamic Art	Prints (15th–20th c.)
Japanese Works of Art	Rugs
Jewelry	Scientific Instruments
Judaica	Sculpture (16th–20th c.)
Maps	Silver
Medieval Works of Art	Toys
Musical Instruments	

Sales are advertised regularly in such daily newspapers as *Frankfurter Allgemeine Zeitung* and *Süddeutsche Zeitung*.

Catalogues for each sale are available singly at the house and by order (DM20–DM30 each). Subscriptions to a season's catalogues cost in 1980: DM130 West Germany, DM150 Western Europe, $120 U.S. (including airmail postage).

Usual viewing procedure: Exhibition begins 8 days prior to sale. Hours are Monday–Friday 9:30 A.M.–1 P.M., 3–6 P.M.; Thursday to 7:30 P.M.; Saturday 9:30 A.M.–1 P.M.

Bidder Information

All auctions are held on premises.

The buyer's premium is 12 percent for registered dealers, 15 percent for all others. The buyer's premium is negotiable. Accounts must be settled within 10 days of the auction. Credit cards are not accepted. Mail order bids will be executed.

The house does not offer buyers packing or shipping services.

The house does not offer guarantees of authenticity, but will accept return of goods that are not as catalogued.

Consignor Information

Those wishing to consign property should contact the house by telephone or in writing; if the latter, a photograph of the property to be consigned should be included. Minimum value for property accepted is DM80.

Commissions generally are 12 percent for dealers; for all others, 15 percent per item to DM1,000 and 10 percent per item over DM1,000. The commission fees are negotiable.

Consignors pay for illustrations in the catalogue (DM170 for one-page reproductions), for insurance on consigned property (depending on value, but usually 3 percent), and for packing and shipping of consigned property. Consignors are not charged for warehousing.

Settlement is made 3 weeks after the property is auctioned.

Consignors must pay to the house DM30 for each item that does not sell.

Reserves are accepted.

Appraisal service is available: the fee for items valued up to DM100,000 is 1.5 percent; thereafter the fee is negotiable.

Neumeister Münchener Kunstauktionshaus is a member of Bundesverband Deutscher Kunstversteigerer.

583. Petzold KG– Photographica

Maximilian Strasse 36   Tel. (0821) 3 37 25
D-8900 Augsburg 11   Telex: 533298

This highly specialized, somewhat unusual auction house offers only photographica and fields it considers related. However, the house casts its nets wide in defining photographica—a typical Petzold sale will offer not only the expected historical and classical camera equipment (including highly desirable Leica items), photographs, daguerreotypes, and photo albums, but also magic lanterns, books about film and photography, graphics touching on photography, such as Daumier caricatures, scientific and optical instruments, posters, such as Kodak wall advertisements, and what one catalogue simply described as "kitsch."

Contact person: Michael Kahan

Days/hours of operation: Mon.–Fri. 9 A.M.– 1 P.M., 3–5:30 P.M.

Frequency of auctions: Four times a year

Areas in which general auctions and special sales are held:

Photographica   Postcards   Stamps

Sales are advertised worldwide in such magazines as *History of Photography: An International Quarterly,* and such newspapers as *Financial Times,* as well as domestically in the daily press, such as *Süddeutsche Zeitung.*

Catalogues are available singly for each sale at the house or by order (DM30 West Germany, DM35 Europe, DM40 U.S.). Subscriptions to a season's catalogues, including postage, cost: DM82.50 Germany, DM85 Europe, DM105 U.S.

Usual viewing procedure: Exhibition begins 1 week prior to the sale date. Hours vary.

Bidder Information

All auctions are held on the premises.

The buyer's premium is 15 percent and not negotiable. Accounts must be settled immediately by buyers present, 14 days after receipt of invoice for written or phone bids. Phone bids have to be confirmed in writing at least a day before the sale. Credit cards are not accepted. Credit is available to museums or institutions. Mail order bids are accepted.

The house offers buyers packing and shipping services for a fee.

The house offers a limited guarantee: items proving to be fakes will be taken back; catalogue errors will be taken back only if the error, to use the house definition, is "basically important"; condition is not a ground for return. Petzold uses a letter grading system (A to E) to inform collectors about the condition of camera equipment and accessories, and bidders are expected to familiarize themselves with that system. Such items are sold as collector's items, and exact function of the shutter or other parts, or particular optical performance, are not guaranteed.

Consignor Information

Those wishing to consign property should write Mr. Kahan, including as complete a list as possible of what is to be consigned. If the collection is very large, the prospective consignor should request a visit in lieu of sending a complete listing.

Commissions are 17.5 percent on the first DM1,000 fetched by an item sold (with a minimum charge of DM20), 15 percent on the next DM19,000, and 12 percent thereafter. Commissions are negotiable on consignments in excess of DM50,000.

Consignors do not have to pay for illustrations in the catalogue, insurance on consigned property, or warehousing. Consignors must pay for shipping and packing.

Goods are usually sold 2–3 months after consignment, and accounts are settled 4–5 weeks after the property is auctioned.

There are no fees if an item does not sell.

Reserves are accepted.

Appraisal service is available; the fee is determined by the costs involved (travel, etc.). If the goods are later consigned to auction at Petzold, the appraisal fee is refunded.

Petzold KG–Photographica buys and sells on its own behalf.

584. Reiss & Auvermann
Zum Talblick 2   Tel. (06174) 69 47/48
D-6246 Glashütten im Taunus 1   Telex: 410643
                              Cable: INTERBUCH KÖNIGSTEIN

Auvermann & Reiss KG is a well-known dealer. The firm's vast stock includes antiquarian books and runs of hard-to-get back numbers of diverse periodicals. Reiss & Auvermann oHG is an affiliated firm which since 1970 has successfully auctioned old and rare books, maps, and decorative prints.

Located in a posh suburb of Frankfurt, Reiss & Auvermann holds 2 auctions a year, in April and in October. These are massive affairs, usually numbering well over 3,500 lots each, which take several days, with morning and afternoon sessions.

The catalogues are carefully prepared. Though a number of valuable items are offered, the average lot goes for around DM500. An indication of the auction house's success is the fact that its annual turnover is approximately DM7 million.

Contact person: G. M. Reiss

Days/hours of operation: Mon.–Thurs. 9 A.M.–5:30 P.M., Fri. 9 A.M.–4 P.M.

Areas in which sales are held:

        Books   Maps   Prints

Sales are advertised in the German daily press, in German and international magazines, and in specialized journals, such as *The Map Collector.*

Catalogues for each sale are available singly at the house and by order, but not by subscription. Cost: DM20 West Germany; $15 U.S. (including airmail postage). Bidders at a previous auction are automatically added to the mailing list announcing availability of catalogues.

Usual viewing procedure: Exhibition begins 2 weeks prior to the sale and takes place during regular business hours, as well as Saturdays.

Bidder Information

All sales are on premises.

The buyer's premium is 12 percent for dealers, 15 percent for private parties. Credit is available upon mutual agreement. Otherwise, all successful bidders must settle accounts immediately, except that institutions have 3 weeks to pay.

Mail order bids are executed.

"Any nonauthentic lot can be returned within 4 weeks," as can any lot that does not prove to be as catalogued, but "claims must be given to auctioneer within 3 days after receipt of goods."

Consignor Information

Anyone interested in consigning should write to the house, providing a detailed list of property to be sold. If necessary, Mr. Reiss will come to view the material without charge ("of course, only if the material is of considerable value"). The minimum value for "any lot" calls for an estimate of at least DM100.

The commission structure for consignors varies, depending on the quantity and quality of the material: 20–25 percent of the hammer price for individuals, 15–20 percent for dealers.

Consignors do not pay for packing/shipping, warehousing, or insurance on consigned property, nor do they pay for catalogue illustrations.

Reserves are accepted, "but only in accordance with the auctioneer's estimate."

Settlement is made within 4 weeks; where the amount is very considerable, payment can be made in 2 parts, usually 3 and 6 weeks after the sale.

There is no cost if the property does not sell.

Appraisal service is available: cost up to DM5,000, 5 percent (at least DM50); up to DM30,000, 3 percent (at least DM200); amounts exceeding DM30,000 no percentage but at least DM1,000.

The house pays finder's fees, the amount depending on the situation.

Reiss & Auvermann belongs to the International League of Antiquarian Booksellers, Verband Deutscher Antiquare, and Bundesverband Deutscher Kunstversteigerer.

585. Gus Schiele Auktions-Galerie
Ottostrasse 7 (Neuer Kunstblock)   Tel. (089) 59 41 92
D-8000 Munich 2

Schiele is the only German-owned auction house operation regularly and actively holding sales in 2 different locations. Gus Schiele München (to use the familiar name) is a new saleroom located in downtown Munich, but although the venue is new, the management is veteran. Gus Schiele has been holding auctions at his saleroom in Stuttgart since the early 1970s. And this operation has proved itself as a good middle-rank general-purpose auction house in terms of turnover, consignments, etc.

However, given the fact that a significant portion of his consignments as well as a goodly number of his bidders came from Munich, Schiele decided to branch out and held his first auction there on July 18, 1980. He intends to continue holding auctions regularly in both Stuttgart and Munich, approximately 3 times a year at each location.

Contact person: Gus Schiele

Days/hours of operation: Mon.–Fri. 9 A.M.–1 P.M., 3–6 P.M.

Areas in which general auctions and special sales are held:

Chinese Works of Art	Jewelry
Clocks and Watches	Paintings
Drawings	Old Masters
Engravings	19th c. European
Etchings	Porcelain
Furniture	Prints
Glass	Rugs
Japanese Works of Art	Silver

Sales are advertised regularly in the local press and in magazines, such as *Weltkunst*.

Catalogues are available singly for each sale. Schiele maintains a large mailing list, to whom announcements of sales are sent, and a catalogue is free upon request.

Usual viewing procedure: Normally, exhibition is a week before the sale during regular business hours, and 10 A.M.–6 P.M. on weekends.

Bidder Information

All auctions are held on premises.

The buyer's premium is 12 percent, and is not negotiable.

Accounts must be settled immediately, or in the case of mail order bids, upon receipt of invoice.

Mail order bids are executed; no mail order bid of less than DM15 will be accepted.

Packing and shipping services are available, but are charged for.

The house does not offer guarantees of authenticity, but will accept return of goods that are not as catalogued.

Consignor Information

Those wishing to consign property should contact the house in writing or by phone. The minimum value for a consignment is DM1,000 (for either an individual property or a bunch).

Commissions are generally 12 percent for dealers, 15 percent for all others.

Reserves are accepted.

Goods are usually sold within 6 weeks after consignment and settlement is between 2 and 6 weeks after the sale.

"No cost at all" for bought-in items.

Consignors are charged for catalogue illustrations, insurance on consigned property, and for packing and shipping. The consignor is not charged for warehousing of property.

Appraisal service is available. There is no charge, but you are asked to make an appointment in advance.

The house does buy and sell on its own behalf, "occasionally but not regularly."

586. Gus Schiele Auktions-Galerie

Paulinen Strasse 47   Tel. (0711) 61 63 77
D-7000 Stuttgart 1

Gus Schiele Stuttgart is an auction house which occasionally buys and sells on its own behalf.

For details, please see description for the Munich operations of this house.

587. J. A. Stargardt

Universitäts Strasse 27   Tel. (06421) 234 52
D-3550 Marburg   Cable: STARGARDT MARBURG

This firm specializes in autographs and manuscripts, as both a dealer and an auctioneer. It is noted in both instances for its wide-ranging, highly prized, interesting properties. The lots sold at auction represent a rich cross section, concentrating on European figures since the Renaissance. The lots can include, as did one recent sale, such disparate items as a musical score by Frederick the Great, a signed photo portrait of Nehru, a letter from Dickens to an English bookseller, a receipt with a message handwritten by Diderot, and a manuscript by García Lorca.

Stargardt's auction catalogues are much admired and in demand, because of the high quality of their cataloguing and the fascinating range of the lots. Indeed, the catalogues sell at a premium after the sale. The firm also publishes books dealing with autographs.

Stargardt holds sales every 8 months (the cycle is February, November, June, February, etc.). Sales are held off premises, usually at the local Kurhotel Ortenberg. Although some items sell for thousands of marks, the average lot sells for less than DM1,000. Founded in Berlin in 1830, since 1885 Stargardt has been in the possession of the Mecklenburg family, which moved the firm from Berlin in 1944. Annual turnover is estimated to be approximately DM3,500,000.

Contact person: Karl Mecklenburg

Days/hours of operation: Mon.–Fri. 9 A.M.–1 P.M., 3–6 P.M.

Areas in which special sales are held:

      Autographs   Manuscripts

Sales are advertised regularly in German and international daily newspapers, as well as in specialized journals, such as *Weltkunst*.

Catalogues for each sale are available singly at the house and by order: DM20 West Germany and Europe, $18.50 U.S. and Latin America (including airmail postage).

Usual viewing procedure: Exhibition is 1 day in the saleroom, and usually 3 weeks prior to sale in Stargardt's offices; business hours in both places.

Bidder Information

Auctions are held off premises (see above).

The buyer's premium is 12 percent for members of the International League of Antiquarian Booksellers, 15 percent for all others. The buyer's premium is not negotiable. Accounts must be settled immediately after the sale, though if prior arrangements have been made, institutions may pay over a period of time. Mail order bids are executed. Credit cards are not accepted.

Bidding during an auction will be raised as follows: by DM2 to DM100, by DM5 to DM500, by DM20 to DM1,000, by DM50 to DM10,000, and thereafter by at least DM500.

The house guarantees the authenticity of the autographs, but claims must be made within 5 years of the sale. Buyers may return for a refund goods that prove to be not as catalogued, provided this return is within 3 days of accepting the goods and no later than 3 weeks after the auction took place.

Consignor Information

Persons wishing to consign property should write to the house, giving as much detail as possible. The minimum value for property accepted is DM500 for a collection and DM100 for a single item.

The commission structure ranges from 10 to 25 percent of the knockdown price, depending on the value of the lot and on prior arrangements. The commission is negotiable, depending on the situation.

Consignors do not pay for warehousing or insuring of consigned property, nor do they pay for catalogue illustrations.

Settlement is made 3–6 weeks after the property is auctioned.

There is no buy-in charge if property fails to sell.

Reserves are accepted subject to mutual agreement.

Appraisal service is available on the following scale: for items valued to DM1,000, 5 percent or at least DM20; for items to DM10,000, 3 percent or at least DM50; for items to DM30,000, 2 percent or at least DM300; for items valued over DM30,000, the fee is negotiable but must be at least DM600. There is no charge if Stargardt buys items for stock or if items are put up at auction.

J. A. Stargardt belongs to Verband Deutscher Antiquare, International League of Antiquarian Booksellers, and Bundesverband Deutscher Kunstversteigerer.

The house deals on its own behalf (see above).

588. Auktionshaus Tietjen & Co.

Spitaler Strasse 30   Tel. (040) 33 03 68/69
D-2000 Hamburg 1

Since 1969, this estimable firm has been holding auctions of coins, paper money, medals, and numismatic literature. The Tietjens, Dagmar and Detlef, not only hold auctions in these specialties but also have a good-sized retail operation, as well as publishing reprints and new books in the numismatic field. Approximately 4 auctions a year are held, in spring and fall, with one given over to numismatic literature. The catalogues are thoroughly indexed, and intelligently scholarly in their forewords to specific groups of objects. It is very understandable that the older catalogues continue to sell. In recent sales, the bulk of the lots have gone for less than DM500.

Tietjen used to hold auctions outside Hamburg, but it has not done so since the early 1970s. In recent years, the auctions have been held in the serviceable but pleasant "Senatorenstube" of the Hotel Europäischer Hof, in downtown Hamburg, a very short walk from the train station.

Contact persons: Detlef Tietjen/Dagmar Tietjen

Days/hours of operation: Mon.–Fri. 9 A.M.–1 P.M., 2:15–5 P.M.

Areas in which general auctions and special sales are held:

      Coins   Medals   Paper Money

Sales are advertised regularly in the German and international press, as well as in specialty magazines, both in West Germany and abroad.

Catalogues for each sale are available singly at the house and by order. Subscription to a season's catalogues is DM20. Catalogues are sent automatically to anyone who buys more than DM200 at any sale.

Usual viewing procedure: Exhibition is at the Tietjen company's premises, Monday–Friday 10 A.M.–5 P.M., and is ongoing until 1 hour before the sale begins. Saturday viewing is by appointment only.

Bidder Information

Auctions are held on the company's premises.

The buyer's premium is 12 percent.

Mail order bids are executed and such bidders have up to a week to settle; all others must settle the day of the auction.

Bidding is by regular jumps: to DM100, DM2; DM100–DM250, DM5; DM250–DM500, DM10; DM500–DM1,000, DM25; thereafter, DM50.

The house offers packing and shipping services, at the buyer's expense.

Authenticity is guaranteed. All claims must be presented in writing within a week after the auction. Lots described as *"Schön"* (Fine) and *"Gering erhalten"* (Very good) are exempt from any claims against the house— these designations are the bottom of a six-numbered scale used for descriptive purposes, which begins with *"Polierte Platte"* (Proof) and *"Stempelglanz"* (Uncirculated).

Consignor Information
Prospective consignors should contact the house in writing or by telephone.
Minimum value for a consignment is DM1,000.
Commissions are generally 12 percent for dealers and 15 percent for all others. But depending on the situation, commissions are negotiable.
Reserves are accepted. There is no charge for buy-ins.
Goods consigned are usually sold within 3 months; settlement is 6 weeks after the auction.

Tietjen is a member of Verband der Deutschen Münzenhändler.
The firm also buys and sells on its own behalf.

West Germany: also worthy of note

589. Aachener Auktionshaus Crott & Schmelzer
Pont Strasse 21   Tel. (0241) 369 00
Aachen

Auctions are held twice a year by Crott & Schmelzer, mainly of CLOCKS AND WATCHES and JEWELRY, for which the respective experts are Dr. Crott and K. Schmelzer. The auctions are usually held on the premises, although when circumstances warrant, they are conducted elsewhere. Catalogues are available for each sale. There is a buyer's premium. The house also buys and sells on its own behalf.

590. Kunstauktionen Rainer Baumann
Obere Woerthstrasse 7-11   Tel. (0911) 20 48 47
Nuremberg

Specializing in DOLLS and TOYS, this house holds auctions 4 times a year. Catalogues are available at DM20 each. Sales are advertised in the national press and in trade journals. There is viewing before each sale. Hours of operation are 10 A.M.–noon, 2–6 P.M. daily.

591. August Bödiger oHG
Oxford Strasse 4   Tel. (0228) 63 69 40
Bonn

Holding sales 3 or 4 times a year, Bödiger is a dealer whose auctions include FURNITURE and ORIENTAL ART. Catalogues for each sale are available from Bödiger for DM20. Information sheets are available free of charge; just write to be put on the mailing list. Exhibitions are held 1 week before the sale (including Saturdays and Sundays). Mail order bids are executed. Reserves are accepted, subject to mutual agreement. Credit terms can be arranged by buyers, in advance of the sale. Bödiger is a member of the Bundesverband Deutscher Kunstversteigerer.

592. Bolland & Marotz
Feldhören 19   Tel. (0421) 32 18 11
Bremen

A general-purpose auction house, the Hanseatisches Auktionshaus Bolland & Marotz oHG (to give its formal title) holds sales 4 times a year. Hours of operation are Monday–Saturday 10 A.M.–6 P.M. Specialties include DUTCH TILES and NORTH GERMAN FOLK ART. Catalogues may be bought for each sale or by subscription (write to Mrs. G. Freerks). Consignor's commission rates are negotiable, as is the buyer's premium. The house accepts reserves on more valuable items, and will make credit available to some buyers, depending on the situation. The person to contact about such matters is Mr. J. Marotz. The house does buy and sell on its own behalf.

593. Bongartz Geigen Auktionen
Münsterplatz 27   Tel. (0241) 206 19
Aachen

This unusual auction house, which specializes in stringed instruments, especially the VIOLIN, holds sales 3 times yearly, usually off premises in venues such as the fashionable Intercontinental Hotel in Cologne. Profusely illustrated, intelligent catalogues are available from the house by annual subscription or for each sale (approximately DM12). The buyer's premium is 10 percent. Buyers must settle up within 2 weeks of the sale unless other conditions have been negotiated. Mail order bids are accepted. There is usually 2 days of viewing before the sale. Anyone wishing to consign property should write to the house. Commission rates are not negotiable and there is no separate rate structure for dealers.

Christie's International Ltd.
594. Düsseldorf: Alt Pempelfort 11a   Tel. (0211) 35 05 77
                 D-4000 Düsseldorf   Telex: 8587599
                 Jörg-Michael Bertz   Cable: CHRISKUNST

595. Hamburg: Wenzelstrasse 21   Tel. (4940) 279-0866
                 D-2000 Hamburg 60
                 Mrs. Isabella von Bethmann Hollweg

596. Munich: Maximilianstrasse 20   Tel. (089) 22 95 39
                 D-8000 Munich 22   Telex: 524177
                 Max Graf Arco

597. Württenburg: Schloss Langenburg
D-7183 Langenburg
Charlotte Fürstin au Hohenlohe-Langenburg

The Christie's agents in West Germany carry on in the best tradition of the firm's representatives and give advice to prospective bidders, as well as soliciting consignments.

598. Kunstauktion Jürgen Fischer
Alexander Strasse 11   Tel. (07131) 785 23
Heilbronn

This general-purpose auction house sells property (sometimes on its own behalf) in a wide variety of areas, including ARMS AND ARMOR, COINS, DRAWINGS (of all periods), JEWELRY, MEDALS, PAINTINGS, PEWTER, PORCELAIN, RUGS, SILVER, and TOYS. One of the approximately 4 auctions held each year is devoted to the specialty of the house, GLASS.

Catalogues of each sale are available either singly for DM12 (that for the glass auction costs a bit more) or by annual subscription for DM40. The house has just moved to attractive new quarters, but sales are usually held in the ballroom of a local hotel.

The buyer's premium of 17 percent includes taxes (some of which are refunded, especially for foreigners who are taking the property out of the country). Mail order bids are executed, and settlement of such bids is expected within 30 days of the auction. All other bids must be settled at once, unless prior arrangements have been made.

In the usual viewing procedure, exhibitions begin 2 days before the sale, 9 A.M.–9 P.M. Occasionally the house has an exhibition after the sale has taken place.

The consignor's commission, ranging from 12 to 20 percent, depends on the situation, the property, and the consignor.

599. Galerie Göbig
Ritterhaus Strasse 5 (am Thermalbad)   Tel. (Frankfurt)
Bad Nauheim   (0611) 77 40 80

A general-purpose auction house which among other things sells FURNITURE, GLASS, and SILVER. Sales are held monthly and catalogues are available from Herr Moser at Ludolfus Strasse 13, Frankfurt. Buyers must settle accounts within 1 week after the sale. The house buys and sells on its own behalf.

600. Knut Günther

Auf der Kömerwiese 19-21   Tel. (0611) 55 32 92/55 70 22
Frankfurt

Doing business by appointment only, Günther holds auctions either "at the estate of vendor or in public venues." Among lots he sells are ART DECO, ART NOUVEAU, FURNITURE, GLASS, JEWELRY, MEDIEVAL WORKS OF ART, PAINTINGS (19th c. European), RUGS, SCIENTIFIC INSTRUMENTS, and SILVER. Catalogues are available upon "written order." Mail order bids are accepted. The buyer's premium is 20 percent. No guarantees of authenticity are offered, nor is the chance to return lots that prove to be not as catalogued. Viewing is a minimum of 2 hours before the sale. Settlement must be made at once. The minimum value for acceptance by Günther of property for auction is DM1,000 per item and/or DM500,000 per consignment. Consignors are charged 20 percent commission. Günther is a member of Fachverband Deutscher Auktionatoren.

601. Antiquitaeten Lothar Heubel

Odenthaler Strasse 371   Tel. (0221) 60 18 25
Cologne   Cable: HEUBEL KÖLN

Auctions are held twice yearly, off premises, usually at the Intercontinental Hotel. Heubel specializes in ARMS AND ARMOR and PRE-COLUMBIAN ART. Catalogues are available singly at the house and by order for each sale. The house accepts reserves, executes mail order bids, has a separate commission structure for dealers, and does not offer buyers the opportunity to return goods that prove to be not as catalogued. Credit terms are available.

602. Hildener Auktionshaus und Kunstgalerie

Klusenhof 12   Tel. (02103) 602 00
Hilden   Cable: HILDENART

This auction house is located in the very small town of Hilden, between the metropolitan areas of Düsseldorf, Essen, Wuppertal, and Cologne. It holds 4–6 auctions a year and specializes, among other things, in CHINESE WORKS OF ART, INDIAN WORKS OF ART, JAPANESE WORKS OF ART, and THAI WORKS OF ART, as well as NETSUKE, PEWTER, and SILVER. The energetic owner, Hans-Dieter Dahmann, has served as president of the German auctioneer association for the Rhineland/Westphalia area. Sales are usually held on the premises. No advance announcements are sent out by the house, but sales are advertised in West Germany, the Benelux countries, and the U.K. There are special catalogues for each auction. Viewing begins 5 days before the auction. Office hours are 9 A.M.–4 P.M.

603. Auktionshaus Julius Jäger oHG
Luisen Strasse 6   Tel. (06121) 30 41 02
Wiesbaden

This general-purpose auction house holds sales 6–8 times a year on and off the premises. These sales are advertised in the Wiesbaden and Frankfurt daily press. There are catalogues for most sales, but they are not available by subscription. Reserves are accepted. Accounts must be settled immediately after the auction.

604. Galerie Wolfgang Ketterer
Prinzregentenstrasse 60   Tel. (089) 47 20 83
D-8000 Munich 80   Cable: KETTERERKUNST MUENCHEN

This important fine arts auction house holds multi-session sales 2–3 times a year, usually in spring and fall. Specialties of the house, which attract an international clientele, include PAINTINGS (Modern Art, Contemporary Art), ART NOUVEAU, and POSTERS. Originally the present owner's brother had run an auction-retail business with some success, but for a variety of reasons he left West Germany some years ago for Switzerland, and the present owner became the Ketterer active on the West German auction scene. Legend has it that Robert Ketterer before he left Germany was responsible for the presentation of a red rose to a successful bidder who broke an existing price record.

The Ketterer catalogues are well done and copiously illustrated. They cost between DM15–50, with postage extra. Absentee bids are accepted as are reserves. Packing and shipping services are available at the buyer's expense. Consignors are charged for catalogue illustrations. Viewing is usually a week before the sale. Ketterer's American representative is

Richard K. Larcada
790 Madison Avenue, Suite 202   Tel. (212) 535-6432
New York, NY 10021

He will help prospective bidders and consignors.

Sales are advertised in West German and Swiss newspapers and trade journals as well as selected international press outlets, such as the *New York Times*.

605. Kunsthandel Klefisch G.m.b.H.
Hardefuststrasse 9   Tel. (0221) 32 17 40
D-5000 Cologne 1   Cable: KLEKUNST COLOGNE

Like so many German auctioneers, Klefisch is also a dealer. The firm specializes in Asiatic arts and the auctions offer very much the same thing, including CHINESE WORKS OF ART, JAPANESE WORKS OF ART, and NETSUKE. Sales are usually held 3 times a year and last for 2 days.

The sales are advertised in the German and international press, as well as in specialty publications. Catalogues are available singly for each sale and by subscription. The more recent catalogues have cost $12/£6 (including airmail postage). A subscription in Germany costs DM40 per annum; for costs elsewhere, please write Mrs. Trudel Klefisch.

The buyer's premium is 15 percent. Absentee bids are accepted. Packing and shipping services are available. Buyers can return goods that prove to be not as described, provided that the firm is notified within 14 days of the sale. Viewing is usually 6 days before the sale, 10 A.M.–1 P.M., 3–6 P.M. Settlement for floor bidders is immediately and for all others within 10 days of receipt of invoice.

The commission structure for consignors varies between 10 and 15 percent. Consignors are charged for catalogue illustrations and for insurance. Consigned goods are usually sold within 2–3 months. Settlement is 4 weeks after the sale. Reserves are accepted.

Appraisal service is available. Contact Mrs. Klefisch.

606. Die Kleine Galerie
Leonhard Strasse 39   Tel. (07321) 446 14
Heidenheim

The popular name for this auction house is Neils, for Norbert Neils, who administers it. Auctions are usually held 4 times a year. Die Kleine Galerie is also a retail operation. Auction specialties include CLOCKS AND WATCHES, DOLLS, GLASS, PAINTINGS (19th c. European), PEWTER, PORCELAIN, and SILVER. Auctions are held off the premises at places such as the Hotel Krone in nearby Tübingen. Catalogues are available, but not by subscription. There is no buyer's premium and the consignor's commission is negotiable. Credit terms are available, depending on the situation. The house buys and sells on its own behalf.

607. D. M. Klinger
Mühlgasse 1   Tel. (0911) 22 76 98
Nuremberg

Self-described as Nuremberg's first auction house, Klinger is a dealer who holds auctions as well. The firm sells a wide variety of goods, including FURNITURE (15th–18th c.), PAINTINGS (various schools, 15th–20th c.), ORIENTAL WORKS OF ART, AFRICAN ART, and RUGS. There are separate dealers' rates both for consignors and for bidders. Klinger has had a buyer's premium since 1972; it is negotiable. Mail order bids are executed. Reserves are accepted. Buyers may not return goods that do not prove to be as catalogued. Consignors pay for catalogue illustrations (DM80 each), packing and shipping of consigned property, and insurance on consigned property (2 percent of reserve if wanted). Catalogues are available singly for each sale and by subscription from Klinger. The house buys and sells on its own behalf.

AUCTION HOUSES

608. Jan R. Kube Militaria Auktion
Oskar von Miller Ring 33   Tel. (089) 28 38 91
Munich

Specializing in MILITARIA, this house also auctions ARMS AND ARMOR and MED-
ALS, but "no Third Reich items!" Kube concentrates on historical military
equipment, helmets, uniforms, especially German 1750–1918. Auctions are
generally held 4 times a year, on premises; the house is open to the public
Monday–Friday, 3–6 P.M. Catalogues are available by subscription ($15 annu-
ally U.S., including airmail postage).
  The buyer's premium is 12 percent and mail order bids are executed. Viewing is possible 2 days before the sale and accounts must be settled within 10
days after the auction unless prior arrangements have been made. The house
also sells on its own behalf.
  Consignors do not pay for warehousing, illustrations in the catalogue, or
insurance on property consigned. Consignors do pay for shipping and packing.
Settlement is made within 6 weeks of the auction. If property goes unsold, the
only charge to consignors is the cost of the return shipment. The consignor's
commission is 20 percent of the knockdown price. There is a separate commission structure for dealers and institutions that wish to consign property; that
structure is negotiable, and depends on the value of the goods to be consigned.

609. Kunst-Auktionshaus Roland Mars
Ludwig Strasse 4   Tel. (0931) 15 56 58
Würzburg

Lots for sale by this firm include CLOCKS AND WATCHES, DRAWINGS, ENGRAV-
INGS, FURNITURE, JEWELRY, PAINTINGS (Old Master, 19th c. European), PEW-
TER, PORCELAIN, and SILVER.
  The auctions, held 3 times a year, are advertised in the German and Swiss
press, as well as in various specialty periodicals, such as *Weltkunst*. All auctions are held on the premises. Catalogues are available for a single sale (approximately DM18) and by subscription.
  There is a buyer's premium. Absentee bids are accepted. Packing and shipping services are available, at the buyer's expense. There are no guarantees of
authenticity, but buyers do have the opportunity within a limited time to return goods that are not as catalogued. Buyers must settle accounts within 8
days after the sale. Viewing is usually Sunday–Wednesday before the auction
(10 A.M.–7 P.M., with a midday break).
  There is a standard consignor's commission, but it is negotiable. Reserves
are accepted. Consigned goods are sold within 5 months. Settlement is after 4
weeks. Consignors are not charged for catalogue illustrations or for insurance
or for warehousing.
  Mars does not pay finder's fees.

610. Kunstund Auktionshaus Peretz

Dudweiler Strasse 9   Tel. (0681) 356 97
Saarbrücken

A good provincial auction house located in a town not far from the French border, Peretz sells CLOCKS AND WATCHES, DOLLS, DRAWINGS, ENGRAVINGS, FURNITURE (especially 18th & 19th c.), GLASS, JEWELRY, PAINTINGS (Old Master, 19th c. European), PEWTER, PORCELAIN, RUGS, and SILVER, as well as various kinds of applied arts, such as ART DECO lamps, sculpture, and utensils. Auctions are held approximately 10 times a year. Catalogues are available singly for each sale or by subscription for a season. There is a buyer's premium of 15 percent. Lots on the whole sell for reasonable prices. The commission structure for consignors fluctuates between 10 and 15 percent. Minimum value for a consignment is DM200. The head of the house, Marc Peretz, is efficient and energetic.

The auction house is a member of the Bundesverband Deutscher Kunstversteigerer.

611. Karl Pfankuch & Co.

Hagenbruecke 19   Tel. (0531) 458 07
Braunschweig

STAMP auctions are held 3 times a year (March, June, November), off premises at Haus Zur Hanse, Guelden Strasse 7, Braunschweig. Catalogues are available free of charge upon application to company proprietor K. J. Tellgmann. There is a buyer's premium of 13 percent. Credit terms are available upon mutual agreement. Mail order bids are executed. The consignor commission structure is 15 percent, "but only 10 percent for single lots or collections fetching over DM500." Reserves are accepted. "What are consignor's costs if property consigned is not sold? Unfortunately nothing." Viewing is possible during regular business hours (8:30 A.M.–1 P.M., 3–6 P.M.), beginning usually about 14 days before the sale. Auctions are advertised in German philatelic papers.

612. Schloss Ricklingen Auktionshaus

Schloss Ricklingen   Tel. (05031) 710 66
D-3008 Garbsen 5

Located in central Germany, not too far from Hannover, this firm—which also has a retail operation—holds 3 auctions a year, under the direction of Werner Kittel. Lots sold include CLOCKS AND WATCHES, FURNITURE, JEWELRY, PORCELAIN, RUGS, and SILVER.

Auctions are held on the premises, which are open for business and viewing Tuesday, Thursday, and Friday 10 A.M.–6 P.M., Wednesday 10 A.M.–8 P.M., and Saturday 10 A.M.–4 P.M. Auctions are advertised in the daily press and in specialized trade journals. Catalogues are available singly for each sale and by

AUCTION HOUSES

subscription (DM40 per annum). The buyer's premium is 15 percent for private parties and 12 percent for dealers. Mail order bids are accepted. Claims must be made within 3 weeks. Buyers must settle immediately after auction or upon receipt of invoice.

Consignor's commission structure: 14 percent up to DM1,000 per lot, beyond that 10 percent. Consignors pay for illustrations in the catalogue (DM400 per half page color, DM100 per half page black and white); consignors do not pay for insurance or for warehousing on consigned property. Reserves are accepted. If property does not sell and reserve was insisted on, cost to consignor is 3 percent of the reserve. The house pays finder's fees: 3 percent of the hammer price. Schloss Ricklingen Auktionshaus buys and sells on its own behalf.

613. Auktionshaus Bernd Rieber
Lazarett Strasse 14-16   Tel. (0711) 23 29 62
Stuttgart

Rieber, who also deals in antiques, holds auctions twice yearly. At these auctions are sold ART DECO and ART NOUVEAU objects, CHINESE WORKS OF ART, CLOCKS AND WATCHES, ENGRAVINGS, ETCHINGS, FURNITURE, JAPANESE WORKS OF ART, JEWELRY, PAINTINGS, PEWTER, PORCELAIN, RUGS, and SILVER.

Rieber holds house sales as well as auctions on premises. Exhibitions are held for 5 days before a sale. Accounts must be settled within 7 days of the sale. The firm buys and sells on its own behalf.

614. Kunstauktion Schenk
Kölner Strasse 30   Tel. (0211) 35 40 99
Düsseldorf

This company holds some 10 relatively large auctions a year. These sales are often categorized by value ("middle range," "lower priced," etc.). The 2-day morning and afternoon sessions are generally held on Schenk's premises, but the company has also held auctions in Wiesbaden and in Bad Homburg.

Catalogues are usually not available "until very shortly before each auction." The cost is DM7–DM8; "smaller lists are approximately DM3.50." Lots for sale include ARMS AND ARMOR, CHINESE WORKS OF ART, CLOCKS AND WATCHES, DRAWINGS, FURNITURE, GLASS, JAPANESE WORKS OF ART, JEWELRY, MUSICAL INSTRUMENTS, PAINTINGS, PEWTER, PORCELAIN, PRINTS, RUGS, and SCULPTURE.

Schenk has a very direct approach to selling goods consigned to it. If a property does not sell at one auction, then as long as the consignor acquiesces, Schenk will put the property up for sale at subsequent auctions. Between auctions, the property is for sale at Schenk's good-sized quarters for a fixed price (agreed upon between Schenk and the consignor). The company's avowed policy is that not everyone learns about auctions in time to participate in them, so why should they be deprived of the chance to obtain something that takes their fancy.

Schenk seems to have had some success with these policies.
Business hours for Schenk are Tuesday–Friday 11 A.M.–1 P.M., 3–7 P.M.;
Saturday 11 A.M.–1 P.M. On the premises is also the company's Cafe Antik,
which offers passers-by and visitors the chance for a light repast amidst goods
consigned for sale.

615. Kunstauktionshaus Schöninger & Co.

Dachauer Strasse 17   Tel. (089) 59 68 72
Munich

This house holds 3 auctions a year, including DRAWINGS (19th–20th c.), EN-
GRAVINGS, ETCHINGS, JAPANESE WORKS OF ART, RUGS, and SILVER. The house
also offers at auction GERMAN PAINTINGS (19th–20th c.). The contact person
is Leonhard Pelloth. Catalogues for each sale are available singly by order;
subscription for the season is DM45. The house charges consignors for catalogue illustrations (a half page is DM85) and insurance on consigned property, but not for warehousing. Reserves are accepted. Mail order bids are
executed. Schöninger & Co. undertakes appraisals, is glad to advise on the
disposal of collections, and will provide color photos of any item in the catalogue that is of interest to a potential bidder.

616. Kunstauktionshaus Schloss Ahlden G.m.b.H.

Schloss   Tel. (05164) 85 75
Ahlden   Telex: 924343

Located midway between Bremen and Hannover, this house is known familiarly as Florian Seidel, after its energetic director. Sales are held 4 times a
year. Specialties of the house include FURNITURE, GLASS, PAINTINGS, PORCE-
LAIN, and SILVER. Catalogues are available by subscription annually: DM70
West Germany; DM110 Europe; DM270 elsewhere (including airmail
postage).
   The house executes mail order bids, but they have to be received 1 day
before the auction takes place. A property may be returned, if not as catalogued, up to "14 days after auction." Consignor's commission is negotiable.
Appraisal service is available; the cost is 6 percent of the value of the item.

617. Bernd Schramm Antiquariat-Buchhandlung

Dänische Strasse 26   Tel. (0431) 943 67
Kiel

A bookseller who since the early 1970s has held at least one auction a year of
BOOKS, ENGRAVINGS, and MAPS. Sales are held on premises. There is a buyer's
premium. Catalogues are DM5. Mail order bids are accepted. Accounts must
be settled within 3 weeks after the auction. Consignor's commission is 15 percent, but it is negotiable, depending on the situation. Reserves are accepted.
Viewing is possible beginning a week before the auction during regular busi-

ness hours (9 A.M.–1 P.M., 3–6 P.M. daily, Saturdays 9 A.M.–1 P.M.). The house
buys and sells on its own behalf.

Sotheby Parke Bernet G.m.b.H.

618. Munich: Odeonsplatz 16   Tel. (089) 22 23 75/6
                    D-8000 Munich 22   Telex: 523443

619. Hamburg: Bellevue 39A   Tel. (040) 270-1202
                    D-2000 Hamburg 60

620. Frankfurt: Steinlestrasse 7   Tel. (0611) 62 20 27
                    D-6000 Frankfurt

The Sotheby representatives in West Germany are Dr. Ernst Behrens, who is
based in Munich, and Ms. Tatiana von Hessen, who is based in Hamburg
("for correspondence only").

Sotheby representatives have for some time been soliciting consignments
and advising bidders, but more recently the firm has decided to test the auction waters in West Germany and in 1980 it held a sale in Frankfurt at a
rented location.

621. Galerie "Unter Den Linden"
Gahngof Strasse 30   Tel. (07121) 408 76
Reutlingen

CLOCKS AND WATCHES are the specialty of this firm, which holds auction sales
every 5 weeks or so. The gallery is very centrally located, just a few footsteps
from the train station in this picturesque South German town.

The sales are normally held on Saturdays, with viewing the 3 previous days
(9 A.M.–noon, 3–6 P.M.; Fridays to 8 P.M.) and the morning of the sale. About
400 lots are sold at a sale, approximately 100 to the hour, according to the
catalogue.

Sales are advertised in the local and international press, as well as in specialty periodicals. All auctions are held on the premises. Each sale is catalogued (individual copies cost DM10). Absentee bids are executed. There is a
buyer's premium. Packing and shipping services are available, at the buyer's
expense. Guarantees of authenticity are not offered. Settlement for floor bidders is immediately and for absentee bidders 3 days after receipt of invoice.

The consignor's commission is negotiable, depending on the situation. Galerie "Unter Den Linden" can provide consignor contracts in English. There
are separate rates for dealers and institutions; these are negotiable. Consignors
are not charged for catalogue illustrations or for warehousing, but do pay
insurance at 4 percent of the value. Reserves are accepted, but according to
owner H. Dreczko, there are "no costs" for buy-ins. Settlement is 4 weeks
after the auction.

The house does buy and sell on its own behalf: "all kinds of watches and
clocks for collectors."

622. Baruch Zandberg

Feldberg Strasse 10   Tel. (0611) 72 20 20
Frankfurt

Holds auctions every month in a wide variety of areas, including JUDAICA. Not all sales are catalogued. Sales are advertised in the national press. Viewing is 2 days before sale, 8 hours a day.

Zimbabwe

Zimbabwe has a 15 percent government sales tax on goods purchased at auction. Because of the somewhat unsettled politics of Zimbabwe, we advise that you check on export regulations before purchasing at auction there.

623. Fitz-Gerald & Company
34 Lobengula Avenue   Tel. 3300/3322
Gwelo   Cable: FITZ

624. Fitz-Gerald & Des Fontaine
8 Second Avenue
Que Que

Fitz-Gerald's is a firm of auctioneers, estate agents, and valuers which holds auctions of general household goods, machinery and vehicles, and livestock, both at its two premises and on site. The weekly sales are advertised in the Gwelo *Times*. Catalogues are not available by subscription, but one can write to B. D. Moore Fitz-Gerald or Maurice Moore Fitz-Gerald for announcements and catalogues of specific sales. Viewing is the day before the sale, and potential buyers will be pleased to learn that packing and shipping services are available, mail order bids are accepted, guarantees of authenticity are obtainable, and goods that prove to be not as catalogued may be returned. The buyer must settle accounts immediately after the sale, and Fitz-Gerald's accepts payment by Barclay Card but does not extend credit.

Consignors pay in commission 15 percent "for goods sold in our premises, 10 percent on household sales, 10 percent on heavy machinery and vehicles sold at our premises." There are no other charges. Fitz-Gerald's is a speedy firm: "We attempt to sell immediately upon receipt. If advertising is necessary, 10 days." Settlement is immediately after the auction. Commissions may be negotiable, but there is no separate rate structure for dealers. Fitz-Gerald's sales are unreserved auctions.

Appraisal service is available, and the rates are as laid down by the Rhodesian Institute of Valuers.

APPENDIXES

I. Conditions of Business: Sotheby's, London

Sotheby's carries on business (whether with actual or prospective buyers and sellers or consignors requiring inspection, appraisal or valuation of property or persons reading catalogues, or otherwise) on the following terms and conditions and on such other terms, conditions and notices as may be set out on pages iii to vi of any relevant catalogue. The definition of words and phrases with special meanings appear in Condition 38.

Conditions mainly concerning buyers

1 *The Buyer.*

The highest bidder shall be the buyer at the "hammer price" and any dispute shall be settled at the auctioneer's absolute discretion. Every bidder shall be deemed to act as principal unless there is in force a written acknowledgement by Sotheby's that he acts as agent on behalf of a named principal.

2 *Minimum Increment.*

The auctioneer shall have the right to refuse any bid which does not exceed the previous bid by at least 5 per cent or by such other proportion as the auctioneer shall in his absolute discretion direct.

3 *The Premium.*

Except in respect of "special category items", the buyer shall pay to Sotheby's a premium of 10% on the "hammer price" together with Value Added Tax at the standard rate on the premium, and agrees that Sotheby's, when acting as agent for the seller, may also receive commission from the seller in accordance with Condition 19.

4 *Value Added Tax (VAT).*

Lots on which Value Added Tax is payable by the buyer on the "hammer price" are indicated in the catalogue with the sign † (where the tax is payable at the standard rate) and with the sign ‡ (where the tax is payable at a different rate). Value Added Tax, the rates of which are subject to alteration by law, is payable at the rates prevailing on the day of the auction.

For wines, spirits and cigars not available for collection from Sotheby's premises, the supply of a release order authorising the release of the lot to the buyer will constitute delivery by Sotheby's.

12 *Buyers Responsibilities for Lots Purchased.*

The buyer will be responsible for loss or damage to lots purchased from the time of collection or the expiry of 5 working days after the day of the auction, whichever is the sooner, and neither Sotheby's nor its servants or agents shall thereafter be responsible for any loss or damage of any kind, whether caused by negligence or otherwise, while any lot is in its custody or under its control.

13

The buyer of a "motor vehicle" is responsible for complying with the provisions of the Road Traffic Act 1972 and all relevant regulations made under section 40 thereof (including the Motor Vehicles (Construction and Use) Regulations 1973) and any statutory modification thereof.

14

The buyer of a firearm is responsible for obtaining a valid firearm certificate, shot gun certificate or certificate of registration as a firearms dealer and for conforming with the regulations in force in Great Britain relating to firearms, notice of which is published in catalogues of firearms. Sotheby's will not deliver lots to buyers without production of evidence of compliance with this condition.

5 Currency Converter.

A currency converter will be operated at some auctions but only for the guidance of bidders. Sotheby's will not accept any responsibility in the event of error on the currency converter whether in the foreign currency equivalent of bids in pounds sterling or otherwise.

6 Payment.

Immediately a lot is sold the buyer shall:—

(a) give to Sotheby's his name and address and, if so requested, proof of identity; and

(b) pay to Sotheby's the "total amount due" (unless credit terms have been agreed with Sotheby's before the auction).

7 Sotheby's may, at its absolute discretion, agree credit terms with the buyer before an auction under which the buyer will be entitled to take possession of lots purchased up to an agreed amount in value in advance of payment by a determined future date of the "total amount due".

8 Any payments by a buyer to Sotheby's may be applied by Sotheby's towards any sums owing from that buyer to Sotheby's on any account whatever without regard to any directions of the buyer or his agent, whether express or implied.

9 Collection of Purchases.

The ownership of the lot purchased shall not pass to the buyer until he has made payment in full to Sotheby's of the "total amount due".

10 (a) The buyer shall at his own expense take away the lot purchased not later than 5 working days after the day of the auction but (unless credit terms have been agreed in accordance with Condition 7) not before payment to Sotheby's of the "total amount due".

(b) The buyer shall be responsible for any removal, storage and insurance charges on any lot not taken away within 5 working days after the day of the auction.

15 Remedies for Non-Payment or Failure to Collect Purchases.

If any lot is not paid for in full and taken away in accordance with Conditions 6 and 10, or if there is any other breach of either of those Conditions, Sotheby's as agent of the seller shall at its absolute discretion and without prejudice to any other rights it may have, be entitled to exercise one or more of the following rights and remedies:—

(a) to proceed against the buyer for damages for breach of contract;

(b) to rescind the sale of that or any other lots sold to the defaulting buyer at the same or any other auction;

(c) to re-sell the lot or cause it to be re-sold by public auction or private sale and the defaulting buyer shall pay to Sotheby's any resulting deficiency in the "total amount due" (after deduction of any part payment and addition of re-sale costs) and any surplus shall belong to the seller;

(d) to remove, store and insure the lot at the expense of the defaulting buyer and, in the case of storage, either at Sotheby's premises or elsewhere;

(e) to charge interest at a rate not exceeding 1.5% per month on the "total amount due" to the extent it remains unpaid for more than 5 working days after the day of the auction;

(f) to retain that or any other lot sold to the same buyer at the same or any other auction and release it only after payment of the "total amount due";

(g) to reject or ignore any bids made by or on behalf of the defaulting buyer at any future auctions or obtain a deposit before accepting any bids in future;

(h) to apply any proceeds of sale then due or at any time thereafter becoming due to the defaulting buyer towards settlement of the "total amount due" and to exercise a lien on any property of the defaulting buyer which is in Sotheby's possession for any purpose.

Appendix I (Cont'd.)

472   APPENDIXES

16 *Liability of Sotheby's and Sellers.*
(a) Goods auctioned are usually of some age. All goods are sold with all faults and imperfections and errors of description. Illustrations in catalogues are for identification only. Buyers should satisfy themselves prior to sale as to the condition of each lot and should exercise and rely on their own judgment as to whether the lot accords with its description. Subject to the obligations accepted by Sotheby's under this Condition, none of the seller, Sotheby's, its servants or agents is responsible for errors of description or for the genuineness or authenticity of any lot, no warranty whatever is given by Sotheby's, its servants or agents, or any seller to any buyer in respect of any lot and any express or implied conditions or warranties are hereby excluded.
(b) Any lot which was executed by someone other than the person described in the catalogue as the artist may be returned by the buyer to Sotheby's within five years of the date of the auction, in the same condition in which it was at the time of the auction, accompanied by a statement of defects, the number of the lot and the date of the auction at which it was purchased. If Sotheby's is satisfied that the lot was so executed and that the buyer has and is able to transfer a good and marketable title to the lot free from any third party claims the sale will be set aside and any amount paid in respect of the lot will be refunded.
(c) A buyer's claim under this Condition shall be limited to any amount paid in respect of the lot and shall not extend to any loss or damage suffered or expense incurred by him.
(d) The benefit of this Condition shall not be assignable and shall rest solely and exclusively in the buyer who, for the purpose of this Condition, shall be and only be the person to whom the original invoice is made out by Sotheby's in respect of the lot sold.

Conditions mainly concerning sellers and consignors

17 *Warranty of title and availability.*
(a) The seller warrants to Sotheby's and to the buyer that he is the true owner of the property or is properly authorised to sell the property by the true owner and is able to transfer good and marketable title to the property free from any third party claims.
(b) The seller of property not held by Sotheby's on its premises or under its control, warrants and undertakes to Sotheby's and the buyer that the property will be available and in a deliverable state on demand by the buyer.
(c) The seller will indemnify Sotheby's, its servants and agents and the buyer against any loss or damage suffered by either in consequence of any breach of (a) or (b) above on the part of the seller.

Sotheby's control and except as previously disclosed to Sotheby's the same are safe if reasonably used for the purpose for which they were designed and free from any defect not obvious on external inspection which could prove dangerous to human life or health, and will indemnify Sotheby's its servants and agents against any loss or damage suffered by any of them in consequence of any breach of the above warranty and undertaking.
22 *Rescission of the Sale.*
If before Sotheby's remit the "sale proceeds" to the seller, the buyer makes a claim to rescind the sale under Condition 16 if appropriate and Sotheby's is of the opinion that the claim is justified, Sotheby's is authorised to rescind the sale and refund to the buyer any amount paid to Sotheby's in respect of the lot.

18 Reserves.
The seller shall be entitled to place prior to the auction a reserve on any lot, being the minimum "hammer price" at which that lot may be treated as sold. A reserve once placed by the seller shall not be changed without the consent of Sotheby's. Where a reserve has been placed, only the auctioneer may bid on behalf of the seller. Where no reserve has been placed, the seller may bid, either personally or through the agency of any one person.

19 Authority to Deduct Commission and Expenses.
The seller authorises Sotheby's to deduct commission at the "stated rates" and "expenses" from the "hammer price" and acknowledges Sotheby's right to retain the premium payable by the buyer in accordance with Condition 3.

20 Insurance.
Unless otherwise instructed, Sotheby's will insure property (other than "motor vehicles") consigned to it or put under its control for sale and may, at its discretion, insure property put under its control for any other purpose. In all cases save where Sotheby's is required to insure, the property shall remain at all times at the risk of the seller or consignor and neither Sotheby's nor its servants or agents will be responsible for any loss or damage whether caused by negligence or otherwise. Such insurance will be at the expense of the seller or consignor, will be for the amount estimated by Sotheby's to be, from time to time, the current value of the property at auction and will subsist until whichever is the earlier of the ownership of the property passing from the seller or the seller or consignor becoming bound to collect the property.

21 Electrical and Mechanical Goods.
The seller or consignor of electrical or mechanical goods warrants and undertakes to Sotheby's that at the date on which the same are consigned to Sotheby's or put under

23 Payment of Sale Proceeds.
Sotheby's shall remit the "sale proceeds" to the seller not later than one month (or, in the case of numismatic items, 14 days) after the auction, but if by that date Sotheby's has not received the "total amount due" from the buyer then Sotheby's will remit the "sale proceeds" within five working days after the day on which the "total amount due" is received from the buyer. If credit terms have been agreed between Sotheby's and the buyer, Sotheby's shall remit to the seller the sale proceeds not later than one month (or, in the case of numismatic items, 14 days) after the auction unless otherwise agreed by the seller: Provided that where in the case of postage stamps Sotheby's has granted an extension it shall remit the "sale proceeds" when a certificate of genuineness is received by Sotheby's or sixty-five days after the auction, whichever is the sooner, but if by then Sotheby's has not received the "total amount due" from the buyer then Sotheby's will remit the "sale proceeds" within five working days after the day on which the "total amount due" is received from the buyer.

24 If the buyer fails to pay to Sotheby's the "total amount due" within 3 weeks after the auction, Sotheby's will notify the seller and take the seller's instructions as to the appropriate course of action and, so far as in Sotheby's opinion is practicable, will assist the seller to recover the "total amount due" from the buyer. If circumstances do not permit Sotheby's to take instructions from the seller, the seller authorises Sotheby's at the seller's expense to agree special terms for payment of the "total amount due", to remove, store and insure the lot sold, to settle claims made by or against the buyer on such terms as Sotheby's shall in its absolute discretion think fit, to take such steps as are necessary to collect moneys due by the buyer to the seller and if necessary to rescind the sale and refund money to the buyer.

Appendix I (Cont'd.)

25 If, notwithstanding that the buyer fails to pay to Sotheby's the "total amount due" within three weeks after the auction, Sotheby's remits the "sale proceeds" to the seller, the ownership of the lot shall pass to Sotheby's.

26 *Charges for Withdrawn Lots.*
Where a seller cancels instructions for sale, Sotheby's reserves the right to charge a fee of 10% of Sotheby's then latest estimate or middle estimate of the auction price of the property withdrawn, together with Value Added Tax thereon and "expenses" incurred in relation to the property.

27 *Rights to Photographs and Illustrations.*
The seller gives Sotheby's full and absolute right to photograph and illustrate any lot placed in its hands for sale and to use such photographs and illustrations and any photographs and illustrations provided by the seller at any time at its absolute discretion (whether or not in connection with the auction).

28 *Unsold Lots.*
Where any lot fails to sell, Sotheby's shall notify the seller accordingly. The seller shall make arrangements

either to re-offer the lot for sale or to collect the lot and to pay the reduced commission under Condition 29 and "expenses". If such arrangements are not made:—
(a) within 7 days of notification, the seller shall be responsible for any removal, storage and insurance expenses;
(b) within 3 months of notification, Sotheby's shall have the right to sell the lot at public auction without reserve and to deduct from the "hammer price" any sum owing to Sotheby's including (without limitation) removal, storage and insurance expenses, the "expenses" of both auctions, reduced commission under Condition 29 in respect of the first auction as well as commission at the "stated rates" on the sale and all other reasonable expenses before remitting the balance to the seller or, if he cannot be traced, placing it in a bank account in the name of Sotheby's for the seller.

29 Sotheby's reserves the right to charge commission up to one-half of the "stated rates" calculated on the "bought-in price' and in addition "expenses" in respect of any unsold lots.

General conditions and definitions

30 Sotheby's sells as agent for the seller (except where it is stated wholly or partly to own any lot as principal) and as such is not responsible for any default by seller or buyer.

31 Any representation or statement by Sotheby's, in any catalogue as to authorship, attribution, genuineness, origin, date, age, provenance, condition or estimated selling price is a statement of opinion only. Every person interested should exercise and rely on his own judgment as to such matters and neither Sotheby's nor its servants or agents are responsible for the correctness of such opinions.

38 In these Conditions:—
(a) "Sotheby's" means Sotheby Parke Bernet & Co.;
(b) "catalogue", includes any advertisement, brochure, estimate, price list and other publication;
(c) "hammer price" means the price at which a lot is knocked down by the auctioneer to the buyer;
(d) "total amount due" means the "hammer price" in respect of the lot sold together with any premium, Value Added Tax chargeable and additional charges and expenses due from a defaulting buyer under Condition 15, in pounds sterling;

32 Whilst the interests of prospective buyers are best served by attendance at the auction, Sotheby's will if so instructed execute bids on their behalf, neither Sotheby's nor its servants or agents being responsible for any neglect or default in doing so or for failing to do so.

33 Sotheby's shall have the right, at its discretion, to refuse admission to its premises or attendance at its auctions by any person.

34 Sotheby's has absolute discretion without giving any reason to refuse any bid, to divide any lot, to combine any two or more lots, to withdraw any lot from the auction and in case of dispute to put up any lot for auction again.

35 (a) Any indemnity under these Conditions shall extend to all actions proceedings costs expenses claims and demands whatever incurred or suffered by the person entitled to the benefit of the indemnity.

(b) Sotheby's declares itself to be a trustee for its relevant servants and agents of the benefit of every indemnity under these Conditions to the extent that such indemnity is expressed to be for the benefit of its servants and agents.

36 Any notice by Sotheby's to a seller, consignor, prospective bidder or buyer may be given by first class mail or airmail and if so given shall be deemed to have been duly received by the addressee 48 hours after posting.

37 These Conditions shall be governed by and construed in accordance with English law. All transactions to which these Conditions apply and all matters connected therewith shall also be governed by English law. Sotheby's hereby submits to the exclusive jurisdiction of the English courts and all other parties concerned hereby submit to the non-exclusive jurisdiction of the English courts.

(e) "special category items" means numismatic items, wines, spirits, cigars and motor vehicles;

(f) "book" means any item included or proposed to be included in a sale of books and includes a manuscript or print;

(g) "deliberate forgery" means an imitation made with the intention of deceiving as to authorship, origin, date, age, period, culture or source which is not shown to be such in the description in the catalogue and which at the date of the sale had a value materially less than it would have had if it had been in accordance with that description;

(h) "sale proceeds" means the net amount due to the seller being the "hammer price" of the lot sold less commission at the "stated rates" and "expenses" and any other amounts due to Sotheby's by the seller in whatever capacity and howsoever arising;

(i) "stated rates" means Sotheby's published rates of commission for the time being and Value Added Tax thereon;

(j) "expenses" in relation to the sale of any lot means Sotheby's charges and expenses for insurance, illustrations, special advertising, packing and freight of that lot and any Value Added Tax thereon;

(k) "motor vehicle" means any item included or proposed to be included in a sale of motor vehicles;

(l) "bought-in price" means 5 per cent more than the highest bid received below the reserve.

39 Special terms may be used in catalogues in the description of a lot. Where terms are not self-explanatory and have special meanings ascribed to them, a glossary will appear before Lot I in the catalogue of the auction.

40 The headings in these Conditions do not form part of the Conditions but are for convenience only.

II. Conditions of Sale: Sotheby Parke Bernet, New York

This catalogue, as amended by any posted notices or oral announcements during the sale, is Sotheby Parke Bernet Inc.'s and the Consignor's entire agreement with the purchaser relative to the property listed herein. The following Conditions of Sale, the Terms of Guarantee and any glossary contained herein are the complete and only terms and conditions on which all property is offered for sale. The property will be offered by us as agent for the Consignor, unless the catalogue indicates otherwise.

1.   The authenticity of the Authorship of property listed in the catalogue is guaranteed as stated in the Terms of Guarantee; except as provided therein all property is sold "AS IS," and neither we nor the Consignor make any warranties or representations of the correctness of the catalogue or other description of the physical condition, size, quality, rarity, importance, provenance, exhibitions, literature or historical relevance of the property and no statement anywhere, whether oral or written, shall be deemed such a warranty or representation. Prospective bidders should inspect the property before bidding to determine its condition, size and whether or not it has been repaired or restored. We and the Consignor make no representation or warranty as to whether the purchaser acquires any reproduction rights in the property.

2.   A premium of 10% of the successful bid price will be added thereto and is payable by the purchaser as part of the total purchase price.

3.   We reserve the right to withdraw any property before sale.

4.   Unless otherwise announced by the auctioneer, all bids are per lot as numbered in the catalogue.

5.   We reserve the right to reject any bid. The highest bidder acknowledged by the auctioneer will be the purchaser. In the event of any dispute between bidders, or in the event of doubt on our part as to the validity of any bid, the auctioneer will have the final discretion either to determine the successful bidder or to reoffer and resell the article in dispute. If any dispute arises after the sale, our sale record is conclusive. Although in our discretion we will execute order bids or accept telephone bids as a convenience to clients who are not present at auctions, we are not responsible for any errors or omissions in connection therewith.

6.   If the auctioneer decides that any opening bid is below the value of the article offered, he may reject the same and withdraw the article from sale, and if, having acknowledged an opening bid, he decides that any advance thereafter is insufficient, he may reject the advance.

7.   On the fall of the auctioneer's hammer, title to the offered lot will pass to the highest bidder acknowledged by the auctioneer, subject to fulfillment by such bidder of all of the conditions set forth herein, and such bidder thereupon (a) assumes full risk and responsibility therefor, (b) will sign a confirmation of purchase thereof, and (c) will pay the full purchase price therefor or such part as

we may require. In addition to other remedies available to us by law, we reserve the right to impose a late charge of 1½% per month of the total purchase price if payment is not made in accordance with the conditions set forth herein. All property must be removed from our premises by the purchaser at his expense nor later than 3 business days following its sale and, if it is not so removed, (i) a handling charge of 1% of the purchase price per month until its removal will be payable to us by the purchaser, with a minimum of 5% for any property not so removed within 60 days after the sale, and (ii) we may send the purchased property to a public warehouse for the account, risk and expense of the purchaser. If any applicable conditions herein are not complied with by the purchaser, in addition to other remedies available to us and the Consignor by law, including without limitation the right to hold the purchaser liable for the total purchase price, we at our option may either (a) cancel the sale, retaining as liquidated damages all payments made by the purchaser or (b) resell the property at public auction without reserve, and the purchaser will be liable for any deficiency, costs, including handling charges, the expenses of both sales, our commission on both sales at our regular rates, all other charges due hereunder and incidental damages. In addition, a defaulting purchaser will be deemed to have granted us a security interest in, and we may retain as collateral security for such purchaser's obligations to us, any property in our possession owned by such purchaser. We shall have all of the rights afforded a secured party under the New York Uniform Commercial Code with respect to such property and we may apply against such obligations all monies held or received by us for the account of, or due from us to, such purchaser. At our option, payment will not be deemed to have been made in full until we have collected funds represented by checks, or, in the case of bank or cashier's checks, we have confirmed their authenticity.

8.   Lots marked with ■ immediately preceding the lot number are offered subject to a reserve, which is the confidential minimum price below which such lot will not be sold. We may implement such reserves by bidding on behalf of the Consignor. In certain instances, the Consignor may pay us less than the standard commission rate where a lot is "bought-in" to protect its reserve. Where the Consignor is indebted to or has a monetary guarantee from us, and in certain other instances, where we or our affiliated companies may have an interest in the offered lots and the proceeds therefrom other than our commissions, we may bid therefor to protect such interests.

9.   Unless exempted by law, the purchaser will be required to pay the combined New York State and local sales tax or any applicable compensating use tax of another state on the total purchase price. The rate of such combined tax is 8% in New York City and ranges from 4% to 8% elsewhere in New York State.

10.   These Conditions of Sale as well as the purchaser's and our respective rights and obligations hereunder shall be governed by and construed and enforced in accordance with the laws of the State of New York. By bidding at an auction, whether present in person or by agent, order bid, telephone or other means, the purchaser shall be deemed to have consented to the jurisdiction of the state courts of, and the federal courts sitting in, the State of New York.

11.   We are not responsible for the acts or omissions of carriers or packers of purchased lots, whether or not recommended by us. Packing and handling of purchased lots by us is at the entire risk of the purchaser.

III. Conditions of Acceptance and Terms: Christie, Manson & Woods, London

Our commission from the Seller is 10 per cent. of the final bid price except for wine, coins and medals for which the commission is 15 per cent. of the final bid price. There is a Buyer's premium of 10 per cent. of the final price (together with any V.A.T. chargeable thereon) except for wine, coins and medals on which there is no Buyer's premium. In the case of Lots failing to reach their reserve a charge of 5 per cent. will be made on the last bid on Lots on which the final price bid is less than £500, and 2½ per cent. on all other Lots.

V.A.T. at the standard rate is payable on all Sellers' commission.
Foreign residents, except those within the E.E.C., are exempt from V.A.T. on Sellers' commission.

1   Christie's act only as agent save as hereinafter appears of the person or persons (in these Conditions called the Seller) sending property to or leaving property with Christie's for sale. The Seller warrants to Christie's that he is entitled to sell.
Christie's accept property for sale only on the basis that if they sell the same they will be entitled in addition to commission from the Seller to retain that part of the purchase price representing the premium payable by the Buyer as set out in Conditions 5 (A) and 10 of their Conditions of Sale as follows:

5(A) The purchase price payable by the Buyer shall be the aggregate of the final bid and a premium of 10% of the final bid (together with any V.A.T. chargeable on the final bid and such premium). "The final bid" means the price at which a lot is knocked down to the Buyer.

10. The property in a lot shall not pass to the Buyer until he has paid the purchase price in full, but the lot shall be at the Buyer's risk in all respects from the fall of the hammer. Notwithstanding that Christie's act only as agents for the Seller, they shall be entitled to retain the premium referred to in Condition 5(A) hereof, irrespective of and in addition to such remuneration as they may receive from the Seller. Christie's shall be entitled to a lien on any lot sold until the purchase price is paid in full by the Buyer.

Similarly in the event of the failure by a Buyer to pay the purchase price, and on a resale there being a surplus over the purchase price after payment of all expenses Christie's shall be entitled to retain the premium. All sums received by Christie's by way of purchase price shall as between the Seller and Christie's be appropriated exclusively to purposes other than the payment of the premium until the Seller's and all other claims upon such sums shall have been fully discharged.

2   Christie's shall have complete discretion as to whether to offer for sale or not and as to:

(a)   whether the property is suitable for sale by them and if so as to the place and date of sale and as to the Conditions of Sale and as to the manner in which such sale is conducted.

(b)   the description of the property in their catalogues or other literature.

(c)   seeking the views of any expert.

(d)   illustrating the property in their catalogues at the expense of the Seller up to a maximum of £35.

3   The Seller shall not bid for his property or employ any person to bid for him save that he may impose a reserve in which case the Auctioneer alone shall have the right to bid on behalf of the Seller. If a reserve is imposed in a currency other than sterling such reserve will be calculated at the closing rate obtainable by Christie's on the London Foreign Exchange Market on the last business day before the sale, the certificate in writing of Christie's as to such rate being conclusive.

4   (a)   The net proceeds of sale less the premium, Christie's commission and any charges to the Seller's debit will become due and payable to the Seller at the expiration of one month after the date of sale provided that Christie's have by then been paid the

purchase price in full by the Buyer and that no notice has been given by the Buyer under Condition 7 of Christie's Conditions of Sale (relating to rescission for forgery).

(b) In the case of overseas Sellers, whose property has been sent to the United Kingdom for sale, the net proceeds of sale will be paid to the Seller in such currency available to Christie's as may be agreed providing that the Seller specifies to Christie's in writing prior to the date of sale the currency required. Such sum shall be calculated at the spot rate available for the net proceeds on the London Foreign Exchange Market on the date of sale, the certificate in writing of Christie's as to such spot rate being conclusive. If no currency is specified as aforesaid the net proceeds will be paid in the currency of the country where the Seller has his address as notified to Christie's or at Christie's discretion in sterling.

5. Once the catalogue including the property has been printed the property may be withdrawn by the Seller but only on payment of 5 per cent. of the reserve, or if there is no reserve on payment of 5 per cent. of the figure at which the property has been valued for insurance (as determined by Christie's).

6. If within 21 days after the sale Christie's have received from the Buyer of any lot notice in writing that in his view the lot is a deliberate forgery and within 14 days after such notification the Buyer where the lot has been taken away, returns it to Christie's in the same condition as at the time of sale and within a reasonable period thereafter by producing evidence, the burden of proof to be upon the Buyer, satisfies Christie's that considered in the light of the entry in the catalogue the lot is a deliberate forgery then Christie's are authorised to rescind the sale of the same and to refund to the Buyer the purchase price thereof. "A deliberate forgery'' means a lot made or substantially made with an intention to deceive, when considered in the light of the entry in the catalogue, and which at the date of the sale had a value materially less than it would have had if it had been in accordance with that description.

7. All property being held by Christie's for sale, and not otherwise covered by insurance, whether on Christie's premises or elsewhere, will automatically be covered for insurance under Christie's own Fine Arts Policy. The rate of premium payable by the Seller on sale is 0.5 per cent. The sums for which the property is covered for insurance under this Condition shall not constitute and shall not be relied upon by the Seller as a representation, warranty or guarantee that the property will, when sold by Christie's, be sold for such amount.

8. Lots bought in and property not being kept for sale must be collected at the Seller's expense within two months after notice requiring the Seller to collect. After such two months Christie's are authorised to sell such property in such manner and on such terms as they think fit. Property returned at the request of the Seller shall be returned at his risk and expense and will not be insured in transit unless Christie's have received special directions.

9. Christie's reserve the right at their discretion to arrange for storage in a warehouse of any property sent to or left with them.

10. The Seller must give Christie's all relevant information as to his V.A.T. status with regard to the article to be sold which he warrants to be correct and upon which Christie's shall be entitled to rely. Once a lot has been designated in the sale catalogue on the basis of such information no alteration so as to affect the liability to V.A.T. can be made.

11. Modern firearms see attached supplement.

12. Any notice given hereunder shall be in writing and if given by post to the address of the Seller any such notice shall be deemed to have been delivered in the ordinary course of post.

13. (a) These Conditions constitute together with the matters set out on the reverse side of this page the entire agreement between Christie's and the Seller.

(b) The respective rights and obligations of the parties shall be governed and interpreted by English law and the Seller hereby submits to the non-exclusive jurisdiction of the English Courts.

IV. Conditions of Acceptance: Christie, Manson & Woods International, New York

1. **CONSIGNMENT:** Seller hereby consigns to Christie's the property identified in the attached schedule (the "Property") which Christie's, as Seller's agent, will offer for sale at public auction subject to provisions set forth below and Christie's standard CONDITIONS OF SALE and INFORMATION FOR INTENDING BUYERS printed in the catalogue.

2. **COMMISSION:** For its services, Christie's will receive and retain from the proceeds of the sale as a commission from Seller (i) an amount equal to 10% of the final bid on each lot sold for over $500 and 15% of the final bid on each lot sold for $500 or less, and (ii) a premium of 10% of the final bid to be collected by Christie's from the buyer.

3. **SALE:** Christie's shall have complete discretion as to (i) the place and date of sale and the manner in which such sale is conducted, (ii) the description of the property in their catalogues or other literature, (iii) seeking the views of any expert, and (iv) the consignment of items with a value of $1,000 or less to its subsidiary gallery, Christie's East, 219 East 67th Street, New York, N.Y. 10021 to be offered on the same terms, but in accordance with the conditions of sale of that gallery.

4. **CERTAIN WARRANTIES:** Seller warrants that he has the right to consign the Property for sale, that the same is free and clear of liens, encumbrances and claims of third parties and that good title will pass to the buyer. If Seller is acting as an agent for an undisclosed principal, Seller and principal, jointly and severally, assume all of the obligations hereunder to the same extent as if Seller were acting as principal.

5. **EXPENSES:** Seller agrees to bear expenses of (i) insurance, (ii) packing and transport to Christie's premises, (iii) gemological tests of jewelry and related items, and (iv) illustration charges.

6. **PACKING AND TRANSPORT:** While Christie's will on request recommend a carrier, it accepts no responsibility therefor and packing and transport will be at Seller's expense and risk. Christie's reserves the right to arrange for storage of the Property in a warehouse.

7. **INSURANCE:** Seller must insure the Property against all risks while being packed and unpacked, in transit from door-to-door and while on Christie's premises or warehouse and in its charge. Insurance coverage of all Property will be furnished by special arrangement with Christie's as follows: (i) Property covered from the time of packing and transport to Christie's until seven days following the sale thereof at the rate of 0.7% of the final bid or, if the Property has not been offered for sale, at the mean of our estimates at the time of loss or damage; (ii) Property received at Christie's galleries will be covered from the time of receipt until seven days following the sale thereof at a rate of 0.5% of the final bid or, if the Property has not been offered for sale, at the mean of our estimates at the time of loss or damage. Christie's liability to Seller resulting from loss or damage of any Property shall not exceed the above mentioned insurance coverage of such Property. Seller may elect to insure the Property under his own policy covering Seller's interest as well as Christie's commission and expenses. In such case Christie's will not be responsible for, and Seller releases Christie's from, any liability for loss or damage of the Property, and Seller will arrange with his insurer to waive any right of subrogation against Christie's, its agents, employees and contractors, and Seller undertakes to otherwise notify his own insurance carrier of the terms of this agreement.

8. **RESERVES:** All Property will be sold subject to a reserve price. Unless another reserve price is mutually agreed between Seller and Christie's and confirmed by Seller in a writing, which is received by Christie's at least five days before the sale, the reserve will be an amount equal to 60% of the printed low presale estimate circulated with the catalogue. The reserve price and the printed presale estimate shall be based upon a bid price and shall not include premium or taxes. Neither Seller, his principal, if any, nor any other representative or agent of Seller or principal shall bid for the Property and all bids to protect reserves will be made by Christie's representative. Should a lot fail to reach its reserve price, there will be a charge of 5% of the bought in price.

9. **WITHDRAWAL:** No Property may be withdrawn after the date of this agreement without Christie's consent. In the event that Christie's consents to such a withdrawal, the Property may be withdrawn upon payment of 20% of the reserve price or 20% of the insurance valuation where the reserve has not been fixed. Christie's reserves the right to withdraw any Property at any time before actual sale if in Christie's best judgment (i) there is doubt as to its authenticity, or (ii) Seller's representations to Christie's concerning it are inaccurate in any respect, or (iii) Seller has breached or is about to breach any provision of this agreement, or (iv) for other just cause.

10. **NO REPRESENTATIONS:** Any appraisal, estimate or other statement of Christie's or its representative with respect to the selling price of any article is a statement of opinion only and may not be relied upon as a prediction of the actual selling price.

11. **SETTLEMENT OF ACCOUNT:** Thirty-five calendar days after the sale, Christie's will pay Seller the net proceeds received and collected from the sale of the Property, after deducting its commission, any expenses incurred for Seller's account and any other amounts due it, unless Christie's shall have received notice of the buyer's intention to rescind the sale or of any other claim or shall for any reason have refunded such proceeds to the buyer prior to the expiration of such thirty-five days.

12. **HOLD HARMLESS:** Christie's as Seller's agent is authorized to accept the return and rescind the sale of any Property at any time if Christie's, in its best judgment, determines that the offering for sale of any Property has subjected or may subject Christie's and/or Seller to any liability, including any liability under warranty of authenticity. In such event Christie's is further authorized to refund or credit to the buyer the purchase price of such returned Property and if Christie's has already remitted to Seller any proceeds of the rescinded sale, Seller agrees to pay Christie's on request an amount equal to the remitted proceeds. Seller further agrees to indemnify Christie's and hold it harmless from and against any and all claims, loss, liabilities and expenses (including reasonable attorneys' fees) relating to the claims of buyers or persons claiming for buyers resulting from Christie's offering for sale or selling any Property consigned hereunder, whether or not it has been returned to Christie's.

13. **NON-PAYMENT BY PURCHASER:** In the event of non-payment by the buyer, Christie's in its discretion may cancel the sale and return the Property to Seller, or enforce payment by the buyer.

14. **UNSOLD PROPERTY:** Any Property bought in and not being kept for sale must be collected at Seller's expense within two months after notice requiring Seller to collect it. Seller shall not be entitled to reclaim any unsold Property until all commissions and expenses owed to Christie's have been paid in full. Any Property not reconsigned for sale or picked up within ten days of such notice to collect may be delivered to

Appendix IV (Cont'd.)

and stored at a public warehouse of Christie's choice at Seller's expense. Two months after such notice to collect, the Property may be sold by Christie's at public auction for the joint account of the warehouse and Christie's as their respective interests may then exist. Seller hereby waives any and all requirements of notice, advertisement and disposition of proceeds with regard to said sale. All sales of uncollected Property will be at Christie's standard commission rates without reserve. The proceeds of such sale shall first be applied to the indebtedness owing to Christie's and the warehouse, including reasonable expenses incurred hereunder, and the excess, if any, will be remitted to Seller, or held by Christie's for Seller's account.

While Christie's undertakes to exercise reasonable care in storing and handling the Property, it shall not be responsible for damage to PLASTER frames.

15. **MISCELLANEOUS:** All prior negotiations, representations, contracts or agreements between the parties hereto relating to the Property, if any, are hereby merged into this agreement and this agreement is complete, entire and the only agreement between us. No modification, alteration, construction, amendment or rescission of or to this Seller's Contract shall be effective or binding unless in writing and executed by a duly authorized officer of Christie's and Seller. This agreement shall be governed by and construed in accordance with the laws of the State of New York. All pronouns and any variations thereof shall be deemed to refer to the masculine, feminine, neuter, singular or plural as the circumstances shall require. The captions appearing herein are for the convenience of the parties only and shall not be construed to affect the meaning of the provisions of this agreement. Any notice given hereunder shall be in writing to the address of Seller and any such notice shall be deemed to have been delivered upon mailing.

Seller agrees to the foregoing by signing below and returning a signed copy of this Seller's Contract to Christie's.

V. Categories Which Certain Houses Emphasize, Listed by Auction House Number

African Art: 32, 75, 534, 535, 607
Americana: 1, 2, 3, 11, 12, 14, 15, 17, 18,
    19, 22, 23, 24, 25, 26, 27, 28, 29, 30,
    32, 34, 36, 37, 38, 40, 41, 42, 55, 57,
    61, 72, 76, 78, 80, 82, 83, 85, 88, 90,
    95, 101, 104, 108, 109, 110, 113,
    117, 118, 125, 126, 127, 128
American Indian Relics and Art: 19, 32,
    95
Antique Ironwork: 570
Antique Tools: 47
Architectural Antiques: 50
Arms and Armor: 7, 8, 14, 19, 21, 24,
    25, 26, 32, 33, 112, 131, 132, 134,
    136, 139, 141, 147, 150, 155, 156,
    158, 167, 191, 198, 225, 263, 275,
    290, 328, 344, 373, 427, 434, 441,
    461, 469, 495, 496, 498, 499, 500,
    501, 534, 545, 555, 556, 578, 582,
    598, 601, 608, 614
Art Deco: 11, 12, 13, 15, 17, 19, 22, 24,
    25, 26, 27, 30, 32, 33, 36, 37, 38, 40,
    41, 67, 76, 88, 105, 111, 113, 121,
    131, 132, 134, 135, 136, 141, 147,
    148, 152, 155, 160, 165, 219, 275,
    427, 434, 438, 441, 446, 460, 461,
    464, 496, 498, 499, 501, 535, 548,
    573, 574, 576, 580, 582, 600, 610,
    613
Art Nouveau: 11, 12, 13, 15, 17, 19, 22,
    24, 25, 26, 27, 30, 31, 33, 36, 37, 38,
    40, 41, 67, 76, 88, 105, 111, 113,
    121, 131, 133, 134, 135, 136, 141,
    147, 148, 152, 155, 160, 165, 219,
    275, 427, 434, 438, 441, 446, 460,
    461, 464, 496, 498, 499, 501, 573,
    574, 581, 582, 613
Australian Colonial Furniture: 347

Autographs: 9, 12, 18, 20, 26, 31, 35, 39,
    70, 71, 72, 114, 134, 151, 216, 355,
    404, 405, 434, 460, 461, 545, 553,
    569, 573, 575, 576, 578, 587
Automobilia: 141
Baxter Prints: 141
Belgian Art: 406
Birds, Dorothy Doughty & Boehm: 1
Bond and Stock Certificates: 216
Books: 2, 7, 8, 9, 11, 12, 15, 16, 18, 24,
    26, 27, 28, 29, 31, 33, 35, 39, 41, 72,
    78, 129, 130, 132, 134, 135, 136,
    137, 140, 141, 144, 145, 147, 148,
    151, 154, 155, 157, 158, 159, 160,
    161, 167, 181, 183, 199, 213, 223,
    224, 239, 240, 241, 248, 249, 250,
    255, 256, 257, 263, 264, 267, 273,
    275, 276, 292, 298, 302, 303, 315,
    317, 318, 326, 328, 350, 355, 379,
    404, 421, 427, 429, 432, 500, 523,
    527, 534, 535, 536, 542, 545, 553,
    556, 558, 562, 569, 571, 573, 574,
    575, 576, 580, 584, 617
Brass: 263
Bronzes: 15, 276, 423, 545
Buttons: 100
Canadiana: 427, 429
Ceramics: 132, 135, 140, 143, 144, 145,
    147, 153, 154, 159, 164, 274, 292,
    314, 328, 427, 500, 574
Chinese Works of Art: 7, 8, 10, 11, 12,
    13, 14, 15, 17, 19, 23, 25, 26, 27, 30,
    32, 33, 36, 37, 38, 82, 88, 110, 124,
    132, 134, 135, 136, 141, 147, 148,
    150, 152, 154, 155, 157, 159, 200,
    413, 419, 423, 427, 428, 431, 434,
    441, 446, 447, 461, 464, 495, 498,
    501, 507, 545, 550, 556, 560, 573,

Stamps: *(cont'd)*
158, 160, 216, 221, 240, 246, 261, 263, 274, 275, 276, 283, 284, 285, 292, 311, 346, 357, 363, 371, 379, 405, 434, 441, 495, 498, 499, 501, 526, 532, 534, 536, 545

Steam Models: 134, 152, 286

Swedish Art: 545

Textiles: 16, 135, 145, 252, 276, 570

Thai Works of Art: 602

Toys: 2, 7, 8, 11, 18, 19, 24, 25, 26, 27, 32, 33, 36, 37, 38, 41, 46, 47, 57, 76, 85, 88, 90, 100, 105, 128, 131, 135, 140, 141, 144, 145, 147, 148, 152, 153, 155, 159, 213, 223, 263, 276, 298, 353, 464, 469, 496, 498, 545, 555, 556, 566, 570, 582, 590, 598

Toy Soldiers: 25, 141, 159, 427, 446

Victoriana: 7, 8, 22, 32, 117, 144, 152, 303

Vintage Cars: 11, 29, 32, 150, 379, 460, 469, 498, 507

Wine: 132, 134, 135, 150, 239, 274, 417, 447, 532, 548, 564

Acknowledgments

No book, especially a work of this kind, is completed in isolation. We depended on the cooperation of hundreds of people and were extremely fortunate in this respect. We owe a great deal of thanks to those many in the auction business who took the time to see us, answered our questionnaires, our written follow-ups, and our telephone calls. We wish that we could thank them all by name but the list would be almost as long as this book. Yet there is no doubt that without them there would be nothing, and we greatly appreciate their help and advice.

However, certain people must be thanked individually. Christie's managing director Paul Whitfield was extraordinarily helpful, as were several of that firm's officers and personnel including Steve Lash, Ray Perman, Elizabeth Shaw, and Brian Cole—who did double duty, since when we first began this book he headed Phillips' North American operations. Others from Phillips who were of assistance include Cintra Huber (USA) and Andrew Clayton-Payne (UK). At Sotheby's we benefited enormously from Tom Norton's wise counsel and received considerable help from Roger Chubb, John Collins, Betsy Pinover, and Wathena Slaughter.

Serge Sabarsky was kind enough to share with us his encyclopaedic knowledge of the continental auction scene. Terry Ingram of the *Australian Financial Review* gave us a different perspective on auction rooms Down Under. Helping us to understand the Japanese auction situation were Sir John Figgess, Richard Weatherhead, and Dennis Yasamoto, as well as several others who prefer to remain anonymous.

Marjorie Stone, Associate General Counsel for Sotheby Parke Bernet Inc., and Doreen Noyes of Jessica Dee Associates, who handled the Morton's account, were of assistance at a time when we needed help fast. Helen G. Kyes shared her particular knowledge of the Midwest auction scene with us. Elizabeth Oliver of the British Universities Film Council helped us to get some vital information.

Our friends and colleagues at *American Book Prices Current*—Jane Mallison, George Milne, Susi Reardon, and Stephen Paul Davis (now with the Library of Congress)—pitched in and gave unstintingly of themselves. Our Connecticut neighbor Lynn Brinton did a fine job in assisting us with the various mailings.

At Harper's we owe a sincere vote of thanks to production editor William Monroe and copy editor Marjorie Horvitz, and we owe even more to our editor Frances Lindley, a consummate professional. Caro Hobhouse at Macmillan spurred us on graciously but firmly and we benefited from her efforts with regard to the manuscript.

Finally we would like to thank our agents, Lois Wallace, who helped to find this book an American home, and Giles Gordon, who persevered in the UK even when bemused.

Daniel J. Leab
Katharine Kyes Leab

Washington, CT